Y0-DYU-171

Wildlife Population Ecology

WILDLIFE POPULATION ECOLOGY

Edited by
James S. Wakeley

The Pennsylvania State University Press
University Park and London

Library of Congress Cataloging in Publication Data

Wildlife population ecology.
   1. Animal populations. 2. Animal ecology.
I. Wakeley, James S., 1950–
QL752.W52   599.05′248   81–83148
ISBN 0–271–00303–0   AACR2
ISBN 0–271–00304–9 (pbk.)

TABLE OF CONTENTS

Note: Although part and section titles do not appear in the text, they are included here as a guide for the convenience of the reader.

PART II: FACTORS AFFECTING POPULATION CHARACTERISTICS

WEATHER

PREDATION AND EXPLOITATION

INTERSPECIFIC COMPETITION

INTRASPECIFIC COMPETITION

BEHAVIOR

PHYSIOLOGICAL STRESS

ASSESSING THE IMPORTANCE OF VARIOUS FACTORS

PREFACE

This selection of readings on wildlife population ecology was developed in response to my own need for an ecologically oriented text appropriate for upper-level undergraduate students in a wildlife-management curriculum. It is intended to fill the gap between available management-oriented texts that cover a range of topics from law enforcement to habitat analysis, and general texts in population biology that draw most heavily from studies of invertebrate groups. Depending upon the orientation of the particular course, this collection would complement such texts as Giles's *Wildlife Management*, Dasmann's *Wildlife Biology*, Boughey's *Ecology of Populations*, Emmel's *Population Biology*, Elseth and Baumgardner's *Population Biology*, Caughley's *Analysis of Vertebrate Populations*, or Tanner's *Guide to the Study of Animal Populations*. Thus it is intended for any course in population ecology that emphasizes vertebrates, whether basic or applied, descriptive or quantitative.

Instructors generally agree that students benefit from direct exposure to the scientific literature. However, recent changes in copyright laws have made it difficult, if not impossible, to make original readings available for use by large classes. Instructors are sometimes forced to reduce the desired reading list, detracting from students' educational experience. This worsening situation makes the published collection of original readings a particularly valuable instructional aid.

Several people helped to develop this collection by suggesting appropriate topics or key articles. I appreciate the advice given by G. M. Kelly, G. L. Storm, W. M. Tzilkowski, and F. B. Samson. I also thank the senior authors and publishers of the original articles who gave their permission to reproduce copyrighted material. In particular, I thank The Wildlife Society, whose publications make up the major part of this collection.

INTRODUCTION

Practical wildlife management may be as much art, politics, or economics as it is science, but management decisions still must be based upon the biological realities of the system being manipulated. Effective management of wildlife populations requires a thorough understanding of ecological principles and detailed knowledge of the population under consideration.

There are only four basic processes affecting the size and structure of any population. *Natality* and *immigration* add new members to a population, while *mortality* and *emigration* subtract old members. All other characteristics of populations—density, age and sex composition, growth, fluctuation—are determined by the balance among these basic processes and by their variation through time.

For example, the dramatic seasonal changes in abundance of wildlife in the temperate zone are due to the restriction of reproduction to the favorable spring and summer period, and the influx and departure of migrants. Mortality rates also vary seasonally and may be highest during winter. In many populations, dispersal of young animals during summer and fall reduces population density from the post-breeding peak. In the same way, long-term trends or variations in sequential annual censuses of a wildlife population are determined by the relative magnitudes of annual rates of natality, mortality, and movements.

Wildlife Population Ecology is designed to introduce the reader to the array of factors that may influence the size or composition of bird and mammal populations. The collection is organized into two parts. The first, "Characteristics of Wildlife Populations," examines the processes that produce numerical changes in populations—natality, mortality, and movements (dispersal)—and investigates their consequences—age/sex composition, growth, and fluctuation. In the first paper under "Natality," Perrins (1965) shows how clutch sizes in birds are influenced by age of the parent, date of laying, density of breeding pairs, habitat type, and a variety of other proximate factors. Ultimate factors responsible for the evolution of clutch and litter sizes are addressed by Cody (1966) and Millar (1973). Cody also examines geographic trends in clutch sizes of birds and offers a theoretical explanation.

In the section on "Mortality," Caughley (1966), Perrins (1966), and Botkin and Miller (1974) analyze the relationship between annual mortality rate and age in birds and mammals. In addition, Caughley (1966) tries to relate the survivorship patterns seen in a variety of mammals to their life histories and ecological roles, and discusses problems in the estimation of mortality rates in wild populations.

"Dispersal" of animals from local populations is the subject of papers by Hawkins et al. (1971) on deer and Storm et al. (1976) on red foxes. These investigators identify sex and age groups that are prone to disperse, and analyze movement patterns of dispersing individuals.

Under "Age and Sex Composition," Howe (1977) and Taber and Dasmann (1954) show how sex ratios in populations are affected by changes in sex ratios of animals at birth and by sex differences in mortality rates of juveniles. Caughley (1974) discusses factors influencing age ratios in populations and cautions about their use as indices of productivity.

In the section on "Population Growth," Klein (1968) analyzes the irruptive growth pattern of an introduced reindeer herd, in one of the few well-documented examples of the growth of a wild vertebrate population. Caughley and Birch (1971) try to end the confusion about various measures of population growth and discuss their estimation for real populations.

The causes of cyclic fluctuations in wildlife populations have been debated among ecologists for decades. Under "Population Fluctuation," Krebs et al. (1973) review the evidence for an intrinsic cause of the four-year cycle in microtine rodents, and Keith and Windberg (1978) summarize their long-running research on the causes of the ten-year cycle in snowshoe hares.

The second division of the book, "Factors Affecting Population Characteristics," examines the biotic and abiotic factors that may affect the size and composition of wildlife populations through their influence on rates of reproduction, mortality, and dispersal. In the first section, Francis (1970) and Meslow and Keith (1971) analyze the relationship between aspects of "Weather" and various population parameters. They find that weather usually affects wildlife populations indirectly, through changes in the habitat upon which populations depend.

The short-term and long-term effects of "Predation and Exploitation" on selected bird and mammal populations are examined in the next selection of papers. Wagner and Stoddart (1972) describe the effects of natural predation on the characteristics of a prey population, while Mosby (1969) and Murton et al. (1974) study the population consequences of hunting by man on a popular game animal (gray squirrel) and an agricultural pest (wood pigeon).

In the section on "Interspecific Competition," Cameron (1964) and Heller (1971) describe how distributional patterns in small mammals may be determined by competitive interactions with other similar species. Orians and Willson (1964) discuss the evolution of interspecific territoriality in birds and attempt to predict the ecological situations in which it may be favored.

The consequences of "Intraspecific Competition" for available food resources are examined by Clark (1972) on coyotes, and Anderson (1977) on sparrows. Both papers examine the impact of natural fluctuations in food supplies on reproduction and survival in the consumer populations.

In the section on "Behavior," Watson and Jenkins (1968) study the role of territoriality in limiting the density and productivity of red grouse populations, while Collias and Jahn (1959) show how productivity of individual pairs of Canada geese in a confined population is related to their position in a dominance hierarchy.

In the following section, Christian and Davis (1956) and Christian and LeMunyan (1958) discuss the possible role of "Physiological Stress" in reducing productivity and increasing mortality in high-density populations. This stress is thought to be produced by the increased frequency of intraspecific interaction that is a consequence of high density.

The final papers use two recent techniques to assess the relative influence of different environmental factors on the size of populations. First, Krebs (1970) applies a k-factor analysis to the years of accumulated data on the Oxford great tit population, in an effort to identify the factors most responsible for limiting and regulating population density. Then, Walters and Gross (1972) use computer simulation to assess the consequences of various harvest strategies and environmental changes on a deer population, and to show how model predictions can assist in management decisions.

Any collection of readings is a compromise between completeness and practicality, and no two compilers would agree on the contents. I have tried to introduce the reader to a variety of topics within wildlife population ecology, and in so doing, I have slighted each one. I hope this selection will stimulate further investigation of the literature. I have provided a list of additional references at the end of this book for readers who wish to follow up on the themes presented here. This list is not meant to be complete; rather, it is a further introduction to a large and fascinating literature.

POPULATION FLUCTUATIONS AND CLUTCH-SIZE IN THE GREAT TIT, *PARUS MAJOR* L.

By C. M. PERRINS

INTRODUCTION

History

This study forms part of a long-term investigation of the factors affecting populations of tits; it was started, under the general direction of Dr D. Lack, in 1947. Emphasis has been on the three species great, blue and coal tit, *Parus major*, *P. caeruleus* and *P. ater*, but this paper is largely concerned with work done by the writer, on the great tit, since 1957. Most of the work has been done in Wytham Wood, an area of mixed deciduous woodland, some 2 miles west of Oxford.

In 1946–47 J. A. Gibb put up nest-boxes in the part of the Wytham Estate known as Marley Wood, an area of 66 ac (*c.* 26 ha), of which about 3 ac are open, marshy, ground, unsuitable for tits and another 8 ac mainly shrubs with no trees. Since the summer of 1947 the number of breeding pairs of great and blue tits has been recorded. The reader is referred to Gibb (1950) for a general description of the breeding biology of these two species.

Since 1957 the writer has used, in addition to Marley, an increasing number of other parts of the wood, as the Marley population was insufficient to provide enough data for various aspects of the study. In addition to those in Wytham there were about 100 boxes in gardens in Oxford from 1958 to 1961, inclusive; the data from gardens provided an interesting comparison with those from Wytham in some respects, but extensive trapping was not practicable in gardens in winter and survival data for the garden birds were not obtained.

Only blue and great tits nest commonly in the boxes in Wytham. For 5 years Gibb (1954a) made careful censuses of the breeding population and found that, while no great tits nested in natural sites, up to one third of the blue tits did so. Hence the population figures for the blue tit, while probably reflecting the numbers present, are not complete.

Wytham Wood

The woodland areas used in this study were all within the Wytham Estate (Fig. 1). The woodland covers some 800 ac, but about 200 ac of this are young plantations, including much conifer, and are less used by the tits. Hence there are some 600 ac (*c.* 250 ha) of woodland suitable for tits. The wood is privately owned by the University; there was little disturbance, apart from forestry operations.

Except for a few small plantations of mature conifers, the wood is broad-leaved deciduous, very mixed in composition, but of two main types. One consists primarily of oak, *Quercus robur* (L.), with an understorey of varying amounts of hawthorn, *Crataegus monogyna* (Jacq.), hazel, *Corylus avellana* (L.), and elder, *Sambucus niger* (L.), and often a thick ground layer of bracken, *Pteridium aquilinum* (L.) and bramble, *Rubus* spp. The other type is predominantly sycamore, *Acer pseudoplatanus* (L.) and ash, *Fraxinus excelsior* (L.), with a rather clearer forest floor owing to the attention of foresters. However, there is much variation, and other areas range from large, old beech, *Fagus sylvatica* (L.), to impenetrable blackthorn, *Prunus spinosa* (L.), scrub.

Wytham is an island of woodland surrounded by agricultural land and urban areas. While many tits must breed in the surrounding areas it is evident that movement in and out of the wood is limited and to some extent the woodland population can be considered a closed one.

Methods

Each nest-box was visited at least once a week during the nesting season; since the great tit lays one egg per day, it was possible from such visits to get the date when each clutch was started and completed. Every great tit nest was visited each day from the eleventh day after completion of the clutch until the first young hatched. Thus the date when each brood hatched was known.

On the day of hatching some of the broods were artificially altered in size. For example, if two broods of nine young hatched, three young might be transferred from one brood to the other, making one brood of six and another of twelve. The down of transferred young was dyed with gentian violet, which was normally visible for at least 10 days. This was done mainly to ascertain whether the foster parents discriminated in any way against the strange chicks; they did not. The reason for manipulating the size of broods was that when studying survival of the young in broods of different sizes, Lack, Gibb & Owen (1957) had very few data on the broods of above the normal size. To give some idea

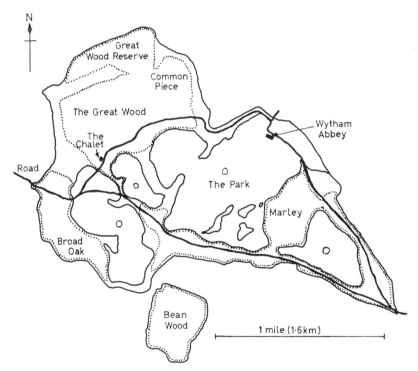

FIG. 1. Wytham Wood. The areas enclosed by dotted lines are those in which there were nest-boxes during this study. Areas marked with an 'O' are open habitats, either fields or young plantations.

of the extent of this operation, some half to one-third of the broods were used for manipulation (excluding late broods); virtually all broods of eleven young or more were artificial.

The young birds were weighed on the fifteenth day after hatching and their weights were recorded against their ring numbers. Thereafter the nests were not visited until well after the time at which the young should have flown (about the nineteenth to twentieth day after hatching) to avoid any possibility of causing the young to leave the nest prematurely. It was nearly always possible at the final visit to ascertain whether the young had fledged successfully or whether they had been attacked by a predator.

From 1961 onwards the females were caught on the nest at night when they were roosting with the young and their age was determined by plumage characteristics.

Temperature

Tollenaar (1922) and Kluijver (1951) have shown that the breeding season of the tits is closely correlated with the spring temperature. Following Kluijver, Fig. 2 shows for the period 1 March to 20 April the warmth average (equal to day-degrees C—calculated by summing the mean temperatures for each day), plotted against the mean date of the first egg in the year. There is a clear, though not very close, correlation between the temperature and the date of breeding. That the correlation is not closer is due partly to the method of analysis; since the mean date of first egg has varied by about a month, the temperature over a fixed period is not a satisfactory way of measuring the earliness of the spring, since in early seasons, e.g. 1948, the birds were all breeding before the end of the period used for the temperature record, and so could not have been influenced by the later temperature concerned. Indeed, since a tit needs about 4 days to produce an egg (Kluijver

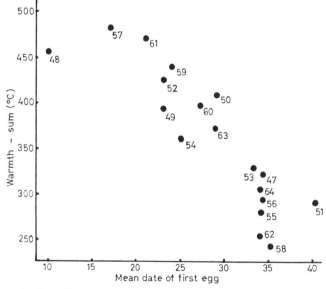

FIG. 2. Great tit: date of breeding in Marley in relation to spring weather. Date of breeding is the mean of the dates of the first egg (1 April = 1, 5 May = 35) laid by each pair in each year; the index of spring weather is the sum of the mean of the maximum and minimum temperatures (°C) for each day from 1 March to 20 April.

1951) many of the birds breeding in 1948 were hardly influenced by any April weather at all. Early April was not warm in this year and so the warmth sum for 1948 appears relatively colder than the actual period which affected the breeding season of the tits. Again, in 1958 there was an exceptionally fine February, and it seems possible that this caused the birds to breed earlier than would have been expected from the March temperatures.

However, the breeding season of the tits can be fairly closely correlated with weather in March and early April and perhaps also in February. The times of appearance of the caterpillars on oaks vary in parallel, and thus are available to the tits for their young earlier in a warmer spring than in a cold one. It seems possible that, as Lack (1954) suggested, the tits come into breeding condition primarily in response to the increase in day-length during the spring, but that their response is modified by temperature so as to bring them into breeding condition at such a time that their young will be in the nest when the caterpillars will be most numerous. However, it is not clear in what way the tits respond to temperature. It seems likely that they do not do so directly. Great tits kept by Suomalainen (1937) in continuous illumination during January and February came into breeding condition (as judged by gonad size), while other tits kept in natural day-length did not. One half of each of these two groups was kept at around 0° C and the other at 15–19° C. The temperature made no apparent difference to gonad size and hence temperature, at that time, probably has no direct effect in bringing the birds into breeding condition in the wild state.

In Germany, Löhrl (1957) has shown that the warmer the weather in April the earlier the collared flycatcher, *Ficedula albicollis*, breeds. The collared flycatcher is a migrant and does not arrive in Europe until late April, and yet its time of breeding is still affected by the temperature on the breeding ground before it gets there. Here the collared flycatcher cannot be responding directly to temperature, but it may be to some phenomenon such as the opening of the leaves or the number of insects available, which may be directly correlated with the temperature of the preceding period. The great tit may well do the same.

Table 1. *Age of female great tits in relation to date of laying*

	Age of bird (years)	No. of birds	Mean date of first egg (April)
1961	1	122	22·4
	2	19	17·7
	3	15	17·8
1962	1	52	33·2
	2	40	32·3
	3	12	30·2
1963	1	54	30·0
	2	32	26·7
	3	28	26·4
	4	8	26·1

The date is counted from 1 April, e.g. 33 = 3 May.

Age of breeding

It is known that, in many species, females breeding for the first time lay slightly later than older birds. For most species these differences have been shown only between birds breeding for the first time and birds that have bred before. However, in some species, e.g. the yellow-eyed penguin, *Megadyptes antipodes* (Hombron & Jacquinot) (Richdale 1957), it is known that the average laying dates become progressively earlier over at least the first 3 years of breeding.

Kluijver (1951) has shown that second-year great tits lay, on average, 2·1 days earlier than those that are breeding for the first time. In addition Kluijver had data for eight 3-year-old birds and these bred 3·8 days earlier than his 2-year-old birds. Comparable data are available for the Wytham great tits only since 1961. Table 1 shows that the first-year birds bred on average 4·7, 0·9 and 3·3 days later than the 2-year-old birds and 3-year-olds 0, 2·1 and 0·3 days earlier than 2-year-olds.

The difference in the date of laying of the different age groups will modify somewhat the mean date of laying of the whole population in different years. If the year is one when there is considerable increase in the breeding population, there will be proportionately more young birds present than in a year when the population has decreased. However, the greatest effect that this is likely to have had on the mean date of laying is to alter it by 1 day either way.

It is not known whether the age of the males influences the date of laying. This could happen if the older males courted more vigorously or started earlier than the younger males and so brought the female to the point of breeding earlier. Unfortunately the data on this point are not available for Wytham. Kluijver notes that he could find no such effect.

Habitat

Lack (1955, 1958) showed that the tits breed at different times in different habitats, in particular that blue and great tits breed earlier in scots pine, *Pinus sylvestris* (L.), than in corsican pine, *P. nigra* (Arnold), and earlier in gardens than in woodland. In both cases the birds bred first in the more open habitat.

Table 2 shows the mean dates of laying in Marley, the Great Wood Reserve and the

Table 2. *Mean date of laying in different areas*

	Mean date of first egg (1 April = 1)		
	Marley	Great Wood	Gardens
Great tit			
1958	35·1	35·8	31·6
1959	23·9	21·2	17·6
1960	27·1	23·0	23·0
1961	21·0	20·1	15·7
1962	34·5	32·1	–
1963	29·7	28·6	–
Blue tit			
1958	34·3	30·7	32·0
1959	21·8	18·4	22·5
1960	19·9	18·9	20·8
1961	18·7	12·4	17·8
1962	32·2	31·0	–
1963	32·4	30·6	–

The date is counted from 1 April, e.g. 33 = 3 May.

gardens at Oxford. The great tits in gardens were the earliest by an average of 3 days over those in the Great Wood Reserve and nearly 5 days over those in Marley. Lack showed that blue tits bred about 2 days earlier in gardens than in woodland, but at Oxford they started about the same time as the birds in Marley and about 3 days later than those in the Great Wood Reserve. The tits laid consistently earlier in the Great Wood Reserve than in Marley (Table 2). The only exception was in the Great Wood Reserve in 1958, perhaps because this was the first year that boxes were provided.

There is some evidence that the caterpillars in the Great Wood Reserve are a little earlier than those in Marley, the average difference being about 1 day (Gibb, in Lack 1955). The only obvious difference between the two areas is that the former lies a little lower, being on average about 250 ft above sea-level whereas Marley is about 350 ft above sea-level. However, the long series of data for Marley, which runs up the side of a hill, shows no variation in date of laying with altitude.

The Great Wood Reserve would seem the best habitat for tits which has been examined during this study. Evidence provided later shows that the clutch-size is highest here and that nestling mortality is lowest. In addition there appears to be a higher density of blue tits here than in Marley.

If the Great Wood Reserve is a habitat with a good food supply then the birds might breed earlier there because they can get into breeding condition earlier. The earlier breeding of the tits in scots pine than in corsican could also be explained on this basis since Gibb (1960) showed that there is usually more insect life in scots pine, endemic in northern Europe, than in the introduced corsican pine.

However, this does not explain why great tits should be able to breed earlier in gardens whereas blue tits do not do so, and a good explanation has not been given.

It is of interest to note that Kluijver (*in litt.*) tried to influence the breeding season of the great tit in Holland by putting out trays of mealworms, *Tenebrio molitor* L., for them in early spring. While the birds ate them in the winter they ignored them in the spring and concentrated on their natural foods. This suggests that the birds did not need the extra food in the spring and thus the supply put out by people in gardens at this time may be similarly unimportant.

CLUTCH-SIZE

While several factors will be shown to affect the size of the great tit's clutch to varying extents, the average clutch in Wytham is usually about nine or ten. Lack (1947) developed the theory that the clutch-size of birds was adapted to the largest number of young which could be raised successfully; Lack *et al.* (1957) gave some evidence that this was true for the great tit. It is now possible to examine the situation further.

Gibb (1955) showed that the larger the brood the more often the parents feed the young, but they are not able to increase the rate of feeding in proportion to the increase in the number of young. 'A member of a small family therefore received more food per day than did one of a larger family' (Gibb 1955). This situation has been recorded for many species of bird (e.g. Moreau 1947; Kendeigh 1952). As might be expected, the result is that the young of the large broods are lighter in weight; Table 3 shows the range. (It will be shown below that young in later broods are lighter than those in early ones and that brood-size decreases with season. Hence large broods occur most commonly when young tend to be heaviest and so the weights in this table are biased in favour of the large broods and the difference, at any given time of the season, is actually greater than that shown.)

In Wytham, omitting nests destroyed by predators, 90–95% of the young leave the nest successfully, regardless of their weight. Many of these young are caught during the following winter and analysis of these in relation to their weight (Fig. 3) shows that more of the heavy than of the light young survive. Hence proportionately more of the young

Table 3. *Great tit—weight in relation to brood-size*

	Brood-size															
	1	2	3	4	5	6	7	8	9	10	11	12	13	14	15	16
1958																
No. of broods	1	–	–	3	3	8	5	2	3	3	7	5	3	–	–	–
Mean of mean weights (g)	17·0	–	–	19·4	20·2	20·1	19·8	19·1	18·6	18·8	17·8	18·5	16·2	–	–	–
1959																
No. of broods	–	1	3	12	12	13	10	6	13	8	9	11	6	1	–	–
Mean of mean weights (g)	–	18·5	19·1	19·8	19·9	19·6	19·6	19·2	19·0	18·7	18·6	18·3	18·2	16·0	–	–
1960																
No. of broods	1	1	4	7	12	17	7	12	4	13	10	3	1	–	–	–
Mean of mean weights (g)	19·0	20·1	20·5	20·0	19·4	19·6	19·5	19·0	19·3	18·9	18·6	18·1	18·2	–	–	–
1961 (Marley)																
No. of broods	–	1	4	4	6	7	5	9	3	–	3	8	9	–	–	–
Mean of mean weights (g)	–	19·9	18·9	19·4	18·4	18·3	18·5	18·0	17·5	–	15·1	17·4	16·9	–	–	–
1961 (rest of Wytham)																
No. of broods	–	4	11	12	15	18	21	17	11	6	8	5	1	–	–	–
Mean of mean weights (g)	–	19·3	19·0	19·1	19·2	18·8	18·6	19·0	19·2	18·3	18·6	17·9	13·6	–	–	–
1962																
No. of broods	2	2	8	10	25	19	14	21	16	11	10	3	1	–	–	–
Mean of mean weights (g)	21·3	20·0	19·1	19·1	19·0	18·5	18·5	18·2	18·3	16·9	16·6	16·5	18·4	–	–	–
1963																
No. of broods	1	1	2	13	8	13	18	21	22	26	14	6	3	–	1	2
Mean of mean weights (g)	19·5	20·5	19·9	19·3	20·1	19·3	19·0	19·1	19·6	19·1	18·8	18·3	18·6	–	18·7	18·5

Brood-size here is the number of young weighed, except for Marley 1961 (where many of the large broods lost several young); there it is the total number of the young originally present.

from the smaller broods survive than those from the large broods. Although an analysis has not been made, heavy young are usually quite plump, and presumably some of their weight is fat which is available as a food store in the difficult period when the birds are learning to fend for themselves.

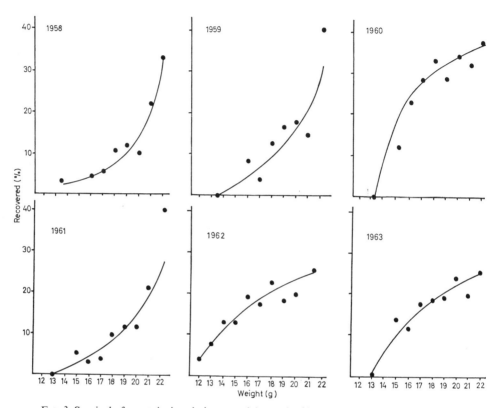

FIG. 3. Survival of great tits in relation to weight on the fifteenth day. Any bird which was known to be alive 3 months after fledging was counted as having survived. Owing to the very small numbers of recoveries of birds of 15 g or less, in most years information for the birds of 12–15 g has been lumped and presented as one point. Since the weights of the young form a normal distribution, data on the very light and the very heavy are fewer than those of the more average weights. The lines are drawn through the points by eye.

Table 4 shows the recoveries in terms of the number of surviving young per brood (the important measure from the evolutionary point of view). The large broods do not always produce proportionately more surviving young than those of normal size. Table 4 shows the survival rate in relation to brood-size for the blue tit, where the same holds true. The figures given here include broods that were taken in the nest by predators since predators tend to take larger broods (Table 5). (The reason for dividing the season into two halves will become apparent in the following section.)

There is little doubt that the large broods are taken more frequently by predators because they are hungrier and calling more. The predators are chiefly weasels, *Mustela nivalis*, grey squirrels, *Sciurus carolinensis*, and great spotted woodpeckers, *Dendrocopus major*. The two mammals enter the box by the hole, the weasel being able to get through a hole large enough for a great tit, the grey squirrel having to enlarge it. The woodpecker provides additional evidence that it is finding the young by sound. It makes a hole into the box through one of the sides just at the level of the calling young, a little less than an inch above the level of the nest. It seems likely that it is gauging the level of the young by ear. In addition to the loss of the young about 20% of the females seem to be taken with their broods, thus increasing the disadvantage of raising a large brood, since these females will not get a further opportunity to breed.

Table 4. *Recoveries of great and blue tits in relation to brood-size*

	Brood-size	Great tit				Blue tit	
		No. broods	No. young	Recovered (%)	No. recovered /brood	No. broods	No. recovered /brood
1958	2–5	4	17	11·7	0·50	1	0
	6–8	16	109	12·5	0·87	9	0·44
	9–11	14	142	8·4	0·85	32	0·69
	12–14	12	153	6·5	0·83	6	1·67
1959	1–5	28	120	15·8	0·63	3	0
	6–8	42	286	13·3	0·90	27	0·59
	9–11	31	308	13·6	1·36	71	0·89
	12–14	21	264	7·5	0·95	16	0·47
1960	1–5	33	124	27·5	1·03	5	0
	6–8	36	257	25·7	1·83	22	0·74
	9–11	21	211	27·9	2·81	67	1·09
	12–16	12	152	30·3	3·83	37	1·49
1961 (All Wytham except Marley)	2–5	41	157	10·2	0·39	10	0·10
	6–8	67	467	8·6	0·60	80	0·28
	9–11	32	312	12·8	1·25	77	0·42
	12–15	8	100	8·0	1·0	8	0·13
1961 (Marley)	2–5	20	80	7·5	0·30	(The above entries
	6–8	28	179	6·7	0·43	(1961) are for Wytham
	9–11	9	91	3·3	0·33	incl. Marley)
	12–13	17	212	1·9	0·23	
1962	1–5	38	168	13·7	0·61	5	0·25
	6–8	44	316	15·8	1·14	18	0·56
	9–11	50	494	12·8	1·26	73	0·67
	12–14	25	349	7·2	1·25	23	0·48
1963	1–5	16	70	20·0	0·88	1	0·00
	6–8	35	262	25·2	1·89	13	0·46
	9–11	75	742	15·4	1·52	85	1·20
	12	7	84	21·4	2·57	43	1·60
	13–16	14	209	12·4	1·86	34	1·12

Table 4 is biased in favour of the large broods. The great majority of the broods of eleven or more in the great tit are artificial in that, as mentioned earlier, the broods were increased by three or more young at hatching. These broods appear to be reared in a perfectly normal way by the parents. However, they differ from natural broods of the same size in that, had the parents laid a clutch of that size, they would either have had to start laying earlier (for which they might not have had enough food) or the clutch would have been completed later, and consequently hatched later, by 3 or 4 days. Such delay would have been accompanied by lower survival since, as will be shown later, the date of hatching markedly affects the survival of the young. Hence the young in these artificially increased broods, had they been natural, would have hatched later and survived less well than the figures show by perhaps 15%.

Hence the commonest brood-size is that which normally produces the most surviving young. A larger brood results, on average, in fewer rather than more surviving young.

Further, I think that the variations in clutch-size which will be demonstrated in the following section can also be looked at in this light.

Table 5. *Predation on great tit nests in Wytham in relation to brood-size and time of season, 1959–63*

	1959						
	Up to 13 May				After 13 May		
Brood-size	No. nests	No. lost	%		No. nests	No. lost	%
3–6	9	0	0		25	1	4·0
7–10	23	0	0		14	3	21·4
11–15	17	0	0		20	5	25·0
	1960						
	Up to 15 May				After 15 May		
Brood-size	No. nests	No. lost	%		No. nests	No. lost	%
2–5	13	1	7·7		20	3	15·0
6–8	24	2	8·3		34	5	14·7
9–14	28	5	17·8		21	6	28·6
	1961						
	Up to 10 May				After 10 May		
Brood-size	No. nests	No. lost	%		No. nests	No. lost	%
2–5	22	2	9·1		33	7	21·2
6–8	43	0	0		43	9	20·9
9–13	35	6	17·1		26	6	23·1
	1962						
	Up to 23 May				After 23 May		
Brood-size	No. nests	No. lost	%		No. nests	No. lost	%
2–7	31	1	3·3		42	5	11·9
8–10	30	3	10·0		26	4	15·4
11–14	20	3	15·0		19	4	21·1
	1963						
	Up to 26 May				After 26 May		
Brood-size	No. nests	No. lost	%		No. nests	No. lost	%
0–9	70	0	0		23	4	17·4
10–16	65	2	3·1		4	1	25·0

Each year is subdivided so that approximately half the data will fall into each half of the season. Similarly brood-sizes are chosen so that similar numbers of nests will fall into small, medium and large broods. The data are biased in favour of large broods as the very late broods suffer the heaviest predation and most of these broods are small. In 1963, with very few losses, the season is not divided into two halves, but into main and late; all four losses of broods of 0–9 occurred after 15 June and were second broods.

FACTORS AFFECTING CLUTCH-SIZE

Date of laying

The size of the clutch becomes progressively smaller as the breeding season progresses, as demonstrated by Tollenaar (1922) and Kluijver (1951). In Marley the reduction in clutch-size is 0·09 eggs (S.E. 0·039) for each day later that breeding begins.

Gibb (1955) showed that the individual young in early broods are fed more often than those in late broods. This is presumably correlated with the food supply, which he showed was abundant for only 2–3 weeks, after which it rapidly diminished. The weight of the young decreases as the season progresses. This fact is partly obscured since brood-size decreases with season, and weight decreases with increasing brood-size. A regression

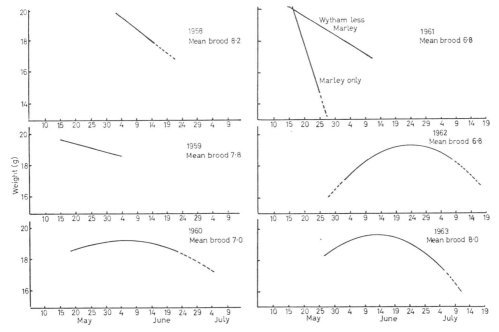

FIG. 4. Regression lines showing differences in weight of young great tits hatched at different times in the season. The weights are plotted against the date of weighing although, of course, they hatched 2 weeks earlier. The lines are dotted where there are particularly few data. The unusually low weights in the early part of 1962 were due to the very cold weather; the females had to brood the small young to keep them warm and so could not go and collect food for them; associated with this, weights were low and mortality in the nest was high (Table 7).

Table 6 . *Nestling mortality of great tits in relation to date of hatching, Marley, 1961, and all Wytham, 1962*

Marley 1961

Date of hatching	No. broods	No. young	Died (%)
3–6 May	3	28	0
7–8 May	9	76	9·2
9–11 May	26	202	10·4
12–14 May	13	83	34·9
15–19 May	2	14	64·3

All Wytham, 1962

Date of hatching	No. broods	No. young	Died (%)
13–27 May	113	916	23·1
28 May to 17 June	27	200	9·0
18–30 June	5	28	39·3

11

analysis in which brood-size was allowed for, made by Dr J. F. Scott, showed that there was usually a highly significant reduction in weight as the season progressed, though the young in the earliest broods were also sometimes lighter than those a little later. The resulting regression lines are shown in Fig. 4. Even by rearing a smaller brood, the parents that breed later are not usually able to feed the young sufficiently well to produce young as heavy as those reared earlier in the season. Hence it seems clear that the reduction in clutch-size with date is an adaptation to a steadily worsening food supply for the young which reduces the chances of raising many well-nourished young.

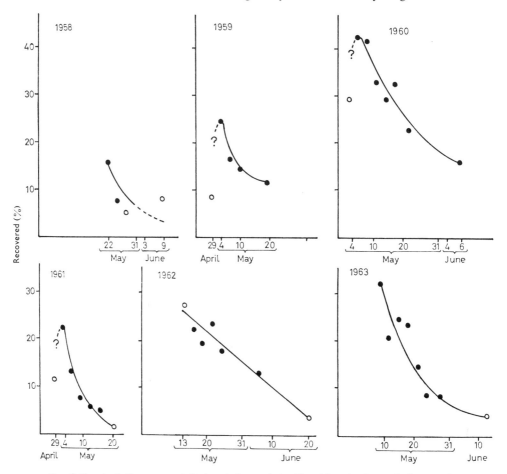

FIG. 5. Survival of young great tits in relation to date of hatching. Again survival means that the birds were known to be alive 3 months after fledging. Data are lumped into 3-day periods at the beginning of the season, but into longer periods at the end when there was less information. Points marked by open circles are based on less than five recoveries. Lines are drawn through the points by eye.

There is a higher proportion of predation in the later part of the season (Table 5). The young of the later broods are lighter and more noisy than the early ones, and this is probably the main reason that they are more vulnerable to predators. It is also possible that predators require more food at the time. In either case there will be selection for earlier breeding since it results in smaller losses of females and young in the nest.

There is some other evidence that the parents cannot easily raise their young later in the season. Table 6 shows the mortality in the nest in relation to date of hatching in 1962 and in Marley in 1961; these are the two instances when more young than usual were lost during the nestling period.

Fig. 5 shows how rapidly the chances of survival for the young decrease from the start of the season. Since the figures are percentages and the earlier broods are larger than the later, the advantages of early breeding in terms of production of young are even more marked than is apparent from this figure.

As might be expected from the data in Fig. 5, there is some evidence that the weight of the chicks is less important to their survival at the beginning of the season than later. Hence while a 17 g young may stand an almost equal chance of survival with a 20 g one if it hatches at the beginning of the season, it has a much lower chance of surviving later in the season. This effect is particularly noticeable in 1962 when many of the early young were quite light, but they survived as well as the heavier young that were raised a little later.

Table 7. *Survival of young great tits in relation to the part of the season in which they hatched*

| | First half of season | | | | | Second half | |
| | Early part | | Remainder | | Total | | |
Year	No. young	Recovered (%)	No. young	Recovered (%)	Recovered (%)	No. young	Recovered (%)
1947	27	7·4	48	14·8	12·9	88	6·8
1948	68	11·8	90	18·6	15·8	209	10·9
1949	46	8·7	231	9·1	9·0	200	7·0
1950	15	6·7	56	3·6	4·2	115	3·5
1951	22	0	51	7·8	5·5	83	7·2
1952	30	16·7	41	2·4	8·4	77	6·5
1953	39	15·4	46	8·7	11·8	89	4·5
1954	35	8·6	95	7·4	7·7	100	2·0
1955	19	5·3	59	3·4	3·8	100	8·0
1956	29	10·3	74	5·4	6·8	70	4·3
1957	28	3·6	89	6·7	6·0	99	4·0
Total	358	9·61	880	8·52	8·80	1230	6·42

Similar results are shown in Table 7 for the years 1947–57, though here, with many fewer data, the breeding season was divided into only two parts. It will be seen that, in general, the young survived better in the first half of the season, while in the two apparent exceptions the data were very sparse. There is no clear evidence that the very first birds to breed in the season are at a disadvantage. Table 7 also shows the success of the earliest broods compared with the rest of the broods in the first half of the season. Overall the survival from the earliest broods was the same as that from the others. Hence the survival figures show that there must be strong selection for breeding in the first part of the season and, in addition, that there is no clear sign that those that breed first of all are at either an advantage or a disadvantage. In 1962, but in no other year, cold weather forced the females to brood and not to feed the young and so caused high mortality and low weights among the early broods. This disadvantage was not enough to outweigh the advantage of early breeding and does not seem to occur at all frequently.

Density of breeding pairs

Clutch-size decreases as the population increases, as shown in Fig. 6. When the population doubles in size the clutch is reduced by 2·02 eggs (S.E. 0·39). In all 69 % of the variation in clutch-size can be accounted for by the effects of date of laying and density. It is difficult to provide evidence that this variation is an adaptive behaviour since feeding conditions and nesting success vary so much from year to year. However, in 1961, there was a considerable difference in the breeding densities in different parts of Wytham. The full reasons for this are not clear, but it may have been due partly to Marley having more than

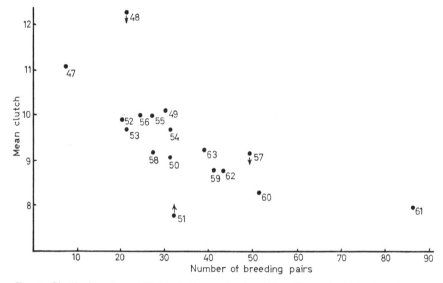

FIG. 6. Clutch-size of great tit in relation to density of breeding pairs in Marley. Arrows mark points which were particularly affected by the date of breeding, i.e. breeding was late in 1951 and clutch-size would have been larger if the birds had bred at the normal time, clutch-size would have been smaller in 1948 and 1957 if the birds had not bred so early.

enough boxes and Great Wood insufficient. There is no reason to suppose that in 1961 the initial food supply was poorer in Marley than in Great Wood, the caterpillar populations tending to be similar over large areas of woodland due to the aerial dispersion of the winter moth in its first instar.

In Marley mortality in the nest was abnormally high (for deciduous woodland) and this was markedly affected by brood-size (Table 8). Fig. 4 shows that in 1961 the

Table 8. *Nestling mortality of great tits in relation to brood-size,*
Marley, 1961

Brood-size	No. broods	No. young	No. died	Died (%)
2–4	9	28	1	3·6
5–7	19	112	9	8·0
8–10	11	93	16	17·2
11–13	14	170	40	23·5

difference in weight between the early and the late young was much more marked in Marley than in the rest of Wytham. In addition breeding stopped earlier in Marley, there being a tendency for birds in other parts of Wytham to lay repeat clutches later than those in Marley. Not only did the young in the nest in Marley fare worse than those in the other parts of Wytham, but there was a significant difference in the survival after fledging between the young in the two areas (Table 9). Even comparing young of equal weight, survival was poorer in Marley than elsewhere.

The reason that the tits raised fewer young in Marley than in Great Wood could well have been that tits have greater difficulty in raising young at high than at low density, because there is less food per pair. I therefore suggest that the habit of laying fewer eggs at a higher density has been selected as a result of the individual birds producing, under these circumstances, more surviving young from small than from large clutches. This is in contrast to the suggestion of Wynne-Edwards (1962) that lower production at

Table 9. *Breeding success of great tits in Marley and Wytham Great Wood, 1961*

	Marley	Wytham Great Wood
Density (pairs/ac)	1·3	0·60
Mean weight of young on fifteenth day	18·0	19·0
Nestlings died (excluding those taken by predators) (%)	16·4	3·0
Broods taken by predators (%)	29	8
Fledged young recovered after 3 months (%)	6·6	12·4
No. young recovered per brood after 3 months	0·44	0·96

high densities is an adaptation which prevents over-population. The reduction in clutch-size is not nearly proportional to the increase in the number of breeding pairs, so that it is difficult to understand how the latter system works in the great tit.

Age of birds

Kluijver (1951) has shown that, on average, birds breeding for the first time have smaller clutches than older birds. Table 10(a) shows that this is also true for Wytham great

Table 10. (a) *Mean clutch-sizes of yearling and older great tits*

	All Wytham, 1961		All Wytham, 1961		Marley, 1961		All Wytham, 1962		All Wytham, 1963	
	No.	Mean	No.	Mean	No.	Mean	No.	Mean	No.	Mean
Yearlings	32	7·9	128	7·7	41	7·9	54	8·5	54	9·4
Older birds	24	8·5	77	8·3	24	8·1	93	9·1	100	9·8

No. = No. clutches; Mean = mean clutch.

(b) *Mean clutch-size and age of great tits in Wytham*

Age	1961		1962		1963	
	No.	Mean	No.	Mean	No.	Mean
Yearlings	128	7·7	54	8·5	54	9·4
2	18	8·5	43	9·0	33	10·0
3	14	8·3	12	8·8	29	9·7
4			5	8·2	9	9·7
5			1	8·0	2	9·5
6					1	9·0

tits. There does not seem to be any further change in clutch-size with further increase in age (Table 10b); rather, the opposite appears to be the case. Older birds breed slightly earlier than the younger ones, thus part of the difference in clutch-size will be due to this. However, the mean difference in laying date is not enough to account for all the difference in clutch-size.

In years of population increase, there will be proportionately more young birds in the population than in years when there has been no increase, since increases occur mainly when large numbers of young birds survive. Hence the reduction in the size of clutch at higher densities will be exaggerated by the higher proportion of young birds, particularly if the change in population is large. The reverse is also likely to be true, in that when the population decreases the proportion of older birds is larger. However, these effects are usually only very small, and unlikely to be greater than 0·2 of an egg.

The figures in Table 11 show that not only did the older birds produce a slightly higher percentage of surviving young, but since their broods were also larger they produced considerably more surviving young per brood. Presumably natural selection must favour the laying of a rather smaller clutch in the first year, since those individuals which do so must, on average, raise more young.

It seems unlikely that the time of year which is most favourable for the breeding of experienced adults would not also be the best time for the younger birds. The most reasonable suggestion is that the birds cannot get into breeding condition earlier, and that

Table 11. *Survival of young great tits in relation to age of female parent*

	1960		1961 (excluding Marley)		1961 (Marley only)		1962		1963	
	Year-ling	Older	Year-ling	Older	Year-ling	Older	Year-ling	Older	Year-ling	Older
No. hatched	160	234	489	359	278	194	349	745	476	875
No. broods	23	29	73	48	37	22	45	87	52	94
Mean brood	6·9	8·1	6·7	7·5	7·5	8·8	7·8	8·5	9·1	9·3
No. recovered	40	75	45	45	11	12	55	110	66	163
Recovered (%)	25·0	32·0	9·2	12·5	4·0	6·2	15·8	14·8	13·9	18·6
No. recovered per brood	1·74	2·59	0·62	0·94	0·30	0·55	1·22	1·26	1·27	1·73

An analysis of variance done by P. H. Leslie, on the above data, showed that the differences in survival between the two age classes were significant at the 5% level.

first-year birds, not being so experienced in collecting food, are unable to get into breeding condition as early as older, more experienced birds.

Habitat

Both Lack (1955) and Kluijver (1951) have shown that the clutch-size of the great tit is affected by the habitat in which the clutch is laid. The same is true for the blue tit (Lack 1955). Since the differences were consistent there can be no doubt that they were due to some aspect of the habitat itself. This argument is strongly supported by the fact that, in both studies, the largest clutches were found in rich oak woodland and the smallest in gardens or open parkland.

These variations in clutch-size can be explained only on the basis of some form of reaction of the bird to the environment. However, the food which the birds utilize for their young is not available at the time of laying so that the birds cannot be responding to this (see also below). Hence it seems more likely that the tits respond to the general appearance of the vegetation in some way, perhaps to the number of large trees in the surroundings or to some other indicator of what the later food supply will be like. It is conceivable, though not known, that those habitats, in which there was most food for the young, were also those in which there was more early spring food for the adults; if this were true then clutch-size could be affected adaptively by the food supply for the parents.

However, since the laying dates and clutch-size do not vary in parallel in different habitats, food supply cannot be the factor influencing both.

Many of the differences shown by Kluijver and Lack were for areas of woodland situated far apart, but even within the Oxford area there is a marked difference between the mean clutch-sizes found in gardens and in woodland (Table 12). These two areas are too close to be seriously affected by different local climatic conditions and are at the same altitude. The smaller clutches in gardens cannot be due to a higher density there, at least for the great tit, since the territory size seems to be about half as large again as that in Marley during the 4 years shown. Even within Wytham, there seem to be consistent differences between the mean clutch-sizes of blue tits laying in areas of oak woodland and those laying in areas of more mixed woodland (Table 12) though this does not hold for the great tit. Perhaps the most significant point about these small differences is that they are in the same direction as those shown by Lack and Kluijver in other woods.

Table 12. *Clutch-size in relation to habitat*

	Gardens		Marley		Great Wood	
	No. pairs	Mean clutch	No. pairs	Mean clutch	No. pairs	Mean clutch
GREAT TIT						
1958	15	7·6	25	9·2	10	9·3
1959	17	7·7	41	8·8	8	8·6
1960	22	7·2	51	8·3	11	8·6
1961	39	7·8	86	8·0	21	7·9
1962	–	–	43	8·8	13	9·1
1963	–	–	39	9·2	9	9·3
Average of means		7·6		8·7		8·8
BLUE TIT						
1958	9	8·3	12	9·5	16	10·6
1959	14	9·3	20	9·6	16	10·9
1960	18	8·8	23	10·2	28	11·1
1961	17	8·9	51	8·5	32	9·8
1962	–	–	21	9·9	14	10·7
1963	–	–	41	10·6	15	12·1
Average of means		8·8		9·7		10·9

Clutches are in fact larger in good oak woodland than in poor woodland and larger in poor woodland than in gardens.

In view of this, the main types of woodland in Marley were mapped with respect to the nest-boxes. When this had been done it proved possible to separate seven areas, each being reasonably homogeneous within itself. Examination of these areas showed that three of them, A, D and G, had a large number of big trees (these being oak in A and G and wych elm, *Ulmus glabra* (Huds.), in D) with much undergrowth of nettles, *Urtica dioica* (L.), bracken and brambles, whereas B, C and E had fewer large trees and were predominantly stands of hazel with dog's mercury, *Mercurialis perennis* (L.), as a herb layer. Area F was, in profile, rather similar to the latter group though the shrub layer was of close stands of hawthorn and elder, some of which had nothing growing under them. At first it was uncertain whether F, which has a few oaks, and G, which has a few stands of blackthorn among the oaks, might not have been grouped together as intermediate between the other two groups.

As it has been shown that both the density of breeding bird and the date of laying influence the mean clutch-size, both of these factors were allowed for in the analysis of the mean clutch-size in these areas; the very large multiple regression analysis was made by Mr J. F. Scott. Using the formula

$$y = a_i + bx + cz$$

where y is the clutch-size, x the number of pairs per ac, z the number of days to the laying date after 30 March, b is $-1·54$, c is $-0·074$ and a_i is a constant specific to the ith area and thus measures the average clutch-size after adjustment for density and date, mean clutch-sizes for the great tit were derived, adjusted for 0·60 pairs per ac (1·48 pairs per ha) and a laying date of 27 April, as follows:

Area	A	B	C	D	E	F	G
Adjusted clutch-size	9·99	9·07	9·28	10·14	8·97	9·13	10·21

It will be seen that the clutch-size in area G suggests that this area is, in fact, similar to areas A and D while the clutch-size in area F suggests that this area is similar to areas B, C and E. Thus the seven areas will be treated as if they form two groups, those with many large trees and those with fewer large trees. It will be seen from the above figures that the latter have average clutch-sizes of 8·97–9·28, whereas the areas with large trees have average clutch-sizes of 9·99–10·21. The differences are highly significant ($P = 0·001$). The complete data are deposited at the Edward Grey Institute.

Apart from the tendency for the areas with larger trees to be those in which the tits lay, on average, larger clutches (as found by Kluijver (1951) and Lack (1958)) there is only one other trend in these data. This is that in areas A and D the birds start to lay slightly later than those in areas B, C and E. No satisfactory reason can be given for this.

One point slightly reduces the validity of the above differences; the analysis was done assuming that each clutch was independent of all the others. This is, of course, not so as many of the birds must have contributed clutches laid in 2 or more years. However, as most of the birds were not individually recognized, this factor could not be allowed for. In any case there are several reasons for believing that it is not important.

Firstly, the analysis extended over 15 years; only about half the adults alive in one year are alive the next, so that very few indeed will have been responsible for clutches in as many as 5 different years. There is no sign that the magnitude of the differences between the areas has altered over the period of the study, as would be expected if the differences were due mainly to particular individuals.

Several factors might produce these results. If, for example, birds bred in the habitats in which they were reared and there were inherited differences in clutch-size, small differences such as those shown might continue to be apparent for a very long period whether they were advantageous or not. Alternatively, older birds lay larger clutches than those breeding for the first time and, if such birds showed a tendency to move into the areas where there were more larger trees, larger clutches would be expected in such places. However, there is no sign that either of these possibilities actually occurs.

Food

The trends in clutch-size discussed have been explained as adaptations which enable the birds to raise the greatest number of young. This must depend on the amount of food that the parents can find for them.

Fig. 7 shows the clutch-size of the great tits in Marley for each year since 1947 and the number of caterpillars per m². A brief glance suggests that there may be some correlation at both the beginning and the end of the period, but little from 1951 to 1958. It seems certain, however, that the apparent correlations were accidental and they can be explained on the basis of trends in clutch-size in relation to the density of pairs and the date of laying that have already been established. Hence clutch-size was high in 1947 because the birds were so sparse, high in 1948 because breeding was so early, low in 1951 because breeding was so late and low in the years 1959–61 owing to the steadily increasing density of breeding birds. This was checked by a regression analysis by Mr J. F. Scott. There was no significant indication that either the caterpillar population or the clutch-size showed a serial correlation. This greatly simplified the analysis as it was then possible to do a straightforward regression on the data. When the clutch-size was adjusted for date of laying and density of pairs (see earlier), the correlation coefficient with the density of caterpillars was only −0·12, which is, of course, nowhere near significance. These findings are in agreement with Lack (1958), correcting Lack (1955).

Survival of parents in relation to the size of brood they rear

The parents which raised the largest broods did not always produce as many surviving offspring as those which raised slightly smaller broods. It was also noted that a proportion of the females were killed when their broods were taken by predatorr and, since more large than small broods were taken by predators, fewer of the parents of such broods would live to breed again.

Kluijver (1952) has shown that both parents lose weight while raising young and that they are at their lightest in June and July. It seems likely that this is due to the strain of raising a brood; similar loss of weight during breeding has been recorded for several

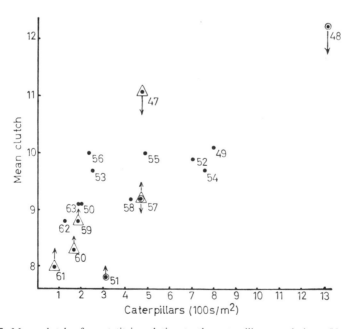

FIG. 7. Mean clutch of great tit in relation to the caterpillar populations. Years when clutch-size was affected particularly by date of breeding season (○) (48, 57 early, 51 late) or density of pairs (△) (47 low, 57, 59, 60, 61 high) are marked, and arrows show direction in which clutch-size would have been altered had conditions been average in these years.

species. The greatest strain presumably will be imposed on those birds which are endeavouring to raise the largest broods, though this point does not seem to have been examined.

Gibb (1955) records 'In the second half of the nestling period, activity was usually maintained or increased at small first broods, but slackened off at large first broods. This strongly suggests that parent great tits feeding large broods were becoming tired and so could not maintain their rate of feeding. Arnold (1952) gives a striking case where a female blue tit disappeared half-way through the nestling period. The male at first almost exactly doubled his rate of feeding to compensate for the female's absence, but after the fifteenth day fed very much more slowly. This may be typical of broods where the parent is straining to feed'.

This might be yet another selective factor favouring a smaller clutch-size. The birds that lay larger clutches would, on average, breed fewer times and thus selection would favour the genotypes of parents which laid slightly smaller clutches, but survived to breed again.

Similarly a differential survival rate of parents might be one of the reasons why the birds do not often have late broods. Gibb (1955) has data to show that the parents of late broods are straining to feed the young, and it will be remembered that the weights of late broods are low and the predation rate is higher. Thus the chances of a parent laying a later clutch and surviving to breed again are lower than those of a parent laying an early clutch. Data to test these factors properly are not yet available, and, while in 1961 there was some evidence that subsequent survival of females laying large or late clutches was lower than that of those laying smaller or early clutches, this did not appear to be true in 1962.

Statistical analysis

Many of the factors affecting clutch-size and survival in the great tit are clearly interacting. A regression analysis was made in an attempt to clarify these interactions, though it does not, of course, show which of the factors are causal. The main points are appended together here rather than scattered through the section.

1. Post-fledging survival of young was more strongly correlated with the mean weight of the brood than with the weight of the individual concerned. This is due to the fact, not mentioned above, that males are heavier than females by about 1 g on the fifteenth day. Since the nestlings could not be sexed, it was not possible to analyse survival of the two sexes separately. Hence a high mean brood-weight means a relatively heavy weight of all young, and a bird below average in such a brood is more likely to be a relatively heavy female with good chance of survival, than a lighter male.

2. The survival of the Marley young was inclined to be different from that of the young from the rest of the wood; this was especially so in 1961. So for these analyses the data for these two areas were kept separate.

3. It was obviously of extreme importance to allow for date while studying survival in relation to brood-size, since both brood-size and survival-rate were smaller later in the season. This is a point that others (e.g. Löhrl 1957; Kluijver 1963) have overlooked. The results of the analysis showed that the larger broods produced more surviving young per brood in 4 of the 6 years in the rest of Wytham and in only 2 of the 6 years in Marley. Since nearly all the large broods were artificial, the data are still biased in their favour, for the reason put forward earlier.

SECOND BROODS

The number of young raised per pair per year is dependent on both the number of young in the brood and the number of broods. Second broods are rare in oak woodland in England, where more than 5% of the pairs raise second broods only exceptionally. In similar (broad-leaved) habitats in Holland the percentage of second broods is about 35 (Kluijver 1951). In pinewoods in both countries there is a higher proportion of second broods, some 28% in England and 76% in Holland (Lack 1958; Kluijver 1951). While the difference between the two countries remains unexplained, the difference between the two habitats is clearly related to the food supply, which is better later in the summer in pinewoods than in oak woodland (see Gibb & Betts 1963).

Kluijver has, therefore, many more data on the occurrence of second broods than it has been possible to obtain in England. He found that second broods occur more frequently (i) in years when the density of breeding pairs is low, (ii) among older birds than younger ones, and (iii) in pinewoods than broad-leaved woods. Under two of these conditions (low density and in pinewoods) second clutches are laid when there is likely to be more food; in the third case they are laid more frequently by the more competent parents. Thus, like larger clutches, more second clutches are laid when there is a better chance of raising them.

The annual percentages of second broods in Wytham (Table 13) shows that some of the years when second broods occur are those when conditions might have been expected to be particularly favourable; in 1947 there was a very low density of breeding pairs and in 1948 there was an exceptionally early start to the breeding season with the highest caterpillar population of the study.

In recent years there also seems to have been a relationship between the proportion of second broods and the seasonal decline in weight of the young. Thus comparison of the seasonal weight decreases shown in Fig. 4 and the percentage of second broods (Table 13) shows a tendency for second broods to occur in those years when there was less difference in weight between the early and the later broods. Thus the parents lay second clutches in those years when they are able to find more food for their broods.

Nevertheless, although the second broods are produced in those years when there is the best hope of raising them, they are still highly unsuccessful in most years compared

Table 13. *Great tit: proportion of second broods in Wytham*

	No. of broods	Second broods (%)
1947	18	5·6
1948	38	13·2
1949	61	0
1950	35	5·7
1951	35	0
1952	20	0
1953	21	0
1954	31	0
1955	27	0
1956	24	0
1957	49	0
1958	55	0
1959	136	0
1960	147	3·8
1961	256	0
1962	184	3·8
1963	169	7·7

with the earlier broods. Thus it seems likely that there is only weak selection for having them at all in deciduous woodland in England.

DISCUSSION

Selective factors affecting breeding

1. *Date of laying*. The data in this paper show that there is great advantage in being an early breeder, but that many of the great tits do not breed early, and this can only be because something prevents them. The most likely factor seems to be that the birds are unable to get sufficient food to manufacture eggs earlier. It will be remembered the older birds breed earlier than yearlings, perhaps because, being more experienced, they are able to get enough food earlier in the season. The food taken is very varied at this time, but composed mainly of small invertebrates.

Emphasis has been laid on the condition of the female because it seems likely that the production of eggs is a greater strain on the female than the formation of sperm by the male. While the male's gonads enlarge greatly in early spring the energy required for this growth is probably much less than that required by the female to lay a clutch of eggs. Great tit eggs weigh about $1\frac{3}{4}$ g each and, since a female may lay ten to twelve eggs, this means that she will have to produce, over a period of 10–12 days, some $17\frac{1}{2}$–21 g of eggs—about her own body weight. Kluijver (1952) has shown that the weight of the female increases by about 2 g between mid-March and mid-April. However, in April the variation in weight of the females is very great; presumably this is because some females are in more advanced breeding condition than others. Since there is a great advantage in being an early breeder and no apparent advantage in breeding later, I suggest that the great tits do not inherit a tendency to breed early or late, but only the tendency to breed as early as they can. Hence presumably the variation in the weights of the females reflects the individual abilities and the local food supplies of these birds.

While I have suggested that at least some element of the spring food is sufficiently scarce to prevent many of the females from getting into breeding condition at the time which would enable them to raise the largest number of young, it must be stressed that the evidence is circumstantial. The earlier the tits breed the more young they rear; the tits are lightest in February and early March, but the females increase rapidly in weight from mid-March onwards and need a considerable amount of food to produce their eggs; finally the older birds manage to breed before the more inexperienced yearlings.

There is one fact which perhaps supports the suggestion that food must be in good supply if the tit is to be able to lay a clutch of eggs. This is that if there is a cold spell after breeding has started those individuals which have not started to lay postpone starting. Those that have started to lay complete their clutches but the rest do not start laying until 4 days after the warmer weather returns.

Insects are likely to be much less active during the cold weather and few emerge during such a period. Thus food supply is much scarcer and collecting enough to make eggs might be difficult. Those individuals that have started to lay continue to do so partly because their behaviour and physiology are arranged so that they tend to complete a clutch once they have started and partly because they have already collected some of the food required to make some of the remaining eggs. It might be expected that those great tits which complete their clutches during a cold spell might lay a slightly smaller clutch. While this is not known, Kendeigh (1952) has shown that house wrens, *Troglodytes aedon* (Vieillot), do lay smaller clutches in cold weather.

In the section on breeding season I noted that there was some difficulty in reconciling the suggestion that the birds were not laying as early as they should with the fact that there is a correlation between the time of the tits' breeding season and that of the caterpillars.

The ultimate factor to which the tits' breeding season is adapted is the food supply for the young, which leave the nest, on average, some 10–12 days after the peak of winter moth abundance. Since those that leave earlier survive much better than those that leave later it is evidently important to leave the nest when food is still plentiful. Yet many of the young leave later than the time when food is most abundant.

Interesting support for this suggestion that the female great tit finds it difficult to collect enough food to manufacture eggs comes from Royama's work in Japan (Royama, in preparation); he observed that the female starts begging for food from the male as soon as she has started laying. From this time onwards the male feeds the female about five times an hour throughout the laying period (i.e. some seventy meals per day and about 30% of the females' daily food). Such feeding has been called courtship feeding, but one would expect selection to have established the habit of the male trying to help the female obtain sufficient food if it is in short supply.

Hence, although there is presumably selective pressure towards breeding at the best time in relation to the caterpillars, the time at which they actually get into breeding condition is not related to the caterpillars' season but to the supply of spring food. (The supply of spring food, like the timing of the caterpillar season, is probably largely affected by the weather. This would explain why the tits' breeding season is approximately correlated to the time of caterpillar abundance since both the spring food supply and the caterpillar season are likely to be similarly affected by the spring weather.)

Many points remain to be elucidated before this suggestion can be considered proved but there is, perhaps, one main reason for treating the idea with caution. This is that many other species vary their clutch in the same way as the great tit, the first clutches being largest and a steady decrease in clutch-size occurring throughout the season. It seems likely that, as in the great tit, the largest clutches are laid at the time at which they can be most easily reared, and that selection has favoured the laying of smaller clutches later in the season because it is not possible to rear quite such large broods at this time. Thus the first birds to lay rear the largest number of young and the others would be more successful if they laid earlier.

Not only do other insectivores vary in their clutch-size in this manner, e.g. the collared flycatcher (Löhrl 1957) and the wood warbler, *Phylloscopus sibilatrix* (E. Lack 1950), but so also do some sea-birds, e.g. the kittiwake, *Rissa tridactyla* (Coulson & White 1958). Thus, if my suggestion is correct, it seems likely that many of the individuals of these species are also not breeding at the time which would result in the production of the maximum number of young, but that they are breeding as early as the females can produce their eggs.

Lack (1958) has suggested that 'it is unlikely that the physical condition of the female tits in April could be so critical as to offset the selective advantage of raising as many young as possible'. Nevertheless it has been shown that many of the tits are not breeding at the most opportune time. While I agree with Lack's suggestion that there will be very strong selection for birds to breed at the most advantageous time for the nestlings, it does seem as if many of the birds may not do so, and I believe that some factor is preventing them. If no birds could get into breeding condition by the most opportune time then those birds which bred closest to this time would be the ones that would produce most young. The difficulty remains of explaining the continued presence in the population of a large number of birds which are breeding when the most advantageous time has passed.

As mentioned earlier, the most reasonable suggestion that I can offer is that the great tit does not inherit a tendency to breed early or late, but merely the tendency to breed as early as it can. In this way it is not necessary to postulate an advantage for late breeding, the late breeders being the birds which, had they been able to do so, would have bred earlier.

As early as 1871 Darwin wrote 'there can also be no doubt that the most vigorous, best nourished and earliest breeders would, on average, succeed in rearing the largest number of fine offspring'. R. A. Fisher (1929), quoting Darwin, goes on to say 'whether this is so or not is difficult to say, but it should be noted that the dates of the breeding phenomena of a species could only be stabilized if birds congenitally prone to breed early did not for this reason produce more offspring. The correlation required by Darwin's theory must be due solely to non-hereditary causes, such as chance variations of nutrition might supply'.

2. *Production of young.* Several factors affect the clutch-size of the tits. Although they may not all be influencing the birds simultaneously, usually several of them are affecting the clutch-size at any one time, either directly, or indirectly through the time of laying. Moreover, apart from the factors established, the reasons why, in Marley, the birds that are in the apparently good habitats lay consistently later than the birds in the poorer ones remain to be explained. Thus there must be at least one further factor which is affecting the time of laying. Nor is it by any means clear that all the different times of laying can be explained in terms of availability of food for the adults prior to laying.

In this paper it has been assumed that the birds inherit the ability to vary the size of the clutch within certain limits, the limits being different in genotypes. Thus, a bird which inherits the tendency to lay a large clutch will lay clutches of different sizes in years of high or low density, in good or poor habitats, etc., but in all these conditions its clutch-size will be above average for the conditions prevailing.

It might be supposed that the clutch-size was limited by the physiological requirements of the birds and that the smaller clutches were laid by those birds which failed to get as much food as those that laid the larger clutches. While food supply might limit the clutch-size under exceptional circumstances, such as for instance, unusually cold weather which started after the birds commenced laying, it seems very unlikely that it normally does so, for the following reasons. Firstly, the later the birds breed the smaller the clutch they lay, in spite of the fact that there is less food for the early breeders and food increases rapidly during the first part of the breeding season. Even if an early breeder (laying a large clutch) loses its clutch and lays a replacement the second clutch is smaller, about the size of the normal for that time of year. Secondly if an early breeder loses its clutch while laying it will move to another box and lay another. The combined total for the two clutches is usually well in excess of the size of a single clutch.

Hence, once food has become sufficiently common for laying to start it seems unlikely that the birds are forced to terminate their clutch by shortage of food, because it is normally becoming progressively more common. It seems more probable that clutch completion is the result of selection for the most productive clutch-size.

From the evolutionary point of view, while it is of selective advantage to rear as many healthy young as possible, in Wytham there is a limit to which clutch-size can be raised without resulting in fewer healthy young being raised (Lack *et al.* 1957). It is believed that a similar situation exists under the other conditions discussed, namely that at some point an increase of one in clutch-size leads, on average, to the production of fewer, rather than more, surviving young. The most productive clutch-size will probably be different in different conditions. At least four factors affect the clutch-size in the Oxford area, namely habitat, date of laying, density of pairs and age of female. In each case, smaller clutches are laid in the conditions that are less suitable for raising a larger one, either when there will be less food or when the parent is less capable.

There is no evidence that the tits can predict the level of the caterpillar populations. It seems likely, therefore, that the tits are not modifying the size of their clutches directly to the food supply for the young, but are adjusting the clutches by reaction to other factors such as, perhaps, the appearance of the habitat. Thus areas of large trees usually carry more food than areas where there are few large trees; nesting at the start of the season means that there will be more food for the young; fewer competitors result in there being more food for each, and so on. By responses of this kind the birds lay clutches which are overall, but not always, well fitted to the conditions.

With this in view it is worth remembering that 1960 was a year in which the overall survival was the best during the study. However, the clutches were only of average size, and it is tempting to suggest that this was a year when the tits could have laid larger clutches, but that they failed to take the opportunity. In 1961 there were exceptionally large numbers of breeding pairs in Marley and although they laid small clutches accordingly, caterpillars were very scarce (the lowest population during the study) and some birds had difficulty in raising even small broods. While the mean clutch was about the normal for oak woodland in Britain, the birds would almost certainly have been more successful with smaller broods still.

Similarly perhaps the great tits in pinewoods, described by Lack (1955) and Gibb & Betts (1963), were responding as they would have in oak woodland. However, they were in pinewood where the food supply is very different from that in oak woodland. In pinewoods caterpillars are relatively scarce at the time when they are most abundant in oak woodland. Nevertheless the pattern of laying of the great tits is the same in pinewoods as it is in oak woods. The first birds to lay have the largest clutches and clutch-size decreases throughout the season. The result is that the first broods are very unsuccessful, the young weighing, on average, 14·4 g on the fifteenth day (as opposed to 19·0 g in Wytham) which is almost certainly too little for many of them to survive. The second broods (more common than in deciduous woodland) fare better partly because they are smaller anyway and partly because there are more caterpillars at this time. Even so, the chicks of these smaller broods are lighter (17·7 g) than those of the larger first broods in oak woodland.

Thus, in pinewoods, the tits vary their clutches in a similar manner to those in deciduous woodland but, because the food supply is so different, they are not nearly so successful in rearing their young. It must be assumed that the birds respond to factors in pinewood in just the same way as they do in deciduous woodland. Pinewoods are not a natural habitat in England and thus, until recently, the English great tit has had no reason to adapt to pinewood and, even now, no areas of pine in England are large enough for a population of great tits to become genetically isolated there.

The data available lead me to the tentative conclusion that, while the spring food may be of chief importance in enabling the birds to get into breeding condition early, it does not affect the size of their clutch. The latter is determined partly by response to the various external factors like the breeding density, the date of laying and the habitat, and partly by the genetic constitution of the bird.

It has not been explained why the tits which breed in a late season should lay a smaller clutch than those breeding in an early season as shown in both Wytham and Holland.

There is no reason to believe that food is shorter in a late season than in an early one, since the caterpillars are as late in hatching as the tits are in starting to lay. Nor is there any evidence that the survival of caterpillars is poorer in a late spring than in an early one. Thus I cannot see any adaptive advantage for laying smaller clutches in a later season. It is possible that there has been such strong selection for reduction of clutch-size within one season that a response has been evolved by which the tits lay a clutch of a certain size at a certain time of year. This might conflict with a possible response which enabled the birds to lay the same size of clutch at the beginning of a season regardless of whether the season was early or late.

Therefore I suggest that there has been strong selection for those birds which could lay a large clutch at the beginning of the season, but laid a smaller clutch if they were not able to start breeding so early. By far the most likely factor to influence the tits is the increase in day-length, a factor well known to stimulate breeding in many species (see Marshall 1961 for review). Indeed Suomalainen (1937) succeeded in getting both sexes of great tits into breeding condition (as judged by gonad size) in February by keeping the birds in artificial light of longer duration than day-length.

In conclusion it is clear that the great tit shows a remarkable series of responses to the external conditions when laying its clutch, although the mechanism by which it does so is not understood. The birds are not able to forecast the food supply directly and their responses are based only on the conditions normal to a given set of circumstances and, while they lay a size of clutch that is reasonably well adapted to local conditions, they sometimes respond inappropriately when these are exceptional. In addition, since conditions for rearing young vary so much from year to year, the most productive clutch-size varies also. Because of this a fairly wide range of clutch-sizes is still found in any population, presumably because each has been the most productive too frequently for it to have been eliminated by natural selection.

REFERENCES

Arnold, G. A. & Arnold, M. A. (1952). The nesting of a pair of Blue Tits. *Br. Birds*, **45**, 175–80.

Betts, M. M. (1955). The behaviour of a pair of Great Tits at the nest. *Br. Birds*, **48**, 77–82.

Betts, M. M. (1955). The food of titmice in oak woodland. *J. Anim. Ecol.* **24**, 282–323.

Coulson, J. C. & White, E. (1958). The effect of age on the breeding biology of the Kittiwake, *Rissa tridactyla*. *Ibis*, **100**, 40–51.

Cramp, S., Pettet, A. & Sharrock, J. T. R. (1960). The irruption of tits in autumn 1957. *Br. Birds*, **53**, 49–77, 99–117, 176–92.

Darwin, C. (1871). *Descent of Man and Selection in Relation to Sex*. (Quoted here from 2nd edn., 1890, London)

Fisher, R. A. (1929). *The Genetical Theory of Natural Selection*. (Quoted here from edition of Dover Publications, 1958.)

Gibb, J. A. (1950). The breeding biology of the Great and Blue Titmice. *Ibis*, **92**, 507–39.

Gibb, J. A. (1954a). Population changes of titmice, 1947–1951. *Bird Study*, **1**, 40–8.

Gibb, J. A. (1954b). Feeding ecology of tits, with notes on treecreeper and goldcrest. *Ibis*, **96**, 513–43.

Gibb, J. A. (1955). Feeding rates of great tits. *Br. Birds*, **48**, 49–58.

Gibb, J. A. (1960). Populations of tits and goldcrests and their food supply in pine plantations. *Ibis*, **102**, 163–208.

Gibb, J. A. & Betts, M. M. (1963). Food and food supply of nestling tits (Paridae) in Breckland pine. *J. Anim. Ecol.* **32**, 489–533.

Haartman, L. von (1954). Clutch-size in polygamous species. *Acta XIth int. orn. Congr.*, 450–3.

Hartley, P. H. T. (1953). An ecological study of the feeding habits of the English titmice. *J. Anim. Ecol.* **22**, 261–88.

Hinde, R. A. (1952). The behaviour of the Great Tit (*Parus major*) and some other related species. *Behaviour*, Suppl. **2**.

Jenkins, D., Watson, A. & Miller, G. R. (1963). Population studies on red grouse, *Lagopus lagopus scoticus* (Lath.) in north-east Scotland. *J. Anim. Ecol.* **32**, 317–76.

Kendeigh, S. C. (1952). Parental care and its evolution in birds. *Illinois biol. Monogr.* **22**, Nos. 1–3, 1–356.

Kluijver, H. N. (1950). Daily routines of the Great Tit, *Parus m. major* L. *Ardea*, **38**, 99–135.

Kluijver, H. N. (1951). The population ecology of the Great Tit, *Parus m. major* L. *Ardea*, **39**, 1–135.

Kluijver, H. N. (1952). Notes on body weight and time of breeding in the Great Tit, *Parus m. major* L. *Ardea*, **40**, 123–41.

Kluijver, H. N. (1963). The determination of reproductive rates in Paridae. *Acta XIIth int. orn. Congr.*, 706–16.

Kratzig, H. (1939). Untersuchungen zur Seidlungsbiologie waldbewohnender Höhlenbrüter. *Dt. Vogelwelt Beihefte*, **1**, 1–96.

Lack, D. (1947). Significance of clutch-size. *Ibis*, **89**, 302–52.

Lack, D. (1954). *The Natural Regulation of Animal Numbers*. Oxford.

Lack, D. (1955). British tits (*Parus* spp.) in nesting boxes. *Ardea*, **43**, 50–84.

Lack, D. (1958). A quantitative breeding study of British Tits. *Ardea*, **46**, 91–124.

Lack, D. (1964). A long-term study of the great tit (*Parus major*). *J. Anim. Ecol.* **33**, (Suppl.), 159–73.

Lack, D., Gibb, J. A. & Owen, D. F. (1957). Survival in relation to brood-size in tits. *Proc. zool. Soc. Lond.* **128**, 313–26.

Lack, E. (1950). Breeding season and clutch-size of the Wood Warbler. *Ibis*, **92**, 95–8.

Löhrl, H. (1957). Populationsökologische Untersuchungen beim Halsbandschnäpper (*Ficedula albicollis*). *Bonn. zool. Beitr.* **2**, 130–77.

Marshall, A. J. (1961). *Biology and Comparative Physiology of Birds*, Vol. II. New York.

Moreau, R. E. (1947). Relations between number in brood, feeding rate and nestling period in nine species of birds in Tanganyika Territory. *J. Anim. Ecol.* **16**, 205–9.

Richdale, L. E. (1957). *A Population Study of Penguins*. Oxford.

Snow, D. W. (1958). *A Study of Blackbirds*. London.

Suomalainen, H. (1937). The effect of temperature on the sexual activity of non-migratory birds, stimulated by artificial lighting. *Ornis fenn.* **14**, 108–12.

Tollenaar, D. (1922). Legperioden en eierproductie bij eenige wilde vogelsoorten, vergeleken met die bij hoenderassen. *Meded. LandbHoogesch. Wageningen*, **23**, (2), 1–46.

Turcek, F. J. (1955). Doplnkyk ekologickej analyze populacie vtakov a cicavcov prirodzeneho lasa na polane. (Slovensko). *Lesn. Sb.* **1**, 23–44.

Ulfstrand, S. (1962). On the nonbreeding ecology and migratory movements of the Great Tit (*Parus major*) and the Blue Tit (*Parus caeruleus*) in Southern Sweden. *Vår. Fågelvärld.* (suppl.) **3**, 1–145.

Ulfstrand, S. (1963). Ecological aspects of irruptive bird migration in northwestern Europe. *Acta XIIIth int. orn. Congr.*, 780–94.

Wynne-Edwards, V. C. (1962). *Animal Dispersion in Relation to Social Behaviour*. Edinburgh.

Reproduced from the *Journal of Animal Ecology* 34:601–648, 1965, with permission of the British Ecological Society. [Shortened]

A GENERAL THEORY OF CLUTCH SIZE

Martin L. Cody

It is possible to think of organisms as having a certain limited amount of time or energy available for expenditure, and of natural selection as that force which operates in the allocation of this time or energy in a way which maximizes the contribution of a genotype to following generations. This manner of treatment of problems concerning the adaptation of phenotypes is called the "Principle of Allocation" (Levins and MacArthur, unpublished), and one of its applications might be the formulation of a general theory to account for clutch size in birds. At this stage we will assume that clutch size is a hereditary phenotypic characteristic which can be affected to a greater or lesser extent by the prevailing environmental conditions and which exhibits the normal variability of such characteristics. Lack (1954) discusses the validity of several hypotheses which attempt to account for clutch size and its variation under different circumstances and conditions, all of which were rejected in favor of his now widely accepted theory that clutch size is adapted to a limited food supply. This paper is an attempt to show that this and other existing hypotheses when taken singly are inadequate in some respect to account for all the data, that each holds for some particular set of conditions, and that each is but a part of the complete explanation. The theories will be dealt with individually and it will be shown that as environment varies so will the factors which determine clutch size.

PRESENTATION OF THE THEORY

It is known that in temperate regions, because periodic local catastrophes reduce and maintain populations below the carrying capacity, K, of the habitat, natural selection is proceeding to maximize r, the reproductive rate (Fisher, 1929, whose fundamental theorem is density independent). In these regions any phenotypic variation which enables parents to leave more offspring will be selected for. Any increase in clutch size, up to a limit determined by natural resources, would suffice to increase the reproductive rate. In the tropics, however, with a more climatically stable environment where the advent of such catastrophes is rare, populations will be at saturation densities, and any adaptive variations which will increase the carrying capacity $\bar{K}$ will usually be favored by natural selection (MacArthur, 1962). Increasing $\bar{K}$ is equivalent to increasing the population density with the same resources, or maintaining the population density with decreased resources. Whereas in unstable regions all energy was perforce utilized to increase r, an individual living in a stable environment well suited to the needs of the species would need to spend much less energy on maximizing r than individuals living elsewhere. By the "Principle of Allocation," maximum contribution to future generations will be achieved by those individuals which utilize, to increase $\bar{K}$, some of the energy conserved by reducing r. Such individuals will be favored by natural selection over others which do not allocate surplus energy to this end. We can guess suitable recipients for the conserved energy, possible candidates for its use being predator avoidance, more successful intraspecific competition (i.e., reduction in resource density necessary for maintained existence), or perhaps devoting more energy per individual to the raising of the young. All these considerations could serve to increase the contribution to future generations. Such energy requirements or drains, together with the number of eggs laid, may

28

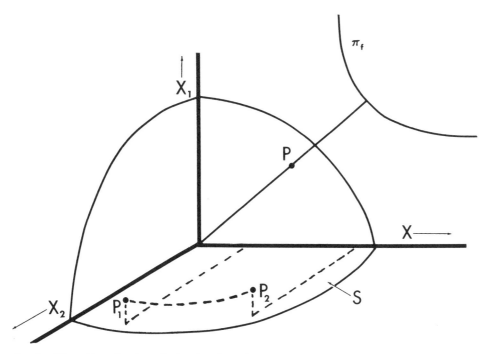

FIG. 1. Three-dimensional graph showing the point of intersection P of the surface of phenotypes S with the "adaptive function" π_f. The phenotype P receives benefits proportional to its intercepts on the axes X, X_1, and X_2, resulting from dividing its energy between clutch size, avoiding predators and competitive ability respectively.

all be operating simultaneously and can be considered as acting along the axes of a multidimensional graph. Distance along the axes represents not the actual amount of energy spent, but the advantage gained by the individual who spends that amount of energy on that particular requirement. Measurable quantities such as clutch size can be substituted as units for the purpose of this argument. Representing increasing clutch size along the X-axis, two other energy drains can be represented along X_1 and X_2 in a three-dimensional figure (Fig. 1). All possible allocations of energy to these three requirements—clutch size, predator avoidance, and competition—can be represented as points comprising a surface S and the volume under it in the figure. Every point of the surface S can be considered as a phenotype having the strategy indicated by the proportions of the available energy to be spent on the factors represented by the three axes. Using the

coordinates shown in the figure, phenotypes at the vertices of the solid farthest out along the axes, will be concentrating their energy on either laying many eggs, avoiding enemies, or competing more efficiently for resources. Since a jack-of-all-trades policy often brings greater returns than a specialist policy, the ability to avoid predators will rise appreciably when a large clutch is sacrificed for a slightly smaller one. Reasoning likewise with the other two combinations of axes, we deduce the convex nature of the surface S which, together with the enclosed space, represents all possible phenotypes. We can now consider the strategy which maximizes the number of descendants for a particular species and environment and is favored by natural selection over the many alternatives as that point where a surface π touches S tangentially. π is an "adaptive function" for the environmental conditions, the position of which varies in relation to the surface as the relative importance of the coordinates changes. π_f consists of all points of equal fitness, f (see Levins, 1962), and the most fit phenotype, or most apt strategy, is that represented by a point P which lies both on S and the π_f with largest f. The fitness or suitability, f, of a phenotype for certain conditions increases with the perpendicular distance of π_f from the origin, because the farther out a point is on lines radiating from the origin, the greater are the advantages obtained along the axes (bigger intercepts) and the more fit becomes the phenotype. So the one point which lies farthest from the origin on S and on the farthest π indicates the best strategy. Different environments will select different optimum phenotypes. As the relative importance of one coordinate, say competitive ability, increases, the adaptive surface π will rotate toward that coordinate, resulting in an optimal phenotype which has sacrificed some egg-laying ability for increased competitive ability. So the position of P and hence clutch size, the intercept of P on the X-axis, will vary with the environmental conditions.

EXISTING THEORIES OF CLUTCH SIZE

That a bird is limited physiologically from laying more eggs is a view which finds little acceptance today. There are numerous instances of birds laying more eggs than their normal clutch when eggs are removed at laying. And yet there are groups, e.g., Procellariiformes, which lay one egg and usually do not replace it if lost. This seems a great waste of reproductive potential, and this theory might be the correct answer to account for the low r, especially as petrels lay eggs notably large for the size of the bird. But then, if natural selection has brought the ruddy duck (*Oxyura jamaicensis*) to lay a clutch three times its own weight (Kortright, 1943), surely the same could apply to a petrel given the same environmental conditions if it were advantageous to the species. It is apparent that this group of birds, living in the most stable coastal environment, are at a fairly constant maximum

density as determined by the resources, and the importance of increasing r is small. Denoting X_1 and X_2 as shown in Fig. 1, large X_2 and small X_1 (predation being low) intercepts indicate strategy P_1 as shown, having a very small X intercept (clutch size).

The second hypothesis, again not a popular one, states that clutch size is limited by the number of eggs a parent can cover. This seems plausible when we consider that many ground-nesting birds have large clutches, this being a nest-site obviously conducive to holding many eggs. However, most of the large clutches of ground-nesters belong to gallinaceous birds, in which the young are not heavily dependent on the parents for food. Therefore, the largest number of eggs which can be covered, or young which can be brooded (shelter probably being very important), whichever is the lower, will determine clutch size. This being a limitation which does not vary with environment, we expect clutch size to be invariably high (large X intercept). Ground-nesters which do feed young have much smaller clutches (*Caprimulgus, Sterna, Alauda*).

A third theory is that clutch size is adjusted "to balance mortality," but it has been pointed out by Lack (1947, 1949, 1954) that there is no proven mechanism to carry out this adjustment, convenient though such a system would be. The "balancing mortality" theory implies altruism, that birds possess a self-regulatory mechanism whereby recruits just compensate for losses. We cannot see how natural selection could operate in successive years to favor that clutch which would bring the population back to its optimum. Birds which laid larger clutches would naturally come to predominate, if conditions allowed the survival of these clutches, to the detriment of any or all altruistic members of the population which lay the supposedly optimal clutch for that season. There is perhaps one conceivable way in which a population could balance its mortality, and that is a behavioral one. There have been certain cases documented in which popula-

TABLE 1. *Effect of variations in food supply on clutch size.*

Species	Conditions average or below	Conditions above average	Reference
Nutcracker, *Nucifraga caryocatactes*	poor nutcrop previous year, av. clutch = c/3	good nutcrop av. clutch = c/4	Swanberg, in Lack, 1954
Barn owl, *Tyto alba*	normal clutch = c/3 in this part of Africa	clutch size during mouse plague = c/7	Fuggles-Couchman, in Moreau, 1944
Ploceus velatus	dry season, 10% c/4, 90% c/3	good rainfall, 90% c/4, 10% c/3	Hoesch, in Moreau, 1944
Bay-breasted warbler, *Dendroica castanea*	non-budworm years 4 c/4, 8 c/5, 5 c/6 av. = c/5.1	budworm years 1 c/4, 5 c/5, 15 c/6, 3 c/7, av. = c/5.8 (significantly higher)	MacArthur, 1958

tion density has been shown to be inversely proportional to clutch size, but it is just as difficult to see how natural selection could accomplish this. Kluijver (1951) showed this relation for *Parus major*, and also that the same inverse relation holds for numbers of broods and density. Given that this relationship obtains, and is adhered to by all members of the population, here is a possible and sufficient mechanism to ensure a constant optimum density, on the average. Thus a greatly depleted population will have a correspondingly high clutch size, and as density increases under the influence of this high clutch, the latter will decrease accordingly. Large or small overwinter losses can be accommodated in this way. Many examples of density-fecundity relationships are given by Wynne-Edwards (1962), observed both in laboratory and field populations. We would now interpret this as follows, that as population density increases, numbers approach $\overline{K}$, and advantage is removed from high r with a corresponding reduction in clutch size. The greatest difficulty in assessing the value of such relationships is that of divorcing density and food supply, and it is undoubtedly the latter which is the more appropriate factor in many cases; the inversely proportional density and clutch size may be an incidental result of the directly proportional food supply and clutch size.

Lack's (1954) views that parents rear the average maximum number of young possible, given the prevailing conditions and food supply, that one clutch size is optimal for a species in a locality in any particular year, and that this is the clutch size that will be favored by natural selection in that year is supported by much data for temperate passerines and near-passerines. It is also supported indirectly by observed variances in clutch size with food supply (Table 1). Evidence does show one optimum clutch size per season, as revealed either by the greatest number of fledglings reared from intermediate clutch size (as in *Apus apus*, Lack and Lack, 1951) or by the greatest post-fledging survival from an intermediate clutch size in those species which show approximately the same fledging success for several clutch sizes (*Sturnus vulgaris* and *Parus major*, Lack, 1954). Examples of variation in clutch size with food supply are assembled in Table 1, which illustrates how independent of rigid genetic control clutch size may become. Influence of food-gathering conditions, not on clutch size but on differential survival, is seen in swifts (Lack and Lack, 1951) in which c/3 and c/2 yield 0.9 and 1.0 fledglings, respectively, in a bad year (below average sunshine) and 2.3 and 1.9 fledglings, respectively, in a good year. Non-passerines are also subject to a food limitation, as is seen in the case of the short-eared owls (*Asio flammeus*), snowy owls (*Nyctea nyctea*) and pomatorhine skuas (*Stercorarius pomarinus*), all of which prey on lemmings (*Dicrostonyx*) in northern Alaska. Population density is one per three to four square miles, one per two to four square miles, and 18 per square mile, respectively, in peak lemming years, zero, one per two to four square miles, and four per square mile in intermediate years, and no breeding takes place in years of low density (Pitelka *et al.*, 1955). It is agreed here that because of the adaptive nature of clutch size, parents are rearing as many young as will maximize their contribution to the next generation and that in the above cases the limiting factor is food.

Clutch Size and Latitude

The increase of clutch size with latitude is a phenomenon which has been recognized by ornithologists for many years (Moreau, 1944, pp. 286–287). The only reasonable attempt to account for this trend is that of Lack (1947) who maintained that food supply is limiting in the tropics as in the temperate zones. He accounted for the increase in clutch size by considering that increasing day length from the equator gave parents a longer time per day to find food, and consequently larger broods could be reared. Support for this was forthcoming from data on the raven (*Corvus corax*) and the crossbill (*Loxia curvirostra*), both of which nest before the March equinox in northern Europe and show an increase in clutch size toward the equator. The theory does not easily account for species which feed young and do not increase clutch size with latitude (many Corvidae, Sulidae, Falconiformes, Charadriiformes), or species which do not feed young and do increase clutch size with latitude (Anatidae —see Fig. 2.4, Rallidae). Even more interesting are the tropical species which nest before the equinox (many tropical Passerines nest in the dry season, January to March). These show a large increase in clutch size from the equator northward, although day length decreases with north latitude (Skutch, 1954, 1960). It is also interesting that nocturnal mammals show increased litter size with latitude (Lord, 1960).

The more stable an environment is for a species, the greater the incidence of selec-

tion for $\overline{K}$ in populations of that species, and the more inter- and intraspecific competition will occupy the time and energy of the species, with a consequent reduction in clutch size. We therefore expect that clutch size will be inversely proportional to the climatic stability of the habitat, and as this stability decreases on moving north or south from the equator, clutch size will increase correspondingly. The latitude/ clutch size graphs in Fig. 2 illustrating this relationship have been compiled from sources listed in the bibliography. A discussion of the individual examples mentioned in the figure footnote will be found below, as well as discussion of differences in the distribution of points and steepness of slopes. We may now relate these graphs to the theoretical model presented earlier. Degree of environmental stability, as we infer this to be directly proportional to energy spent on competition, may be represented along the X_2 axis in Fig. 3, and all points of equal stability on S are given by the intersection of S and a plane perpendicular to X_2 and parallel to X and X_1.

Before we can denote the path described on S by the optimal phenotype as the adaptive function changes from one suitable at high latitudes to one suitable at low latitudes, we need to know the relationship between X_2 and X_1, the axis along which energy spent avoiding predation is represented. Students of tropical birds have often remarked on the heavy predation losses sustained by their subjects at breeding. Skutch (1949, 1954, 1960), perhaps the most experienced observer in this field, emphasized that nest predation in the tropics is far greater than in temperate counterparts, to the extent that he has postulated the necessity for a reduced number of trips to the nest with food for the young, and hence a better chance of escaping the detection of a watching predator, as a possible reason for low clutch size in the tropics. He further observed that the habit, apparently widely developed among forest birds, of bringing to the nest large morsels seldom and thereby cutting visits to a minimum, might be an adaptation

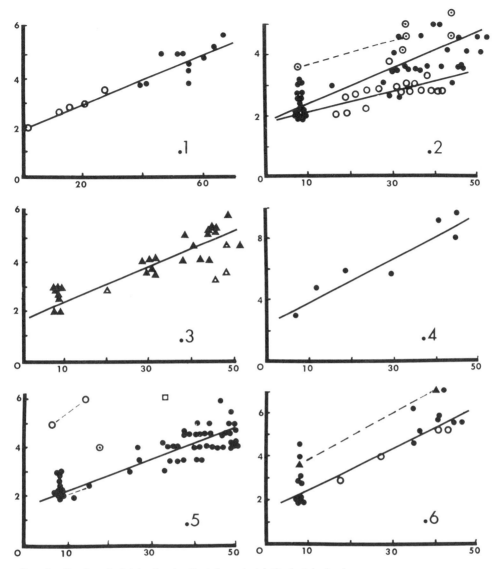

FIG. 2. Graphs of clutch size (ordinate) against latitude (abscissa).

2.1—the genus *Emberiza*. ◯ = species nesting in Africa south of the equator; ● = species nesting in Europe and Asia. The two sets of points fit the same line.

2.2—the family Tyrannidae. ◯ = South American species; ● = North American species ($p \ll$ 0.001 that the lines fitting these two sets of points have the same slope); ☉ = the genus *Myiarchus* (hole nesters); ☉---☉ = *Myiarchus tuberculifer*.

2.3—the family Icteridae. ▲ = North American species; △ = South American species.

2.4—the genus *Oxyura* (family Anatidae), worldwide distribution.

2.5—the "superfamily" Thraupidae plus Parulidae, in Central and North America. ●---● = *Myioborus miniatus*; ◯---◯ = *Tanagra lauta* (hole nester); ☉ = *Tanagra luteicapilla* (niche nester); ☐ = *Prothonotaria citrea* (hole nester).

2.6—the family Troglodytidae. ◯ = South American species; ● = North American species; ▲---▲ = *Troglodytes aedon*.

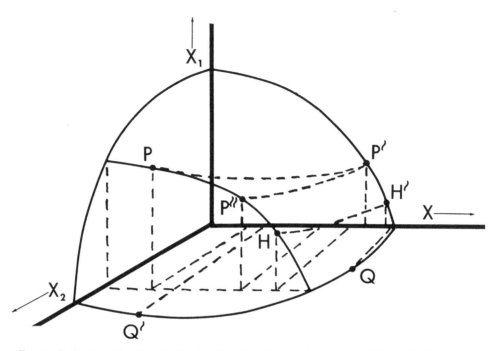

FIG. 3. Paths traced by the adaptive function from temperate to tropical latitudes for mainland open-nesting passerines ($P'----P$), predation-free species ($P'----P''$), hole-nesters ($H'----H$) and island-nesting species ($Q----Q'$).

to reduce nest predation. The work of Snow (1962) on *M. manacus*, in which the young of only 19 per cent of 227 nests reached fledgling over five years of observation confirms this high rate of loss to nest enemies, as at least 158 of these failures could be attributed to predation. Such losses from this cause are not nearly so great in temperate regions (Lack, 1954). If we now let P' be the strategy of a species nesting in the temperate, with low predation, low stability, and therefore a high clutch, the optimal phenotype will describe a curve PP', where P represents the strategy in the tropics, a region of high predation and high stability, resulting in a small intercept on X and a low clutch size.

PREDICTIONS FROM THE THEORY

Let us first consider stable environments. We have asserted above that reduced clutches in the tropics are the indirect result of climatic stability. If this is indeed so, and we have correctly deduced the most pertinent factors involved, then we should be able to predict that reduced clutch sizes will be found in any environment characterized by its stable conditions. Moreau (1944), when comparing species inhabiting evergreen forests in equatorial Africa with close relatives occupying more seasonal habitats at the same latitude (and therefore receiving the same amount of light per day), found that in eight cases the forest birds had lower clutches, in two cases the opposite, and in 12 instances no change in clutch size could be detected (by t-test, these data have a 75 per cent probability of significance). Specifically, a caprimulgid which nests in the forest lays one egg, while all other members of its family in the Old World and in North America lay two eggs.

Oceanic islands, well known for the great climatic stability they enjoy, ought to show decreased clutches from the mainland at the same latitude, and indeed this is the case (Table 2). See also Lack (1947, pp.

34

TABLE 2. *Differences between island and mainland clutch sizes at the same latitude.*

Species or genus	For temperate islands off the coast of New Zealand[1] Average mainland clutch	Average island clutch	Species or genus	For tropical islands in the Caribbean[2] Average mainland clutch	Average island clutch
Anas	8 (3 sp.)	3.5(1 sp.)	Saltator albicollis	2.0	2.5
Bowdleria punctata	3.1	2.5	Tangara gyrola	2.0	2.0
Gerygone	4.5(1 sp.)	4.0(1 sp.)	Habia rubica	2.3	2.0
Petroica macrocephala	3.5	3.0	Cacicus cela	2.0	2.0
Miro australis	2.6	2.5	Coereba flaveola	2.5	2.5
Anthornis melanura	3.5	3.0	Empidonax euleri	2.0	3.0
Cyanoramphus novaezelandeae	6.5	4.0	Elaenia flavogaster	2.3	2.5

[1] Species considered were either indigenous to the offshore islands and had a mainland relative in the same genus, or were subspecifically distinct on the island. The difference between the mainland and island means is 90 per cent significant, by *t*-test.

[2] Species on isolated West Indian islands are compared to the mainland, and also the extreme southerly Lesser Antillean islands (isolated) are compared to Trinidad, which is very close to the mainland. The means are not significantly different.

308–309). To exhibit an "island effect" (i.e., reduced clutch size), the island must be sufficiently isolated that mainland immigrants, which lay a larger clutch, do not swamp the island population, and the typical island clutch size is kept at the lower level. I have taken the subspeciation of island forms as an indication of sufficient isolation to fulfill this requirement. As well as possessing an impoverished fauna in general, most islands have no predators whatsoever, either on adult birds (most island bird lists are without accipiters or falcons) or on nests (snakes and mammals, among the chief nest predators at lower latitudes, are poor colonizers and are absent from most islands), a fact which probably accounts for the evolution of many flightless species (rails and ducks) on islands. Lack of predation puts island strategies in the XX_2 plane in the figure, and if Q represents the strategy on an island at the same latitude as the temperate mainland but having a much milder, fairly stable climate, and Q' the strategy on a tropical island, perhaps even more stable than the opposite mainland, $Q'Q$ is the path of optimum strategies of island birds from high latitudes to the equator. Consequently, although temperate islands should have reduced clutch sizes, tropical island clutch sizes, if different at all, will be only slightly

higher or slightly lower than those on the mainland, depending on the relative increase of predation on the mainland which determines the X-intercept of P, or the relative increase of stability on the island which will alter the X-intercept of Q. This prediction is also verified in Table 2 which shows that in some cases lack of predation permits a larger clutch size on tropical islands not compensated for by increased stability on the island. In many others the difference in clutch size will be perhaps only fractional (of an egg), requiring a detailed study of many nests to reveal it.

Coastal areas of continents are more stable climatically than central regions, and as we would expect if the theory is correct, clutch size increases from the coast inland (Lack, 1947, for Europe). This phenomenon is well observed in the United States, which has an extremely mild west coast, in contrast to the center of the continent where violent storms are of common occurrence. Thus, many birds (see, for example, Bent, 1938, p. 302, for the great horned owl, *Bubo virginianus*) lay their largest clutches in the midwest (between about 86° and 96° east longitude), an area which includes those states most familiar with severe winters and storms. A study by Johnston (1960) of clutch size in song sparrows, *Melospiza melodia*, revealed not only a gradual latitudinal increase from Baja California (3.05 eggs) to Alaska (4.17), but an increase from the Pacific coast east to Ohio (4.15) at which latitude the coastal sparrows lay 3.65 eggs. Presumably by taking advantage of the coastal climate, a few hummingbirds (Trochilidae) reach British Columbia, while one species, *Selasphorus rufus*, reaches Alaska (61° N). Mountainous areas are more unstable and unpredictable in their climate than adjacent lowlands, which accounts for the general trend for species nesting at high altitudes to lay larger clutches. In the Sierra Nevada, song sparrows (Johnston, 1960) at a median latitude of 38° N lay an average clutch of 3.99 eggs, which would not be found on the coast south of about 58° N.

A further instance of climatic stability affecting clutch size is found in South America, whose narrow and tapered configuration, especially below the tropics, where the influence will be most important, allows the closer proximity of inland areas to the surrounding oceans and results in a considerably milder more stable climate in this country compared to similar latitudes in North America. The Humboldt current up the west coast will have an additional ameliorating influence. We expect that the slope of the latitude clutch size graph will be steeper in North America than in the southern half of the continent, and this is exactly the situation which exists (Fig. 2). Africa, on the other hand, has a much larger and wider land mass, and Fig. 2 shows an equal slope for both north and south of the equator there. Large sea-birds live in coastal and hence quite stable environments, and have few predators, and so in tropical and temperate waters alike there will be a tendency to increase $\bar{K}$ not r, because of the stable conditions in which these birds live. Implications that this might be the case come from the work of Nelson (1964) on *Sula bassana*, which suggests (but does not prove as yet) that food is not the limiting factor of clutch size. It is possible that the X_2 axis in Fig. 1 might more appropriately denote effort spent on an individual chick, measurable as weight at fledging, as even slightly smaller chicks at fledging would perhaps be at a disadvantage in its competitive ability during the next few years.

The Peruvian booby, *Sula variegata*, is a guanay-producing species which feeds in the waters of the Humboldt current off western South America. Every seven years or so the cold waters of this current are met by warm waters ("El Niño") from the northeast at a time when these birds are feeding young, and a food shortage results during which colonies are abandoned and the young boobies starve (Murphy, 1936). So far as this species is concerned conditions are unstable, and selection will be proceeding for r. In fact this species lays one to four eggs, and six out of seven years rears three young as often as two (other species of *Sula* which lay two eggs seldom rear both young). This is no doubt made possible by the rich food supply of the Humboldt current, and is seen graphically as equivalent to moving from P_1 to P_2 in Fig. 1.

The bay-breasted warbler, *Dendroica castanea*, Cape May warbler, *D. tigrina*, and the Tennessee warbler, *Vermivora peregrina*, are the North American warblers which depend on an unstable food supply. These species are largely dependent on irregular spruce-budworm outbreaks (MacArthur, 1962) for food during their breeding season, and as we would expect lay larger clutches (of five to six, five to seven, and five to six eggs, respectively) than other member of the Parulidae (normal clutch size four, rarely five, eggs). Another exception to the usual four eggs is the prothonotary warbler, *Prothonotaria citrea*, which is a hole-nester and lays a six-egg clutch.

A second prediction concerns predation-free species. It can be seen from Fig. 3 that if a species does not experience the increased predation in the tropics that most passerines do, the line $P'P$ would be altered to $P'P''$, P'' having the same X_2-intercept as P, but an intercept on X_1 equal or nearly equal to that of P' and an X-intercept closer to that of P'. Thus we can predict that species which are relatively free from predators will have a smaller temperate-tropical increase in clutch size. This is exactly the situation observed by Lord (1960) in North American mammals, in which no statistically significant increase in litter size with latitude could be found in predatory species (*Vulpes, Felis, Mustela*).

Hibernating animals would manage to avoid predation during winter and showed a less steep slope than did non-hibernating prey species, all these being statistically significant.

A third and final prediction may be made for hole nesters. Hole-nesting birds would escape much of the predation suffered by species nesting in open or exposed situations. For instance in the red-breasted merganser (*Mergus serrator*), which in Europe commonly nests in holes in banks, rocks, and tree roots, 91 per cent of hatched young survived, whereas for six species of open-nesting ducks this figure averages 58 per cent (from data in Lack, 1954). We can predict not only that clutch size will be higher in the tropic and temperate zones alike, but also that, as nest predation is higher in the tropics and the relative advantage of hole-nesting over open nests is greater there, the latitude/clutch size slope will be less steep for these hole nesters than for the open nesters. As this has been represented in Fig. 3, P and P' move down curves of points of equal stability to strategies H and H', but PH will be greater than $P'H'$ due to the greater relative advantage gained in the more stable-greater predation region. Lack (1948) showed not only that hole nesters lay a larger clutch by nearly two eggs on the average, for mid-European passerines, but that strategies between P' and H' exist, as intermediate stages of nest exposure, i.e., roofed and niche sites, between hole and open sites, which expose the nest to more predation and a higher chance of failure, result in intermediate clutch sizes. Tropical hole nesters also have higher clutches. The genus *Myiarchus* comprises the only tyrannid flycatchers to nest in holes in decayed stumps (Skutch, 1960, p.

398), and these species are responsible for the higher clutches of the family (Fig. 2.2). Similarly, of the Central American Thraupidae the only member for which clutch data exist and which nests in a hole is the Bonaparte euphonia, *Tanagra lauta*. While the other members of its genus, and indeed its family, lay two to three and rarely more eggs in this region (Skutch, 1954, p. 249), this species lays five to six eggs. The hole-nesting Ramphastidae (toucans) lay three to four eggs, compared to the two eggs which comprise a full clutch for the vast majority of tropical birds and likewise with the jacamars Galbulidae laying an average of 2.6 eggs (Skutch *et al., in litt.*). Indications that the slope of the graphs for hole-nesters is more gradual are obtained from limited data, but hole-nesting Alcenidae increase their clutch size from four to five or six (ratio 1 : 1.4) from Central America to the United States, while most of the graphs given show a ratio of 1 : 2.5 for that range of latitude.

SUMMARY

The principle of allocation of time and energy is used to formulate a general theory to account for clutch size in birds. "Advantages" are figured as the axes of a three-dimensional graph, and phenotypes allocating their energy in particular ways as points in space forming a surface and enclosed solid.

In the temperate zones most energy is used to increase the reproductive rate r. In the tropics the carrying capacity of the habitat is more important, resulting in a smaller clutch size. Different phenotypes will be more fit in different environments, as optimum allocation of energy differs.

Previous theories of clutch size are discussed, and incorporated into this general theory. Increase of clutch size with latitude is analyzed, and accounted for by the theory.

Predictions are made that all stable environments, the tropics, islands, coasts, will favor reduced clutches. Examples are quoted in which instability of conditions results in increased clutch size. The situation of predation-free species is examined, and it is predicted that the clutch size of such species will remain relatively unchanged with latitude changes. These predictions seem to be verified in all cases where data are available to test them.

ACKNOWLEDGMENTS

I am deeply indebted to Dr. Robert MacArthur for his assistance throughout the preparation of this paper. I am also grateful to Dr. Mike Rosensweig and Dr. Harry Recher for reading the manuscript and offering many useful suggestions.

LITERATURE CITED

BENT, A. C. 1938. Life histories of North American birds of prey (Part 2). Bull. U. S. Nat. Mus., **170**: 1–482.

BOND, J. 1947. A field guide of birds of the West Indies. Macmillan, New York.

CAYLEY, N. W. 1956. What bird is that? Angus and Robertson, Sydney.

DELACOUR, J. 1959. The waterfowl of the world. Country Life, London.

FISHER, R. A. 1929. Genetical theory of natural selection. Oxford Press.

GOODALL, J. D., A. W. JOHNSON, AND R. A. PHILIPPI. 1946. Las aves de Chile. Buenos Aires.

HERKLOTS, G. A. C. 1961. The birds of Trinidad and Tobago. Collins, London.

JOHNSTON, R. F. 1960. Variation in breeding season and clutch size in song sparrows of the Pacific coast. Condor, **56**: 268–273.

KORTRIGHT, F. H. 1943. The ducks, geese and swans of North America. Amer. Wildlife Inst., Washington.

KLUIJVER, H. N. 1951. The population ecology of the Great Tit *Parus m. major* L. Ardea, **39**: 1–135.

LACK, D. 1947. The significance of clutch size. Parts I and II. Ibis, **87**: 302–352.

——. 1948. The significance of clutch size. Part III. Ibis, **90**: 25–45.

——. 1949. Comments on Mr. Skutch's paper on clutch size. Ibis, **91**: 455–458.

——. 1954. The natural regulation of animal numbers. Clarendon Press, Oxford.

LACK, D., AND E. LACK. 1951. The breeding biology of the swift *Apus apus*. Ibis, **93**: 501–546.

LEVINS, R. 1962. Theory of fitness in a heterogeneous environment. 1. The fitness set and adaptive function. Amer. Nat., **96**: 361–373.

LORD, R. D. JR. 1960. Litter size and latitude in North American mammals. Amer. Midl. Nat., **64**: 488–499.

MACARTHUR, R. H. 1958. Population ecology of some warblers of Northeastern coniferous forests. Ecology, **39**: 599–619.

——. 1962. Some generalized theorems of natural selection. Proc. Nat. Acad. Sci., **48**: 1893–1897.

MOREAU, R. 1944. Clutch size: A comparative study, with special reference to African birds. Ibis, **86**: 286–347.

MURPHY, R. C. 1936. Oceanic birds of South America. Macmillan, New York.

NELSON, B. 1964. Factors influencing clutch size and chick growth in the North Atlantic gannet *Sula bassana*. Ibis, **106**: 63–77.

OLIVER, W. R. B. 1955. New Zealand birds. Reed, Wellington.

PITELKA, F. A., P. Q. TOMICH, AND G. W. TREICHEL. 1955. Ecological relations of jaegers and owls as lemming predators near Barrow, Alaska. Ecol. Monogr., **25**: 85–117.

POUGH, R. H. 1949. Audubon land bird guide. Doubleday, New York.

——. 1957. Audubon water bird guide. Doubleday, New York.

SKUTCH, A. F. 1949. Do tropical birds rear as many young as they can nourish? Ibis, **91**: 430–455.

——. 1954. Life histories of Central American birds. Pacific Coast Avifauna, **31**: 1–448.

——. 1960. Life histories of Central American birds. II. Pacific Coast Avifauna, **34**: 1–593.

SNOW, D. 1962. Field study of the black and white manakin *Manacus manacus*. Zoologica, **47**: 65–104.

WYNNE-EDWARDS, V. C. 1962. Animal dispersion in relation to social behaviour. Oliver and Boyd, Edinburgh.

EVOLUTION OF LITTER-SIZE IN THE PIKA, *OCHOTONA PRINCEPS* (RICHARDSON)

John S. Millar[1]

Attempts to explain the evolutionary significance of litter-size have been relatively few, but varied in approach and scope. Lack (1948) considered that natural selection favors those animals producing the most offspring because they leave the most descendants. He suggested that an "upper limit is set by the number of young which the parents can successfully raise" but recognized that "there is an evolutionary alternative between producing more young, or fewer young which are better nourished and better protected." Several hypotheses have been based on Lack's basic premise that natural selection favors the production of maximum number of offspring. These generally view litter-size as only part of an overall reproductive strategy, but differ in the parameters considered important in determining litter-size. For example, "resources," length of breeding season, food supply, body size, altitude, latitude, mortality, population stability, and competition have all been suggested to influence litter-size directly or indirectly (Lord, 1960; Cody, 1966; Gibb, 1968; Smith and McGinnis, 1968; Spencer and Steinhoff, 1968).

During a study of the pika *Ochotona princeps* (Richardson) in southwestern Alberta, data on reproduction, mortality, and population density were obtained. Here these data are used to evaluate the significance of litter-size in pikas. Several aspects of the biology of these animals have been reported by Millar (1972*a*, *b*) and Millar and Zwickel (1972*a*, *b*).

METHODS

A total of 667 animals were collected from several study areas by shooting throughout the breeding seasons of 1968, 1969 and 1970. Ovaries of mature females were fixed in A.F.A. (alcohol-formalin, acetic acid), embedded in paraffin, and serially sectioned at 7–10μ. Corpora lutea and corpora albicantia were counted microscopically, and these counts were considered to be the litter-size at conception, or potential litter-size. Such counts may be biased by twinning of ova or polyovulation. Polyovulation and twinning of ova would result in females having more embryos than corpora lutea, but this situation was not observed. Twinning of ova would result in some embryos sharing a chorion with another, but again, none were found. Stage of gestation was determined from the size of embryos in collected females, and all embryonic losses occurred prior to mid-pregnancy (Millar, 1972*b*). The number of healthy embryos in late gestation was considered to be the litter-size at birth; the difference between the number of corpora lutea and healthy embryos in late stages of pregnancy provided an estimate of prenatal losses.

Discrete fat bodies were present in the interscapular, cardiac, and splenic regions of collected animals. These were removed and weighed, and mg fat per 100 gm body wt was used as an index of condition.

Age of collected animals was determined from histological sections of lower jaws. Adult mortality rates were based on age structure of the populations (Millar and Zwickel, 1972*a*).

Several marked populations were followed on one area during the three years

TABLE 1. *Litter-size and number of litters per season of North American pikas. Litter-size based on counts of embryos.*

Region	Litter-size					Litters per Season	Source
	1	2	3	4	5		
California	1	6	8	2	1	3–4	Severaid, 1955
		2	3			–	Grinnell et al., 1930
Nevada		1	5	2		–	Hall, 1946
Oregon				2		2‡	Bailey, 1936
			2			–	Roest, 1953
Colorado	1	2	1			2	Johnson, 1967
		1	2				Anderson, 1959
			1†				Dice, 1927
		3		1		2‡	Present study
Colorado and Utah		3	4	5		2	Hayward, 1952
Utah			1			–	Long, 1940
Washington					1	2‡	Dice, 1926
British Columbia			1†			–	Underhill, 1962
Alberta	8	38	33	1		2	Present study
Alaska*				1			Dixon, 1938
			2	1		2‡	Rausch, 1961, 1970

* *O. collaris.*

† born.

‡ based on scanty evidence.

of the study. Animals on 10 discrete rock slides were live-trapped and individually marked. Certain females were retrapped and observed as often as possible throughout each breeding season. Young pikas emerging from nests beneath the rocks were associated with particular females, counted, and marked. The number of young associating with a particular female was considered to be the litter-size at weaning.

Total populations were marked on 4 slides that were measured and mapped. Number of adults per unit area of rock slide provided estimates of population density.

RESULTS

Pikas in southwestern Alberta matured as yearlings (the spring followed their birth) and all females had the potential to produce two litters each breeding season. A comparison of breeding parameters among pikas throughout North America (Table 1) indicates that litter-size varies little and most populations (with the exception of California) have two litters per

year. Presumably, populations in areas with short summers do not have a sufficiently long period of favorable conditions to have animals maturing during the season of their birth (assuming growth rates similar to those in Alberta). A comparison of breeding parameters among several species of Asian pikas (Table 2) indicates that different species have quite different breeding patterns, and that most Asian species have higher fecundity than pikas in North America.

Mortality of Litters

Entire litters were frequently lost prior to independence (48% of 67 females known to be pregnant failed to produce weaned young), but females that were successful had a constant pattern of fecundity. For example, potential litter size did not vary in relation to season, year, age and type of habitat. It is the steady erosion of potential litter-size that is examined here. Mean litter-size was 2.64 at ovulation, 2.33 at birth, and 1.83 at weaning (Fig. 1). Thirteen per cent of all ova shed were lost

TABLE 2. *Summary of reproductive parameters of Ochotonidae.*

Species	Approximate Weight (grams)	Litters per Season	Mean embryo Counts	First Breeding	Source
1) *O. alpina*	130	2	2.2		Revin, 1968
2) *O. alpina*		2–3	3 *	yearling	Khmelevskaya, 1961
3) *O. alpina*		2	2–3**	yearling	Yergenson, 1939‡
4) *O. alpina*	115	1–2	2–6**		Kistchinsky, 1969
5) *O. daurica*		2	7.0	summer of birth	Nekypelov, 1954‡
6) *O. hyperborea*	110	1	4.8	yearling	Kapitonov, 1961
7) *O. macrotis*	180	2–3	5.0	yearling	Zimina, 1962
8) *O. macrotis*		2–4	6.0	summer of birth	Bernstein, 1964
9) *O. pallasi*		2–3	8.0	summer of birth	Shubin, 1956‡
10) *O. pallasi*			5.8	summer of birth	Chergenov, 1961‡
11) *O. pallasi*		3	6.0	summer of birth	Tarasov, 1950‡
12) *O. pusilla*	200	3–5	9.0	summer of birth	Shubin, 1965
13) *O. rufescens*	250		6.0		Puget, 1971
14) *O. rutila*	275	2–3	4.2	yearling	Bernstein, 1964
15) *O. princeps*	135	2	2.3	yearling	Present study
16) *O. princeps*	135	3–4	2.8	yearling	Severaid, 1955

* mode.

** range.

‡ not seen; cited by Bernstein, 1964.

before birth while losses between birth and weaning were estimated at 21% (Millar, 1972*b*). The extent of losses in litters of different size was evaluated by comparing the frequencies of litter-sizes at conception, birth and weaning. Prenatal mortality almost always involved only one embryo per litter, except when whole litters were lost. Assuming losses in all successful litters to involve only one offspring, an expected frequency was calculated by applying a constant loss to each litter-size at the preceding stage. This expected frequency was then compared statistically (x^2) to the observed frequency. Prenatal, but not postnatal losses were compared directly in relation to initial litter size.

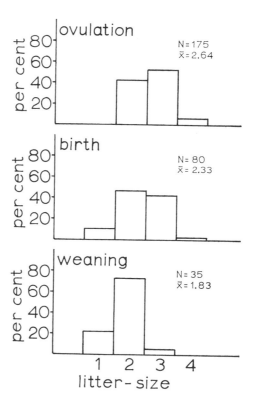

FIG. 1. Frequencies of litter-size of pikas in southwestern Alberta at ovulation (based on counts of corpora lutea and corpora albicantia), birth (based on counts of healthy embryos after day 13 of gestation), and weaning (based on counts of young emerging from the rocks).

TABLE 3. *Mortality of embryos between conception and birth in relation to initial litter-size at conception based on counts of corpora lutea and corpora albicantia. Observed litter-size at birth based on counts of healthy embryos in late gestation. Expected frequencies at birth based on a uniform 13% loss in all litters during gestation and assumes that only one embryo is lost from any one litter.*

	Litter-size				
	1	2	3	4	Total
A. Observed Frequency at Conception	0	75	89	11	175
B. Percent Frequency at Conception	0	42.9	50.8	6.3	100
C. 13% loss [(13/100) $\times$ B]	0	5.6	6.6	0.8	13
D. Remaining (B – C)	0	37.3	44.2	5.5	87
E. Gain From Next Largest Litter (C)	5.6	6.6	0.8	0.0	13
F. Adjusted Frequency (D + E)	5.6	43.9	45.0	5.5	100
G. Expected Frequency at Birth [(F/100) $\times$ 80]	4.5	35.1	36.0	4.4	80
H. Observed Frequency at Birth	8	38	33	1	80
χ^2	2.7222	0.2396	0.2500	2.6272	5.8390; $P > .100$; N.S.

A comparison of frequency of litter-sizes between conception and birth (Table 3) indicated that the frequency of litters at birth was not significantly different from the frequency expected if mortality was equal among all litter-sizes. However, a direct comparison of prenatal losses in relation to potential litter-size (Table 4) indicated that although there were no differences between females ovulating two and three ova, those producing four ova suffered significantly greater losses than those shedding three. Potential litters of four were uncommon, and heavy losses resulted

TABLE 4. *Prenatal losses in successful pregnancies in relation to initial litter-sizes, based on differences between counts of corpora lutea and healthy embryos after day 13 of gestation (see Millar, 1972b). Tabulated as a percentage of females that have losses and a percentage of ova that are lost. Sample sizes in parentheses.*

Initial Litter-size	Prenatal Losses	
	% Females	% Ova
2	21.2 (33)	10.6 (66)
3	28.2 (39)	10.2 (117)
4	87.5* (8)	28.1** (32)

*Significantly higher than in females shedding 3 ova ($\chi^2 = 6.1871$, $P < .025$).
**Significantly higher than in females shedding 3 ova ($\chi^2 = 5.2825$; $P < .025$).

in almost no litters of four at birth. Similar differences in rates of mortality were apparent between birth and weaning. The frequency of litters at weaning was significantly different than expected if mortality was equal among all litter sizes at birth (Table 5). Litters of three were less common at weaning than expected, while litters of one and two were more common, indicating that greater mortality occurs in litters of three. Litters of three were common at birth (41% of 80 litters contained three young), but rare at weaning (6% of 35 weaned litters contained three young) indicating that most females could raise only two young. Conceiving more offspring than can be raised may be advantageous in case an offspring is lost for some other reason.

The fate of missing young is not known; only one dead nestling, estimated to be two weeks of age, was found.

Index of Fat

The sizes of particular fat bodies are difficult to relate to the condition of animals because different fat bodies may be deposited or mobilized in response to changes in environmental (temperature, food supplies) conditions or physiological status (sex, age, breeding status) (Flux, 1971). The generalized fat index used here

TABLE 5. *Mortality of nestling pikas in relation to litter-size at birth. Observed litter-size at birth based on counts of healthy embryos in late gestation. Observed litter-size at weaning based on counts of young emerging from the rocks. Expected frequencies at weaning based on a uniform loss of 21% in all litters and assumes that only one nestling is lost from any one litter.*

| | Litter-size | | | | |
	1	2	3	4	Total
A. Observed Frequency at Birth	8	38	33	1	80
B. Percent Frequency at Birth	10.0	47.5	41.2	1.3	100
C. 21% Loss $[(21/100) \times B)]$	2.1	10.0	8.6	0.3	21
D. Remaining (B − C)	7.9	37.5	32.6	1.0	79.0
E. Gain From Next Largest Litter (C)	10.0	8.6	0.3	0	18.9
F. Adjusted Frequency (D + E)	17.9	46.1	32.9	1.0	97.9
G. Adjusted Percent Frequency $[(F/97.9) \times 100]$	18.3	47.1	33.6	1.0	100
H. Expected Frequency at Weaning $[(G/100) \times 35]$	6.4	16.5	11.8	0.3	35
I. Observed Frequency at Weaning	8	25	2	0	35
χ^2	0.4000	4.3787	8.1389	0.3000	13.2176; $P < .005$

(mg cardiac, splenic, interscapular fat per 100 gm body weight) presumably reflects general fat levels. Fat animals are not necessarily healthy animals, but fat animals must be obtaining, or at least storing, more energy in relation to their requirements than thin animals. In the pika, females enter the breeding season with much higher fat indexes than males, but lose these reserves over the breeding season. A comparison of fat reserves in relation to pregnancy and lactation (Fig. 2) indicates that fat is deposited during pregnancy and drained during lactation. These drains occurred despite the presence of abundant food during the period of lactation, and did not vary in relation to littering period or type of habitat.

Population Density

This parameter is difficult to estimate, but pikas in southwestern Alberta exhibit several characteristics that indicate they are at or near saturation level.

For instance, overall population levels were relatively stable over the three years of the study. Although individual populations varied considerably (Table 6), yearly averages of adults per ha of rock were 7.5 in 1968, 5.8 in 1969 and 6.5 in 1970 (based on 0.8, 8.5 and 8.5 ha, respectively). Secondly, pikas appeared relatively immune to variations in environmental conditions; no "catastrophes" were recorded. Thirdly, although few populations were dense enough to exhibit responses to density, low populations produced more offspring per female to weaning than high populations, and any

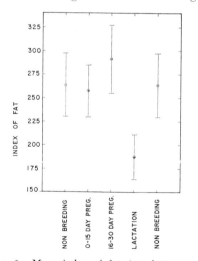

FIG. 2. Mean index of fat (mg interscapular, cardiac and splenic fat per 100 gm body wt) of mature female pikas in southwestern Alberta in relation to stages of pregnancy and lactation. Vertical lines denote two standard errors each side of the mean.

TABLE 6. *Population parameters for five discrete populations of pikas in southwestern Alberta. Density based on number of adult pikas per hectare of rock slide. Number of weaned young based on counts of young animals emerging from the rocks. Emigrants include only animals born in the populations and whose final location was known. Transients and immigrants include all young animals caught on the area that were known not to be born there.*

Popu-lations	Density	No. Ad. ♀♀	No. Weaned Young	No. Weaned Young per Female	No. Known Emigrants	No. Known Transients and Immigrants
1	4.0	5	9	1.80	3	1
2	4.1	6	14	2.33	–	1
3	5.4	6	14	2.33	3	7
4	10.9	12	13	1.08	–	–
5	22.0	6	2	0.33	–	1

populations that were still low after the breeding season could easily be replenished with immigrants (Table 6). These data indicate that the populations studied were probably at or near saturation level at all times.

DISCUSSION

Each female appears to be producing as many offspring as she can support. Females drain their energy reserves during lactation and large litters (three) appear to suffer higher mortality prior to independence than small litters (one and two). This limit of two offspring supported during lactation could be considered a local phenomena, but data from Colorado and Utah indicate that the same limit exists there. Counts of embryos from that area (Table 1) indicate that many females (16 of 26) gave birth to three or four young, while Krear (1965) noted that the number weaned was usually two.

The limit imposed on litter-size during lactation did not appear related to environmental conditions since weather was relatively mild and food was abundant during the breeding season. The limit was more likely physiological; possibly based on one or more of three factors: energy assimilation, drainage of energy reserves, and the rate of growth of the young. Small mammals such as bank voles (*Clethrionomys glareolus*), common voles (*Microtus arvalis*), mice (*Mus musculus*) and red squirrels (*Tamiasciurus hudsonicus*) increase their food intake during pregnancy and

lactation (Kaczmarski, 1966; Migula, 1968; Myrcha et al., 1969; Smith, 1968, respectively) and pikas likely do the same. Pikas also drain their reserves during lactation and apparently cannot support offspring through increased assimilation alone. Possibly, rather than draining their reserves below a critical level, or decreasing the size of each offspring, they sacrifice the size of the litter. The difference in energy expenditure between a female (mean weight 133 gm) supporting two and three offspring (weaning weight approximately 50 gm) would be considerable.

Few studies were found where survival of young or condition of females was documented for natural populations. Le Resche (1968) found greater mortality of twin moose calves (*Alces alces*) than single calves, and data collected by Markgren (1969) indicates a similar trend. Tree mice (*Phenacomys longicaudus*) support only a certain biomass of offspring, even when fed an abundance of natural foods (Hamilton, 1962) and young rabbits (*Oryctolagus cuniculus*) in small litters grow faster than those in large litters (Myers and Poole, 1963), indicating that milk is limited.

In general, the differential mortality in litters of different size during lactation appear to be related to the female's ability to support offspring. Prenatal mortality, however, occurred early in gestation when embryos were very small in relation to the size of the female, and mortality at that time was not likely related to any nutritional stress on

44

the female. A possible explanation is that litter-size has been reduced over evolutionary time by limiting the capacity of the uterus, rather than by reducing the number of ova shed. This could operate by limiting the number of embryos implanted, as in the elephant shrew (*Elephantulus myurus*) (Horst and Gillman, 1941) or through limiting the number of implanted embryos carried to term, as in the alpaca (*Lama pecos*) (Fernandex-Baca et al., 1970). Although most evolved reductions in litter-size undoubtedly arise through changes in ovulation rates, some sort of restriction placed on litter-size by the uterus may be relatively common. Greater prenatal losses in large litters have been noted in white-tailed deer (*Odocoileus virginianus*) (Ransom, 1967) and European rabbits (*Oryctolagus cuniculus*) (Poole, 1960), and the trend is evident in other data presented for European rabbits (Brambell, 1942; Lloyd, 1963; McIlwaine, 1962), European hares (*Lepus europaeus*) (Flux, 1967) and snowshoe hares (*Lepus americanus*) (Newson, 1964).

Lack's (1948) hypothesis that females produce as many offspring as they can support appears to hold true for the pika. However, his suggestion that the most frequent litter-size at birth is the most productive is not supported by my data, and has been criticized on theoretical grounds by Mountford (1968). Litters of three were common at birth, but were generally reduced to two young at weaning. Such a system may appear inefficient, but the "wastage" of one offspring would be selected against only if the wastage contributed in some way to the death of the parent or surviving offspring. Perhaps, in pikas, there is an advantage in having an extra nestling available in case one is lost for some other reason before the critical period of lactation.

Spencer and Steinhoff (1968) suggested that animals with restricted breeding seasons have larger litters than those with extended breeding seasons to maximize the number of offspring produced during the

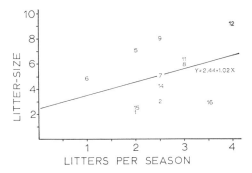

FIG. 3. Regression of mean litter-size against number of litters per breeding season of several species of pikas. Numbers refer to data in Table 2. A significant proportion of the variance of y is not explained by regression on x. ($F = 1.4289$; $P > .25$.)

females life span. From this, populations with short breeding seasons (hence fewer litters per year) should have the largest litters. A comparison of pika populations indicates no such trend (Fig. 3), while there is a trend (not significant) for large litters to be associated with long breeding seasons. Their assumption that maternal mortality varies directly with the size of the litter may be invalid (Tinkle, 1969). All behavioral or physiological attributes of a species can be related to the ability to survive or to reproduce. Since survival is a prerequisite to reproduction, it is likely that requirements for survival take priority over requirements for reproduction, and that females will sacrifice their litters before threatening their own survival. In the pika, this is seen as a loss of total litters at high population densities and under other adverse conditions (Millar, 1972b).

The trend in litter-size among species may be attributed, at least in part, to body size. Species with large litters are generally larger than those with small litters (Table 2).

Lord (1960) predicted a positive correlation between litter-size and latitude in non-hibernating prey species. This is not true of the pika; litter-size is relatively constant in North America (Table 1). My data do not, however, refute his suggestion

TABLE 7. *Reproduction and adult mortality in populations of pikas.*

Population	Adult Mortal-ity*	Litter-size	Litters/ season	Sources
O. princeps (Colorado and Utah)	43.4	2.9	2	Present study; Johnson, 1967; Hayward, 1952
O. princeps Alberta	46.0	2.3	2	Present study
O. macrotis	58.2	6.0	2–4	Bernstein, 1964
O. rutila	64.8	4.2	2–3	Bernstein, 1964

* Based on per cent yearlings in mature populations (see Millar and Zwickel, 1972a).

that populations suffering low mortality produce relatively small litters because resources are limited. Mortality in Alberta was relatively low and litters were small (Table 7). The problem of determining the limited resource remains. Gibb (1968) considered food to be the important resource, but pikas are herbivores that feed on a wide variety of plants, and food appeared abundant in Alberta.

Cody (1966) suggested that successful offspring in saturated populations must be larger in order to be competitive. This may explain the partitioning of available maternal resources into only two offspring (rather than three or four smaller offspring). Perhaps the resource in question is space. Pikas are territorial (Kilham, 1958; Krear, 1965) and although detailed behavioral studies have not yet been done, competition for space likely occurs.

SUMMARY

Potential litter-sizes, mortality of embryos and nestlings, maternal fat reserves during pregnancy and lactation, and population parameters of pikas in southwestern Alberta are documented and used to evaluate several hypotheses on the significance of litter-size. Two, three, or sometimes four ova are shed at conception. Relatively

heavy losses in litters of four occur during gestation. These losses are not likely caused by any nutritonal stress on females, and may be related to an evolutionary reduction in litter-size by limiting the capacity of the uterus. Relatively heavy losses in litters of three between birth and weaning, and low maternal fat reserves during lactation indicate that females produce as many offspring as they can support. Population appeared at or near saturation level, and the advantage in partitioning maternal resources into two, rather than three or four smaller offspring may be that the better nourished offspring are more successful at competing for space.

ACKNOWLEDGMENTS

This study was conducted under the supervision of Dr. F. C. Zwickel and was supported by funds from the National Research Council of Canada and the Department of Zoology and the R. B. Miller Biological Station, University of Alberta. R. A. MacArthur and H. Reynolds provided assistance during 1969 and 1970, respectively. Special thanks are due to F. C. Zwickel, J. O. Murie, S. C. Tapper, J. P. Ryder, A. E. Aubin and C. D. Ankney, for many valuable comments, suggestions, criticisms and heated arguments.

LITERATURE CITED

ANDERSON, S. 1959. Mammals of the Grand Mesa, Colorado. Univ. Kansas Publs. Mus. Nat. Hist. 9:405–414.

BAILEY, V. 1936. The mammals and life zones of Oregon. North Amer. Fauna No. 55:112–117.

BERNSTEIN, A. D. 1964. The reproduction by red pika (*Ochotona rutila* Sev.) in the Zailijsk Alutau (In Russian). Bull. Mosc. Soc. Nat., Biol. 69:40–48.

BRAMBELL, F. W. R. 1942. Intra-uterine mortality of the wild rabbit. *Oryctolagus cuniculus* (L.). Proc. Roy. Soc. B. 130:462–479.

CODY, M. L. 1966. A general theory of clutch size. Evolution 20:174–184.

DICE, L. R. 1926. Pacific coast rabbits and pikas. Occ. Papers Mus. Zool., Univ. Mich. 166:1–28.

——. 1927. The Colorado pika in captivity. J. Mammal. 8:228–231.

DIXON, J. S. 1938. Birds and Mammals of

Mount McKinley National Park, Alaska. Nat. Park Service, Fauna Ser. 3, 236 p.

FERNANDEZ-BACA, S., W. HANSEL, AND C. NOVOA. 1970. Embryonic mortality in the alpaca. Biol. Reprod. 3:243–251.

FLUX, J. E. C. 1967. Reproduction and body weights of the hare, *Lepus europaeus* Pallas, in New Zealand. N.Z.J. Sci. 10:357–401.

———. 1971. Validity of the kidney fat index for estimating the condition of hares: a discussion. N.Z.J. Sci. 14:238–244.

GIBB, J. A. 1968. The evolution of reproductive rates: are there no rules? Proc. N.Z. Ecol. Soc. 15:1–6.

GRINNEL, J., J. DIXON, AND J. M. LINSDALE. 1930. Vertebrate natural history of a section of northern California through the Lassen Peak region. Univ. Cal. Publ. Zool. 35:1–594.

HALL, E. R. 1946. Mammals of Nevada. Univ. Calif. Press. 710 p.

HAMILTON, W. J. 1962. Reproductive adaptations in the red tree mouse. J. Mammal. 43:486–504.

HAYWARD, C. L. 1952. Alpine biotic communities of the Uinta Mountains, Utah. Ecol. Monogr. 22:93–102.

HORST, C. J. V. D., AND J. GILLMAN. 1941. The number of eggs and surviving embryos in *Elephantulus*. Anat. Rec. 80:443–452.

JOHNSON, D. R. 1967. Diet and reproduction of Colorado pikas. J. Mammal. 48:311–315.

KACZMARSKI, F. 1966. Bioenergetics of pregnancy and lactation in the bank vole. Acta Theriol. 11:409–417.

KAPITONOV, V. I. 1961. Ecological observations on *Ochotona hyperborea* Pall. in the lower part of the Lena River. (In Russian; English summary). Zool. Zh. 40:922–933.

KHMELEVSKAYA, N. V. 1961. On the biology of *Ochotona alpina* Pallas. (In Russian; English summary). Zool. Zh. 40:1583–1585.

KILHAM, L. 1958. Territorial behavior in pikas. J. Mammal. 39:307.

KISTSCHINSKY, A. A. 1969. The pika (*Ochotona alpina hyperborea* Pall.) in the Kolyma highlands. (In Russian; English summary). Bull. Mosc. Soc. Nat. Biol. 74:134–143.

KREAR, H. R. 1965. An ecological and ethological study of the pika (*Ochotona princeps saxitilis* Bangs) in the Front range of Colorado. Ph.D. Thesis, Univ. of Colorado, Boulder. 329 p.

LACK, D. 1948. The significance of litter-size. J. Anim. Ecol. 17:45–50.

LE RESCHE, R. E. 1968. Spring-fall calf mortality in an Alaska moose population. J. Wildlife Manage. 32:953–956.

LLOYD, H. G. 1963. Intra-uterine mortality in the wild rabbit, *Oryctolagus cuniculus* (L.) in populations of low density. J. Anim. Ecol. 32:549–563.

LONG, W. S. 1940. Life histories of some Utah mammals. J. Mammal. 21:170–180.

LORD, R. D. 1960. Litter-size and latitude in North American mammals. Am. Midl. Nat. 64:488–499.

MARKGREN, G. 1969. Reproduction of moose in Sweden. Viltrevy 6:127–299.

McILWAINE, C. P. 1962. Reproduction and body weights of the wild rabbit *Oryctolagus cuniculus* (L.) in Hawke's Bay, New Zealand. N.Z.J. Sci. 5:324–341.

MIGULA, P. 1969. Bioenergetics of pregnancy and lactation in the European common vole. Acta Theriol. 14:167–179.

MILLAR, J. S. 1972a. Timing of breeding of pikas in southwestern Alberta. Can. J. Zool. 50:665–669.

———. Success of reproduction in pikas (*Ochotona princeps* Richardson) Fecudity of pikas in relation to the environment. (in preparation).

MILLAR, J. S., AND F. C. ZWICKEL. 1972a. Determination of age, age structure, and mortality of the pika, *Ochotona princeps* (Richardson). Can. J. Zool. 50:229–232.

———, AND ———. Characteristics and ecological significance of hay piles of pikas. Mammalia (*in press*)

MOUNTFORD, M. D. 1968. The significance of litter-size. J. Anim. Ecol. 37:363–367.

MYERS, K., AND W. E. POOLE. 1963. A study of the wild rabbit *Oryctolagus cuniculus* (L.) in confined populations. V. Population dynamics. C.S.I.R.O. Wildlife Research. 8:166–203.

MYRCHA, A., L. RYSZKOWSKI, AND W. WALKOWA. 1969. Bioenergetics of pregnancy and lactation in white mouse. Acta. Theriol. 14:161–166.

NEWSON, J. 1964. Reproduction and prenatal mortality of snowshoe hares on Manitoulin Island, Ontario. Can. J. Zool. 42:987–1005.

POOLE, W. E. 1960. Breeding of the wild rabbit, *Oryctolagus cuniculus* (L.) in relation to the environment. C.S.I.R.O. Wildlife Research 5: 21–43.

PUGET, A. 1971. *Ochotona r. rufescens* (Gray 1842) in Afghanistan and its breeding in captivity. (In French; English summary). Mammalia 35:24–37.

RANSOM, A. B. 1967. Reproductive biology of white-tailed deer in Manitoba. J. Wildl. Manage. 31:114–123.

RAUSCH, R. L. 1961. Notes on the collared pika, *Ochotona collaris* (Nelson), in Alaska. Murrelet. 42:22–24.

———. 1970. Personal communication, College, Alaska.

REVIN, Y. N. 1968. A contribution to the biology of the northern pika (*Ochotona alpina* Pall.) on the Olekmo-Charskoe highlands (Yukatia). (In Russian; English summary). Zool. Zh. 47:1075–1082.

ROEST, R. I. 1953. Notes on pikas from the Oregon Cascades. J. Mammal. 34:132–133.

SEVERAID, J. H. 1955. The natural history of the pika (Mammalian genus *Ochotona*). Ph.D. Thesis, Univ. of Calif. 820 p.

SHUBIN, I. G. 1965. Reproduction of *Ochotona pusilla* Pall. (In Russian; English summary). Zool. Zh. 44:917–924.

SPENCER, A. W., AND H. W. STEINHOFF. 1968. An explanation of geographical variation in litter-size. J. Mammal. 49:281–286.

SMITH, C. C. 1968. The adaptive nature of social organization in the genus of three squirrels *Tamiasciurus*. Ecol. Monographs 38:31–63.

SMITH, M. H., AND J. T. McGINNIS. 1968. Relationships of latitude, altitude, and body size to litter size and mean annual production of offspring in *Peromyscus*. Res. Popul. Ecol. X:115–126.

TINKLE, D. W. 1969. The concept of reproductive effort and its relation to the evolution of life histories of lizards. Amer. Natur. 103:501–516.

UNDERHILL, J. E. 1962. Notes on pika in captivity. Can. Field Nat. 76:177–178.

ZIMINA, R. P. 1962. The ecology of *Ochotona macrotis* Gunther dwelling in the area of the Tersky-Alutau mountain range. (In Russian; English summary). Bull. Mosc. Soc. Nat., Biol. 67:5–12.

MORTALITY PATTERNS IN MAMMALS

GRAEME CAUGHLEY

Abstract. Methods of obtaining life table data are outlined and the assumptions implicit in such treatment are defined. Most treatments assume a stationary age distribution, but published methods of testing the stationary nature of a single distribution are invalid. Samples from natural populations tend to be biased in the young age classes and therefore, because it is least affected by bias, the mortality rate curve (q_x) is the most efficient life table series for comparing the pattern of mortality with age in different populations.

A life table and fecundity table are presented for females of the ungulate *Hemitragus jemlahicus*, based on a population sample that was first tested for bias. They give estimates of mean generation length as 5.4 yr, annual mortality rate as 0.25, and mean life expectancy at birth as 3.5 yr.

The life table for *Hemitragus* is compared with those of *Ovis aries, O. dalli,* man, *Rattus norvegicus, Microtus agrestis,* and *M. orcadensis* to show that despite taxonomic and ecological differences the life tables have common characteristics. This suggests the hypotheses that most mammalian species have life tables of a common form, and that the pattern of age-specific mortality within species assumes an approximately constant form irrespective of the proximate causes of mortality.

INTRODUCTION

Most studies in population ecology include an attempt to determine mortality rates, and in many cases rates are given for each age class. This is no accident. Age-specific mortality rates are usually necessary for calculating reproductive values for each age class, the ages most susceptible to natural selection, the population's rate of increase, mean life expectancy at birth, mean generation length, and the percentage of the population that dies each year. The importance of these statistics in the fields of game management, basic and applied ecology, and population genetics requires no elaboration.

The pattern of changing mortality rates with age is best expressed in the form of a life table. These tables usually present the same information in a variety of ways:

1) Survivorship (l_x) : this series gives the probability at birth of an individual surviving to any age, x (l_x as used here is identical with P_x of Leslie, Venables and Venables 1952). The ages

49

are most conveniently spaced at regular intervals such that the values refer to survivorship at ages 0, 1, 2 etc. yr, months, or some other convenient interval. The probability at birth of living to birth is obviously unity, but this initial value in the series need not necessarily be set at 1; it is often convenient to multiply it by 1,000 and to increase proportionately the other values in the series. If this is done, survivorship can be redefined as the number of animals in a cohort of 1,000 (or any other number to which the initial value is raised) that survived to each age x. In this way a kl_x series is produced, where k is the constant by which all l_x values in the series are multiplied.

2) Mortality (d_x): the fraction of a cohort that dies during the age interval x, x + 1 is designated d_x. It can be defined in terms of the individual as the probability at birth of dying during the interval x, x + 1. As a means of eliminating decimal points the values are sometimes multiplied by a constant such that the sum of the d_x values equals 1,000. The values can be calculated from the l_x series by

$$d_x = l_x - l_{x+1}$$

3) Mortality rate (q_x): the mortality rate q for the age interval x, x + 1 is termed q_x. It is calculated as the number of animals in the cohort that died during the interval x, x + 1, divided by the number of animals alive at age x. This value is usually expressed as $1,000q_x$, the number of animals out of 1,000 alive at age x which died before x + 1.

These are three ways of presenting age-specific mortality. Several other methods are available— e.g. survival rate (p_x), life expectancy (e_x) and probability of death (Q_x)—but these devices only present in a different way the information already contained in each of the three series previously defined. In this paper only the l_x, d_x and q_x series will be considered.

METHODS OF OBTAINING MORTALITY DATA

Life tables may be constructed from data collected in several ways. Direct methods:

1) Recording the ages at death of a large number of animals born at the same time. The frequencies of ages at death form a kd_x series.

2) Recording the number of animals in the original cohort still alive at various ages. The frequencies from a kl_x series.

Approximate methods:

3) Recording the ages at death of animals marked at birth but whose births were not coeval. The frequencies form a kd_x series.

4) Recording ages at death of a representative sample by ageing carcasses from a population that has assumed a stationary age distribution. Small fluctuations in density will not greatly affect the results if these fluctuations have an average wave length considerably shorter than the period over which the carcasses accumulated. The frequencies form a kd_x series.

5) Recording a sample of ages at death from a population with a stationary age distribution, where the specimens were killed by a catastrophic event (avalanche, flood, etc.) that removed and fixed an unbiased sample of ages in a living population. In some circumstances (outlined later) the age frequencies can be treated as a kl_x series.

6) The census of ages in a living population, or a sample of it, where the population has assumed a stationary age distribution. Whether the specimens are obtained alive by trapping or are killed by unselective shooting, the resultant frequencies are a sample of ages in a living population and form a kl_x series in certain circumstances.

Methods 1 to 3 are generally used in studies of small mammals while methods 4 to 6 are more commonly used for large mammals.

TESTS FOR STATIONARY AGE DISTRIBUTION

Five methods have been suggested for determining whether the age structure of a sample is consistent with its having been drawn from a stationary age distribution:

a) Comparison of the "mean mortality rate," calculated from the age distribution of the sample, with the proportion represented by the first age class (Kurtén 1953, p. 51).

b) Comparison of the annual female fecundity of a female sample with the sample number multiplied by the life expectancy at birth, the latter statistic being estimated from the age structure (Quick 1963, p. 210).

c) Calculation of instantaneous birth rates and death rates, respectively, from a sample of the population's age distribution and a sample of ages at death (Hughes 1965).

d) Comparison of the age distribution with a prejudged notion of what a stationary age distribution should be like (Breakey 1963).

e) Examination of the "l_x" and "d_x" series, calculated from the sampled age distribution, for evidence of a common trend (Quick 1963, p. 204).

Methods a to c are tautological because they assume the sampled age distribution is either a kl_x or kd_x series; method d assumes the form of the life table, and e makes use of both assumptions. These ways of judging the stationary nature of a population are invalid. But I intend something more general than the simple statement that these five methods do not test what they are supposed to test. Given no information other than a single age distribution, it is theoretically impossible to prove that the distribution is from a stationary population unless one begins from the assumption that the population's survival curve is of a particular form. If such an assumption is made, the life table constructed from the age frequencies provides no more information than was contained in the original premise.

Mortality Samples and Age Structure Samples

Methods 4 to 6 for compiling life tables are valid only when the data are drawn from a stationary age distribution. This distribution results when a population does not change in size and where the age structure of the population is constant with time. The concept has developed from demographic research on man and is useful for species which, like man, have no seasonally restricted period of births.

Populations that have a restricted season of births present difficulties of treatment, some of which have been discussed by Leslie and Ranson (1940). Very few mammals breed at the same rate throughout the year, and the stationary age distribution must be redefined if it is to include seasonal breeders. For species with one restricted breeding season each year, a stationary population can be defined as one that does not vary either in numbers or age structure at successive points in time spaced at intervals of 1 yr. The stationary age distribution can then be defined for such populations as the distribution of ages at a given time of the year. Thus there will be an infinite number of different age distributions according to the time of census, other than in the exceptional case of a population having a constant rate of mortality throughout life.

The distribution of ages in a stationary population forms a kl_x series only when all births for the year occur at an instant of time and the sample is taken at that instant. This is obviously impossible, but the situation is approximated when births occur over a small fraction of the year. If a population has a restricted season of births, the age structure can be sampled over this period and at the same time the number of live births produced by a hypothetical cohort can be calculated from the number of females either pregnant or suckling young. In this way a set of data closely approximating a kl_x series can be obtained.

If an age distribution is sampled halfway between breeding seasons, it cannot be presented as a kl_x series with x represented as integral ages in years. With such a sample (making the usual assumptions of stability and lack of bias) neither l_x nor d_x can be established, but q_x values can be calculated for each age interval x + ½, x + 1½. The age frequencies from a population with a continuous rate of breeding are exactly analogous; they do not form a kl_x series but can be treated as a series of the form

$$k \, (l_x + l_{x+1}) \, / 2$$

This series does not allow calculation of l_x values from birth unless the mortality rate between birth and the midpoint of the first age interval is known.

Because a sample consists of dead animals, its age frequencies do not necessarily form a mortality series. The kd_x series is obtained only when the sample represents the frequencies of ages at death in a stationary population. Many published samples treated as if they formed a kd_x series are not appropriate to this form of analysis. For instance, if the animals were obtained by shooting which was unselective with respect to age, the sample gives the age structure of the living population at that time; that the animals were killed to get these data is irrelevant. Hence unbiased shooting samples survivorship, not mortality, and an age structure so obtained can be treated as a kl_x series if all other necessary assumptions obtain. Similarly, groups of animals killed by avalanches, fires, or floods—catastrophic events that preserve a sample of the age frequencies of animals during life—do not provide information amenable to kd_x treatment.

A sample may include both l_x and d_x components. For instance, it could consist of a number of dead animals, some of which have been unselectively shot, whereas the deaths of others are attributable to "natural" mortality. Or it could be formed by a herd of animals killed by an avalanche in an area where carcasses of animals that died "naturally" were also present. In both these cases d_x and l_x data are confounded and these heterogeneous samples of ages at death can be treated neither as kd_x nor kl_x series.

Even if a sample of ages at death were not heterogeneous in this sense, it might still give misleading information. If, for instance, carcasses attributable to "natural" mortality were collected only on the winter range of a population, the age frequencies of this sample would provide ages at death which reflected the mortality pattern during only part of the year. But the d_x series gives the proportion of deaths over contiguous periods of the life span and must reflect all mortality during each of these periods.

It has been stressed that the frequencies of ages in life or of ages at death provide life-table information only when they are drawn from a population with a stationary age distribution. This age distribution should not be confused with the stable distribution. When a population increases at a constant rate and where survivorship and fecundity rates are constant, the age distribution eventually assumes a stable form (Lotka 1907 a, b; Sharpe and Lotka 1911). Slobodkin (1962, p. 49) gives a simple explanation as to why this is so. A stable age distribution does not form a kl_x series except when the rate of increase is zero, the season of births is restricted, and the sample is taken at this time. Hence the stationary age distribution is a special case of the stable age distribution.

THE RELATIVE USEFULNESS OF THE l_x, d_x AND q_x SERIES

Most published life tables for wild mammals have been constructed either from age frequencies obtained by shooting to give a kl_x series, or by determining the ages at death of animals found dead, thereby producing a kd_x series. Unfortunately, both these methods are almost invariably subject to bias in that the frequency of the first-year class is not representative. Dead immature animals, especially those dying soon after birth, tend to decay faster than the adults, so that they are underrepresented in the count of carcasses. The ratio of juveniles to adults in a shot sample is usually biased because the two age classes have different susceptibilities to hunting. With such a bias established or suspected, the life table is best presented in a form that minimizes this bias. An error in the frequency of the first age class results in distortions of each l_x and d_x value below it in the series, but q_x values are independent of frequencies in younger age classes. By definition, q is the ratio of those dying during an age interval to those alive at the beginning of the interval. At age y the value of q is given by

$$q_y = d_y/l_y$$

but

$$d_y = l_y - l_{y+1}$$

therefore

$$q_y = (l_y - l_{y+1})/l_y \ .$$

Thus the value of q_y is not directly dependent on absolute values of l_x but on the differences between successive values. If the l_x series is calculated from age frequencies in which the initial frequency

is inaccurate, each l_x value will be distorted. However, the difference between any two, divided by the first, will remain constant irrespective of the magnitude of error above them in the series. Thus a q_x value is independent of all but two survivorship age frequencies and can be calculated directly from these frequencies (f_x) by

$$q_x = (f_x - f_{x+1})/f_x$$

if the previously discussed conditions are met.

The calculation of q from frequencies of ages at death is slightly more complex:

by definition $\qquad q_y = d_y/l_y$

but $\qquad l_y = \sum_{x=0}^{\infty} d_x - \sum_{x=0}^{y-1} d_x$

therefore $\qquad q_y = d_y/(\sum_{x=0}^{\infty} d_x - \sum_{x=0}^{y-1} d_x)$

$$= d_y/\sum_{x=y}^{\infty} d_x$$

but the frequencies of ages at death (f'_x) are themselves a kd_x series and so $\qquad q_y = f'_y/\sum_{x=y}^{\infty} f'_x \ .$

Thus the value of q at any age is independent of frequencies of the younger age classes. Although the calculated value of q for the first age class may be wrong, this error does not affect the q_x values for the older age classes.

The q_x series has other advantages over the l_x and d_x series for presenting the pattern of mortality with age. It shows rates of mortality directly, whereas this rate is illustrated in a graph of the l_x series (the series most often used when comparing species) only by the slope of the curve.

A LIFE TABLE FOR THE THAR,

Hemitragus jemlahicus

The Himalayan thar is a hollow-horned ungulate introduced into New Zealand in 1904 (Donne 1924) and which now occupies 2,000 miles^2 of mountainous country in the South Island. Thar were liberated at Mount Cook and have since spread mostly north and south along the Southern Alps. They are still spreading at a rate of about 1.1 miles a year (Caughley 1963) and so the populations farthest from the point of liberation have been established only recently and have not yet had time to increase greatly in numbers. Closer to the site of liberation the density is higher (correlated with the greater length of time that animals have been established there), and around the point of liberation itself there is evidence that the population has decreased (Anderson and Henderson 1961).

The growth rings on its horns are laid down in each winter of life other than the first (Caughley 1965), thereby allowing the accurate ageing of specimens. An age structure was calculated from a sample of 623 females older than 1 yr shot in the Godley and Macaulay Valleys between November 1963 and February 1964. Preliminary work on behavior indicates that there is very little dispersal of females into or out of this region, both because the females have distinct home ranges and because there are few ice-free passes linking the valley heads.

As these data illustrate problems presented by most mammals, and because the life table has not been published previously, the methods of treatment will be outlined in some detail.

Is the population stationary?

Although it is impossible to determine the stationary nature of a population by examining the age structure of a single sample, even when rates of fecundity are known, in some circumstances a series of age structures will give the required information. This fact is here utilized to investigate the stability of this population.

The sample was taken about halfway between the point of liberation and the edge of the range. It is this region between increasing and decreasing populations where one would expect to find a stationary population. The animals came into the Godley Valley from the southwest and presumably colonized this side of the valley before crossing the 2 miles of river bed to the northeast side. This pattern of establishment is deduced from that in the Rakaia Valley, at the present edge of the breeding range, where thar bred for at least 5 yr on the south side of the valley before colonizing the north side. Having colonized the northeast side of the Godley Valley, the thar would then cross the Sibald Range to enter the Macaulay Valley, which is a further 6 miles northeast. The sample can therefore be divided into three subsamples corresponding to the different periods of time that the animals have been present in the three areas. A 10 × 3 contingency test for differences between the three age distributions of females 1 yr of age or older gave no indication that the three subpopulations differed in age structure ($\chi^2 = 22.34$; $P = 0.2$).

This information can be interpreted in two ways: either the three subpopulations are neither increasing nor decreasing and hence are likely to have stationary age distributions, or the subpopulations could be increasing at the same rate, in which case they could have identical stable age distributions. The second alternative carries a

TABLE I. Relative densities of thar in three zones

Zone	Number females autopsied	Mean density index[a]	Standard error
Godley Valley south........	258	2.19	0.56
Godley Valley north........	240	1.67	0.53
Macaulay Valley..........	115	2.66	0.69

$F_{2,56}$ for densities between valleys = 1.74, not significant
[a]Density indices were calculated as the number of females other than kids recorded as autopsied in a zone each day, divided by the number of shooters hunting in the zone on that day.

corollary that the subpopulations would have different densities because they have been increasing for differing periods of time. But an analysis of the three densities gives no indication that they differ (Table I). This result necessitates the rejection of the second alternative.

The above evidence suggesting that the sample was drawn from a stationary age distribution is supported to some extent by observation. When I first passed through the area in 1957, I saw about as many thar per day as in 1963-64. J. A. Anderson, a man who has taken an interest in the thar of this region, writes that the numbers of thar in 1956 were about the same as in 1964 (Anderson, pers. comm.). These are subjective evaluations and for that reason cannot by themselves be given much weight, but they support independent evidence that the population is stationary or nearly so.

Is the sample biased?

A sample of the age structure of a population can be biased in several ways. The most obvious source of bias is behavioral or range differences between males and females. For instance, should males tend to occupy terrain which is more difficult to hunt over than that used by females, they would be underrepresented in a sample obtained by hunting. During the summer thar range in three main kinds of groups: one consists of females, juveniles and kids, a second consists of young males and the third of mature males. The task of sampling these three groupings in the same proportions as they occur throughout the area is complicated by their preferences for terrain that differs in slope, altitude and exposure. Consequently the attempt to take an unbiased sample of both males and females was abandoned and the hunting was directed towards sampling only the nanny-kid herds in an attempt to take a representative sample of females. The following analysis is restricted to females.

Although bias attributable to differences in behavior between sexes can be eliminated by the simple contrivance of ignoring one sex, some age classes of females may be more susceptible than others to shooting. To test for such a difference, females other than kids were divided into two groups: those from herds in which some members were aware of the presence of the shooter before he fired, and those from herds which were undisturbed before shooting commenced. If any age group is particularly wary its members should occur more often in the "disturbed" category than is the case for other age groups. But a χ^2 test ($\chi^2 = 7.28$, df $= 9$, $P = 0.6$) revealed no significant difference between the age structures of the two categories.

The sample was next divided into those females shot at ranges less than 200 yards and those shot out of this range. If animals in a given age class are more easily stalked than the others, they will tend to be shot at closer ranges. Alternatively, animals which present small targets may be underrepresented in the sample of those shot at ranges over 200 yards. This is certainly true of kids, which are difficult to see, let alone to shoot, at ranges in excess of 200 yards. The kids have therefore not been included in the analysis because their underrepresentation in the sample is an acknowledged fact, but for older females there is no difference between the age structures of the two groups divided by range which is not explainable as sampling variation ($\chi^2 = 9.68$, df $= 9$, $P = 0.4$). This is not to imply that no bias exists—the yearling class for instance could well be underrepresented beyond 200 yards—but that

no bias could be detected from a sample of this size.

The taking of a completely representative sample from a natural population of mammals is probably a practical impossibility, and I make no claim that this sample of thar is free of bias, but as bias cannot be detected from the data, I assume it is slight.

Construction of the life table

The shooting yielded 623 females 1 yr old or older, aged by growth rings on the horns. As the sampling period spanned the season of births, a frequency for age 0 cannot be calculated directly from the number of kids shot because early in the period the majority had not been born. In any case, the percentage of kids in the sample is biased.

The numbers of females at each age are shown in Table II, column 2. Although the ages are given only to integral years each class contains animals between ages x yr $- \frac{1}{2}$ month and x yr $+ 2\frac{1}{2}$ months. Variance owing to the spread of the kidding season is not included in this range, but the season has a standard deviation of only 15 days (Caughley 1965).

Up to an age of 12 yr (beyond this age the values dropped below 5 and were not treated) the frequencies were smoothed according to the formula

$$\log y = 1.9673 + 0.0246x - 0.01036 x^2,$$

where y is the frequency and x the age. The linear and quadratic terms significantly reduced

TABLE II. Life table and fecundity table for the thar *Hemitragus jemlahicus* (females only)

1 Age in years x	2 Frequency in sample	3 Adjusted frequency	4 No. female live births per female at age x m_x	5 $1,000\ l_x$	6 $1,000\ d_x$	7 $1,000\ q_x$
0	—	205[a]	0.000	1,000	533	533
1	94	95.83	0.005	467	6	13
2	97	94.43	0.135	461	28	61
3	107	88.69	0.440	433	46	106
4	68	79.41	0.420	387	56	145
5	70	67.81	0.465	331	62	187
6	47	55.20	0.425	269	60	223
7	37	42.85	0.460	209	54	258
8	35	31.71	0.485	155	46	297
9	24	22.37	0.500	109	36	330
10	16	15.04	0.500	73	26	356
11	11	9.64	}0.470	47	18	382
12	6	5.90		29		
13	3		}0.350			
14	4					
15	3					
16	0					
17	1					

[a]Calculated from adjusted frequencies of females other than kids (column 3) and m_x values (column 4).

G. Caughley

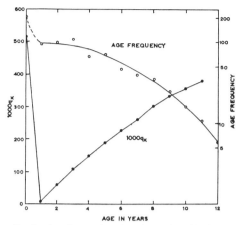

Fig. 1. Age frequencies, plotted on a logarithmic scale, of a sample of female thar, with a curve fitted to the values from ages 1 to 12 yr, and the mortality rate per 1,000 for each age interval of 1 yr ($1,000q_x$) plotted against the start of the interval.

variance around the regression, but reduction by the addition of a cubic term was not significant at the 0.05 level. There are biological reasons for suspecting that the cubic term would have given a significant reduction of variance had the sample been larger, but for the purposes of this study its inclusion in the equation would add very little. The improved fit brought about by the quadratic term indicates that the rate of mortality increases with age. Whether the rate of this rate also increases, is left open. The computed curve closely fitted the observed data (Fig. 1) and should greatly reduce the noise resulting from sampling variation, the differential effect on mortality of different seasons, and the minor heterogeneities which, although not detectable, are almost certain to be present. The equation is used to give adjusted frequencies in Table II, column 3.

The frequency of births can now be estimated from the observed mean number of female kids produced per female at each age. These are shown in column 4. They were calculated as the number of females at each age either carrying a foetus or lactating, divided by the number of females of that age which were shot. These values were then halved because the sex ratio of late foetuses and kids did not differ significantly from 1:1 (93 ♂ ♂ : 97 ♀ ♀). The method is open to a number of objections: it assumes that all kids were born alive, that all females neither pregnant nor lactating were barren for that season, and that twinning did not occur. The first assumption, if false, would give rise to a positive bias, and the second

and third to a negative bias. However, the ratio of females older than 2 yr that were either pregnant or lactating to those neither pregnant nor lactating did not differ significantly between the periods November to December and January to February ($\chi^2 = 0.79$, $P = 0.4$), suggesting that still births and mortality immediately after birth were not common enough to bias the calculation seriously. Errors are unlikely to be introduced by temporarily barren females suckling yearlings, because no female shot in November that was either barren (as judged by the state of the uterus) or pregnant was lactating. Errors resulting from the production of twins will be very small; we found no evidence of twinning in this area.

The products of each pair of values in columns 3 and 4 (Table II) were summed to give an estimate of the potential number of female kids produced by the females in the sample. This value of 205 is entered at the head of column 3. The adjusted age frequencies in column 3 were each multiplied by 4.878 to give the $1,000l_x$ survivorship values in column 5. The mortality series (column 6) and mortality-rate series (column 7) were calculated from these.

Conclusions

Figure 1 shows the mortality rate of females in this thar population up to an age of 12 yr. Had the sample been larger the graph could have been extended to an age of 17 yr or more, but this would have little practical value for the calculation of population statistics because less than 3% of females in the population were older than 12 yr.

The pattern of mortality with age can be divided into two parts—a juvenile phase characterized by a high rate of mortality, followed by a postjuvenile phase in which the rate of mortality is initially low but rises at an approximately constant rate with age.

Table II gives both the l_x and m_x series, and these two sets of values provide most of the information needed to describe the dynamics of the population. Assuming that these two series are accurate, the following statistics can be derived: generation length (i.e. mean lapse of time between a female's date of birth and the mean date of birth of her offspring), T:

$$T = \frac{\Sigma l_x m_x x}{\Sigma l_x m_x} = 5.4 \text{ yr};$$

mean rate of mortality for all age groups, $\bar{q}_x$:

$$\bar{q}_x = 1/\Sigma l_x = 0.25 \text{ per female per annum};$$

life expectancy at birth, e_0:

$$e_0 = \Sigma l_x - \tfrac{1}{2} = 3.5 \text{ yr}.$$

55

The last two statistics can also be expressed conveniently in terms of the mortality series by

$$\bar{q}_x = 1/\Sigma \ (x+1) \ d_x$$

and

$$e_0 = \frac{\Sigma \ (2x+1) \ d_x}{2} \, .$$

The relationship of the two is given by

$$\bar{q}_x = 2/(2e_0 + 1).$$

LIFE TABLES FOR OTHER MAMMALS

The difficulty of comparing the mortality patterns of animals that differ greatly in life span can be readily appreciated. To solve this problem, Deevey (1947) proposed the percentage deviation from mean length of life as an appropriate scale, thereby allowing direct comparison of the life tables of, say, a mammal and an invertebrate. For such comparisons this scale is obviously useful, but for mammals where the greatest difference in mortality rates may be at the juvenile stage the scale often obscures similarities.

By way of illustration, Figure 2 shows $1,000q_x$ curves for two model populations which differ only in the mortality rate of the first age class. When the values are graphed on a scale of percentage deviation from mean length of life the close similarity of the two sets of data is no longer apparent. Thus the use of Deevey's scale for

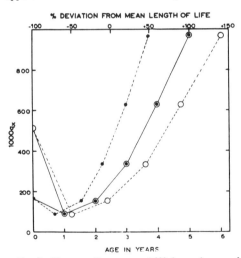

FIG. 2. The mortality rate per 1,000 for each year of life for two model populations that differ only in the degree of first-year mortality. These $1,000q_x$ values are each graphed on two time scales: absolute age in years (continuous lines) and percentage deviation from mean life expectancy (broken lines).

comparing mortality patterns in mammals might result in a loss rather than a gain of information. In this paper, absolute age has been retained as a scale in comparing life tables of different species, although this scale has its own limitations.

Domestic sheep, Ovis aries.—Between 1954 and 1959, Hickey (1960) recorded the ages at death of 83,113 females on selected farms in the North Island of New Zealand. He constructed a q_x table from age 1½ yr by "dividing the number of deaths which have occurred in each year of age by the number 'exposed to risk' [of death] at the same age." An age interval of 1 yr was chosen and the age series 1½, 2½, 3½ etc. was used in preference to integral ages.

The q_x series conformed very closely to the regression: log $q_x = 0.156x + 0.24$, enabling him in a subsequent paper (Hickey 1963) to present the interpolated q_x values at integral ages. He also calculated q for the first year of life from a knowledge of the number of lambs dying before 1 yr of age out of 85,309 (sexes pooled) born alive.

These data probably provide the most accurate life table for any mammal. The $1,000q_x$ curve is graphed in Figure 3.

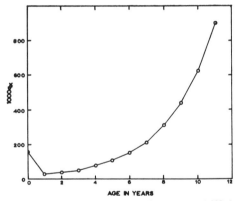

FIG. 3. Domestic sheep: mortality rate per 1,000 for each age interval of 1 yr ($1,000q_x$), plotted against the start of the interval. Data from Hickey (1963).

Dall sheep, Ovis dalli.—During his study on the wolves of Mount McKinley National Park, Murie (1944) aged carcasses of dall sheep he found dead, their ages at death being established from the growth rings on the horns. This sample can be divided into those that died before 1937 and those that died between 1937 and 1941. The former sample was used by Deevey (1947) to construct the life table presented in his classic paper on mortality in natural populations. Kurtén (1953) constructed a life table from the same

G. CAUGHLEY

data, but corrected the underrepresentation of first-year animals resulting from the relatively greater perishability of their skulls by assuming that adult females produce 1 lamb per annum from about their second birthday. Taber and Dasmann (1957) constructed life tables for both males and females from the sample of animals dying between 1937 and 1941, and adjusted both the 0 to 1- and 1 to 2-year age frequencies on the assumption that a female produces her first lamb at about her third birthday and another lamb each year thereafter, that the sex ratio at birth is unity and that the loss of yearlings is not more than 10%.

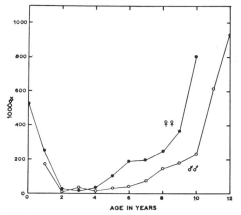

FIG. 4. Dall sheep: mortality rate per 1,000 for each age interval of 1 yr ($1,000q_x$), plotted against the start of the interval. Data from Murie (1944).

Figure 4 shows a version of this table constructed from the pre-1937 sample. The mortality of the first year class has been adjusted by assuming that the sex ratio at birth is unity, that 50% of females produce their first kids at their second birthday and that thereafter 90% produce kids each year. The figure of 50% fecundity at age 2 is borrowed from Woodgerd's (1964) study on the closely related *Ovis canadensis*, and the subsequent 90% fecundity is based on Murie's (1944) statement that twins are extremely rare. To allow for temporarily or permanently barren animals, 10% is subtracted from the potential fecundity.

This life table must be taken as an approximation. As Deevey (1947) has pointed out, the pre-1937 and 1937–41 samples differ significantly in age structure. The obvious conclusion is that the mortality rate by age was changing before and during the period of study. Consequently the age structure of the sample is likely to be only an approximation of the kd_x series. Furthermore,

the q_x values for age 1 yr are likely to have been biased by differential perishability of skulls, but no arbitrary adjustment has been made.

Man.—Most of the life tables available for man show that males have a higher rate of mortality than females. However, Macdonell's (1913) tables for ancient Rome, Hispania and Lusitania suggest that this might not always have been so and that in some circumstance the reverse can be true.

A $1,000q_x$ curve for Caucasian males and females in the United States between 1939 and 1941 is shown in Figure 5. The values are taken from Dublin, Lotka, and Spiegelman (1949).

Rat, Rattus norvegicus.—Wiesner and Sheard (1935) gave the ages at death of 1,456 females of the albino rat (Wistar strain) in a laboratory population. Their table begins at an age of 31 days, but Leslie et al. (1952) calculate from Wiesner and Sheard's data that the probability of dying between birth and 31 days was 0.316. Figure 6 gives a q_x curve constructed from these data.

Short-tailed vole, Microtus agrestis.—The ages at death of 85 males and 34 females were reported by Leslie and Ranson (1940) from a laboratory population of voles kept at the Bureau of Animal Population, Oxford. Frequencies for both sexes were pooled and the data were smoothed by the formula $f_x = f_0 e^{-bx^2}$ where f is the frequency of animals alive age x, and b is a constant. The computed curve closely fitted the data ($P = 0.5$ to 0.7). Figure 6 shows the $1,000q_x$ curve derived from the authors' sixth table.

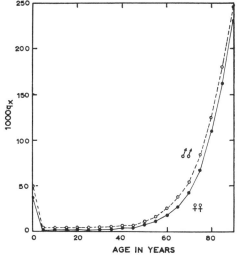

FIG. 5. Man in U.S.: mortality rate per 1,000 per year of age ($1,000q_x$). Data from Dublin et al. (1949).

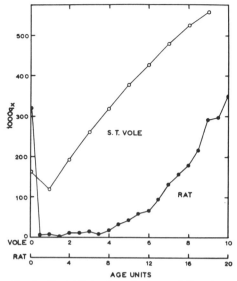

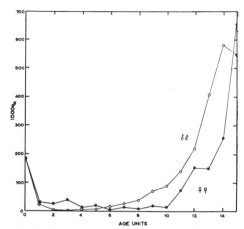

Fig. 7. Orkney vole: mortality rate per 1,000 for each age interval of 56 days $(1,000q_x)$, plotted against the start of the interval. Data from Leslie et al. (1955).

Fig. 6. Short-tailed voles and rats: mortality rate per 1,000 for each age interval $(1,000q_x)$, plotted against the start of the interval. Age interval is 56 days for voles and 50 days for rats. Rat data from Wiesner and Sheard (1935); vole data from Leslie and Ranson (1940).

The pooling of mortality data from both sexes is strictly valid only when the two q_x series are not significantly different. Studies on differential mortality between sexes are few, but those available for man (Dublin et al. 1949, and other authors), dall sheep (Taber and Dasmann 1957, and this paper), the pocket gopher (Howard and Childs 1959) and Orkney vole (Leslie et al. 1955) suggest that although mortality rates certainly differ between sexes, the trends of these age-specific rates tend to be parallel. Consequently, this life table for voles, although based on presumably heterogeneous data, is probably quite adequate for revealing the gross pattern of mortality with age.

Orkney vole, Microtus orcadensis.—Leslie et al. (1955) gave a life table for both males and females in captivity from a base age of 9 weeks. In addition they gave the probability at birth of surviving to ages 3, 6, and 9 weeks, but did not differentiate sexes over this period. The q_x curve given here (Fig. 7) was constructed by calculating survivorship series for both males and females from these data, drawing trend lines through the points, and interpolating values at intervals of 8 weeks.

Proposed life tables not accepted

In the Discussion section of this paper the life tables discussed previously are examined in an attempt to generalize their form. Only a small proportion of published life tables are dealt with, and any generalization from these could be interpreted as an artefact resulting from selection of evidence.

To provide the reader with the information necessary for reaching an independent conclusion, the published life tables not selected for comparison are listed below with the reason for their rejection. Only those including all juvenile age classes are cited. These tables are rejected only for present purposes because comparison of mortality patterns between species demands a fairly high level of accuracy for individual tables. The inclusion of a table in this section does not necessarily imply that it is completely inaccurate and of no practical value.

Tables based on inadequate data (i.e. less than 50 ages at death or 150 ages of living animals): *Odocoileus hemionus* (Taber and Dasmann 1957), *Ovis canadensis* (Woodgerd 1964);

Probable sampling bias: *Lepus americanus* (Green and Evans 1940), *Rupicapra rupicapra* (Kurtén 1953), fossil accumulations (Kurtén 1953, 1958; Van Valen 1964), *Balaenoptera physalus* (Laws 1962);

Age structure analyzed as a kd_x series: *Sylvilagus floridanus* (Lord 1961), *Odocoileus virginianus* and *Capreolus capreolus* (Quick 1963);

Death and emigration confounded: *Peromyscus maniculatus* (Howard 1949), *Capreolus capreolus* (Taber and Dasmann 1957, Quick 1963);

Sample taken between breeding seasons: *Odocoileus virginianus* (Quick 1963);

Form of life table, or significant portion of it, based largely on assumption: *Callorhinus ursinus* (Kenyon and Scheffer 1954), *Myotis mystacinus* (Sluiter, van Heerdt, and Bezem 1956), *Cervus elaphus* (Taber and Dasmann 1957), *Rhinolophus hipposideros, Myotis emarginatus,* and *Myotis daubentonii* (Bezem, Sluiter, and van Heerdt 1960), *Halichoerus grypus* (Hewer 1963, 1964);

Sample from a nonstationary population: *Sylvilagus floridanus* (Lord 1961);

Inadequate aging: *Gorgon taurinus* (Talbot and Talbot 1963);

Confounding of l_x and d_x data: *Rangifer arcticus* (Banfield 1955).

Discussion

The most striking feature of the q_x curves of species accepted for comparison is their similarity. Each curve can be divided into two components: a juvenile phase where the rate of mortality is initially high but rapidly decreases, followed by a postjuvenile phase characterized by an initially low but steadily increasing rate of mortality. The seven species compared in this paper all produced q_x curves of this "U" or fish-hook shape, suggesting that most mammals share a relationship of this form between mortality rate and age. This conclusion, if false, can be invalidated by a few more life tables from other species. It can be tested most critically by reexamining some of the species for which life tables, although published, were not accepted in this paper. Those most suitable are species that can be adequately sampled, and accurately aged by growth rings on the horns or growth layers in the teeth (chamois, Rocky Mountain sheep, and several species of deer), or those small mammals that can be marked at birth and subsequently recaptured.

High juvenile mortality, characterizing the first phase of the q_x curve, has been reported also for several mammals for which complete life tables have not yet been calculated (e.g. for *Oryctolagus cuniculus* (Tyndale-Biscoe and Williams 1955, Stodart and Myers 1964), *Gorgon taurinus* (Talbot and Talbot 1963), *Cervus elaphus* (Riney 1956) and *Oreamnos americanus* (Brandborg 1955). Kurtén (1953, p. 88) generalized this phenomenon by stating that "the initial dip [in the survivorship curve] is a constitutional character in sexually reproducing forms at least . . .". This phase of mortality is highly variable in degree but not in form. Taber and Dasmann (1957) and Bourlière (1959) have emphasized the danger of

considering a life table of a population in given circumstances as a typical of all populations of that species. Different conditions of life tend to affect life tables, and the greatest differences between populations of a species are likely to be found at the juvenile stage. For example, the rate of juvenile mortality in red deer (Riney 1956) and in man differ greatly between populations of the same species.

The second phase—the increase in the rate of mortality throughout life—is common also to the seven species compared in this paper. However, although the increase itself is common to them, the pattern of this increase is not. Mortality rates have a logarithmic relationship to age in domestic sheep and to a less marked extent in the rat, the Orkney vole, and the dall sheep, whereas the relationship for the thar and the short-tailed vole appears to be approximately arithmetic. However, this difference may prove to be only an artefact resulting from the smoothing carried out on the data from these two species.

Despite these differences, the characteristics common to the various q_x curves dominate any comparison made between them. The similarities are all the more striking when measured against the ecological and taxonomic differences between species. Taxonomically, the seven species represent three separate orders (Primates, Rodentia, and Artiodactyla), and ecologically they comprise laboratory populations (rats and voles), natural populations (thar, dall sheep and man) and an artificial population (domestic sheep). The agents of mortality which acted on these populations must have been quite diverse. Murie (1944) reported that most of the dall sheep in the sample had been killed by wolves; most mortality in the thar population is considered to result from starvation and exposure in the winter; mortality of domestic sheep seems to be largely a result of disease, physiological degeneration, and possibly iodine deficiency in the lambs (Hickey 1963); whereas the deaths in the laboratory populations of voles and rats may be due to inadequate parental care and cannibalism of the juveniles, and perhaps disease and physiological degeneration in the adults. These differences suggest that the q_x curve of a population may assume the same form under the influence of various mortality agents, even though the absolute rate of mortality of a given age class is not the same in all circumstances. This hypothesis is worth testing because it implies that the susceptibility to mortality of an age class, relative to that of other age classes, is not strongly specific to any particular agent of mortality. A critical test would be to compare the life tables of two stationary populations of the same species, where only one population is subjected to predation.

Although no attempt is made here to explain the observed mortality pattern in terms of evolutionary processes, an investigation of this sort could be informative. A promising line of attack, for instance, would be an investigation of what appears to be a high inverse correlation between the mortality rate at a given age and the contribution of an animal of this age to the gene pool of the next generation. Fisher (1930) gives a formula for the latter statistic.

Bodenheimer (1958) divided expectation of life into "physiological longevity" ("that life duration which a healthy individual may expect to live under optimum environment conditions until dying of senescence") and "ecological longevity" (the duration of life under natural conditions). This study suggests that such a division is inexpedient because no clear distinction can be made between the effect on mortality rates of physiological degeneration and of ecological influences.

It is customary to classify life tables according to the three hypothetical patterns of mortality given by Pearl and Miner (1935). These patterns can be characterized as: 1) a constant rate of mortality throughout life, 2) low mortality throughout most of the life span, the rate rising abruptly at old age, and 3) initial high mortality followed by a low rate of mortality. Pearl (1940) emphasizes that the three patterns are conceptual models having no necessary empirical reality, but a few subsequent writers have treated them as laws which all populations must obey. None of these models fit the mortality patterns of the seven species discussed in this paper although Pearl's (1940) later modification of the system provides two additional models (high–low–high mortality rate and low–high–low mortality rate), the first of which is an adequate approximation to these data. For mammals at least, the simple three-fold classification of mortality patterns is both confusing and misleading. The five-fold classification allows greater scope; but do we yet know enough about mortality patterns in mammals to justify the construction of any system of classification?

ACKNOWLEDGMENTS

This paper has greatly benefited from criticism of previous drafts by M. A. Bateman, CSIRO; P. H. Leslie, Bureau of Animal Population; M. Marsh, School of Biological Sciences, University of Sydney; J. Monro, Joint FAO/IAEA Div. of Atomic Energy; G. R. Williams, Lincoln College, and B. Stonehouse, Canterbury University, New Zealand; and B. B. Jones and W. G. Warren of this Institute. The equation for smoothing age frequencies of thar was kindly calculated by W. G. Warren. For assisting in the shooting and autopsy of specimens, I am grateful to Chris Challies, Gary Chisholm, Ian Hamilton, Ian Rogers and Bill Risk.

LITERATURE CITED

Anderson, J. A., and J. B. Henderson. 1961. Himalayan thar in New Zealand. New Zeal. Deerstalkers' Ass. Spec. Publ. 2.

Banfield, A. W. F. 1955. A provisional life table for the barren ground caribou. Can. J. Zool. **33**: 143-147.

Bezem, J. J., J. W. Sluiter, and P. F. van Heerdt. 1960. Population statistics of five species of the bat genus *Myotis* and one of the genus *Rhinolophus*, hibernating in the caves of S. Limburg. Arch. Néerlandaises Zool. **13**: 512-539.

Bodenheimer, F. S. 1958. Animal ecology today. Monogr. Biol. 6.

Bourlière, F. 1959. Lifespans of mammalian and bird populations in nature, p. 90-102. *In* G. E. W. Wolstenholme and M. O'Connor [ed.] The lifespan of animals. C.I.B.A. Colloquia on Ageing **5**.

Brandborg, S. M. 1955. Life history and management of the mountain goat in Idaho. Idaho Dep. Fish and Game, Wildl. Bull. 2.

Breakey, D. R. 1963. The breeding season and age structure of feral house mouse populations near San Francisco Bay, California. J. Mammal. **44**: 153-168.

Caughley, G. 1963. Dispersal rates of several ungulates introduced into New Zealand. Nature **200**: 280-281.

――――. 1965. Horn rings and tooth eruption as criteria of age in the Himalayan thar *Hemitragus jemlahicus*. New Zeal. J. Sci. **8**: 333-351.

Deevey, E. S. Jr. 1947. Life tables for natural populations of animals. Quart. Rev. Biol. **22**: 283-314.

Donne, T. E. 1924. The game animals of New Zealand. John Murray, London.

Dublin, L. I., A. J. Lotka, and M. Spiegelman. 1949. Length of life. Ronald Press, New York.

Fisher, R. A. 1930. The genetical theory of natural selection. Clarendon Press, Oxford.

Green, R. G., and C. A. Evans. 1940. Studies on a population cycle of snowshoe hares on the Lake Alexander area. II. Mortality according to age groups and seasons. J. Wildl. Mgmt. **4**: 267-278.

Hewer, H. R. 1963. Provisional grey seal life table, p. 27-28. *In* Grey seals and fisheries. Report of the consultative committee on grey seals and fisheries. H. M. Stationary Office, London.

――――. 1964. The determination of age, sexual maturity, longevity and a life table in the grey seal (*Halichoerus grypus*). Proc. Zool. Soc. Lond. **142**: 593-623.

Howard, W. E. 1949. Dispersal, amount of inbreeding, and longevity in a local population of prairie deermice on the George Reserve, Michigan. Contrib. Lab. Vertebrate Biol. Univ. Michigan, 43.

Howard, W. E., and H. E. Childs Jr. 1959. The ecology of pocket gophers with emphasis on *Thomomys bottae mewa*. Hilgardia **29**: 277-358.

Hickey, F. 1960. Death and reproductive rate of sheep in relation to flock culling and selection. New Zeal. J. Agric. Res. **3**: 332-344.

――――. 1963. Sheep mortality in New Zealand. New Zeal. Agriculturalist **15**: 1-3.

Hughes, R. D. 1965. On the composition of a small sample of individuals from a population of the banded hare wallaby, *Lagostrophus fasciatus* (Peron & Lesueur). Austral. J. Zool. **13**: 75-95.

Kenyon, K. W. and V. B. Scheffer. 1954. A population study of the Alaska fur-seal herd. United States Dep. of the Interior, Special Scientific Report—Wildlife No. 12: 1-77.

Kurtén, B. 1953. On the variation and population dynamics of fossil and recent mammal populations. Acta Zool. Fennica 76: 1-122.

———. 1958. Life and death of the Pleistocene cave bear: a study in paleoecology. Acta Zool. Fennica 95: 1-59.

Laws, R. M. 1962. Some effects of whaling on the southern stocks of baleen whales, p. 137-158. In E. D. Le Cren and M. W. Holdgate [ed.] The exploitation of natural animal populations. Brit. Ecol. Soc. Symp. 2. Blackwell, Oxford.

Leslie, P. H., and R. M. Ranson. 1940. The mortality, fertility and rate of natural increase of the vole (Microtus agrestis) as observed in the laboratory. J. Animal Ecol. 9: 27-52.

Leslie, P. H., U. M. Venables, and L. S. V. Venables. 1952. The fertility and population structure of the brown rat (Rattus norvegicus) in corn-ricks and some other habitats. Proc. Zool. Soc. Lond. 122: 187-238.

Leslie, P. H., T. S. Tener, M. Vizoso and H. Chitty. 1955. The longevity and fertility of the Orkney vole, Microtus orcadensis, as observed in the laboratory. Proc. Zool. Soc. Lond. 125: 115-125.

Lord, R. D. 1961. Mortality rates of cottontail rabbits. J. Wildl. Mgmt. 25: 33-40.

Lotka, A. J. 1907a. Relationship between birth rates and death rates. Science 26: 21-22.

———. 1907b. Studies on the mode of growth of material aggregates. Amer. J. Sci., 4th series, 24: 199-216.

Macdonell, W. R. 1913. On the expectation of life in ancient Rome, and in the provinces of Hispania and Lusitania, and Africa. Biometrika 9: 366-380.

Murie, A. 1944. The wolves of Mount McKinley. Fauna Nat. Parks U.S., Fauna Ser. 5.

Pearl, R. 1940. Introduction to medical biometry and statistics. 3rd ed. Philadelphia: Saunders.

Pearl, R., and J. R. Miner. 1935. Experimental studies on the duration of life. XIV. The comparative mortality of certain lower organisms. Quart. Rev. Biol. 10: 60-79.

Quick, H. F. 1963. Animal population analysis, p. 190-228. In Wildlife investigational techniques (2nd ed). Wildlife Soc., Ann Arbor.

Riney, T. 1956. Differences in proportion of fawns to hinds in red deer (Cervus elaphus) from several New Zealand environments. Nature 177: 488-489.

Sharpe, F. R., and A. J. Lotka. 1911. A problem in age-distribution. Phil. Mag. 21: 435-438.

Slobodkin, L. B. 1962. Growth and regulation of animal populations. Holt, Rinehart and Winston, New York.

Sluiter, J. W., P. F. van Heerdt, and J. J. Bezem. 1956. Population statistics of the bat Myotis mystacinus, based on the marking-recapture method. Arch. Néerlandaises Zool. 12: 63-88.

Stodart, E., and K. Myers. 1964. A comparison of behaviour, reproduction, and mortality of wild and domestic rabbits in confined populations. CSIRO Wildl. Res. 9: 144-59.

Taber, R. D., and R. F. Dasmann. 1957. The dynamics of three natural populations of the deer Odocoileus hemionus columbianus. Ecology 38: 233-246.

Talbot, L. M., and M. H. Talbot. 1963. The wildebeest in western Masailand, East Africa. Wildl. Monogr. 12.

Tyndale-Biscoe, C. H., and R. M. Williams. 1955. A study of natural mortality in a wild population of the rabbit Oryctolagus cuniculus (L.). New Zeal. J. Sci. Tech. B 36: 561-580.

Van Valen, L. 1964. Age in two fossil horse populations. Acta Zool. 45: 93-106.

Wiesner, B. P., and N. M. Sheard. 1935. The duration of life in an albino rat population. Proc. Roy. Soc. Edinb. 55: 1-22.

Woodgerd, W. 1964. Population dynamics of bighorn sheep on Wildhorse Island. J. Wildl. Mgmt. 28: 381-391.

SURVIVAL OF YOUNG MANX SHEARWATERS *PUFFINUS PUFFINUS* IN RELATION TO THEIR PRESUMED DATE OF HATCHING

C. M. Perrins.

More young Manx Shearwaters *Puffinus puffinus* have been ringed on Skokholm Island, Pembrokeshire than at all other places combined. Some 17,794 were ringed as young on the surface, just prior to fledging, in the years 1947–61 inclusive. Of these, 1,076 are known to have been alive the year after ringing, since they have been recovered subsequently, mostly in later breeding seasons on Skokholm itself.

The young were ringed when they were found out of their burrows on the surface at night. They may sit about on the surface for several nights, exercising their wings, before finally departing. Hence the date of ringing indicates approximately, but not exactly, the date of departure from the colony, but the approximation does not seriously affect the statistical comparisons made in this paper. In some years considerable numbers of young were ringed as nestlings in burrows, but since the date of their departure was not recorded, the results for these young have been omitted from Fig. 1. In Fig. 1 the totals of young ringed and recovered in each 5-day period in each year were converted to percentages, and the means of all these percentages have been plotted for each 5-day period. Since the intention was to study fledging and post-fledging success, all birds recovered after the year of ringing were included, regardless of where, or how many years later, they were recovered. Only the very few birds recovered as " ring found on skeleton " early in the year subsequent to that of ringing were excluded. Since it is unusual for many one-year-old birds to visit the colony, it is probable that these were birds that had failed to fledge.

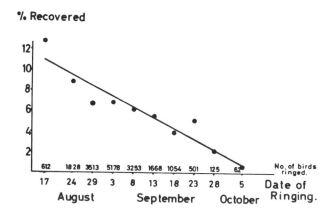

FIGURE 1. The percentage of young Manx Shearwaters *Puffinus puffinus* that are known to have survived until the following year in relation to date of ringing. The points are the means of the percentage recoveries for each 5-day period in all years (1947–1961). The total ringed in each period is also given on the graph. The regression line through the points is highly significant (p=0·001).

Since all the young in Fig. 1 were ringed at about the same stage of growth, the date of ringing gives a good indication of the date of hatching, and it can be seen that there was a strong tendency for fledglings hatched earliest in the breeding season to survive better than the later ones. Overall, it is clear that early breeding is more successful than late breeding; however, the data in Fig. 1, being derived from the amalgamation of the data for all years, mask the fact that there were considerable variations in survival between years. In six of the 15 years, later chicks survived hardly less well than earlier ones, but only small numbers were ringed in these six years. Fig. 2 shows the results for one of these years—1960, in which the largest number were ringed. In 1960 only the very late young may not have been so successful; in addition, the earlier young were not more successful than those which were ringed in the first two weeks in September. Also plotted in Fig. 2 are the data for 1948, when there was the most extreme selection against the later young.

The sample of years is too small for conclusions to be drawn, and data for more years are required before it will be possible to say how regularly the earliest young survive better than the later ones. This is of particular interest in relation to the paper by Harris (1966, ' Ibis ' 108 : 17-33) who found, during the time the chicks were in their burrows, no trends towards poorer survival of the later young in 1963 and 1964. Only in 4-5 years' time will there be sufficient recoveries from these years to see whether .there were seasonal differences in survival. At present there is no evidence as to the cause of such variation. However, Richdale (1963, Proc. Zool. Soc. Lond. 141: 1-117) recorded high mortality in young Sooty Shearwaters *P. griseus* prior to fledging, apparently due to food shortage, and it was highest among those which hatched later.

Discussion

I have shown elsewhere (Perrins 1963, ' Proc. 13th Int. Orn. Congr.': 717-728; 1965, ' J. Anim. Ecol.' 34: 601-647): that young Great Tits *Parus major* stand a much better chance of surviving if they hatch early in the season than if they hatch later; the earlier they are hatched the more of the short period of food abundance of caterpillars is available to them. Great Tits have large clutches, but the size of the clutch decreases steadily throughout the season. I suggested that this was an adaptation on the part of the parents, who are able, later in the season, to raise more young of heavier mean weight from a smaller than from a larger brood. I argued that there must be considerable natural selection acting on the parents to breed earlier since, by doing so, they leave more progeny. I concluded that the Great Tits were probably breeding as early in the year as possible, and that the date of laying was determined by the condition of the female.

I think that similar conclusions may also apply to the Manx Shearwater. The birds .that breed earliest apparently leave the most surviving offspring and there must therefore be strong selection for them to breed as early in the year as possible. The Shearwater, unlike the Great Tit, has a clutch of only one egg, which obviously is irreducible at whatever time it breeds, and if those birds that breed at the beginning of the season lay only one egg presumably this is because it is the most productive clutch-size (and Harris provides evidence that this is so).

Wynne-Edwards (1954, ' Proc. 11th Int. Orn. Congr.': 540-547) postulated that the failure of many sea-birds to replace their clutch if it was lost, was one of the ways in which recruitment of young was kept below that level at which the population would over-exploit its food supply. I think that, for the Manx Shearwater at least, another explanation of the failure to lay a replacement clutch is possible. This is that a replacement cannot be made until late in the season and by such a time there is not a good enough chance of raising a chick for the parents to endanger their own survival by ·coming ashore and so being vulnerable to predation.

63

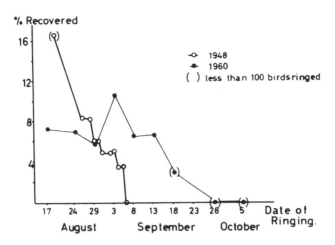

FIGURE 2. Contrasts in survival of young Manx Shearwaters *Puffinus puffinus* in two different years. For 1960 the data (see Fig. 1 for explanation) are lumped in 5-day periods (or longer at each end of the season). For 1948 each day of ringing is represented by a separate point except that two days with very small samples are lumped in the first point. 1942 chicks were ringed in 1948 and 104 recovered. In 1960 the figures were 2,265 ringed and 156 recovered.

There is only one record of a replacement egg in the Manx Shearwater and this was laid 28 days after the original which was lost at laying (see Harris). This might be a longer interval than normal, but Marshall & Serventy (1956, ' Proc. Zool. Soc. Lond.' 127 : 489–510) have shown that the Short-tailed Shearwater *P. tenuirostris* takes about three weeks on the feeding grounds to collect the extra food materials necessary for producing an egg. Hence it seems likely that a Manx Shearwater might also take this long, and Harris's data in his Table 1 suggest that this is so.

In the case of the Short-tailed Shearwater, the spread of the laying period for the whole colony is short, only about 13 days. This means that a replacement egg could not be laid less than a week later than the normal laying period. In the Manx Shearwater on the other hand, an egg laid three weeks after an early loss would still be within the spread of the main laying period which is usually 4–5 weeks. Less than 10% of the young are on the surface before 26 August, so that if an early breeding pair lost their egg at laying and replaced it in three weeks, the chick from the replacement egg would be on the surface about 15 September. From Fig. 1 it can be seen that the chances of such a replacement egg producing a surviving chick would be less than half as good as that of the first egg, and later replacements would of course have considerably less chance than that.

There must be a point at which this slight advantage (to the genotype) of the possibility of raising a chick is outweighed by the dangers to the parents of breeding again (such as strain on the parents, predation by gulls, delay in leaving for winter quarters, etc.). This is particularly true for so long-lived a bird as a Manx Shearwater with its low annual mortality (Harris, in prep.), where the chance of returning to breed in the following year is great. Natural selection may well favour those individuals that do not attempt a replacement clutch rather than those that try to breed at an unfavourable time with little prospect of raising their young.

It is not known what factors cause the death of the young, but, whatever they are, there will be strong selection in favour of those birds breeding earlier. Why then do only 20–30% of the parents succeed in raising their chicks (Fig. 1) to the point of fledging in August and the rest reduce even further their chance of raising a chick by being later?

64

Whatever the reason may be, it cannot be a direct consequence of selection for the production of young. The most likely reason is that most females do not get into breeding condition early enough. It seems at least possible, in view of the large supplies of food required to make the egg, that the female cannot get enough food, as early in the season as would be most advantageous. Possibly daylight is too short or plankton (and hence the small fishes) of the surface layers is too scarce.

In conclusion, it is necessary to stress that these suggestions must be considered tentative, since they are based on deductions only from the data on the survival of the young as there is no direct evidence on the type or amount of food of breeding Manx Shearwaters and its effect on the timing of the breeding season. However, in addition to the Great Tit and the Manx Shearwater, it seems likely that earlier breeding produces more surviving young in other species such as the Kittiwake *Rissa tridactyla* (Coulson & White 1958, ' Bird Study ' 5: 74–83—though the age of the parent is also involved here) and the phenomenon may prove to be more widespread.

Reproduced from *Ibis* 108:132–135, 1966, with permission of the British Ornithologists' Union.

MORTALITY RATES AND SURVIVAL OF BIRDS

DANIEL B. BOTKIN AND RICHARD S. MILLER

Adult birds are assumed to have a constant mortality rate in most bird population studies. Here we analyze mortality and survivorship of several species of birds for which data are reasonably good, and we conclude that a constant mortality is an unreasonable assumption. Alternative models of age-dependent mortality are discussed.

In his classic study of life tables for natural populations, Deevey (1947) reviewed available data on avian mortality and concluded, "All natural populations so far investigated in detail appear . . . to be alike in suffering a constant risk to death from early adult life to the end of the life span." This hypothesis, first introduced by Nice (1937), has been almost universally accepted in subsequent studies of avian mortality and survival (Lack 1943a, 1943b; Davis 1951; Hickey 1952; Gibb 1961; Slobodkin 1966; and others). In other words, birds are generally assumed to have a constant annual rate of adult mortality and the type III survivorship described by Slobodkin (1966), in which a constant fraction of the cohort dies during each age interval. This type of survivorship, given average annual mortality rates reported for several species of birds, would result in potential natural longevities of 100 years or more in many cases. With an annual mortality of 3%, the best present estimate, there is one chance in 1,000 that a royal albatross (*Diomedea epomorhora*) breeding in New Zealand today was 25 years old when Captain Cook made his first visit to the island in 1769! If the initial cohort were 10,000 birds, a 302-year-old bird might live in the colony today.

Fish are also believed to have an approximately constant adult mortality throughout life (Ricker 1958; Beverton and Holt 1958), but this conclusion is based on better data and more reasonable biological assumptions. Ages of most bony fish can be determined directly by counts of the annular rings on their scales, and complete samples of all age classes of a fish population can often be obtained at an instant in time, or a cohort can be followed through several years of sampling. Consequently, detailed and accurate life tables are available for many species of fish. Moreover, fish are of indeterminate size and age, they do not have the high metabolic antithermal cost of birds, and the nature of the aging process in fish would seem to be more conducive to extreme old age. Nevertheless, there are few authenticated records of fish living for more than 40 or 50 years in natural environments. The record is apparently a lake sturgeon (*Acipenser transmontanus*) that lived for 152 years (Altman and Dittmer 1962).

66

One possible approach to the question of potential natural longevity in animals is through records of captive animals, but these are often suspect. Because of the popularity and public-relations value of old animals in zoos, officials have sometimes replaced one individual with another to perpetuate a tradition, and there is reason to doubt many, if not most, popular accounts of very old animals. Flower (1947) examined records of ages of captive animals and found that the famous elephant, "Princess Alice," which was supposed to have lived for 157 years, changed from an African to an Indian elephant in the process! Among authenticated records of animals reaching very old age in captivity, the oldest appear to be two tortoises (*Testudo elephantopus* and *T. sumeirei*) which lived for 100–150 and 152 years, respectively. Hann (1953) listed nine species of birds with authenticated records of old age in captivity, and only three species lived for more than 50 years; the oldest was an eagle owl (*Bubo bubo*) that lived for 68 years. More recently, Davis (1969) reported a Siberian crane (*Grus leucogeranus*) that lived for 61 years and 9 months in the National Park Zoo in Washington, D.C.

Obviously, factors affecting survival in natural populations differ from those of captive animals, and few species are likely to have natural longevities approaching the maximum life spans they would reach in captivity. The record for natural longevity among wild birds is a herring gull (*Larus argentatus*), banded as a chick and recovered 36 years later (Pettingill 1967). A blackbrowed albatross (*Diomedea melanophrys*), first seen in a colony of gannets (*Sula bassana*) on Myggaenaes Holm in the Faeroe Islands in 1860, was shot in 1894, after apparently having lived in the colony for 34 years. Clapp and Hackman (1969) reported a natural longevity of 34 years for a great frigatebird (*Fregata minor*), and several records of sea birds living for 20–30 years exist (Bergstrom 1952, 1956; Clapp and Sibley 1966; Serventy 1970).

For reasons discussed later, band returns probably provide serious underestimates of natural longevity in birds, but in view of the fact that only two animals, a fish and a reptile, have been known to live for more than 150 years and only four birds have lived for longer than 50 years in captivity, a constant adult mortality rate that would result in a potential natural longevity of more than 100 years is improbable for most species of birds, and an age-dependent mortality is a more likely description of avian survivorship.

Although it seems entirely reasonable that adult avian mortality should be in some way age dependent, this possibility has been almost universally ignored in the literature. Perhaps this has occurred because few, if any, data seem to suggest an age-dependent rate and because, as Austin (1942) has written, it seems "of little importance biologically speaking how long members of a species live providing their life span is long enough for a generation to reach and maintain sexual maturity in order to duplicate the achievement of its predecessors." We contend that the assumption of age-independent mortality (1) leads to unreasonable predictions contradictory to observation, (2) is a poor conceptual hypothesis, and (3) has non-trivial consequences in regard to bird species threatened with extinction or subject to hunting.

We compiled a list of species (table 1) for which published records provide a range of adult mortality rates from 0.72 for the blue tit (*Parus caeruleus*) to 0.03 for the royal albatross (*Diomedea epomorpha*). We used these rates to calculate (1) the average expectation of life after a specified initial age, (2) the predicted maximum age reached by one individual in 1,000, usually known as the potential natural longevity or maximum life span, and (3) the predicted maximum age for one individual in 100,000. We use these data to develop models of age-dependent mortality which are consistent with different assumptions about the potential natural longevities of each species.

Estimates of Mortality

Life tables for birds are usually constructed from estimates of mortality and survival obtained from one or more of the following methods: (1) an annual census of banded individuals returning to breed each year in a local area or colony; (2) the age at death of birds banded as nestlings, or as young of known age, and subsequently recovered; (3) retraps of banded individuals of known age; or (4) in a stationary population, the number of new individuals breeding each year is assumed to be equal to the death rate. Various sources of error in these methods are described in detail by Davis (1951), Hickey (1952), Kadlec and Drury (1968), and others. In general, errors in these methods almost invariably result in overestimates of mortality, and we can probably assume that most published mortality rates for birds are higher than true rates (Kadlec and Drury 1968, Lack 1966).

Band Returns

Most life tables and almost all records of longevity for natural populations of birds are obtained from band returns. Table 2 shows bandings and recoveries for some of the species in table 1. These records are for birds banded in Britain from 1909 through 1969 (Spencer 1971).

Recovery rates of banded birds are usually less than 4%, and the cumulative average for 6,898,046 birds banded in Britain over the period of 60 years is 2.7%. The probability of recovery of a banded bird is influenced by factors such as its size and conspicuousness, the source and place of mortality, and whether recoveries are due to chance or deliberate search and retrieval. For example, investigators studying a particular species may systematically search for dead birds, and many returns shown in table 2

TABLE 1

Adult Survivorship Characteristics for Several Avian Species

Species	Average Annual Adult Mortality	Maximum Recorded Longevity (Years)	Life Expectancy (Years)	Potential Natural Longevity		
				(1/1,000)	(1/10,000)	(1/100,000)
Blue tit (*Parus caeruleus*)	0.72[a]	9[b]	0.9	6	7	10
European robin (*Erithacus rubecula*)	0.62[c]	12[c]	1.1	8	10	12
Redstart (*Phoenicurus phoenicurus*)	0.56[a]	...	1.3	9	11	15
Starling (*Sturnus vulgaris*)	0.52[d]	20[b]	1.4	10	13	16
Blackbird (*Turdus merula*)	0.63[d]	...	...	...	...	...
	0.42[e]	7[b]	1.9	13	17	21
Lapwing (*Vanellus vanellus*)	0.34[a]	16[b]	2.4	17	22	28
Grey heron (*Ardea cinerea*)	0.31[f]	24[b]	2.7	19	25	31
Alpine swift (*Apus melba*)	0.18[a]	16[b]	5.1	35	46	58
Common swift (*Apus apus*)	0.18[a]	21[b]	5.1	35	46	58
Yellow-eyed penguin (*Megadyptes antipodes*)	0.10[a]	...	9.5	66	87	109
Sooty shearwater (*Puffinus griseus*)	0.07[g]	27[a]	13.8	96	127	159
Fulmar (*Fulmaris glacialis*)	0.06[h]	10[i]	16.2	102	149	186
Gannet (*Sula bassana*)	0.06[j]	17[b]	16.2	102	149	186
Herring gull (*Larus argentatus*)	0.09[k]	36[j]	...	...	...	...
Royal albatross (*Diomedea epomophora*)	0.04[k]	10[b]	24.5	170	226	282
	0.09[m]	...	...	...	...	...
	0.03[a]	...	32.8	228	302	378

NOTE.—Potential natural longevity is expressed as the expected number of years for a cohort of size *n* (*n* = 1,000, 10,000, and 100,000) to be reduced to one and only one individual, assuming an age-independent mortality rate.

[a] Lack 1954.
[b] Rydzewski 1962.
[c] Lack 1943b.
[d] Lack and Schifferli 1948.
[e] Lack 1943a.
[f] Lack 1949.
[g] Richdale 1963.
[h] Dunnett, Anderson, and Cormack 1963.
[i] Thomson & Leach 1952.
[j] Nelson 1964.
[k] Kadlec and Drury 1968.
[l] Pettingill 1967.
[m] Westerskov 1963.

TABLE 2

RECOVERIES OF BIRDS BANDED IN BRITAIN FROM 1909 THROUGH 1969 (SPENCER 1971)

Species	Total Banded	Total Recovered	Recovery Rate (%)
Manx shearwater (*Puffinus puffinus*) ...	175,745	2,356	1.3
Fulmar (*Fulmaris glacialis*)	17,993	206	1.1
Gannet (*Sula bassana*)	33,785	1,821	5.4
Heron (*Ardea cinerea*)	6,411	986	15.4
Lapwing (*Vanellus vanellus*)	89,662	1,976	2.2
Herring gull (*Larus argentatus*)	99,718	3,928	3.9
Kittiwake (*Rissa tridactyla*)	31,053	762	2.4
Common swift (*Apus apus*)	66,309	1,404	2.1
Blue tit (*Parus caeruleus*)	340,399	5,430	1.6
Blackbird (*Turdus merula*)	509,983	19,662	3.8
Redstart (*Phoenicurus phoenicurus*) ...	28,625	168	0.6
European robin (*Erithacus rubecula*) ...	167,308	3,769	2.2
Starling (*Sturnus vulgaris*)	549,802	20,880	3.8

are also of birds recaptured and released at some time after their initial bandings. These factors are undoubtedly important in the relatively high recovery rate for the gannet, as compared with the rates for other sea birds in this list. Waterfowl have relatively high recovery rates because they are hunted and retrieved; only 582 white-fronted geese (*Anser albifrons*) were banded in Britain but 190 were recovered, for a return rate of 32.6%. The recovery rate of 15.4% for the heron is undoubtedly due to the fact that it is a very large, conspicuous bird, and populations of this species have been investigated for many years (Lack 1966). Recovery rates for small, inconspicuous birds are, however, often quite low (many species have recovery rates of less than 1%). Of 161,809 willow warblers (*Phylloscopus trochilus*) banded in Britain through 1969, 417 were recovered, for a return rate of only 0.2%. Because of the number of years required for long-lived birds to express their maximum life spans and the low recovery rates and high mortality rates of short-lived birds, a very large number of individuals must be banded, in either case, to have a reasonable expectation of recovering a bird of maximum natural longevity.

This problem is further complicated by the fact that the majority of bandings of all species have been made in recent years, and records of maximum longevity of long-lived birds presently depend on relatively small initial cohorts. The history of herring gull (*Larus argentatus*) bandings in the United States shows this. There is no record of when the first herring gulls were banded—there are references to bandings in the early 1920s but this species was probably banded when the banding program was begun by the American Bird Banders' Association in 1909 (B. Sharp, personal communication). Records of the U.S. Fish and Wildlife Service Bird Banding Laboratory show that 18,567 herring gulls had been banded in the United States by 1931 and that bandings have increased almost exponentially since then, except for the decrease in banding activity during the decade of World War II (1941–1950). As a result of this trend, 46% of the total of 646,055 herring gulls banded in the United States were banded in the past decade (1961–1970), and approximately 68% of the total were banded after 1950. The bandings up to and including 1931 constitute only 3% of the total, and this cohort of 18,567 birds banded over a period of about 15 years is the only one that might reveal a gull that had reached an age of 40 years or more. Kadlec and Drury (1968) estimate that 30%– 70% of banded chicks die in their first year and that the adult mortality rate of the New England herring gull population is between 4% and 9% per year. The recovery rate of banded herring gulls in the United States is almost identical with that in Britain, about 4% (Kadlec and Drury 1968), so that the probability of recovering an individual banded before 1931 is quite low.

Another important factor, especially for relatively long-lived birds that frequent salt water, is that aluminum bands become corroded and worn and may be lost before the death of the bird. Several authors (Kadlec and Drury 1968; Ashmole 1971; and others) have suggested that mortality tables based on band recoveries are unreliable and bear little relation to real patterns of mortality and survivorship. Band loss undoubtedly reduces the probability of recovering very old birds, at least in some species, but this factor may not be serious enough to eliminate the possibility of some long-lived birds reaching their maximum potential natural longevity with intact and legible bands. Harris (1964) studied wear and loss of bands on manx shearwaters (*Puffinus puffinus*) and concluded that 4 years is the useful life of bands on most of these birds. Kadlec and Drury (1968) estimated band loss in herring gulls by calculating the amount of loss required to adjust mortality tables derived from banding to data of assumed mortality rates in censused populations. They concluded that band loss does not start until the third or fourth year and reaches a constant rate after about the sixth year. According to their calculations, which assume a constant true rate of adult mortality, band loss might be as high as 20% per year after the sixth year, and almost all bands would be lost after about 20 years.

Earlier we mentioned many records of birds recovered with their bands intact and legible after 20 or 30 years, but the probability of such returns could be quite low; thus, we do not yet know whether longevity records of long-lived species will increase substantially with time and additional bandings, or whether banding data more often measure the life of the band rather than the bird. In either case, considering various sources of error in band returns and the fact that a very large proportion of the total bandings are fairly recent, the potential natural longevities of many species listed in table 1 are undoubtedly much greater than present records indicate.

Life Tables

Deevey (1947) and Hickey (1952) described different methods used to construct life tables for birds. As juvenile mortality is considerably higher than adult mortality in birds (Lack 1954), the conventional practice is to calculate the rate of mortality for those individuals which survive after a selected initial age and to use this value to describe the survivorship characteristics of the species. The selected initial age is usually 0.5 years, but may be 1.5 years or greater, depending upon the breeding behavior of the species.

Average Annual Adult Mortality

Average annual adult mortality is often calculated as a simple arithmetic mean of all years for which mortality is observed, but most authorities use weighted annual mortality rates which usually are calculated as $M_w = (D_1 + D_2 + D_3 \ldots D_n)/(D_1 + 2D_2 + 3D_3 \ldots + nD_n) = \Sigma D_i/\Sigma i D_i$, where $D_1, D_2, D_3, \ldots D_n$ are the number of deaths in each year and M_w is the weighted mean annual mortality rate. Here we accept the mortality rates published by several authors and do not attempt to distinguish between weighted and arithmetic means, both of which are noted simply as M.

Expectation of Life

Given that M is known and mean annual mortality rates for each age group do not differ appreciably from the overall mean for the population, expectation of life from the specified initial date can be calculated as $e_1 = (1/M) - (1 - p)$, where e_1 is expectation of life, from time t, and p is the mean period survived during the year of death. However, a uniform mortality rate throughout the year is a reasonable approximation, and expectation of life can be calculated more simply as $e_1 = (2 - M)/2M$.

Potential Natural Longevity

Assuming annual mortality is age independent, the probability, P, that an individual will survive a given number of years, A, is $(1 - M)^A = P$ or $A = \ln P/\ln(1 - M)$, where ln is the logarithm to the base e. Potential natural longevity is usually defined in terms of $P = 1/1,000$, but this is a convention in which the actual sample size is adjusted to 1,000 to allow comparisons between different populations. We used values for M in table 1 to calculate A for $P = 1/1,000$, $1/10,000$, and $1/100,000$ to show a range of potential natural longevities for different sized cohorts.

RESULTS

Table 1 shows average annual mortality rates and maximum recorded life spans for selected species. The authority shown for each annual mortality rate calculated and reported this rate, but is not necessarily the author of the original research. Because of potential errors in estimating mortality rates referred to above, we used the lowest reported rate for each species. Rates shown in table 1 were used to calculate the potential natural longevities that would result from the assumption of a constant, age-independent mortality.

For birds with reported annual mortality rates of 30% or more and life expectancies of less than 5 years, the reported maximum longevity is often greater than the predicted potential natural longevity as it is currently defined $(P = 1/1,000)$. The observed life span of the starling, for example, exceeds the predicted lifetime of $1/100,000$. This suggests perhaps that the observed annual mortality is too high or that survival improves with age for some age classes of this species. The observed longevities for the blue tit and European robin exceed the predicted lifetimes of $1/100,000$ and also suggest that estimated annual mortalities for these species may be too high. The recorded maximum lifespans of 21 years for the common swift (*Apus apus*) and 16 years for the alpine swift (*Apus melba*) are somewhat less than their potential natural longevities of 35 years, but the latter value might be a reasonable approximation of real survivorship.

Deevey's (1947) conclusion that there is an approximately constant annual mortality in adult birds was based on a limited number of available life tables for species with life expectancies of from 1.0 years for the European robin to 2.4 years for the lapwing, and average annual adult mortality rates of 0.34 or more. For the lapwing, a constant annual mortality of 0.34 results in a $1/1,000$ survival probability of 17 years, which agrees well with the recorded lifespan of 16 years for this species. The remaining species, with average annual adult mortality rates of 12% or less and theoretical life expectancies of over 50 years, show increasingly large differences between their potential natural longevities predicted from age-independent mortality rates and recorded maximum longevities, as well as with lifespans that are reasonably consistent with the records of old age in animals.

For example, the predicted probable lifetime of one sooty shearwater in 1,000 is $3\frac{1}{2}$ times the longest observed. For the fulmar, the ratio is 10:1, for the gannet 6:1, the herring gull about 5:1, and the royal albatross 23:1. Since the total populations of these species in the last few centuries could easily have been 10,000 or 100,000 or more birds, the assumption of age-independent mortality leads to possible lifetimes even more at variance with observation. Clearly, the following three statements cannot be true simultaneously, and one or all of them must be false: recorded maximum longevity accurately reflects true longevity, recorded annual mortality accurately measures true mortality, and adult mortality is age independent.

As suggested above, recorded maximum longevities are very likely too low, but it is unreasonable to expect, on the basis of observations of reptiles and mammals as well as birds, that the longevity of even the longest-lived species would exceed 150 years.

The problem would be trivial if the assumption of age-independent mortality led to the prediction that only a few individuals in a cohort would remain alive at the time of observed maximum longevity. Then one could say that adult mortality was age independent until that final year, when the remaining few individuals would die of senility. However, using the table 1 values for M, 23% of the original cohort of herring gulls would remain alive at year 36 and 8% of the population at year 60. If we assume a pure death process (Chiang 1968), the probability that 1,000 sooty shearwaters would be reduced to 10 individuals or less in 30 years is vanishingly small.

Age-dependent Mortality

In light of the previous discussion, it seems only reasonable to assume that mortality increases with age at least in older individuals. Lacking further evidence, nothing definite can be said regarding the kind of age-dependent effects that might occur, and indeed those who hope to understand the population dynamics of birds clearly must obtain more information regarding these effects.

The simplest assumption regarding mortality and age is that the rate of mortality increases linearly with age so that m_i, the mortality rate of age class i, is $m_i = \alpha + m_{i-1}$, where α is a constant and m_{i-1} is the mortality rate of the previous age class. Adding only this assumption to previous ones, we constructed hypothetical cohorts for a number of species and determined the age-dependent rate required to reduce 1,000 birds in year 1 to one bird at the maximum reported age (table 3). Here the reported annual mortality rate is taken as the initial rate. Figure 1 shows the resulting survivorship curve for the sooty shearwater assuming a maximum longevity (1/1,000 probability) of 30 years and an initial adult mortality of 0.07. While the curve for age-independent mortality leaves approximately 12% of the birds alive at their observed maximum age, the simple assumption of a constant increase in mortality of 0.01 per year leads to a reduction in 30 years to one individual in 1,000.

Table 3 shows that comparatively small age-dependent rates are required to fulfill expected real lifetimes. It is therefore not surprising that age-dependent rates have not been observed. In fact, the kind of studies that have been made tend to obscure the existence of such rates. Given the stochastic properties of a real population and the difficulty of observing

TABLE 3

AVERAGE ANNUAL MORTALITY RATES, ASSUMED POTENTIAL NATURAL LONGEVITIES, AND REQUIRED AGE-DEPENDENT MORTALITY RATE FOR SOME SPECIES

Species	Reported Average Annual Mortality	Assumed Maximum Lifetime	Required Age-dependent Rate
Blue tit	0.72	9	0.0
Lapwing	0.34	17	0.0
Common swift	0.18	25	0.006
Sooty shearwater	0.07	30	0.01
Herring gull	0.04	40	0.00636
Royal albatross	0.03	60	0.00284

NOTE.—The age-dependent rate is the constant annual increase in mortality necessary to decrease a cohort of 1,000 at the start of adulthood to one or less by the assumed maximum age.

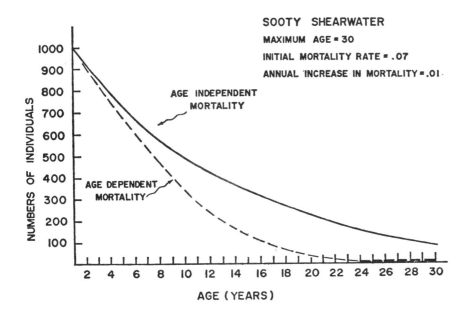

FIG. 1.—Theoretical survivorship curves for the sooty shearwater assuming age-independent and age-dependent mortality. The age-dependent factor was chosen to reduce an initial cohort of 1,000 birds in their first year of adulthood to one or less in 30 years, the reported maximum lifetime.

such a population, one would expect age-dependent rates to be revealed most clearly in long-term studies of stationary populations. As we have pointed out, even the best banding studies have not existed long enough or involved enough individuals to provide such data. Furthermore, the species most often banded, the herring gull, has been rapidly expanding during the twentieth century. The rapid expansion of this population would greatly obscure age-dependent mortality factors. Finally, the "mortality" of inert objects such as the bands themselves would tend to follow an age-independent rate. Studies heavily dependent on banding would for this reason also tend to obscure the existence of age-dependent mortality in the birds.

An age-independent mortality clearly must be rejected. What should replace it? The only justification for assuming a constant age-dependent factor is its simplicity. No doubt those familiar with the study of avian physiology or populations can suggest other kinds of age-varying mortality more consistent with their own understanding and intuition. For example, a plausible argument could be made that long-lived species would have a survivorship curve similar to that reported by Jordan, Botkin, and Wolf (1971) for moose (*Alces alces*). In this curve, annual mortality reaches a minimum in midadulthood, increasing afterward. The reduction of mortality in the early stages of adulthood in birds might occur through learning behavior, for example, in regard to avoidance of predation.

With the use of current knowledge, perhaps more conceptually satisfactory models of avian population dynamics could be generated and used to construct hypothetical populations, which could then be compared with observed ones.

SUMMARY

Birds have been assumed to have a constant adult mortality rate in which a constant fraction of a cohort dies in each age interval. Average annual mortality rates reported for many species would result in exceedingly long potential life spans, and it seems more reasonable to assume that avian mortality is age dependent. Data on the mortality and survivorship of several species of birds are analyzed and alternative models of age-dependent mortality are discussed.

ACKNOWLEDGMENTS

We thank N. P. Ashmole, W. H. Drury, Jr., R. Mendelssohn, and I. C. Nisbett for helpful comments.

LITERATURE CITED

Altman, P. L., and D. S. Dittmer, eds. 1962. Growth. Federation American Society Experimental Biology, Washington, D.C. 608 pp.

Ashmole, N. P. 1971. Sea bird ecology and the marine environment. Avian Biol. 1:223–286.

Austin, O. L. 1942. The life span of the common tern. Bird-banding 13:150–176.

Bergstrom, E. A. 1952. Extreme old age in terns. Bird-banding 23:72–73.

———. 1956. Extreme old age in birds. Bird-banding 27:128–129.

Beverton, J. H., and S. J. Holt. 1958. On the dynamics of exploited fish populations. Fishery Investigations, Ser. 2. Vol. 19. Her Majesty's Stationery Office, London. 533 pp.

Chiang, C. L. 1968. An introduction to stochastic processes in biostatistics. Wiley, New York. 313 pp.

Clapp, R. B., and C. D. Hackman. 1969. Longevity record for a breeding great frigatebird. Bird-banding 40:47.

Clapp, R. B., and F. C. Sibley. 1966. Longevity records of some Central Pacific seabirds. Bird-banding 37:193–197.

Davis, D. E. 1951. The analysis of population by banding. Bird-banding 22:103–107.

Davis, M. 1969. Siberian crane longevity. Auk 86:347.

Deevey, E. S., Jr. 1947. Life tables for natural populations of animals. Quart. Rev. Biol. 22:238–314.

Dunnet, G. M., A. Anderson, and R. M. Cormack. 1963. A study of survival of adult fulmars with observations on the pre-laying exodus. Brit. Birds 56:2–18.

Flower, S. S. 1947. Further notes on the duration of life in mammals. V. The alleged and actual ages to which elephants live. Proc. Zool. Soc. London 117:680–688.

Gibb, J. A. 1961. Bird populations. Pages 413–446 in A. J. Marshall, ed. Biology and comparative physiology of birds. Academic Press, New York.

Hann, H. W. 1953. The biology of birds. Edwards, Ann Arbor, Mich. 153 pp.

Harris, M. P. 1964. Ring loss and wear of rings on marked Manx shearwaters. Bird Study 11:39–46.

Hickey, J. J. 1952. Survival studies of banded birds. USDI, Fish and Wildlife Serv. Spec. Sci. Rep., Wildlife No. 15, Washington, D.C. 117 pp.

Jordan, P. A., D. B. Botkin, and M. L. Wolf. 1971. Biomass dynamics in a moose population. Ecology 52:147–152.

Kadlec, J. A., and W. H. Drury. 1968. Structure of the New England herring gull population. Ecology 49:644–676.

Lack, D. 1943a. The age of the blackbird. Brit. Birds 36:166–172.

———. 1943b. The age of some more British birds. Brit. Birds 36:193–197, 214–221.

———. 1949. The apparent survival-rate of ringed Herons. Brit. Birds 42:74–79.

———. 1954. The natural regulation of animal numbers. Clarendon, Oxford. 343 pp.

———. 1966. Population studies of birds. Clarendon, Oxford. 341 pp.

Lack, D., and A. Schifferli. 1948. Die Lebensdauer des Stares. Ornithologische Beobachter 45:107–114.

Nelson, J. B. 1964. Factors affecting clutch-size and chick growth in the North Atlantic gannet *Sula bassana*. Ibis 106:63–77.

Nice, M. M. 1937. Studies in the life history of the song sparrow. Vol. I. A population study of the song sparrow. Dover, New York. 246 pp.

Pettingill, O. S., Jr. 1967. A 36-year old wild herring gull. Auk 84:123.

Richdale, L. E. 1963. Biology of the sooty shearwater *Puffinus griseus*. Proc. Zool. Soc. London 141:1–117.

Ricker, W. E. 1958. Handbook of computations for biological statistics of fish populations. Bull. Fisheries Reserve Board Canada 119:1–300.

Rydzewski, W. 1962. Longevity of ringed birds. Ring 3:147–152.

Serventy, D. L. 1970. Longevity records and banding data on short-tailed shearwaters. Australian Bird-Bander 8:61–62.

Slobodkin, L. B. 1966. Growth and regulation of animal populations. Holt, Rinehart, & Winston, New York. 184 pp.

Spencer, R. 1971. Report on bird-ringing for 1969. Brit. Birds 64:137–186.

Thomson, A. L., and E. P. Leach. 1952. Report on bird-ringing for 1951. Brit. Birds 45:265–277.

Westerskov, K. 1963. Ecological factors affecting distribution of a nesting royal albatross population. Pages 795–811 in American Ornithologist's Union, Proc. 13th Internat. Ornith. Congr. Baton Rouge, La.

Reproduced from the *American Naturalist* 108:181–192, 1974, with permission of the University of Chicago Press.

DISPERSAL OF DEER FROM CRAB ORCHARD NATIONAL WILDLIFE REFUGE

R. E. HAWKINS

W. D. KLIMSTRA

D. C. AUTRY

Abstract: Six hundred one of 687 white-tailed deer (*Odocoileus virginianus*), marked and released on Crab Orchard National Wildlife Refuge during 1962–68, were subsequently observed one or more times on the study area. Eighty of the deer subsequently observed (13 percent) were killed off the area. Over 50 percent of the marked deer killed off the area were yearling bucks. For all years, 22 percent of the marked yearling bucks known to be alive from field observations moved from the study area and were killed an average of 5 miles from initial capture sites. The percentage of deer moving off the study area annually appeared to be directly related to population levels. November was the principal time of dispersal. Data indicated that substantial numbers of the deer harvested annually in Williamson County were furnished by the study area.

Little information has been published on the contribution of a nonyarding, white-tailed deer population from a refuge to surrounding areas subjected to annual deer harvests. Study of the Crab Orchard National Wildlife Refuge (CONWR) deer herd from July 1962 through December 1968 afforded an opportunity to evaluate such conditions. Most of the dispersal information was obtained from study of hunter harvests and road-kills of marked deer.

Parameters studied included: (1) percentage of marked deer, known to be alive, in each sex- and age-class that moved from the study area and were killed each year; (2) principal time of year of such movement; (3) distances moved from capture sites; and (4) distribution of mortality in relation to the study area.

The study area was the 18,000-acre inviolate portion of CONWR. The four major habitat types previously described (Hawkins 1967:3) included cropland and fallow areas (27 percent), pasture (17 percent), brush (27 percent), and timber (29 percent). These types formed a well-dispersed pattern throughout the refuge. A population estimate, based on the Lincoln Index, was made after a controlled hunt in January 1966; a prehunt herd of approximately 2,250 deer (one deer per 8.0 acres) was indicated (Autry 1967:8).

The assistance of the following is acknowledged: graduate students of the Cooperative Wildlife Research Laboratory, particularly J. Davis, G. Fooks, K. Thomas, J. Schwegman, and L. Lamely, for field assistance; conservation officers, especially J. Yates, Williamson County, Illinois, for reporting marked deer that were road-killed; and L. Mehrhoff, R. Personius, M. Duncan, and D. Uptegrafft, all of CONWR, for collaboration and access to records on road-killed deer in the vicinity of the refuge. This research was supported in part by the McIntire-Stennis Cooperative Forestry Research Program, USDA.

METHODS

Deer were captured and marked by various methods (Hawkins et al. 1967*a*,*b*, 1968), which made field recognition of individuals possible. Determination of age was according to Severinghaus (1949). Four hundred sixty-three (67 percent) of the 687 deer marked during this study were 1.5 years of age or younger when marked. All deer were arbitrarily assigned a birthday of June 1.

Kill locations of hunter-harvested deer were ascertained and plotted on maps at compulsory check stations operated in counties surrounding the study area. The accuracy of these plots was probably not greater than 0.5 mile in most cases. Data on road-killed marked deer were obtained through reports by state conservation officers and CONWR personnel; since traffic is assumed to be uniform throughout the year, these deer serve as an indicator of seasonal movement from the study area.

RESULTS

Six hundred eighty-seven deer were marked and released on the study area; 601 of these (74 adult males, 125 adult females, 74 yearling males, 95 yearling females, 130 male fawns, and 103 female fawns) were subsequently observed in the field one or more times. Eighty of the 601 (13 percent) were killed by hunters or cars off the inviolate area of the refuge. The percentage of deer observed on the refuge and killed off the study area the same year varied from 1 percent in 1962 to 17 percent in 1965 (Table 1), suggesting an increasing population pressure until a controlled public hunt was conducted on the refuge in January 1966 (Roseberry et al. 1969). During the controlled hunt, 1,109 deer were harvested, of which 154 were marked. After the controlled hunt, the population apparently again increased. The increase seems probable because of the high reproductive rate of the deer herd (Roseberry and Klimstra 1970) and the increasing percentage of deer moving off the refuge and getting killed from 1967 to 1968 (Table 1).

The 80 kills recorded included 41 yearling males, 20 adult males, 1 female fawn, 7 yearling females, and 11 adult females. Thus, over 50 percent of the marked deer killed outside the study area were yearling bucks. Of the 20 adult males, 14 were last

Table 1. Mortality of marked deer off the study area as a percentage of the total number of marked deer observed each year on the study area.

Year	Number Mortalities/ Number Marked[a]	Mortality (percent)
1962	1/79	1
1963	6/105	6
1964	20/185	11
1965	19/113	17
1966	—	—
1967	3/34	9
1968	11/86	13

[a] Only deer killed the year they disappeared from the study area are included in the mortality figures; however, all marked deer observed on the study area in a given year are included in the number marked regardless of the date of marking.

observed on the study area as yearlings or younger; many of these probably moved from the study area at about that age.

Mortality of marked deer off the study area by sex- and age-classes at the time of death is expressed in Table 2 as a percentage of the total number of marked deer in each age-class observed on the study area the same year they were killed off the area. These data show that 22 percent of all the marked yearling bucks (many were originally marked as fawns) were killed off the study area; the next highest percentage was 8 for 2-year-old bucks. Only 3 percent of the marked yearling does observed on the study area were killed off the study area the same year.

Based upon any substantial change in area utilized as shown by analyses of field observations, the annual dispersal rate for fawns was less than 4 percent, slightly over 80 percent for yearling bucks, about 13 percent for yearling does, and less than 7 percent for adult does (unpublished data, Cooperative Wildl. Research Lab.). Dispersal of adult males at 2 years of age or older was slightly over 10 percent. Reasons for such high dispersal rates for some classes of deer are not fully understood and are receiving more study. However, it is certain

Table 2. Mortality of marked deer[a] off the study area by sex- and age-class, when killed, as a percentage of the total number of marked deer observed in each sex- and age-class, 1962–68.

AGE (years)	MALE Number Mortalities/ Number Observed	MALE Mortality (percent)	FEMALE Number Mortalities/ Number Observed	FEMALE Mortality (percent)
0–1	0/132	0	1/109	1
1–2	39/177	22	5/173	3
2–3	7/ 91	8	2/169	1
3–4	2/ 49	4	1/130	1
4–5	0/ 18	0	1/ 94	1
5–6	0/ 11	0	2/ 55	4
6–7	0/ 9	0	0/ 27	0
7–8	0/ 6	0	0/ 15	0
8–9	0/ 1	0	0/ 2	0
9–10	0/ 0	0	0/ 1	0

[a] Each deer included in this table was observed on the study area the same year it was killed off the area.

Table 3. Road-kills of marked deer off the study area, 1962–68.

MONTH[a]	MALES Adults	MALES Yearlings	MALES Fawns	FEMALES Adults	FEMALES Yearlings	FEMALES Fawns	TOTAL
January		2	1				3
February	2	1					3
March				3	1		4
April	4	1				1	6
May			1	1	1	1	4
July	2			1			3
September		1					1
October		2		1	1		4
November	4	5		1			10
Totals	12	12	2	6	4	2	38

[a] Months not listed had no road-kills.

that lack of food or a deteriorating habitat are not factors. Social pressure is a possible explanation, but the mechanisms involved are not known.

November was indicated as the principal month of dispersal, when road-kills were used as an index to the time of such movement (Table 3), but dispersal may not always have occurred during the month in which the death was recorded. However, unpublished radio-tracking data (Cooperative Wildl. Research Lab.) also indicates November as the principal time of dispersal. This month is just preceding and during the main part of the rut on CONWR. Sixteen of 20 (80 percent) of the deer killed on roads during October through February (the entire rutting period) were yearling or older bucks. Mortality of yearling bucks was recorded an average of 5 miles (Table 4) from initial capture sites; this average was slightly higher than those for the other sex- and age-classes except in the case of adult males.

The estimated herd was 2,250 deer in the winter of 1965. The population structure of the herd was derived from the January 1966

controlled hunt (Unpublished data, Cooperative Wildl. Research Lab.). The structure as projected to the total population was as follows: buck fawns, 372; yearling bucks, 209; adult bucks, 2–3 years old, 159; adult bucks, 3 years old or older, 278; doe fawns, 358; yearling does, 251; and adult does, 623. (These figures have certain biases, but the biases do not significantly affect the calculations that follow.) Applying the dispersal rates according to sex and age (Table 2) gives an estimate of 91 deer dispersing from the study area and getting killed. Thus, an average of about three deer per square mile was provided by the 28-square-mile study area to the legal harvest outside the area. This was approximately 27 percent of the deer harvested (331) in the entire 441 square miles of Williamson County in 1965.

Distribution of all deer harvested within 4 miles of the boundary of the study area from 1962 through 1968 is presented in Fig. 1. Fifteen hundred thirty-four deer were harvested within this area; 685 of these (45 percent) were harvested within 1 mile of the boundary of the study area. According to the Spearman rank correlation coef-

Table 4. Distances from capture sites on the study area to mortality sites off the study area, 1962–68.

SEX AND AGE[a] OF MARKED DEER	NUMBER	AVERAGE DISTANCE (miles)	RANGE (miles)
Males			
Adults	20	5	1–11
Yearlings	41	5	2–22
Females			
Adults	11	4	2– 7
Yearlings	7	4	2– 6
Fawns	1	4	—

[a] Age when killed.

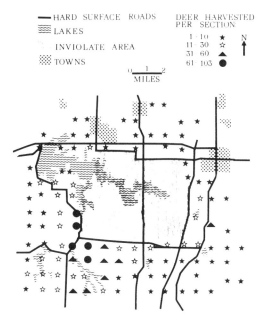

Fig. 1. Distribution of deer harvested by hunters in relation to the study area, 1962–68.

ficient (Siegel 1956:202–213), the total number of deer harvested annually was significantly correlated with the percentage dispersal from the refuge ($P < 0.01$; $r_s = 0.978$, $N = 6$). Also, after the controlled public hunt on Crab Orchard in January 1966, when an estimated 65 percent of the herd was removed (Autry 1967:40), the harvest in the surrounding county the following winter declined 32 percent from the previous year. At the same time, the hunter pressure increased about 15 percent (personal communication, J. C. Calhoun, Illinois Dept. of Conservation). There were no major differences in weather, length of season, and hunting methods from 1966 to 1967.

Another indirect index to the contribution of the study area to the Williamson County deer harvest is shown by a comparison of the number of yearling bucks (the major dispersers) in the November–December 1965 Williamson County harvest with the same group in the January 1966 controlled hunt on CONWR. Of 102 yearlings in the 1965 harvest, 66 (64.7 percent) were bucks, compared with 90 bucks of a total of 206 (43.7 percent) yearlings in the 1966 hunt. Chi-square analysis revealed this difference to be significant ($P < 0.01$; $X^2 = 12.05$, 1 df), suggesting that many of the yearling bucks had moved from the study area prior to the controlled hunt.

DISCUSSION

As early as 1960 Crawford (1962:25) believed that movement of deer from the study area increased the annual harvest outside the refuge; our data clearly support this observation and suggest that yearling males especially contribute considerably to the population of the surrounding area. The probability of movement into the refuge because of hunter pressure does not seem significant in light of Autry's (1967) study of the response of the CONWR deer herd during a special controlled hunt. Even though hunting pressure on the refuge was considerably greater than during the regular state hunting season, Autry found (p. 41) no increased use of nonhunted areas. The deer responded to harassment by hiding or decreasing diurnal activity.

To appreciate the management of the deer herd on the study area, one should understand the uniqueness of CONWR. Because of the food-planting program for wintering Canada geese, there is an almost unlimited food supply except during late winter and early spring. The chief population regulatory mechanism seems to be social pressure manifesting itself in dispersal of yearling bucks, which are the most expendable in terms of population dynamics. Also, relatively mild winters and little snow alleviate yarding; thus the entire habitat is available to the herd on a year-round basis. Further, the hunting pressure in the area surrounding the refuge is heavy; therefore, the surplus animals leaving the refuge are cropped, preventing overpopulation.

This management program seems to have worked well, resulting in an apparently healthy deer herd with little detriment to the habitat. Only one controlled harvest has been held since the herd began in 1942–43. However, we do not suggest that this type of management would necessarily be successful under other circumstances. The crash of the Kaibab North deer herd (Russo 1964), to name just one, is proof of this.

LITERATURE CITED

AUTRY, D. C. 1967. Movements of white-tailed deer in response to hunting on Crab Orchard National Wildlife Refuge. M.S. Thesis. Southern Illinois Univ., Carbondale. 44pp.

CRAWFORD, G. J. 1962. A preliminary investigation of the white-tailed deer on Crab Orchard National Wildlife Refuge. M.A. Thesis. Southern Illinois Univ., Carbondale. 43pp.

HAWKINS, R. E. 1967. Social organization of the white-tailed deer on Crab Orchard National Wildlife Refuge. M.S. Thesis. Southern Illinois Univ., Carbondale. 180pp.

———, D. C. AUTRY, AND W. D. KLIMSTRA. 1967a. Comparison of methods used to capture white-tailed deer. J. Wildl. Mgmt. 31(3): 460–464.

———, W. D. KLIMSTRA, G. FOOKS, AND J. DAVIS. 1967b. Improved collar for white-tailed deer. J. Wildl. Mgmt. 31(2):356–359.

———, L. D. MARTOGLIO, AND G. G. MONTGOMERY. 1968. Cannon-netting deer. J. Wildl. Mgmt. 32(1):191–195.

ROSEBERRY, J. L., D. C. AUTRY, W. D. KLIMSTRA, AND L. A. MEHRHOFF, JR. 1969. A controlled deer hunt on Crab Orchard National Wildlife Refuge. J. Wildl. Mgmt. 33(4):791–795.

———, AND W. D. KLIMSTRA. 1970. Productivity of white-tailed deer on Crab Orchard National Wildlife Refuge. J. Wildl. Mgmt. 34(1):23–28.

RUSSO, J. P. 1964. The Kaibab North deer herd, its history, problems and management. Arizona Game and Fish Dept. Wildl. Bull. 7. 195pp.

SEVERINGHAUS, C. W. 1949. Tooth development and wear as criteria of age in white-tailed deer. J. Wildl. Mgmt. 13(2):195–216.

SIEGEL, S. 1956. Nonparametric statistics for the behavioral sciences. McGraw-Hill Book Company, Inc., New York and Toronto. 312pp.

MORPHOLOGY, REPRODUCTION, DISPERSAL, AND MORTALITY OF MIDWESTERN RED FOX POPULATIONS

Gerald L. Storm,   Ronald D. Andrews,   Robert L. Phillips,
Richard A. Bishop,   Donald B. Siniff,   and John R. Tester

INTRODUCTION

Red foxes *Vulpes vulpes* are distributed locally north of Mexico throughout the United States and Canada (Hall and Kelson 1959). Hoffmann et al. (1969) reported that this species was extending its range in the western United States. Macpherson (1964) reported on range expansion in and around Baffin Island, northeastern Canada. It appears that the red fox extended its range in the United States where forests have been cleared and where wolves *Canis lupus* and coyotes *Canis latrans* have been reduced or eliminated.

Interest in hunting and trapping foxes for pelts has continued and perhaps increased during the past 5 years in the north-central United States. Besides its commercial value, the red fox is valued for its ecological role as a carnivore and the esthetic and recreational opportunities it provides in North America (Scott 1955).

Researchers have concentrated more on feeding habits than on most other aspects of the life history of foxes. Errington (1935), Scott (1943), Latham (1950), Scott and Klimstra (1955), and others (see Englund 1965 and Knable 1970 for reviews) have documented the wide variety of plant and animal foods taken by foxes and the adjustments these canids make to changes in the availability of prey.

Reproductive patterns, particularly natality, have also been well studied for red foxes. However, a recent report by Englund (1970) pointed out the lack of knowledge concerning the factors related to annual changes in productivity of foxes in some local areas. Likewise, little is known about the causes of mortality in wild foxes; there have been no detailed reports on mortality of red foxes in general, and only a few reports on mortality caused by specific agents, mange (Pryor 1956) and rabies (Cowan 1949).

Dispersal of individual red foxes was documented by Errington and Berry (1937), Sheldon (1950, 1953), Longley (1962), and others (Phillips et al. 1972), but no intensive study of dispersal in foxes has been reported. In fact, little research seems to have been reported on dispersal for most mammals. Howard (1949) was one of the first to study dispersal in small mammals. Since then, other workers have described certain aspects of dispersal in mule deer *Odocoileus hemionus* and white-tailed deer *O. virginianus* (Robinette 1966, Hawkins et al. 1971), marmots *Marmota flaviventris* (Shirer and Downhower 1968), old field mice *Peromyscus polionotus* (Smith 1968), and Kangaroo rats *Dipodomys merriami, D. microps,* and pocket mice *Perognathus formosus, P. longimembris* (French et al. 1968). However, descriptive data on dispersal are still needed for many species, and are essential to better understand the functions and mechanisms of dispersal in mammals in general.

Dispersal has been explained as a response to overcrowding (Elton 1927, Wynne-Edwards 1962, Errington 1963a), an innate tendency unrelated to population density (Andrewartha and Birch 1954), and a response regulated by both intrinsic and extrinsic factors (Bovbjerg 1964, Howard 1960). Elton (1933, 1949) was one of the first to recognize the importance of dispersal in population dynamics of mammals. Errington (1956) emphasized its importance in regulating muskrat *Ondatra zibethicus*

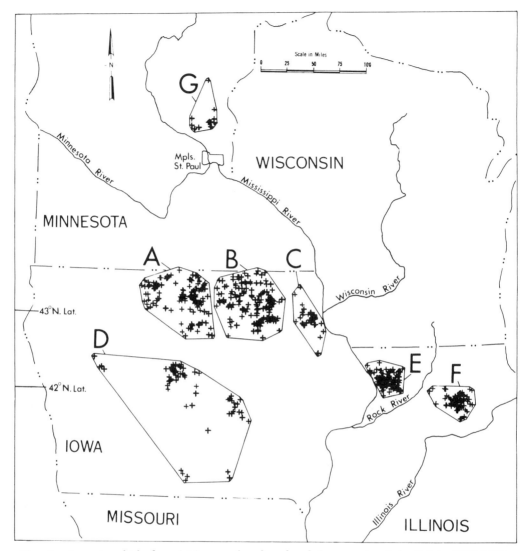

Fig. 1. Areas in which dens (+) were found and red foxes captured April–July 1965–1970.

populations, and Krebs et al. (1969) reported that it was important in regulating microtine rodent populations.

This paper reports on field research conducted from 1962 to 1971 to assess the role of reproduction, dispersal, and mortality in the population dynamics of red foxes in the north-central United States. The objectives were to: (1) describe the morphology of red foxes in Illinois, Iowa, and Minnesota and relate differences to dispersal within the 3-state area; (2) determine the reproductive patterns of red foxes in the north-central

United States; (3) describe the dispersal of red foxes with emphasis on seasonal timing, proportion of each sex dispersing, and distances, directions, and rates of travel; (4) study the possible effects of age, hormonal changes, and social interaction on initial dispersal; and (5) determine the cause and rates of mortality relative to age, sex, season, and geographic regions of Illinois and Iowa.

DISPERSAL

Dispersal is usually defined as the process

in which an animal moves from its birthplace to another locality. Udvardy (1969: 91) stated: "Dispersal, in the wide sense, means shifting of domicile. Two kinds of spatial shifts have different biological meaning for the species. Dispersion within the distribution area means spacing of individuals, a concept of population ecology. Dispersal, in the stricter sense, spreads individuals outside the limits of the range of the species and expands the area of population—this is the zoogeographical concept."

Dispersal in mammals is common at puberty (Burt 1940, Howard 1960, Robinette 1966, Hawkins et al. 1971). Beer and Meyer (1951) noted that most muskrats in Wisconsin were transient in March, when there also was an increase in gonadotropic activity and in development of the gonads. Although the relative importance of internal and external factors remains uncertain, it is likely that a certain physiological state must be attained before mammals disperse. The idea that physiological changes are associated with migration in birds was discussed by Farner (1955) and Weise (1967).

Howard (1960) suggested that the tendency to disperse was an inherited trait. Others (Burt 1949, Blair 1953, Dice and Howard 1951) have suggested that, in some mammals, an inherent tendency to disperse may be stimulated by physiological changes. The idea that parents frequently drive the young from their home range has been documented in numerous publications (Wynn-Edwards 1962, Jewell and Loizos 1966). Dispersal rates also may increase in response to increased social pressure or limited food, or both associated with increased animal density (Snyder 1961, Errington 1963a:77, Van Vleck 1968, Christian 1971).

We considered a movement of over 5 air miles (8 km) between first and last captures as dispersal. This arbitrary limit was based on data that indicate home ranges of nondispersing red foxes are less than 5 miles (8 km) in diameter (Murie 1936, Scott 1943:443–444, Storm 1965, Ables 1969b, Sargeant 1972).

Time of Dispersal and Factors Influencing Onset

Subadult red foxes did not start to dis-

TABLE 1. — STRAIGHT-LINE DISTANCES IN MILES (1.61 KM) BETWEEN FIRST AND LAST CAPTURES OF RED FOXES TAGGED AND RELEASED AT POINT OF CAPTURE AND RECOVERED DURING THEIR FIRST YEAR OF LIFE, ILLINOIS AND IOWA. FOXES WERE TAGGED DURING 1963–1970 IN ILLINOIS AND DURING 1966–1970 IN IOWA

Month Recaptured	Males			Females		
	No. Foxes	Distance		No. Foxes	Distance	
		Mean	Range		Mean	Range
April	2	0.0	0.0–0.0	5	0.0	0.0–0.0
May	16	0.5	0.0–1.9	5	0.1	0.0–0.3
June	16	0.6	0.0–1.4	12	0.9	0.0–2.8
July	11	1.2	0.0–7.9	8	1.0	0.0–4.4
August	6	1.9	0.4–4.5	7	0.8	0.0–2.1
September	2	0.8	0.4–1.1	7	1.6	0.0–5.8
October	21	11.8	0.0–45.4	11	5.2	0.0–25.4
November	60	19.3	0.0–98.5	48	5.8	0.0–45.1
December	89	22.1	0.0–94.1	48	6.5	0.0–49.2
January	102	27.3	0.4–130.6	69	9.2	0.0–54.3
February	25	22.7	0.0–85.3	28	11.9	0.0–67.0
March	1	51.5	51.5–51.5	2	10.8	3.6–17.9
Total	351			250		
Mean		19.4			6.7	
Median		13.3			1.9	
Range			0.0–130.6			0.0–67.0

perse until late September or early October, when about 7 months old and nearly full grown. Of 97 earmarked juveniles and sub-adults recovered during April–September, only 2 (a male in July and a female in September) died more than 5 miles (8 km) from their natal ranges (Table 1).

The radiotracking results also indicated that few red foxes in the north-central states disperse before October. Of 22 Iowa foxes (14 males and 8 females) and 35 Minnesota foxes (20 males and 15 females) with functional radios, none left its natal range before 1 October. Radio contact was lost with 2 foxes in Iowa during September 1970. They may have dispersed, but failure to locate them by aerial search suggested that their transmitters had stopped functioning.

The only fox known to have dispersed be-fore October was a large juvenile male (4.1 kg) marked and released 5 miles (8 km) southeast of the CCHNA by A. B. Sargeant (pers. comm.) on 30 July 1965. This fox was recaptured 8 September 1965 near Buffalo, Minnesota, 35 air miles (56 km) away.

By mid-October, some subadult males had moved more than 20 miles (32 km) from their natal ranges. During October, the average recovery distance was 12 miles (19 km) for 22 subadult males and 5 miles (8 km) for 11 subadult females (Table 1).

Dates of departure from natal areas were obtained for 14 radiotagged foxes, 8 in Iowa and 6 in Minnesota. In Iowa, the earliest departure dates were 1 October 1970 for a subadult male and 6 October 1970 for a subadult female, and 7 subadults had left before 18 October. Dispersal was later in Minnesota; the earliest departure date was 21 October 1969, for both a subadult female and a subadult male. Since whelping tended to be earlier in Iowa than in Minne-sota, the onset of dispersal apparently was related to the fox's stage of development and maturation. In Minnesota, the first subadults to disperse were the largest (presumably the oldest) when captured in early September.

If date of dispersal is related to age, one might expect similar departure dates among littermates. Radiotracking in Minnesota showed that a subadult male and a sub-adult female of 1 litter both departed on 21 October 1969. In 3 litters in Iowa, the maximum difference in departure times be-tween littermates was 21 to 44 days. How-ever, this variation is small compared with the total dispersal period, which is 4 to 5 months (see below).

The radiotracking results indicated that males disperse earlier than females. This difference may be related to seasonal changes in reproductive activity. According to Venge (1959), male foxes are sexually mature in late November and December, whereas estrus does not begin in females until January or February. McIntosh (1963) reported that testes begin enlarging about 3 months before the height of the breeding season, whereas ovaries do not begin to enlarge until about 2 months later.

Since the cyclic pattern of gonadal activ-ity was similar in subadult and adult males (see "Minimum Breeding Age"), the timing of dispersal in red foxes corresponds to the time of puberty and to increased gonadal activity in both ages. This correlation of dispersal and increased gonadal activity supports the idea that physiological state influences dispersal in red foxes. Such physiological change apparently takes place over a period of several weeks, since foxes in Minnesota were known to disperse throughout a 4-month period (October–February). Although the latest dispersal recorded for a radiotagged male in Iowa was 1 November, in Minnesota, 2 radiotagged, subadult male littermates were still in their natal area on 5 February. However, both had been killed more than 15 miles (24 km) away by 12 March.

In Iowa, 38 foxes were castrated in 1968 and 16 in 1970 to gain some insight into the effect of altered testicular activity on dis-persal in males. Each year, 16 littermates of the castrates were used as controls. Of these 86 males, 18 castrates and 11 controls were recovered between October and March within a year after tagging. Ten of the 11 controls and only 8 of the 18 castrates were recovered more than 5 miles (8 km) from their natal areas, a statistically significant difference. However, 6 of the castrate males were recovered more than 20 miles (32 km) from their natal area, indicating that testicular activity was not the only factor affecting dispersal.

Since foxes were seldom observed for extended periods in late summer and early fall, it was difficult to determine whether dispersal was initiated by social behavior, such as overt aggression, changes in odor released during scent marking, or a combination of several such factors. However, little is known about the modes of communication among foxes and how to define and interpret contact between foxes in groups. Although no controlled experiments on the effect of social interaction on dispersal were attempted in this study, some of the observations and results obtained in the field may be pertinent.

Radiotracking data obtained by Sargeant (1972) and during the present study indicated a tendency toward avoidance between individuals, even among family members, beginning after August and increasing through early fall when dispersal begins. Thus, there was no apparent increase in the amount of contact between individuals at the time radiotagged foxes left their natal ranges. These observations do not support the idea that socially dominant individuals drive subordinate ones through overt aggression.

Two other observations argue against the idea that aggression by dominant adults is a major factor in subadult dispersal. First, was the pattern of travel during dispersal. It was common for dispersing foxes to move at least 6 miles (9.7 km) the first night, or well beyond the limits of their parents' range. If a subordinate dispersed merely to avoid aggression, one would expect it not to move much beyond the dominant's range. Second, was the fact that subadults were not the only foxes dispersing. One adult male (No. 432) radiotracked in Iowa in the fall regularly moved over a 2-square-mile (5.2-km²) area. His range bordered that of another adult male radiotracked at the same time. There was no evidence of overlap in

areas used by the males, and their movement patterns seemed typical of resident adult foxes. Nevertheless, on 16 October, No. 432 left his range and apparently settled in a new area about 36 miles (58 km) away.

It also seems unlikely that limited food initiates dispersal in foxes, at least in the Midwest. Food for foxes, both plant and animal, is not scarce there during late summer and early fall; in fact, prey and certain fruits may be at the annual peak locally during early fall.

Proportion Dispersing

The proportion of radiomarked and earmarked foxes known to have dispersed during the present study is shown in Fig. 2. Of the earmarked subadults recovered between October and March in their first year, 80 percent of the males but only 37 percent of the females had traveled more than 5 miles (8 km) from their natal ranges; this difference was significant. However, the proportion increased to 96 percent for males and 58 percent for females if they survived another year (Fig. 2).

The tendency to disperse was less pronounced in adults. Of 22 adult males and 49 adult females earmarked, only 30 percent of the males and 21 percent of the females were recovered more than 5 miles (8 km) from the release points during October–March (Fig. 2). These data support Sheldon's (1953) report that a few foxes disperse as adults. Of the 26 adults that dispersed, only 2 were recovered more than 15 miles (24 km) away suggesting that most adults did not travel long distances. In some cases, the extensive movements of adults may have resulted from mating behavior rather than dispersal. We do not know whether dispersing adults had also dispersed in their first year. In either case, it is clear that not all red foxes set up permanent residence during their first year of life and remain there until they die.

Previous studies indicated that adults did not disperse during spring and summer (Storm 1965, Ables 1969b). Apparently, adults, like subadults, disperse during fall

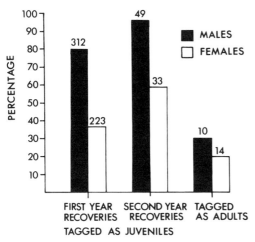

FIG. 2. Percentages of red foxes recovered more than 5 miles (8 km) from the point of release; 1 group was tagged as juveniles and the other as adults. The number above each bar is the total number of recoveries, October through March.

and winter. The only radiotagged adult followed during dispersal was No. 432, who started dispersing 16 October.

Dispersal Distance

The straight-line distance between points of first and last captures for each eartagged fox (all tagged as juveniles) recovered at various distances from their natal ranges varied by sex, month of recovery, and age at last capture (Fig. 3). Part A of Fig. 3 represents the straight-line distances of juveniles and subadults based on recoveries for all months. Twice as many females as males were recovered less than 10 miles (16 km) from the natal range, and more males traveled more than 10 miles (16 km) in their first year. The recovery distances for juvenile and subadult males for all months ranged from 0.0 to 130.6 miles (211 km) with a mean of 19.4 miles (31 km) and a median of 13.3 miles (22 km). Recovery distances for juvenile and subadult females ranged from 0.0 to 67.0 miles (108 km) with a mean of 6.7 miles (11 km) and a median of 1.9 miles (3 km). Recoveries of subadults from October through March only (Part B, Fig. 3) showed lower percentages within 10 miles (16 km) of the

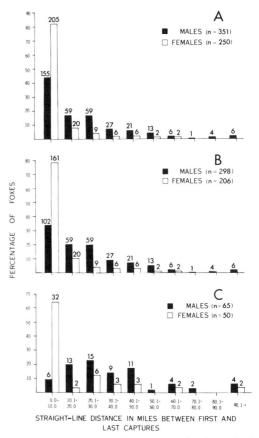

STRAIGHT-LINE DISTANCE IN MILES BETWEEN FIRST AND LAST CAPTURES

FIG. 3. Straight-line distance in miles (1.61 km) between the first and last captures for male and female red foxes marked as juveniles, Illinois and Iowa. A. Last capture occurred during all months of the year and foxes were in their first year at the time of last capture. B. Last capture occurred during October through March and foxes were in their first year at the time of last capture. C. Last capture occurred during all months of the year and foxes were adults in their second, third, or fourth year at the time of last capture.

natal range than in Part A, because they excluded predispersal juvenile mortality, most of which occurred on the natal range.

Part C of Fig. 3 shows recoveries of tagged juveniles recovered as adults (after 1 year). Of these, 96 percent of the males and 50 percent of the females were recovered more than 5 miles (8 km) from their natal ranges, and 71 percent of the males and 32 percent of the females were beyond 20 miles (32 km).

A more detailed picture of subadult dis-

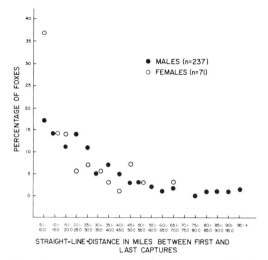

FIG. 4. A comparison of the proportion of male and female red foxes captured after dispersal at various distances in miles (1.61 km) from the point of first capture. All foxes were marked and released as juveniles and were recaptured during their first year of life.

persal is given in Fig. 4, which shows percentages of males and females recovered throughout their first year beyond 5 miles (8 km) from their natal areas. The sample

size of females is small, because 72 percent of the original sample was recovered within 5 miles. However, the females' tendency to move less is still apparent; 64 percent of the dispersing females were recovered 5 to 35 miles (8 to 56 km) from their birthplace, and only males moved farther than 70 miles (113 km).

The percentage of males recovered decreased as the distance from the natal range increased from 5 to 75 miles (8 to 121 km), but increased slightly beyond 75 miles (121 km) (Fig. 4). An upward trend in the proportion of animals moving the long distances has also been observed with small mammals (Dice and Howard 1951, Howard 1960) and has been used to support the hypothesis that certain individuals are genetically endowed to make long and directed movements (Johnston 1956, French et al. 1968).

Recovery distances for subadult males increased significantly between October and January (Fig. 5). The smaller distances for males in October and November may reflect mortality before or during dispersal. If this is true and if dispersal ends in March,

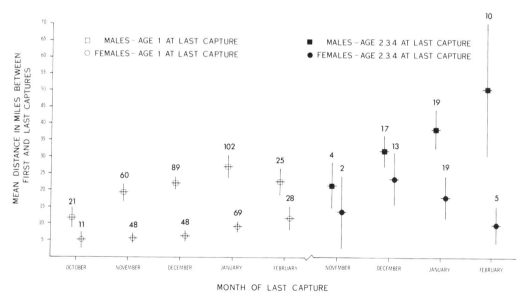

FIG. 5. A monthly comparison of the mean distance in miles (1.61 km) between first and last captures for foxes less than 1 year old and those more than 1 year old at the time of last capture. All foxes were tagged as juveniles during April through July in Illinois and Iowa. Horizontal and vertical lines represent the mean and 1 standard error of each side of the mean, respectively. The number above each symbol is the sample size.

the January and February recovery data provide the best estimate of the distribution of dispersal distances because these animals had survived through the peak dispersal period and settled in a new area. The January and February data for subadult males (Fig. 6) shows that there was no significant difference between these 2 months in the proportion recovered in comparable distance categories (the first 4 shown).

Unlike the data from subadult males, those from subadult females did not show a significant increase in the mean dispersal distance between October and December, but the means did increase in January and February (Fig. 5). These results indicate that the proportion of transient animals during different times of the dispersal period was less variable for females than for males.

The mean distances between first and last captures for adults recovered during November through February are also shown in Fig. 5. Since these foxes were tagged as juveniles and killed as either 2, 3, or 4 year olds, the time of dispersal was unknown. Some, or most, may have dispersed during their first year and survived 2 to 4 years.

There was an increase in the recovery distances of adult males from November to February (Fig. 5). After November, the recovery distances of adult males exceeded those of subadult males. These results probably reflect dispersal by some males in their first year and again in subsequent years. If so, this suggests a tendency for individuals to disperse in the same direction in successive years, thereby increasing the distance moved from the natal area.

Like males, adult females were recovered farther from their natal ranges than subadult females (Fig. 5). However, the difference between adults and subadults was not as pronounced as with males, again showing that long-distance dispersal is not as common in females as it is in males.

The maximum straight-line distances recorded for foxes tagged as juveniles were 67 miles (108 km) for a subadult female, 159 miles (256 km) for a 5-year-old female, 130 miles (209 km) for a subadult male, and 215 miles (346 km) for a 2-year-old male. The maximum distances for foxes tagged as adults were 36 miles (58 km) for a male and 104 miles (167 km) for a female, both recovered within a year after being tagged. Ables (1965:102) reported that a male fox traveled a straight-line distance of 245 miles (395 km) between Wisconsin and Indiana.

Dipersal Direction

The recovery locations of 418 foxes that moved more than 5 miles (8 km) from the release points showed that more were killed north than south of the release sites (Fig. 7). This tendency was also evident in data reported for foxes in Michigan (Arnold and Schofield 1956:95). The number of foxes recovered north of release points increased as the dispersal distance increased beyond 5 miles; those recovered within 5 miles showed no such northerly tendency (Fig. 8).

The higher proportion of tagged foxes killed in the 2 northern quadrants does not necessarily mean more foxes moved north from natal areas. There may be more hunters and trappers in the northern areas, and because snow is more frequent north of release points in Illinois and Iowa, fox hunting conditions may be better in the north. The latter view is supported by the yearly winter recovery data. In January 1971, snow covered broad areas of both southern and northern Iowa and presumably provided better conditions for shooting foxes over a

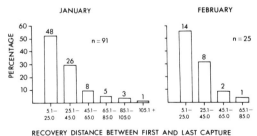

Fig. 6. The number and proportion of subadult males recovered at various distances in miles (1.61 km) from their natal range during January and February within 1 year of tagging; n = total number recovered each month.

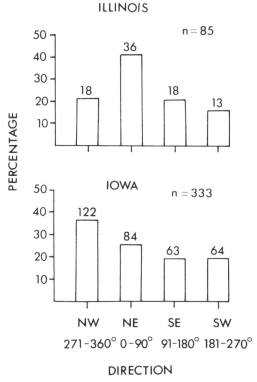

ILLINOIS

n = 85

IOWA

n = 333

NW   NE   SE   SW
271-360° 0-90° 91-180° 181-270°

DIRECTION

FIG. 7.   Distribution of recoveries in the 4 directional quadrants for 418 tagged foxes recovered more than 5 miles (8 km) from point of release.

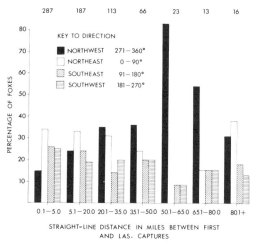

FIG. 8.   Distribution of dispersal distances of foxes in the 4 directional quadrants. Numbers across the top are the totals recovered in each distance category; all foxes were first captured in Illinois or Iowa, 1966–1970.

wider area than from 1967 through 1969. Although the recovery rate in the winter of 1971 was again higher for the northern quadrants, the ratio of the northern to southern zones was 54:46, the smallest recorded for any year of this study.

First-year recovery data for all years in Illinois and Iowa showed 64 percent of the males and 59 percent of the females recovered north of their natal ranges, versus 36 percent of the males and 41 percent of the females recovered south. Because the travel distances of subadults were significantly less for females than for males, this difference between the sexes may again reflect the increased vulnerability to the north.

There was no difference in travel direction between foxes recaptured as subadults and those recaptured as adults. In each group, 63 percent were recovered north and 37 percent south of their release points.

There were no reports of eartagged foxes crossing the Mississippi River along the Illinois–Iowa boundary (Figs. 9, 10). The river in this area usually is not frozen during October and November, but some years it is covered with ice and snow by late December or early January. Nevertheless, it does appear to be at least a partial barrier to dispersing foxes.

Only 2 eartagged foxes were known to have crossed major waterways. One female tagged 6 May 1967 north of the Illinois River was recovered south of the river 20 April 1968. Another female tagged 6 June 1967 in Iowa was recaptured near St. Cloud, Minnesota, 16 January 1972, on the other side of the Minnesota River (Fig. 10). The time of dispersal was not known for either female and both could have crossed when the rivers were frozen, or even used bridges.

The proportion of foxes recaptured in the 4 directional quadrants from the points of release are presented in Fig. 11. Of the foxes tagged within 40 miles (64 km) of the Mississippi River in Iowa, only 11 percent of those recovered were recovered northeast (0–90°), and only 16 percent of those recovered in the Illinois sample were re-

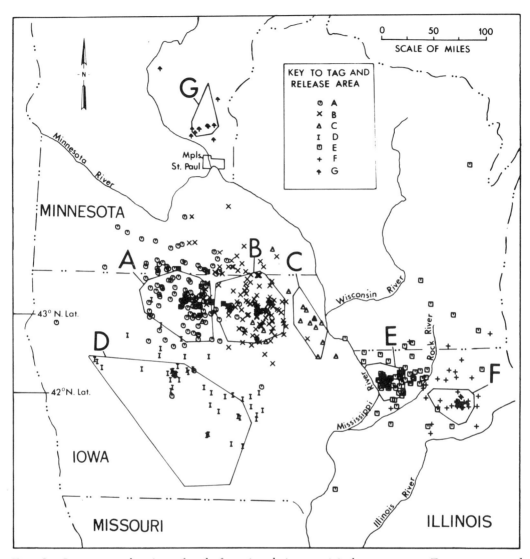

Fig. 9. Last capture locations of male foxes in relation to original capture area. Foxes were tagged and released within 1 of the 7 areas marked A–G, and each fox is represented by a symbol corresponding to the area where it was tagged.

covered northwest (271–360°). In contrast, foxes tagged and released more than 40 miles (64 km) from the river showed a fairly even distribution in the 4 quadrants, providing further evidence that the river was a barrier to foxes.

Male foxes commonly dispersed during October, and 80 percent or more dispersed in their first year. The present study produced 3 things that apparently contradict the hypothesis that young foxes are "forced"

from natal ranges by their parents: (1) spacing between family members increased during summer, and by dispersal in fall, direct contact among members appeared minimal; (2) foxes traveled 6 to 10 miles (10–16 km) in 1 general direction during the first night of dispersal, which seems excessive merely to avoid agonistic behavior of a resident fox; and (3) some adults with established home ranges in summer also dispersed in fall or winter.

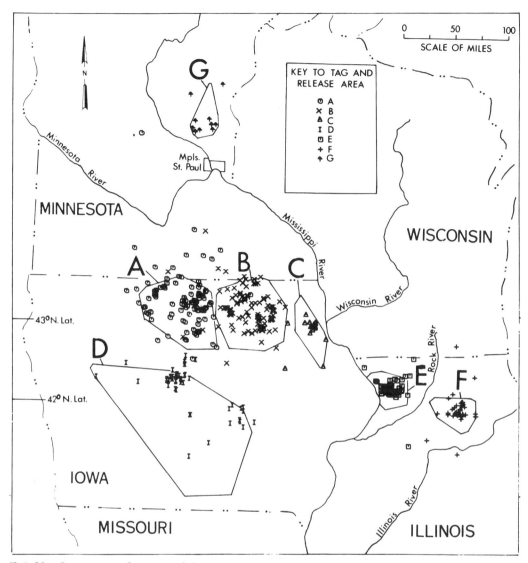

Fig. 10. Last capture locations of female foxes in relation to original capture area. Foxes were tagged and released within 1 of the 7 areas marked A–G, and each fox is represented by a symbol corresponding to the area where it was tagged.

Behavioral interactions among parents and offspring vary among mammals (Harper 1970). One pattern emphasized by Wynne-Edwards (1962) is that adults drive off their offspring when they reach sexual maturity. Conversely, in other species such as the prairie dog *Cynomys ludovicianus* (King 1955) and tree squirrels *Tamiasciurus douglasii* and *T. hudsonicus* (Smith 1968) the offspring may stay on the natal ground, but the adults emigrate. Red foxes apparently do not follow either of these patterns. Studies of the social systems in mammals have not received much attention until recent years (Crook 1970), but hopefully more research will be directed toward understanding how parent–offspring interactions relate to dispersal.

In the northern hemisphere, foxes begin dispersing in early fall when the rate of decrease in daylight maximizes and gonadal activity increases. The results of our study

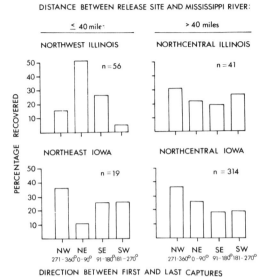

DISTANCE BETWEEN RELEASE SITE AND MISSISSIPPI RIVER:

≤ 40 mile·   > 40 miles

DIRECTION BETWEEN FIRST AND LAST CAPTURES

FIG. 11. The proportion of foxes recovered in 4 directional quadrants from the point of release indicating the influence of a major river on movements. Figures on the left represent data for foxes first captured and released in northwestern Illinois (1962–1970) and northeastern Iowa (1966–1970), less than 40 miles (64 km) from the Mississippi River. Figures on the right represent foxes first captured and released in north-central Illinois and Iowa (1967–1970), more than 40 miles (64 km) from the Mississippi River.

to determine the influence of testicular activity on male dispersal were not conclusive, despite the indication that fewer castrates than controls dispersed. Perhaps experiments dealing with the pituitary and adrenals would provide more insight into the role of endocrines in dispersal mechanisms.

It appears unlikely that a single factor is responsible for initiating dispersal. Sprugel (1951:74) noted that temperature, snow cover, sexual maturity, and social intolerance apparently influenced the initiation and rate of spring dispersal in muskrats, but cited no one factor as the prime force to start the general movement. Still more obscure are the factors that operate in the evolution of mammalian dispersal. Since dispersal probably evolved under different conditions, the factors that now stimulate

dispersal in present-day populations may not be the same factors that stimulated dispersal in earlier populations.

This study showed that foxes' daily dispersal routes usually were directional. This pattern is efficient in terms of energy and of time spent in unfamiliar terrain, to distribute foxes throughout local areas and to find areas vacant of other foxes. The present study did not show what mechanisms or cues are used to orient, but the data on travel routes provided evidence that dispersing foxes recognized previously used areas.

Whether circular travel, usually at the end of dispersal, reflected a response to other foxes or somehow served to "turn off" dispersal is not known. Likewise, it is not clear why certain individuals settled in an area for 1 to 6 days and then continued to disperse. It does not seem likely that it took this amount of time for the resident in these cases to detect the transients, or vice versa. Sargeant (1972:227) noted that "Boundaries of territories were not patrolled, yet there appeared to be an acute awareness of the presence and a mutual avoidance between family members holding adjacent territories."

French et al. (1968:279) indicated that their data on dispersal of desert rodents "May be interpreted to support the hypothesis that dispersal is not due to random movements but to purposeful directed moves by certain individuals." Our data on dispersing foxes also indicate directed travel that apparently was independent of the distances traveled. Thus, the 10- to 15-mile (16–24 km) dispersal routes seemed as directed as the 20- to 30-mile (32–48 km) routes.

The actual distances traveled by dispersing foxes are most likely regulated by a combination of genetic, social, and physical environmental factors that may vary locally. Murray (1967:977) stated, "It seems possible that individuals differing in the distance they disperse differ in their ability to procure a suitable breeding site rather than in a predisposition to disperse a particular distance." We believe that both

94

these factors as well as the availability of vacant fox ranges are involved in the distances traveled by dispersing foxes. Most of their travel probably is regulated by nonsocial factors, but as dispersal ends and the transients integrate with their new environment, additional shifts probably result from social interactions.

Dispersal of red foxes is not necessarily from place of birth to a new locality where the animal remains until it dies. This type of movement may be true in some cases, but some foxes emigrate as adults from areas where they bred successfully. Nevertheless, once foxes disperse from their natal ranges, the probability of returning appears extremely low.

Dispersal begins in late September or early October and may continue through February, during the breeding season. Lidicker (1962:29) suggested that, because transient animals are more likely to make more contact with other members of their species than resident animals, they may mate more than residents. This type of mating would be advantageous to the species by increasing genetic exchange. We were not able to follow any transient foxes during the breeding season.

There were no reports indicating that tagged foxes crossed the Mississippi River along the Illinois and Iowa boundary. The river in that region is about 0.3 to 0.5 mile (0.5 to 0.8 km) wide and usually is not frozen during November; in some years it may be frozen and covered with snow by late December or early January, but by that time many foxes have dispersed. Thus, the river acts as a partial barrier to gene flow between these local populations. This barrier apparently was reflected in the cranial morphology among red foxes from Illinois, Iowa, and Minnesota.

Cranial measurements were significantly different between each 2- and 3-state comparison made. There was also some indication that skulls in Minnesota were more like those in Iowa than those in Illinois, although the data were not conclusive. This comparison suggests that isolation, by distance, physiographic barriers, or both, was more pronounced between populations on opposite sides of the Mississippi River than between those on the same side. Perhaps more intensive sampling on both sides of the river from the southern United States to Canada would provide data on the influence of isolation on morphological differences in red foxes. Ehrlich and Raven (1969) suggested that considerable local differentiation may occur even in highly mobile species and that local populations may be changed rapidly by selection. A different view is that differentiation of populations is prevented by gene flow (Mayr 1963).

Literature Cited

Ables, E. D. 1965. An exceptional fox movement. J. Mammal. 46(1):102.

———. 1969a. Activity studies of red foxes in southern Wisconsin. J. Wildl. Manage. 33(1):145–153.

———. 1969b. Home range studies of red foxes (*Vulpes vulpes*). J. Mammal. 50(1):108–120.

Andrewartha, H. G., and L. C. Birch. 1954. The distribution and abundance of animals. Univ. Chicago Press, Chicago, Ill. 782 pp.

Andrews, R. D., G. L. Storm, R. L. Phillips, and R. A. Bishop. 1973. Survival and movements of transplanted and adopted red fox pups. J. Wildl. Manage. 37(1):69–72.

Archer, J. 1970. Effects of population density on behavior in rodents. Pp. 169–210. *In* Crook, J. H., (Ed.). Social behaviour in Birds and Mammals, Essays on the Social Ethology of Animals and Man. Academic Press Inc., London, Eng. 492 pp.

Arnold, D. A. 1956. Red foxes of Michigan. Mich. Dept. Cons., Lansing, Mich. 48 pp.

———, and R. D. Schofield. 1956. Home range and dispersal of Michigan red foxes. Pap. Mich. Acad. Sci., Arts Lett. 41:91–97.

Asdell, S. A. 1964. Patterns of mammalian reproduction. 2nd Edition. Cornell Univ. Press, Ithaca, N. Y. 670 pp.

Bailey, E. D. 1969. Immigration and emigration as contributory regulators of populations through social disruption. Can. J. Zool. 47(6):1213–1215.

Baker, J. R., and R. W. Ranson. 1932–1933. Factors affecting breeding of the field mouse (*Microtus agrestis*). I. Light. Proc. Roy. Soc. London B110:313–322. II. Temperature and food. Proc. Roy. Soc. London B112:39–46.

Beer, J. R., and R. K. Meyer. 1951. Seasonal changes in the endocrine organs and behavior patterns of the muskrat. J. Mammal. 32(2):173–191.

BELLROSE, F. C. 1967. Orientation in water-fowl migration. Pp. 73–99. *In* Storm, R. M., (Ed.). Animal orientation and navigation. Proc. 27th Ann. Biol. Coll. Oregon St. Univ. Press, Corvallis, Ore. 134 pp.

BISSONNETTE, T. H. 1935. Modification of mammalian sexual cycles. IV. Delay of oestrus and induction of anoestrus in female ferrets by reduction of intensity and duration of daily light periods in the normal oestrus season. J. Exp. Biol. 12:315–320.

BLACKWELL, T. L., AND P. R. RAMSEY. 1972. Exploratory activity and lack of genotypic correlates in *Peromyscus polionotus*. J. Mammal. 53(2):401–403.

BLAIR, W. F. 1953. Population dynamics of rodents and other small mammals. Pp. 1–41. *In* Demerec. M., (Ed.). Advances in genetics Vol. 5. Academic Press, New York, N. Y. 331 pp.

BOVBJERG, R. V. 1964. Dispersal of aquatic animals relative to density. Verh. Int. Ver. Limnol. 15:879–884.

BRAY, J. R., D. B. LAWRENCE, AND L. C. PEARSON. 1959. Primary production in some Minnesota terrestrial communities for 1956. Oikos 10(1):38–49.

BURT, W. H. 1940. Territorial behavior and populations of some small mammals in southern Michigan. Misc. Publ. Mus. Zool. Univ. Mich. 45:1–58.

———. 1949. Territoriality. J. Mammal. 30 (1):25–27.

CARR, A. 1965. The navigation of the green turtle. Sci. Amer. 212(5):78–86.

CAUGHLEY, G. 1966. Mortality patterns in mammals. Ecology 47(6):906–918.

CHAPMAN, D. G., AND D. S. ROBSON. 1960. The analysis of a catch curve. Biometrics 16(3):354–368.

CHIASSON, R. B. 1953. Fluctuations of some Illinois fox populations. Ecology 34(3):617–619.

CHRISTIAN, J. J. 1970. Social subordination, population density, and mammalian evolution. Science 168(3927):84–90.

———. 1971. Fighting, maturity and population density in *Microtus pennsylvanicus*. J. Mammal. 52(3):556–567.

CHURCHER, C. S. 1959. The specific status of the new world red fox. J. Mammal. 49(4):513–520.

CLARK, C. H. D. 1940. A biological investigation of the Thelon Game Sanctuary. Natl. Mus. Can. Bull. 96. 135pp.

COCHRAN, W. W., AND R. D. LORD, JR. 1963. A radio-tracking system for wild animals. J. Wildl. Manage. 27(1):9–24.

CONAWAY, C. H. 1968. Influence of weather on mammalian reproduction. Pp. 131–144.

In Lowry, W. P., (Ed.). Biometeorology. Ore. St. Univ. Press, Corvallis, Ore. 171 pp.

COWAN, I. M. 1949. Rabies as a possible population control of arctic canidae. J. Mammal 30(4):396–398.

CREED, R. F. S. 1960a. Gonad changes in the wild red fox (*Vulpes vulpes crucigera*). J. Physiol. (London) 151:19–20.

———. 1960b. Observations on reproduction in the wild red fox (*Vulpes vulpes*). An account with special reference to the occurrence of fox–dog crosses. Brit. Vet. J. 116:419–426.

CROOK, J. H. (Ed.). 1970. Social behavior in birds and mammals: essays on the social ethology of animals and man. Academic Press. New York, N. Y. 492 pp.

DAVIS, D. E. 1970. Evaluation of technics for measuring mortality. J. Wildl. Diseases 6(4):365–375.

DICE, L. R., AND W. E. HOWARD. 1951. Distance of dispersal by prairie deermice from birthplace to breeding sites. Univ. Mich. Cont. Lab. Vert. Biol. 50:1–15.

DOUGLAS, M. J. W. 1965. Notes on the red fox (*Vulpes vulpes*) near Braemar, Scotland. Notes on British Mammals–No. 12. J. Zool. 147:228–233.

EBERHARDT, L. L. 1969. Population analysis. Pp. 457–495. *In* Giles, R. H. Jr., (Ed.). Wildlife management techniques. 3rd Edition. Edwards Brothers, Inc., Ann Arbor, Mich. 623 pp.

EHRLICH, P. R., AND P. H. RAVEN. 1969. Differentiation of populations. Science 165:1228–1232.

ELTON, C. 1927. Animal ecology. Sidgwick and Jackson, Ltd., London, Eng. 209 pp.

———. 1933. Animal ecology and evolution. Clarendon Press, London, Eng. 97 pp.

———. 1949. Movements of arctic fox populations in the region of Baffin Bay and Smith Sound. Polar Rec. 27(38):296–305.

EMLEN, S. T. 1970. The influence of negative information on the orientation of the Indigo bunting, *Passerina cyanea*. Anim. Behav. 18:215–224.

ENDERS, R. K. 1938. Fur animal reproductive cycles and their relation to management. Trans. N. Amer. Wildl. Conf. 3:515–517.

ENGLUND, J. 1965. Studies on food ecology of the red fox (*Vulpes v.*) in Sweden. Viltrevy (Swedish Wildlife) 3(4):377–485.

———. 1970. Some aspects of reproduction and mortality rates in Swedish foxes (*Vulpes vulpes*), 1961–63 and 1966–69. Viltrevy (Swedish Wildlife) 8(1):1–82.

ERRINGTON, P. L. 1935. Food habits of midwest foxes. J. Mammal. 16(3):192–200.

———. 1943. An analysis of mink predation

upon muskrats in north-central United States. Iowa Agr. Exp. Sta. Res. Bull. 320:797–924.

———. 1954. The special responsiveness of minks to epizootics in muskrat populations. Ecol. Monogr. 24:377–393.

———. 1956. Factors limiting higher vertebrate populations. Science 124:304–307.

———. 1963a. Muskrat populations. Iowa St. Univ. Press, Ames, Ia. 665 pp.

———. 1963b. The phenomenon of predation. Amer. Sci. 51(2):180–192.

———, AND R. M. BERRY. 1937. Tagging studies of red foxes. J. Mammal. 18(2): 203–205.

FAIRLEY, J. S. 1969. Survival of fox (*Vulpes vulpes*) cubs in northern Ireland. J. Zool., Lond. 159:532–534.

———. 1970. The food, reproduction, form, growth, and development of the fox *Vulpes vulpes* (L.) in northeast Ireland. Proc. R. Irish Acad, 69, Section B, No. 5:103–137.

FARNER, D. S. 1955. The annual stimulus for migration: experimental and physiologic aspects. Pp. 198–237. *In* Wolfson, A., (Ed.). Recent studies in avian biology. Univ. Ill. Press, Urbana, Ill. 479 pp.

FREESE, F. 1964. Linear regression methods for forest research. U. S. For. Serv. Res. Pap., Forest Products Lab. 17, Madison, Wis. 137 pp.

FRENCH, N. R., T. Y. TAGAMI, AND P. HAYDEN. 1968. Dispersal in a population of desert rodents. J. Mammal. 49(2):272–280.

FRIEND, M. 1968. History and epidemiology of rabies in wildlife in New York. N. Y. Fish and Game J. 15(1):71–97.

———, AND S. B. LINHART. 1964. Use of the eye lens as an indicator of age in the red fox. N. Y. Fish Game J. 11(1):58–66.

GABRIEL, K. R. 1964. A procedure for testing the homogeneity of all sets of means in analysis of variance. Biometrics 20:459–477.

———, AND R. R. SOKAL. 1969. A new statistical approach to geographic variation analysis. Syst. Zool. 18:259–278.

GEIS, A. D., AND R. D. TABER. 1963. Measuring hunting and other mortality. Pp. 284–298. *In* Mosby, H. S. (Ed.). Wildlife investigational techniques. 2nd Edition. Edwards Brothers, Inc., Ann Arbor, Mich. 419 pp.

GERASIMOFF, Y. A. 1958. Mange in wild foxes. Translations of Russian Game Reports. Vol. 3 (Arctic and red foxes, 1951–55). The Queen's Printer, Ottawa, Can. 214 pp.

GOULDEN, C. H. 1952. Methods of statistical analysis. Ed. 2. John Wiley & Sons, New York, N. Y. 467 pp.

GROOT, C. 1965. On the orientation of young sockeye salmon (*Oncorhynchus nerka*) during their seaward migration out of lakes. Leiden: E. J. Brill. Suppl. Behav. 14, 198 pp.

HALL, E. R., AND K. R. KELSON. 1959. The mammals of North America. The Ronald Press Co., New York, N. Y. Vol. II:547–1083.

HAMILTON, W. J. 1943. The mammals of eastern United States. Comstock Co., New York, N. Y. 432 pp.

HAMMOND, J., JR. 1951. Control by light of reproduction in ferrets and mink. Nature 167:150–151.

HARPER, L. V. 1970. Ontogenetic and phylogenetic functions of the parent-offspring relationships in mammals. Pp. 75–117. *In* Lehrman, Hinde, and Shaw (Eds.). Advances in the study of behavior. Vol. 3. Academic Press, New York, N. Y. 263 pp.

HASLER, A. D. 1966. Underwater guideposts. Univ. Wis. Press, Madison, Wis. 155 pp.

HATTINGH, I. 1956. Measurements of foxes from Scotland and England. Proc. Zool. Soc. Lond. 127:191–199.

HAWKINS, R. E., W. D. KLIMSTRA, AND D. C. AUTRY. 1970. Significant mortality factors of deer on Crab Orchard National Wildlife Refuge. Trans. Ill. St. Acad. Sci. 63(2): 202–206.

———, ———, AND ———. 1971. Dispersal of deer from Crab Orchard National Wildlife Refuge. J. Wildl. Manage. 35(2):216–220.

HENNY, C. J. 1969. Geographical variation in mortality rates and production requirements of the barn owl (*Tyto alba* spp.). Bird-Banding 40(4):277–290.

HOFFMAN, R. A., AND C. M. KIRKPATRICK. 1954. Red fox weights and reproduction in Tippecanoe County, Indiana. J. Mammal 35(4): 504–509.

HOFFMANN, R. S., P. L. WRIGHT, AND F. E. NEWBY. 1969. The distribution of some mammals in Montana. I. Mammals other than bats. J. Mammal. 50(3):579–604.

HOWARD, W. E. 1949. Dispersal, amount of inbreeding, and longevity in a local population of prairie deermice on the George Reserve, Southern Michigan. Univ. Mich. Cont. Lab. Vert. Biol. 43:1–50.

———. 1960. Innate and environmental dispersal of individual vertebrates. Amer. Midl. Nat. 63(1):152–161.

———. 1965. Interaction of behavior, ecology, and genetics of introduced mammals. Pp. 461–480. *In* Baker, H. G., and G. L. Stebbins (Eds.). The genetics of colonizing species. Academic Press, New York, N. Y. 588 pp.

JENSEN, B. 1968. Preliminary results from the marking of foxes (*Vulpes vulpes* L.) in Denmark. Dan. Rev. Game Biol. 5(4):1–8.

———, AND L. B. NIELSEN. 1968. Age determination in the red fox (*Vulpes vulpes* L.) from canine tooth sections. Dan. Rev. Game Biol. 5(6):1–15.

JEWELL, P. A., AND C. C. LOIZOS (Eds.). 1966. Play, exploration and territory in mammals. Symp. Zool. Soc. Lond., No. 18. Academic Press, New York, N. Y. 280 pp.

JOHANSSON, I. 1938. Reproduction in the Silver Fox. Ann. Agri. Coll. Sweden 5:179–200.

JOHNSON, H. N. 1945. Fox rabies. J. Med. Assoc. Ala. 14:268–271.

JOHNSTON, D. H., AND M. BEAUREGARD. 1969. Rabies epidemiology in Ontario. Bull. Wildl. Disease Ass. 5(3):357–370.

JOHNSTON, R. F. 1956. Population structure in salt marsh song sparrows. Part I. Environment and animal cycle. Condor 58(1):24–44.

KEITH, L. B., O. J. RONGSTAD, AND E. C. MESLOW. 1966. Regional differences in reproductive traits of the snowshoe hare. Can. J. Zool. 44:953–961.

KING, J. A. 1955. Social behavior, social organization, and population dynamics in a black-tailed prairiedog town in the Black Hills of South Dakota. Univ. Mich. Cont. Lab. Vert. Biol. No. 67. 123 pp.

KNABLE, A. E. 1970. Food habits of the red fox (Vulpes fulva) in Union County, Illinois. Trans. Ill. Acad. Sci. 63(4):359–365.

KRAL, J. 1969. Tlumeni vztekliny (Rabies Control). Myslivost 4:76–77.

KREBS, C. J., B. L. KELLER, AND R. H. TAMARIN. 1969. Microtus population biology: Demographic changes in fluctuating populations of M. ochrogaster and M. pennsylvanicus in southern Indiana. Ecology 50:587–607.

LATHAM, R. M. 1950. The food of predaceous animals in northeastern United States. Final Report Pittman–Robertson Project 36-R, Pa. Game Comm. 69 pp.

LAYNE, J. N., AND W. H. MCKEON. 1956a. Some aspects of red fox and gray fox reproduction in New York. N. Y. Fish Game J. 3(1):44–74.

——— AND ———. 1956b. Notes on red fox and gray fox den sites in New York. N. Y. Fish Game J. 3(2):248–249.

LEVER, R. A. 1963. Weights of fox cubs. Proc. Zool. Soc. Lond. 140:337–338.

LIDICKER, W. Z. 1962. Emigration as a possible mechanism permitting the regulation of population density below carrying capacity. Amer. Nat. 46(886):29–33.

LINHART, S. B. 1959. Sex ratios of the red fox and gray fox in New York. N. Y. Fish Game J. 6(1):116–117.

LLOYD, H. G. 1968. The control of foxes (Vulpes vulpes L.). Ann. Appl. Biol. 61:334–345.

LONGLEY, W. H. 1962. Movements of red fox. J. Mammal. 43(1):107.

LORD, R. D., JR. 1959. The lens as an indicator of age in cottontail rabbits. J. Wildl. Manage. 23(3):358–360.

———. 1960. Litter size and latitude in North American mammals. Amer. Midl. Nat. 64(2): 488–499.

LUND, M. K. 1959. The red fox in Norway. Pap. Norwegian Game Res. 5(2):1–57.

LYMAN, C. P. 1943. Control of coat color in the varying hare Lepus americanus Erxleben. Bull. Mus. Comp. Zool. Harvard Coll. 93(3): 393–461.

MACPHERSON, A. H. 1964. A northward range extension of the red fox in the eastern Canadian arctic. J. Mammal. 45(1):138–140.

———. 1969. The dynamics of Canadian arctic fox populations. Can. Wildl. Serv. Rept. Ser. No. 8. 52 pp.

MARCSTRÖM, V. 1968. Tagging studies on red fox (Vulpes v.) in Sweden. Viltrevy (Swedish Wildlife) 5(4):103–117.

MATTHEWS, G. V. T. 1968. Bird navigation. Cambridge Univ. Press, London, Eng. 197 pp.

MAYR, E. 1963. Animal species and evolution. Harvard Univ. Press, Cambridge, Mass. 797 pp.

———. 1970. Populations, species, and evolution. Harvard Univ. Press, Cambridge, Mass. 453 pp.

MCCABE, R. A., AND A. S. LEOPOLD. 1951. Breeding season of the Sonora white-tailed deer. J. Wildl. Manage. 15(4):433–434.

MCINTOSH, D. L. 1963. Reproduction and growth of the fox in the Canberra District. C.S.I.R.O. Wildl. Res. 8(2):132–141.

MCNAB, B. K. 1971. On the ecological significance of Bergmann's rule. Ecology 52(5): 845–854.

MECH, L. D. 1966. The wolves of Isle Royale. Fauna of the National Parks of the United States, Fauna Series 7, Washington, D. C. 210 pp.

———. 1970. The wolf: the ecology and behavior of an endangered species. Natural History Press, Garden City, N. Y. 384 pp.

MERRELL, D. J. 1970. Migration and gene dispersal in Rana pipiens. Amer. Zool. 10:47–52.

MERRIAM, C. H. 1900. Preliminary revision of the North American red foxes. Proc. Wash. Acad. Sci. 2:661–676.

METZGAR, L. H. 1967. An experimental comparison of screech owl predation on resident and transient white-footed mice (Peromyscus leucopus). J. Mammal. 48(3):387–391.

MYERS, J. H., AND C. J. KREBS. 1971. Genetic, behavioral, and reproductive attributes of dispersing field voles Microtus pennsylvanicus and Microtus ochrogaster. Ecol. Monogr. 41(1):53–78.

MOHR, C. O. 1947. Major fluctuations of some Illinois mammal populations. Trans. Ill. Acad. Sci. 40:197–204.

MULLER, J. 1966. The reappearance of rabies in Denmark. Bull. l'Off. Int. Epizootics 65 (1–2):21–29.

Murie, A. 1936. Following fox trails. Univ. Mich. Mus. Zool. Misc. Publ. 32. 45 + [12] pp.

———. 1961. A naturalist in Alaska. Devin–Adair Co., New York, N. Y. 302 pp.

Murray, B. G., Jr. 1967. Dispersal in vertebrates. Ecology 48:975–978.

Norris, K. S. 1967. Some observations on the migration and orientation of marine mammals. Pp. 101–125. In Storm, R. M. (Ed.). Animal orientation and navigation. Proc. 27th Ann. Biol. Coll. Ore. St. Univ. Press, Corvallis, Ore. 134 pp.

North Dakota Game and Fish Department. 1949. The red fox in North Dakota. No. Dak. Game Fish Dept. P-R Rept., Project 7-R, 31 pp.

Olive, J. R., and C. V. Riley. 1948. Sarcoptic mange in the red fox in Ohio. J. Mammal. 29(1):73–74.

Parker, R. L., J. W. Kelly, E. L. Cheatum, and D. J. Dean. 1957. Fox population densities in relation to rabies. N. Y. Fish Game J. 4(2):219–228.

Pearson, O. P., and C. F. Bassett. 1946. Certain aspects of reproduction in a herd of silver foxes. Amer. Nat. 80:45–67.

Phillips, R. L. 1970. Age ratios of Iowa foxes. J. Wildl. Manage. 34(1):52–56.

———, R. D. Andrews, G. L. Storm, and R. A. Bishop. 1972. Dispersal and mortality of red foxes. J. Wildl. Manage. 36(2):237–248.

Pitzschke, H. 1966 (1965). Epizootiology of rabies in Europe. Internatl. Symp. Rabies, Symposia Series in Immunobiological Standardization, 1:231–236. (S. Karger, Basel, Switz., New York, N. Y.).

Powers, D. M. 1970. Geographic variation of red-winged blackbirds in Central North America. Univ. Kans. Publ. Mus. Nat. Hist. 19(1):1–83.

Pryor, L. B. 1956. Sarcoptic mange in wild foxes in Pennsylvania. J. Mammal. 37(1):90–93.

Richards, S. H., and R. L. Hine. 1953. Wisconsin fox populations. Wis. Cons. Dept. Tech. Wildl. Bull. No. 6. 78 pp.

Robinette, W. L. 1966. Mule deer home range and dispersal in Utah. J. Wildl. Manage. 30(2):335–349.

Rongstad, O. J., and J. R. Tester. 1969. Movements and habitat use of white-tailed deer in Minnesota. J. Wildl. Manage. 33(2):366–379.

Ross, J. G., and J. S. Fairley. 1969. Studies of disease in the red fox (Vulpes vulpes) in northern Ireland. J. Zool. 157:375–381.

Rowlands, I. W., and A. S. Parkes. 1935. The reproductive processes of certain mammals VIII. Reproduction in foxes (Vulpes spp.). Proc. Zool. Soc. Lond.:823–841.

Sargeant, A. B. 1972. Red fox spatial characteristics in relation to waterfowl predation. J. Wildl. Manage. 36(2):225–236.

Savage, R. M. 1935. The influence of external factors on the spawning date and migration of the common frog, Rana temporaria temporaria. Proc. Zool. Soc. Lond.:49–98.

Schnurrenberger, P. R., and R. J. Martin. 1970. Rabies in Illinois foxes. J. Amer. Vet. Med. Ass. 157(10):1331–1335.

Schofield, R. D. 1958. Litter size and age ratios of Michigan red foxes. J. Wildl. Manage. 22(3):313–315.

Schoonmaker, W. J. 1938. Notes on mating and breeding habits of foxes in New York State. J. Mammal. 19(3):375–376.

Scott, T. G. 1943. Some food coactions of the northern plains red fox. Ecol. Monog. 13(4):427–479.

———. 1955. An evaluation of the red fox. Ill. Nat. Hist. Surv. Biol. Notes No. 35:1–16.

———, and W. D. Klimstra. 1955. Red foxes and a declining prey population. Monogr. Ser. No. 1, So. Ill. Univ., Carbondale, Ill. 123 pp.

Sheldon, W. G. 1949. Reproductive behavior of foxes in New York State. J. Mammal. 30(3):236–246.

———. 1950. Denning habits and home range of red foxes in New York State. J. Wildl. Manage. 14(1):33–42.

———. 1953. Returns on banded red and gray foxes in New York State. J. Mammal. 34(1):125–126.

Sheppe, W. 1965. Dispersal by swimming in Peromyscus leucopus. J. Mammal. 46(2):336–337.

Shirer, H. W., and J. F. Downhower, 1968. Radio tracking of dispersing yellow bellied marmots. Trans. Kans. Acad. Sci. 71(4):463–479.

Slobodkin, L. B. 1961. Growth and regulation of animal populations. Holt, Rinehart and Winston, New York, N. Y. 184 pp.

Smith, C. C. 1968. The adaptive nature of social organization in the genus of tree squirrels Tamiasciurus. Ecol. Monogr. 38:31–63.

Smith, G. E. 1939. Growth of fox foetus and length of the gestation period. Canadian Silver Fox and Fur (March).

Smith, M. H. 1968. Dispersal of the old-field mouse, Peromyscus polionotus. Bull. Ga. Acad. Sci. 26(1):45–51.

Snyder, R. L. 1961. Evolution and integration of mechanisms that regulate population growth. Proc. Natl. Acad. Sci. 47:449–455.

Southern, H. N. 1964. The handbook of British mammals. Oxford, Eng. 465 pp.

Spencer, A. W., and H. W. Steinhoff. 1968. An explanation of geographic variation in litter size. J. Mammal. 49(2):281–286.

SPRUGEL, G., JR. 1951. Spring dispersal and settling activities of central Iowa muskrats. Iowa St. Coll. J. Sci. 26(1):71–84.

STANLEY, W. C. 1963. Habits of the red fox in northeastern Kansas. Univ. Kans. Misc. Publ. No. 34:1–31.

STEWART, M. E., AND W. G. REEDER. 1968. Temperature and light synchronization experiments with circadian activity rhythms in two color forms of the rock pocket mouse. Physiol. Zool. 41(2):149–156.

STONE, W. B., JR., E. PARKS, B. L. WEBER, AND FRANCES J. PARKS. 1972. Experimental transfer of sarcoptic mange from red foxes and wild canids to captive wildlife and domestic animals. N. Y. Fish Game J. 19(1):1–11.

STORM, G. L. 1965. Movements and activities of foxes as determined by radio tracking. J. Wildl. Manage. 29(1):1–13.

———, AND E. D. ABLES. 1966. Notes on newborn and full-term wild red foxes. J. Mammal. 47(1):116–118.

———, AND K. P. DAUPHIN. 1965. A wire ferret for use in studies of foxes and skunks. J. Wildl. Manage. 29(3):625–626.

STRECKER, R. L. 1954. Regulatory mechanisms in house-mouse populations: the effect of limited food supply on an unconfined population. Ecology 35:249–253.

SWITZENBERG, D. F. 1950. Breeding productivity in Michigan red foxes. J. Mammal. 31(2):194–195.

TESTER, J. R., D. W. WARNER, AND W. W. COCHRAN. 1964. A radio-tracking system for studying movements of deer. J. Wildl. Manage. 28(1):42–45.

THORNTON, P. L., AND J. T. MORGAN. 1959. The forest resources of Iowa. U. S. Forest Service, For. Surv. Release No. 22:1–46.

TRAINER, D. O., AND J. B. HALE. 1969. Sarcoptic mange in red foxes and coyotes of Wisconsin. Bull. Wildl. Disease Ass. 5(4):387–391.

UDVARDY, M. D. F. 1969. Dynamic zoogeography—with special reference to land animals. Van Nostrand Reinhold Co., New York, N. Y. 445 pp.

ULBRICH, F. 1967. Uber Regelmassigkeiten beim Auftreten der Tollwut in Bezirk Dresden. Arch. Exp. Veterinarmed. Bd. 20, H. 4/67:1073–1084.

VAN VLECK, D. B. 1968. Movements of *Microtus pennyslvanicus* in relation to depopulated areas. J. Mammal. 49(1):92–103.

VENGE, O. 1959. Reproduction in the fox and mink. Anim. Breed. Abstr. 27(2):129–145.

VERTS, B. J. 1963. Equipment and techniques for radio-tracking striped skunks. J. Wildl. Manage. 27(3):325–339.

———. 1967. The biology of the striped skunk. Univ. Ill. Press, Urbana, Ill. 218 pp.

———, AND G. L. STORM. 1966. A local study of prevalence of rabies among foxes and striped skunks. J. Wildl. Manage. 30(2):419–421.

WEISE, C. M. 1967. Castration and spring migration in the white-throated sparrow. Condor 69(1):49–68.

WESTELL, W. P. 1910. The book of the animal kingdom. J. M. Dent and Sons, Ltd., London, Eng. 367 pp.

WETMORE, S. P., C. H. NELLIS, AND L. B. KEITH. 1970. A study of winter coyote hunting with use of snowmobiles. Alberta Dept. Lands For. Wildl. Tech. Bull. No. 2. 22 pp.

WILLIAMS, T. C., AND J. M. WILLIAMS. 1970. Radio tracking of homing and feeding flights of a neotropical bat, *Phyllostomus hastatus*. Anim. Behav. 18(2):302–309.

WOOD, J. E. 1958. Age structure and productivity of a gray fox population. J. Mammal. 39(1):74–86.

WYNNE-EDWARDS, V. C. 1962. Animal dispersion in relation to social behaviour. Oliver and Boyd, Edinburgh, Scot., London, Eng. 653 pp.

Reproduced from *Wildlife Monographs* number 49, 82 pp., 1976, with permission of The Wildlife Society. [Shortened]

A SEX DIFFERENCE IN MORTALITY IN YOUNG COLUMBIAN BLACK-TAILED DEER[1]

Richard D. Taber and Raymond F. Dasmann

The understanding of big game populations which is necessary for successful management is based largely on a knowledge of population dynamics. The three factors which interact to constitute the dynamics of a given population are production, mortality and movement. The present paper deals with mortality in a population of Columbian black-tailed deer (*Odocoileus hemionus columbianus* [Richardson]).

The region of study lies in the north coast ranges of California, about five miles west of the town of Lakeport, in Lake County. The cover consists of a mixture of fire-tolerant shrubs—the chaparral. The climate is Mediterranean, characterized by cool, wet winters and hot, dry summers. The average rainfall is about 28 inches, but deviations of almost fifty percent occasionally occur. Various aspects of relations of deer to vegetational cover in this area have been reported upon in previous publications (Biswell *et al.*, 1952; Taber, 1953b).

The deer with which the present study deals are resident, usually living out their lives on rather restricted ranges. Fawns are dropped in late May and early June; the bucks lose their velvet about the first of August; the rut begins in early October and most of the breeding takes place during the first two weeks of November. Does usually breed for the first time at 17 months of age but occasionally do not breed until they are 29 months old. There is no evidence of breeding of fawns during their first fall (Taber, 1953b).

Data concerning mortality rates in young deer were gathered in three ways: (1) by noting the age and sex of any deer found dead; (2) by determining the sex ratio in fawns and yearlings in winter herd composition counts and (3) by intensive studies of a deer population on about 400 acres. Carcasses were aged by dentition, pelage and season of death (with respect to known average molting and fawning dates). They were sexed by examination of the external genitalia or, if these were no longer present, by a study of the secondary sex characters of the skeleton.

Since carcasses are generally found when sex can no longer be determined from external genitalia, the study of sex characters in the skeleton is the most important source of information on sex. Secondary sex characters develop in response to the action of sex hormones, and their appearance is not synchronous in all individuals. Small swellings at the antler site may be detected on the skulls of some males at two months of age, but in others these do not appear until the fourth month.

[1] Contribution from Federal Aid in Wildlife Restoration Project California W 31 R and the Museum of Vertebrate Zoology, University of California.

This means that the presence or absence of antler swellings may not be considered diagnostic of sex in all individuals until the age of four months. Aside from skull characters, the best indicator of sex so far discovered is the shape of the pubic symphysis. Like the presence or absence of antler swellings, the distinctive male and female shapes of the pubic symphysis are reflections of sex hormone levels. Again, satisfactory sex determination is not always possible when age is less than four months. Thus there is at present no reliable method of discovering the true sex ratio in weathered fawn carcasses under four months of age by direct observation. Fawn carcasses under four months of age (in Table 1) are omitted from the calculation of the sex ratio in fawn carcasses.

TABLE 1.—139 CARCASSES OF YOUNG DEER TALLIED BY AGE AND SEX

Age class	Males	Females	Unsexed
0–3 months.......	16	11	10
4–12 months......	46	33	*16
13–19 months.....	6	0	* 1

* Remains too fragmentary for sexing.

In the case of carcasses of fawns four months old or older which could not be sexed because of the fragmentary nature of the remains, it is assumed that the same sex ratio prevails as is found in members of the same group which could be sexed.

Between April, 1949 and April, 1953, 139 carcasses of young deer were found. Of these 132 were fawns (0-12 months old) and 7 yearlings (13-19) months old.

The ratio between the sexes in carcasses of four months and older indicates that more males than females succumbed. Before one can say that this represents a differential mortality between the sexes, however, it is necessary to establish the proportions of the sexes at birth. A recent review of this subject, including data from deer of the present study, indicates that the sex ratio at birth is probably about $120\,\male\,\male$: : $100\,\female\,\female$ (Taber, 1953a). The carcass data for fawns (Table 1) indicate a still higher proportion of males, namely $139\,\male\,\male$: : $100\,\female\,\female$. When the carcass data for yearlings are included the ratio is $162\,\male\,\male$: : $100\,\female\,\female$. It seems apparent that differential mortality did occur.

It is possible to check this conclusion by recourse to records of herd composition. Winter herd composition counts are taken in December and January when deer have quieted after the rut and before all bucks have dropped their antlers. It has been found practicable for an experienced observer, working from a vantage point with binoculars and telescope, to classify almost all deer seen. The classification consists of five categories: adult bucks; yearling (19-month-old) bucks; adult does; yearling does; fawns. From these counts it is possible to derive a yearling buck-doe ratio. Data from fifteen counts, taken so as to sample evenly the time and region from which carcasses were derived, are presented in Table 2.

The ratio derived from these herd composition counts is $64\,\male\,\male$: : $100\,\female\,\female$. Thus, the evidence from herd composition counts strengthens the conclusion that between birth and eighteen months of age bucks suffer a higher mortality than does.

Table 2.—Numbers of Yearling Deer Observed During Winter Herd Composition Counts

Count No.	Yearling Bucks	Yearling Does
1	4	8
2	1	6
3	3	5
4	5	4
5	6	9
6	4	4
7	2	3
8	4	6
9	5	5
10	2	4
11	1	5
12	7	6
13	2	6
14	6	7
15	2	6
Total	54	84

In part of the area more intensively studied, further evidence of differential mortality was obtained. The fawn crop in this 400-acre area in July, 1951 was 35. Assuming a ratio of $120 \,\sigma\sigma$: : $100 \,♀♀$, this would be 19 male to 16 female fawns. After the male fawns had grown their button antlers a fawn sex ratio count was made. Of the 14 animals surviving to this time (December) 5 were males, 6 were females, while 3 could not be classified. By June, 1952 only 9 of the original 35 fawns survived. These were in a ratio of $2 \,\sigma\sigma$: : $7 \,♀♀$. This indicates a loss of 17 males and 9 females from the original population. Twenty-two fawn carcasses were found in this area. Of these 9 were males, 4 females, and 9 could not be classified.

The cause of this mortality is important. Unfortunately, it cannot be determined in every case. Among those for which the probable cause of death could be determined, the majority of deer died of starvation, occasionally complicated by disease.

Accidents, including rattlesnake bites, drowning, and being caught in fences, were the second most common cause of death. Predation accounted for very few deaths.

It seems pertinent to understand how young bucks and young does differ from each other, and how these differences might contribute to the observed differential mortality.

We notice that young bucks have a tendency to stray further from the mother than do young does. This is reflected in the sex-ratio of live-trapped fawns. During October and November, in 1951 and 1952, eleven fawns were trapped. Ten were bucks and one was a doe. Eight buck fawns were trapped without any accompanying adult doe; two buck and the single doe fawn were each accompanied by an adult doe when caught. This illustrates the tendency for male fawns to investigate new situations without waiting for the mother's experienced leadership. Again, during winter herd composition counts, a record was kept of whether or not yearling deer were associated with other members of a family group. Forty-nine yearling bucks and 72 yearling does were classified in this respect. Of the yearling does, 47 per cent accompanied adult does, presumably their mothers; of the yearling bucks only 16 per cent accompanied adult does. In a smaller population under intensive observation, 6 yearling males were present in 1951. Of these, only two were closely attached to family groups. The other four tended to travel independently most of the time, and in some cases could not be related to any doe group. Even the two definitely belonging to family groups spent much more time away from the group than did yearling does in similar associations. A more pronounced antagonism of the mother toward the yearling male than toward the yearling female, during the time when fawns are young, may be in part responsible for the loose family ties of young males. The result is that young does spend a longer period learning their way around in their environment. It is plain that this might well result in a greater mortality of bucks through accidents and predation, but it is by no means obvious that the same would apply to losses through starvation.

To understand the mechanism of differential mortality through starvation, it is necessary to investigate the food-economy of young deer as it is influenced by sex hormones. It was previously stated that the deer of this study display secondary sex characters from about four months of age; the presence of these characters indicates the secretion of sex hormones. Numerous experiments on effects of male sex hormones (androgens) on metabolism of mammals show that they include increased growth of bone and muscle, reduced accumulation of fat and an accompanying rise in basal metabolism (Kenyon, Knowlton and Sandiford, 1944; Kochakian, 1946). This increased metabolism would necessarily imply a greater food requirement for males. Applied to the present data this would indicate a lessened chance for survival when food supplies are low in either quality or quantity. An example of this may be taken from the literature on sheep; a young ram must be fed about 15 per

cent more total digestible nutrients than a ewe of equal age and weight (Morrison, 1948).

Another investigation of Columbian black-tailed deer is being carried out near Hopland, California, by W. M. Longhurst. From November, 1951, through April, 1952, a season of unusually heavy mortality, he found 76 fawns dead. Most of them were victims of starvation through parasitism. Of these, 52 were males and 24 were females. The following year, November, 1952, through February, 1953, a season of low mortality, he found only four male and four female fawns dead (Longhurst and Douglas 1953).

Looking farther afield, one finds that the literature on deer contains many instances of unbalanced sex ratios. These may be caused, in part, by differential sex mortality of the type described above.

Gunvalson, Erickson and Burcalow (1952) reporting on deer populations in Minnesota, point out that on good ranges the sex ratio tends to be about equal, while (p. 130), "In areas which have been protected from hunting for a long time and where the deer population has increased beyond the sustained carrying capacity and resulting in known starvation losses, (a) adult does are greatly in excess of adult bucks . . . . ."

Similarly, Cowan (1950, p. 587) states, "National parks of Canada between 1943 and 1946 supported over-capacity populations of big game in which moose, elk, mule deer and bighorn were in direct competition for a declining food supply on winter ranges. Under these conditions, sex ratios among adult animals favored females in all species except moose, although bighorn and goats were near equality."

Mohler, Wampole and Fichter (1951) reporting on overstocked deer ranges in the Nebraska National Forest, state that pre-hunt counts showed an adult sex ratio of one buck to two does. They give detailed kill records for the first hunt, which was an intensive any-deer harvest. These figures show that while the sex ratio among fawns was nearly even ($30\,\male\,\male$ :: $31\,\female\,\female$), the sex ratio among yearlings was heavily in favor of does ($18\,\male\,\male$ :: $27\,\female\,\female$). This gives a ratio of $67\,\male\,\male$ :: $100\,\female\,\female$, a value quite similar to the $64\,\male\,\male$ :: $100\,\female\,\female$ found in the yearlings of our California population (from data in Table 2).

Within the supposition that poor range conditions are reflected in an unbalanced sex ratio is the implication that good range conditions should result in a balanced sex ratio. This is indeed what Gunvalson, *et al.* reported. In addition, Halloran (1943) working in the Aransas National Wildlife Refuge, Texas, found a ratio of $93\,\male\,\male$ :: $100\,\female\,\female$ (yearling and older deer) on range which he considered to be good.

The famous hoof and mouth disease eradication campaign in the Stanislaus National Forest, California, took place in 1924-6, at the end of a period during which deer had increased rapidly because of fortuitous range improvements. Deer were shot and poisoned indiscriminately in an effort to clear the area, and over 22,000 were actually tallied. The ratio for all age classes together was $92\,\male\,\male$ :: $100\,\female\,\female$ (Leopold, Riney, McCain and Tevis, 1951).

In Massachusetts, where range damage has been avoided by means of a heavy any-deer harvest for many years, a total kill of 74,887 was reported between 1910 and 1950. The sex ratio was $118\,\male\,\male$ :: $100\,\female\,\female$ (Shaw and McLaughlin, 1952).

These examples support the thesis that under good range conditions sex ratios tend to be about equal, or heavy in males, while under poor range conditions the reverse is true, if one leaves out the effects of selective shooting. This could be explained on the basis of a heavier mortality in young male deer where range conditions are poor then on areas where the food supply is adequate.

It must not be concluded, however, that all of the evidence points in this direction, nor that differential sex mortality in fawns is the only factor influencing adult sex ratios in unhunted herds. Thus, in the Jawbone deer herd the sex ratio in the Cherry unit, with relatively poor range conditions and poor survival of fawns was $95\,\male\,\male$ :: $100\,\female\,\female$ for adults and yearlings in the winter of 1949 (Leopold, *et al., op. cit.*). In the portion of our area under intensive observation differential sex mortality resulted in a sex ratio in fawns surviving to the summer, 1952, of $29\,\male\,\male$ :: $100\,\female\,\female$. Yet at the same time the ratio among adults and yearlings was $54\,\male\,\male$ :: $100\,\female\,\female$ despite the fact that only bucks are taken during the hunting season. In the preceding summer, 1951, the yearling sex ratio was $60\,\male\,\male$ :: $100\,\female\,\female$, and the adult sex ratio $70\,\male\,\male$ :: $100\,\female\,\female$. These ratios suggest a possible differential sex loss in older deer, with females succumbing more frequently. Carcasses of adult and yearling deer recovered in this area were $2\,\male\,\male$ :: $11\,\female\,\female$, if hunting losses are excluded.

The entire subject of differential sex

mortality among various age classes of deer is one requiring further investigation in different areas with animals subjected to differing environmental pressures before any broad conclusions can be accepted. In Lake and Mendocino Counties, California, where there is strong evidence for a proportionately heavy loss of male fawns, the protein content of the food supply declines sharply in late summer. Heavy losses through malnutrition may occur from August through October. Winter losses may be of importance, but frequently winter is a period of relatively abundant green herbaceous feed and losses are negligible. In migratory herds, to the contrary, summer and fall months are periods when food supplies are usually adequate; whereas losses from malnutrition occur in late winter and spring. The season when the population is subjected to the greatest environmental stress may be found to have a direct bearing on the type of mortality that occurs.

The normal tendency in a lightly harvested deer population is to increase to the limits of food supply. This tendency is particularly strong in populations from which only bucks are harvested, because there is no control of the production rate. Viewed in the light of data presented here we may expect a lowered survival of male fawns in populations hunted under the buck law, whereas an any-deer harvest may result in a higher proportional survival of male fawns.

SUMMARY

In a study of black-tailed deer it has been found that there is a differential mortality among deer under eighteen months of age, appreciably more males dying than females. This is manifested in the sex ratio of carcasses ($139 \male\male :: 100 \female\female$) and in the sex ratio of surviving yearling (19-month-old) deer in the winter herd ($64 \male\male :: 100 \female\female$). Most mortality was connected with starvation; accidents caused a moderate number of deaths. It is suggested that the higher metabolic rate of the male, reflected in its greater activity, curiosity, independence, etc. results in an increased male mortality due to starvation, disease and accidents. Examples drawn from the literature seem to demonstrate that under poor conditions the adult sex ratio tends to be heavier in females, while under good range conditions the sex ratio tends to be about equal. The possibility is suggested, however, that the adult sex ratio may be influenced in the opposite direction by a heavier differential loss among adult females. It is pointed out that the type of differential sex loss which occurs may be affected by the season at which the population is subjected to the most severe environmental stress.

LITERATURE CITED

BISWELL, H. H., R. D. TABER, D. W. HEDRICK and A. M. SCHULTZ. 1952. Management of chamise brushlands for game in the north coast region of California. Calif. Fish and Game, **38**: 453–484.

COWAN, I. McT. 1950. Some vital statistics of big game on overstocked mountain range. Trans. N. Amer. Wildl. Conf., **15**: 581–588.

GUNVALSON, V. E., A. B. ERICKSON and D. W. BURCALOW. 1952. Hunting season statistics as an index to range conditions and deer population fluctuations in Minnesota. Jour. Wildl. Mgt., **16**: 121–131.

Halloran, A. F. 1943. Management of deer and cattle on the Aransas National Wildlife Refuge, Texas. Jour. Wildl. Mgt., **7**: 203–216.

Kenyon, A. T., K. Knowlton and I. Sandiford. 1944. The anabolic effects of the androgens and somatic growth in man. Ann. Int. Med., **20**: 632–654.

Kochakian, C. D. 1946. The protein anabolic effects of steroid hormones. *In* Vitamins and Hormones, vol. IV. *ed.* by R. S. Harris and K. V. Thimann. Academic Press, New York. Pp. 225–310.

Leopold, A. S., T. Riney, R. McCain and L. Tevis, Jr. 1951. The Jawbone deer herd. California Dept. of Fish and Game, Game Bull. No. 4.

Longhurst, W. M. and J. R. Douglas. 1953. Parasite interrelationships of domestic sheep and Columbian black-tailed deer. Trans. N. Amer. Wildl. Conf., **18**: 168–188.

Mohler, L. L., J. H. Wampole and E. Fichter. 1951. Mule deer in Nebraska National Forest. Jour. Wildl. Mgt., **15**: 129–157.

Morrison, F. B. 1948. Feeds and feeding. 21st Ed. Morrison Pub. Co., Ithaca, New York.

Shaw, S. P. and C. L. McLaughlin. 1952. The management of white-tailed deer in Massachusetts. Mass. Div. of Fisheries and Game, Res. Bull. No. 13.

Taber, R. D. 1953a. The secondary sex ratio in *Odocoileus*. Jour. Wildl. Mgt., **17**: 95–97.

———. 1953b. Studies of black-tailed deer reproduction on three chaparral cover types. Calif. Fish and Game, **39**: 177–186.

Reproduced from the *Journal of Wildlife Management* 18:309–315, 1954, with permission of The Wildlife Society.

INTERPRETATION OF AGE RATIOS

GRAEME CAUGHLEY

Abstract: The extent to which age ratios reflect the dynamics of a population was examined by simulation. The results indicate that age ratios often provide ambiguous information and that their facile interpretation can lead to serious management blunders. A sudden rise or fall in mortality rate that affects all age classes equally has no effect on the age ratio. It remains constant at the level prevailing before the demographic change. Even when the ratio responds to a change in rate of increase there are circumstances in which its trend is the same for two populations, one of which is erupting and the other plunging to extinction. Age ratios cannot be interpreted, even in a general way, without additional demographic information, particularly on the population's rate of increase. But since the ratios are themselves usually collected to gauge rate of increase, the direct measurement of this rate renders them largely redundant.

This paper explores the extent to which age ratios reflect a population's dynamics, and in particular whether they signal changes in rate of increase.

Most animals can be classified as juveniles, subadults, or adults. These classes are defined here by Hanson's (1963) criteria: "(1) juveniles are less than fully grown animals; (2) subadults are essentially fully grown, but the majority of their cohort have not completed their first breeding season; (3) adults are fully grown and the majority of their cohort have completed one or more breeding seasons." When adults and subadults are combined in one class they are called mature animals. Two age ratios will be considered. The primary age ratio is the ratio of juveniles to mature animals. The secondary age ratio is that of subadults to adults.

Although most papers on wildlife populations provide age ratios, these are seldom interpreted. One's curiosity over why these data were collected or what they reveal about the population is usually left unsatisfied by the author. Occasionally he confides that the reported ratio indicates that the population is in good heart, or that the ratio gives cause for concern, but never have I seen spelled out the logical steps by which these judgments are reached. Age ratios unsupported by other information seem to be statistics in search of an application. My purpose in the following investigation is to determine what age ratios reveal about the dynamics, as opposed to the statics, of a population.

INVESTIGATION

Population models were used to examine the effect on age ratios of abruptly changing rate of increase. The fecundity and survival schedules of a simulated population with stationary age distribution and zero rate of increase were modified in four ways to effect a rapid increase in numbers. These schedules were also modified in the reverse direction to bring about steep declines. Age ratios were monitored across the demographic change.

METHODS

A standard population with stationary age distribution and zero rate of increase was manufactured with the statistics of age frequency, survival, and fecundity listed in Table 1. They are f_x, the frequency of animals aged x in the population; l_x, the probability at birth of surviving to age x; p_x, the probability at age x of surviving to age $x + 1$; and m_x, the mean number of off-

Table 1. Statistics of the first standard population.

x	f_x	l_x	p_x	m_x
0	499.25	1.000	0.400	0.0
1	199.70	0.400	0.800	0.6
2	159.76	0.320	0.600	1.2
3	95.86	0.192	0.401	1.4
4	38.44	0.077	0.1818	1.3
5	6.99	0.014	0.000	0.5
6	0.00	0.000		
	1000.00			

spring produced by an animal aged x. The population is of the birth-pulse type which produces births over a restricted season of the year, the ages of all animals at the birth pulse being taken as an integral number of years.

This population was run in the computer for the equivalent of 4 years of real time. A yearly cycle comprised an aging of each class by one year ($f_{x+1} = f_x p_x$) and a season of births that loaded a new cohort into the zero age class ($f_0 = \Sigma f_x m_x$). Population size, age distribution, and age ratios were retrieved after the birth pulse but before onset of the year's mortality. This simple process of growing a population could have been duplicated by using a Leslie-Lewis matrix, but that method would require modified values of age-specific survival and fecundity because the two analyses require that these statistics are defined differently (Leslie 1945:184–185).

The statistics of this population were then modified to achieve a continuous increase in numbers. The four different manipulations listed below were used to bring about a common outcome—an exponential rate of increase that would converge to $r_s = 0.2$ as the population's age distribution converged to its stable form. The required changes in the statistics of the population were calculated by successive approximation to satisfy the equation $\Sigma l_x e^{-r_s x} m_x = 1$, where r_s was set at 0.2 and p_x was related to l_x by $p_x = l_{x+1}/l_x$.

Models of Increase

A. A general rise in survival was applied by multiplying all p_x by 1.22. The modification could reflect a reduction in hunting pressure when the hunting is unselective with respect to age.

B. A general rise in fecundity was brought about by multiplying all m_x by 1.54. An improvement in food supply might produce such an effect.

C. Survival in the 1st year of life was improved by multiplying p_0 by 1.54. A decrease in the depth of winter snow might be the cause.

D. The effect of reducing hunting pressure directed towards only the mature animals was approximated by multiplying all p_x other than the first by 1.70. If the multiplication pushed p_x beyond unity it was set at unity.

Models of Decrease

Four analogous models were constructed as mirror images of those leading to increase in numbers. Each was a modification of the standard population's statistics leading to a decline at the rate of $r_s = -0.20$.

A. General decline in survival (all p_x divided by 1.22).

B. General decline in fecundity (all m_x divided by 1.60).

C. First year survival declines (p_0 divided by 1.60).

D. Survival of mature animals declines (p_x for $x = 1, 5$ divided by 1.45).

Short-lived Species

A second standard population with zero rate of increase was set up with the statistics of survival and fecundity listed in Table 2. It is based on the demographic pattern usually found in short-lived species such as

Table 2. Statistics of the second standard population.

x	f_x	l_x	p_x	m_x
0	869.56	1.00	0.1	0.000
1	86.96	0.10	0.5	6.667
2	43.48	0.05	0.0	6.667
3	0.00			
	1000.00			

Model	Manipulation
A^+	$1.2215\,p_x$
B^+	$1.3000\,m_x$
C^+	$1.3000\,p_0$
D^+	$2.000\,p_1$
A^-	$p_x/1.2215$
B^-	$m_x/1.3115$
C^-	$p_0/1.3115$
D^-	$p_1/2.6766$

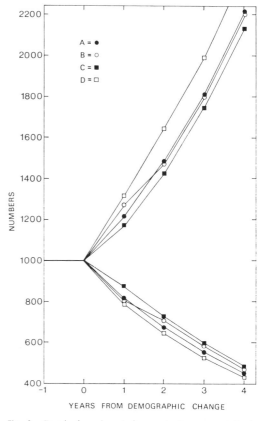

Fig. 1. Trend of numbers before and after a population's demography has been altered by modification of A, survival rate over all age classes; B, fecundity rates; C, juvenile survival; D, survival of mature animals. These rates are increased for the upper set and decreased for the lower set.

rats, voles, and small birds. This population was treated (Table 2) in the same kind of way as the first to achieve $r_s = 0.2$ by the four different manipulations, and $r_s = -0.2$ by those four methods in reverse.

RESULTS

Fig. 1 shows for the first standard population the trajectory of number resulting from the demographic change. One set of manipulations leads to increase whereas the other set produces a decrease. Within a set each population has the same survival-fecundity rate of increase r_s, but trends differ in detail because each population is hunting for a different stable age distribution appropriate to its unique survivorship schedule. Each increasing population is paired with its decreasing analogue. Trends in age ratios across the demographic change are graphed in Fig. 2 for the increasing populations and in Fig. 3 for the decreasing populations.

Manipulation of the second standard population (Table 2) produced trends in the secondary age ratio very similar to those figured for the first standard population. The primary age ratio, however, was less sensitive. Only the increase and decrease of fecundity (models B^+ and B^-) produced a response, the six manipulations of survival having no effect on the trend of the primary age ratio as the population crossed from one demographic regime to the other.

DISCUSSION

The first standard population has statistics of survival and fecundity that are a compromise between what might be expected for a medium-sized mammal and a large bird. The second standard population

110

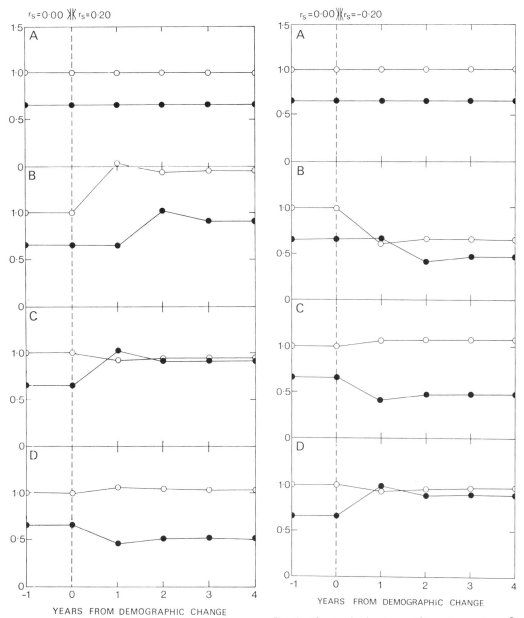

Fig. 2. The trend of primary (○) and secondary (●) age ratios before and after a population's demography has been altered by increasing A, survival rate over all age classes; B, fecundity rates; C, juvenile survival; D, survival of mature animals.

Fig. 3. The trend of primary (○) and secondary (●) age ratios before and after a population's demography has been altered by decreasing A, survival rate over all age classes; B, fecundity rates; C, juvenile survival; D, survival of mature animals.

111

simulates short-lived but highly fecund animals.

Results from the modeled longer-lived animals will be considered first. Although the four increasing populations grew at about the same rate, the trends of their age ratios (Fig. 2) are very different. Neither primary nor secondary ratios changed at all when the dynamics of the standard population were modified by treatment A. The reason for the lack of response lies in the mode of demographic change, an across-the-board rise in the rate of survival. It is well established (Leslie 1948) that a change in survival affecting all age classes equally has no effect on the age distribution. A wildlife manager, using only age ratios to monitor a population, would come completely unstuck if faced by a massive increase or decrease of numbers brought about through a general change in rate of survival. This comment is particularly relevant to waterfowl management. Changes in hunting pressure need have no effect on age ratios where the rate of hunting mortality is independent of age.

The primary and secondary age ratios of the second population (Fig. 2B) respond to the demographic change, a general rise in fecundity. The two peaks are obvious in the example, but they reflect a change (from $r_s = 0.0$ to $r_s = 0.2$) far in excess of that usually encountered. In most cases the peaks would be much less prominent in data from the field.

The primary ratio of the third example (Fig. 2C) declines as the secondary ratio increases, reflecting a rise in juvenile survival. In the last example (Fig. 2D) the trend reverses, the primary ratio increasing and the secondary decreasing, a reflection of enhanced survival amongst mature animals.

Trends in age ratios show a similar variability between the decreasing populations

(Fig. 3). Again the ratios of population A fail to respond to a general change in survival rates, even though the population halves every 3.5 years. The decline initiated by reduced fecundity depresses both age ratios (Fig. 3B), whereas these diverge when juvenile survival is lowered (Fig. 3C) and converge with a decline in the survival of mature animals (Fig. 3D).

Not only can a massive increase or decrease in numbers go completely unmarked by the age ratios, but the same change in rate of increase can produce quite different age-ratio trends according to how the increase was brought about. Even more bothersome is the coincidence between two populations, one of which may be increasing and the other decreasing. A comparison of Fig. 2C with Fig. 3D demonstrates that a rise in rate of increase occasioned by improved juvenile survival, yields trends in age ratios indistinguishable from those of a population declining because of lowered survival amongst mature animals. Conversely, Fig. 2D and Fig. 3C show age ratio trends coinciding between a population increasing at $r_s = 0.2$, under the influence of increased survival of mature animals, and one declining at $r_s = -0.2$, after juvenile survival slipped.

Simulation of the dynamics of short-lived animals (Table 2) produced trends in the secondary age ratio that were similar in form to those resulting from analogous treatments of the longer-lived animals (Table 1). Amplitudes differed but the pattern was duplicated, even to the extent of preserving the ambiguity of C^+ with D^- and D^+ with C^-.

But with short-lived animals the secondary age ratio is largely of theoretical interest; in practice only the primary ratio can be measured. In these models the ratio responded to a change in fecundity in a similar way to that figured for the longer-

G. Caughley

lived animals. In contrast it was inert to an increase or decrease of population size caused by any manipulation of survival. The second result is not general. It stems from the model's constant fecundity rate over ages 1 and 2 (Table 2). Had there been a differential the primary age ratio would have reacted, the strength of the response being determined by the size of the difference in fecundity between the two age classes. But with differential fecundity the problem of detecting a change in survival shifts only from the state where no interpretation is possible because no change in ratio occurs, to the state exemplified by the models of longer-lived animals where trends in age ratios are ambiguous and their interpretation difficult.

These cautions against the naive interpretation of age ratios are illustrated rather than predicated by the simple models used in this investigation. The general conclusion, that age ratios contain little extractable information, is independent of the special characteristics of the models and holds whether a population is of a birthflow or birth-pulse type. The problem is even less tractable than the simple models suggest. The mechanism by which a real population increases or decreases is seldom referable to a single parameter. Both fecundity and survival are affected. And instabilities in age distribution compound the problem by producing demographic noise that has no necessary relationship to the population's current statistics of survival and fecundity. Age ratios are a resultant of all these factors and cannot be broken down to reveal the component effects. This is not to say that a sudden change in an age ratio should be ignored—it indicates that something has happened—but that more information is needed to find out what has happened. Conversely, the fact

that an age ratio remains constant does not imply that the population has maintained a constant rate of increase.

The interpretation of age ratios is obviously a hazardous undertaking. Of themselves they reveal little about the demography of a population, and their unsupported use can lead to serious blunders of interpretation. Only when age ratios are supported by estimates of rate of increase and of survival or fecundity can they be interpreted critically. But rate of increase itself is what we are usually seeking. It tells more about what the population is actually doing than does any other single statistic. Since age ratios are usually estimated in the hope of learning something about this rate a direct estimate of increase renders them largely redundant. There are few short cuts to determining a population's demographic vigor as reflected in its rate of increase, a conclusion that has been discussed at greater length elsewhere (Caughley 1971). Age ratios are not adequate substitutes for accurate estimates of relative or absolute density from which rate of increase can be measured. Nor do they assist in calculation of this rate.

To sum up: age ratios cannot be interpreted without a knowledge of rate of increase, and if we have an estimate of this rate we do not need age ratios.

LITERATURE CITED

Caughley, G. 1971. Demography, fat reserves and body size of a population of red deer *Cervus elaphus* in New Zealand. Mammalia 35(3):369–383.
Hanson, W. R. 1963. Calculation of productivity, survival and abundance of selected vertebrates from sex and age ratios. Wildl. Monogr. 9: 1–60.
Leslie, P. H. 1945. On the use of matrices in certain population mathematics. Biometrika 33(3):183–212.
———. 1948. Some further notes on the use of matrices in population mathematics. Biometrika 35(2):213–245.

Sex-Ratio Adjustment in the Common Grackle

HENRY F. HOWE

Abstract. *From the nestling period through maturity, female grackles are distinctly smaller than males and presumably cost less to rear. Individual birds nesting early in the season lay more female eggs than those nesting later, and in large broods, mortality after hatching consistently favors female fledglings. The first result suggests an adaptive nonrandom meiosis that anticipates seasonal conditions of food availability; the second implies a brood reduction strategy consistent with Fisher's prediction that differential mortality in sexually dimorphic species should favor the less expensive sex.*

Fisher (*1*) hypothesized that natural selection will favor equal parental expenditure on each sex until the end of parental care. If individual males cost as much to rear as individual females, selection should result in population sex ratios of unity at the end of parental care. If one sex costs less to raise than the other, a numerical excess of that sex would be expected at independence. Unless extreme inbreeding occurs (*2*), the hypothesis should apply to all diploid organisms in which reproductive investment in one offspring diminishes parental ability to invest in another.

Despite its generality, Fisher's hypothesis has not been adequately tested with birds. This is surprising because females contribute the sex-determining chromosome in this group (*3*). Nonrandom deviations in primary sex ratio must result from maternal control and cannot reflect conflicting maternal and paternal influences. In principle it is possible to compare initial with subsequent sex ratios produced by heterogametic females, thereby separating the mechanisms of segregation distortion from differential mortality. Dual maternal and paternal influences obscure such comparisons in mammals and other organisms in which males contribute the sex-

determining chromosome (*4*). I now report that adjustment of both primary and subsequent sex ratios occurs in a species of bird and interpret these results in an evolutionary context.

Sex-ratio control consistent with Fisher's hypothesis may come about through parental manipulation of either primary or later sex ratios. The least interesting case concerns organisms in which it costs as much to raise one sex as the other. In such species, the primary population sex ratio should be unity and should be maintained until the end of parental care. More interesting are organisms among which one sex costs more for the parents to raise than the other, as might occur in species with strong sexual size dimorphism. The simplest situation is a hypothetical population for which fu-

Table 1. Embryonic sex ratios among common grackles from two seasons at Dexter, Michigan.

Clutch size	Nests (No.)	Males (No.)	Females (No.)
3	4	4	8
4	25	51	43
5	63	151	143
6	4	5	5
Total	96	211	199

114

ture conditions of parental care are the same for all adults about to breed: the population sex ratio should favor the less expensive sex from conception through independence. A more likely circumstance is that different breeding adults face different conditions of parental care, so that some are more capable of rearing the "expensive" sex than others. Proximate factors might be differences in physical condition, weather, or assistance from mates. If individuals can predict the conditions under which they will later care for young, primary sex ratios should anticipate their future ability to invest. Such anticipation may occur when females know their physical condition relative to others in the population (5) or, more likely, when individuals breeding early in a highly seasonal environment consistently face circumstances different from those breeding later. If parents cannot predict future conditions when they commence breeding, the sex ratio after conception may be adjusted by selectively resorbing embryos or by killing the young in a manner adaptive for the parents (1, 5). Such a method might be expected in a bird in which an adaptive pattern of brood reduction permits parents to cope with seasonal conditions that frequently deteriorate during breeding attempts (6, 7).

Common grackles (*Quiscalus quiscula*, Icteridae) are likely candidates for studies of sex-ratio adjustment. Female fledglings weigh 82 percent as much as males of a similar age, a dimorphism maintained through maturity (8). Thus, one expects a sex ratio at the end of parental care that favors female young requiring less food than males. Preliminary evidence indicates that fledgling males of female size suffer disproportionate mortality after leaving the nest (7). Parents should be selected to produce large healthy males under particularly favorable food conditions but to allocate resources to smaller females when food is scarce. Finally, the species breeds early in the spring in a highly seasonal environment. Individuals nesting earlier than others consistently face severe condi-

tions of freezing temperatures, snow, and cold rains when nestlings require invertebrate food collected by parents. Under such circumstances of predictable food shortage, early breeders should produce female young less costly to rear than males. Birds nesting later in the season sometimes face food shortage due to climatic changes, but at other times encounter early flushes of insects and other invertebrates used as food for young. A late female probably cannot predict which extreme her nestlings are most likely to encounter at the time she lays eggs (2 weeks before hatching); under such conditions, a brood reduction strategy is likely to be adaptive (6, 7).

Sex ratios were determined by inspecting the gonads of embryos, newly hatched young, and nestlings about to fledge (12 to 13 days after hatching) at two sites in southern Michigan. At Dexter, 50 clutches (220 eggs) in 1976 and 46 clutches (200 eggs) in 1977 were collected for dissection 12 days after the onset of incubation (9). In addition, sex ratios at fledging were determined by surgery and gonadal inspection [23 nests (81 birds) in 1975 at Dexter and 22 nests (55 birds) in 1976 at Ann Arbor] (10).

The proportion of females declines with laying date for clutches of five eggs for which the laying date of the first egg of the clutch and the sex of each egg are known (Fig. 1) (1976: 24 clutches, $r = -.45$, $P < .03$; 1977: 18 clutches, $r = -.43$, $P = .07$); pooled data: $r = -.44$, $P < .005$ (11). Trends are similar in samples including nests in which some eggs failed to develop (12). No trends are evident in smaller clutches. In both years, these seasonal trends balanced to produce overall sex ratios slightly in favor of males, but not significantly so. Embryo sex-ratio data are summarized in Table 1.

Sex ratios near the end of parental care (at fledging) are shown in Table 2 (13). Differential mortality consistently favors females in the most common clutches of five and in the overall sex ratio. Pooled data show that sex ratios deviate from unity unequivocally in the di-

Table 2. Fledgling sex ratios among common grackles.

Clutch size	Nests (No.)	Males (No.)	Females (No.)	P*
		Dexter, 1975		
3	3	2	7	
4	2	1	3	
5†	16	24	37	.062
6	2	3	4	
Total†	23	30	51	.013
		Ann Arbor, 1976		
3	2	2	4	
4	9	11	12	
5	10	8	17	.055
?	1	0	1	
Total	22	21	34	.053
		Pooled data		
3	5	4	11	
4	11	12	15	
5	26	32	54	.012
6	3	3	4	
?	1	0	1	
Total	45	51	85	.005

*One-tailed binomial test. †Corrected from Howe (7).

rection predicted by Fisher's hypothesis. As fledgling ratios also differ from embryo ratios ($\chi^2 = 6.81$, d.f. = 1, $P < .01$), this deviation may be attributed to differential mortality rather than to unbalanced primary sex ratios.

The results of this study lead to several intriguing evolutionary interpretations.

1) A seasonal pattern of primary sex ratio change suggests adaptive control. The mechanism is probably nonrandom segregation of the sex chromosomes, a cytological phenomenon well documented in some insects (2, 14) but hitherto undetected in vertebrates. With regard to common grackles, the most plausible evolutionary explanation for the seasonal pattern is that females nesting at different times during the spring face different conditions of food abundance. Early breeders favor smaller females when the chances of raising larger males are remote.

2) The overall primary sex ratio of unity suggests a statistical mean produced by conflicting selective pressures on individuals rather than a population "optimum." Where such variation ex-

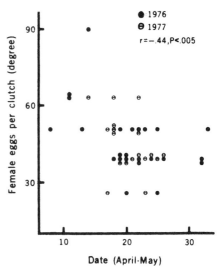

Fig. 1. Proportion of females per complete clutch of five plotted against the date the first egg was laid. The proportion of females per clutch significantly decreases as the season progresses from early April into May. Proportions are expressed in degree units of the angular transformation $\Theta = \arcsin \sqrt{p}$, where p is a proportion from 0 to 1. $\Theta_{1.0} = 90.00$, $\Theta_{.8} = 63.43$, $\Theta_{.6} = 50.77$, $\Theta_{.4} = 39.23$, $\Theta_{.2} = 26.57$ (11).

ists, the mean must be considered an effect of selection and not an evolved adaptation itself (15).

3) Differential mortality of male young occurs as part of a conditional brood reduction strategy (7). The proximate reason for male-versus-female starvation is that males cannot sustain high growth rates under the stress of food shortage. From an evolutionary perspective, the key point is that this shortage is largely under parental control. A considerable body of theory suggests that parents should select which of their offspring receive resources (16); evidence from the common grackle indicates that parents do allocate investment differentially to their young (17). The result of differential mortality is a population sex ratio favoring the less expensive sex, as predicted from Fisher's hypothesis (18).

References and Notes

1. R. A. Fisher, *The Genetical Theory of Natural Selection* (Dover, New York, 1958), p. 158; for a mathematical formulation, see W. Bodmer and A. Edwards, *Ann. Hum. Genet.* **24**, 239 (1960).

2. W. D. Hamilton, *Science* **156**, 477 (1967).
3. A. L. Romanoff, *The Avian Embryo* (Macmillan, New York, 1960). The sex-determining meiotic division occurs less than 36 hours before the egg is laid.
4. K. G. McWhirter, *Nature (London)* **178**, 870 (1956); E. Novitski. *Science* **117**, 531 (1953); W. T. J. Russell, *J. Hyg.* **36**, 381 (1936); J. A. Weir, *J. Hered.* **46**, 277 (1955); *ibid.* **49**, 233 (1958); *ibid.* **55**, 187 (1964); _____ H. Haubenstock, S. L. Beck, *ibid.* **49**, 217 (1958).
5. R. L. Trivers and D. E. Willard, *Science* **179**, 90 (1973).
6. D. Lack, *Ibis* **89**, 302 (1947); R. E. Ricklefs, *Condor* **67**, 505 (1965).
7. H. F. Howe, *Ecology* **57**, 1195 (1976).
8. At fledging, females average 60.0 ± 1.0 g and males 73.5 ± 1.7 g (*N* = 51 and 30, respectively). The same relative dimorphism occurs in adults. Of the first 20 of each sex netted in Ann Arbor in 1976, females weighed 102 ± 10.5 g and males 124.7 ± 6.2 g.
9. The 1976 set includes two nests of five and one of four for which clutch size, but not laying date, are known. The 1977 set includes one nest of five and two of four for which laying dates are unknown. Nestlings from these nests were dissected. No nests of unknown initial clutch sizes are included.
10. Laparotomies were performed on etherized nestlings by means of an 8-mm incision anterior to the left femur. Gonadal inspection is the essential method of sexing nestlings where malnutrition renders size comparisons unreliable [R. K. Selander, *Condor* **62**, 34 (1960)]. Small population sizes precluded sampling both embryo and fledgling sex ratios at the same place during a season.
11. The angular transformation is required for parametric analysis of proportional data [R. R. Sokal and F. J. Rohlf, *Biometry* (Freeman, San Francisco, 1969), p. 386; F. J. Rohlf and R. R. Sokal, *Statistical Tables* (Freeman, San Francisco, 1969), p. 129]. Correlations are also significant for 1976 and for combined analyses without the extreme clutch of five females in 1976 (*r* = − .42, *P* < .05 and *r* = − .40, *P* < .01, respectively).
12. For samples including clutches in which some eggs failed to develop, negative correlations are significant for 1976 (*r* = −.34, *P* = .05, *N* = 33), for 1977 (*r* = −.41, *P* < .03, *N* = 29), and for pooled data (*r* = − .33, *P* < .01). It is not known whether embryonic mortality favors either sex, as data from domestic fowl are inconsistent [W. Landauer, *The Hatchability of Chicken Eggs as Influenced by Environment and Heredity* (Univ. of Connecticut Agricultural Experimental Station, Storrs, 1961), p. 170].
13. Parental care decreases after the young fledge, but it is not known how long or variable this period is in this or comparable species. Trends set during maximal parental effort may be accentuated after fledging but are unlikely to be reversed.
14. E. Novitski, *Genetics* **32**, 526 (1947); *ibid.*, **36**, 267 (1951); _____, W. J. Peacock, J. Engel, *Science* **148**, 516 (1965); E. Novitski and I. Sandler, *Proc. Natl. Acad. Sci. U.S.A.* **43**, 318 (1957); W. J. Peacock and J. Erickson, *Genetics* **51**, 313 (1965); R. Lewontin, *Annu. Rev. Ecol. Syst.* **1**, 1 (1970).
15. G. C. Williams, *Adaptation and Natural Selection* (Princeton Univ. Press, Princeton, N.J., 1966).
16. R. L. Trivers, in *Sexual Selection and the Descent of Man, 1871-1971*, B. Campbell, Ed. (Aldine-Atherton, Chicago, 1972), pp. 136-179; *Am. Zool.* **14**, 249 (1974); R. D. Alexander, *Annu. Rev. Ecol. Syst.* **5**, 325 (1974).
17. H. F. Howe, thesis, Univ. of Michigan (1977).
18. Trivers and Willard (*5*) hypothesized correlations between female condition and investment in offspring and between this investment and the future reproductive success of potentially polygynous male offspring. This grackle is sometimes polygynous, but early breeders (likely to be the healthiest in a bird population) are most likely to produce female young. In this species, a correlation between differential investment in the sexes and future reproductive success of offspring is likely to be an artifact of parental need to ensure that males attain a fast enough rate of growth and a high enough fledging weight to make survival to reproductive age possible. This is a separate hypothesis. It does not require that female condition and parental investment covary with the reproductive success of that small subset of males that does survive to reproductive age. Nor does it confuse the origin of sexual dimorphism—which may well have evolved in response to sexual selection (*1*)—with selection on sex ratio. Reproductive consequences of parental condition have been discussed by D. Lack [*Population Studies of Birds* (Oxford Univ. Press, London, 1966)], C. M. Perrins [*Ibis* **112**, 242 (1970)], and R. E. Ricklefs [in *Avian Energetics*, R. Paynter, Jr., Ed. (Publ. No. 15, Nuttall Ornithological Club, Cambridge, Mass., 1974), pp. 152-297]. Polygyny in this species has been reported by R. H. Wiley [*Z. Tierpsychol.* **40**, 59 (1976)], and Howe (*7, 17*).
19. I thank Dr. and Mrs. W. Burns of Dexter, Michigan, for the use of their property and the staff of the University of Michigan Botanical Gardens for their cooperation. This research was accomplished in partial completion of the Ph.D. requirements at the University of Michigan. I am grateful for useful criticisms of the manuscript from R. D. Alexander, D. De Steven, K. Fiala, D. H. Janzen, L. Masters, J. Maynard Smith, R. B. Payne, and D. W. Tinkle. This work was supported by a Walker Scholarship of the Museum of Zoology and the Graduate School, University of Michigan.

Reproduced from *Science* 198:744–746, 18 November 1977, with permission of the American Association for the Advancement of Science.

THE INTRODUCTION, INCREASE, AND CRASH OF REINDEER ON ST. MATTHEW ISLAND[1]

DAVID R. KLEIN

Abstract: Reindeer (*Rangifer tarandus*), introduced to St. Matthew Island in 1944, increased from 29 animals at that time to 6,000 in the summer of 1963, and underwent a crash die-off the following winter to less than 50 animals. In 1957, the body weight of the reinder was found to exceed that of reindeer in domestic herds by 24–53 percent among females and 46–61 percent among males. The population also responded to the high quality and quantity of the forage on the island by increasing rapidly due to a high birth rate and low mortality. By 1963, the density of the reindeer on the island had reached 46.9 per square mile and ratios of fawns and yearlings to adult cows had dropped from 75 and 45 percent respectively, in 1957 to 60 and 26 percent in 1963. Average body weights had decreased from 1957 by 38 percent for adult females and 43 percent for adult males and were comparable to weights of reindeer in domestic herds. Lichens had been completely eliminated as a significant component of the winter diet. Sedges and grasses were expanding into sites previously occupied by lichens. In the late winter of 1963–64, in association with extreme snow accumulation, virtually the entire population of 6,000 reindeer died of starvation. With one known exception, all of the surviving reindeer (42 in 1966) were females. The pattern of reindeer population growth and die-off on St. Matthew Island has been observed on other island situations with introduced animals and is believed to be a product of the limited development of ecosystems and the associated deficiency of potential population-regulating factors on islands. Food supply, through its interaction with climatic factors, was the dominant population regulating mechanism for reindeer on St. Matthew Island.

St. Matthew Island, 128 square miles in area and located in the Bering Sea Wildlife Refuge in the north central Bering Sea (Fig. 1), supports a poorly developed land fauna. Native land mammals are restricted to a vole (*Microtus abbreviatus*) and the arctic fox (*Alopex lagopus*), although a resident population of polar bears (*Thalarctos maritimus*) existed there in Recent times (Elliot 1882). The reindeer on St. Matthew Island were the result of the release of 24 females and 5 males on August 20, 1944, by the U. S. Coast Guard (Klein 1959). Shortly afterwards, the Coast Guard loran station on the island was abandoned and the island has been uninhabited since then. Specimens taken for

study purposes and those shot by Coast Guard personnel as a recreational pursuit have been the only harvest from the herd. With the exception of 10 in 1966, these were all taken during 1957–63, and totaled 105 animals. This paper reports on the population dynamics and range interrelationships of this island reindeer herd from the time of introduction through its rapid increase and crash die-off until July, 1966.

I appreciate the field cooperation of colleagues Dr. Francis H. Fay, Dr. Vernon L. Harms, Jack Manley, and Gerry Cowan, and the assistance of James Whisenhant and Dr. Detlef Eisfeld. Dr. Eisfeld also did the analyses of the reindeer ovarian material and, through discussion, provided useful suggestions for the interpretation of the data. Sam Harbo provided advice in the statistical treatment of data.

[1] This study of the Alaska Cooperative Wildlife Research Unit was financed by the U. S. Bureau of Sport Fisheries and Wildlife, and in 1963 and 1966 additional support was available from a National Science Foundation Institutional Grant and the U. S. Bureau of Land Management. Transportation to the island was provided by the U. S. Coast Guard.

METHODS

In a preliminary study made during the summer of 1957, a total reindeer count was

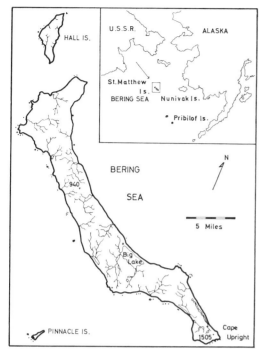

Fig. 1. Map of St. Matthew Island with inset showing its relative location.

surements were taken of the antlers and long bones of the hind leg.

Except in 1963, the total counts of reindeer involved a systematic search on foot of the entire island in as short a time as possible to reduce the chance of reindeer movements confusing the counts. Observations usually were made with binoculars and a spotting scope from the ridge tops which divide the island transversely into several broad valleys. Sex and age composition counts were made in conjunction with the total counts and at other times when conditions were favorable for relatively close observation, which was essential for this work. Sex of adults was determined on the basis of the external genitalia and the relative size of the antlers, and fawns, yearlings, and adults were determined on the basis of size and body conformity, although yearlings and adult cows could be differentiated only under the best of circumstances. In 1963, the total count was obtained by completely covering the island with two U. S. Coast Guard helicopters.

Animals taken as specimens were shot from randomly encountered bands, although some selection was involved in attempting to secure representatives of all sex and age groups. Weights were taken with a 200-lb spring scale, which necessitated weighing heavier animals in segments. Standard body measurements were taken and samples of the rumen contents were preserved in formalin for later chemical analysis. The hide, pharyngeal pouches, and nasal cavities were examined for evidence of warble fly larvae (*Oedemagena* sp.) and nasal bots (*Cephenemyia* sp.), and internal organs were examined for parasites. The entire digestive tract was examined only when the animals were killed close to a supply of water, which was necessary for a thorough examination.

made, sex and age composition of a sample of the population was determined, specimens were collected, and range studies were conducted. Results of this work have been published (Klein 1959). During the summer of 1963 additional work on St. Matthew Island supplemented the initial study and completed the picture of the course of population growth during the interim 6 years, when population density was high and pressure on the range vegetation was extreme. An attempt was made to visit the island during the summer of 1965, but transportation could not be arranged. In 1966 I again visited the island for 3 weeks in late June and July, during which the surviving reindeer were counted and specimens shot and examined. Skeletal remains from the die-off were identified by sex and age, where possible, and mea-

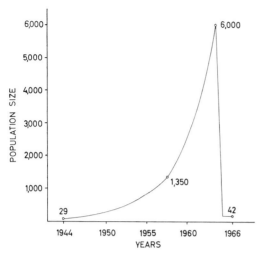

Fig. 2. Assumed population growth of the St. Matthew Island reindeer herd. Actual counts are indicated on the population curve.

Skeletal remains of reindeer encountered during our work on the island were sexed on the basis of the relative size of the antlers and the character of the pelves. The pelves of adult males had characteristic tuberosities on the posterior border of the ischium and the pubic symphyses were thicker than in the females. Age was determined on the basis of tooth development and wear.

The vegetation of the island was studied through the use of point intercept transects and meter-square quadrats in 1957 and has been reported on earlier (Klein 1959). Quantitative evaluation of the effects of the reindeer on the vegetation of the island was possible through the use of two groups of meter-square quadrats located in the dry flats, which originally supported the most extensive lichen stands. Each group of quadrats included two which were fenced to protect them from grazing by reindeer and two unprotected plots. Vegetation within the plots was recorded on the basis of the percentage of the total ground cover occupied by each species.

RESULTS AND DISCUSSION

Population Dynamics

The original reindeer were obtained from Nunivak Island and were all yearlings; that is, just over 1 year of age. Under the assumed ideal range conditions on St. Matthew Island at the time of the release, the introduced nucleus herd probably increased at a rate approaching the theoretical maximum during the years immediately following. This rate could have been as high as 83 percent the first year if all females bred and produced one fawn each. Under optimum range conditions, reindeer have been known to conceive during their first year and have their first fawns when they are 1 year of age (Palmer 1934, Davey 1963, Skuncke 1967). The actual rates of increase cannot be obtained since data on a yearly basis are not available. Fig. 2 shows the population growth from known counts, from the time of introduction to the summer of 1966.

Age composition counts made in 1963 indicate that the reindeer were experiencing a deceleration in their rate of population growth at that time. In the 1957 counts, the ratio of fawns to adult females was obtained from a sample of 910 animals and the ratio of yearlings to adult females from a sample of 218 reindeer. In these samples there were 75 fawns and 45 yearlings per 100 adult females. In the 1963 counts the ratios were 60 fawns and 26 yearlings per 100 females in samples of 1,652 and 705, respectively. It would be expected that deterioration of the range, with associated reduced physical welfare of the reindeer, would lead to poor fawn survival through their first winter, resulting in low yearling to adult ratios. Calculation of the actual annual rate of increase from these ratios is dependent upon knowledge of the adult sex ratio which was not available in either 1957 or 1963. It was often not possible to

120

distinguish sex and age in the total counts; therefore our composition counts were based on samples of the total population. Because bulls were segregated from females and young when we were on the island, the composition counts did not reflect the true proportion of bulls in the population. However, if one assumes a ratio of 57 bulls: 100 cows in the adult segment of the population (the sex ratio of animals over 1½ years of age among the skeletal material from the die-off), the net annual increment to the population, after the winter but before the spring fawning period, would have been in the neighborhood of 29 percent in 1957 and 17 percent in 1963.

In 1963 the excessive population on the range was not only reflected in reduced fawn survival, but physical characteristics of the reindeer had changed as well, and the range vegetation had been significantly altered. There was ample evidence of over-population and the stage was apparently set for the wholesale die-off that followed. Although no one was present on the island, there is strong presumptive evidence that the die-off occurred during the winter of 1963–64 and apparently largely in the February–April period.

On May 18, 1964, a flight was made over the island in a P2-V Navy ice reconnaissance plane in the hope of obtaining a population count of the reindeer through the use of aerial photography. The island was snow-covered with small patches of bare ground visible on wind-swept ridges and south exposures. No reindeer were seen and, even though large groups of reindeer should have been visible under these conditions, we believed that we failed to see them because of the relatively high speed of the plane and reluctance of the pilot to fly at a low altitude over the mountainous terrain. We were not aware, of course, that a die-off had already taken place.

The first realization of the die-off came when Coast Guard personnel went ashore on St. Matthew Island on August 14–16, 1965, to hunt reindeer for recreation. The men hunted in several parties and made a fairly systematic search of the island during three days of unusually favorable weather. On the third day, one group of reindeer, estimated at about 40, was observed near the southeastern end of the island. No other reindeer were seen and the men felt that these were probably the only reindeer remaining on the island. These men also reported that many reindeer skeletons were scattered about, bleached white with no flesh or hide remaining (personal communication). It seems unlikely that, if the die-off had occurred during the winter of 1964–65 rather than 1963–64, the skeletons would have been bleached and free of meat and hide to the extent that this report indicated. When we were on the island during 1966, moss had already begun to grow on many of the bones where they were in contact with moist soil, and the skeleton sites, when soil moisture conditions were favorable, were also characterized by lush growth of certain grasses and forbs which have high nitrogen requirements. These plants are normally restricted to areas adjacent to the bird cliffs which are fertilized by bird droppings, and to disturbed soil near fox burrows and vole colonies. The growth forms of these plants indicated that they had been present for more than one season of growth.

Forty-two live reindeer were on the island when we arrived in 1966. These were counted from the ground in a thorough search of the island and this count (minus 10 animals which were shot) was confirmed from the air on the day we left the island. No fawns or yearlings were present among them and the sample of 10 reindeer also indicates that there had been either no reproduction or no fawn survival since the die-off. Fawns born in the spring of 1964 would have been just over 2 years of age in 1966, and the youngest animal in the sample was just over 4 years of age. The absence of reindeer in the 3-year-old category was also consistent with an assumed 1963–64 die-off since animals in their first winter at the time of the die-off would have been more subject to mortality than prime-age animals.

The winter of 1963–64 on the islands of the Bering Sea was one of the most severe on record from the standpoint of amount and duration of snow on the ground and extreme cold. Weather data were available from the two locations, Mekoryuk on Nunivak Island and St. Paul in the Pribilof Islands, about 250 miles to the east and southeast respectively (U. S. Weather Bureau 1964, 1965). Winter weather conditions on St. Matthew Island are generally milder than on Nunivak which is under a stronger continental influence, and St. Matthew Island has more snow and cold than the Pribilofs which lie almost four degrees of latitude farther south. On Nunivak Island the greatest snow accumulation on the ground during the following months was: January, 31 inches; February, 42 inches; March, 47 inches; and April, 48 inches. This amount of snow for each of these months in 1964 was the greatest during the 20-year record. The average temperature for February was also the coldest on record for that month. At St. Paul Island snow accumulation during the following months was: February, 33 inches; March, 32 inches; and April, 27 inches, also records for this station. Temperatures during February at St. Paul were 7.8 degrees below the monthly mean and were the second coldest in the 20-year record for that month.

With this weather pattern, it is likely that the availability of forage was greatly restricted in late January and February, and the most acute situation was reached sometime after the turn of the year and probably in February or March. That starvation was the cause of death of the reindeer during this period was verified by examination of the medullae of the long bones among the skeletal material. Without exception the cavities were hollow, indicating that no fat was present in the marrow at the time of death. The fat, when present, is resistant to decomposition and will be present in the bones 5 or more years after the death of the animal. This criterion for evaluating physical condition at the time of death has been used successfully among other cervids (Cheatum 1949).

Bones of fetuses were found among the remains of several female reindeer that succumbed during the die-off and they provided a basis for measuring the size of the fetuses at the time of death. Estimated body length of four fetal remains varied from 380 to 480 mm. Davey (1963) obtained body length measurements from 11 fetuses recovered from reindeer shot on St. Paul Island during January and February, 1963, and these varied in size from 8 to 9 inches (203–229 mm) on January 19 to 12 to 15 inches (305–381 mm) on February 15. Since the St. Matthew Island fetuses were only slightly larger than the St. Paul specimens of February 15, it appears that the four adult females carrying the fetuses died in late February and March.

The fact that the reindeer skeletons tended to be grouped suggests that the animals died over a very short period of time; perhaps they were members of a larger band and died during the course of a bedding period. Frequently 10 or more skeletons were found in such close proximity.

The skeletons or other remains of 31 reindeer were found in 1957 and 25 in 1963 and, when possible, they were sexed and aged. No significant differences in the sex

D. R. KLEIN

Table 1. Sex and age composition of skeletal remains of St. Matthew Island reindeer following the die-off (from skeletal remains examined in 1966).

| | FAWNS | AGE | | | | | | | SAMPLE SIZE |
		1½	2½	3½	4½	5½	6½	7½+	
Both sexes (%)	19.9	23.2	19.1	15.4	6.2	4.1	4.6	7.5	241
Exclusive of fawns (%)									
Males		35.4	25.3	17.7	7.6	5.1	2.5	6.3	79
Females		24.6	22.8	20.2	7.9	5.3	7.9	11.4	114
Both sexes		29.0	23.8	19.2	7.8	5.2	5.7	9.3	193

and age characteristics were found between the two samples. In both years, animals over 5 years old predominated and males outnumbered females two to one, although some sampling bias undoubtedly existed because the large bleached antlers of bulls are more visible from a distance than are those of cows.

In 1966, skeletal remains of 241 reindeer that had succumbed during the die-off were examined for sex, age, and other characteristics. Only those skeletons from which sex and age could be recorded were included. In the case of animals less than 1 year of age, sex could not be accurately determined. In the overall sample there was a tendency for the small bones of fawns to become scattered and broken and thus less apparent among the tundra vegetation than the skeletons of older reindeer and this probably contributed to a sample bias.

The possibility of a bias among adult animals because of the different methods of sex determination was considered. However, the sex ratio of the subsample identified on the basis of the pelvis was the same as that identified by antlers. Among the sample of 193 animals over 1 year of age which were identified by sex, 41 percent were males and 59 percent females, which is a significant alteration from the assumed equal sex ratio at birth (X^2 test; $P < 0.02$). However, when examined by individual age-classes (Table 1) it is apparent that the sex ratio, essentially equal in the 1½-year class, shifts in favor of fe-

males among the 6½ and older animals. This disproportionate adult sex ratio is consistent with the heavier mortality of males indicated by the 1957 and 1963 natural mortality data, and is also consistent with findings among other cervid populations (Gunvalson et al. 1952 and Klein 1965).

Physical Condition

The physical condition of the reindeer during 1957, 1963, and 1966 showed a pronounced difference. The 1963 animals, in comparable sex and age-classes, were considerably smaller in both body mass and skeletal proportions than the 1957 reindeer. The differences are illustrated in Tables 2 and 3. In Table 3, slopes and elevations of regressions of body characters against age are compared between 1957 and 1963 for the St. Matthew Island reindeer. The significant differences in elevation of regression lines between the two periods indicate that body size differences between the two years are consistent for all age-classes. The differences in slopes, on the other hand, reflect actual differences in growth rates of the reindeer in 1957 and 1963.

In 1957 the St. Matthew Island reindeer were in excellent condition, exceeding weight ranges of reindeer in domestic herds, including average weights from the Nunivak Island herd which was the source of the original animals introduced to St. Matthew Island (Table 4). The large size of the reindeer in 1957 was undoubtedly the result of their recent establishment

Table 2. Physical characteristics of St. Matthew Island reindeer (mean values).

Sex, Age, and Year	Sample Size	Total Weight (lb)	Hind Foot (mm)	Total Length (mm)	Length Longest Antler Beam (mm)
Males					
Fawns					
1957	0	—	—	—	—
1963	2	67	381	1,186	117
1966	0	—	—	—	—
1 Year					
1957	2	227	467	1,578	727
1963	3	150	450	1,439	455
1966	0	—	—	—	—
3+ Years					
1957	2	404	515	2,023	1,149
1963	2	282	476	1,700	886
1966	1	286	510	1,920	450
Females					
Fawns					
1957	2	102	403	1,321	289
1963	1	62	372	1,146	133
1966	0	—	—	—	—
1 Year					
1957	2	199	448	1,530	562
1963	1	150	426	1,494	455
1966	0	—	—	—	—
3+ Years					
1957	4	246	464	1,743	565
1963	5	175	459	1,623	388
1966	9	208	456	1,644	444

on a very favorable range and the decrease in body weight and skeletal size in 1963 was undoubtedly the product of poorer nutrition, as a result of increased population pressure. However, it is noteworthy that adult weights in 1963, although greatly reduced from 1957, were nonetheless comparable with those from domestic herds, suggesting that in most cases domestic reindeer exist under conditions considerably less than optimal.

Christian (1963) and other workers in the area of physiological mammalogy relate decreasing body size in situations of population increase with density-dependent physiological stress. While there is evidence to support growth depression resulting from stressful situations in laboratory populations of rats and mice (Crew and Mirskaia 1931, Calhoun 1950, Strecker and Emlen 1953), growth of wild ungulates appears to be more directly related to the qualitative and quantitative aspects of the food supply which may not necessarily be related to the density of the population (Riney 1955, Cowan and Wood 1955, Klein 1964).

The reindeer shot in 1966, all 4 years old or older, represent animals that were alive in 1963 before the die-off. All but one were at least 3 years old in 1963 and therefore had attained essentially all of their growth before the die-off. One would therefore not expect to see any growth response in these animals to the reduced competition for high quality range vegetation, and the body measurements confirm this. The weight of the females in 1966, however, substantially exceeds the average weight for the 1963 adult females. Probably this resulted from reduced competition for high quality forage after the winter of 1963–64 and because the 1966 females had not produced young since the die-off. The absence of the burden of gestation and lactation undoubtedly resulted in a substantial conservation of energy.

The reproductive status of females has been used as an index to physiological welfare (Cheatum and Severinghaus 1950, Myers and Poole 1962). The reproductive history of female reindeer collected in 1963 and 1966, as determined from ovarian examination, is given in Table 5. Unfortunately, ovaries from the 1957 collections were lost in storage. In drawing conclusions from the ovaries, it should be borne in mind that identifying the various ovarian bodies was difficult, owing to variation in their stage of development or retrogression

Table 3. Comparison between 1957 and 1963 of slopes and elevations of regressions of body weights and measurements against the logarithm of age of St. Matthew Island reindeer (*t* test for differences in slopes and elevations after Steel and Torrie 1960).

Body CHARACTER	CORRELATION COEFFICIENT r	ELEVATION a	SLOPE b	t$_a$	t$_b$	PROBABILITY LEVEL t$_a$	t$_b$
MALES							
Weight							
1957	0.9983	100.3	430.8	5.23	5.50	0.001	0.001
1963	0.9946	62.3	305.6				
Hind foot							
1957	0.9329	408.8	157.5	2.16	0.18	0.100	ns*
1963	0.9248	386.5	155.2				
Total length							
1957	0.9880	1304.0	1009.5	3.60	2.34	0.005	0.050
1963	0.9921	1180.3	812.8				
Antler length							
1957	0.9773	314.5	1221.4	3.00	0.24	0.025	ns
1963	0.9773	112.4	1182.0				
FEMALES							
Weight							
1957	0.9596	113.4	216.9	2.91	5.26	0.025	0.001
1963	0.9589	70.9	162.3				
Hind foot							
1957	0.8144	410.8	81.9	2.61	1.77	0.025	0.100
1963	0.9799	380.6	122.8				
Total length							
1957	0.9632	1335.2	603.8	10.62	2.33	0.001	0.050
1963	0.9753	1191.1	666.8				
Antler length							
1957	0.8130	335.6	430.2	1.57	0.28	ns	ns
1963	0.6537	169.6	364.5				

* Not significant at the 0.100 level.

and the lack of suitable reference material; consequently, misinterpretation may have resulted. Also, reconstructing the reproductive history of an animal depends upon accurate aging, and while aging the animals by tooth eruption and wear yielded results consistent with other findings, the method was not based on known-age animals.

Among the females collected in 1963 over 1 year of age, two had corpora albicantia corresponding in number to their age. This may indicate that they conceived as fawns and gave birth to their first young at 1 year of age, although an error may have been made in estimating their age, or one or more of the "corpora albicantia" may have been accessory corpora albicantia of pregnancy similar to those observed among elk (Halazon and Buechner 1956). Two other females over 1 year of age and the 1-year-old female had apparently not conceived in their first year. The one nonlactating 1963 adult female showed no indication of previous pregnancies although follicular development appeared normal

Table 4. Average weights in pounds and weight ranges of the St. Matthew Island reindeer with some comparative data from other herds.

HERD	FAWNS		YEARLINGS		ADULTS	
	Males	Females	Males	Females	Males	Females
St. Matthew Is. (12)* (July–Aug. 1957)	—	102 (97–107)	227 (219–235)	199 (186–211)	404 (404)	246 (245–247)
St. Matthew Is. (15)* (July 1963)	67 (63–70)	62 (62)	150 (139–161)	150 (150)	282 (282)	171 (150–193)
St. Matthew Is. (10)* (July 1966)	—	—	—	—	286 (286)	208 (190–222)
Nunivak Is. (113)* (August 1965)	—	—	—	—	251	198
MacKenzie Delta (134)* (Krebs and Cowan 1962–July)	88 (56–115)	78 (34–104)	163 (142–179)	152 (130–162)	283 (252–312)	189 (151–210)
Russian herds (Krebs and Cowan 1962–June)	—	—	134 (94–193)	132 (72–170)	225 (181–292)	161 (115–225)
Swedish Lapland (Skuncke 1968–Sept.)	88	84	123	121	275	198

* Sample sizes.

and brown spots, interpreted as scars of erupted follicles, were present throughout the ovaries. There was no apparent explanation for the reproductive failure of this animal as it was in good condition with abundant fat reserves. The fact that two of the 1963 females appeared to have conceived as fawns is surprising. Although breeding of fawns quite likely contributed to the high rate of increase during the early years after the introduction on St. Matthew Island, it seems doubtful that it could have been common during the period of high density when rates of increase were much lower.

The 1966 females apparently produced young before the die-off, with two exceptions: the 4-year-old animal which was a yearling in 1963, and one whose reproductive history is questionable. However, there was no indication that conception took place in any of these animals after the die-off. The appearance and number of ovarian brown spots, which were interpreted as scars from erupted follicles, suggest that several ovulations took place without con-

ception occurring during the years following the die-off. It does not appear likely that their failure to breed resulted from nutritional factors. Also physiological stress caused by excess population density, which has been implicated in reproductive failure in rodents and inferred in other mammals (Christian and Davis 1964), should not carry over after the die-off.

Perhaps the most plausible explanation of the lack of reproduction lies among the males rather than the females. In the 1966 sample only one male was collected. No other males were observed among the remaining 32 reindeer although admittedly one or more may have been overlooked owing to small antler size. Normally at this time males would have substantially larger antlers than females, but the antlers of the one male collected were smaller than the average size of the female antlers. It can be speculated, however, that because reproductively active males are more susceptible to winter mortality than females, none of them survived the extreme conditions that brought about the nearly com-

126

plete annihilation of the herd. If this is true, the absence of pregnancies after the die-off may have been due to the lack of reproductively capable males. The one male known to survive may not have been reproductively active after the die-off. Its relatively low weight and smaller antler growth under conditions which brought about opposite effects in the surviving females tend to support this assumption.

Twelve reindeer specimens in 1957, 15 in 1963, and 10 in 1966 were examined for parasitism. While sample sizes are too small to enable statistical comparisons, lung worms (*Dictyocaulus* sp.) were found in three of the 1963 animals and in none of the 1957 or 1966 reindeer. None of these infestations were acute. Skin warbles, which commonly infest reindeer and caribou on the mainland, apparently did not establish in the St. Matthew Island herd, for none of these parasites nor the characteristic scars they leave on the skin of the host were found in any of the animals examined.

Lung worm, which has been implicated in mass mortality among other cervids (Cowan 1951), may have contributed to reduction of the St. Matthew herd, but it certainly was not present in epizootic proportions during the summer preceding the die-off. Although parasitism may be the actual agent of death in many instances among wild ungulate populations, it is usually associated with debilitation of the animals from other causes such as malnutrition.

The Vegetation

The vegetation on St. Matthew Island is of the arctic tundra type and is of a more xeric nature than that of the Pribilof Islands to the southeast. All plants are low growing and the annual growth of only a few forbs and grasses exceed 30 cm in height. Willows (*Salix* spp.), the only shrubs com-

monly present, are decumbent in form.

Winter reindeer range on St. Matthew Island is necessarily restricted to windswept areas which are blown free, or nearly free, of snow. Drifted snow collects in stream valleys, depressions, and on the lee side of hills, and greatly restricts availability of vegetation. By nature of their exposure and lack of significant snow cover, the windswept areas support xeric plant communities adapted to the harsh microclimate. A lichen–willow–sedge complex predominated on the winter range through 1957.

Until 1957, the greatest concentration of winter use by reindeer was on the two large dry flats and adjacent low ridges on the southeastern end of the island. Late winter aerial observations made by Rhode in 1955 revealed large numbers of reindeer in these areas (personal communication).

Vegetation on the heavily utilized wintering areas adjacent to Big Lake and Cape

Table 5. Ovarian characteristics of female reindeer collected on St. Matthew Island in 1963 and 1966.

Speci-men No.	Age (Yrs.)	Lac-tating	No. Follicles over 2 mm	Corpora Albicantia Current Year	Total	Brown Spots*
1963						
1	4	+	7	+	4	1
4	3	+	7	+	2	0
6	2	+	5	+	2	0
12	3	–	7	–	0	5
14	4	+	5	+	3	2
15	1	–	5	–	0	0
1966						
3	6	–	17	–	4	9
4	6	–	15	–	0†	7
6	8	–	3	–	3	8
7	6	–	2	–	1	14
8	8	–	7	–	4	11
9	6	–	6	–	4	18
10	6	–	5	–	5	19
11	4	–	2	–	0	12
12	6	–	5	–	2	9

* Brown spots were assumed to be scars of erupted follicles which did not result in pregnancies.

† White opaque structures on the ovaries of this animal may be corpora albicantia.

127

Table 6. Percent changes in vegetation densites between 1957 and 1963 in four fenced and four unfenced meter-square study plots.*

PLOT	GRASSES		SEDGES		WILLOWS	
	Enclosed	Unprotected	Enclosed	Unprotected	Enclosed	Unprotected
A	19.0	9.0	34.0	65.0	−2.5	4.0
B	4.5	8.5	60.0	47.0	−7.0	−6.0
C	6.0	2.0	3.5	5.0	27.5	−9.0
D	0.0	0.0	10.0	2.5	48.0	−6.5
Totals	29.5	19.5	107.5	119.5	66.0	−17.5
Mean change per plot	7.4	4.9	26.9	29.9	16.5	−4.4

* Positive values indicate an increase and negative values a decrease in density over the 1957 condition.

Upright showed the pronounced effect of heavy reindeer use as early as 1957. Lichen growth had been seriously depleted through the combination of winter grazing, trampling, and shattering, and actual removal of the dry, shattered pieces of lichen by the persistently strong winds. With wind velocities often averaging more than 20 miles an hour during winter months, the potential for plant desiccation and erosion is great. By 1963, lichen growth, which formerly occupied slight depressions between raised hummocks of prostrate willows, had been almost completely eliminated. In the past, lichen growth apparently was quite similar to ungrazed areas on reindeer-free Hall Island where the lichen mat was 8–12 cm deep.

In 1963 the lichen mat on the old winter range areas seldom exceeded 1 cm in depth and was composed of badly shatterd lichens usually unattached to the ground. These same areas showed little change when examined in 1966. The fractured parts of lichens remaining on the ground surface consisted in large part of the nonliving basal parts from which regrowth is not possible. However, there may have been enough living material present to allow for renewal of the lichen mat, but any regrowth will be exceedingly slow. The preferred lichen species, such as *Cladonia rangiferina,* are the most vulnerable to shattering through trampling, while the more resilient forms which resist shattering, such as *Thamnolia vermicularis,* are less palatable to reindeer and apparently made up a smaller percentage of the original stands.

Willows fared better than lichens under the heavy reindeer use but by 1963 the willows had begun to show signs of deterioration as a result of heavy winter browsing. It is apparent from observations made in 1957 and on adjacent Hall Island that in the original lichen–willow–sedge stands the willows and sedges were suppressed by the engulfing growth of lichens. The removal of lichens by the reindeer stimulated the growth of willows, sedges, grasses, and some forbs but by 1963 the reindeer were forced to rely heavily on the willows. Comparison of vegetation in fenced and unfenced plots showed an apparent increase in density of willows in the plots that were protected while in the unprotected plots they decreased, but these differences are not statistically significant.

Sedges and grasses continued to increase in density under the continued and increasing grazing pressure. Statistically significant increases in both sedges and grasses were apparent in the fenced and unfenced vegetation plots in 1963 (Tables 6 and 7). Evidence from other reindeer ranges indicates that when lichens are depleted, grasses and sedges are grazed extensively during the winter (Palmer 1929). At the time of the die-off, crowberry (*Empetrum nigrum*) was apparently the only vegetation available in any volume as evidenced by ruminal material still present among the skeletons.

Summer forage use by reindeer did not result in significant alteration of the vegetation complex. During the 1957 summer field studies, reindeer were observed to make almost exclusive use of the well-drained sedge meadows and bog meadows where sedges were very common and were the predominant plants eaten by the reindeer. On the drier, better-drained meadows, *Carex nesophila* was the most abundant sedge and received the brunt of summer use. The wetter, boggy sites support a wider variety of sedges, but *C. aquatilis* is usually the dominant form and in these sites it received the heaviest use during 1957. Other sedges, grasses, leaves stripped from willows, and forbs were also important components of the summer diet of the reindeer. All vegetation types received some summer use by reindeer; however, the types with a high proportion of sedges and grasses appeared to support the brunt of summer grazing.

During the 1963 studies, heavy reindeer pressure on the summer forage was evident but no significant lasting damage was noted. Closely cropped sedges and grasses were present in all vegetation types supporting these plants but were most extensive in moist but well-drained meadows, on lake shores and lake floodplains, and on the drier slopes of hills. There appeared to be sufficient summer forage on the island, but competition for the most nutritious and palatable plants was undoubtedly keen. Evidence from other reindeer ranges in Alaska indicates that summer range seldom suffers from overutilization, while winter range condition varies with population pressure and appears to be the most im-

Table 7. Changes in density of grasses and sedges during the 6-year interval 1957–63.

VEGETATION	YEAR	NO. PLOTS	MEAN DENSITY (% GROUND COVER)	t
Grasses	1957	8	0.26	2.56*
	1963	8	1.31	
Sedges	1957	8	12.80	3.07*
	1963	8	16.50	

* Significant at the 0.05 confidence level utilizing Snedecor's (1956) *t* test for paired replications.

portant factor in population control. However, the importance of summer range in the ecology of the reindeer may be greater on an island where opportunity for movement is restricted.

Summer grazing is apparently seldom permanently destructive to moist subarctic tundra. In fact, indications are that limited grazing of the annual growth of sedges, grasses, and some forbs is actually beneficial in stimulating forage production. Harmful effects on summer range are limited to trampling vegetation and compacting loose, moist soil where movements of large numbers of animals are constricted by narrow valleys and other terrain features. Throughout the spring and summer, when actively growing, plants are able to withstand considerable trampling and still recover rapidly. In addition, the high humidity which accompanies the persistent spring and summer fogs on St. Matthew Island keeps the lichens moist and resilient and less subject to shattering than in a drier atmosphere.

The nutritive quality of the low-growing plants which make up the summer forage for reindeer on St. Matthew Island can apparently be very high. This is indicated by the excellent physical status of the reindeer in 1957. On St. Matthew Island the variations in exposure resulting from irregularities in terrain account for a wide range in plant development and maturity. Also, the cool moist summers delay maturity and

Table 8. Nutritive quality of forage and washed rumen samples (dry-weight basis).

Sample	% Nitrogen	% Protein	% Crude Fat	% Crude Fiber	% Ash
ST. MATTHEW ISLAND					
Forage samples (1963)					
Carex nesophila	4.02	25.14	2.76	22.28	5.11
Arctagrostis latifolia	3.52	22.03	2.64	24.93	6.69
Artemisia arctica	3.74	23.37	2.52	10.74	11.46
Rumen samples (1963)					
Mean (N = 4)	2.86	17.94	3.49	33.95	5.30
Range	2.61–3.29	16.36–20.61	2.73–4.51	32.07–35.34	4.74–5.73
Rumen samples (1966)					
Mean (N = 4)	3.2	19.8	3.1	31.6	3.3
Range	2.7–3.5	17.1–21.7	2.6–4.1	30.8–32.1	3.1–3.7
ADAK ISLAND					
Rumen samples (1966)					
Mean (N = 2)	4.7	29.1	6.0	28.1	4.4
Range	4.5–4.8	28.2–30.0	4.9–7.0	27.4–28.7	4.4

curing of vegetation. Consequently, during its most nutritious period, the early stages of growth, vegetation is being produced over an extended period. Under the heavy stocking of the range in 1963, competition was apparently great enough to restrict the consumption of highest quality forage by individual reindeer to a minimal portion of their diet.

Selected forage samples collected in 1963 were analyzed chemically for nutritive value and were found to be of relatively high quality. Rumen samples from reindeer shot during 1963 and 1966 were washed to remove the microorganisms and ruminal fluid components and then analyzed chemically as a basis for judging the quality of the forage consumed (Klein 1962). Table 8 shows that for 1963, nutritive values of the washed forage from rumen contents were much lower than the selected forage samples, and apparently reflect the limitation upon the reindeer to select forage qualitatively which was imposed by the high population density. In the 1966 rumen samples, percent protein had increased and percent fiber decreased in comparison with the

1963 samples, apparently as a result of the absence of significant competition among reindeer for the highest quality forage. It is interesting to note in Table 8 that comparative rumen samples from caribou on Adak Island, where these introduced animals are exhibiting remarkable growth rates, show protein and fiber levels even more favorable than those in the 1966 St. Matthew Island samples. In Table 9, comparisons are made between protein and fiber levels of gross rumen samples from St. Matthew Island reindeer and reindeer in a domestic herd on the Seward Peninsula, near Nome. Significantly higher protein levels and lower fiber levels among the St. Matthew Island material, both before and after the die-off, than among rumen samples from the managed reindeer herd emphasize that present domestic reindeer herding practices are seldom based on a knowledge of range ecology.

Range Carrying Capacity

With regard to ungulate range, it can perhaps be stated that forage quantity acts primarily to govern population size while

D. R. KLEIN

Table 9. Comparison of analyses of protein and fiber content of gross rumen samples from reindeer on St. Matthew Island and the Seward Peninsula (dry-weight basis).

| SAMPLE | DATE COLLECTED | SAMPLE SIZE | PROTEIN | | FIBER | |
			Mean	SE	Mean	SE
A. St. Matthew Island	July 20–23, 1963	4	29.4	0.965	21.7	0.310
B. St. Matthew Island	July 2–13, 1966	6	32.9	1.341	27.0	1.538
C. Seward Peninsula	June 13–Aug. 7, 1966	6	24.7	1.574	39.4	1.440

Comparison of differences at 0.05 level of significance utilizing Kramer's (1956) modification of Duncan's New Multiple Range Test

COMPARISONS	PROTEIN	FIBER
A & B	not significant	significant
A & C	significant	significant
B & C	significant	significant

quality determines the size of the individual. Further, in northern regions, food limitation is most critical during the winter period while qualitative variations in the food supply make themselves felt during summer when the physiological demands of animals are highest and growth is most rapid (Klein 1964). Thus range carrying capacity involves two quite different criteria: the winter component which governs the upper limit of the population, and the summer component which determines the physical stature of the individual. Of course, seasonal components of the annual physiological cycle of growth and maintenance in ungulates are not completely independent of one another. Physiological welfare in summer affects reproductive success and winter survival and, hence, rate of population increase; physiological status at the end of winter can influence growth and survival of young and rate and time of initiation of summer fat accumulation in adults.

Various authors have made estimates of grazing capacity for reindeer. Palmer (1929) listed 16–18 reindeer per square mile as the maximum for safe range use and he later (1934) suggested that this might be too high a density for most ranges. Hustich (1951) gave a figure of 13 reindeer to the square mile for the lichen woodland of

Labrador. These estimates presumably are for winter range. The density of reindeer on St. Matthew Island in 1957 was 10.5 per square mile and by 1963 it had increased to 46.9 per square mile. It is noteworthy that on St. Paul Island, reindeer reached a density of 49 per square mile just before the "crash die-off" there in the 1940's (Scheffer 1951).

Estimates of desirable stocking on the summer range are generally lacking in the Russian, Scandinavian, and North American literature. Palmer (1934:23–24) listed 6 acres (107 reindeer per square mile) as the combined spring and summer range requirement of reindeer on the basis of studies of fenced reindeer but suggested lower stocking levels on open range. This is not directly comparable to the St. Matthew Island densities because utilizable range is much less than the total land area on the island. Probably as much as half of the island is covered by rock scree which is completely unvegetated except for widely scattered crustose lichens. In addition much of the area utilized as winter range was not used by reindeer in summer.

Mechanisms of Population Control

The reindeer population on St. Matthew Island increased rapidly to a peak which was followed by a crash. This pattern has been observed among other animal populations under varying conditions, but most often among introduced species on islands. Population "explosions" and ensuing die-offs on islands have been reported for reindeer on the Pribilof Islands (Scheffer 1951), cottontail rabbits (*Sylvilagus floridanus*) on Fishers Island, New York (Smith and Cheatum 1944), and moose (*Alces alces*) on Isle Royale in Lake Superior following their arrival there (Mech 1966). Explanations for this type of response of introduced animals may lie in the characteristics of the new environment or in the lack of plasticity of the introduced species. It is conceivable that an environment containing several diverse potential population-regulating mechanisms (for example, food supply, predators, interspecific competition) would bring about a more gradual control of an introduced species than an environment with only one limiting mechanism such as food supply. Therefore, one would expect that the more complex the environment in terms of the flora and fauna present, the more graded would be the response of the introduced species. This explanation has been used, of course, to account for the prevalence of cyclic species in northern regions where ecosystems are characteristically less complex than in temperate or tropical regions. Island ecosystems also tend to be less complex than continental ones. Environmental limitations on islands, especially small ones, are finite. There is no continuum from favorable to less favorable habitat for a species occupying an entire island. Island ecosystems, although sparse from a species standpoint owing to restricted access, tend to be younger than continental ecosystems, with the result that there has been less time for the development of complex interrelationships.

Certain species appear less inclined to wide population fluctuations than others when introduced to new environments. The wolves of Isle Royale are a classic example of a new and successful species stabilizing at a level commensurate with the food supply (Mech 1966). There are innumerable instances of the Norway rat, the house mouse, and other species associated with man, gaining access to islands in temperate and tropical regions and, once established, maintaining relatively stable populations. Reindeer have also been introduced to islands without experiencing the wide fluctuations that occurred on St. Matthew Island and the Pribilofs. On Atka and Umnak Islands in the Aleutians, introduced reindeer appear not to have undergone large scale die-offs although accurate records of their population levels are not available. In the Southern Hemisphere the introduced reindeer of South Georgia have apparently stabilized at about 4,000 (Bonner 1958). However, winter climatic conditions are not as severe in the Aleutians or on South Georgia as on St. Matthew Island or the Pribilofs.

There appears to be a relationship between the self-regulatory ability of animal populations and the relative stability of the environments within which they have evolved. For example, the North American deer that are adapted to early successional stages of vegetation, which are of a transitory nature, appear not to have well developed self-regulatory mechanisms and are characterized by wide population fluctuations. On the other hand the roe deer (*Capreolus capreolus*) in Europe (Andersen 1963) and some bovids, such as the Uganda kob (*Adenota kob thomasi*) (Beuchner 1963), that are found on relatively stable vegetation types, appear to have evolved behavioral mechanisms that tend to contribute to the stability of their popu-

D. R. Klein

lations. The caribou appear to be inter-mediate in this respect. The tundra and open subarctic lichen forests, which are their native habitat, are climax vegetation types of a very stable nature. Mobility and the development of the migratory habit appear to be compensating mechanisms which prevent destruction of the food resource. In addition, the wolf is an effective preda-tor on caribou and the two species have evolved a relationship that appears mu-tually beneficial at the level of the popula-tion.

On St. Matthew Island and the Pribilof Islands (Scheffer 1951), reindeer were in-troduced to restricted ranges free of preda-tors and subjected to insignificant annual harvests. The normal migratory habit of the species could offer no relief to the pres-sure of the animals on the range because of the restricted sizes of the islands. The populations expanded rapidly under the good range conditions and winter mortality at first was light because of the abundant lichen forage. Increasing at geometric rates, the populations passed from moderate levels, with respect to the food supply, to excessive populations in only a few years. On St. Matthew Island, and possibly on the Pribilofs as well, the rapid increase to the peak population was coincident with favor-able winter climatic conditions.

The large scale die-off of reindeer on St. Matthew Island during the winter of 1963–64 was apparently the result of a combina-tion of the following factors: (1) over-grazing of lichens on the island, which are normally the most important winter forage, by the large numbers of reindeer; (2) ex-cessive numbers of reindeer during the win-ter of the die-off competing for the very limited available forage; (3) the relatively poor condition of the reindeer going into the winter as a result of competition for high quality summer forage during the

summer of 1963; and (4) extreme weather conditions, particularly deep snow accumu-lation, during the winter of 1963–64, fur-ther restricting the availability of the al-ready depleted winter forage. These same factors, jointly operative, were apparently responsible for the reindeer die-off on the Pribilof Islands in the 1940's (Scheffer 1951). That weather conditions were not the sole factor in the die-off of reindeer on St. Matthew Island is demonstrated by the good survival of the reintroduced reindeer on St. Paul Island during the same period (F. Wilke in correspondence 1966). Also, on Nunivak Island, although considerable mor-tality occurred among the reindeer there during the winter of 1963–64, no large die-off resulted.

Food supply then, through interaction with climatic factors, was the dominant population-regulating mechanism for rein-deer on St. Matthew Island. Other factors of population control, such as disease or parasites and predation, can be ruled out and there is insufficient evidence to sug-gest that self-regulatory mechanisms of a behavioral (Wynne-Edwards 1965), a ge-netic (Chitty 1960), or a behavioral-physio-logical nature (Christian and Davis 1964) were involved in the die-off.

LITERATURE CITED

ANDERSEN, J. 1963. Populations of hare and roe-deer in Denmark. Proc. 16th Internatl. Congr. Zool. 3:347–351.

BONNER, W. N. 1958. The introduced reindeer of South Georgia. Falkland Islands Dependen-cies Survey Sci. Rept. 22. 11pp.

BUECHNER, H. K. 1963. Territoriality as a be-havioral adaptation to environment in Uganda kob. Proc. 16th Internatl. Congr. Zool. 3:59–63.

CALHOUN, J. B. 1950. The study of wild animals under controlled conditions. Annals N. W. Acad. Sci. 51:1113–1122.

CHEATUM, E. L. 1949. Bone marrow as an index of malnutrition in deer. New York State Con-servationist 3(5):19–22.

———, AND C. W. SEVERINGHAUS. 1950. Variations in fertility of white-tailed deer related to range conditions. Trans. N. Am. Wildl. Conf. 15:171–190.

CHITTY, D. 1960. Population processes in the vole and their relevance to general theory. Canadian J. Zool. 38(1):99–113.

CHRISTIAN, J. J. 1963. Endocrine adaptive mechanisms and the physiologic regulation of population growth. Pp. 189–353. In W. V. Mayer and R. G. van Gelder (Editors), Physiological mammalogy. Vol. I. Academic Press, New York. 381pp.

———, AND D. E. DAVIS. 1964. Endocrines, behavior, and population. Science 146(3651): 1550–1560.

COWAN, I. McT. 1951. The diseases and parasites of big game mammals of western Canada. Proc. Annu. British Columbia Game Convention 5:37–64.

———, AND A. J. WOOD. 1955. The growth rate of the black-tailed deer (Odocoileus hemionus columbianus). J. Wildl. Mgmt. 19(3):331–336.

CREW, F. A. E., AND L. MIRSKAIA. 1931. The effects of density on an adult mouse population. Biol. Generalis 7:239–250.

DAVEY, S. P. 1963. Reindeer and their management on St. Paul Island, Alaska. Unpub. report, U. S. Bur. Commercial Fisheries. Seattle, Washington. 34pp.

ELLIOT, H. W. 1882. Report on the seal islands of Alaska. U. S. Commercial Fish and Fisheries Spec. Bull. 176. 176pp.

GUNVALSON, V. E., A. B. ERICKSON, AND D. W. BURCALOW. 1952. Hunting season statistics as an index to range conditions and deer population fluctuations in Minnesota. J. Wildl. Mgmt. 16(2):121–131.

HALAZON, G. C., AND H. K. BUECHNER. 1956. Postconception ovulation in elk. Trans. N. Am. Wildl. Conf. 21:545–554.

HUSTICH, I. 1951. The lichen woodlands in Labrador and their importance as winter pastures for domesticated reindeer. Acta Geog. 12(1): 1–48.

KLEIN, D. R. 1959. Saint Matthew Island reindeer-range study. U. S. Fish and Wildl. Serv. Spec. Sci. Rept.: Wildl. 43. 48pp.

———. 1962. Rumen contents analysis as an index to range quality. Trans. N. Am. Wildl. and Nat. Resources Conf. 27:150–164.

———. 1964. Range-related differences in

growth of deer reflected in skeletal ratios. J. Mammal. 45(2):226–235.

———. 1965. Ecology of deer range in Alaska. Ecol. Monogr. 35(3):259–284.

KRAMER, C. Y. 1956. Extension of multiple range tests to group means with unequal numbers of replications. Biometrics 12(3):307–310.

KREBS, C. J., AND I. McT. COWAN. 1962. Growth studies of reindeer fawns. Canadian J. Zool. 40(5):863–869.

MECH, L. D. 1966. The wolves of Isle Royale. Fauna of the Natl. Parks of the U. S., Fauna Series 7. 210pp.

MYERS, K., AND W. E. POOLE. 1962. A study of the biology of the wild rabbit, Oryctolagus cuniculus (L.) in confined populations. III. Reproduction. Australian J. Zool. 10(2):225–267.

PALMER, L. J. 1929. Improved reindeer handling. U. S. Dept. Agr. Circ. 82. 18pp.

———. 1934. Raising reindeer in Alaska. U. S. Dept. Agr. Misc. Publ. 207. 41pp.

RINEY, T. 1955. Evaluating condition of free-ranging red deer (Cervus elaphus), with special reference to New Zealand. New Zealand J. Sci. and Technol. 36(5):429–463.

SCHEFFER, V. B. 1951. The rise and fall of a reindeer herd. Sci. Monthly 73(6):356–362.

SKUNCKE, F. 1968. Reindeer ecology and management in Sweden. (In press.) Biol. Papers Univ. Alaska.

SMITH, R. H., AND E. L. CHEATUM. 1944. Role of ticks in decline of an insular cottontail population. J. Wildl. Mgmt. 8(4):311–317.

SNEDECOR, G. W. 1956. Statistical methods. 5th ed. Iowa State University Press, Ames. 534pp.

STEEL, R. G. D., AND J. H. TORRIE. 1960. Principles and procedures of statistics. McGraw-Hill Book Co., Inc., New York. 481pp.

STRECKER, R. L., AND J. T. EMLEN, JR. 1953. Regulatory mechanisms in house-mouse populations: the effect of limited food supply on a confined population. Ecology 34(2):375–385.

U. S. WEATHER BUREAU. 1964. Climatological data Alaska. Vol. 49 (1–13):1–228.

———. 1965. Climatological data Alaska. Vol. 50(1–13):1–244.

WYNNE-EDWARDS, V. C. 1965. Self-regulating systems in populations of animals. Science 147(3665):1543–1548.

Reproduced from the *Journal of Wildlife Management* 32:350–367, 1968, with permission of The Wildlife Society. [Figures 3, 4, 5, and 6 in original article have been omitted and figures renumbered.]

RATE OF INCREASE

GRAEME CAUGHLEY

L. C. BIRCH

Abstract: We outline the differences between three notions of *rate of increase*: r, the observed rate of increase; r_s, the rate implied by the prevailing schedules of survival and fecundity; and r_m, the maximum rate at which a population with a stable age distribution can increase in a specified environment. Several mammalogists recently calculated r_s for natural populations under the misapprehension that they were calculating r_m. However, their calculated values are usually defective even as r_s estimates because they have used life tables constructed from age distributions or from distributions of age at death. The estimates are thereby infiltrated by the unrecognized but implicit assumption that $r_s = 0$, and the calculated values of r_s are therefore assumptions retrieved as conclusions. If r_m, the *intrinsic rate of increase*, is to be determined for a natural population of mammals, it is best calculated either by measuring the rate at which a newly established population initially increases or by fitting a curve to the growth of a population after its density has been artificially reduced.

Over about the last 10 years mammalogists have become increasingly interested in population dynamics, and they have begun using concepts and analyses hitherto restricted almost entirely to the demography of man and insects. This is a welcome trend that should be continued, but at the same time a warning is necessary against uncritically using special methods of analysis that may not be appropriate to field studies of mammals. By this we do not imply that the demography of mammals differs essentially from that of insects; we suggest only that some parameters, whose estimation is relevant to questions that entomologists ask, may be extremely difficult to estimate for natural populations of mammals. In addition, the parameters may be irrelevant to the problem in hand. The reverse is also true. Mammalogists ask questions on conservation and harvesting, for example, that entomologists seldom consider, and they must therefore estimate parameters that entomologists ignore.

In this paper we examine some of the ways in which rate of increase can be measured and point out that some mammalogists, using equations that are valid and widely used in insect ecology, are estimating it incorrectly.

KINDS OF RATE OF INCREASE

Because populations tend to grow geometrically, rate of increase is best expressed in exponential form. A population of 100 animals that increases to 200 over a year has been multiplied by 2 or increased by 100 percent, however one prefers to express it. Its exponential rate of increase, r, is given by

$$e^r = 2$$

and $\qquad r = 0.69,$

e being the base of natural logs, taking the value 2.71828. When the population halves instead of doubles, dropping from 100 to 50 over a year, we say either that the population has multiplied by 0.5 or that it has decreased by 50 percent; hence,

$$e^r = 0.5$$

and $\qquad r = -0.69.$

The observed rate of increase, r, is the slope of $\log_e$ numbers on time. It can be changed from one unit of time to another by simple multiplication or division. When $r = 0.69$ on a yearly basis, $r = 0.69/365$ when expressed as increase per day. In the material that follows, we give all rates of increase in exponential form. The symbol

r should not be confused with r used by Hairston et al. (1970). They employ it to symbolize the statistic we call r_m.

A population's observed rate of increase at a given time is determined by age-specific survival, age-specific fecundity, sex ratio, and age distribution. Sometimes we wish to eliminate the variation in age distribution from the estimate of r because the variation reflects previous influences rather than the population's current ability to increase. If we are interested in the slightly abstract concept of a population's potential to increase at a given density in a given environment, rather than in its actual rate of increase, which is influenced by whatever age distribution has been imposed by events that happened previously, we estimate the rate at which it would increase if it had a *stable age distribution*. This is the distribution of ages that would eventually form if the prevailing life table and fecundity table remained unchanged. Rate of increase at any given density, estimated in such a way as to eliminate the effect of an unstable age distribution, will be symbolized by r_s. Depending on whether survival and fecundity acting together would cause an increase or a decrease, r_s is positive, zero, or negative.

A special case of r_s is provided by the rate of increase at very low density, such that the population has the maximum rates of survival and fecundity attainable in that environment. This rate is r_m, the maximum rate at which a population with a stable age distribution can increase when no resource is limiting. Andrewartha and Birch's (1954) definition of r_m stipulates that the rate is measured in the absence of predators. Although accepting the validity of this constraint, we are inclined to exclude it from a definition of r_m for vertebrates because its inclusion greatly increases the

already daunting technical difficulties of estimating r_m in the field. Rate r_m is not a constant for a species but is specific to the particular environment in which it was measured. It is determined by the climate and by the quality of food, shelter, and other environmental influences interacting with the animal's genetically determined capacity to survive and reproduce. Rate r_m can be positive, zero, or negative. Within the range of a species it will tend to be positive, zero at the natural boundary of distribution, and negative beyond it. A negative r_m measured for a particular combination of environmental variables implies that if animals were introduced into such an environment the population would not survive.

Many names have been given r_m. It has been called the true, the real, the incipient, the inherent, and the intrinsic rate of increase or of natural increase, the Malthusian parameter, the natural rate of increase, and the innate capacity for increase. In this paper we will use *intrinsic rate of increase* when we mean r_m.

Estimating Rate of Increase

So far, we have informally defined three variants of rate of increase—r, the observed rate of increase; r_s, the rate implied by the life table combined with the fecundity table; and r_m, the special case of r_s, which obtains when all individuals have access to more food, shelter, water, and other requirements than they need.

Rate r is measured by regressing $\log_e$ of population size (or a linear index of population size) on time. The slope of this line estimates r, which will be positive, zero, or negative depending on whether the population was increasing, stable, or declining over the period it was observed.

Rate r_s must be calculated from a life

Table 1. Two methods of constructing a life table: from the age distribution of living animals (A) and from the distribution of ages at death (B), assuming that the population is stable.

(A)	AGE (x)	NUMBER SAMPLED (f_x)	$\dfrac{f_x}{f_0}$ $(l_x)^a$	$l_x - l_{x+1}$ $(d_x)^b$	$\dfrac{d_x}{l_x}$ $(q_x)^c$
	0	100	1.00	0.50	0.50
	1	50	0.50	0.20	0.40
	2	30	0.30	0.20	0.67
	3	10	0.10	0.10	1.00
	4	0			

(B)	AGE (x)	NUMBER FOUND DEAD (f_x')	$\dfrac{f_x'}{\Sigma f_x'}$ (d_x)	$\overset{\infty}{\underset{x}{\Sigma}} d_x$ (l_x)	$\dfrac{d_x}{l_x}$ (q_x)
	0	50	0.50	1.0	0.50
	1	20	0.20	0.5	0.40
	2	20	0.20	0.3	0.67
	3	10	0.10	0.1	1.00
	4	0			

ᵃ l_x = probability at birth of surviving to age x.
ᵇ d_x = probability at birth of dying in age interval x, $x+1$.
ᶜ q_x = probability at age x of dying before age $x+1$.

table and a fecundity table. In practice, we consider only the female segment of the population and assume that the male segment increases at about the same rate. When l_x is the probability at birth of a female surviving to age x and m_x is the mean number of female offspring she produces in the age interval pivoted at age x,

$$\Sigma \, l_x e^{-r_s x} m_x = 1 \qquad (1)$$

and r_s can be estimated by inserting trial values into the equation until it balances. When r_s lies between about plus and minus 0.1, an approximate but reasonably accurate direct solution is possible from

$$r_s = \frac{\log_e R_o}{T_c} \qquad (2)$$

in which $R_o = \Sigma \, l_x m_x$

and $T_c = \dfrac{\Sigma \, l_x m_x x}{\Sigma \, l_x m_x}$.

These solutions of r_s require a life table (l_x) covering all ages of females. Most life tables of mammals are constructed either from the age distribution of a shot sample or the distribution of ages at death of animals found dead (Deevey 1947, Caughley 1966). These calculations are outlined in Table 1. However, in both cases the construction of life tables from these distributions is based on the assumptions that the population has a stable age distribution and that $r_s = 0$. Consequently, such a life table, although providing a valid approximation to the mortality pattern, cannot be used to calculate r_s. The resultant estimate of r_s will be very close to zero because the calculation simply retrieves an assumption and disguises it as a conclusion. Logically, such a solving returns an estimate of the r_s within parentheses in

$$\Sigma \, l_x e^{-r_s x} (e^{-r_s x}) m_x = 1 \qquad (3)$$

and not the r_s of equation (1). Equation (1) being true by definition, equation (3) is true only when the parenthesized term equals 1 and therefore only when the value of r_s contained within it is equal to 0. Even when age distribution and fecundity rates are independently calculated, the equation returns an estimate of zero as a logical necessity, and this estimate has no relationship whatsoever to the true value of r_s.

Equations (1) and (2) cannot, therefore, be used on an age distribution or on a distribution of ages at death, but several mammalogists have used them on just such data. The equations have been used incorrectly both to estimate r_s (for example, Lowe 1969, Watson 1969, 1970) and in modified form to test the hypothesis that $r_s = 0$ (for example, Kurtén 1953, 1958, Quick 1963, Hughes 1965, Thomas et al. 1968, Macpherson 1969). In addition, we have recently seen four drafts of papers,

Table 2. Age distributions of female red deer on the island of Rhum—data from Lowe (1969).

YEAR	AGE IN YEARS													
	0	1	2	3	4	5	6	7	8	9	10	11	12	13
1957	154	129	113	113	81	78	59	65	55	25	9	8	7	2
1958	131	129	129	110	107	69	75	51	59	43	12	5	6	3
1959			123	122										
1960				96	98									
1961					75	66								
1962						52	40							
1963							37	25						
1964								23	18					
1965									19	4				

and know of two others, in which mammalogists have used this tautological analysis. Nothing is wrong with the equations. They can be used to estimate r_s for any species, given appropriate data. However, they do not provide an estimate of r_s if a single age distribution or a single distribution of ages at death is used to give the life table for the calculations.

As an example, part of an array presented by Lowe (1969) of age distributions of female red deer (*Cervus elaphus*) on the island of Rhum, Scotland, is given in Table 2. Lowe compiled these age distributions by aging deer found recently dead, thereby obtaining an estimate of date of birth and period of life for each specimen. Because he found almost all deer that died, he was able to reconstruct the number alive in each age-class in each of several years.

Four life tables could be constructed from the frequencies in Table 2: (1) from the 1957 age distribution if the population had a stable age distribution at the time and if r_s equalled zero; (2) from the 1958 age distribution, given the same assumptions; (3) from the yearly decline between 1957 and 1965 of the cohort born in 1957 (the lower diagonal of frequencies); and (4) from the difference between the number in a given age-class in 1957 and the number in the next age-class a year later.

Although four separate life tables could be constructed, they cannot each be combined with the m_x values of a fecundity table to provide four estimates of r_s. Only life tables 3 and 4 can be used in this way, the others being constructed on the assumption that $r_s = 0$.

Lowe (1969) made two estimates of r_s. The first used the age distribution of 1957, the l_x schedule being constructed as the probability of surviving from 1 year of age. The resultant $r_s = 0.047$ is meaningless both because of the $r_s = 0$ assumed in constructing the life table and because Lowe's calculated l_x is not the probability of surviving from birth, as required by the logic of the analysis. It is a probability of surviving from 1 year of age. His second estimate of r_s uses a life table tracing the fortunes of the cohort that was 1 year of age in 1957, the data being the upper diagonal of frequencies in Table 2. The resultant estimate of $r_s = -0.017$ is again meaningless. Although $r_s = 0$ is no longer an implicit assumption, survival is still incorrectly measured from 1 year of age.

In only very special cases is an estimate of r_s needed in the study of a mammalian population. It is a statistic having little relevance to the problems that a field study is usually expected to solve. In most cases, we need only the observed rate of increase,

r, which we calculate by regressing $\log_e$ numbers on time. Estimating r_s in addition is seldom worth the extra labor. For populations of large mammals, r_s will usually be so close to r that any difference will be swamped by sampling variation. Rate r is useful and relatively easy to calculate; r_s is less likely to be relevant and is more difficult to calculate.

Why, then, have several mammalogists recently tried to estimate r_s? It is apparent from their papers or drafts that in each case they confused r_s with r_m. Now r_m is really worth calculating, particularly if the study is aimed at estimating a sustained-yield harvest. It is a statistic needed to estimate how fast a population will build up after being reduced to any particular density. This induced rate of increase is the cropping rate most likely to hold the population stable at the reduced density. However, r_m cannot be estimated from survival and fecundity schedules unless the population is at minimal density.

We suspect that the confusion has arisen because mammalogists, in extrapolating to mammals the equations used by entomologists, have failed to appreciate that their data are of a different kind from those gathered from insects. Entomologists measure r_m by determining life tables and fecundity tables of insects held at low density in bottles or cages (Birch 1948). They substitute this information into equations (1) or (2) to estimate r_m for a particular combination of temperature and humidity. Leslie and Ranson (1940) estimated a value of r_m for the vole (*Microtus agrestis*) in this manner, but obviously the method cannot be adapted to the study of naturally occurring populations of mammals. In these circumstances, r_m is best approximated by measuring the rate of increase of a newly

established population, at which time $r \approx r_s \approx r_m$ in the initial stages.

This opportunity seldom arises, and we are usually forced to calculate r_m indirectly by deducing the rate of increase at minimal density from rate of increase at a much higher density. If the population's pattern of growth is known, a curve of this form can be fitted to successive estimates of the logged size of the growing population, and the curve can be extrapolated backward to minimal population size. The initial slope of this curve is an estimate of r_m.

In fact, the characteristic pattern of growth is seldom known and can only be guessed. Of the multiplicity of curves that might be applicable, we have chosen the logistic curve to demonstrate the general method. Although it is unlikely to provide an exact fit, since the assumptions on which it is based are biologically improbable, it may mimic the growth of some populations closely enough to yield a realistic estimate of r_m. The logistic is a flexible curve; when r_m is below about 0.3 it often provides a good empirical fit to the growth of a population whose dynamics are entirely different from those implied by the derivation of the logistic equation. It can therefore be justified as a first approximation on pragmatic grounds, as long as a tolerable fit is not misinterpreted to indicate that population processes and logistic assumptions are congruent.

Suppose a population that has been fluctuating around a mean of 1,000 animals for some time is suddenly reduced artificially to 800 and that by the following year it has increased to 850 and in the year after that to 890. The intrinsic rate of increase, that rate at which the population would increase if it were reduced to very low density, can be calculated from these totals if we are willing to assume that growth

Table 3. Calculating the intrinsic rate of increase by fitting a logistic curve.

YEAR (t)	NUMBERS (N)	$\frac{K-N}{N}$	$\log_e \frac{K-N}{N}$ (y)
0	800	0.250	−1.39
1	850	0.176	−1.74
2	890	0.123	−2.10

$$-r_m = \frac{\Sigma ty - (\Sigma t)(\Sigma y)/n}{\Sigma t^2 - (\Sigma t)^2/n}$$

$K = 1000 \qquad\qquad n = 3$

$\Sigma t = 3 \qquad\qquad \Sigma y = -5.23$

$\Sigma t^2 = 5 \qquad\qquad \Sigma ty = -5.94$

$\Sigma t^2 - (\Sigma t)^2/n = 2 \qquad \Sigma ty - (\Sigma t)(\Sigma y)/n = -0.710$

$-r_m = \text{slope} = -0.71/2 = -0.355; \; r_m = 0.355$

is approximately logistic and that the original population size was asymptotic. Symbolizing the prereduction (asymptotic) population size as K and the subsequent totals as N,

$$\log_e \frac{K-N}{N} = a - r_m t$$

and r_m can be estimated by linear regression of the left side of the equation ($\log_e (K-N)/N$) on time t. The slope of this regression estimates $-r_m$. The calculation is summarized in Table 3.

The logistic curve is unlikely to describe the growth of a population, even in an approximate way, if environmental conditions fluctuate markedly between years, or if the population responds slowly to a change in the availability of a resource, or if an artificial reduction in density disrupts the organization of social groups within the population. Estimation of r_m from the logistic curve is at best a stopgap procedure that should be abandoned as soon as a population's pattern of growth is established empirically.

LITERATURE CITED

ANDREWARTHA, H. G., AND L. C. BIRCH. 1954. The distribution and abundance of animals. The University of Chicago Press, Chicago. 782pp.

BIRCH, L. C. 1948. The intrinsic rate of natural increase of an insect population. J. Animal Ecol. 17(1):15–26.

CAUGHLEY, G. 1966. Mortality patterns in mammals. Ecology 47(6):906–918.

DEEVEY, E. S., JR. 1947. Life tables for natural populations of animals. Quart. Rev. Biol. 22(4):283–314.

HAIRSTON, N. G., D. W. TINKLE, AND H. M. WILBUR. 1970. Natural selection and the parameters of population growth. J. Wildl. Mgmt. 34(4):681–690.

HUGHES, R. D. 1965. On the age composition of a small sample of individuals from a population of the banded hare wallaby, Lagostrophus fasciatus (Peron & Lesueur). Australian J. Zool. 13(1):75–95.

KURTÉN, B. 1953. On the variation and population dynamics of fossil and recent mammal populations. Acta Zoologica Fennica 76. 122pp.

———. 1958. Life and death of the pleistocene cave bear: a study in paleoecology. Acta Zoologica Fennica 95. 59pp.

LESLIE, P. H., AND R. M. RANSON. 1940. The mortality, fertility and rate of natural increase of the vole (Microtus agrestis) as observed in the laboratory. J. Animal Ecol. 9(1):27–52.

LOWE, V. P. W. 1969. Population dynamics of the red deer (Cervus elaphus L.) on Rhum. J. Animal Ecol. 38(2):425–457.

MACPHERSON, A. H. 1969. The dynamics of Canadian arctic fox populations. Canadian Wildl. Serv. Rept. Ser. No. 8. 52pp. (French and Russian summaries.)

QUICK, H. F. 1963. Animal population analysis. Pages 190–228. In H. S. Mosby [Editor], Wildlife investigational techniques. 2nd ed. revised. The Wildlife Society, Washington, D.C. 419pp.

THOMAS, D. C., G. R. PARKER, J. P. KELSALL, AND A. G. LOUGHREY. 1968. Population estimates of barren-ground caribou on the Canadian mainland from 1955 to 1967. Canadian Wildl. Serv. Progr. Notes 3. 4pp.

WATSON, R. M. 1969. Reproduction of wildebeest, Connochaetes taurinus albojubatus Thomas, in the Serengeti region, and its significance to conservation. J. Reprod. and Fert. Suppl. 6:287–310.

———. 1970. Generation time and intrinsic rates of natural increase in wildebeeste (Connochaetes taurinus albojubatus Thomas). J. Reprod. and Fert. 22(3):557–561.

Population Cycles in Small Rodents

Demographic and genetic events are closely coupled
in fluctuating populations of field mice.

Charles J. Krebs, Michael S. Gaines, Barry L. Keller,
Judith H. Myers, Robert H. Tamarin

Outbreaks of small rodents were recorded in the Old Testament, in Aristotle's writings, and in the pages of European history. Charles Elton (1) summarized the colorful history of rodent plagues, and described the general sequence of outbreaks, from rapid multiplication to the destruction of crops and pastures, and the decline of the plague into scarcity. This cycle of abundance and scarcity is a continuing rhythm in many small rodents, although not all high populations reach plague proportions. The population cycles of small rodents have always been a classic-problem in population ecology, and speculation on the possible causes of rodent outbreaks has long outstripped the available scientific data. Both for practical reasons and because of our innate curiosity we would like to understand the mechanisms behind the rise and fall of these rodent populations.

Population cycles present an ideal situation in which to study population regulation. One question that has occupied biologists since the time of Malthus and Darwin has been this: What stops population increase? Cyclic populations, which follow a four-step pattern of increase–peak–decline–low, are thus useful in presenting a sequence of contrasting phases and then repeating the phases again and again. In small rodents the period of this cycle (2) is usually 3 to 4 years, although 2-year and 5-year cycles sometimes occur.

Since Charles Elton first kindled interest in population cycles in 1924 (3),

a great amount of effort has been expended in trying to describe and to explain these fluctuations. Two general facts have emerged from this work. First, many species of microtine rodents (lemmings and voles) in many different genera fluctuate in numbers. These species have not all been studied for long time-periods, but it is striking that in no instance has a population been studied in detail and found to be stable in numbers from year to year. Second, these cycles are found in a variety of ecological communities: lemmings on the tundras of North America and Eurasia, red-backed voles in the boreal forests of North America and Scandinavia, meadow voles in New York, field voles in coastal California, New Mexico, Indiana, Britain, Germany, and France. The list grows long and includes rodents from north temperate to arctic areas. No cyclic fluctuations have been described for tropical rodents or for South American species, but almost no population studies have been done on these species.

The phenomenon of population cycles is widespread but there is disagreement about whether we should seek a single explanation for the variety of situations in which it occurs. We adopt here the simplest hypothesis, that a single mechanism underlies all rodent cycles, from lemming cycles in Alaska to field vole cycles in southern Indiana. The only empirical justification we can give for this approach is that demographic events are similar in a variety of species living in different climates and in different plant communities; but the expectation of a single explanation for rodent cycles is only an article of faith.

There are two opposing schools of thought about what stops population increase in small rodents. One school looks to extrinsic agents such as food supply, predators, or disease to stop populations from increasing. The other looks to intrinsic effects, the effects of one individual upon another. We have abandoned a search for extrinsic agents of control for reasons discussed elsewhere (4, 5). This is not to say that extrinsic factors such as weather and food are not influencing microtine populations to varying degrees, but we believe that more important than the variable effects of extrinsic factors are the intrinsic factors which act in a common way in cycling rodents. We have turned our attention toward intrinsic effects, particularly those of behavior and genetics hypothesized by Chitty (6). Two essential elements of Chitty's hypothesis are (i) that the genetic composition of the population changes markedly during a cycle in numbers; and (ii) that spacing behavior (or hostility) is the variable which drives the demographic machinery through a cycle.

The suggestion that genetical mechanisms might be involved in the short-term changes in rodent populations has opened a new area of investigation. Population ecologists have traditionally been concerned with quantity rather than quality, and have only recently begun to realize the importance of individual variation (7). The genetical basis of the control of population size was discussed as early as 1931 by Ford (8) but most geneticists have assumed that population control is an ecological problem and not a genetic one. Lerner (9) attempted to bridge the gap between genetics and ecology by showing how the solution of ecological problems might be helped by genetical insights. Although population genetics and population ecology have developed as separate disciplines, we have tried to utilize both

these disciplines in our attempts to determine the causes of population cycles in rodents.

From 1965 to 1970 we studied the relationships among population dynamics, aggressive behavior, and genetic composition of field vole populations in southern Indiana. The two species of *Microtus* (*M. pennsylvanicus* and *M. ochrogaster*) that we studied fluctuate strongly in numbers with peak densities recurring at intervals of 2 or 3 years (10). The purposes of our investigations were to (i) describe the mechanics of the fluctuations in population size, (ii) monitor genetic changes with polymorphic marker loci, and (iii) measure changes in male aggressive behavior during a population fluctuation. We here synthesize our findings on the demography and genetic composition of *Microtus* populations, and summarize the results of our behavioral studies that have been reported elsewhere (11).

Demographic Changes

In *M. pennsylvanicus* changes in population size can be grouped into three phases, each of which lasts several months or more: an increase phase in which the rate of population increase (r) is greater than 0.03 per week (maximum observed, 0.13 per week); a peak phase in which the rate of increase is zero (between −0.02 and +0.03 per week) and density is high and essentially constant; and a decline phase in which r is negative (−0.03 per week or less; maximum observed, −0.12 per week). Figure 1 illustrates these phases for one population of *M. pennsylvanicus*.

Detailed information on changes in population size is available for several species of voles (4, 5, 10, 12). The increase phase is typically the most constant phase of the cycle, and once begun may continue through the winter, as shown in Fig. 1. The peak phase often begins with a spring decline in numbers, and a summer or fall increase restores the population to its former level. The

Table 1. Components of population fluctuations in *M. pennsylvanicus* in southern Indiana, 1965 to 1970. The data are expressed as mean values for more than 2000 individuals from four populations. The survival of early juvenile animals is determined from the number of unmarked young per lactating female; survival of subadults and adults is measured as a probability of survival per 14 days.

Phase	Birth rate (% lactating females)	Survival		
		Early juveniles	Subadult and adult	
			Males	Females
Increase	45	1.31	0.78	0.86
Peak	29	0.96	0.79	0.85
Decline	27	0.88	0.71	0.72

decline phase is most variable. It may begin in the fall of the peak year or be delayed until the next spring. The decline may be very rapid, so that most of the population disappears over 1 to 2 months, but often the decline is gradual and prolonged over a year or more. A phase of low numbers may or may not follow the decline, and little is known of this period, which may last a year or longer.

Changes in birth and death rates are the immediate cause of the population fluctuations in *M. pennsylvanicus* in Indiana. Table 1 shows that the birth rate, measured by the percentage of adult females captured that are visibly lactating, is reduced both in the peak phase and in the decline phase. The principal reason for this is that the breeding season is shortened in the peak and decline phases. Changes in weight at sexual maturity also contribute to a reduced birth rate in peak populations (*13*).

The death rate of small juvenile animals seems to increase dramatically in the peak and declining populations of

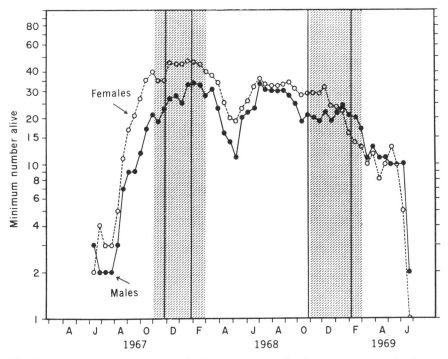

Fig. 1. Population density changes in *Microtus pennsylvanicus* on one grassland area in southern Indiana. Winter months are shaded. Vertical lines separate "summer" breeding period from "winter" period. An increase phase occurred from June to October 1967, and a decline phase from November 1968 to June 1969. [By permission of the Society for the Study of Evolution]

143

M. pennsylvanicus. By contrast, the death rate of subadult and adult animals is not increased in peak populations but is increased in declining populations. Thus, in a peak population, if an animal is able to survive through the early juvenile stage, it has a high survival rate as an adult. Declining populations suffer from a low birth rate and a high mortality rate of both juveniles and adults (*14*).

What is the nature of the mortality factor acting during the population decline? The older animals seem to bear the brunt of the increased mortality during the population decline. Also, periods of high mortality during the decline are not always synchronous in males and females (see Fig. 2). Therefore, the mortality factors that are affecting the age groups and sexes during the population decline can be very selective, which argues against the overwhelming influence of extrinsic agents such as predation and disease.

These changes in birth and death rates are not unique to *M. pennsylvanicus.* Birth rates are higher in the phase of increase for all vole and lemming populations that have been studied (*5, 12, 13, 15*). The most common method of increasing the reproductive rate is by extending the breeding season, which may continue through the winter in both lemmings and voles. Extended breeding seasons are also accompanied by lowered ages at sexual maturity in some species. These trends are reversed in peak and declining populations, and the breeding season may be particularly short in some peak populations. Litter sizes seem to be essentially the same during the increase phase and the decline phase.

Death rate measurements are available for relatively few small rodent populations (*4, 5, 10, 16*). Juvenile losses are often high in peak populations and especially high in declining populations. Adult death rates are not unusually high in dense populations, but may be very high during the decline

phase. The demographic changes which cause these rodent populations to fluctuate are thus a syndrome of reproductive shifts and mortality changes. Reproduction and early juvenile survival seem to deteriorate first, and only later is adult survival impaired. This syndrome of changes is common to situations as diverse as lemmings in northern Canada, voles in England, and field voles in Indiana.

Growth rates of individual animals are also affected by the population fluctuations. Both males and females in increasing populations grow more rapidly than individuals in peak populations, who in turn grow more rapidly than individuals in declining populations. Figure 3 illustrates this change in growth for *M. pennsylvanicus* from southern Indiana. The higher growth rates of individuals in increasing populations, coupled with higher survival rates, produce animals of larger than average body size in increasing and peak populations (*10*). These large animals are characteristic of all peak populations of small rodents.

Fencing Experiments

The first hint we obtained about how the demographic changes are brought about in field populations came from an experiment designed to answer the question: Does fencing a population of *Microtus* effect its dynamics? We constructed three mouse-proof enclosures in the field, each measuring 2 acres (0.8 hectare), and used these to study populations constrained by the fence, which allowed no immigration or emigration of *Microtus.* Figure 4 shows population changes on two adjacent fields, one of which was fenced in July 1965. Both populations increased in size but diverged sharply in the early peak phase. The fenced population (grid B) continued to increase in the summer of 1966 to 310 animals on the 2-acre plot, a density about three times as high as that on control

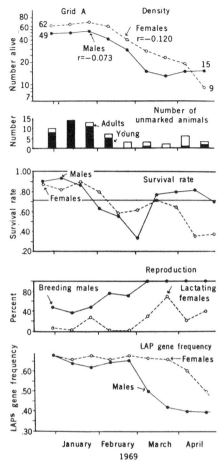

Fig. 2. Detailed breakdown of a population decline in *M. pennsylvanicus* during the spring of 1969. The critical observation is the difference in timing of male losses (highest in early March) and female losses (highest in mid-April). This timing is reflected in the gene frequency changes shown on the lowest graph (r is the instantaneous rate of population increase).

grid A. The overpopulation of the fenced *M. pennsylvanicus* on grid B resulted in habitat destruction and overgrazing, and led to a sharp decline with symptoms of starvation. The result was the same with enclosed populations of *M. ochrogaster* (*10*), and during the course of our studies four introductions of *M. ochrogaster* to the fenced areas resulted in abnormally high densities. Thus we conclude that fencing a *Mi-*

crotus population destroys the regulatory machinery which normally prevents overgrazing and starvation.

Dispersal (immigration and emigration) is the obvious process which is prevented by a fence, and we suggested that dispersal is necessary for normal population regulation in *Microtus*. We could see no indication that predation pressure was changed by the small fence around the large areas we studied. Foxes, cats, weasels, and snakes were known to have entered the fenced areas, and hawks and owls were not deterred.

Dispersal Experiments

If dispersal is important for population regulation, how might it operate? We could envisage two possible ways. First, dispersal might be related to population density, so that more animals would emigrate from an area in the peak phase and especially in the decline phase. These emigrants we would presume to be at a great disadvantage from environmental hazards such as other voles, predators, and bad weather. Second, the number of dispersers might not be as important as the quality of the dispersers. If only animals of a certain genetic type are able to tolerate high densities, dispersal may be one mechanism for sorting out these individuals.

We measured dispersal by maintaining two areas free of *Microtus* by trapping and removing all animals caught for 2 days every second week. Voles were free to colonize the areas for 12 days between each episode of trapping. We defined dispersers as those animals colonizing these vacant habitats (*17*). We thus determined the loss rate of individuals from control populations and the number of colonizers entering the trapped areas, and could calculate the fraction, in control populations, of losses attributable to dispersal.

Dispersal was most common in the increase phase of a population fluctua-

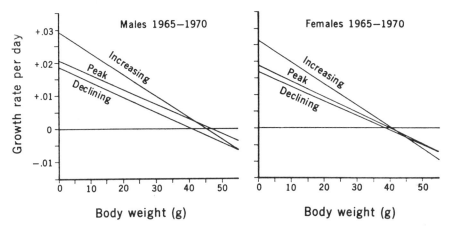

Fig. 3. Instantaneous relative growth rates for *M. pennsylvanicus* in southern Indiana. Regression lines for increase, peak, and decline phases are based on 691, 1898, and 333 observations for males and 776, 1696, and 322 observations for females (all pregnant animals excluded). Slope and elevation of the three regression lines are significantly different ($P < .01$) in both sexes.

tion and least common in the decline phase (Fig. 5). Most of the loss rate in increasing populations seems to be due to emigration (Table 2). Conversely, little of the heavy loss in declining populations is due to animals dispersing into adjacent areas, and hence most losses must be deaths in situ.

Thus dispersal losses from *Microtus* populations were not heaviest during the peak and decline, which supports the view that the role of dispersal is related to the quality of dispersing animals. We present evidence of genetic differences in dispersing *Microtus* in the next section.

Genetic Changes

Polymorphic serum proteins have been used as genetic markers to study the possible role of natural selection in population fluctuations of *Microtus*. We have used the genes *Tf* (transferrin) and *LAP* (leucine aminopeptidase) as markers (*18, 19*). The electrophoretically distinguishable forms of the products of these genes are inherited as if controlled by alleles of single autosomal loci.

We have found evidence of large changes in gene frequency at these two loci in association with population changes. Some of these changes are repetitive and have been observed in several populations (*18, 19*). Figure 2 shows the details of one decline in *M. pennsylvanicus* in the late winter and early spring of 1969. The survival rate of males during this decline dropped to a minimum in early March; female survival dropped 6 weeks later. These periods of poor survival coincided with the onset of sexual maturity in many of the adult males and the approximate dates of weaning first litters in adult females. The frequency of the *LAP^s* allele (distinguished by slow electrophoretic mobility) dropped about 25 percent in the males beginning at the time of high losses, and 4 to 6 weeks

Table 2. Percentage of losses known to be due to dispersal for control populations of *M. pennsylvanicus* in southern Indiana. Total numbers lost are shown in parentheses.

Population phase	Males (%)	Females (%)
Increase	56(32)	69(16)
Peak	33(157)	25(127)
Decline	15(53)	12(42)

146

later declined an equal amount in the females. This type of observation supports strongly the hypothesis that demographic events in *Microtus* are genetically selective and that losses are not distributed equally over all genotypes. Because we may be studying linkage effects and because we do not know how selection is acting, we cannot describe the mechanisms which would explain the associations shown in Fig. 2. We cannot therefore assign cause and effect to the observations.

We have also used the *Tf* and *LAP* variation to investigate possible qualitative differences between dispersing *Microtus* and resident animals. Since dispersal is particularly important in the increase phase (Fig. 5, Table 2), we looked for qualitative differences at this time. Figure 6 shows the genotypic frequencies at the locus of the *Tf* gene for control populations and dispersing animals during an increase phase. Heterozygous females (Tf^C/Tf^E, where *C* and *E* are alleles of the *Tf* gene) are much

more common in dispersing *Microtus* than in resident populations and 89 percent of the loss of heterozygous females from the control populations during the population increase was due to dispersal. Certain genotypes thus show a tendency to disperse, a possibility suggested by several authors (20) but not previously demonstrated in natural populations.

The polymorphic genes that we have used for markers in *M. pennsylvanicus* and *M. ochrogaster* are subject to intensive selection pressure, but we have not been able to determine how these polymorphisms are maintained. For example, let us consider the *Tf* polymorphism in *M. ochrogaster*. Two alleles are found in Indiana populations. The common allele Tf^E has a frequency of 97 percent in female and 93 percent in male *M. ochrogaster*. This polymorphism does not seem to be maintained by heterosis. We have not found any component of fitness (survival, reproduction, or growth) in which heterozygote voles (Tf^E/Tf^F) are superior to

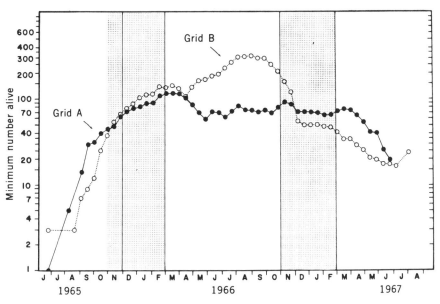

Fig. 4. Changes in population density of *M. pennsylvanicus* on unfenced grid A (control) and fenced grid B. Both are 2-acre (0.8-hectare) grassland fields. Grid B is surrounded by a mouse-proof fence extending 2 feet (0.6 meter) into the soil and projecting 2 feet above the ground. Signs of severe overgrazing were common on grid B by August 1966. [By permission of the Ecological Society of America]

147

homozygote voles (Tf^E/Tf^E), except in declining and low populations when the male heterozygotes survive better than the homozygotes. Increasing populations are always associated with strong selection for the Tf^E allele (18, 19). Homozygote Tf^F/Tf^F females had higher prenatal mortality in field experiments (21). We do not know if this Tf polymorphism is maintained by density-related changes in fitness or by frequency-dependent variations in fitness (22).

An alternative explanation for the associations we have described between population density changes and gene frequency changes has been provided by Charlesworth and Giesel (23). Population fluctuations result in continual shifts in age structure. Genotypes with differing ages at sexual maturity and differing survival rates will thus change in frequency as a result of population fluctuations, and genetic changes could thus be the side effect of population cycles caused by any mechanism. We do not know whether the genetic changes we have described are causally related to population changes or merely side effects, but we question whether they are adequately explained by the Charlesworth and Giesel model. The size of the changes in gene frequency we observed (for example, Fig. 2) is several times larger than the size of the changes obtained in the Charlesworth and Giesel model (1 to 9 percent). Also, Charlesworth and Giesel obtained relatively little effect on gene frequencies by changing death rates in their model; we have found that changes in death rates of different genotypes are a major component of shifts in gene frequency (11, 19). We suggest that field perturbation experiments may help to resolve these alternative explanations (24).

Behavioral Changes

If behavioral interactions among individual voles are the primary mechanism behind population cycles, the be-

havioral characteristics of individuals would change over the cycle. We have tested this hypothesis only for male *M. pennsylvanicus* and *M. ochrogaster* in our Indiana populations. Males were tested by paired round-robin encounters in a neutral arena in the laboratory. Males of both species showed significant changes in aggressive behavior during the population cycle, so that individuals in peak populations were most aggressive (11). Male *M. pennsylvanicus* which dispersed during periods of peak population density tended to be even more aggressive than the residents on control areas (17).

Laboratory measurements of behavior can be criticized because we have no way of knowing how such measures might apply to the field situation. There is no doubt that aggression does go on in field populations of voles and lemmings because skin wounds are found, particularly in males (5, 25). Field experiments could be designed to test the effects of aggression on mortality and growth rates, but none has been done yet on lemmings or voles. In the deer

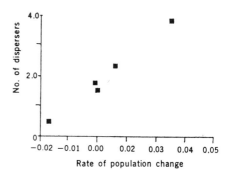

Fig. 5. Rate of population change in *M. pennsylvanicus* control population from southern Indiana in relation to dispersal rate from that population, 1968 to 1970. Rate of population change is the instantaneous rate of change per week, averaged over "summer" and "winter" periods shown in Fig. 1. Dispersal rate is the mean number of voles dispersing from the control population to the trapped grid per 2 weeks, averaged over the same time periods. Populations increasing rapidly show the highest dispersal rates.

148

C. J. Krebs et al.

mouse (*Peromyscus maniculatus*) field experiments have demonstrated that aggressive adult mice can prevent the recruitment of juveniles into the population (26).

Conclusions

We conclude that population fluctuations in *Microtus* in southern Indiana are produced by a syndrome of changes in birth and death rates similar to that found in other species of voles and lemmings. The mechanisms which cause the changes in birth and death rates are demolished by fencing the population so that no dispersal can occur. Dispersal thus seems critical for population regulation in *Microtus*. Because most dispersal occurs during the increase phase of the population cycle and there is little dispersal during the decline phase, dispersal is not directly related to population density. Hence the quality of dispersing animals must be important, and we have found one case of increased dispersal tendency by one genotype.

The failure of population regulation of *Microtus* in enclosed areas requires an explanation by any hypothesis attempting to explain population cycles

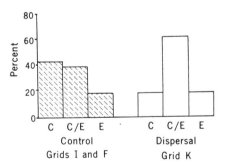

Fig. 6. The increase phase of *M. pennsylvanicus*, fall 1969. Transferrin genotype frequencies of dispersing females on trapped grid K ($N = 39$) compared with those of resident females on control grids immediately adjacent in the same grassland ($N = 224$). Dispersing voles in the increase phase are not a random sample from the control population. C, CIE, and E represent the three transferrin genotypes.

in small rodents. It might be suggested that the fence changed the predation pressure on the enclosed populations. However, the fence was only 2 feet (0.6 meter) high and did not stop the entrance of foxes, weasels, shrews, or avian predators. A striking feature was that the habitat in the enclosures quickly recovered from complete devastation by the start of the spring growing season. Obviously the habitat and food quality were sufficient to support *Microtus* populations of abnormally high densities, and recovery of the habitat was sufficiently quick that the introduction of new animals to these enclosed areas resulted in another population explosion. Finally, hypotheses of population regulation by social stress must account for the finding that *Microtus* can exist at densities several times greater than normal without "stress" taking an obvious toll.

We hypothesize that the prevention of dispersal changes the quality of the populations in the enclosures in comparison to those outside the fence. Voles forced to remain in an overcrowded fenced population do not suffer high mortality rates and continue to reproduce at abnormally high densities until starvation overtakes them. The initial behavioral interactions associated with crowding do not seem sufficient to cause voles to die in situ.

What happens to animals during the population decline? Our studies have not answered this question. The animals did not appear to disperse, but it is possible that the method we used to measure dispersal (movement into a vacant habitat) missed a large segment of dispersing voles which did not remain in the vacant area but kept on moving. Perhaps the dispersal during the increase phase of the population cycle is a colonization type of dispersal, and the animals taking part in it are likely to stay in a new habitat, while during the population decline dispersal is a pathological response to high density, and the animals are not attracted to settling even in a vacant habitat. The alternative to this suggestion is that animals are dying in situ during the decline because of physiological or genetically determined behavioral stress.

Thus the fencing of a population prevents the change in rates of survival and reproduction, from high rates in the increase phase to low rates in the decline phase, and the fenced populations resemble "mouse plagues." A possible explanation is that the differential dispersal of animals during the phase of increase causes the quality of the voles remaining at peak densities in wild populations to be different from the quality of voles at much higher densities in enclosures. Increased sensitivity to density in *Microtus* could cause the decline of wild populations at densities lower than those reached by fenced populations in which selection through dispersal has been prevented. Fencing might also alter the social interactions among *Microtus* in other ways that are not understood.

The analysis of colonizing species by MacArthur and Wilson (27) can be applied to our studies of dispersal in populations of *Microtus*. Groups of organisms with good dispersal and colonizing ability are called r strategists because they have high reproductive potential and are able to exploit a new environment rapidly. Dispersing voles seem to be r strategists. Young females in breeding condition were over-represented in dispersing female *Microtus* (*17*). The Tf^C/Tf^E females, which were more common among dispersers during the phase of population increase (Fig. 6), also have a slight reproductive advantage over the other Tf genotypes (*19*). Thus in *Microtus* populations the animals with the highest reproductive potential, the r strategists, are dispersing. The segment of the population which remains behind after the selection-via-dispersal are those individuals which are less influenced by increasing population densities. These are the individuals which maximize use of the habitat, the K strategists in MacArthur and Wilson's terminology, or voles selected for spacing behavior. Thus we can describe population cycles in *Microtus* in the

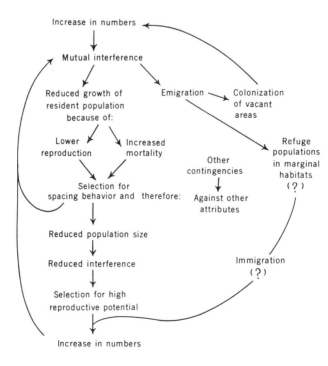

Fig. 7. Modified version of Chitty's hypothesis to explain population fluctuations in small rodents. Density-related changes in natural selection are central to this hypothesis. Our data indicate that selection through dispersal is more important than originally proposed by Chitty.

same theoretical framework as colonizing species on islands.

Our work on *Microtus* is consistent with the hypothesis of genetic and behavioral effects proposed by Chitty (*6*) (Fig. 7) in that it shows both behavioral differences in males during the phases of population fluctuation and periods of strong genetic selection. The greatest gaps in our knowledge are in the area of genetic-behavioral interactions which are most difficult to measure. We have no information on the heritability of aggressive behavior in voles. The pathways by which behavioral events are translated into physiological changes which affect reproduction and growth have been carefully analyzed by Christian and his associates (*28*) for rodents in laboratory situations, but the application of these findings to the complex field events described above remains to be done.

Several experiments are suggested by our work. First, other populations of other rodent species should increase to abnormal densities if enclosed in a large fenced area (*29*). We need to find situations in which this prediction is not fulfilled. Island populations may be an important source of material for such an experiment (*30*). Second, if one-way exit doors were provided from a fenced area, normal population regulation through dispersal should occur. This experiment would provide another method by which dispersers could be identified. Third, if dispersal were prevented after a population reached peak densities, a normal decline phase should occur. This prediction is based on the assumption that dispersal during the increase phase is sufficient to ensure the decline phase 1 or 2 years later. All these experiments are concerned with the dispersal factor, and our work on *Microtus* can be summarized by the admonition: study dispersal.

References and Notes

1. C. Elton, *Voles, Mice and Lemmings: Problems in Population Dynamics* (Clarendon Press, Oxford, 1942).
2. The term "cycle" is used here as a convenient shorthand for the more technically correct term "periodic fluctuation." We do not mean to imply a physicist's meaning of the word "cycle" because both the amplitude and the period of population fluctuations in small rodents are variable.
3. C. S. Elton, *Brit. J. Exp. Biol.* **2**, 119 (1924).
4. D. Chitty, *Phil. Trans. Roy. Soc. London Ser. B* **236**, 505 (1952); *Can. J. Zool.* **38**, 99 (1960).
5. C. J. Krebs, *Arctic Inst. N. Amer. Tech. Pap. No. 15* (1964).
6. D. Chitty, *Proc. Ecol. Soc. Aust.* **2**, 51 (1967).
7. L. C. Birch, *Amer. Natur.* **94**, 5 (1960); W. G. Wellington, *Can. J. Zool.* **35**, 293 (1957); *Can. Entomol.* **96**, 436 (1964).
8. E. B. Ford, *Mendelism and Evolution* (Methuen, London, 1931).
9. I. M. Lerner, *Proc. Int. Congr. Genet. 11th* **2**, 489 (1965).
10. C. J. Krebs, B. L. Keller, R. H. Tamarin, *Ecology* **50**, 587 (1969).
11. C. J. Krebs, *ibid.* **51**, 34 (1970); *Proceedings of the NATO Advanced Study Institute, Oosterbeek, 1970*, P. J. den Boer and G. R. Gradwell, Eds. (Center for Agricultural Publishing and Documentation, Wageningen, Netherlands, 1971), pp. 243–256.
12. D. Chitty and H. Chitty, in *Symposium Theriologicum, Brno, 1960*, J. Kratochvil and J. Pelikan, Eds. (Czechoslovak Academy of Sciences, Prague, 1962), pp. 67–76; F. B. Golley, *Amer. Midland Natur.* **66**, 152 (1961); O. Kalela, *Ann. Acad. Sci. Fenn. Ser. A* **4**, 34 (1957); C. J. Krebs, *Ecol. Monogr.* **36**, 239 (1966); E. P. Martin, *Univ. Kans. Publ. Mus. Natur. Hist.* **8**, 361 (1956); J. Zejda, *Zool. Listy* **13**, 15 (1964); G. O. Batzli and F. Pitelka, *J. Mammalogy* **52**, 141 (1971).
13. B. L. Keller and C. J. Krebs, *Ecol. Monogr.* **40**, 263 (1970).
14. We describe here our findings on *M. pennsylvanicus*. We have similar results for *M. ochrogaster* in Indiana, but we do not present these data here because they provide essentially the same conclusions.
15. G. S. Greenwald, *Univ. Calif. Publ. Zool.* **54**, 421 (1957); W. J. Hamilton, Jr., *Cornell Univ. Agric. Exp. Stat. Mem.* **237** (1941); T. V. Koshkina, *Bull. Moscow Soc. Nat. Biol. Sect.* **71**, 14 (1966); G. O. Batzli and F. A. Pitelka, *J. Mammal.* **52**, 141 (1971).
16. D. Chitty and E. Phipps, *J. Anim. Ecol.* **35**, 313 (1966); G. O. Batzli, thesis, Univ. of California, Berkeley (1969).
17. J. H. Myers and C. J. Krebs, *Ecol. Monogr.* **41**, 53 (1971).
18. R. H. Tamarin and C. J. Krebs, *Evolution* **23**, 183 (1969).
19. M. S. Gaines and C. J. Krebs, *ibid.* **25**, 702 (1971).
20. W. E. Howard, *Amer. Midland Natur.* **63**, 152 (1960); W. Z. Lidicker, *Amer. Natur.* **96**, 29 (1962).
21. M. S. Gaines, J. H. Myers, C. J. Krebs, *Evolution* **25**, 443 (1971).
22. Density-related changes in fitness might be mediated by dispersal. The very rare Tf^F/Tf^F homozygote in *M. ochrogaster* occurred more frequently among dispersing males than in resident populations (*17*).
23. B. Charlesworth and J. T. Giesel, *Amer. Natur.* **106**, 388 (1972).
24. R. P. Canham and D. G. Cameron (personal communication) have obtained evidence for selection against certain *Tf* genotypes in declining populations of *Clethrionomys* and *Peromyscus* which have discrete annual generations in northern Canada. The Charles-

worth and Giesel model (23) can apply only to species with overlapping generations.

25. J. J. Christian, *J. Mammal.* **52**, 556 (1971).
26. R. M. F. S. Sadleir, *J. Anim. Ecol.* **34**, 331 (1965); M. C. Healey, *Ecology* **48**, 337 (1967).
27. R. H. MacArthur and E. O. Wilson, *The Theory of Island Biogeography* (Princeton Univ. Press, Princeton, N.J., 1967).
28. J. J. Christian, *Biol. Reprod.* **4**, 248 (1971); J. J. Christian, J. A. Lloyd, D. E. Davis, *Recent Progr. Hormone Res.* **21**, 501 (1965); J. J. Christian, *Proc. Nat. Acad. Sci. U.S.A.* **47**, 428 (1961).
29. J. R. Clarke, *Proc. Roy. Soc. London Ser. B* **144**, 68 (1955); P. Crowcroft and F. P. Rowe, *Proc. Zool. Soc. London* **129**, 359 (1957);

J. B. Gentry, *Res. Population Ecol.* **10**, 21 (1968); W. Z. Lidicker, *ibid.* **7**, 57 (1965); K. Petrusewicz, *Ekol. Pol. Ser. A* **5**, 281 (1957); R. L. Steecker and J. T. Emlen, *Ecology* **34**, 375 (1953).
30. The population of *M. californicus* on Brooks Island in San Francisco Bay may be acting in the same way as a fenced population, maintaining densities higher than mainland populations (W. Z. Lidicker, personal communication).
31. This research was conducted when all of us were at Indiana University. We thank the National Science Foundation and the Public Health Service for financial support of the research.

A DEMOGRAPHIC ANALYSIS OF THE SNOWSHOE HARE CYCLE

Lloyd B. Keith and Lamar A. Windberg

INTRODUCTION

Cyclic fluctuations of snowshoe hares *Lepus americanus* have persisted for at least 200 years in North America's boreal forests (Keith 1963). These conspicuous, regular, and broadly synchronous changes in population have evoked much speculation and discussion, but their long-term perodicity of mainly 8 to 11 years has tended to discourage field studies of sufficient duration to determine causation. The notable exception was R. G. Green's work in northern Minnesota during the 1930s. Although handicapped by inadequate field techniques and relatively low hare densities even in "peak" years, Green and his colleagues obtained the first really quantitative demographic information on a cyclic population. Subsequent short-term studies have yielded additional demographic data, usually relating to peak or near-peak situations.

Our own work on the "10-year cycle" began in June 1961 and continued through August 1976, spanning 2 periods of population decline and 1 of increase, with peak numbers in 1961 and 1970. Study areas were near Rochester, in central Alberta, a region where hare fluctuations are pronounced and where much of the natural ecosystem is still intact.

In an earlier paper, Meslow and Keith (1968) outlined demographic changes in snowshoe hare populations from 1961 through summer 1967, a period of population decline and initial recovery. The aim of the present paper is twofold: (1) to describe the set of demographic events that characterized 15 years (1.5 cycles) of population change on our Rochester study areas; this analysis is more comprehensive than that published earlier, and the data from 1961–1967 have been reanalyzed and integrated with those from 1968–1976; and (2) to compare and collate information from Rochester with what has been found elsewhere, in an effort to identify those demographic elements that are consistently involved in the snowshoe hare cycle over large geographic areas. This paper is restricted in scope to the problem of the hare cycle, and makes no attempt to summarize demographic data for snowshoe hare populations generally or to review population dynamics of other lagomorphs.

ACKNOWLEDGMENTS

Many graduate students and their laboratory and field assistants made important contributions to this study during its 15-year duration. While some were directly concerned with hare population dynamics, others worked chiefly on ancillary problems but gave freely of their time as members of the research team. We wish to thank the following former students: T. M. Yuill, O. J. Rongstad, J. O. Iverson, C. H. Nellis, E. C. Meslow, D. H. Rusch, D. A. Rusch, S. P. Wetmore, S. Luttich, P. D. Doerr, M. Grandlund, G. L. Hoff, D. C. Surrendi, G. A. Kemp, R. G. Weatherill, G. J. Davis, M. J. Dorrance, R. C. Vowels, C. A. Fischer, W. B. McInvaille, C. J. Brand, J. L. Pease, J. R. Cary, A. W. Todd, R. L. Zarnke, R. S. Adamcik, and M. R. Vaughan. We are especially grateful to a number of competent young women who worked extremely hard in our field laboratory: D. Keith, L.

Munsterman, D. Mathison, J. Keith, R. Munsterman, E. Anderson, and B. Kuhs. Our field assistants also did an excellent job and deserve much credit: B. Keith, D. Wood, C. Bitzer, G. Saunders, N. Saunders, S. Saunders, R. Saunders, G. Munsterman, E. Munsterman, H. Johnson, J. Gorham, T. Smith, G. Anderson, G. Mathison, T. Vowel, B. Slonowski, O. Pall, H. Shopland, J. Jorgenson, and D. Wing.

Financial support came mainly from 4 sources: the Research Council of Alberta provided an annual grant for 15 consecutive years and administered other funds, we particularly appreciate the help and encouragement of N. Grace, E. Wiggins, D. Irwin, and H. Kay of that agency; the College of Agricultural and Life Sciences, University of Wisconsin, Madison, salaried the principal investigator and provided assistantships for graduate students throughout the study; the Fish and Wildlife Division, Alberta Department of Lands and Forests, gave us logistic support and research funds for 11 consecutive years; successive National Science Foundation grants covered a period of 9 years; other organizations and agencies that assisted us financially, and to whom we are also heavily indebted are: the Veterinary Services Branch, Alberta Department of Agriculture; the Research Committee of the Graduate School, University of Wisconsin; the Canadian Wildlife Service; and the Wildlife Management Institute.

A major portion of this paper was written by the senior author during a 1-year study leave in Sweden. His salary and travel expenses at that time were paid jointly by the College of Agricultural and Life Sciences, and the Research Committee of the Graduate School, University of Wisconsin; the National Science Foundation; and the National Swedish Environment Protection Board.

We thank F. H. Wagner and C. J. Krebs for reviewing the manuscript and making numerous suggestions for improvement. The computer programming skills of J. R. Cary were helpful on many occasions.

Lastly, we wish to offer a heartfelt thanks to the many local families whose kindnesses over the years did much to make life pleasant for all of us. We must especially single out the Halls at Dapp, the Hansons and Saunders at Tawatinaw, and the Munstermans, Shoplands, and Gerlachs at Rochester.

STUDY AREAS AND METHODS

The study areas near Rochester and the various field and laboratory techniques employed by us have been described in several previous papers (Meslow and Keith 1968, Keith et al. 1968, Keith and Surrendi 1971). Some of that information is reiterated here, but only briefly. Two aspects of methodology are, however, discussed in considerably more detail because of their importance in understanding population change, viz., estimations of numbers and survival rates of hares.

Description of Region and Study Areas

The Rochester district of central Alberta (Fig. 1) lies within a sector of the boreal forest where aspen *Populus tremuloides* predominates on upland sites due to recurrent fires. The latter have effectively suppressed succession to a white spruce *Picea glauca* climax. The soils have been formed on calcium-rich glacial deposits and generally support a dense growth of herbaceous plants and such woody understory species as hazel *Corylus cornuta* and lowbush cranberry *Viburnum edule*. Jackpine *Pinus banksiana* stands are confined to sandy soils, and there, ericaceous species provide most of the ground cover, with alder *Alnus* spp. as the principal understory shrub. Bogs are scattered throughout the region; stands of dense black spruce *Picea mariana* occur along the bog edges. Tamarack *Larix laricina* and scrub birch *Betula glandulosa* usually grow on the mat of *Sphagnum* and *Carex* that cover wetter areas. About half the land within 3 km of our intensive study areas is agricultural, approximately equal portions being cleared cropland

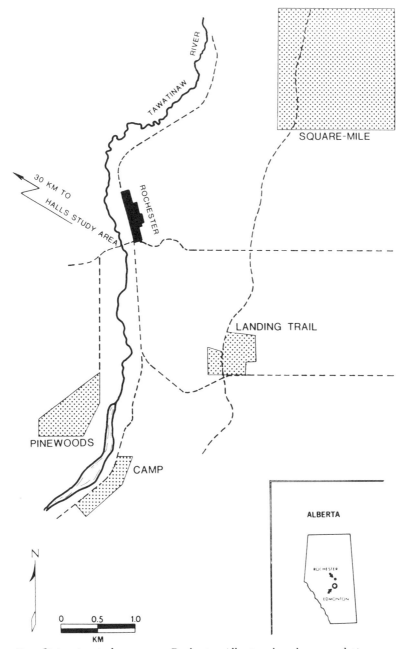

FIG. 1. Location of intensive study areas near Rochester, Alberta, where hare populations were monitored.

and woodland pasture. The country is flat to gently rolling, with the Tawatinaw River valley and several associated coulees providing the only notable topographic relief. The climate is typically northern continental: annual precipitation (water equivalent) totals 45 cm, about one-third of which falls as snow; July and January mean temperatures are 17 and −16 C, respectively.

Three study areas (Square-mile, Pinewoods, Landing Trail) were established

155

within 4 km of Rochester during 1962, and a fourth (Camp) was added in 1963. A fifth study area (Halls) was set up in 1965 about 30 km to the northwest (Fig. 1). Natural demographic changes were monitored seasonally by livetrapping on each area until August 1976. Hares were collected for postmortem examination from many additional sites in the vicinity of Rochester, and other study areas were at times set up for more specific short-term investigations (see Windberg and Keith 1976a, 1976b).

The 5 study areas on which populations were monitored were selected initially as representative of snowshoe hare habitat in the region. There was no notable disturbance to 4 of the areas during our investigations, and their sizes remained constant: Pinewoods 34 ha, Landing Trail 28 ha, Camp 16 ha, Halls 26 ha. The Square-mile study area was, on the other hand, wholly or partly burned 5 times, and, consequently, hare habitat there varied over the years from 259 ha (1 mile²) to 16 ha. Earlier fires had created a spectrum of habitat quality on Square-mile that allowed us to relate changes in habitat occupancy to cyclic changes in the hare population. The eastern third of Square-mile was largely bog and tended to be least affected by fire. Vegetation on Pinewoods consisted mainly of open stands of mature jackpine having little or no brushy undergrowth, grass and sedge meadows devoid of trees, and dense patches of alder and stunted aspen; it was the latter areas that were most frequented by hares. Landing Trail was entirely covered by 20- to 40-year-old aspen, balsam poplar *Populus balsamifera*, and white birch *Betula papyrifera*; the understory was dominated by dense clones of hazel. The Camp study area was in a mature stand of balsam poplar and aspen, with scattered white spruce and white birch. It was situated on a northwest-facing slope of the Tawatinaw River valley; lower sites had extensive thickets of dogwood *Cornus stolonifera* in the understory while hazel predominated elsewhere. Halls study area, 30 km northwest of Rochester, was a mixture of upland and bog. Aspen, balsam poplar, and white spruce occurred on the upland, and lowbush cranberry and buffalo berry *Shepherdia canadensis* were the most conspicuous woody shrubs. Black spruce, often small and very dense, covered much of the lowland, but there were also sedge meadows with willow *Salix* spp. and alder.

Field Techniques

Hares were taken at all times of the year in National live traps set on well-used runways and checked each morning. Traps were baited with good quality alfalfa hay in spring and winter, but were unbaited in summer. Trap densities on the 5 intensive study areas consistently averaged just under 1/ha. Collections of hares from other areas were also mainly with National live traps, although snaring, shooting, and netting were sometimes employed.

In the routine field processing of all hares, we recorded weight, hindfoot length, sex, age, and reproductive status. The latter included pregnancy, lactation, suckling, and teat length, and testis size and position, and penis characteristics. Individuals taken on intensive study areas, and hence released immediately after field processing, were marked with numbered fingerling tags set between the toes of the hindfeet. Toes were clipped from juveniles caught during May–September as an assured permanent identification; all adult hares, and juveniles taken after September, were ear tattooed. Various dyes were used to color the fur during October–April, the most satisfactory being picric acid (yellow) and rhodamine-B (red).

A more complete description, and an evaluation of the above-mentioned techniques, has been provided by Keith et al. (1968).

Laboratory Techniques

Procedures for handling hares in the laboratory depended on the primary aim

156

of specific collections. Information of major importance to demographic studies that could only be obtained postmortem included: (1) paunched body weight and organ weights (mainly adrenal, liver, spleen, and heart); (2) reproductive performance and status as reflected in corpora lutea and embryo counts, and testis weights; and (3) age of adult-sized animals as determined from eye lens weights. During 1962–1975, we obtained lens weights from approximately 50 wild snowshoe hares marked as juveniles and recaptured 6 months to 4 years later. Lens weights were also obtained from another 40 individuals that had been marked as adults and recaptured up to 3 years later. Those lens data provided an excellent basis for segregating yearlings, 2 year olds, and older animals, and will be summarized in a future publication.

RESULTS AND CONCLUSIONS

Numerical Trends (Local)

Initial estimates of snowshoe hare numbers on the Square-mile study area at Rochester were obtained in April 1962, on Pinewoods and Landing Trail in July 1962, and on Camp in April 1963. Censuses on Halls study area (30 km northwest) began in August 1965. As previously discussed, the accuracy of such population estimates varied seasonally and between estimators, due mainly to bias from ingress (midwinter and spring estimates) and perhaps also from trappability (summer estimates).

Meslow and Keith (1968) described field observations that suggested a general upward trend in the regional hare population from 1959 to 1961. They also presented indexes to snaring success on sites adjacent to the Rochester study areas during 1961–1964, that, together with the earlier observations, indicated a peak in late summer 1961.

The spring and midwinter means of all population estimates for each study area were plotted (Fig. 2) to show trends in hare numbers. Spring populations de-

clined to a low level by April 1964 on the 4 study areas nearest Rochester, were lowest during 1965–1966, and thereafter increased markedly to a peak in 1970 on the Camp area, and in 1971 on Square-mile, Pinewoods, and Landing Trail. The same increasing trend occurred during 1968–1971 on Halls study area, 30 km away. Spring populations on all 5 areas declined in 1972 and continued to do so through 1974 or 1975. Midwinter trends largely paralleled those of spring, with all study areas experiencing a midwinter peak in 1970–1971.

The amplitude of the increase phase of that fluctuation, as gauged from the above indexes, ranged from about 17- to 50-fold for spring populations on the different study areas. The subsequent decline reduced numbers below those recorded during the previous low, and hence the amplitude of change during the decrease phase was even greater. If we consider only those spring population estimates from unbiased estimators (reobservation and trapping efficiency), and exclude the Square-mile area because of habitat disturbance by fire, the amplitude of change from low to high on the 3 other study areas at Rochester averaged 23-fold. There was a 29-fold change on Halls.

Conclusions about absolute densities of hares at different stages in this cyclic fluctuation are complicated by our inability to state precisely the size of the area occupied by the estimated population. The problem arises because the home range of some hares trapped within designated study areas lay partly outside the arbitrarily established boundaries, which, in fact, simply represent limits of trap distribution.

A crude and undoubtedly maximum approximation of the area to which the population estimates apply can be made through records of hare movements on the Square-mile study area. During 1962–1964 we trapped over the entire 259 ha with extreme distances between traplines of 1,600 m; 95 percent of all (265) recaptures of hares during the first year after marking occurred within 300 m of the initial cap-

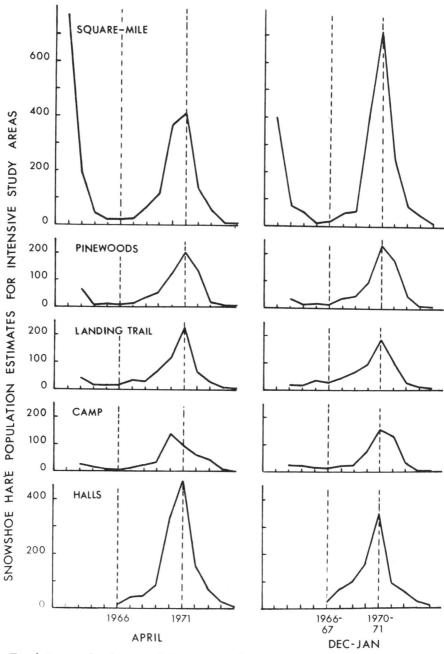

FIG. 2. Trends in snowshoe hare populations on 5 study areas near Rochester, Alberta. The amount of hare habitat on Square-mile varied greatly due to wildfires: i.e., April 1962–May 1964 (259 ha), June 1964–May 1968 (40 ha), June 1968–June 1969 (16 ha), July 1969–April 1976 (61 ha). There were no fires on the other 4 study areas: Pinewoods (34 ha), Landing Trail (28 ha), Camp (16 ha), and Halls (26 ha). Numbers plotted for each study area are means of all available time-specific population estimates (Appendixes 1 and 2), but must be considered as indexes only because some estimates were inflated by ingress as discussed in text.

ture site (Meslow and Keith 1968). If 300 m is taken as the maximum distance beyond study area boundaries from which hares taken in traps would range, and hare habitat within a strip of that width is added to each study area, the effective size of all 5 areas is about doubled.

On that basis, and again using only the unbiased estimates from reobservation and trapping efficiency, absolute densities during the cyclic low in April 1966 lay between 13 and 26 hares/100 ha on the combined Pinewoods, Landing Trail, and Camp areas. The highest absolute density on those areas was recorded in November 1970, and lay between 588 and 1,177 hares/100 ha (1,525–3,049/mi²). The measured amplitude of increase from the lowest spring population to the highest early winter population thus averaged 46-fold. On the Square-mile study area, the lowest absolute density of 17 to 33 hares/100 ha occurred in April 1965, and the highest of 1,145 to 2,291/100 ha (2,968–5,936/mi²) in November 1970. The amplitude of increase there was about 70-fold. Such peak densities on the Square-mile study area existed in ideal habitat that had had 3 growing seasons to regenerate following a wildfire in May 1968 (Keith and Surrendi 1971).

The peak November densities cited above were not, of course, the maxima attained on the study areas; using age ratio and age-specific survival data given later in this paper, we calculated that hare numbers in early September would have been 1.8 times greater. If spring 1966 marked the hare low on Halls study area, the low absolute density lay between 27 and 54 hares/100 ha, and the high between 769 and 1,538/100 ha (1,993–3,986/mi²) in April 1971. The amplitude of increase was thus 29-fold.

During the 5 consecutive springs of population (P) growth from 1966 to 1971, annual finite rates of increase ($\lambda = P_2/P_1$) based on reobservation and trapping efficiency estimators averaged 2.0 on the combined Pinewoods, Landing Trail, and Camp study areas; the lowest rate of increase was 1.1 and the highest was 3.0.

The greatest rate of increase (4.0) was observed on the Square-mile area between April 1969 and 1970. On Halls, λ also averaged 2.0 during 1966–1971, and ranged from 1.5 to 2.4. Rates of numerical change could be calculated for 4 years of spring population decrease (1963–1964, 1971–1974) on Pinewoods, Landing Trail, and Camp. Those rates of change averaged 0.35, with a range of 0.18 to 0.55. In 5 years of measured population decrease on Square-mile (includes 1962–1963) the rate of change averaged 0.29, and ranged from 0.13 to 0.48. On Halls, the mean rate during 1971–1974 was 0.33, varying only between 0.33 and 0.39.

The foregoing analysis indicates that hare populations tended to decrease more rapidly than they increased, falling in successive springs to about one-third previous levels during the decline phase of the cycle, but about doubling each year during the increase phase. This means that 3 successive years of population decline would negate a 5- to 6-year period of increase.

Our data suggest that peak hare populations occurred at Rochester after the breeding seasons in 1961 and 1970, a 9-year interval. Measured low populations on the 4 Rochester study areas combined occurred in the springs of 1965 and 1966, and 1975, also a 9-year interval.

DISCUSSION
Demography of Cyclic Snowshoe Hare Populations

This 15-year study of cyclic snowshoe hare populations spanned 2 periods of decline and 1 of increase, and the initial stages of a second period of increase. Thus, the sequence of demographic events underlying major numerical change was largely replicated. On that basis, it seems reasonable to designate the following conditions as being predictably associated with the hare cycle at Rochester, Alberta:

1. A marked reduction in overwinter survival of juveniles beginning in the

peak year and continuing for 4 or 5 years of declining numbers.

2. Some improvement in juvenile survival during the last year or 2 of low survival rates, without any resulting numerical increase.

3. An average overwinter survival rate for juveniles during years of population increase 3 to 4 times higher than during years of decline, but still extremely variable.

4. A reduction in late winter survival of adults 1 year after the population peak, that continues through the low.

5. A pronounced rise in average weight loss between winter (November–January) and spring (April) during the winter immediately preceding the peak summer and fall, and a return to lesser weight losses after 3 or 4 years and prior to the cyclic low.

6. Mean growth rates of young hares in summer that are inversely correlated with mean adult weight losses during the previous winter to spring, and hence tend to decrease in the peak summer and rise again before the population reaches a low.

7. Annual changes in average November–January weights of juvenile hares that reflect the previous summer's growth rates.

8. A potential natality (young born per adult female surviving the breeding season) that begins to drop in the peak summer, drops further during the first 2 or 3 summers of population decline, and starts to recover before the cyclic low.

9. Changes in ovulation rate, third and fourth litter pregnancy rate, and length of breeding season that are primarily responsible for annual changes in potential natality; annual values of all 4 of those reproductive parameters being inversely correlated with mean weight losses during previous winters.

10. As a consequence of conditions 1, 2, 4, and 8, there is a sharp decrease in the proportion of yearlings in spring and summer, and juveniles in fall and

winter, during the year following the peak, and a rise again at the low before any numerical increase.

It seems to us that 2 very significant aspects of this demographic picture are the chronological sequences: (1) lower winter–spring weight loss, increased reproduction, increased juvenile growth rate, increased juvenile survival over winter; and (2) higher winter–spring weight loss, decreased reproduction, decreased juvenile growth rate, decreased juvenile survival over winter. The first sequence began about 3 years after the peak winter and slowed the rate of decline; the second preceded the peak winter by 1 year and slowed the rate of increase. In neither case was the existing population trend immediately reversed because adult survival was unaffected and juvenile survival only partially so.

Those weight, reproductive, growth, and survival changes are consistent with the conceptual model of cyclic fluctuations presented by Keith (1974), who suggested that 2 different but related interactions are involved, both of which contain strong delayed density dependent elements. The first is between the hare and its winter food supply (woody browse); this initiates the population decline and sets the stage for the second, a hare–predator interaction, that extends it. Thus the nutritional problems that beset the hare population as it approaches peak densities are reflected first in winter to spring weight loss, and then in lower reproduction and growth of young. The reduced overwinter survival of juveniles that follows is, to begin with, mainly related to severe food shortage compounded by the normally lower survival of lightweight individuals. After the initial major decline in the hare population, predation becomes increasingly important as an immediate mortality factor on both juveniles and adults, and adult survival then also decreases. Termination of the critical nutritional phase is signalled by reduced winter to spring weight loss and a subsequent rise in reproductive and growth

Table 1.—Relationship between overwinter food supplies for hare populations on 2 study areas at Rochester, Alberta, and winter to spring weight change

Winter	Population trend or status	Ratio of total food available in late Nov to total food required by the November hare population over winter[1]		Change in mean weight of males between win and spr[3] (%)
		Telemetry study area[2]	Landing Trail study area	
1970–1971	Peak	0.48	0.97	−8.9
1971–1972	Decreasing	0.71	0.98	−10.3
1972–1973	Decreasing	1.8	2.7	−8.5
1973–1974	Decreasing	13.2	6.6	−5.8
1974–1975	Low	(26.4)[4]	(53.3)	−3.0
1975–1976	Increasing	22.5	8.8	−5.4

[1] Data from Pease (1977, unpublished thesis).

[2] The telemetry study area consisted of the southeastern portion of Square-mile plus an eastward extension and totalled about 40 ha (see Brand et al. 1975).

[3] Based on data from the 5 intensive study areas: Square-mile, Landing Trail, Pinewoods, Camp, and Halls

[4] Data for 1974–1975 indicate conditions in January–February as no browse measurements were made in November of that winter.

rates. Juvenile survival only partially recovers because high predation caused mortality continues; adult survival likewise remains depressed through predation. It is, therefore, not until the predator population has declined and such losses cease that survival rates improve sufficiently to permit another period of numerical increase for the hares. By this time, too, the browse will have largely recovered from its previous overutilization.

A major weakness in our data set is that measurements of winter food supplies cover only 6 years, from 1970–1971 to 1975–1976. This was, however, an important period as it began with a population peak and ended with the first year of recovery from a low, thus theoretically spanning the transition from food shortage to sufficiency. The data in fact fit the above conceptual model, since highest winter to spring weight losses occurred in 1970–1971 and 1971–1972 when food shortage was most severe, and decreased markedly by 1973–1974 when food supplies apparently were adequate (Table 1). That lower weight loss was followed immediately by improved reproduction

and juvenile survival (we have insufficient data to check growth rates).

We do not claim that all variance in mean winter weight losses nor in subsequent reproductive and growth rates is attributable solely to varying overwinter nutrition. Indeed, Cary and Keith (1978) demonstrated significant correlations between winter–spring weather and important elements of reproduction; while Keith (1974) suggested, and Pease (1977, unpublished master's thesis, University of Wisconsin, Madison, Wisconsin) showed experimentally, that winter temperatures can interact significantly with nutritional stress to determine survival. What we do believe is that a hare–food interaction in concert with a hare–predator interaction provide the basic intrinsic mechanism that generates the predominant cyclic pattern of population change.

If the preceding account of population demography is broadly representative of events elsewhere in North America where cyclic fluctuations of snowshoe hares have occurred, one might logically expect to see evidence of this in earlier studies. We found 5 studies of cyclic populations in which 1 or more demographic variables could be related to some measurement or index of numbers. When noting litter size changes in the following review, we exclude the first litter of the breeding season whose size averages only about half that of the 2 or 3 later litters, and whose year-to-year changes at Rochester and elsewhere are largely unrelated to the population cycle (Cary and Keith 1978).

The first and longest investigation was the pioneering work of Green and Evans (1940) in northern Minnesota. They concluded that reproduction remained essentially unchanged from a population peak to a low. We have reanalyzed their data in light of more recent information on synchrony of littering and the consistent tendency for first litters to be smaller. Contrary to Green and Evan's (1940) initial conclusion, reproduction appears to have declined in the peak year (1932) and remained relatively low for 3 more years

TABLE 2.—REPRODUCTIVE AND AGE RATIO DATA FROM 5 REGIONS WITH CYCLIC SNOWSHOE HARE POPULATIONS. ASTERISK DESIGNATES YEAR IN WHICH PEAK NUMBERS ATTAINED; SAMPLE SIZES IN PARENTHESES[1]

Study area location and reference	Year (starting 1 Apr)	Mean size of 2nd, 3rd, and 4th litters	Potential natality (R)[2], or max. litters/female (L)	Time and type of population estimate or index	Population estimate or index	Juveniles in fall or winter population (%)
Minnesota:	1931–1932			Feb census	275	
Lake	*1932–1933	4.0 (11)	8.9 (R)	(hares/mile²)	478	
Alexander	1933–1934	3.6 (12)	5.8		374	64
(Green and	1934–1935	3.2 (23)	6.3		356	66
Evans 1940)	1935–1936	2.9 (22)	7.0		246	56
	1936–1937	3.3 (17)	5.7		151	44
	1937–1938		9.4		32	85
	1938–1939				73	82
Alberta:	1949–1950	4.4 (21)	4 (L)	May–Apr	220	
Anzac	*1950–1951	4.4 (30)	3	(hares	365	
(Rowan and	1951–1952	3.8 (6)	3	collected by	105	
Keith 1956)	1952–1953	2.2 (5)	3	snares	65	
	1953–1954			and rifle)	5	
	1957–1958	4.9 (13)	4		>58	
Newfoundland:	1958–1959	4.4 (8)		Oct–Dec	242	86 (242)
Humber and	1959–1960	3.7 (10)		(humeri	548	87 (548)
St. Barbes	*1960–1961	4.1 (22)		collected	996	74 (996)
(Dodds 1965)	1961–1962	3.3 (6)		for age	114	61 (114)
	1962–1963	3.3 (3)		determination)		
	*1960–1961	5.5 (13)				94 (162)
	1961–1962	3.2 (11)				
	1962–1963	3.8 (10)				
Ontario:	*1959–1960	3.8 (45)		Fall (general		54 (98)
Manitoulin I.	1960–1961	3.1 (79)		observations)		47 (49)
east and west	1961–1962	3.0 (66)				32 (40)
(Newson 1964,						
Newson and	1959–1960	4.2 (80)		Fall (general		69 (159)
De Vos 1964)	*1960–1961	3.5 (54)		observations)		52 (317)
	1961–1962	3.4 (109)				61 (132)
Alaska:	1970–1971	5.8 (34)	11.6 (R)	Aug–Nov	400	
Central and	*1971–1972	6.0 (21)	11.3	census	960	
Fairbanks	1972–1973	5.1 (20)	9.2	(hares on study	fewer	
(Ernest 1974)				areas)		
	*1971–1972	5.6 (16)	10.1		788	
	1972–1973	4.1 (19)	8.2		257	
	1973–1974	4.8 (20)	9.1		140	

[1] Reproductive data from the studies of Green and Evans (1940) and Rowan and Keith (1956) were reanalyzed in light of more recent information on synchrony of littering and the consistent tendency for first litters to be smaller than later litters. Mean litter sizes given by Dodds (1965) probably contain some first litters.
[2] The average number of young born to each adult female that survived throughout the breeding season.

(Table 2). Rowan and Keith's (1956) data from Anzac, Alberta, were also reanalyzed, and strongly suggest that reproduction fell in the peak year (1950) when the number of litter groups decreased from 4 to 3, and declined further in the next 2 years when litter size was also reduced. By 1957, litter size had risen markedly at Anzac and the population was increasing. Mean litter size likewise declined in the 2 years immediately following a 1960 population peak in 2 districts of Newfoundland (Table 2). Litter size data from 1 section of Manitoulin Island, Ontario, where hares allegedly peaked in 1960 showed a decline between 1959 and 1961; and data from another section that allegedly peaked in 1959 also showed the same declining trend. There was decreased reproduction following a population peak in 1971 on 2 study areas in Alaska (Table 2); both litter size and pregnancy rate reductions were implicated (Ernest 1974).

Two additional sets of observations seem relevant: Aldous (1937) reported a decline in mean litter size after the 1932 peak in Minnesota; and MacLulich (1937) similarly noted that mean litter size was greater during 1933 in a high population at Smoky Falls, Ontario, than 2 years later when hare numbers had decreased.

Thus, the available information, from our own work at Rochester, and from previous studies of cyclic hare populations elsewhere, ties a lowering of reproduction to the transition from numerical increase to decrease. Unfortunately, the other potential indicators of nutritional stress—annual winter to spring weight changes, and growth rates of young— were not measured by earlier workers.

The only previous study that attempted to estimate survival rates was that of Green and Evans (1940). They, like we, found a sharp reduction in juvenile survival associated with a major decline in population, but there was no sign of a partial recovery of survival rates prior to the low. Adult survival varied little during the first 4 years of population decline, dropped during the fifth and final year, and together with juvenile survival rose in the sixth year. As at Rochester, it took a marked increase in both adult and juvenile survival to initiate an increase in numbers. Green and Evans (1940) calculated a combined survival rate for adults and juveniles of only 50–57 percent during January–February in 2 successive years of decrease, and concluded that by far the greatest mortality among adult-sized hares occurred in winter. This agrees with our own findings, as do most of the general field observations on the time of "crash" mortality (Keith 1963:142).

Because changes in age ratios may reflect variations in reproductive rate and/or ratios of juvenile to adult survival, they

are of limited value in identifying the immediate demographic causes of numerical change. The proportion of juveniles in fall and winter populations was given in 3 of the previously mentioned studies (Table 2). The major shifts in age composition tend, predictably, to be associated with changes in reproduction. At Lake Alexander, Minnesota, as at Rochester, Alberta, a rise in percentage of juveniles preceded that in numbers (Green and Evans 1940). In each instance, we know that an increase in both reproduction and the ratio of juvenile to adult survival happened beforehand. The data from Newfoundland and Ontario suggest higher proportions of juveniles in prepeak and peak populations. Those observations too are in line with ours at Rochester.

There is no evidence from time- and age-specific sex ratios that differential mortality plays a significant role in the hare cycle. The tendency toward slightly more males than females has been seen in most other studies with large sample sizes (Aldous 1937, Webb 1937, Newson and De Vos 1964, Dodds 1965). While this may indicate a minor imbalance in the population, a more likely explanation is that it depicts sampling bias caused by the larger home range and greater activity of males (Meslow and Keith 1968). On the other hand, obvious sampling bias favoring females has occurred during roadside shooting in summer (Philip 1939, Newson and De Vos 1964). The highly unbalanced sex ratios (31:69, sample of 280) in snares reported by Rowan and Keith (1956) during the prepeak summer and winter of 1949–1950 at Anzac, Alberta, are still puzzling because they were followed by an approximately balanced ratio (46:54, sample of 190) in that same cohort during the peak summer of 1950. Since the sampling method did not change, we now believe that there were either extensive differential movements in the prepeak year that biased the sample, or that the apparent imbalance was simply due to normal variance in random sampling.

It has often been stated that during population highs snowshoe hares become almost ubiquitous, occupying even the most marginal of habitats. This is certainly a valid description of conditions at Rochester during the peak winter of 1970–1971, when hares utilized small woodlots and hedge rows in cultivated fields, and suddenly appeared in shelter belts and gardens on open farmland. One must, of course, avoid the circularity of defining habitat quality in terms of density changes and then explaining density changes in terms of habitat quality. We pointed out earlier that hare distribution is discontinuous during periods of scarcity, even within a matrix of apparently acceptable habitat. Our calculations suggested that cyclic variations in density were 2 to 10 times greater within hare habitat as a whole than on continuously occupied sites. MacLulich's (1937:66) data indicated fluctuations for the countryside in general that were about 30 times greater than in the swamps where hares persisted during periods of scarcity.

The conspicuous distributional changes of hares, especially noticeable at peak densities, imply large-scale movements; and these have indeed been observed occasionally (Keith 1963:89). In 1970, Windberg and Keith (1976b) began measuring dispersal by intensive removal trapping in good hare habitat at Rochester. They found a direct relationship between numbers of dispersing individuals and densities on surrounding areas. That disperal was density dependent only to the extent that rates of ingress (number of ingressing hares/unit time/unit density) were higher in the peak winter than during the following 3 winters of decreasing populations. We have shown that lighter weight individuals had higher disappearance rates in winter, and that among juveniles those rates were disproportionately increased during peak and decline years. It is likely that a substantial fraction of such losses was caused by egress from our study areas rather than by immediate onsite mortality, as the dispersing animals intercepted by Windberg and Keith (1976b) in winter were significantly lighter than average and were predominantly juveniles. The significantly smaller ad-

renals and greater incidence of body scars that also characterized the dispersing cohort during the peak winter may well have been symptomatic of intraspecific competition for the then inadequate food supply.

To sum up, certain demographic events appear to be predictably associated with cyclic fluctuations of snowshoe hares. Declines are precipitated by decreased reproduction and greatly reduced juvenile survival over winter. Numbers increase only after maximization of reproduction and major rises in both adult and juvenile survival. The sequencing of those and other variables constitutes a demographic pattern consistent with the hypothesis that winter food shortage provokes the initial population decline, and thereby leads to higher predation rates that extend it.

Comparative Demography of Snowshoe Hare and Microtine Cycles

The largely 3- to 4-year fluctuations of arctic and temperate zone microtines have been studied widely, but there is still no consensus on what ultimately generates such extreme instability. It is now well established, however, that certain demographic traits are invariably linked with major numerical changes. These were summarized from a number of sources by Keith (1974:40) as:

1. "A reproductive rate that is highest during the increase phase, due mainly to lower breeding age, and longer breeding season.
2. "A major decrease in juvenile survival and in reproduction precipitates the cyclic decline.
3. "Lower survival of all age classes during the decline than during the increase phase.
4. "A greater proportion of large-size adults in peak populations.
5. "Reduced growth rates of juveniles with the onset of population decline.
6. "Dispersion of individuals throughout all available habitats during peak years."

164

Following their major review of population cycles in small mammals, Krebs and Myers (1974:387–388) concluded additionally that:

1. "There is no systematic difference between increasing populations and declining populations in (1) litter size, (2) percentage of adult females pregnant during the breeding season, or (3) sex ratios.
2. "Prenatal mortality may vary slightly over the cycle but is not a serious loss even in declining populations.
3. "Dispersal is most frequent from increasing populations, and relatively infrequent from declining populations."

Except for the relative inflexibility of initial breeding age among snowshoe hares, and the fact that hare litter sizes and pregnancy rates do vary systematically, the demography of hare and microtine cycles seems to be identical. It is tempting to speculate that these demographic processes are evoked by some common cause, as argued by Christian et al. (1965) and Chitty (1967). An alternative view was expressed by Keith (1974:42): "Perhaps those similar patterns of birth, death and movements which constitute the immediate basis of population change are part of a 'General Demographic Syndrome' among small mammals in response to a variety of intraspecific and environmental stressors."

Much might be learned by comparing the dynamics of cyclic or highly fluctuating populations with noncyclic or more stationary populations of the same species. Stationary microtine populations evidently are uncommon, or at least have not been well studied, but Krebs et al. (1969) reported that an increased amplitude of fluctuation, obvious devastation of food supply, and starvation were consequences of restricting dispersal of an otherwise natural vole population. That observation could prove especially important, because it suggests that environmental differences affecting ingress and egress can significantly alter population dynamics (Krebs and Myers 1974:311–312). Is it then likely, for example, that microtine fluctuations within large continuous blocks of range, where movements of dispersing individuals are mainly through natural habitat, have the same etiology as fluctuations within small discontinuous units, where dispersal is inevitably through nonhabitat? It seems much less reasonable to equate dispersal and death in the first case than in the second, and hence one might anticipate higher growth rates and peak densities in the former.

This question is relevant as well to snowshoe hare fluctuations, because decreased amplitude and regularity are characteristic of insular habitats, both natural and man-made (Keith 1963:67–68, 73). Dolbeer and Clark (1975) studied relatively stationary populations of hares in insular habitat in the mountains of Colorado and Utah. The lower recapture rates of juveniles frequenting open and sparsely forested areas (presumably poorer habitats) were interpreted as signifying lower survival. Dolbeer and Clark then suggested that density induced dispersal into marginal habitats was a regulatory mechanism that could partly explain the stability of those disjunct populations. Although we had no direct means of measuring the survival of dispersing individuals at Rochester, an experiment by Windberg and Keith (1976b) clearly illustrated the potential advantage of dispersal through continuous habitat. The resident hare population was removed from an area in December 1971, and 20 ingressing animals were marked and released there in mid-January 1972. Subsequent recapture rates of those immigrants indicated that they had settled in the vacant habitat, and experienced survival comparable to that of hares on our regular study areas.

A Conceptual Model of the 10-Year Cycle

A conceptual model of the 10-year cycle was developed in 1971, and later published by Keith (1974). Subsequent trends in hare demography and other variables monitored in the system have not necessitated revision of the initial model. Very briefly, we believe that the cycle is repeatedly generated intrinsically through a hare–vegetation interaction (dominant herbivore vs. winter food supply) that triggers the population decline. This elevates the predator–hare ratio, thereby intensifying a second interaction that extends the period of decline and drives the hare population still lower. The grouse are cyclic due to varying rates of predator induced mortality—a spin-off from the hare–predator interaction. Interregional synchrony is caused basically by mild winters that moderate mortality in peak hare populations, and permit others that are lagging to attain peak densities. Such synchrony is reinforced by highly mobile predator populations. The reader will recognize that key ideas in this model have been expressed in previous cycle theories; their origins were fully credited and discussed by Keith (1974:46–48).

The consistency between certain recurrent features of hare demography and the above model has been noted already. The hare–grouse–predator interaction was partially quantified by Keith et al. (1977), and a thesis on the hare–vegetation interaction has been written (Pease unpublished thesis). We were, of course, concerned with those and other ecologically relevant components of the ecosystem during our long-term investigation of the hare cycle, and will utilize that information in a summary mathematical model.

It was hypothesized initially that food shortage would likely occur in winter rather than summer because: (1) highest densities of hares would be reached in late August when the last litter group was born, and immediately before the annual transition to the winter diet of woody browse; (2) such browse is the hare's staple diet for 7 to 9 months of the year; and (3) there would be no regeneration of that food supply during its seasonal utilization. Although no attempt was made to measure summer food supplies of natural hare populations, our work with artificially created high densities on islands (Windberg and Keith 1976a) suggests that food shortages probably did not occur on our regular study areas in summer. The islands were populated with adult hares in spring 1971–1973 at densities approximating those measured during the peak fall of 1970, and by mid-July food was in short supply. There were 2 highly conspicuous population responses to this midsummer food shortage: (1) the hares turned to their usual winter food of woody stems and browsed them heavily, and (2) survival of young became extremely low. Neither event was observed at Rochester where the highest natural densities in summer were only about one-third those on the islands.

Although our conceptual model contains a number of testable components, its cornerstone is the nutritional interaction and its alleged consequences on hare demography. Here then is the first place to seek evidence with which to reject the model. It could, for example, be forcibly argued that those demographic changes largely ascribed by us to varying nutrition are a more direct consequence of density changes per se; i.e., the result of a self-regulatory process involving social interactions which affect hare physiology and behavior—phenotypically and/or genotypically (Christian et al. 1965, Chitty 1967, Krebs and Myers 1974:353–384).

Our first attempt to isolate density effects was by manipulating hare populations on islands (Windberg and Keith 1976a). We were unable to identify any impact of density as such, and the overwhelming evidence pointed to food shortage as causing the observed reductions in juvenile survival and reproduction. Those results, while highly suggestive, were insufficient to reject density as an alternative to winter nutrition in the conceptual model because the experiments could only be conducted during the ice-free period, May–October.

In fall 1974, we began to work with artificial populations of hares in 8 4-ha en-

166

closures in natural habitat. The idea was to replicate high and low densities under food abundant and food short conditions, so as to evaluate the individual and joint effects of each factor. Those experiments are still in progress, with density, survival, weight, reproductive parameters, and juvenile growth rates being monitored most closely.

SUMMARY

This paper summarizes 15 years of demographic changes in cyclic snowshoe hare populations near Rochester, Alberta, and relates such information to that from other sections of North America where the hare also exhibits an approximate "10-year cycle" of abundance. Rochester hare populations peaked in late summer 1961 and 1970; lowest numbers were recorded in the springs of 1965 and 1966, and 1975. Similar trends characterized regional populations elsewhere in Alberta. The mean amplitude of change from lowest to highest spring densities was 23-fold. In November 1970, there were between 1,100 and 2,300 hares/100 ha (3,000–5,900/mi^2) on the highest density study area; densities on other areas reached about half that level. Finite rates of increase (λ) averaged 2.0 and 0.35 during years of population growth and decline, respectively.

Survival of adult hares was lower during the cyclic decline than during the increase; the seasonal change in survival that was significantly correlated with annual numerical change occurred between midwinter and spring. Extremely low birth to spring survival (0.01 to 0.06) of juveniles accompanied years of marked population decline; survival during increase years was much higher but extremely variable. Annual numerical changes were most closely associated with juvenile survival from early fall to midwinter. Overwinter survival was lowest among lighter weight adults and juveniles; such differential survival was accentuated among juveniles in years of peak and declining populations.

Growth rates of young hares varied greatly between years, and were negatively correlated with mean weight losses of adults during the previous winter to spring. Highest growth rates occurred in years of low and increasing populations, 1965 to 1969. Higher growth rates resulted in heavier terminal weights, and trends in mean weight of juveniles between successive winters reflected trends in growth rates between successive summers. Thus, the general pattern of changes in juvenile winter (November–January) weights followed that of hare numbers, but with a well-defined peak in the winter preceding the population peak. When yearlings comprised more than half of the adult cohort, winter weights of adults were highly correlated with juvenile weights during the preceding winter. The same-year correlation between adult and juvenile winter weights was greatest during population declines, suggesting that while growth rates and terminal weights of juveniles 1 year earlier were the major determinants of adult weight in increase years, some other variable acting on both adults and juveniles, had an important effect in decrease years.

Years of high reproduction corresponded with years of population increase, low reproduction with decline, and intermediate reproduction with peak years. Potential natality during increase years (15–18 young/female) was at least double that of the worst decrease years immediately preceding the low. Key reproductive parameters of both males and females were negatively correlated with mean weight loss during the previous winter to spring.

Net ingress rates at Rochester were highest during midwinter to early summer of years of population increase. Egress rates also were apparently greater in growing populations. The rate of dispersal (individuals/unit time/unit density) was higher in the winter of peak densities than during the decline. Hares became much more widely distributed during years of high population. In those disjunct sections of hare habitat that continued to hold hares during low years, densities fell to 10 or 20 percent of peak densities, as compared to 2 to 6 percent in acceptable habitat as a whole.

The occurrence of unbalanced sex ratios in about 16 percent of the seasonal samples was in no systematic way related to population density or cycle phase. Yearlings averaged 78 percent of the adult cohort in 5 increase years, 51 percent in 2 peak years, 28 percent in 5 major decline years, and 64 percent in 3 years of lowest population. Changes in age ratios indicated that the lower survival of younger animals persists well into their second year of life, and that survival differential is greatest in peak and declining populations. Annual changes in juvenile survival, adult survival, and reproduction were independently capable of generating numerical trends that closely parallel those of study area populations. But it was juvenile survival that had the greatest impact on both numbers and age structure.

The main demographic events associated with fluctuations at Rochester have also occurred in other cyclic hare populations. The sequencing of such variables is consistent with the hypothesis that winter food shortage provokes the initial population decline, and thereby leads to higher rates of predation that extend it.

LITERATURE CITED

ALDOUS, C. M. 1937. Notes on the life history of the snowshoe hare. J. Mammal. 18(1):46–57.

BRAND, C. J., R. H. VOWLES, AND L. B. KEITH. 1975. Snowshoe hare mortality monitored by telemetry. J. Wildl. Manage. 39(4):741–747.

CARY, J. R., AND L. B. KEITH. 1978. Reproductive change in the 10-year population cycle of snowshoe hares. Can. J. Zool. In press.

CHAPMAN, D. G. 1948. A mathematical study of confidence limits of salmon populations calculated from sample tag ratios. Internatl. Pac. Salmon Fish. Comm. Bull. 2:69–85.

CHITTY, D. 1967. The natural selection of self-regulatory behavior in animal populations. Proc. Ecol. Soc. Aust. 2:51–78.

CHRISTIAN, J. J., J. A. LLOYD, AND D. E. DAVIS. 1965. The role of endocrines in the self-regulation of mammalian populations. Recent Prog. Hormone Res. 21:501–571.

DODDS, D. G. 1965. Reproduction and productivity of snowshoe hares in Newfoundland. J. Wildl. Manage. 29(2):303–315.

DOLBEER, R. A., AND W. R. CLARK. 1975. Population ecology of snowshoe hares in the central Rocky Mountains. J. Wildl. Manage. 39(3):535–549.

ERNEST, J. 1974. Snowshoe hare studies. Alaska Dept. Fish Game. 46 pp. (mimeographed).

GREEN, R. G., AND C. A. EVANS. 1940. Studies on a population cycle of snowshoe hares on the Lake Alexander area. J. Wildl. Manage. 4(2):220–238, 4(3):267–278, 4(4):247–258.

KEITH, L. B. 1963. Wildlife's ten-year cycle. Univ. Wisconsin Press, Madison, Wis. 201 pp.

———. 1966. Habitat vacancy during a snowshoe hare decline. J. Wildl. Manage. 30(4):828–832.

———. 1968. Estimation of census date for Lincoln-index calculations. 7 pp. (mimeographed).

———. 1974. Some features of population dynamics in mammals. Proc. Internatl. Cong. Game Biol. 11:17–58.

———, E. C. MESLOW, AND O. J. RONGSTAD. 1968. Techniques for snowshoe hare population studies. J. Wildl. Manage. 32(4):801–812.

———, AND D. C. SURRENDI. 1971. Effects of fire on a snowshoe hare population. J. Wildl. Manage. 35(1):16–26.

———, A. W. TODD, C. J. BRAND, R. S ADAMCIK, AND D. H. RUSCH. 1977. An analysis of predation during a cyclic fluctuation of snowshoe hares. Proc. Internatl. Cong. Game Biol. 13.

KREBS, C. J. 1966. Demographic changes in fluctuation populations of *Microtus californicus*. Ecol. Monogr. 36(3):239–273.

———, B. L. KELLER, AND R. H. TAMARIN. 1969. *Microtus* population biology: demographic changes in fluctuating populations of *M. ochrogaster* and *M. pennsylvanicus* in southern Indiana. Ecology 50(4):587–607.

———, AND J. H. MYERS. 1974. Population cycles in small mammals. Pp. 267–399. In MacFadyen A. (Ed.). Advances in Ecological Research. Academic Press, London, England.

MACLULICH, D. A. 1937. Fluctuations in the numbers of the varying hare (*Lepus americanus*). Univ. Toronto Stud., Biol. Ser. No. 43, 136 pp.

MESLOW, E. C., AND L. B. KEITH. 1968. Demographic parameters of a snowshoe hare population. J. Wildl. Manage. 32(4):812–834.

NEWSON, J. 1964. Reproduction and prenatal mortality of snowshoe hares on Manitoulin Island, Ontario. Can. J. Zool. 42(6):987–1005.

NEWSON, R., AND A. DE VOS. 1964. Population structure and body weights of snowshoe hares on Manitoulin Island, Ontario. Can. J. Zool. 42(6):975–986.

O'FARRELL, T. P. 1965. Home range and ecology of snowshoe hares in interior Alaska. J. Mammal. 46(3):406–418.

PHILIP, C. B. 1939. A parasitological reconnaissance in Alaska with particular reference to varying hares. J. Mammal. 20(1):82–86.

POOLE, R. W. 1974. An introduction to quantitative ecology. McGraw-Hill Book Co., New York, N.Y. 532 pp.

RICKER, W. E. 1958. Handbook of computations for

biological statistics of fish populations. Fish Res. Bd. Can. Bull. No. 119:1–300.

ROWAN, W., AND L. B. KEITH. 1956. Reproductive potential and sex ratios of snowshoe hares in northern Alberta. Can. J. Zool. 34(4):273–281.

RUSCH, D. H., AND L. B. KEITH. 1971. Ruffed grouse–vegetation relationships in central Alberta. J. Wildl. Manage. 35(3):417–429.

SEBER, G. A. F. 1973. The estimation of animal abundance. Hafner Press, New York, N.Y. 506 pp.

WEBB, W. L. 1937. Notes on the sex ratio of the snowshoe rabbit. J. Mammal. 18(3):343–347.

WINDBERG, L. A., AND L. B. KEITH. 1976a. Snowshoe hare population response to artificial high densities. J. Mammal. 57(3):523–553.

———, AND ———. 1976b. Experimental analyses of dispersal in snowshoe hare population. Can. J. Zool. 54(12):2061–2081.

Reproduced from *Wildlife Monographs* number 58, 70 pp., 1978, with permission of The Wildlife Society. [Shortened]

THE INFLUENCE OF WEATHER ON POPULATION FLUCTUATIONS IN CALIFORNIA QUAIL

WILLIAM J. FRANCIS

Abstract: Age ratios of quail (*Lophortyx californicus*) in San Luis Obispo County, California, were available for 14 consecutive years. Ratios were based on hunter-shot samples averaging 672 birds per year. Weather data were compiled and a multiple linear regression of quail productivity on selected weather parameters revealed a close relationship ($P < 0.01$). Quail productivity seemed to be a function, in order of importance, of (1) soil moisture in late April calculated from temperature and rainfall data, (2) proportion of breeding females over 1 year old, and (3) the seasonal rainfall from September to April.

Three geographically isolated wild quail populations and one penned population were observed during two breeding seasons that were very different in productivity. In 1963, quail produced many young. The breeding period was characterized by intense activity and persistence of breeding effort extending, in captive birds, to production of second broods. Vegetation that year included many annual forbs growing vigorously during the breeding season. In 1964, production of quail was very low on all areas. The birds seemed to lack reproductive drive, and breeding effort terminated early. Forb vegetation that year was sparse.

Reproductive success and the resultant population levels of California quail are known to vary considerably from year to year. As far back as 1887, quail were observed to remain in coveys and to fail to breed in unfavorable years (Grinnell et al. 1918; Sumner 1935). Storer et al. (1942), Raitt and Genelly (1964), and McMillan (1964) have reported large annual variations in the proportion of juvenile birds in California quail populations in the fall. Among California quail introduced into New Zealand, the ratio of juvenile to adult birds was found by Williams (1963:444) to vary from 0.17 to 1.15:1 over a 14-year period.

In the reports cited the variation in production of young is frequently attributed to weather, sometimes directly, but more often indirectly through its influence on the vegetation. The description of the weather is often in such general terms as "a dry winter," "spring wetter than usual," etc., but sometimes more specific, as "October to March rainfall."

The present study was undertaken: to investigate the particular weather factors relating to reproductive success; to determine the joint effect of such weather factors on biological parameters affecting population levels; and to find combinations of weather factors which would be significant in predicting quail production.

Several departments of the University of California provided facilities and assistance: the Animal Behavior Laboratory, the Survey Research Center, the Public Health Computer Laboratory, the Department of Entomology and Parasitology, and the Mu-

170

Table 1. Distribution of quail by sex and age in fall hunting samples, Shandon area.

Year	Adult Males	Immature Males	Adult Females	Immature Females	Immature Adult Ratio	Total Number
1949	80	164	59	158	2.32	461
1950	65	127	52	130	2.20	374
1951	178	16	180	13	0.08	387
1952	87	365	86	377	4.30	915
1953	176	94	149	90	0.57	509
1954	140	333	86	339	3.00	898
1955	185	302	136	309	1.90	932
1956	151	203	86	198	1.70	638
1957	149	214	131	207	1.50	701
1958	157	311	80	272	2.46	820
1959	205	86	145	71	0.45	507
1960	116	157	91	161	1.54	525
1961	192	119	152	105	0.65	568
1962	195	431	131	416	2.60	1173
1963	250	292	161	264	1.35	967
1964	167	6	129	5	0.04	307

Data from McMillan (1964, and personal communications).

seum of Vertebrate Zoology. I am indebted to I. McMillan for permission to work on his ranch and for other assistance, to J. Davis and K. White for assistance and facilities at Hastings Reservation, to Catherine Pyle for assistance in maintaining quail in the enclosure, to W. F. Taylor for guidance in statistical analysis, and to G. M. Christman for assistance with graphs. A. S. Leopold gave advice and assistance throughout the study and constructively criticized the manuscript. R. F. Labisky also read the manuscript and offered suggestions.

METHODS AND MATERIALS

Study Areas

Quail populations were studied in three principal areas in California. These will be referred to as *Berkeley* in Contra Costa and Alameda Counties; the *Hastings Reservation* in Monterey County; and *Shandon* in San Luis Obispo County, especially on the McMillan Ranch. Some additional observations were made in Kern and Monterey Counties.

Population Records

Data on sex and age ratios in quail populations for previous years were available for all three areas (Raitt and Genelly 1964; McMillan, 1964; and original banding records at Hastings Reservation.) The length of record and size of samples at both Berkeley and Hastings Reservation were too small to permit adequate statistical anaylsis, and correlations are reported only for Shandon data. Field observations in all areas are included in the discussion. Table 1 shows data on quail sex and age-classes in fall hunting samples taken at Shandon and reported by McMillan (1964: 705), supplemented by his unpublished field notes.

Weather Station Records

Temperature and rainfall data for Paso Robles (USWB Station 6730), 18 miles west of Shandon, were made available on punched cards by the National Weather Records Center, Asheville, North Carolina. Rainfall data for Cholame (USWB Station 1743), 8 miles east of Shandon, were ex-

171

tracted from U.S. Weather Bureau climatological publications; no temperature data for Cholame were available. Additional data were obtained from the hourly weather observations of the F.A.A. station at the Paso Robles Airport for the period February, 1963 to May, 1964.

Weather instruments were installed to record temperature, humidity, and rainfall data within the quail habitats in the three study areas during the 2 years of field study. A comparison of the data from the Shandon installation with official data from Paso Robles and Cholame showed the day-to-day variations to be similar and indicated that the official data could be accepted as indicating weather variations in the Shandon quail areas.

The volume of data in these records—maximum and minimum temperature and amount of precipitation for each day—required some reduction. Means of weather elements were calculated for 10-day periods (referred to hereafter as "decades") numbered consecutively beginning with September 2 of each year. Previous studies have found periods of this order to be desirable (Nice 1937, Allison 1962, Errington 1942). The days remaining after 36 decades were ignored.

Captive Quail

In early March, 1963, four male and four female wild quail (half adults and half yearlings) were trapped, marked with colored leg bands, and placed in a 100- × 100-ft enclosure on the Animal Behavior Station, Berkeley campus (Francis 1965:541). One female was killed by collision with the fence on April 19, leaving a breeding population of three pairs and one extra male.

On February 24, 1964, I reduced the population to four pairs by trapping and releasing excess birds. The remaining birds were one pair over 2 years old, one pair in

the second breeding season, and two pairs of yearlings hatched in the enclosure the previous year.

An observation hut built into one side of the enclosure allowed close observation of the birds with a minimum of disturbance. I observed behavior and breeding phenology throughout two breeding seasons. Supplementary food (poultry chow) and water were supplied.

Trapping

Trapping programs were carried out to obtain sex and age ratios in the quail populations, and to estimate population size, in the Berkeley Hills, at Hastings Reservation, and at the McMillan Ranch in the Shandon area. Wire mesh, funnel-type traps were used at all locations.

Field Observations

Observations during 1963 and 1964 included amount and species composition of vegetation, breeding behavior of quail, breeding phenology of both captive and wild quail, and examination of 22 specimens. Observed ratios of young to adult quail were very different during these 2 years; 1963 was a year of good production, while production in 1964 was almost a complete failure.

RESULTS

Vegetation

Berkeley quail enclosure.—In 1963, a variety of annual forbs were present in abundance, the more prominent species in the spring including *Erodium cicutarium, Medicago apiculata, Medicago hispida, Geranium dissectum, Anagallis arvensis, Vicia sativa, Brassica campestris,* and *Ranunculus californicus.* Grasses, thistles, and other Compositae were also present (Plant names follow Jepson 1960).

Medicago and *Erodium* are among im-

172

portant natural foods for quail (Sumner 1935:172–173) and presumably are highly nutritious; green leaves of *Vicia* were also extensively used by the quail in the enclosure.

In 1964, forbs decreased greatly and grasses increased, in comparison with the previous year. None of the spring-blooming forbs were present, but thistles increased noticeably. Observations of feeding birds showed a greater use of grain supplements, compared to natural foods, than in 1963.

Hastings Reservation.—A heavy growth of grasses in the open meadows in 1963 remained in 1964, although with little new growth. *Erodium cicutarium* was common in both years, but other forbs were less numerous in 1964 than in 1963.

Shandon.—At McMillan's Ranch, growth of vegetation was exceptionally good in 1963. Interspersed with pasture grasses were abundant forbs of several species of *Eriogonum* and *Lupinus*, *Medicago hispida*, *Amsinckia douglasiana* and widespread and abundant *E. cicutarium*. These are all quail food (Sumner 1935; Glading et al. 1940), and probably important sources of essential nutrients. Poorer growth was evident in 1964, and the forbs found the preceding year were scarce or absent. Close examination of a pasture in which quail were observed feeding showed many very small *Erodium* plants, and the quail in this area showed no signs of malnutrition in the quantitative sense.

Breeding Behavior

Berkeley quail enclosure.—Observations were made for a total of 60 hours on 58 days from March 14 to June 19, 1963. Normal pairing may have been disrupted by trapping, but three pairs formed by April 28. Little aggressive behavior was noted among the birds in the enclosure, but the males reacted to "squill" calls (Sumner 1935:200–205) from wild birds outside by running along the fence, looking out, and answering. The wild birds seemed to be strongly attracted to those in the enclosure, and in many cases would follow a feeding pair or group by walking across the top of the enclosure. "Cow" calls were frequent among the wild birds, and were occasionally answered by males in the enclosure. Copulation by the captive birds was observed on nine occasions.

In 1964, observations were made for a total of 23 hours on 34 days from March 2 to June 13. Pair formation was first noted on March 8. No aggressive behavior was observed among the eight captive birds; there was little calling of any kind either in the enclosure or from birds outside, and copulation was not observed at any time. The birds fed frequently in a group rather than in separate pairs. An occasional male outside the enclosure approached the fence. On April 13, a male inside exchanged "squill" calls with a bird outside and seemed to attempt an attack through the fence. "Cow" and "squill" calls were heard outside the enclosure on about four occasions in May, but no "cow" calls were given by any bird inside. The birds were less active than during the previous year, spending more time resting in cover of the brush.

Hastings Reservation.—Pairing began in early March, 1963, and by the first part of May, the one covey observed had broken up completely into mated pairs and single birds. "Cow" calls were heard regularly. In 1964, in early March, there were no signs of pair formation in a covey of 25 birds; in April, however, most birds appeared to be paired, and a short cockfight, accompanied by "squill" calls was observed on one occasion. No "cow" calls were heard during the spring.

Shandon.—In early March, 1963, pair formation was well underway, with loose pair-bonds evident in about one half of 500 birds seen; pairing was virtually complete by March 27. By May, at least 90 percent of the population, estimated at 1,500 birds, was distributed in pairs over the McMillan Ranch. "Cow" calls were heard frequently from late March through May; in one case, two birds kept up a steady exchange of calls lasting 15 minutes. Aggressive behavior, including chases, "squill" calls, and cockfights, was observed throughout the spring.

In 1964, pairing appeared to reach about the same stage in early March as it did in 1963, with loose pair-bonds evident in about half of 465 birds seen. In April, however, most of the 500 observed quail were still in loosely associated groups, with many birds remaining in pairs within the group while feeding. About one fourth of the birds showed no signs of being paired. By early June, the five principal coveys had reformed, with only 6 to 7 percent of the birds remaining paired. The only chicks seen during the entire season were a group of 11 accompanying two pairs of adults, and a single chick with an adult male. The other birds seemed to have abandoned all nesting attempts; 57 adults trapped on June 8–9, 1964, were all molting, and had no young birds with them. Aggressive behavior was observed only in April, when I observed one cockfight, with accompanying "squill" calls, and two chases; no "cow" calls were heard at any time during the spring of 1964. The general impression, except for the pairing of birds in March, was that of absence of reproductive activities; by June, the behavior was that of fall coveys in a sexually inactive state.

In summary, the behavior of quail during the breeding season showed that initial pair formation took place in about the same way and at the same time in the 2 years. In the productive year of 1963, however,

Table 2. Ratio of immature to adult quail in trapping samples (T), direct counts (C), and hunters' bags (H) by locality, 1963 and 1964.

LOCALITY	1963 Ratio	Number	1964 Ratio	Number
Berkeley	2.83 (T)	92	0.17 (T)	42
Hastings Reservation	3.38 (T)	35	0.71 (C)	58
Shandon Area	1.35 (H)	967	0.04 (H)	307
Hunter Liggett Military Reservation	3.08 (H)	653	0.64 (H)	479

the intensity of the pair bond increased as the season progressed, aggressiveness was high and remained so during the spring, and the "cow" calls typical of the breeding season were frequent. In 1964, the intensity of the pair bond decreased early in the season, and in the Shandon area the bond had dissolved entirely with the formation of coveys in May and early June. Little aggressive behavior was noted at any time, and no "cow" calls were heard except among wild birds in Berkeley. The difference in reproductive drive between the 2 years was evident in April, before nesting began.

Reproductive success

Reproductive success (production and survival of young) was measured by brood counts, by the proportion of young birds in trapped samples, and by the proportion of young birds in hunting bags. The differences were similar in all study areas; the ratios of immature to adult birds are given in Table 2. A brief summary of the observations in each area is given below.

Berkeley.—Ninety-two quail, almost the entire covey, were trapped, marked, and released in the fall of 1963 in the area adjacent to the quail enclosure; the ratio of juveniles to adults in this covey was 2.83:1. In 1964, fall trapping in the same area, plus birds trapped in the winter of

1964–65 by R. Jones and R. Fletcher, yielded 42 birds, with a juvenile:adult ratio of 0.17:1.

Among the captive quail, in 1963, two adult females hatched 33 eggs in their first nests, and one subadult female hatched none. Some of the chicks escaped from the enclosure when only a few days old; of the 15 remaining, nine grew to adult size, a survival rate of 60 percent. Second nests by both these females (each with a new mate) hatched a total of 19 chicks of which only four (21 percent) survived. The age ratio of these captive birds, after making corrections for those which escaped, was 3.14:1 compared to 2.83:1 in the wild covey trapped in the same area.

In 1964, with four pairs of quail in the enclosure, half adult and half yearling birds, five nests were located, containing a total of 74 eggs; five additional eggs were found on the ground, all but one close to one of the nests. Only two of these nests, containing 19 and 13 eggs, respectively, were incubated, both by the adult females, and all eggs but one hatched in each nest. Three abandoned nests contained 14 eggs each. The contents of one of these, plus three of the eggs found on the ground, were incubated artificially and 14 hatched; fertility was probably high in all clutches. Of the 30 eggs hatched by the adult females, only eight chicks were alive at the age of 2 weeks, and only three survived to adult size. The productivity for 1964 (allowing for the escape of one quail) was 0.50 young per captive adult, and 0.17 young per wild-trapped adult. The similarity suggests influences of the common environment.

The observations of captive quail show clearly that the failure of reproduction in 1964 was not attributable to clutch size or to fertility, which changed only slightly from 1963 to 1964.

Hastings Reservation.—In December,

1963, 35 birds, of a population estimated at 49, were trapped; the juvenile:adult ratio was 3.38:1. In August, 1964, close observation of a covey of 58 birds permitted an accurate age count. The juvenile:adult ratio was 0.71. Only six out of 17 adult pairs were accompanied by young, with an average of four young birds per successful pair.

Shandon.—On three occasions in the summer of 1963, I observed quail at close range from a blind near a water hole. Over 2,500 observations of individuals were recorded with an average of about four observations on each bird, and age estimated on the basis of size and plumage development. The average age ratio, combining young of all ages, was computed to be 3.28 young per adult. Hunting bags in the 1963 season totaled 967 birds, with a juvenile-adult ratio of 1.35:1.

In June and August, 1964, 12 young were observed among a population of 600 quail, a ratio of 0.02 juveniles per adult. Only 11 of 307 quail killed by hunters were young, a ratio of 0.04 young per adult. This represents the most complete failure of reproduction ever documented in this area, not excepting the 1951 case described by McMillan (1964:707).

On the Hunter Liggett Military Reservation in Monterey County, a ratio of 3.08 young per adult was found in a sample of 653 hunter-killed quail in 1963; among 479 quail checked in 1964, the ratio was only 0.64 young per adult.

Specimens

Five males collected in May, 1963, in the Shandon area and nearby Kern County all had fully developed testes (calculated volumes 266 to 496 mm³). Of four females collected at the same time, two had ovaries with developing eggs; one had completed laying, with regressed ovary; and one was apparently not breeding, with an ovary weighing only 0.05 g.

In 1964, three males, collected June 8 on the McMillan Ranch, all had undeveloped testes (calculated volumes 18 to 35 mm^3) and were molting, having dropped the 5th, 6th, and 7th primaries respectively. Of the three females collected at this time, one appeared to have a regressed ovary, the other two were undeveloped. They were also molting, having dropped the 5th, 6th, and 7th primaries respectively.

The livers of 14 specimens were frozen, and later analyzed for vitamin A content by a commercial laboratory. Mean vitamin A levels and standard errors for groups of specimens were as follows:

Shandon area, August, 1963: 4 birds—132±62 IU/g.

Berkeley, September, 1963: 3 birds—692±97 IU/g.

Hastings Reservation, Dec. 1963: 1 bird—1331 IU/g.

Shandon area, June 1964: 6 birds—793±140 IU/g.

Vitamin A levels in molting birds in the Shandon area in August, 1963, were low compared to the high levels in molting birds in Berkeley in September, both populations having produced approximately normal numbers of young. Vitamin A levels were also high in the birds from Shandon which were molting in June, 1964, following an apparent failure to breed.

ANALYSIS OF SEX AND AGE DATA

Data on the composition of quail populations shown in Table 1 were obtained from hunting bags. Although it has been generally accepted that such samples represent population sex, and age ratios, comparisons of hunting samples from different areas and at different times, and comparisons of trapping samples with hunting samples in the same area were made. This was done to determine if such factors as differential susceptibility to hunting introduced any significant bias into the samples.

Significant differences were found in two cases. In one sub-area, the immature sex-ratio at the end of the hunting season differed significantly from the early-season sex ratio ($P < 0.05$) and also from the expected 1:1 ratio ($P < 0.01$). All other sub-samples showed immature sex-ratios very close to 1:1. In another sub-area, the adult sex-ratio at the end of the hunting season differed ($P < 0.05$) from that at the beginning of the hunting season, with fewer adult females in the late season.

Combining data for the two sexes, and looking at the age ratios only, I found no significant differences between areas, between early and late season hunting, or between hunting and trapping. The lack of a difference between hunting and trapping samples can mean only (1) that both methods of sampling give an unbiased estimate of the population composition, or (2) that both trapping and hunting are biased in the same way with respect to age groups. The latter hypothesis would be difficult to justify. Trapping of marked birds showed no consistent bias in frequency of capture of young versus old birds. The assumption is made, therefore, that the hunting samples give unbiased estimates of the proportion of young and old birds in the population sampled. There is more doubt as to how well the sex ratios are estimated.

Population Model

In order to make a quantitative evaluation of changes in sex and age ratios, a population model was constructed with the same observable parameters as the observed samples in the Shandon area (Table 1). If a population does not increase or decrease

Table 3. Numbers of California quail, by sex and age, in a model population with a constant male survival rate and in proportions identical to those of hunting samples in the Shandon area for corresponding years.

Year	Adult Males	Immature Males	Adult Females	Immature Females	Total
1949	155	362	140	343	1000
1950	219	428	175	438	1260
1951	274	25	277	20	596
1952	127	533	125	550	1335
1953	279	149	236	141	805
1954	181	430	111	438	1160
1955	259	423	190	432	1304
1956	289	389	165	382	1225
1957	287	412	252	398	1349
1958	296	586	151	513	1546
1959	373	156	264	129	922
1960	224	304	176	311	1015
1961	223	138	177	122	660
1962	153	338	103	326	920
1963	208	243	134	220	805
1964	191	7	148	6	352

during a year, it is evident that the number of young birds of the current year's brood must equal the number of older birds that died during the year. The percentage of young birds in the fall population would, therefore, be equal to the mortality rate of the adults for the past year (Burkitt 1926, Farner 1955). Even with large year-to-year fluctuations in population, if the

population size is the same at the end as at the beginning of a period of years, the total number of young must equal the total number of deaths, and the average mortality rate is given by the sum of the yearly numbers of young as a percentage of the sum of the total population each year. The proportions of young among hunter-killed birds gives the same result.

If hunting methods and intensity do not change on the average over a period of years, as in the Shandon area according to notes kept by McMillan (Personal communication) during the hunting seasons from 1951 to 1962, it is reasonable to assume that any progressive change in population size would be reflected in a parallel change in kill statistics. Year-to-year variations in both population and kill would tend to average out in a few years. The kill on the Shandon area for the 6 years, 1951–1956, totalled 4,279 birds, an average of 713 per year; and for the following 6 years, 1957–1962, 4,294 birds, or 716 per year. No appreciable change in the population is indicated, and the data may, therefore, be used to estimate average survival rates.

Table 4. Contributions to changes in a model population attributable to mortality rates different in females than in males, and to reproductive rates different from the rate required to replace losses. (See text for definitions).

Year	Adult Females			Immatures			Total Change in Population	
	Pot. No.	Calc. No.	Diff.	Repl. No.	Calc. No.	Diff.	Number	Percent
1950	204	175	− 29	577	866	+289	+260	+ 26.0
1951	259	277	+ 18	727	45	− 682	− 664	− 52.7
1952	126	125	− 1	344	1083	+739	+738	+123.8
1953	286	236	− 50	770	290	− 480	− 530	− 39.7
1954	160	111	− 49	464	868	+404	+355	+ 44.2
1955	232	190	− 42	669	855	+186	+144	+ 12.5
1956	263	165	− 98	752	771	+ 19	− 79	− 6.1
1957	231	252	+ 21	707	810	+103	+124	+ 10.1
1958	275	151	−124	778	1099	+321	+197	+ 14.6
1959	281	264	− 17	892	285	− 607	− 624	− 40.4
1960	166	176	+ 10	532	615	+ 83	+ 93	+ 10.1
1961	206	177	− 29	585	260	− 325	− 354	− 34.9
1962	127	103	− 24	381	664	+283	+259	+ 39.2
1963	182	134	− 48	531	463	− 68	− 116	− 12.6
1964	150	148	− 2	464	13	− 451	− 453	− 56.3

177

Construction of the model population also requires some assumption as to survival rates. Because the number of adult males is generally greater than the number of adult females (Table 1), it appears that variations in the adult sex ratio are the result of variations in female mortality. The assumption is made that the survival of adult males each year is constant, and equal to the mean survival rate of 0.424 derived from the total numbers of adult and immature males in hunting samples from 1952–1962. The model population is calculated by starting with a cohort of 1,000 birds, and dividing it into sex and age-classes in the same proportion as the observed hunting sample in the initial year. The total number of males is then multiplied by the assumed survival rate to give the number of adult males the following year. The numbers of adult females and immature males and females are then calculated to give the same ratios to adult males as in the hunting sample. This procedure was carried out in successive years to give the model population shown in Table 3.

From this survival table, a further analysis was made to show the contributions of differential female mortality and production of young to the total population change. This analysis is shown in Table 4. The "Potential Number" of females (column 2) is the number that would be present if the survival rate were the same as that assumed for males; the difference (column 4) from the calculated number given in Table 3 (column 3) is the number of females which die in excess of the expected number (negative sign); the three cases with a small positive difference probably represent sampling errors, since differences of about 20 are not significant in a population of the postulated size. The "Replacement Number" of immature birds (column

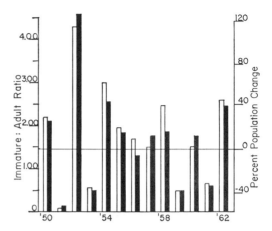

Fig. 1. Population indices of California quail populations in the Shandon area, 1950–1962. White bars—ratio of immature to adult birds in fall hunting samples; black bars—percentage change in the model population size.

5) is the number required to maintain the population on the assumption of a constant mortality rate for adults. The estimated numbers calculated in Table 3 are shown in column 6, and the difference from the "Replacement Number" in column 7. The final columns show the total population change in numbers and as a percentage of the previous population. Fig. 1 shows the percentage population change as computed by this method, as well as the immature: adult ratios from the hunting records; the scales have been adjusted to be equivalent.

To test the agreement of the model population with the observed sample, the population totals were summed for the years 1951–1956, and for 1957–1962. In the earlier period, numbers totalled 6,425, and in the latter period 6,412. The model population, therefore, not only has the proportions of the sex and age-classes for each year equal to the proportions in the hunting samples, but also remains at the same level over a period of years, with annual variations superimposed, as do the hunting samples.

The total change in the model population

Table 5. Correlation of hunting–kill statistics with population model parameters.

KILL STATISTICS	POPULATION MODEL PARAMETERS FROM TABLE 4			
	IMMATURE[a] :FEMALES	PERCENT[b] CHANGE	"EXCESS"[c] YOUNG	FEMALE[d] SURVIVAL
Imm:Adults	0.983	0.974	0.988	−0.260
Imm:Adult Males	0.989	0.995	0.998	−0.123
Imm:Adult Females	0.921	0.892	0.922	−0.454

[a] Ratio of immature birds to potential breeding females (Col. 6/Col. 2).
[b] Percent annual change in model population (Col. 9).
[c] "Excess" young produced (Col. 7).
[d] Excess of adult females surviving (Col. 4).

is due almost entirely to reproduction greater or less than that required to replace losses, and differential female mortality is of minor quantitative importance (Table 4).

Parameters of the model population are correlated ($P < 0.01$) with kill statistics (Table 5). The immature-adult ratio in the fall has, therefore, been taken as the measure of productivity in the populations studied.

Age and Density Factors

Population parameters such as population size, sex ratio, and age ratio may themselves affect productivity and population size. In both the Shandon and Berkeley areas (the only ones with unbroken records), every case of abnormally high reproductive success followed a year in which reproduction was lower than normal. This may have resulted from increased reproduction due to lower population densities; from higher reproductive rates in older females as compared to those in their first breeding season; or from a combination of these effects. Smaller populations, following a year of poor reproduction, have a higher proportion of old birds in the following season's breeding population. Observations of the birds in captivity suggest that the breeding efficiency of older females is more impor-

Table 6. List of independent variables tested for correlation with productivity index.

A. Proportion of adults among females the previous fall.
B. Relative size of model population.
C. Total seasonal rainfall through decade 24.
D. Total rainfall decades 13–21.
E. Total evapotranspiration decades 13–24.
F. Total rainfall decades 17–20.
G. Total evapotranspiration decades 17–20.
H. Soil moisture (computed) decade 24.
I. Rainfall amount decade 24.
J. Accumulated evapotranspiration decade 24.
K. Rain index decade 20.
L. Rain index decade 19–21 minus rain index decade 22–24.
M. Temperature index minus rain index decade 20.
N. Temperature index minus rain index decades 25–27.
O. Drought index decades 16–20.
P. Accumulated temperature above 55 F, decades 19–27.
Q. Departure of minimum temperature, decades 21–22.
R. Mean temperature range decades 17–20.
S. Date of new moon after March 6.

tant than density. In the 2 years in which breeding was observed in Berkeley, with essentially no difference in population density, four adult females hatched 83 chicks in six nests, while three yearling females failed to hatch any chicks at all. There does not appear to be any correlation between reproduction and sex ratio, which was near unity in field data for both 1951 with very poor reproduction, and 1952, with the highest reproduction rate observed (Table 1).

Two population parameters were, therefore, calculated for the Shandon area for use in regression analysis. These were:

A. The percentage of adults among females in the preceding fall hunting sample.
B. The size of the model population.

WEATHER PARAMETERS

To use weather data meaningfully, parameters bearing a biological relation to the quail population must be developed from the temperature and precipitation data. Climatic data are used only as an index to the total weather pattern. In order to develop such parameters, the biological effects of various weather conditions on quail, both as reported in the literature, and suggested by field observations in this study, were considered, and working hypotheses formulated as to the possible relations between weather parameters and the subsequent quail reproduction. Development of rainfall parameters are discussed below in some detail, and other factors are treated more briefly.

Rainfall

Both the amount and distribution of rain have been frequently noted to affect the reproductive rate of quail and other birds. In semi-arid regions, low rainfall is associated with reduced reproduction, and above normal rainfall with good reproduction (Grinnell et al. 1918, Gullion 1960, Sowls 1960, Gallizioli and Webb 1961, Hungerford 1964). Williams (1959:212–215) found that a wet spring delayed the onset of breeding in California quail in New Zealand by 2 weeks. Raitt (1960) found no correlation of precipitation with productivity of California quail, but noted variations in vegetation corresponding to year-to-year differences in rainfall.

The effect of rainfall on quail reproduction may depend on the response of vegetation to rainfall (Sumner 1935, Lehmann 1946, MacGregor and Inlay 1951, Hungerford 1964). Similarly, field observations in my study showed good productivity of California quail in 1963, when green vegetation and annual forbs were abundant following high winter and spring rainfall. Poor quail productivity occurred in 1964 when vegetative growth was poor following low rainfall. The drier Shandon area pro-

Table 7. Immature-adult quail ratios in three areas of different rainfall.

AREA	MEAN RAINFALL	IMMATURE ADULT	
		1963	1964
Berkeley	32.80	2.83	0.17
Hastings	19.33	3.38	0.71
Shandon	9.56	1.35	0.04

duced fewer young than the wetter Berkeley and Hastings areas in both years (Table 7). The hypothesis is suggested that rainfall effect on quail productivity may operate through its effect on vegetation. Nutritional deficiencies (Vitamin A or other yet unidentified factors) and variations in cover are two mechanisms which have been suggested.

Vegetation growth depends on the amount of rainfall, its distribution during the year, and the temperature at the time water is available to the plants. The joint effect of rainfall and temperature on vegetative growth was studied by Thornthwaite (1948) and Thornthwaite and Mather (1955), who developed an empirical formula for "potential evapotranspiration" (Thornthwaite 1948:89–94). Potential evapotranspiration is defined as the amount of water which will be evaporated and transpired under the temperature regime of a given locality with an unlimited water supply. The value is calculated from the temperature data for the locality. The actual (computed) evapotranspiration is determined by a "bookkeeping" method, in which the potential evapotranspiration is compared with the amounts of water available from rainfall and from soil moisture storage (Thornthwaite and Mather 1957, Francis 1967). Although the concept has certain theoretical drawbacks (Pelton et al. 1960), evapotranspiration has proved, for practical purposes, to be an excellent indicator of vegetative growth in California and elsewhere (Arkley and Ulrich 1962, Arkley 1963, Major 1963).

On the hypothesis that quail reproduction is influenced by vegetative growth, which is controlled by the accumulated evapotranspiration from September to some critical period in the breeding season, I calculated the Thornthwaite evapotranspiration by 10-day periods for each year considered. Preliminary calculations indicated that the evapotranspiration effect was greatest when summed through decade 24 (late April); accumulated evapotranspiration for that period was then selected as the weather parameter with which to test the particular hypothesis.

Similar methods were used to examine other possible effects of rainfall amount and distribution. The weather parameters testing these effects were chosen as follows:

C. Total seasonal rainfall through decade 24 (late April).

D. Total rainfall decades 13–21 (January–March).

E. Total evapotranspiration decades 13–24 (January–April).

F. Total rainfall decades 17–20 (mid-February–mid-March).

G. Total evapotranspiration decades 17–20 (mid-February–mid-March).

H. Computed available soil moisture decade 24 (late April).

I. Rainfall amount in decade 24 (late April).

J. Accumulated evapotranspiration through decade 24 (late April).

Rain may also act as a trigger or a deterrent to breeding if it occurs at a critical time, without regard to the total amount except in a broad sense. Lehmann (1946: 112) noted that breeding was resumed by Texas bobwhites when summer rains occurred, but that during incubation, birds left their nests at the first sign of a shower.

Drought, or the continued non-occurrence of rain, has often been cited as an inhibitor of breeding (for example, Errington 1945: 14, Lehmann 1953:221); Nice (1937:210) noted that drought has an indirect effect via the food supply. Marshall (1959:468) found rainfall to be a powerful regulator of breeding in birds, especially in arid regions. "Bad weather," which in context usually refers to a combination of rain and low temperatures, has been frequently mentioned as a cause of delayed breeding or reduced productivity. Lewin (1963:259) found earlier breeding in California quail when a rainy March was followed by a dry April than in the reverse situation. Low temperatures in conjunction with rainy days have been related to population levels; Allison (1962), using paired factors of temperature and precipitation, found New England grouse (*Bonasa umbellus*) populations fluctuate with degree-days above 65 F, and with the total rainfall for the last 2 weeks of May.

The effects of the occurrence or non-occurrence of rain, with or without accompanying cold, were tested by the use of the following weather parameters:

K. Rain index at decade 20 (mid-March).

L. Sum of rain indices for decades 19–21 (March) less the sum of rain indices for decades 22–24 (April).

M. Temperature index minus rain index for decade 20 (mid-March).

N. Temperature index minus rain index for decades 25–27 (May).

O. Drought index for decades 16–20 (early February to mid-March).

Temperature

Quail may be killed directly by cold (Grinnell et al. 1918, Kendeigh and Baldwin 1937) or by exposure to the heat of the sun (Sumner 1935). Hatchability of eggs may

WEATHER

be affected by temperature (Hickey 1955, Landy 1962, Romanoff 1934, Yeatter 1950). Timing of the breeding cycle and variations in reproductive physiology and behavior are related to temperature (Nice 1937, Lehmann 1946, Marshall 1949, 1959:467; Marshall and Coombs 1957, Buss and Swanson 1950, Lewin 1963, Crawford 1962, Somes 1962).

Field observations in this study do not provide any evidence of mortality due to extreme temperature, or of temperature effects on eggs. In fact, very little mortality from any cause was noted, the few cases being caused by accident or predation. Fertility and hatchability of 95 eggs found and tested was 92 percent, with no difference between 1963 and 1964. Temperature may have affected the time of onset of breeding behavior, with some effect on productivity; and temperature during the breeding season may have affected the vigor of the laying hen and indirectly the viability of the chicks.

Weather parameters selected to test temperature effects were as follows:

P. Accumulated temperature excess above 55 F for decades 19–27 (March, April, May).

Q. Departure of minimum temperature from the mean of the two preceding years, for decades 21–22 (late March–early April).

Light

The photoperiod, or length of day, is an important factor controlling the onset of reproductive activity of birds (Rowan 1925, 1926, 1938; Burger 1949). While the astronomical day length on a given date does not vary from year to year, it is evident that in nature there must be a threshold of light intensity that delimits the end of the light period, and a threshold that delimits the end of the dark period. Threshold intensities may be reached at different times with

respect to astronomical sunrise and sunset (Sumner 1935, Davis 1958, Emlen 1937, Leopold and Eynon 1961, Shaver and Walker 1931). The variations are related to cloudy versus clear skies, and to the brightness of moonlight. The few days immediately following the full moon have a small increment of light in the early morning that, in effect, produces an earlier daybreak and a longer length of day. The total variation may be as much as 40 minutes between a cloudy and a clear day (Bartholomew 1949:465). Such differences in effective day length are equivalent to several weeks advance or delay in the season, and may affect the reproductive success.

Cloudy days are characterized by lower maximum temperatures, as a result of reduced solar radiation reaching the surface during the day, and by higher minimum temperatures from reduced net outgoing radiation from the surface during the night. The daily range of temperature, the difference between the maximum and the minimum, is closely correlated with the duration of cloudy weather. Light effects on reproduction may thus be tested by cloudiness, expressed in terms of daily temperature range, and by the moon phase, expressed as the date of full moon. The parameters selected were the following:

R. Mean temperature range (maximum minus minimum) for decades 17–20 (mid-February–mid-March).

S. Number of days after March 6 that full moon occurs.

Table 6 lists the independent variables used in the regression analysis which may be causative factors in quail population changes.

STATISTICAL ANALYSIS

The relationship between the juvenile: adult ratios (Y) in the Shandon area (Table

182

1) and the variables shown in Table 6 was analyzed by a stepwise multiple linear regression, using an IBM 1620 computer with a program written by Boles (1963). At each step, coefficients for the multiple regression equation, the standard error of Y on X, the squared correlation coefficient, the sum of the squares of the residuals, the standard error of each coefficient, and the t-ratio for each coefficient were computed.

Simple Correlation

High correlations ($P < 0.01$) were found between the juvenile:adult ratio and the following variables:

A. Proportion of adults among females the previous fall.
B. Relative size of model population.
C. Total seasonal rainfall through April.
D. Total rainfall January–March.
E. Total evapotranspiration January–April.
H. Soil moisture (computed) late April.
J. Accumulated evapotranspiration late April.
M. Temperature index minus rain index mid-March.

Some correlations were found which statistically would appear to be significant but cannot logically have any causal connection. For example, the percent of adult females in the preceding fall sample is significantly correlated ($P < 0.01$) with the occurrence of rain in the middle of March ($r = 0.677$). High correlation ($P < 0.01$) is also found between the date of the new moon (S), and both mean temperature range in decades 17–20 (R) and the occurrence of rain and low temperature in mid-March (M). Although the first inclination is to dismiss these as spurious or accidental, there is a possibility that there may be a real, if undefined, relationship. Brier and Bradley (1964:387–388) have shown a sig-

nificant ($P < 0.001$) cycle of 14.765 days in precipitation data for the United States, equal to exactly one half of a lunar month, and they suggest that the causal factor is lunar. Lund (1965) found a lunar period in sunshine observations in the United States, and Siivonen and Koskimies (1955) have shown population fluctuations in phase with the lunar cycle.

Multiple Regression Analysis

In view of the correlation existing between most of the weather variables being considered, only a limited amount of information can be gained from the above simple correlations. Multiple linear regression of the juvenile:adult ratio (Y) on the 19 variables of Table 6 (17 weather parameters and two population parameters) for the years 1949–1962 yielded the following regression equation for the quail reproductive index in this area:

$$Y = 0.929\,H + 0.021\,A - 0.120\,C - 0.975,$$
$$R^2 = 0.988$$

All of the coefficients in the above equation are significantly different from zero ($P < 0.01$). The goodness of fit to the observed value of Y is measured by the squared correlation coefficient R^2, which is equal to $1 - $ (the ratio of the residual variance to the total variance of the dependent variable Y).

The quantitative importance of the additional variable added in each step is indicated by the amount by which R^2 is increased and the residual variance is decreased. With the single variable H (soil moisture), $R^2 = 0.831$; addition of variable A (proportion of adults among females) increases R^2 by 0.124; variable C (seasonal rainfall) by 0.033.

In brief, the variance of the productivity index Y is due to all three factors which account for almost 99 percent of the variance

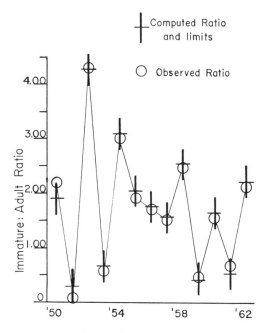

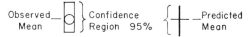

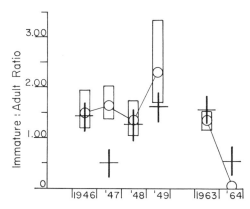

Fig. 2. Observed ratios of immature to adult birds in fall hunting samples in the Shandon area and ratios calculated from the regression equation $Y = 0.929 H + 0.021$ A $- 0.120$ C $- 0.975$. Data from hunting records for the period 1950–1962.

Fig. 3. Ratio of immature to adult quail predicted from independent data by the regression equation $Y = 0.929$ H $+ 0.021$ A $- 0.120$ C $- 0.975$, and observed ratios in the hunting samples for 6 years.

of the reproductive index. A fourth variable, seasonal evapotranspiration to the end of April, contributes very little more, reducing the variance by less than 1 percent.

The closeness of fit of the values of Y calculated from the above equation, indicated by the R^2 value of 0.988, is illustrated in Fig. 2, in which the vertical bars represent the calculated values plus or minus two standard errors, and the observed values are indicated by circles. The fit is striking, since only three independent variables have been used in this case to calculate the 13 points.

Details on the methods of calculation and the results of tests on independent data have been previously reported (Francis 1967). The close agreement found between observed indices of reproductive success and those computed from independent data

(Fig. 3) is convincing evidence that the factors in the above regression equations determine population levels in the Shandon area for all but a few exceptional years.

The apparent discrepancy for 1964 is attributed to the observed ratio being nearly zero. In this case, confidence limits could not be computed, and it is also reasonable to expect departure from linearity. The 1947 discrepancy remains unexplained. The incomplete data for this year required that the proportions of adults among females be estimated, and the estimate may have been in error.

DISCUSSION

The mechanisms by which these weather factors affect quail reproduction can only be conjectured. Direct observations of both captive and wild birds suggest that a proximate factor is the behavior of the birds during the breeding season. Differences were very noticeable in pair formation, incubation behavior, and care of the young, between the 2 years of the study. In the clutches which were successfully hatched in the enclosure at Berkeley, survival of the young made the difference between the 2 years. Parental care appeared, from my observations, to be responsible for the greater survival in 1963, but neither viability of the chicks due to an influence of earlier conditions on the parents' physiology, or a more direct influence of the quality of food available to the chicks, can be ruled out.

Evidence that the differences in reproduction in the Shandon area were related to hormone levels is given by the gonadal development of specimens. Of nine specimens examined in 1963, eight were in breeding condition, while in 1964 only one of six was in possible breeding condition in early June ($P < 0.05$). Early molt gives stronger evidence, with all of 57 trapped birds molting on June 8.

The effect of Vitamin A remains obscure. Hungerford (1964) related quail productivity to vitamin A storage in the liver in Gambel quail. His June specimens showed lower vitamin A levels in a year of good production of young, while specimens in my study had relatively high vitamin A levels in June when almost no young were produced. In view of the rapid change in vitamin A storage that occurs after precipitation (Hungerford 1964:145), my data cannot be compared with his for other months.

It seems likely that differences in reproductive success are related to the plant species which are abundant under the different rainfall regimes, and to the time of year when they are growing most vigorously and have a high nutritive value. Observations in the present study, both in the field and in the enclosure, showed striking differences in the vegetation composition, years of good

quail reproduction being those with an abundance of annual forbs, including legumes, known to be important as quail foods. Species of plants and growth stage may be more important to quail nutritionally than the production of food in quantity.

As a working hypothesis, it appears that the temperature and rainfall regime in a given year is responsible for the production, prior to the beginning of the quail breeding season, of highly nutritious plant foods which, under optimum conditions, supply all the elements (protein, vitamins, and other) necessary for vigorous reproductive behavior. An appropriate photoperiod will trigger the beginning of the reproductive season; if nutrients are present in an adequate amount, gonadotropic secretions of the pituitary will lead to full gonadal development, as evidenced by pairing, aggressive behavior, vocalizations, mating, etc., followed by nesting and egg-laying. Normal environmental stimuli, and perhaps gonadal feed-back to the pituitary, will then stimulate the production of prolactin and other hormones associated with incubation and with parental behavior; such hormones are more readily elicited in experienced females than in those breeding for the first time. With deficiencies of essential nutrients, the pituitary will produce subnormal amounts of both gonadotropins and prolactin, and both reproductive and parental behavior will be expressed at a low level, resulting in poor hatches of eggs and poor survival of young.

There remains a wide field of inquiry in many aspects of the system here postulated. It would be desirable to determine the variations in species, and in the timing of growth of plants under different weather conditions; the nutrient value of both seeds and vegetative parts of these plants; the levels of vitamins and other nutrients in quail feeding on particular plants; the development of the gonads and the accompanying reproductive behavior; the normal changes in vitamin levels and in endocrine production at each stage of the breeding cycle, and their variation with weather conditions; and the complex neuroendocrine relations involved in behavior at all stages of the reproductive cycle.

LITERATURE CITED

ALLISON, D. G. 1962. Factors affecting grouse population changes. New Hampshire Statewide Wildl. Survey, Job Completion Rept. No. III, Proj. No. W-9-R-15.

ARKLEY, R. J. 1963. Relationships between plant growth and transpiration. Hilgardia 34 (13):559–584.

———, AND R. ULRICH. 1962. The use of calculated actual and potential evapotranspiration for estimating potential plant growth. Hilgardia 32(10):443–462.

BARTHOLOMEW, G. A., JR. 1949. Effect of light intensity and day length on reproduction in the English Sparrow. Harvard Univ. Bull. Museum Comp. Zool. 101(3):431–476.

BOLES, J. N. 1963. 80-series multiple linear regression system, program manual. California Agr. Expt. Sta., Giannini Foundation Agr. Econ., Univ. of California, Berkeley. 48pp. Mimeo.

BRIER, G. W., AND D. A. BRADLEY. 1964. The lunar synodical period and precipitation in the United States. J. Atmospheric Sci. 21 (4):386–395.

BURGER, J. W. 1949. A review of experimental investigations on seasonal reproduction in birds. Wilson Bull. 61(4):211–230.

BURKITT, J. P. 1926. A study of the Robin by means of marked birds. British Birds 20(4): 91–101.

BUSS, I. O., AND C. V. SWANSON. 1950. Some effects of weather on pheasant reproduction in southeastern Washington. Trans. N. Am. Wildl. Conf. 15:364–378.

CRAWFORD, R. D. 1962. Recent findings in the inhibition of avian sperm sustentation. Pp.3–22. In D. K. Wetherbee (Editor), Some recent findings in the inhibition of avian reproductivity. U. S. Fish and Wildl. Serv. Spec. Sci. Rept., Wildl. 67. 97pp.

DAVIS, J. 1958. Singing behavior and the gonad cycle of the Rufous-sided Towhee. Condor 60(5):308–336.

EMLEN, J. T., JR. 1937. Morning awakening time of a mockingbird. Bird-Banding 8(2): 81.

ERRINGTON, P. L. 1942. On the analysis of productivity in populations of higher vertebrates. J. Wildl. Mgmt. 6(2):165–181.

———. 1945. Some contributions of a fifteen-year local study of the northern bobwhite to a knowledge of population phenomena. Ecol. Monographs 15(1):1–34.

FARNER, D. S. 1955. Birdbanding in the study of population dynamics. Pp.397–449. In A. Wolfson (Editor), Recent studies in avian biology. Univ. Illinois Press, Urbana. 479pp.

FRANCIS, W. J. 1965. Double broods in California quail. Condor 67(6):541–542.

———. 1967. Prediction of California quail populations from weather data. Condor 69 (4):405–410.

GALLIZIOLI, S., AND E. WEBB. 1961. The influences of hunting upon quail populations. Arizona Game and Fish Dept., Phoenix. Completion Rept. W-78-R-5, Work Plan 4, Job 3. 18pp.

GLADING, B., H. H. BISWELL, AND C. F. SMITH. 1940. Studies on the food of the California quail in 1937. J. Wildl. Mgmt. 4(2):128–144.

GRINNELL, J., H. C. BRYANT, AND T. I. STORER. 1918. The game birds of California. Univ. of California Press, Berkeley. 642pp.

GULLION, G. W. 1960. The ecology of Gambel's quail in Nevada and the arid southwest. Ecology 41(3):518–536.

HICKEY, J. J. 1955. Some American population research on gallinaceous birds. Pp.326–396. In A. Wolfson (Editor), Recent studies in avian biology. Univ. Illinois Press, Urbana. 479pp.

HUNGERFORD, C. R. 1964. Vitamin A and productivity in Gambel's quail. J. Wildl. Mgmt. 28(1):141–147.

JEPSON, W. L. 1960. A manual of the flowering plants of California. Univ. of California Press, Berkeley. 1238pp.

KENDEIGH, S. C., AND S. P. BALDWIN. 1937. Factors affecting yearly abundance of passerine birds. Ecol. Monographs 7(1):91–123.

LANDY, M. J. 1962. Recent findings in the inhibition of avian embryogenesis. Pp.35–51. In D. K. Wetherbee (Editor), Some recent findings in the inhibition of avian reproductivity. U. S. Fish and Wildl. Serv. Spec. Sci. Rept., Wildl. 67. 97pp.

LEHMANN, V. W. 1946. Bobwhite quail reproduction in southwestern Texas. J. Wildl. Mgmt. 10(2):111–123.

———. 1953. Bobwhite population fluctuations and vitamin A. Trans. N. Am. Wildl. Conf. 18:199–246.

LEOPOLD, A., AND A. E. EYNON. 1961. Avian daybreak and evening song in relation to time and light intensity. Condor 63(4):269–293.

Lewin, V. 1963. Reproduction and development of young in a population of California quail. Condor 65(4):249–278.

Lund, I. A. 1965. Indications of a lunar synodical period in United States observations of sunshine. J. Atmospheric Sci. 22(1):24–39.

MacGregor, W., Jr., and M. Inlay. 1951. Observations on failure of Gambel quail to breed. California Fish and Game 37(2):218–219.

Major, J. 1963. A climatic index to vascular plant activity. Ecology 44(3):485–498.

Marshall, A. J. 1949. Weather factors and spermatogenesis in birds. Proc. Zool. Soc. of London, Ser. A. 119:711–716.

———. 1959. Internal and environmental control of breeding. Ibis 101(3–4):456–478.

———, and C. J. F. Coombs. 1957. The interaction of environmental, internal and behavioral factors in the Rook, *Corvus f. frugilegus* Linnaeus. Proc. Zool. Soc. of London. 138:545–589.

McMillan, I. I. 1964. Annual population changes in California quail. J. Wildl. Mgmt. 28(4):702–711.

Nice, Margaret Morse 1937. Studies in the life history of the Song Sparrow. I. A population study of the Song Sparrow. Trans. Linnaean Soc. of New York, Vol. 4. 247pp.

Pelton, W. L., K. M. King, and C. B. Tanner. 1960. An evaluation of the Thornthwaite and mean temperature methods for determining potential evapotranspiration. Agron. J. 52(7):387–395.

Raitt, R. J. 1960. Breeding behavior in a population of California quail. Condor 62(4):284–292.

———, and R. E. Genelly. 1964. Dynamics of a population of California quail. J. Wildl. Mgmt. 28(1):127–141.

Romanoff, A. L. 1934. Study of artificial incubation of game birds. New York State Agr. Expt. Sta. at Cornell Univ., Bull. 616, 39pp.

Rowan, W. 1925. Relation of light to bird migration and developmental changes. Nature 115(2892):494–495.

———. 1926. On photoperiodism, reproductive periodicity, and the annual migrations of birds and certain fishes. Proc. Boston Soc. Nat. Hist. 38(6):147–189.

———. 1938. Light and seasonal reproduction in animals. Biol. Rev. 13(4):374–402.

Shaver, Jesse M., and Ruby Walker. 1931. A preliminary report on the influence of light intensity upon the time of ending of the evening song of the robin and mockingbird. Wilson Bull. 38(1):9–18.

Siivonen, L., and J. Koskimies. 1955. Population fluctuations and the lunar cycle. Helsinki, Finland. Papers on Game Research 14. 22pp.

Somes, R. G., Jr. 1962. Recent findings in the inhibition of avian oogenesis. Pp.52–72. *In* D. K. Wetherbee (Editor), Some recent findings in the inhibition of avian reproductivity. U. S. Fish and Wildl. Serv. Spec. Sci. Rept., Wildl. 67. 97pp.

Sowls, L. K. 1960. Results of a banding study of Gambel's quail in southern Arizona. J. Wildl. Mgmt. 24(2):185–190.

Storer, T. I., F. P. Cronemiller, E. E. Horn, and B. Glading. 1942. Studies on Valley quail. The San Joaquin Exptl. Range. Univ. of California Agr. Expt. Sta. Bull. 663:130–135.

Sumner, E. L., Jr. 1935. A life history study of the California quail, with recommendations for its conservation and management. Part 1. California Fish and Game 21(3):167–256.

Thornthwaite, C. W. 1948. An approach toward a rational classification of climate. Geog. Rev. 38(1):55–94.

———, and J. R. Mather. 1955. The water balance. Drexel Inst. of Technol. Lab. of Climatology, Pub. in Climatology. 8(1):1–86.

———, and ———. 1957. Instructions and tables for computing potential evapotranspiration and the water balance. Drexel Inst. of Technol., Lab. of Climatology, Pub. in Climatology. 10(3):185–311.

U. S. Weather Bureau. Hourly precipitation data, California.

———. Monthly Climatological Data, California.

———. Monthly Hydrologic Bulletins, South Pacific District.

Williams, G. R. 1959. Aging, growth rate, and breeding season phenology of wild populations of California quail in New Zealand. Bird-Banding 30(4):203–218.

———. 1963. A four-year population cycle in California quail, *Lophortyx californicus* (Shaw) in the South Island of New Zealand. J. Animal Ecol. 32(3):441–459.

Yeatter, R. E. 1950. Effects of different pre-incubation temperatures on the hatchability of pheasant eggs. Science 112(2914):529–530.

187

A CORRELATION ANALYSIS OF WEATHER VERSUS SNOWSHOE HARE POPULATION PARAMETERS[1]

E. CHARLES MESLOW
LLOYD B. KEITH

Abstract: Computer facilities were utilized to examine five snowshoe hare (*Lepus americanus*) population parameters for correlations with 12 weather factors in a wide array of time periods. Intensity of illumination in midwinter, as measured by cloud cover, was highly significantly correlated with the date of onset of breeding the following spring. No significant correlations between weather and the date of testis regression were disclosed. Between-year differences in litter size were significantly correlated with temperatures and snow depth. The colder the temperatures in the 250 days preceding mid-February, and the deeper the winter's accumulation of snow, the larger the litters the next spring. Adult survival in the period January through April 25 was highly significantly correlated with both temperatures and snowfall; the critical periods were the 80 days preceding April 25, and January 5 to March 26, respectively. Colder temperatures and deeper snow in these periods correlated with poorer adult survival. Relative survival of first-litter young during their first 45 days of life was highly significantly enhanced by brighter days and warmer temperatures throughout the 45-day survival period. Relative survival of second-litter hares was highly significantly negatively correlated with rainfall. Both total rainfall and the number of days with rainfall throughout almost the entire 45-day survival period were involved. Relationships expressed by the correlations were compared with the findings of other investigators; possible biological mechanisms operative in the correlations were outlined.

In a previous paper (Meslow and Keith 1968) we documented demographic changes in a snowshoe hare population between 1961 and 1967 at Rochester, Alberta. Fluctuating rates of adult survival, juvenile survival, and birth all contributed to observed numerical changes. The present paper examines, through correlation analysis, relationships between weather and elements of the previously documented population parameters.

Incorporation of unpublished hare data from 1968 gave us population statistics spanning 6 to 8 years. We limited investigations of weather factors to those standard observations of temperature, precipitation, and cloud cover recorded by most climatological reporting stations. An IBM 1620 computer facilitated the correlation of population statistics versus weather data. While the resulting correlations may imply cause and effect relationships, in themselves they prove nothing.

We used the data-processing facilities of the College of Agricultural and Life Sciences, University of Wisconsin, and gratefully acknowledge Arden Hardie, Department of Dairy Science, for computer programming and James Torrie, Department of Agronomy, for statistical advice.

[1] A contribution of the Department of Wildlife Ecology, University of Wisconsin, and the Research Council of Alberta; study supported by the Research Council of Alberta; the College of Agricultural and Life Sciences, University of Wisconsin; the National Institutes of Health (Grant A104-725); the Ford Foundation (Grant 63-505); and the National Science Foundation (Grant GB-7744).

Table 1. Population parameters of Rochester, Alberta, snowshoe hares used, for correlation with weather factors.

Year	Hares/1,000 Acres in Spring[a]	Mean Date of Initiation of Breeding	Litter Size (Mean of Litters 2–4)	Mean Date of Testis Regression[b]	Adult Survival Rate (Jan.–Apr.)	Relative Juvenile Survival Rate (birth to age 45 days[c])	
						Litter 1	Litter 2
1961	Peak Population[d]	March 30	4.88	July 26	—	0.20 (May 4)[e]	0.18 (June 9)[e]
1962	972	April 9	4.52	July 3	—	0.12 (May 14)	0.10 (June 19)
1963	399	April 15	3.55	July 10	0.46	0.17 (May 20)	0.32 (June 26)
1964	82	April 9	3.75	July 24	0.24	0.17 (May 14)	0.15 (June 18)
1965	51	April 9	6.00	August 4	0.18	0.09 (May 14)	0.12 (June 17)
1966	60	March 31	5.77	August 5	0.37	0.04 (May 5)	0.22 (June 9)
1967	123	April 10	5.44	August 3	0.31	0.11 (May 15)	0.36 (June 20)
1968	217	March 25	5.16	August 10	0.57	0.16 (April 29)	0.24 (June 2)

[a] Based on population estimates and acreages of the study areas (Meslow and Keith 1968, and unpublished).
[b] Date on which the average testis weight fell below 4 grams.
[c] Based on the ratio of juvenile/adult captures; corrected for litter size.
[d] Hare density estimated as greater than the densities of 1960 and 1962 (Meslow and Keith 1968:815).
[e] Mean date of birth.

METHODS

Of the hare population parameters available (Meslow and Keith 1968, and unpublished), only five (Table 1) were amenable to examination for possible correlations with annual weather: (1) date of initiation of breeding; (2) date of testis regression; (3) litter size; (4) adult survival, January to April 25; and (5) early juvenile survival, birth to age 45 days. The latter two incorporate survival periods and measurements not discussed in our 1968 paper.

Weather data were from the Meanook Meteorological Observatory, 16 miles north of Rochester. The 12 weather factors used were: mean temperature, mean maximum temperature, mean minimum temperature, cloud cover (1–4 scale), mean depth of snow on the ground, number of days with snow on the ground, total rainfall, total snowfall, total precipitation, and number of days with recorded rainfall, snowfall, and precipitation. Cloud cover provided the only measure of radiation. There was no measurement of wind available.

In searching for significant correlations between weather and population parameter change, we first established a broad time period within which weather might be expected to act on each hare parameter. With survival, this period was simply the time over which survival was measured; with reproduction, the problem was more difficult. For instance, how long before conception might weather act to modify ovulation rates? This problem was approached by coupling prior biological evidence with trial-and-error explorations.

The broad time periods above were then sampled intensively in a stepwise fashion by what we term weather periods (Fig. 1). Both the length of the weather periods and

189

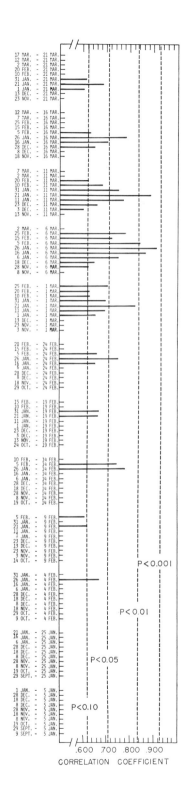

the stepwise increments of sampling were designed to fit realistically each population parameter. For instance, because (1) it seemed that juvenile hares in their first few weeks of life would be more responsive to the survival effects of weather than would adults, and (2) because juvenile survival was measured over a shorter time span than adult survival (45 versus 115 days), we used both a shorter minimal weather period and stepwise increment of sampling: 5 versus 10 days.

Use of a computer allowed us to maximize the number of weather periods examined, and also to employ small stepwise increments in sampling. We could inspect each of the 12 weather factors in relation to each of the population parameters. This approach resulted in disclosure of significant correlations that never would have been examined with less automated data analysis.

Types of Weather Periods

We utilized two different types of weather periods in the investigation. The first, a calendar weather period, was based on the same calendar dates each year; the second, a biological weather period, was related to the date of occurrence of a demographic event. For example, weather in periods affecting the early survival of young hares (birth to age 45 days) could not be based on the same calendar dates each year because the date of birth of the same litter group varied up to 20 days between years. Hence, only biological weather periods, keyed yearly to mean birth dates, were appropriate for investigating early survival of juveniles.

←

Fig. 1. Correlation coefficients, $r > -0.600$, between mean date of initiation of breeding of snowshoe hares and cloud cover in 120 calendar weather periods.

Superficially, it would seem desirable to utilize biological weather periods for all correlations with population parameters of varying dates. Biological weather periods, however, can not be employed where the population variable is (1) expressed as a date (initiation of breeding, testis regression), or (2) where it is substantially correlated with the date establishing the weather period (litter size which tends to be correlated, $r = -0.514$, with the date of conception of the second litter). In such cases, biological weather periods reduce or remove potential correlations with weather.

Suppose, for example, that a mean temperature of 55 F maintained for 10 days triggers onset of breeding. Can we then demonstrate a significant correlation between temperature and the onset of breeding by using a 10-day biological weather period immediately preceding the mean date of initiation of breeding? No, a correlation coefficient of 0.00 would result because the same mean temperature (55 F) is paired with each of the various breeding dates.

As a result of the two restrictions above, only early survival of juvenile hares was amenable to investigation using biological weather periods.

Weather Period Sampling

As an example of a selected pattern of weather periods investigated relative to a demographic parameter, the calendar weather periods for initiation of breeding were typical (Fig. 1). The following were examined yearly: 5-, 10-, 20-, 30-, 40-, 50-, 60-, 80-, 100-, and 120-day periods prior to each of the following dates (numbered days of the year in parentheses): March 21 (80), March 16 (75), March 11 (70), March 6 (65), March 1 (60), February 24 (55), February 19 (50), February 14 (45),

February 9 (40), February 4 (35), January 25 (25), and January 5 (5). Thus, weather periods of 10 different lengths were paired with each of 12 dates, yielding a total of 120 weather periods for examination. Each weather factor (12) in each weather period (120) of each year was paired with the mean date of initiation of breeding in that year, and a correlation coefficient for the 8 years (1961–68) computed. In this example there were 1,440 correlations (12 weather factors $\times$ 120 weather periods) testing the effect of weather on initiation of breeding. For the other hare parameters (Table 1) we examined from 312 to 864 weather factor correlations in from 52 to 72 weather periods.

Biological weather periods were sampled in a pattern similar to calendar weather periods. But, instead of basing the periods on calendar dates, we based them on the occurrence of a demographic event such as mean date of birth.

Types of Error

We employed simple linear correlation analysis. Some of the relationships between weather factors and hare population parameters might better have been expressed through nonlinear correlation; such a relationship, however, can not be developed on the basis of data for only 6 or 8 years (points). Linear correlation analysis assumes sampling from a bivariate normal distribution. The types of weather data we utilized tend to be normally distributed (Jenkinson 1957, Thom 1968). The hare data (Table 1) span too short a period to speculate as to their distribution.

Four types of error of a statistical nature were encountered during our investigations. Those peculiar to our study we termed *Type A* and *Type B* errors. We also faced the problem of dealing with Type I (α) and

Type II (β) errors common to tests of significance (Steel and Torrie 1960:70).

Type A Error.—Some significant correlations resulted from the interrelationships of weather factors. Total precipitation in winter was almost entirely a function of snowfall; there was also an obligate but less well defined relationship between cloud cover and all forms of precipitation. Other weather-factor relationships, such as those between temperatures and cloud cover were more difficult to interpret. We attempted to reject any significant correlations stemming from an obligate relationship of weather factors which forced significant correlations during the same or closely allied weather periods. We termed such forced correlations Type A errors.

To minimize Type A errors we used partial correlations to determine the relative contribution of pairs of weather factors in the same or closely allied weather periods. For instance, cloud cover was found to be significantly correlated with the earliness of breeding (Fig. 1). But the same weather periods during which cloud cover was significant also frequently (13 times) exhibited significant correlations with precipitation (days with recorded snowfall and total snowfall). Testing with partial correlations disclosed that cloud cover was the more important determinant of the pair; when tested by partials, cloud cover remained significant while snowfall dropped to nonsignificance.

Type B Error.—Type B errors occurred when correlations with rain or snow were significant at the time of year when that form of precipitation ceased to occur and the weather periods spanned that date. For example, as a series of weather periods going back in time from December 1 begins to include days prior to September 15, there was practically no chance of more snow being recorded as the length of the weather periods increased. Therefore, if snowfall was significantly correlated during the September 15–December 1 weather period, then all longer weather periods (August 15–December 1, July 15–December 1) were forced to be significant.

Type I and Type II Errors.—Examining a large number of correlation coefficients, we found that a potentially important problem was Type I error: the rejection of the null hypothesis when it is true. Raising the level of significance required for rejection of the null hypothesis is the method of reducing Type I errors. In many cases we could decrease the probability of Type I errors by relying heavily on only those correlations that were significant at the $P \leq 0.01$ level.

Type I errors should also have been more or less randomly distributed among the 12 weather factors investigated. We found, however, that the preponderance of significant correlations, after Type A and B errors were eliminated, was with a single weather factor.

Significant correlations between a weather factor and a hare parameter also generally exhibited a progressive climb to and decline from significance over time. This pattern in time would not be expected from Type I errors, which should have been scattered randomly. But because most weather periods overlapped, each correlation was seldom totally independent of all others. Thus, any apparently meaningful pattern over time was to a large extent a function of overlapping weather periods. In examining discrete non-overlapping weather periods, however, we likewise found no tendency for significant correlations to be scattered randomly through time.

The fact that correlation coefficients can

192

be either positive or negative was of further help in recognizing Type I errors. If both positive and negative significant correlations were associated with the same weather factor, we felt confident that Type I error was involved. The lack of any plausible biological hypothesis for a significant correlation likewise strongly suggested involvement of Type I error. In this paper, however, we have not rejected any significant correlations solely because we could offer no acceptable hypothesis for the relationship implied.

A significant correlation was rejected as Type I error if: (1) it appeared singly as an abrupt jump to significance, or (2) both positive and negative significant correlations were associated with the same weather factor. It appears to us that the observed correlations were in general remarkably free of Type I errors.

Type II error, accepting the null hypothesis when it is false, increases in probability as the level of significance demanded for rejection of the null hypothesis is increased. We have erred in the direction of conservatism and make no attempt to identify situations where Type II errors may have been involved.

Error Summary.—All significant correlations, $P \leq 0.05$, were stringently screened and those which could definitely be attributed to errors of Type A, B, or I were rejected. These rejected correlations receive no elaboration or description in the text. By the same token, we have been careful not to use the various forms of error as an excuse to reject significant correlations that seem biologically suspect. Where we can only surmise that error produced a significant correlation, we so state, but document the correlation briefly in the text. We feel that the remaining correlations, $P \leq 0.05$, are real, not error-produced; we

present these correlations both graphically and in the text. We do not have the same confidence that our efforts disclosed all relevant correlations.

INITIATION OF BREEDING

The mean date of initiation of breeding (conception of the first litter) varied between years from March 25 to April 15, but was closely synchronized in any one year. Dates of initiation of breeding presented here (Table 1) differ from those presented earlier (Meslow and Keith 1968:Fig. 4) by 1 day at most and utilize all conceptions rather than only first-litter conceptions to establish the mean date of initiation of breeding. We assumed immediate postpartum mating (Severaid 1945) and a gestation period of 34.5 days to backdate litter 2–4 conceptions to those of litter 1. We used the mean interval between birth of successive litter groups (Meslow and Keith 1968:Fig. 4) to obtain the 34.5-day gestation period.

Of 1,440 correlations examined, 29 (two percent) were significant at the $P \leq 0.05$ level ($r \geq 0.707$). Of these 29, 13 were rejected as Type A errors and 2 as Type I errors. The remaining 14, including 4 at the $P \leq 0.01$ level, were significant positive correlations between earliness of breeding and decreased cloudiness (Fig. 1). Thus, less cloud cover (more sunshine) between about January 6 and March 16 was associated with earlier initiation of breeding. The highest correlation, $r = 0.911$ ($P < 0.01$), was in the period January 26 to March 6.

Flux (1967:397) singled out photoperiod as "presumably the most important proximate factor controlling the breeding season." He then went on to document a temperature effect superimposed on the basic photoperiod control in the European hare (*Lepus europaeus*). Flux alluded to other "minor or immediate proximate factors" such as heavy rain or soft snow that may delay mating.

Studies in Missouri (Wight and Conaway 1961, Conaway and Wight 1962) led to the conclusion that photoperiod was the over-all synchronizing stimuli for breeding in the cottontail (*Sylvilagus floridanus*); behavioral stimuli furthered this synchrony. These authors showed that in wild populations, abnormally heavy snowfalls or prolonged cold delayed the onset of breeding, and that high densities under pen conditions had the same effect.

Lyman (1943:452), working with captive snowshoe hares, concluded that breeding condition was brought about by the combination of photoperiod and a "rhythm inherent in the animal." He could detect no effect of temperature superimposed on the photoperiod effect. The apparent relationship between cloud cover and initiation of breeding, as disclosed by our studies, suggests that intensity of illumination was influential. Lord's (1961:29–30) data tend to support our findings. Lord showed that increased pregnancy rates among cottontails in Illinois were correlated with increased sunshine during the breeding season. This correlation was not statistically significant, however, probably because of small sample size.

The mid- to late-winter period, January to March, during which the apparent sunshine effect is operative, appears biologically reasonable. Marshall (1951) pointed out that in birds inhabiting countries with a relatively dull winter, sunshine, as distinct from temperature or photoperiod, is an important breeding stimulus. The following observation (Marshall 1951:250) could explain the operation of a cloud cover correlation such as ours: "A long succession of days suitable to reproductive develop-

ment [sunny] will heighten sexuality irrespective of day-length; and a period of adverse weather, even when days are lengthening, will depress it, thus delaying the sexual season."

TESTIS REGRESSION

The mean date of testis regression varied 39 days (July 3–August 10) between years (Table 1). An index of regression was arbitrarily established as the day each year on which average testis weight, as indicated by a regression curve, fell below 4 grams (Meslow and Keith 1968:Fig. 5, and unpublished).

We examined 720 correlations in 60 calendar weather periods ranging back in time from July 4. This initial exploration indicated highly significant correlations between earliness of testis regression and snowfall. The highest correlation, $r = -0.936$ ($P < 0.001$), indicated that greater snowfall in the 50 days preceding June 19 was followed by earlier testis regression.

Further investigation, however, disclosed that these high correlations were almost totally dependent on two snowstorms: May 3–4, 1962, and May 1, 1963. If only the first 5 days of May in each year were used, a correlation of -0.913 ($P < 0.01$) resulted; snowfall during this 5-day period in all years except 1962 and 1963 was 0. The high correlations in periods extending beyond May 5 we interpreted as Type B errors since not enough snow fell after May 5 in any year to materially affect the correlation. Because the basic correlation between testis regression and snowfall involved such a short time period and resulted from only two records of snowfall in an 8-year period, we rejected it as Type I error.

Testis regression, marking the end of the breeding season, has received little attention compared to initiation of breeding.

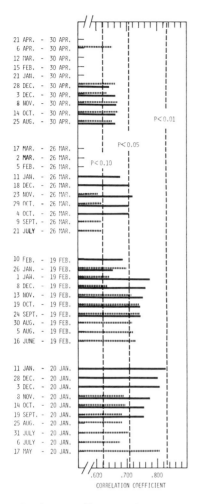

Fig. 2. Correlation coefficients, $r > \pm\ 0.600$ between snowshoe hare litter size and mean maximum temperatures (negative correlation, dashed line) and mean depth of snow on the ground (positive correlation, solid line), in 40 calendar weather periods.

Lyman (1943:453) credited a refractoriness developed in the testes and a rapid decrease in illumination (photoperiod) as the factors leading to regression in the snowshoe hare. With the observed 39-day difference in mean date of regression, photoperiod was obviously not the only factor operative at Rochester. Our investigations, however, failed to disclose any weather variable that could be satisfactorily hypothesized as modifying what is evidently basic photoperiodic control of testis regression.

LITTER SIZE

Changes in litter size between 1961 and 1968 were a prime factor in changing birth rates, which markedly affected the snowshoe hare population level at Rochester. The snowshoe is a multi-littered species, and during 1961–68 either three or four litter groups were born annually. Significant yearly differences occurred in the mean size of both first and later litters; between-year differences were most pronounced in litters 2 through 4 (Meslow and Keith 1968:Table 14, and unpublished). There was no demonstrable within-year difference in the mean size of litters 2 through 4. We chose to use the mean size of litters 2 through 4 (Table 1) to explore correlations between weather and litter size. Any weather factors influencing the mean size of these litters must have been prior to conception of litter 2 (birth date of litter 1) because changes in litter size primarily represented changing ovulation rates; pre-implantation and intrauterine loss were consistently low (Keith, unpublished).

We initially examined 672 correlations in 56 calendar weather periods. Sixteen of these 56 periods, falling completely within the previous calendar year, were later dropped from consideration because all significant correlations disclosed in these periods were attributable to error.

Among the remaining 480 correlations, 44 were significant at the $P \leq 0.05$ level. One was rejected as Type A error, 9 were rejected as Type B errors, and 6 as Type I errors. Six significant negative correlations with minimum and mean temperatures were ignored in favor of 7 negative correlations of a higher order with maximum temperatures (Fig. 2). The highest correlation in this group, $r = -0.804$ ($P < 0.05$), was in the 250-day period preceding January 20, indicating that colder temperatures during this period were associated with larger litter size in the subsequent breeding season.

The remaining 15 significant correlations were all positive associations between litter size and the mean depth of snow on the ground (Fig. 2); thus the deeper the snow the larger the litters. Weather periods of various lengths between late September and late March were involved. The highest associations were in fairly short weather periods centered about January 1.

Support in the literature for these temperature and snow depth correlations is essentially limited to the well-documented relationship between litter size and latitude. Rowan and Keith (1956) and Keith et al. (1966:956) demonstrated a positive correlation ($r = 0.80$, $P < 0.01$) between litter size and latitude for the snowshoe hare. Lord (1960) further explored this relationship between litter size and latitude and concluded that it applied generally to nonhibernating, nonfossorial rodents and lagomorphs. We submit that "latitude" is an imperfect but acceptable index to winter temperatures and snow depths found within the snowshoe's range.

That temperature is an important constituent of the complex of environmental factors expressing themselves in latitude was shown by Flux (1967:378). He demonstrated that mean litter size in the European hare was significantly correlated ($r = -0.91$, $P < 0.01$) with mean annual temperatures in seven locations ranging from Poland to New Zealand.

Each of the references above deals with interregional comparisons, however, and not with between-year changes in litter size on the same area in relation to weather. Furthermore, Keith et al. (1966) showed that latitudinal differences in snowshoe hare litter sizes have a genetic basis. Variation in litter size may thus have two components: (1) an interpopulation, genetically fixed increase with latitude; and (2) an intrapopulation, phenotypic response to temperature and snow depth stimuli.

It is difficult to envision any direct cause-and-effect relationship between litter size (ovulation rate) and temperatures or snow depth. This is especially so because the correlations indicate increasing litter size with increased snow depth and cold temperatures—weather conditions usually considered harsh. A review of the literature of reproductive physiology was not helpful. Indirect pathways, operating through the food supply, can be envisioned but supportive evidence is equally lacking; thus any relationships postulated are highly speculative.

As snow depth increases, the height above ground level at which a hare feeds also increases. A workable hypothesis arises if the nutritive value of this "higher" food is such that it promotes a greater ovulation rate. Keith (unpublished) found that winter food of the snowshoe hare in Alberta consists primarily of the buds, twigs, and bark of aspen (*Populus tremuloides*), willow (*Salix* spp.), birch (*Betula* spp.), and rose (*Rosa* spp.), and that deeper snow would tend to make younger and presumably more nutritious portions of these plants available.

ADULT SURVIVAL

Adult survival rates for the period January 1 through April 25 were calculated by the survival series method (Ricker 1958: 128). Only 6 years of data were available

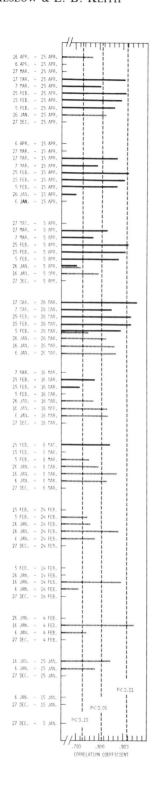

Fig. 3. Correlation coefficients, $r > \pm$ 0.700, between snowshoe hare adult survival rates (January–April 25) and the number of days with recorded snowfall (negative correlation, dashed line) and mean minimum temperatures (positive correlation, solid line) in 72 calendar weather periods.

(Table 1), thus raising the correlation coefficient required for $P \leqq 0.05$ to 0.811. Survival-rate trends during this winter period tended to parallel the annual adult survival rates presented previously (Meslow and Keith 1968:Table 7).

A total of 864 correlations in 72 calendar weather periods were examined; 71 (eight percent) were significant at the $P \leqq 0.05$ level. Seven of these were rejected as Type A errors and 5 as Type I errors. Two positive correlations, $P < 0.01$, between decreasing cloudiness and increasing survival in the periods January 16 to February 4 and January 16 to February 14 are suspect as Type I errors.

There were 12 negative correlations, $P \leqq 0.05$, between the number of days with recorded snowfall and adult survival. The more frequently it snowed in the general period January 6 through March 26, the lower the adult survival rate. The highest correlation in this group, $r = -0.945$ ($P < 0.01$), was in the period January 16 through February 4 (Fig. 3).

A total of 45 positive correlations, $P \leqq 0.05$, between temperatures and adult survival were disclosed. Because more and higher correlations in the same weather periods were found with minimum than with maximum or mean temperatures, only the 18 correlations with minimum temperatures are considered (Fig. 3). These 18 include 5 at the $P \leqq 0.01$ level. Apparently the warmer the temperatures, especially minimum temperatures, the greater the adult survival. The critical period lies in the 80

197

days preceding April 25, with the highest correlations, $r > 0.933$ ($P < 0.01$), in the period February 15 through March 26.

We could find no comparable studies of leporids where adult survival rates in winter were examined for correlations with weather. There is a general paucity of quantitative survival measurements, especially for seasonal periods. There is a reference to decreased European hare populations following cold or abnormally snowy winters in Finland (Siivonen 1956). The time period during which our correlations between survival and snow and temperature were operative corresponded to the late-winter and early-spring period implicated in the mass die-offs of hares associated with population crashes (Keith 1963: 119). Green and Evans (1940:275) also indicated that by far the greatest mortality among snowshoes occurred during the winter months.

Irving et al. (1957) and Hart et al. (1965) examined cold stress in snowshoe hares from near Anchorage, Alaska, and Ottawa, Ontario, respectively. Both found that winter temperatures ranged below the hares' zone of thermoneutrality; both agreed, however, that behavioral and insulative adjustments by the hares permitted the expenditure of little more than basal metabolic energy to maintain body heat under winter conditions. This information argues against direct mortality from winter weather.

We noted at Rochester a marked decrease in hare activity (as evidenced by fresh tracks) associated with both bitter cold and fresh snowfall. Severaid (1942) observed the same phenomenon, which was accompanied by a noticeable reduction in food consumption. It thus seems possible that low temperatures and frequent snowfalls, which limit feeding movements, create nutritional problems for the hares.

JUVENILE SURVIVAL

Litter 1

The relative survival rate of juvenile hares during their first few weeks of life was derived from age ratios in traps. We used the ratio of first-litter young to adults during the period 30 to 60 days following the mean birth date of the litter. This ratio was corrected for yearly differences in litter size to yield a relative survival rate for the 45 days following birth (Table 1). Because of the comparatively short period over which survival was measured, and the 20-day difference between years in mean date of birth of litter 1, only biological weather periods were suitable for analysis.

A total of 624 correlations in 52 weather periods were examined; 92 (15 percent) were significant at the $P \leq 0.05$ level. Seventeen of the 92 were rejected as Type A errors; 18 significant correlations with mean and minimum temperatures were dropped from consideration because in the same weather periods higher correlations existed with maximum temperatures.

There were 27 positive correlations, $P \leq 0.05$, between maximum temperatures and first-litter survival, including 10 at the $P \leq 0.01$ level (Fig. 4). Here, the warmer the temperatures, especially the maximum temperatures, the higher the survival of first-litter young. These significant correlations lay in weather periods extending throughout the 45-day period following the mean date of birth. The highest correlation, $r = 0.893$, was in the period of birth plus 15 to birth plus 40 days.

Correlations between cloud cover and relative survival of first-litter young revealed 28 instances where the level of significance attained at least the $P \leq 0.05$ level (Fig. 4); 13 of these were at $P \leq 0.01$. The distribution in time of these correlations in-

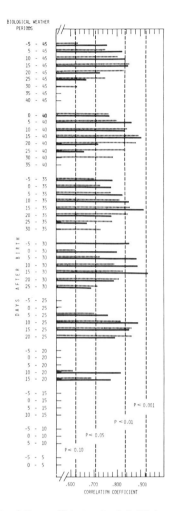

Fig. 4. Correlation coefficients, $r > \pm 0.600$, between relative survival rates of first-litter snowshoe hares (birth to age 45 days) and mean maximum temperatures (positive correlation, dashed line) and cloud cover (negative correlation, solid line) in 52 biological weather periods.

identify summer, and specifically the first few weeks of life, as the period of highest mortality for young snowshoes. Andersen (1952) reported for Denmark an association between warm, dry weather in the breeding season and high fall populations of European hares. He indicated that warm temperatures were the weather factors, operative in the early portion of the breeding season (February to May), which acted either to reduce juvenile mortality or to increase the fertility of the adults.

Orrin Rongstad (unpublished data) learned from radiotelemetry studies of snowshoe hares in Minnesota that the young are left unattended by the female soon after birth. The female's only contact with her litter is apparently thereafter limited to a single brief nursing period daily. Young hares of each litter dispersed over a considerable area and litter mates moved independently of one another. While dispersal and nonassociation of young may have survival value for the litter in the face of predation, it is difficult to envision how such behavior might ameliorate the adverse effects of weather.

Thus, it seems entirely reasonable that survival of first-litter young would be enhanced by warm temperatures; especially since daily minimum and maximum temperatures for the month of May, while highly variable, average only about 40 F and 60 F, respectively.

The correlation between increasing survival and decreasing cloudiness was at first suspect as Type A error resulting from an obligate relationship between warm temperatures and clear skies in the spring. Testing with partial correlations, however, indicated that despite a high correlation ($P < 0.01$) between cloud cover and temperatures, both weather factors were influencing survival.

dicating increasing survival with decreasing cloudiness was similar to that for maximum temperature. The highest correlation, $r = -0.933$ ($P < 0.001$), was in the period of birth plus 15 to birth plus 30 days.

As with adult survival in winter, the literature yielded no comparable studies of early juvenile survival in the snowshoe hare. Green and Evans (1940) did, however,

Litter 2

The relative survival rates for second-litter juveniles (Table 1) were derived as those for litter 1. Because rain was the only form of precipitation recorded during the relevant weather periods, the six weather factors dealing with snow could be ignored; this left 312 correlations for examination.

Of these 312 correlations, 41 (13 percent) were significant at the $P \leq 0.05$ level. Except for 6 rejected as Type I errors, all were negative correlations between rainfall and survival (Fig. 5). These correlations were with both total rainfall and days with recorded rainfall, and spanned the entire period from 5 days before the mean date of birth of the second litter to 45 days following birth. The more rain and rainy days, the poorer the survival. Several of the highest correlations in this group approached, and one exceeded the $P \leq 0.001$ level.

Andersen's (1952) correlation between dry summers (June and July) and large fall European hare populations offers some corroboration of our results. The summer months of June through August comprise the period during which most of the annual rainfall occurs in the Rochester area. Both the amount and distribution of rainfall within this period are highly variable. Such variability, coupled with the lack of maternal care, provides an ideal situation for interaction between juvenile survival and weather. With both maximum and minimum temperatures averaging about 10 F warmer than those earlier found critical to first-litter survival, it is not surprising to find rainfall a dominant influence on early survival of second-litter young.

DISCUSSION

Andersen (1952), Siivonen (1956), and Larsen and Lahey (1958), among many

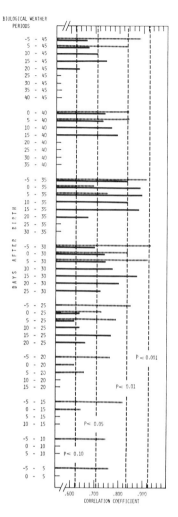

Fig. 5. Correlation coefficients, $r > -0.600$, between relative survival rates of second-litter snowshoe hares (birth to age 45 days) and total rainfall (negative correlation, dashed line) and the number of days with recorded rainfall (negative correlation, solid line) in 52 biological weather periods.

investigators examining population responses to weather, have had available only annual population estimates or indices. That any of these studies succeeded in demonstrating meaningful correlations between population level and weather depended on either: (1) the overriding influence of a single population parameter on the population level and a strong correlation between this parameter and weather; or (2) weather simultaneously influencing several parameters which jointly determined population level.

Correlation analyses, even when specific population statistics are examined with weather, are of limited use in diagnosing weather effects. Perhaps the most important limitation is that this method assumes the same time period is critical each year. Secondly, weather may act indirectly with the resultant time lag obscuring the true relationship. For example, initiation of breeding in the black-tailed jack rabbit (*Lepus californicus*) and the wild rabbit (*Oryctolagus cuniculus*) is delayed until the advent of the wet season, and then the availability of green plants is apparently a necessary prerequisite for breeding (Lechleitner 1959:79, Poole 1960, and Hughes and Rowley 1966). Finally, investigators too often fail to measure the appropriate weather factors. Our investigations, for example, lacked the potentially important weather factor of wind, and our only measure of radiation was a 1–4 index of cloud cover.

We were unable to detect a dominant influence of any one weather variable on the several population parameters considered here. Cold winter weather was the only factor that even hinted at a dominant influence. Adult survival decreased in cold, snowy winters while litter size increased the following spring. Increased litter size thereby constitutes a compensatory response to the same weather, cold and snow, which evidently increased mortality among adults over winter.

Despite the potential insensitivity of correlation analyses, the present investigation produced numerous statistically significant correlations with weather. Because only 6

to 8 years of population data were available, all statistically significant correlations had high correlation coefficients and hence high coefficients of determination (> 0.5). The significant correlations disclosed by this investigation, after implementation of error guidelines, generally formed the basis for reasonable biological hypotheses.

The high coefficients of determination, frequently > 80 percent, force us at this time to accept as highly significant the impact of weather. We wish, however, to await data covering at least one complete 10-year cycle of abundance before attempting to appraise the role of weather in that population phenomenon. Present information spans only a portion of the cyclic decline and the initial recovery from a population low.

LITERATURE CITED

Andersen, J. 1952. Fluctuations in the field hare population in Denmark compared with certain climatic factors. Papers Game Research 8:41–43.

Conaway, C. H., and H. M. Wight. 1962. Onset of the reproductive season and first pregnancy of the season in cottontails. J. Wildl. Mgmt. 26(3):278–290.

Flux, J. E. C. 1967. Reproduction and body weights of the hare *Lepus europaeus* Pallas, in New Zealand. New Zealand J. Sci. 10(2):357–401.

Green, R. G., and C. A. Evans. 1940. Studies on a population cycle of snowshoe hares on the Lake Alexander Area. II. Mortality according to age groups and seasons. J. Wildl. Mgmt. 4(3):267–278.

Hart, J. S., H. Pohl, and J. S. Tener. 1965. Seasonal acclimatization in varying hare (*Lepus americanus*). Canadian J. Zool. 43(5):731–744.

Hughes, R. L., and I. Rowley. 1966. Breeding season of female wild rabbits in natural populations in the Riverina and Southern Tablelands Districts of New South Wales. C.S.I.R.O. Wildl. Research 11(1):1–10.

Irving, L., J. Krog, Hildur Krog, and Mildred Monson. 1957. Metabolism of varying hare in winter. J. Mammal. 38(4):527–529.

Jenkinson, A. T. 1957. Relations between standard deviation of daily, five-day, ten-day and thirty-day mean temperatures. Meteorol. Mag. 86:169–176.

KEITH, L. B. 1963. Wildlife's ten-year cycle. The University of Wisconsin Press, Madison. 201pp.

————, O. J. RONGSTAD, AND E. C. MESLOW. 1966. Regional differences in reproductive traits of the snowshoe hare. Canadian J. Zool. 44(5):953–961.

LARSEN, J. A., AND J. F. LAHEY. 1958. Influence of weather upon a ruffed grouse population. J. Wildl. Mgmt. 22(1):63–70.

LECHLEITNER, R. R. 1959. Sex ratio, age classes and reproduction of the black-tailed jack rabbit. J. Mammal. 40(1):63–81.

LORD, R. D., JR. 1960. Litter size and latitude in North American mammals. Am. Midland Naturalist 64(2):488–499.

————. 1961. Magnitudes of reproduction in cottontail rabbits. J. Wildl. Mgmt. 25(1):28–33.

LYMAN, C. P. 1943. Control of coat color in the varying hare Lepus americanus Erxleben. Harvard College, Museum Comp. Zool. Bull. 93(3):393–461.

MARSHALL, A. J. 1951. The refractory period of testis rhythm in birds and its possible bearing on breeding and migration. Wilson Bull. 63(4):238–261.

MESLOW, E. C., AND L. B. KEITH. 1968. Demographic parameters of a snowshoe hare population. J. Wildl. Mgmt. 32(4):812–834.

POOLE, W. E. 1960. Breeding of the wild rabbit, Oryctolagus cuniculus (L.), in relation to the environment. C.S.I.R.O. Wildl. Research 5(1):21–43.

RICKER, W. E. 1958. Handbook of computations for biological statistics of fish populations. Fisheries Research Board Canada Bull. 119. 300pp.

ROWAN, W., AND L. B. KEITH. 1956. Reproductive potential and sex ratios of snowshoe hares in northern Alberta. Canadian J. Zool. 34(4):273–281.

SEVERAID, J. H. 1942. The snowshoe hare; its life history and artificial propagation. Maine Dept. Inland Fisheries and Game. 95pp.

————. 1945. Breeding potential and artificial propagation of the snowshoe hare. J. Wildl. Mgmt. 9(4):290–295.

SIIVONEN, L. 1956. The correlation between the fluctuations of partridge and European hare populations and the climatic conditions of winters in south-west Finland during the last thirty years. Papers Game Research 17:1–30.

STEEL, R. G. D., AND J. H. TORRIE. 1960. Principles and procedures of statistics. McGraw-Hill Book Company, Inc., New York. 481pp.

THOM, H. C. S. 1968. Standard deviation of monthly average temperature. Environmental Data Service Technical Report, EDS-3, U. S. Dept. Commerce, Washington, D. C. 10pp.

WIGHT, H. M., AND C. H. CONAWAY. 1961. Weather influences on the onset of breeding in Missouri cottontails. J. Wildl. Mgmt. 25(1):87–89.

THE INFLUENCE OF HUNTING ON THE POPULATION DYNAMICS OF A WOODLOT GRAY SQUIRREL POPULATION[1]

HENRY S. MOSBY

Abstract: This investigation compared the vital statistics of an exploited gray squirrel (*Sciurus carolinensis*) population in a 17.9-acre woodlot with similar data from an unshot population in a neighboring 7.9-acre woods. Calculations based on trap-retake techniques resulted in population estimates which were smaller than the number of squirrels known, from time-specific data, to be present. Frequency-of-capture estimates appeared unrealistically high. Therefore, the vital statistics and population ratios for the populations in both woodlots included only data from animals actually handled. During this 6-year study, an average of 37.4 percent of the fall population of the experimental area was harvested by hunting and an average of 17.3 percent of the control population was lost to "shock" and trap accidents. The control woodlot supported an average of 5.7 squirrels per acre as compared with 4.5 per acre in the harvested woods but the average number of young per female (r_1) was lower (1.18) in the unshot population than it was for the experimental group (1.53). Composite dynamic life table calculations indicated a slightly higher average annual mortality rate ($m_a = 47.6$ percent) for the exploited population than was observed with the control group ($m_a = 42.4$ percent). The turnover period was longer (7.2 years) for the shot population than was calculated for the control group (6.2 years). The percent immature (j) in the harvested squirrels was 41.3 percent as compared with 35.0 percent for the controls. However, the mean life expectancy ($e_x.^5$) was slightly greater (1.86 years) for the controls as compared with the harvest squirrels (1.60 years) but this difference was significant only at the 0.10 level. Based on the average annual mortality and the average percentage of animals removed from each woodlot, "natural" losses accounted for 25.2 percent of the annual attrition in the control population but only amounted to 10.2 percent in the exploited group. This study suggests that about 40 percent of the fall gray squirrel population may be exploited, using *minimal* (time-specific) population estimates as a basis for calculating removal.

In several states, the gray squirrel is ranked as the game animal hunted by most sportsmen (Redmond 1953, Gale 1954, Florida Game Commission 1962, Uhlig 1956) and in other states it ranks second in popularity only to the cottontail (Sharp 1959:386).

The primary objective of the present investigation was to test the influence of removing various proportions of the fall squirrel population upon the population dynamics. It was assumed that such information would be useful for squirrel-management purposes and, in addition, might be helpful in arriving at a better understand-ing of the impact of hunter-harvest on an important game species.

Two woodlots, separated by open pasture or cultivated fields (Fig. 1), were the areas utilized in the present investigation. These two woodlots were selected on the assumption that there would be minimal movement between woodlots and that, therefore, each woodlot population might be treated as an individual entity. The woodlots, the 7.9-acre North Crumpacker Woods, the control area, and the 17.9-acre Crumpacker Woods, the experimental or exploited area were prime squirrel habitat supporting fall populations that varied from 4 to 7 squirrels per acre. They contained uncut, over-mature oak-hickory hardwoods with diameters up to 50 inches.

Den sites were abundant. All of the Virginia Polytechnic Institute Farm was designated as a research area and no public hunting was permitted; thus, we had con-

[1] Release #68-1 of the Virginia Cooperative Wildlife Research Unit, Virginia Polytechnic Institute, Virginia Commission of Game and Inland Fisheries, Wildlife Management Institute, and U. S. Fish and Wildlife Service, cooperating. This investigation was financed largely by Project S040 of the Virginia Agricultural Experiment Station through the Department of Forestry and Wildlife.

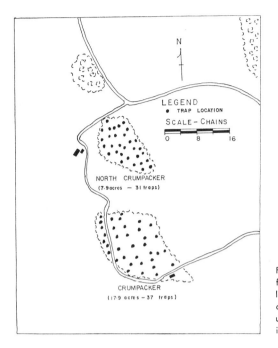

N

LEGEND
● TRAP LOCATION
SCALE – CHAINS
0   8   16

NORTH CRUMPACKER
(7·9 acres — 31 traps)

CRUMPACKER
(17·9 acres – 37 traps)

Fig. 1. The two woodlots are separated by open cultivated fields, minimizing movements between the two squirrel populations. The smaller woodlot (North Crumpacker) was used as the control area and the larger woods (Crumpacker) was used as the exploited area. Permanent trap locations are indicated in each woodlot.

trol over all squirrels removed from these areas.

Squirrels in both the control and experimental woodlots were trapped and tagged at least semiannually beginning in 1952. Similar trapping and marking operations had been undertaken intermittently in these and neighboring woodlots since 1937. The hunting-removal experiment reported in this paper began in the fall of 1954 and continued for 6 years, terminating with the removal of squirrels in the fall of 1959. Semiannual or more frequent trapping was continued in these two woodlots up to the present (1967). Thus population data are available for the period 1952–1966. For purposes of this investigation, the records for all individual year-classes 1952–1966 have been utilized. This was done so that vital facts for the turnover period for each of the six year-classes 1954–1959 would be available.

The influence of hunting was tested by comparing population dynamics data ob-tained from the control population with information taken in an identical manner from the experimental group. The comparisons of the population characteristics for the two groups of squirrels involved (1) changes in density, (2) recruitment rates, (3) mortality-survival, (4) mean life expectancy, and (5) population structural changes.

The writer assumed personal responsibility for the field collection of data for the period 1954–1959 but acknowledges with gratitude the assistance of many graduate students prior to, during, and following this investigational period. Jan E. Riffe assisted in the statistical evaluation of the data.

MATERIALS AND METHODS

The two woodlots used in this study were selected because (1) they afforded excellent squirrel habitat which supported high densities, thus affording populations of practical workable size; (2) each woodlot was isolated from neighboring woods by exten-

204

sive open pasture or cropland; (3) previous live-trapping and other work with the squirrel populations in these two woodlots resulted in the accumulation of considerable background data on each population; and (4) it was possible to keep these areas under constant surveillance. Sex, age, movement, survival, and "census" data were collected by live-trapping in early fall, normally in early October or later, and again in early spring, normally in March or April before the spring litters were out of the nest. Trapping during July and August was done during several years. Squirrels were live-trapped, removed for examination and tagging by means of a cloth-wire funnel, and tagged in the lower leading edge of both ears (#1, model 1005, serially numbered tags available from National Band and Tag Co., Newport, Kentucky). They were then sexed and aged, and the data recorded at the trap site. Also recorded was the date, trap number in which captured, the woodlot, and any other data on the condition of the animal. When first captured, squirrels were sexed by an examination of the external genitalia and the sex was redetermined on each subsequent capture to minimize errors. Accurate aging proved to be difficult for there is no known field technique that does not involve considerable judgment. The more exact X-ray, eye-lens, and baculum-aging procedures were not suited for field application. Therefore, the three criteria used in designating age in the field included (1) weight and body size, which proved to be valid measures for immature individuals; (2) development and condition of the testes and scrotum of males and the mammae of females (Taber 1963: 169, 170); and, for squirrels in winter pelage (3) the fur condition and pelage pattern of the tails (Sharp 1958). Using these criteria, three age categories were designated: immature—less than 6 months of age; sub-

adult—6 to 16 months of age; and adult—over 16 months of age. Immature individuals were the easiest to identify; it was more difficult to distinguish between subadult and adult age-classes. Unfortunately the pelage technique developed by Barrier and Barkalow (1967) was not available at the time of the present investigation.

If trapping was being carried out in the fall of 1955, then an immature individual (less than 6 months of age) captured at that time was assumed to have been born in the spring of 1955; a subadult (6 to 16 months of age) was assumed to be 12 months of age and to have been born in the fall of 1954; all adults (more than 16 months of age) were assumed to be 2 years of age and to have been born in the fall of 1953. This technique of placing individuals in year-classes is likely to underestimate the age (season and year of birth) of adults.

Population estimates were calculated in several ways. Lincoln Index estimates involving trap-retrap data (the first half of the trapping period designated as the precensus period, and the latter half considered as the census period) were made for each trapping endeavor. In the experimental woods, Lincoln Index estimates were calculated using the entire trapping period as the precensus section and the hunting harvest data as the census period. The Schnabel (Krumholtz) procedure (Davis 1963:109 example) also was used in preparing estimates for each trapping effort. The number of squirrels trapped and recaptured was not adequate to calculate sound estimates for many trapping periods. Strandgaard (1967:650), in working with roe deer, concluded that the trap-recapture procedures seldom provide acceptable population estimates unless 50 percent or more of the calculated population was handled. Our experience indicates that this was likely true for squirrels. It was possible to approximate

CONTROL AREA SQUIRREL POPULATION

7.9 Acres

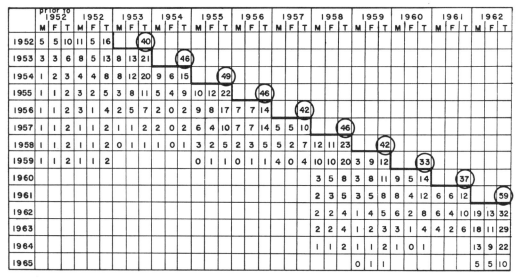

	prior to 1952			1952			1953			1954			1955			1956			1957			1958			1959			1960			1961			1962		
	M	F	T	M	F	T	M	F	T	M	F	T	M	F	T	M	F	T	M	F	T	M	F	T	M	F	T	M	F	T	M	F	T	M	F	T
1952	5	5	10	11	5	16	(40)																													
1953	3	3	6	8	5	13	8	13	21	(46)																										
1954	1	2	3	4	4	8	8	12	20	9	6	15	(49)																							
1955	1	1	2	3	2	5	3	8	11	5	4	9	10	12	22	(46)																				
1956	1	1	2	3	1	4	2	5	7	2	0	2	9	8	17	7	7	14	(42)																	
1957	1	1	2	1	1	2	1	1	2	2	0	2	6	4	10	7	7	14	5	5	10	(46)														
1958	1	1	2	1	1	2	0	1	1	1	0	1	3	2	5	2	3	5	5	2	7	12	11	23	(42)											
1959	1	1	2	1	1	2							0	1	1	0	1	1	4	0	4	10	10	20	3	9	12	(33)								
1960																						3	5	8	3	8	11	9	5	14	(37)					
1961																						2	3	5	3	5	8	8	4	12	6	6	12	(59)		
1962																						2	2	4	1	4	5	6	2	8	6	4	10	19	13	32
1963																						2	2	4	1	2	3	3	1	4	4	2	6	18	11	29
1964																						1	1	2	1	1	2	1	0	1				13	9	22
1965																									0	1	1							5	5	10

Fig. 2. Vital facts for the gray squirrel population in the control area (North Crumpacker) for the years 1952–1962. The encircled figure indicates the annual time-specific population estimate, secured by summing the number of individuals in each age-class present for the given year.

EXPERIMENTAL AREA SQUIRREL POPULATION

17.9 Acres

	prior to 1952			1952			1953			1954			1955			1956			1957			1958			1959			1960			1961			1962		
	M	F	T	M	F	T	M	F	T	M	F	T	M	F	T	M	F	T	M	F	T	M	F	T	M	F	T	M	F	T	M	F	T	M	F	T
1952	19	11	30	15	14	29	(68)																													
1953	14	5	19	11	11	22	17	10	27	(98)																										
1954	8	2	10	9	10	19	17	10	27	23	19	42	(74)																							
1955	2	2	4	3	5	8	8	4	12	11	9	20	16	14	30	(88)																				
1956	1	2	3	0	1	1	6	2	8	3	7	10	12	10	22	19	25	44	(87)																	
1957							1	1	2	1	2	3	8	1	9	14	21	35	22	16	38	(82)														
1958							1	0	1	1	0	1	4	0	4	7	13	20	14	12	26	14	16	30	(57)											
1959													0	3	3	8	5	13	12	10	22	11	8	19	(36)											
1960													0	1	1				5	2	7	5	5	10	10	8	18	(55)								
1961													0	1	1				1	0	1	3	4	7	9	7	16	17	13	30	(43)					
1962													0	1	1				1	0	1	1	1	2	5	3	8	4	8	12	13	6	19			
1963													0	1	1							1	0	1	1	0	1	2	5	7	12	5	17			
1964																						1	0	1	1	0	1	1	3	4	9	1	0			
1965																						1	0	1				0	2	2	1	1	2			

Fig. 3. Vital facts for the gray squirrel population for the exploited area (Crumpacker Woods) for the years 1952–1962. The encircled figures indicate the annual time-specific population estimate, secured by summing the number of individuals in each age-class present for the given year.

Table 1. Comparison of several trap-recapture, frequency-of-capture, and time-specific methods of estimating squirrel populations for 1954, 1955, and 1957. These 3 years were the only periods during the investigation in which about 50 percent of the population was taken in the fall trapping effort.

YEAR	NUMBER OF SQUIRRELS		TRAP-RECAPTURE ESTIMATES			FREQUENCY-OF-CAPTURE ESTIMATE[d]	TIME-SPECIFIC ESTIMATE[e]
	Trapped	Recaptured	Lincoln Index		Cumulative capturesᶜ		
			Retrap[a]	Kill[b]			
Control Population							
1954	38	62	47	—	72	107	46
1955	28	61	38	—	32	126	49
1957	23	34	36	—	33	64	42
Experimental Population							
1954	63	93	102	104	105	222	98
1955	40	61	54	72	63	123	74
1957	41	54	82	57	70	164	87

[a] Calculated by taking first half of trapping period as precensus marking interval, with latter half as the census period.
[b] Calculatd with entire marking period as precensus, and kill data as census interval.
[c] Using cumulative-capture procedure of Krumholtz as illustrated in Davis 1963:109.
[d] Using linear regression method of Edwards and Eberhardt 1967.
[e] Summing totals in each age-class in time-specific vital facts (Figs. 3 and 4).

this rate of capture-recapture in only three fall trapping periods, 1954, 1955, and 1957. The frequency-of-capture technique (Edwards and Eberhardt 1967) was used to estimate the population for the above 3 years; this method of population estimation also appears to require that about 50 percent or more of the population be taken once, and with a 1½–2 times total captures, to provide suitable data (Edwards and Eberhardt 1967:95). Finally, population estimates were tabulated from time-specific data. These population estimates were based on records of squirrels actually handled or known to be present in the population each year (Figs. 2 and 3). Our experience agrees with that of other workers (Edwards and Eberhardt 1967:94, Nixon et al. 1967:99) in that the Lincoln Index and Schnabel procedures tended to underestimate the population (time-specifically determined). Our frequency-of-capture estimates were unrealistically higher than was indicated by time-specific data and extensive field observations (Table 1). Therefore, the time-specific estimates were used as the basis for our examination of the in-

fluence of hunting on the demography of these two populations. It should be emphasized, however, that time-specific data result in *minimal* squirrel-density estimates.

The primary objective of all trapping operations was to capture the maximum number of squirrels. Therefore, the traps were not gridded but were placed where the most captures could be made. Each trap site was located on the map made for each woodlot and the number of the trap site was painted on the bole of the nearest tree. In Crumpacker Woods (the exploited area) there were 37 trap stations in the 17.9 acre woods (2.1 traps per acre); there were 31 trap stations (3.9 traps per acre) in the 7.9 acre control area (North Crumpacker Woods). Thus every squirrel in both woodlots was exposed, in its normal movements, to more than one trap. The degree of bias which may have been introduced owing to the difference in trap density is unknown.

Not all squirrels present in each woodlot were handled each year. It was assumed that if a squirrel was captured in 1955 but not handled again until 1957 that he was also present, but not handled, in 1956.

Likewise, any squirrel not captured for two or more trapping periods was assumed to have disappeared from the population at the mid-point between the date of his last capture and the next trapping period.

The experimental design called for the removal of squirrels only from the experimental woodlot, with no squirrels being taken in the control area. The objective was unattainable in practice owing to the loss of squirrels during trapping operations. Most of these losses were due to "shock," especially in the control woodlot (Guthrie et al. 1967), but a few individuals died as a result of trap-induced wounds.

Movement data, both within and between woodlots, were recorded by denoting the location of the trap each time the individual was captured. Minimum home-range information and between-woods movements were calculated from these data.

The procedures as detailed by Deevey (1947), Barclay (1958), and Quick (1963) were utilized in the construction and interpretation of life tables calculated for each woodlot. Life table analyses were used in examining such population characteristics as average annual mortality rates, survival by age-classes, mean life expectancies, recruitment rates, and turnover periods.

The vital facts assembled during this study are among some of the most detailed data for a wild game population known to the writer but they suffer significant defects. Movements into and out of the investigational woodlots, the arbitrary methods used in designating the year-class of adults, the weakness of all methods of age determination, and the virtual certainty that all individuals in each woodlot were not handled each year are some of the more important sources of bias in these records. Identical techniques of capturing, handling, recording, and calculating population phenomena were employed in both woodlots.

RESULTS

Vital Facts

Figs. 2 and 3 present the vital facts for the turnover periods for all cohorts of squirrels "prior to" 1952 through 1962 for the control and experimental woodlot populations, respectively. These records include only those data secured from individuals actually handled and undoubtedly represent the minimal populations present on each woodlot. The primary purpose of these figures is to present the dynamic (vertically read) and time-specific (horizontally read) information for individual year-classes 1954 through 1959.

Young squirrels normally remain in or near the nest for about 10 weeks (Shorten 1951, Uhlig 1956) and thus are not exposed to ground-placed traps. Therefore, the information shown in Figs. 2 and 3 for each year-class entering the population relates only to those squirrels which were about 3 months of age or older. For convenience in calculations made from these vital facts, all immature squirrels were assumed to be 0.5 year of age.

Population Density

Table 1 presents population estimates calculated by several Lincoln Index procedures, by the frequency-of-recapture technique, and by the time-specific method for the years 1954, 1955, and 1957. These 3 years were the only periods when acceptable quantities of capture and recapture data were obtained. The trap-retrap estimates were generally lower than the minimal estimates indicated by time-specific information in 1955 and 1957. In all 3 years, the frequency-of-capture estimates were unrealistically high. Therefore, the time-specific population estimates, though minimal, were judged by the writer to be the most acceptable density measurements.

Table 2. Trap-retake and time-specific population estimate and number of squirrels removed by year for the control and experimental areas, 1954 through 1959. General mast conditions are noted for each year.

| YEAR | CONTROL POPULATION ESTIMATES | | REMOVED | | EXPERIMENTAL POPULATION ESTIMATES | | REMOVED | | GENERAL MAST CONDITIONS |
	Trap-retrap	Time-specific	No.	%	Trap-retrap	Time-specific	No.	%	
1954 Fall	65	46	15	33	105	98	55	56	Average
1955 Spring	18				40				
1955 Fall	30	49	5	10	63	74	18	24	Poor
1956 Spring	20				45				
1956 Fall	40[a]	46	7	15	60[a]	88	23	26	Poor
1957 Spring	35				35				
1957 Fall	35	42	12	28	70	87	26	30	Good
1958 Spring	28				40				
1958 Fall	40[a]	46	6	13	60[a]	82	31	38	Good
1959 Spring	30				30[a]				
1959 Fall	35[a]	42	2	5	50[a]	57	29	51	Average
Total/Avg.	245	271	7.8	17.3	408	486	30.3	37.4	

[a] Inadequate number of captures and recaptures to provide satisfactory trap-retake population estimate.

The inability to secure satisfactory fall and spring population estimates by the trap-retake techniques made it necessary to reject the estimates of total numbers present in each woodlot as calculated by this procedure. Table 2 presents the trap-retrap estimates, the number of animals removed from the populations, and the total number of squirrels present as indicated by time-specific vital facts (Figs. 2 and 3). The trap-retrap population estimates were consistently lower than the time-specific records indicate except for the fall 1954 period. The information presented in Table 1 shows why little confidence was placed in the population estimates calculated from trap-retrap records. The population figures derived from the time-specific vital facts table, on the other hand, probably are more nearly correct. They undoubtedly are conservative, for field observations and hunting samples indicate that we did not trap and mark every squirrel in these woodlots each year.

During the 6-year period, an average of 37.4 percent (1.69 sq./acre) of the time-specific determined population was removed from the experimental area, primar-

ily by hunting, and 17.8 percent (0.97 sq./acre) of the control woods population was lost, largely as a result of trap-confinement "shock."

Mast conditions were extremely poor in 1956 and 1957 but this fact had little or no measured influence on the average number of young produced or on the total squirrel population in each woodlot. Conversely, the good to excellent mast conditions in 1958 did not result in a population increase in 1959. Agricultural crops, which might serve as supplemental food, were not available in adjacent fields. These observations are in contradiction to the results of other workers (Smith and Barkalow 1967) who report that poor mast years normally result in lowered productivity the succeeding year whereas good mast years show an increase in the number of young produced the following year. Thus, no influence of mast upon population density was detected.

At the initation of our squirrel investigations, general observations indicated that the control and exploited woodlots were comparable gray squirrel habitat because they were of essentially the same forest

209

cover type and age and because each area supported a population of about 5 squirrels per acre in 1954. For the period 1954–1959, the average number of squirrels-per-acre was 4.52 for the experimental area and 5.72 for the control population. This difference in density was highly significant (t test $P < 0.01$). For the 10-year period 1953–1962, the average squirrels-per-acre was 3.84 for the exploited population and 5.57 for the control woods ($P < 0.01$). The results of the population density calculations indicate, therefore, that the control area was more desirable squirrel habitat than was the experimental area, a fact not known at the beginning of this investigation.

It was anticipated that the open area around each of the woodlots would reduce to a minimum the movements of squirrels into and out of the two woodlots. However, the two study areas were separated only by 220 yards of open pasture at their closest point (Fig. 1). Most previous workers agree (Sharp 1959, Flyger 1960) that the minimum home range of the gray squirrel in excellent habitat normally is under 3 acres and the squirrels are fairly sedentary except during infrequent "migratory" movements when Sharp (1959:384) records an exceptional movement of 62 miles.

Intermittent live-trapping has been carried out in many of the woodlots on the V. P. I. Farms since 1937. Records from 1947–1966 are available for a total of 812 tagged squirrels from these wood lots. Out of this total, there were 45 records (5.5 percent) of between-woods movements involving 30 males and 15 females. The average distance traveled between-woods by the males was 2,882 ft (0.55 miles); the females averaged 2,016 ft (0.38 miles). There was no significant difference in distances moved by males and females (t-test, $P > 0.40$).

In the control and exploited woodlots, a total of 296 records are available of individ-

ually tagged squirrels for the period 1954–1959. Out of 25 between-woods movements recorded during the 6-year investigational period, 7 squirrels moved out of the exploited area but 8 squirrels entered the woods from other areas. In the control woods, 7 squirrels left the area and 11 individuals moved into this woods. Six of the 7 squirrels leaving the control area moved into the exploited woods and 5 of the 7 squirrels which left the exploited area took up residence in the control woods. The remaining 3 between-woods movements recorded involved squirrels which left the exploited woods, were captured in adjoining woodlots, but later returned to their home woods. Therefore, the gains and losses in number of individuals resulting from these movements was a gain of one in the hunted area and four in the control woodlot. The sex-age of the individuals involved in these 25 between-woods movements were 15 males and 10 females; 5 immature, 10 subadults, and 10 adults.

If a squirrel left one woodlot but later returned, he was recorded with the population of his original, or home, woodlot. However, if he left his home woodlot and remained in the other investigational woods, he was counted with the population in the second woods. If he left his home woodlot for any area other than the two study areas, he was considered removed (lost) from the home-woodlot population.

Little evidence exists for territoriality in the gray squirrel (except for the female with nestlings) but a social hierarchy (Bakken 1952, Flyger 1955, Taylor 1966) was demonstrated in these two populations (Pack et al. 1967).

In both woodlots, the average minimum home range was less than 2 acres. For example, in the control woods, the average minimum home range for squirrels ranked linearly in the social hierarchy was 1.45

Table 3. Composite life tables for the squirrel population in the control woodlot, 1954 through 1959. Base data presented in Fig. 2.

x	l'_x	d_x	l_x	1000_{qx}	L_x	e_x	
AGE	No. Surviving in Age-Class x	No. Dying in Age Interval per 1000	No. Surviving at Beginning of Age-Class per 1000	Mortality Rate per 1000 at Beginning of Age Interval	Average No. Living Between Two Age Intervals	Mean Expectation of Life Remaining	Age as % Deviation from e_{x_1}
			Composite Dynamic—Both Sexes				
0.5–1	93	204	1000	204	898	1.86	−73
1–2	74	452	796	568	570	1.21	−46
2–3	32	193	344	561	248	1.13	+ 8
3–4	14	97	151	642	103	0.94	61
4–5	5	43	54	796	33	0.72	115
5–6	1	11	11	1000	6	0.50	169
			$m_a = 42.4$	$T = 6.18$			
			Composite Time Specific—Both Sexes				
0.5–1	96	094	1000	094	953	2.33	− 78
1–2	87	489	906	540	662	1.51	− 57
2–3	40	177	417	429	328	1.70	− 14
3–4	23	136	240	567	172	1.59	+29
4–5	10	52	104	500	78	2.02	72
5–6	5	10	52	192	47	2.54	115
6–7	4	00	42	000	42	2.02	158
7–8	4	21	42	500	32	1.02	200
8–9	2	21	21	1000	11	0.50	243
			$m_a = 35.4$	$T = 9.57$			

acres with the more dominant individuals ($P < 0.01$) having the larger home range (Pack et al. 1967). No evidence was secured in this present study which would suggest that the normal daily movements or behavioral characteristics influenced the population dynamics of these two squirrel populations. A possible, but *unproven*, exception to this statement might be higher losses due to "shock" at higher per acre population densities as observed in the control woods.

Recruitment—Mortality

This investigation was concerned primarily with the determination of general population characteristics and the influence of hunter-harvest on these properties. Therefore, it seemed desirable to examine composite (entire 6-year period) life tables rather than individual year-class tables. Further, dynamic data seemed more meaningful, other than for calculating recruitment rates, than did time-specific information. For this reason, dynamic and composite life table characteristics will be emphasized. The vital facts presented in Figs. 2 and 3 may be cast into both dynamic (vertically read) and time-specific (horizontally read) life tables for each individual year-class.

Tables 3 and 4 present composite dynamic and time-specific life tables, including both sexes, for the control and exploited squirrel populations, respectively. It should be emphasized that these calculations incorporate all mortality including death by trap loss, hunter removal, as well as "nat-

Table 4. Composite life tables for the squirrel population in the exploited woodlot, 1954 through 1959. Base data present in Fig 3.

x	l'_x	d_x	l_x	1000_{q_x}	L_x	e_x	x'
AGE	NO. SURVIVING IN AGE-CLASS PER 1000 x	NO. DYING IN AGE INTERVAL PER 1000	NO. SURVIVING AT BEGINNING OF AGE-CLASS PER 1000	MORTALITY RATE PER 1000 AT BEGINNING OF AGE INTERVAL	AVERAGE NO. LIVING BETWEEN TWO AGE INTERVALS	MEAN EXPECTATION OF LIFE REMAINING	AGE AS % DEVIATION FROM e_{x_1}
Composite Dynamic—Both Sexes							
0.5–1	203	335	1000	335	833	1.60	− 69
1–2	135	340	665	511	495	1.15	− 38
2–3	66	261	325	803	195	0.83	+25
3–4	13	44	64	688	41	1.20	88
4–5	4	10	20	500	15	1.80	150
5–6	2	000	10	000	10	2.10	213
6–7	2	5	10	500	8	1.10	275
7–8	1	5	5	1000	3	0.50	338
		$m_a = 47.6$		$T = 7.20$			
Composite Time Specific—Both Sexes							
0.5–1	203	251	1000	251	875	1.89	− 74
1–2	152	340	749	454	579	1.36	− 47
2–3	83	232	409	567	293	1.08	+ 6
3–4	36	138	177	780	108	0.84	58
4–5	8	19	39	487	30	1.03	111
5–6	4	20	20	1000	10	0.50	164
		$m = 41.8$		$T = 6.55$			

ural" mortality. As indicated previously, movements into and out of these populations also influenced these calculations.

Recruitment.—Most American investigators have found that the average litter size for the gray squirrel varies from 2.25 to 3.0, with summer litter size averaging slightly higher than spring litters (Hibbard 1935). In England, Shorten (1951:441) reports the average of 148 spring litters as 2.50 and for 55 autumn litters, the average was 3.23.

Redmond (1953:383) expressed the opinion that Mississippi gray squirrels averaged 1.6 litters per year but other investigators (Donohoe 1965, Uhlig 1956) think that the average number of litters per female per year is closer to one. Information presented in Table 5 suggests that the squirrels in the two woodlot populations probably average

closer to one litter per year. These data do not refer to litter size, of course, but include only young squirrels which survived to approximately 0.5 year of age, were feeding on the ground and thereby were exposed to the live-traps. If these two squirrel populations did average more than one litter per year, the mortality from birth to 0.5 year of age was much higher than similar mortality calculations reported by other investigators.

Robinson and Cowan (1954:278) found the average number of young-per-female to be 1.6. Donohoe (1965) records an average of 2.07 immature-per-adult-female from hunter-harvest samples for five game management regions in Ohio. The information shown in Table 5 suggests that there is considerable variation between years as well as between woodlot populations. The range in the immature: adult female ratio (r_i)

Table 5. Immature : adult female ratio, percentage of immatures, and time-specific populations of squirrels on the control and experimental woodlots, 1953–1962.

YEAR	CONTROL WOODS			EXPERIMENTAL WOODS		
	Immature: Adult Female Ratio (r_i)	Percentage of Immature (j)	Time-specific Population (P)	Immature: Adult Female Ratio (r_i)	Percentage of Immature (j)	Time-specific Population (P)
1953	2.625	52.5	40	1.687	65.8	68
1954	0.833	32.6	46	1.909	42.8	98
1955	1.467	44.8	49	1.500	40.5	74
1956	0.933	30.4	46	2.000	50.0	88
1957	0.714	23.8	42	1.520	43.7	87
1958	2.300	50.0	46	1.200	37.5	82
1959	0.857	28.6	42	1.056	33.3	57
1960	1.075	42.5	33	2.250	50.0	36
1961	1.000	32.4	37	2.500	54.5	55
1962	2.666	54.2	59	1.461	45.2	43
$\bar{x}_{10}$	1.336	38.2	44	1.646	46.3	69
$\bar{x}_6$	1.184	35.0	45	1.530	41.3	81

was from 0.71 to 2.60. The 6-year average was 1.53 young-per-adult-female for the exploited woodlot population and 1.18 for the control area. These ratios were not significantly different between populations (t-test, $P > 0.30$).

The attained recruitment rate for an animal population often is indicated, in addition to r_i, by the percentage of immature individuals in the population (j). The percentage of immatures in these two populations varied, for the 6-year period, from 24 percent to a high of 50 percent. The average value of j was 35 percent for the control area and 41 percent for the exploited woods. These percentages are lower than the average 47 percent reported for Ohio (Donohoe 1965:78). Both Uhlig (1956) in West Virginia and Allen (1943) in Michigan state that 60 percent or more of a thriving gray squirrel population should be composed of immature individuals.

Intuitive reasoning suggests that both r_i and j might be directly correlated to the total animal population from which these ratios are derived for any given year. A

simple correlation test was made between r_i and the annual population for the control woodlot. The correlation, if any, between these two statistics was very weak ($r = 0.46$). The results of this investigation suggest, therefore, that values for r_i and j may not be used to indicate directly the size of the animal population from which they are derived.

Mortality—Survival.—Petrides (1949) has suggested that the turnover period, the interval required for complete replacement of a cohort by its progeny, be calculated as the time required for a population of 100 to be reduced to 0.5, which would be a fractional individual. When the theoretical population is raised to a cohort of 1,000, it seemed reasonable to calculate the turnover period as that time when the population is reduced to 9 (l_x column of life table calculations) since this would constitute a fraction of one individual. This method has been employed in the calculations of the turnover period (T_9) in this investigation.

Survival is the complement of mortality. The average survival rates (l_x values from

Table 6. Average annual mortality rate, turnover period, and mean life expectancy calculated from composite dynamic data for the gray squirrel populations of the control and experimental areas, 1954 through 1959.

Area	Average Annual Mortality Rate (m_a)	Turn-over Period—Years (T_g)	Mean Life Expectancy—Years ($e_x^{0.5}$)	Significance of Difference in Survival (l_x)
Both Sexes				
Control	42.4	6.2	1.86	$P < 0.10$
Experimental	47.6	7.2	1.60	
Males Only				
Control	43.1	4.6	1.82	$P < 0.30$
Experimental	47.7	5.1	1.60	
Females Only				
Control	41.9	6.5	1.89	$P < 0.20$
Experimental	47.8	8.1	1.60	

Table 7. Calculation of the average "natural" losses which occurred in the exploited and control gray squirrel populations during the 6-year period 1954–1959.

Population	Average Annual Mortality (m_a—%)	Removed by Hunting (%)	Removed by Trap Loss (%)	"Natural" Loss (%)
Control population	42.4		17.3	25.2
Exploited population	47.6	37.4		10.2

Tables 3 and 4) for the control and exploited populations for the 6-year investigational period are presented in Fig. 4. This figure indicates that the survival of the control population was slightly higher for the first 6 years of life than was true for the exploited population. However, the turnover period for the control group was 6.2 years as compared with 7.2 for the exploited population. Differences between populations in survival of "both sexes" were marginally significant (t-test; $0.10 < P < 0.05$). Differences for "males only" and "females only" were not significant ($P > 0.30$ and $0.20 < P < 0.10$, respectively).

Based on composite dynamic life table data, the average annual mortality rate ($ma = \Sigma d_x/\Sigma l_x$) for the 6-year investigational period was 42.4 percent for the control population and 47.6 percent for the exploited gray squirrel population (Table 6). Both of these average statistics incorporate all mortality, including trap losses, hunting removal, and "natural" losses. Table 7 summarizes the average annual mortality rate, the percentage removed by hunting and trap losses, and the resultant calculation of the "natural" loss which must

have occurred in each squirrel population. Using these average removal and mortality calculations, natural losses accounted for 25.2 percent of the average annual mortality for the control population and only 10.2 percent for the exploited population. These calculations suggest that, within limits which are below the average annual mortality rate, hunting removed a proportion (37.4 percent) of the annual population recruitment that would have been lost to "natural" causes.

The m_a calculations discussed above relate only to those squirrels about 0.5 year of age or older. The trees in both woodlots were over-mature hardwoods, with numerous den sites which were difficult to reach and almost impossible to examine. Therefore, in this investigation no effort was made to collect data on litter size or on survival-mortality of young squirrels from birth to 0.5 year. Assuming an average litter size of 2.72 (Uhlig 1956) and the validity of the r_i values calculated for both populations during the investigational period, these data suggest that the survival from birth to 0.5 year of age was about 56 percent for the exploited population and only 43 percent for the control woodlot population.

The dynamic life table calculated mean life expectancy (e_x column, Tables 3 and 4) of squirrels old enough to be taken in ground-placed traps was 1.86 years in the control population and 1.60 years in the

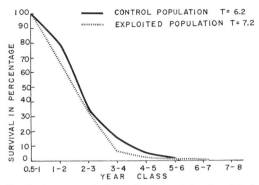

Fig. 4. Average survival rates for the control and exploited woodlot gray squirrel populations, 1954–1959.

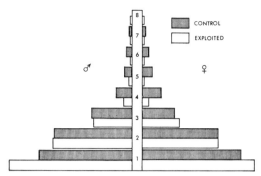

Fig. 5. Sex-age pyramid based on composite time-specific data, 1954–1959, for the control and exploited gray squirrel populations.

hunted group. Mean life expectancy as calculated by Burkitt's formula ($e_x = 2-m_a/2m_a$) resulted in identical mean life expectancies as those derived from life table analysis (Davis 1960:345).

Population Structure

Exploitation, of course, may change both the numerical and structural status of a population. Sex-age pyramids have been employed (Allee et al. 1955:281) to indicate graphically the gross recruitment rate as well as the crude sex-age structure of a given wild animal population. Fig. 5 represents the sex-age structure for both the control and exploited populations based on composite dynamic vital facts (Fig. 2 and 3) for the 6-year investigational period. The average sex ratios were 48.9:51.1 for the control area and 51.6:48.4 for the exploited population. No difference of significance is apparent in the sex ratios for the several year-classes; the small difference observed in the average sex ratios could be due to chance.

The general shape of the age pyramid has been used to indicate crudely the recruitment and subsequent survival, by sex, attained by a given population (Alexander 1958). Exploitation of a wild game population frequently may lower the height

(age) of the pyramid by removing the older age group and may widen the base due to increased recruitment.

Fig. 5 suggests that exploitation of the experimental population did increase slightly the width of the base of the age pyramid. The fortuitous survival of several individuals in both populations extended the height (age) of both pyramids. As pointed out previously, however, the difference in number of young produced per adult female in these two woodlots was not statistically significant. Therefore, the apparent graphic difference between the sex-age pyramids for these two populations may be more apparent than real.

SUMMARY

An average of 37.4 percent of the squirrels were removed from the exploited population during the 6-year study period. The percentage of the population removed each year varied from a high of 56 percent to a low of 24 percent.

The removal of about 38 percent of the exploited population resulted, on the *average*, in a slightly greater r_i, j, m_a, and T_9 in the exploited group of squirrels. The differences in these population measurements between the exploited and control populations, however, were not statistically

215

significant. Exploitation did widen the base slightly of the sex-age pyramid and did decrease somewhat the average survival.

A plot of the percentage of the population removed in hunting against the following year's population indicated an inverse relationship, which suggests that hunting might have depressed the population in the exploited woodlot. However, the population in both the control and hunted woods was below normal for 2 years following the termination of the experiment in the fall of 1959. The significance of the apparent depression by hunting of the following year's population is unknown.

The writer concludes, based on time-specific vital facts, that the removal by hunting of about 38 percent of the time-specific determined squirrel population did not adversely affect recruitment in the exploited population, had no significant influence on the average annual mortality rate, and probably removed a segment of the population that would normally be lost to "natural losses." The magnitude of the percentage removed (38 percent) must be accepted with caution, however, as the time-specific population calculations are conservative estimates. If they were appreciably lower than the true populations, then the removal percentage would be correspondingly lower.

LITERATURE CITED

ALEXANDER, M. M. 1958. The place of aging in wildlife management. Am. Scientist 46(2): 123–137.

ALLEE, W. C., A. E. EMERSON. O. PARK, T. PARK, AND K. P. SCHMIDT. 1955. Principles of Animal Ecology. W. B. Saunders Co., Philadelphia. 837pp.

ALLEN, D. L. 1943. Michigan Fox Squirrel Management. Michigan Dept. Conserv., Lansing. 404pp.

BAKKEN, A. 1952. Interrelationships of *Sciurus carolinensis* (Gmelin) and *Sciurus niger* (Linnaeus) in mixed populations. Ph.D. Thesis. Univ. of Wisconsin, Madison. 188pp.

BARCLAY, G. W. 1958. Techniques of Population Analysis. John Wiley & Sons, Inc., New York. 311pp.

BARKALOW, F. S., JR. 1967. A record gray squirrel litter. J. Mammal. 48(1):141.

BARRIER, M. J., AND F. S. BARKALOW, JR. 1967. A rapid technique for aging gray squirrels in winter pelage. J. Wildl. Mgmt. 31(4):715–719.

DAVIS, D. E. 1960. A chart for estimation of life expectancy. J. Wildl. Mgmt. 24(3):344–348.

———. 1963. Estimating the numbers of game populations. Pp. 89–118. *In* H. S. Mosby (Editor), Wildlife Investigational Techniques. The Wildlife Society, Washington. 419pp.

DEEVEY, E. S., JR. 1947. Life tables for natural populations of animals. Quart. Rev. Biol. 22: 283–314.

DONOHOE, R. W. 1965. Squirrel harvest and population studies in Ohio. Pp. 65–93. *In* K. W. Laub (Editor), Game Research in Ohio. Vol. 3. Ohio Dept. Nat. Resources, Columbus. 220pp.

EDWARDS, W. R., AND L. EBERHARDT. 1967. Estimating cottontail abundance from livetrapping data. J. Wildl. Mgmt. 31(1):87–96.

FLORIDA GAME AND FRESH WATER FISH COMMISSION. 1962. Florida squirrels. #Pl.-16. Tallahassee. 6pp.

FLYGER, V. F. 1955. Implications of social behavior in gray squirrel management. Trans. 20th Am. Wildl. Conf. Pp. 381–389.

———. 1960. Movements and home range of the gray squirrel *Sciurus carolinensis* in two Maryland woodlots. Ecol. 41(2):365–369.

GALE, L. R. 1954. The effect of season changes on hunting effort and game kill. Proc. Annual Conf. Southeastern Game and Fish Commissioners 7:117–120.

GUTHRIE, D. R., J. C. OSBORNE, AND H. S. MOSBY. 1967. Physiological changes associated with shock in confined gray squirrels. J. Wildl. Mgmt. 31(1):102–108.

HIBBARD, C. W. 1935. Breeding seasons of gray squirrel and flying squirrel. J. Mammal. 16(4):325–326.

NIXON, C. M., W. R. EDWARDS, AND L. EBERHARDT. 1967. Estimating squirrel abundance from livetrapping data. J. Wildl. Mgmt. 31(1):96–101.

PACK, J. C., H. S. MOSBY, AND P. B. SIEGEL. 1967. Influence of social hierarchy on gray squirrel behavior. J. Wildl. Mgmt. 31(4):720–728.

PETRIDES, G. A. 1949. Viewpoints on the analysis of open season sex and age ratios. Trans. 14th N. Am. Wildl. Conf. Pp. 391–410.

QUICK, H. F. 1963. Animal population analysis. Pp. 190–228. *In* H. S. Mosby (Editor), Wildlife Investigational Techniques. The Wildlife Society, Washington. 419pp.

REDMOND, H. R. 1953. Analysis of gray squirrel

breeding studies and their relation to hunting season, gunning pressure, and habitat conditions. Trans. 18th N. Am. Wildl. Conf. Pp. 378–389.

Robinson, D. J., and I. McT. Cowan. 1954. An introduced population of the gray squirrel (*Sciurus carolinensis* Gmelin) in British Columbia. Canadian J. Zool. 32(3):261–282.

Sharp, W. M. 1958. Aging gray squirrels by use of tail-pelage characteristics. J. Wildl. Mgmt. 22(1):29–34.

———. 1959. A commentary on the behavior of free-running gray squirrels. Pp. 382–387. *In* V. Flyger (Editor), Symp. on the Gray Squirrel. Contrib. 162. Maryland Dept. Research and Education. Annapolis.

Shorten, Monica. 1951. Some aspects of the biology of the gray squirrel (*Sciurus carolinensis*) in Great Britain. Proc. Zool. Soc. London. 121:427–459.

Smith, N. B., and F. S. Barkalow, Jr. 1967. Precocious breeding in the gray squirrel. J. Mammal. 48(2):328–330.

Strandgaard, H. 1967. Reliability of the Petersen Method tested on a roe-deer population. J. Wildl. Mgmt. 31(4):643–651.

Taber, R. D. 1963. Criteria of sex and age. Pp. 119–189. *In* H. S. Mosby (Editor), Wildlife Investigational Techniques. The Wildlife Society, Washington. 419pp.

Taylor, J. C. 1966. Home range and agonistic behaviour in the grey squirrel. Pp. 229–235. *In* P. A. Jewell and Caroline Loizos (Editors), Play, Exploration and Territory in Mammals. Academic Press, New York. 280pp. (Symp. Zool. Soc. London, No. 18).

Uhlig, H. G. 1956. The gray squirrel in West Virginia. Conserv. Comm. West Virginia. Div. Game Mgmt. Bull. 3, Charleston, 83pp.

Reproduced from the *Journal of Wildlife Management* 33:59–73, 1969, with permission of The Wildlife Society.
[Fig. 2 in original article has been omitted and figures renumbered.]

INFLUENCE OF COYOTE PREDATION ON BLACK-TAILED JACKRABBIT POPULATIONS IN UTAH

FREDERIC H. WAGNER
L. CHARLES STODDART

Abstract: This report presents data pointing to the possible influence of coyote (*Canis latrans*) predation on the latter years of decline and first 3 years of increase in a population of black-tailed jackrabbits (*Lepus californicus*) in northern Utah from 1962 to 1970. The study was conducted in the southern half of Curlew Valley, a 1,200-square-mile desert area dominated by sagebrush vegetation. The density index for jackrabbits in fall in Curlew Valley increased from 40 in 1962 to 61 in 1963, declined to 21 in 1967, and increased again to 185 in 1970. Eighty-five percent of the observed variation in the annual changes in density can be explained by the observed changes in October-to-October mortality rates of adults and by the birth-to-October mortality rates of juveniles. Mortality rates, calculated on a monthly basis, have been quite similar within years among the three life-history stages—juveniles from birth to October, adults from October to March, and adults from March to October—perhaps due to a common mortality factor operative throughout the year. These rates have undergone similar year-to-year variation, also possibly due to a common, extrinsic mortality source such as predation. Mortality rates have been correlated with coyote:rabbit ratios in the area. These correlations, plus extrapolations of the regression lines to zero coyote predation, suggest that coyote predation has been a major source of rabbit mortality from 1962 to 1970. This hypothesis is supported by telemetry data and speculative estimates on the proportion of jackrabbits taken by coyotes. The data indicate that 69 percent of the observed variation in rabbit numbers is associated with variation in the coyote:rabbit ratio. Accordingly, we postulate that coyote predation played an important role in the jackrabbit population trends from 1962 to 1970: hastening, if not primarily causing, the decline from 1963 to 1967 by its impact, and largely, or in part, permitting the increase in rabbits in 1968–70 by its relaxation. In the process, predation pressure on rabbits eased as both populations declined, because the coyotes declined more rapidly (coyote density decreased 87 percent, rabbit density 66 percent). This pattern may have followed a classical, Lotka–Volterra predator–prey oscillation during the studied phase of population change. We surmise that the Lotka–Volterra pattern will not hold for the initial population decline.

The objective of this report is to present data gathered from 1962 to 1970 in northern Utah and southern Idaho—data that provide evidence on the possible influence of coyote predation on black-tailed jackrabbit population trends during this period. Jackrabbit populations in this region fluctuate sharply through what local residents sometimes refer to as a 7-year *cycle*. However, there are no critical, long-term data (spanning several decades) from which one can make judgments about the regularity or geographic synchrony of these fluctuations. The period of study herein reported witnessed the latter 4 or 5 years of a population decline (1962 to 1967) and 3 successive years of population increase. Subjective observations by local residents in the region place the last period of high population density approximately during the years

1958–60. Thus, this study was initiated in about the second or third year of a protracted period of decline.

Furthermore, the trends observed in our study area appear, again largely on the basis of subjective reports, to have been paralleled by jackrabbit populations over a broad area of southern Idaho, western Utah, and northern Nevada. French et al. (1965) observed a population *high* in southeastern Idaho in 1959. Synchrony has not been perfect, however, for we observed populations, which were 1 or 2 years out of phase with each other, in intermountain valleys in this region.

The tentative hypotheses that we propose must relate only to the latter period of decline and to the first years of recovery, because our research was confined to this period. The relationships and the influential factors probably are different in the later years of increase and the initial years of decline. Hence, additional years of data are needed to disclose the processes under way in these unstudied periods of change and, in general, to test the hypotheses herein proposed.

Many individuals helped in these studies, including the crews of students who conducted the drive counts on the study area and those who aided in population collections and telemetry. C. R. Baird, H. G. Goulden, Betty L. Gross, D. Martinsen, R. A. Stefanski, and J. E. B. Stuart all served as laboratory or field technicians, or both.

We acknowledge the financial support of the Environmental Sciences Branch, Division of Biology and Medicine of the U. S. Atomic Energy Commission through Contract No. AT(11-1)-1329. We also acknowledge financial aid of National Institutes of Health Predoctoral Fellowship 5FL GM 20803-02, and the Utah State University Research Council and Ecology Center. The coyote and raptor studies were supported by the Research Divison of the U. S. Bureau of Sport Fisheries and Wildlife and by the National Science Foundation Undergraduate Research Participation Program (Project GY–6131, 1969), respectively.

METHODS

Study Area

Our studies were conducted in Curlew Valley, an intermountain basin of roughly 1,200 square miles (Clark 1972). The Utah–Idaho boundary divides the valley into approximately equal north–south halves. The jackrabbit study was conducted in the Utah portion of the valley, from which monthly collections of 50–150 animals were taken. Population censuses were made in 350 square miles of the total (Clark 1972, Fig. 1).

Climate, vegetation, and topography have been described in detail by Rusch (1965) and Gross (1967). Vegetation and climate patterns are summarized by Clark (1972), who also showed the area of overlap between the coyote and jackrabbit study areas.

Census Methods

The two census methods used for jackrabbits were described and analyzed in detail by Gross (1967) and Gross et al. (1972). In brief, the first was a network of 1-mile transects, distributed at random through the 350-square-mile area, and traversed by an observer on foot, once in March and once in October of each year. The number of transects declined from the original 78 in 1962 to 72 in the latter years of study because of advancing cultivation in the valley. All rabbits flushed on the transects were counted and the results expressed on a purely relative index basis as rabbits per lineal mile of transect.

A second census method consisted of

systematic drives by crews of students on 1 square mile in the middle of the rabbit study area, once in March and once in October. The purpose was to obtain estimates of rabbit numbers on this area. In addition, four 1-mile transects were run in and near the square mile on the mornings prior to the drives, to develop a regression relating relative transect results to actual densities on the area. Strictly speaking, the regression is applicable only to vegetative cover structurally like that of the square mile; however, this area was chosen because its vegetation was similar to that over much of the valley. Hence we believe the regression can be used with the results of counts on transects to provide crude estimates of actual numbers over the valley.

Census methods for coyotes have been described by Clark (1972).

Mortality Estimates

The methods of estimating jackrabbit mortality rates were described in detail by Gross (1967). In brief, postnatal mortality estimates at three stages of the life history were possible:

1. October-to-March mortality of the entire population was measured by comparing October and March censuses.

2. March-to-October mortality of adults (all animals become adults on January 1 by our criteria) was measured by comparing March and October censuses and by deducting the proportion of juveniles in the fall population from the October census to allow a March-to-October comparison of adults in the censuses. Fall age composition was determined by random samples of 200–300 animals in September and October, collected at night with spotlight and shotgun from the 350-square-mile area.

3. Birth-to-October mortality of young was measured by estimating the number of young born per lineal mile of transect as

described in the following paragraph and comparing this number with the number of young counted in October. The number of young counted in October was determined from the October censuses and the percentage of young in these censuses as disclosed by the September and October collections.

The number of young born per transect mile was derived in several steps:

1. Adult female mortality was assumed to be constant (on a monthly basis) between March and October, in the absence of any evidence to the contrary. The March census was, therefore, halved (assuming a 50:50 sex ratio) to provide an estimate of female numbers and reduced by a constant monthly rate derived from the March-to-October mortality estimate for the year in question. The monthly winter mortality rate was assumed to apply to the month of February, and the March female population was appropriately increased to estimate February numbers. In this way, we estimated numbers of female breeders per mile of transect for each month of the breeding season.

2. Adult females were collected monthly during the breeding season to determine the extent and timing of their breeding effort. Ages of fetuses were determined by criteria only slightly modified from those of Bookhout (1964) for the snowshoe hare (*Lepus americanus*). The dates of birth of the fetuses were projected accordingly.

3. The products of the numbers of adult females present per month and their reproductive output per month provided monthly estimates of the number of young born per mile of transect. Summing these monthly values for the year provided estimates of the total number of young produced per transect mile per year. Summer and fall juveniles were distinguished from adults by unpublished eye lens–weight criteria.

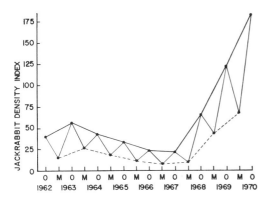

Fig. 1. October and March jackrabbit population trends in Curlew Valley based on population indices.

RESULTS

Role of Mortality in Jackrabbit Population Changes

Jackrabbit Population Changes from 1962 to 1970.—The population trends shown by semiannual censuses (Fig. 1) indicate an increase between the autumns of 1962 and 1963, a continuous decline thereafter from 1963 through 1967, and increases in 1968, 1969, and 1970. Since general, subjective reports of observers in this region place the last high-density population approximately in late 1959 or early 1960, we assume that the increase in 1963 was a temporary reversal in an otherwise continuous 1960 to 1967 population decline. The population in 1963 was substantially (59 percent) above that of 1962, but its level was still relatively low in comparison with our measured values in 1969 and 1970. It is likely that a *high* involves densities that are higher than those of 1969–70. Thus, we consider 1963 to have been one of a series of low years, dating at

Observations on the magnitude, timing, and apparent causes of mortality between September 1967 and January 1970 were studied by using radiotelemetry as described by Stoddart (1970).

least as far back as 1962 and extending as late as 1967.

Jackrabbit Mortality Rates.—Mortality rates estimated for the three life-history stages described above and shown in Table 1 have been calculated in two ways. First, the percentage of animals alive at the beginning of each time interval that die during the interval is shown in the first of the two columns for each life-history stage. Thus, the 8-year mean of the October-to-March mortality of the entire population was 56 percent of animals alive in October. The 8-year mean of March-to-October adult mortality was 57 percent, and the 8-year mean of birth-to-October juvenile mortality was 58 percent.

These three seasonal values are not directly comparable, however, because each represents a time interval different in length from the others. The March-to-October adult mortality occurs over a 7-month period and the October-to-March population mortality over a 5-month period. The birth-to-October juvenile mortality covers, on the average, a period intermediate between the summer-adult and winter mortality periods. In most years, jackrabbits in this area produce four synchronous and immediately consecutive litters (Stoddart 1972). The first is born in mid- or late February, the last in early July. May 1 represents an approximate midpoint of the litter season, and the period from this date to the October censuses encompasses roughly 6 months.

The three seasonal mortality estimates can be made comparable by two different means. The first is by converting them to instantaneous rates (Ricker 1958:24–25) and comparing these. The other, as was done for the second columns of Table 1, is to divide the period over which the seasonal figure is estimated by the number of months in the period—5, 7, and 6, respectively, in

Table 1. Jackrabbit mortality rates for different life-history stages by years, 1962–71.[a]

Year	PERCENTAGE OF MORTALITY						
	Total Population		Adults		Juveniles		Annual
	Oct.–Mar.	Monthly[b]	Mar.–Oct.	Monthly[b]	Birth–Oct.	Monthly	Oct.–Oct.[c]
1962–63	65	19					
1963			70	16	22	4	89
1963–64	57	16					
1964			87	25	69	18	94
1964–65	58	16					
1965			74	18	69	18	89
1965–66	65	19					
1966			70	16	67	17	89
1966–67	69	21					
1967			65	14	67	17	89
1967–68	56	15					
1968			9	1	38	8	60
1968–69	33	8					
1969			60	12	61	15	73
1969–70	46	12					
1970			23	4	68	17	58
Mean	56	16	57	13	58	14	80

[a] These values vary slightly, for the periods concerned, from those reported by Stoddart (1970) because of recent reanalyses and refinement of the census technique reported by Stoddart (1972).

[b] See text for derivation of monthly values.

[c] This value is based on the October–March total population value plus the following March–October adult loss. The two values are combined with Thompson's (1928) equation $M = a + (1 - a)b$ where M is the value for the entire year and a and b are the rates for the two subintervals of the year.

Table 1. We then used the method of Thompson (1928, 1955), who showed that mortality rates for subintervals of a longer period could not be added to provide the rate for the entire period. Rather, the rate for the period is given by the equation

$$M = a + (1 - a)b + (1 - a)(1 - b)c + (1 - a)(1 - b)(1 - c)d$$

where M is the rate for the period, and a, b, c, and d are the fractions of the population alive at the beginning of each subinterval that die during that subinterval. If the rates for the subintervals are the same (a, b, c, and d are equal), and the subintervals are of equal length, the equation can be simplified and the notation altered to give

$$M = 1 - (1 - m)^n$$

where M is again the mortality rate for the period, m the rate for each subinterval, and n the number of intervals (months, in this case). We calculated monthly rates for the three time periods in Table 1 by this method by assuming that the mortality was constant over the total time periods.

Two generalizations about these rates merit attention. First, the adult and juvenile mortality rates in the warm season appear very similar. There is some year-to-year divergence, but the two monthly means for the 8-year period (13 and 14 percent per month) are essentially the same. The mean monthly rate for the entire population during the October-to-March period (16 percent) is not statistically different from the other two.

The second generalization is that these three sets of mortality rates have undergone approximately parallel year-to-year variations during the period of study. This is best shown by correlating the three sets of seasonal rates with one another (Fig. 2). Summer-adult and subsequent overwinter

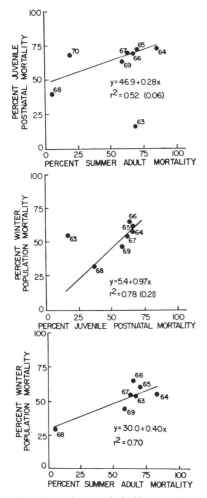

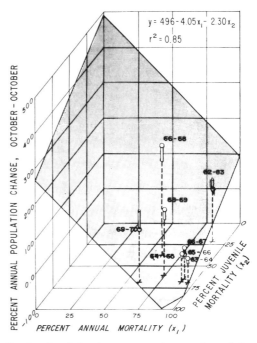

Fig. 3. Correlation between annual rates of population change and the annual and postnatal mortality rates. The relationship is significant ($P < 0.05$).

Fig. 2. Correlations between jackrabbit mortality rates at different stages of the life history. The values are from Table 1. The lower correlation is significant at the 0.05 probability level. The middle and upper correlations are significant at the 0.10 and 0.05 levels, respectively, without the 1963 values; but neither is significant with the 1963 included. In the latter two cases the r^2 values in parentheses are those for which the 1963 values are included; the others are calculated without 1963.

mortality are significantly correlated ($P < 0.05$). Adult and juvenile mortality in summer are not significantly correlated. But without the 1963 value, which we suspect is aberrant, the relationship approaches significance ($0.10 > P > 0.05$). The juvenile losses in summer and in subsequent winter

are not significantly correlated when the 1963 value is included but attain significance ($P < 0.05$) with the 1963 value excluded. The overall impression, however, seems to be that the two summer and the winter mortality rates followed similar year-to-year variations—relatively high in the first 5 years of study, lower in the latter 3.

Influence of Mortality Rates on Jackrabbit Population Trends.—Gross et al. (1972), at the end of their first 4 years of study, reported that the population changes observed during that period were largely due to annual variations in mortality, the reproductive rate having remained essentially constant during the same time. Since that time, the same generalization has continued to hold. Thus, a three-dimensional test (Fig. 3) of annual rates of population change against October-to-October annual mortality rates and postnatal juvenile rates produces a significant correlation ($P <$ 0.05) and an r^2 value of 0.85. This implies that 85 percent of the variation in population change has been associated with variations in the mortality rate during this period. The October-to-October mortality (Table 1) is derived by combining the overwinter population mortality for any given year with the ensuing adult loss in summer, and by using Thompson's (1928) equation $M = a + (1-a)b$ where M is the annual rate and a and b the rates for the successive sub-intervals.

Influence of Coyote Predation on Jackrabbit Populations

Correlations Between Coyote Density and Rabbit Mortality.—Clark (1972) presented density indices of coyote populations for the period 1963 to 1970. These may be correlated directly with jackrabbit mortality rates, except that it seems desirable to plot mortality as a function of the ratio of coyotes to rabbits. One can conceive of a substantial coyote population, which, because the rabbit density is so extremely high by comparison, cannot make significant inroads into rabbit numbers. The result would be a high coyote density associated with low rates of predation.

Annual indices of coyote populations (Clark 1972) were divided by fall indices of jackrabbit populations (Fig. 1) of the same year. The three sets of jackrabbit mortality rates (Table 1) were then plotted as functions of these coyote:rabbit ratios (Fig. 4).

All of these plots suggest a positive relationship. Since the Y values for each of the three functions cannot exceed 100 percent, some form of curvilinear relationship probably exists in each case. However, the data were few at this stage of the study, and we used the simplest equations that appeared to fit the points reasonably well. In the case

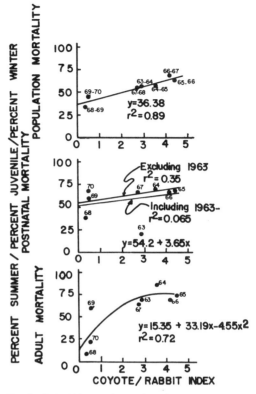

Fig. 4. Jackrabbit mortality rates at three life-history stages plotted as functions of the coyote:rabbit index (see text for derivation). The lower relationship is highly significant ($P <$ 0.01) and the upper relationship is significant ($P <$ 0.05). The middle test is significant ($P <$ 0.10) without the 1963 value but short of significance with 1963 included. Coyote data are from Clark (1972).

of the adult mortality in summer, the data appear well represented by the parabolic equation $Y = a + bX + cX^2$. In the other two cases, a straight line appears to give a good preliminary fit.

The relationship of coyote population indices with the adult mortality in summer was highly significant ($P < 0.01$), and that with the fall-to-spring mortality was significant ($P < 0.05$). The postnatal relationship was not significant but when tested without the 1963 value approached significance ($P < 0.10$).

Radiotelemetry Evidence.—Stoddart

(1970) followed 75 jackrabbits telemetrically between October 1967 and October 1969. The estimated mean semiannual mortality rate of telemetered animals during this period was identical with rates calculated demographically, as in Table 1. Nearly two-thirds of the mortality was concluded to have been due to mammalian predation, primarily that of coyotes.

Estimating the Proportion of Jackrabbits Killed by Coyotes.—The data at hand permit crude approximations of the proportions of rabbits taken by coyotes if we can derive (1) annual estimates of the number of rabbits per unit area in Curlew Valley, (2) the number of coyotes per unit area, and (3) the number of rabbits killed by a coyote per unit of time. These proportions can then be compared with the measured mortality rates to test the implication developing from the demographic and telemetric evidence previously discussed that coyote predation was a major part of jackrabbit mortality, at least during the decline period.

1. Gross (1967) derived a regression equation, later modified by Gross et al. (1972), to equate jackrabbit transect indices with absolute jackrabbit densities. This relationship estimates the five successive 1965-to-1969 October values at 48, 34, 30, 93, and 176 rabbits per square mile as an average for Curlew Valley. We may use the monthly mortality rates in Table 1 to reduce these to 31, 22, 21, 79, and 132 at the beginning of each January 1966 to 1970.

By means discussed in the methods section, Gross et al. (1972) estimated total young born in each year per mile of transect. These estimates were converted to numbers born per square mile in the same manner as the conversion above of the October indices and were 85, 80, 127, 375, and 580 young rabbits born per square mile respectively, in 1966 to 1970. The total number of individual animals per square mile in each of these years then were the sum of the adults in January and the young born and for the same years were 116, 102, 148, 454, and 712.

The number of rabbits per square mile in October (transects corrected by regression, as above) in the same years (1966 to 1970) were 34, 30, 93, 176, and 373. These can be reduced by the monthly mortality rates in Table 1 to year-end values of 22, 21, 79, and 132 for 1966 to 1969. (The overwinter rates for 1970–71 are not yet available.) Comparison of these year-end densities with the total rabbits per mile for the respective years suggested an overall loss of 82, 80, 47, and 71 percent for adults and young alive per square mile in 1966 to 1969—values that can be compared with the estimated percentage of rabbits killed by coyotes.

2. Clark (1972) explored the problems of estimating realistic values for actual coyote densities from among the May population estimates he had made. His subjective estimates apparently were closest to reality, although even these could be conservative.

Coyote pups in Curlew Valley were whelped about April 1, as an average date. Although the new pups may not themselves be hunting until mid- or late summer, their food demands exist and undoubtedly place an increased hunting load on the adults. Hence the April-through-October population (7 months) may in a sense be considered a hunting population.

A major part of the coyote mortality appears to be man-induced in this region, and most of it apparently occurs between fall and spring (Clark 1972). A few animals are killed incidentally by game bird and big game hunters afield in the fall. Stations baited with 1080 poison are placed in the field by personnel of the Division of Wildlife Services in fall and removed in spring.

Aerial hunting is primarily a winter practice, whereas trapping for bounties and pelts is a fall and winter operation.

For these reasons, the coyote population may be roughly stable in numbers during the 7-month period, April to October. It then probably declines from November through March, once again to recover through reproductive recruitment in April. The population estimate for May would therefore appear to be somewhat high as as an average for the year. If the population triples between March and April, remains roughly stable from April through October, then declines to one-third of the summer value between October and March, the mean for the year would be approximately three-fourths of the April-to-October value.

Because the actual May population is probably higher than the mean number of animals present through the year, and because the subjective May estimates may be lower than the true value for that month, the subjective May estimates may serve as a reasonable approximation of the mean population value for the year. We will take them as such for the present exercise. These values for the period of 1966 to 1970 on the 700-square-mile coyote study area were 192, 173, 164, 201, and 260.

3. Calculating the frequency with which a coyote kills a jackrabbit poses a final problem. Our only empirical data were those of Clark (1972), who reported that jackrabbit remains were present in about three-fourths of the year-round coyote dietary samples. These constituted instantaneous samples of the daily diet and, as such, reflected food consumption by the animal concerned only for a period of some hours prior to collection of the animal or prior to his defecation.

We were not aware of any data reporting the length of time that a meal remains in a coyote stomach. It is well known, however, that an animal caught in a trap during the night will have an empty stomach by morning and is therefore useless for food habits information. Thus, a coyote's stomach may evacuate within 8–10 hours after a meal, quite probably within 12. It therefore follows that, when 75 percent of a random population sample contains rabbit in the stomach, no fewer than 75 animals of 100 eat jackrabbit each day. A similar sample taken from the same population 12 hours earlier would presumably have shown the same frequency, but these samples would represent different meals and different prey animals. Hence, nearly every coyote in the population must eat rabbit every day, and doubtless some portion of the population eats rabbit more than once a day. If each dietary representation of jackrabbit constituted an individual rabbit, 100 coyotes might eat $2 \times 75 = 150$ rabbits per day, or 1.5 rabbits per coyote per day.

F. W. Clark (unpublished data) studied the feeding behavior of captive coyotes. By 6 weeks of age, a pup was physically capable of consuming a rabbit carcass completely without leaving any remains. By 3 to 4 months of age and thereafter, captive coyotes characteristically consumed an entire rabbit at a single meal, and frequently two entire animals. Clark believed that by this age (by June or July), young coyotes have essentially the same food needs as the adults. Hence, many instances of rabbit remains in a coyote stomach probably constitute an entire prey animal, and some may represent two animals.

However, coyotes hunting together probably share a kill on many occasions, and rabbit remains in a stomach do not invariably represent entire animals. The problem of scavenging, a potential variable, has been discussed by Stoddart (1970). Rabbits killed by automobiles, winter weather, starvation, or disease, when picked up by coyotes,

Table 2. Calculated annual jackrabbit kills by coyotes in 700-square-mile Utah–Idaho study area.[a]

	RABBIT NUMBERS		NUMBER OF COYOTES IN 700 SQUARE MILES (C)	PREDATION RATE AT ONE RABBIT KILL PER 2 DAYS		PERCENTAGE KILLED AT ONE KILL PER DAY (2E)	TOTAL PER-CENTAGE OF MORTALITY OF INDIVIDUAL RABBITS ALIVE DURING YEAR
YEAR	Mean Number per Square Mile (A)	Number in 700 Square Miles (B = A × 700)		Number Killed (D = C × 183)	Percentage Killed (E = D/B × 100)		
1966	116	81,200	192	35,136	43	86	82
1967	102	71,400	173	31,659	44	88	80
1968	148	103,600	164	30,012	29	58	47
1969	454	317,800	201	36,783	12	24	71
1970	712	498,400	260	47,580	10	20	—

[a] See text for sources and derivations of the parameters.

appear in the diet but do not constitute predation. We had no evidence that these were significant causes of jackrabbit loss during our study. Some animals were killed on highways traversing the area, but they constituted an infinitesimal fraction of the rabbits in this remote 1,200-square-mile valley. Although rabbits congregated in winter in concentration areas and applied heavy pressure to the shrubby vegetation with their browsing, we found no evidence of winter malnutrition or starvation.

One other behavior pattern places the estimation of kill frequency from dietary data on the conservative side. We observed examples in the field where coyotes killed rabbits in winter under snowy conditions and left them uneaten. This behavior produced carrion; however, Stoddart's (1970) data indicated that carrion was most often gleaned by birds.

Bearing all of these contingencies in mind and recognizing that we may have minimized the duration of small portions of a rabbit meal in the stomach, prevalence of scavenging, and frequency with which one animal feeds on a single rabbit, we estimated the kill frequency at something less than 1.5 rabbits per coyote per day, perhaps somewhere between 0.5 and 1.0. Saunders (1963), on the basis of 73 percent frequency of snowshoe hare in the lynx (*Lynx canadensis*) diet, concluded that his lynx killed a hare every other day.

We projected total annual rabbit-kill values using these estimated kill rates and population densities (Table 2). The results suggested that in the first 3 years with data (1966–68), coyote predation may have ranged somewhere between half of and all of the mortality. In 1969 and 1970, the proportion appeared lower.

DISCUSSION

A basic aim in population ecology is to understand the pattern of influences operating on any species with which one may be concerned. That pattern must be described mathematically so that quantitative consequences of measured changes in the pattern may be predicted. Predation is one influence in the pattern, and we desire to learn its quantitative influence on prey density.

As Wagner (1969:293) pointed out, environmental factors do not operate directly on density but rather on reproductive and mortality rates. These, in turn, are the components of the rates of population change, which ultimately influence density. Thus, statements describing the impact of environmental factors on populations must relate those factors to changes in the rates of reproduction, mortality, and population change. The rates, viewed as dependent variables, are expressed as functions of the environmental variables that affect them. The best examples of this approach in populations of free-living animals are the predictive models for insect populations described by Watt (1961) and Morris (1963) and some of the production and exploitation models developed for fishery populations (Ricker 1946).

Consequently, our needs in predation studies are measurement of the percentage of prey populations taken by predators, how these percentages influence mortality rates, and ultimately, how they affect rates of change in the prey populations. Since predation is almost never observed directly as a statistical phenomenon—telemetry is currently the closest approach to direct observation—the approach is correlative. The percentage of prey removed by predators is measured under varying values for predator, prey, and buffer numbers, and of other environmental variables.

The present study is of this kind. The evidence is largely circumstantial and indirect and is adequate only to permit formulation of hypotheses. The 8 years of accumulated data provide no more than seven points for a functional plot, perhaps only a quarter or a third of the number needed to approach the true form of the relationship. Nevertheless, at this stage of our research, preliminary hypotheses need to be developed.

We observed 4 years of population increase and 4 years of population decline during the period we studied jackrabbits in Curlew Valley. Although we observed some variation in reproductive rates during this period, the observed, annual population changes were largely due to year-to-year variations in mortality (Fig. 3).

Mean monthly mortality rates (Table 1) of adults during the warm season (13 percent), of juveniles between birth and October (14 percent), and of the entire population between fall and spring (16 percent) were similar. This similarity could occur if

the same factor or factors primarily responsible for mortality were operative throughout the year and on all age-classes.

That the postnatal loss of young and the summer loss of adults should proceed at the same rate may give some pause. At this stage of our studies we do not know the temporal pattern of postnatal loss. At first glance, the young might seem most vulnerable in their first few weeks of life. Probably their small size makes them potentially vulnerable to more species of predators. However, these very young animals are extremely secretive in their behavior and in our experience do not begin to move about until they are approximately 6 weeks of age. During nocturnal collecting with spotlights, we rarely saw rabbits younger than 6 weeks of age. Furthermore, the young are characteristically precocial. They can make sizable leaps within a few hours after birth, and, on those rare occasions when very small animals are seen in the field, they scurry with great speed from one bush to another. Hence, we do not regard it as being self-evident that the young hares are most vulnerable to mortality.

The parallel year-to-year changes in mortality between age-classes and seasons (Fig. 2) could also occur if the mortality were importantly affected by some common, probably extrinsic, influence. Predation could be such an influence, and the parallel changes between summer and winter could suggest year-round, resident predatory species.

The coyote is clearly the dominant predator on jackrabbits in Curlew Valley, both in terms of the degree to which it utilizes the species in its diet and its numerical abundance relative to other predatory species. There are other carnivorous species that prey on jackrabbits. Bobcats (*Lynx rufus*) are individually effective, but we believe their numbers to be low (Stoddart

228

1970). Badgers (*Taxidea taxus*) are present in numbers comparable to those of the coyote but seem to be of doubtful total impact. Long-tailed weasels (*Mustela frenata*) are present, perhaps in substantial numbers. They seem to be capable of taking young rabbits, but their influence is unknown.

A number of raptorial species have been seen feeding on jackrabbits in the valley, or jackrabbit remains have been found in their nests or pellets. These include golden eagle (*Aquila chrysaëtos*), ferruginous hawk (*Buteo regalis*), red-tailed hawk (*B. jamaicensis*), Swainson's hawk (*B. swainsoni*), harrier (*Circus hudsonius*), and great horned owl (*Bubo virginianus*). None of these species is nearly as abundant as the coyote. In 1969, J. Platt (unpublished data) surveyed the numbers of these species and determined that collectively their numbers perhaps approached the order of 150 in the same area in which coyotes may have numbered 201. The disparity is much greater on a biomass basis, if one compares the body weights of the raptors—ranging from the smallest (and most numerous) harrier (1.0–1.5 lb) to the heaviest (and least numerous) eagle (12 lb)—with the 20-lb weights of the coyotes. Platt's food habits studies showed jackrabbits to be important dietary items only for the eagle and ferruginous hawk. Rodents, birds, reptiles, and invertebrates made up the majority of food items in the other species. Add to these considerations the migratory status of the raptors, and it seems quite probable that the raptors are moving far less energy from the jackrabbit food base than are the coyotes.

The correlation between jackrabbit mortality rates and coyote:rabbit ratios (Fig. 4) suggests that coyote predation constitutes a major part of the total rabbit mortality and of the predation operating on rabbits. This same conclusion is suggested by the limited telemetry data and by the speculative estimates on the proportion of rabbits killed by coyotes in Curlew Valley (Table 2).

A preliminary indication of the proportion of the total mortality rate caused by coyote predation can be gained by extrapolating the regression lines in Fig. 4 to zero coyote numbers (zero coyote:rabbit ratio) and calculating the mortality rates with the regression equations. The resulting values imply the mortality rates occurring in the absence of coyotes and due to all other causes. This technique has been used to estimate mortality rates of waterfowl in the absence of hunting, the procedure being to plot annual mortality rates against first-year recovery rates (indices of the level of hunting kill) and to extrapolate the resulting regression line to the Y-intercept and zero hunting kill (Hickey 1952:156, Geis and Taber 1963:291, Moisan et al. 1967:116–119).

The Y-intercept for adult mortality in summer (Fig. 4) is about 15 percent, whereas that for the overwinter population loss is 36 percent. The high mortality rates in the early 1960's (Table 1) may therefore have been substantially the result of coyote predation. The Y-intercept for juvenile mortality (Fig. 4)—54 percent—is not greatly increased with higher coyote:rabbit ratios. Although this intercept and that for the overwinter loss will probably be lowered when the correct curvilinear equation is fitted to the data, the sources of mortality affecting the young are probably more numerous than those in the other life-history stages, and substantial losses may occur with or without heavy coyote densities.

Nevertheless, three partially or wholly independent sources of evidence—the correlations in Fig. 4, the telemetry data, and the predation-rate calculations in Table 2— are consistent in pointing to coyote predation as a major portion of the mortality encountered by the rabbit population in the period from 1963 to 1970. Because the changes in rabbit population during this period largely resulted from variations in mortality, we suggest as a first hypothesis that coyote predation, and changes therein, may have played a major role in the observed rabbit trends by hastening, if not primarily causing, rabbit declines between 1963 and 1967, and largely, or in part, permitting rabbit increase in 1968–70. This hypothesis tends to be supported by a plot of rabbit population change on the coyote: rabbit ratio (Fig. 5). The 0.69 r^2 value suggests that roughly two-thirds of the variation in rabbit numbers has been associated with variation in the coyote:rabbit ratio.

If these patterns continue to hold, they resemble the classical Lotka–Volterra predator–prey oscillations (Volterra 1931, Lotka 1956), an implication of which is a gradual relaxation of predator pressure as both predator and prey decline until prey is released once again.

Predator pressure would not remain the same if rabbits became relatively less vulnerable by contracting into environmental refugia wherein they were more difficult to catch, a common prerequisite for the realization of predator–prey oscillations (Slobodkin 1961:148), or if coyote populations declined faster than rabbit populations.

The regressions in Fig. 4 suggest one or both of these alternatives. As coyotes follow rabbits down, their impact on rabbits, as measured by the mortality rates of the latter, appears to decline. It is, however, the second of the above alternatives that appears responsible for this changing impact. Clark's (1972) data show coyote indices declining from 174 in 1963 to 23 in 1968, and 87 percent decline. In the same period, the jackrabbit indices (Fig. 1) declined by 66 percent.

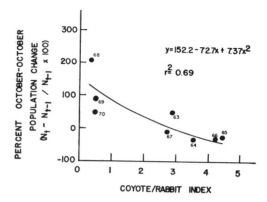

Fig. 5. Correlation between annual rates of jackrabbit population change and the coyote:rabbit index. The relationship is significant ($P < 0.05$).

Continuation of a Lotka–Volterra oscillation now demands that the impact of coyotes on rabbits increase as rabbits increase, until predators once again start the prey into decline. For this to occur, coyotes must increase faster than rabbits in the years ahead. If this happens, the relationship of coyote density and rabbit mortality will continue to follow the pattern represented in Fig. 4 for 1963 to 1970, a relationship that developed during a late decline and an initial period of increase.

We surmise that this is unlikely. The jackrabbit has a higher potential rate of increase than the coyote. If the coyote were the major source of mortality for the jackrabbit, then the disparity in their population trends in the late 1960's will have released the rabbit to the point where it will increase faster than the coyote, and the rate of coyote predation should decline as rabbits increase. Other mortality sources—disease, exhaustion of the food supply or pituitary–adrenal stress, or both—will presumably be needed to reverse the population trend, induce decline, and enable the now-abundant coyotes once again to assume dominance over the prey.

One might then ask what the long-range

effect is of predator on prey, both in terms of mean prey density and of the phase and amplitude of prey fluctuation, and what the pattern might be in the absence of, or with greater numbers of, predators. Answers to these tempting questions could be explored by further deduction, but they are best left until the data are at hand for all stages of population change.

LITERATURE CITED

Bookhout, T. A. 1964. Prenatal development of snowshoe hares. J. Wildl. Mgmt. 28(2):338–345.

Clark, F. W. 1972. Influence of jackrabbit density on coyote population changes. J. Wildl. Mgmt. 36(2):343–356.

French, N. R., R. McBride, and J. Detmer. 1965. Fertility and population density of the black-tailed jackrabbit. J. Wildl. Mgmt. 29(1):14–26.

Geis, A. D., and R. D. Taber. 1963. Measuring hunting and other mortality. Pages 284–298. In H. S. Mosby [Editor], Wildlife investigational techniques. 2nd ed. revised. The Wildlife Society, Washington, D. C. 419pp.

Gross, J. E. 1967. Demographic analysis of a northern Utah black-tailed jackrabbit population. Ph.D. Thesis. Utah State Univ. 127pp.

———, L. C. Stoddart, and F. H. Wagner. 1972. Demographic analysis of a northern Utah jackrabbit population. Wildl. Monographs. (In press.)

Hickey, J. J. 1952. Survival studies of banded birds. U. S. Fish and Wildl. Serv. Spec. Sci. Rept.: Wildl. No. 15. 177pp.

Lotka, A. J. 1956. Elements of mathematical biology. Dover Publications, Inc., New York. 465pp.

Moisan, G., R. I. Smith, and R. K. Martinson. 1967. The green-winged teal: its distribution, migration, and population dynamics.

U. S. Fish and Wildl. Serv. Spec. Sci. Rept.: Wildl. No. 100. 248pp.

Morris, R. F. 1963. The development of a population model for the spruce budworm through the analysis of survival rates. Memoirs Entomol. Soc. Canada 31(pt. 2):30–32.

Ricker, W. E. 1946. Production and utilization of fish populations. Ecol. Monographs 16(4):373–391.

———. 1958. Handbook of computations for biological statistics of fish populations. Fisheries Research Board Canada Bull. 119. 300pp.

Rusch, D. H. 1965. Some movements of black-tailed jackrabbits in northern Utah. M.S. Thesis. Utah State Univ. 43pp.

Saunders, J. K., Jr. 1963. Food habits of the lynx in Newfoundland. J. Wildl. Mgmt. 27(3):384–390.

Slobodkin, L. B. 1961. Growth and regulation of animal populations. Holt, Rinehart and Winston, New York. 184pp.

Stoddart, L. C. 1970. A telemetric method for detecting jackrabbit mortality. J. Wildl. Mgmt. 34(3):501–507.

———. 1972. Population biology of northern Utah black-tailed jackrabbits. Ph.D. Thesis. Utah State Univ. In preparation.

Thompson, W. R. 1928. A contribution to the study of biological control and parasite introduction in continental areas. Parasitology 20(1):90–112.

———. 1955. Mortality factors acting in a sequence. Canadian Entomologist 87(6):264–275.

Volterra, V. 1931. Variations and fluctuations of the number of individuals in animal species living together. Pages 409–448. In R. N. Chapman, Animal ecology with especial reference to insects. McGraw-Hill Book Company, Inc., New York and London. 464pp.

Wagner, F. H. 1969. Ecosystem concepts in fish and game management. Pages 259–307. In G. M. Van Dyne [Editor], The ecosystem concept in natural resource management. Academic Press, New York and London. 383pp.

Watt, K. E. F. 1961. Mathematical models for use in insect pest control. Canadian Entomologist 93(Suppl. 19):1–62.

A STUDY OF WOOD-PIGEON SHOOTING: THE EXPLOITATION OF A NATURAL ANIMAL POPULATION

By R. K. MURTON, N. J. WESTWOOD and A. J. ISAACSON

INTRODUCTION

Since the late 18th century the wood-pigeon (*Columba palumbus* L.) has been recognized as a potential pest of the arable farmer, a status which was emphasized when war made it imperative to conserve home-produced food stocks (Colquhoun 1951; Murton 1965). Yet the wood-pigeon has been favoured by sportsmen, especially by those unable to shoot partridges (*Perdix perdix* L.) and pheasants (*Phasianus* sp.). As a result of studies sponsored by the Agricultural Research Council (1941–43), it was concluded that the pigeon problem could best be solved by reducing total population size, based on the false assumption that a positive correlation must exist between the incidence of real crop damage and pigeon numbers. It seemed likely that the objective of killing large numbers of pigeons could be achieved by encouraging sportsmen, and to this end, a Government subsidy was introduced in 1953 which contributed half the cost of cartridges. This bonus scheme was administered via the Divisional Pest Service of the Ministry of Agriculture.

Two main methods of shooting pigeons were adopted.

(1) 'Lone-wolf' gunners attracted the birds with artificial pigeon decoys displayed near a camouflaged hide situated by a vulnerable field crop. These sportsmen were considered the elite and their efforts effective.

(2) During February and March, after the pheasant shooting season, local gunners collaborated in roost shooting; the birds were shot as they returned to their roosting places at dusk. Such co-ordinated battue shoots were popular with Pests Officers as they could be readily organized and cartridges distributed according to the number of men participating or to the number of pigeons killed. When it was shown that battue shoots did not reduce the pigeon population below the level attained naturally and that real savings in crop damage were not achieved, Government financial support was withdrawn in early 1965 in spite of dissension from shooting advocates (Murton, Westwood & Isaacson 1964). Half-price cartridges could still be obtained through the Rabbit Clearance Societies, providing that shooting was confined to sites where pigeons caused damage. Particularly in eastern England, a shortage of rabbits (*Oryctolagus cuniculus* L.) in the mid-1960s caused farmers to relinquish their support for Rabbit Clearance Societies and to demand more action against pigeons. It was, therefore, an expediency to make it necessary to belong to a Rabbit Society before cartridges could be obtained as this helped keep societies active. However, a change in Government policy regarding financial support to the farming community led in 1969 to the abolition of Rabbit Clearance

Societies and subsidies for cartridges. This paper examines the effects of these policy changes and demonstrates the extent to which the ubiquitous wood-pigeon is amenable to rational exploitation.

METHODS

A population study of the wood-pigeon was undertaken from 1958 to 1970 at Carlton, Cambridgeshire (1061 ha) and at nearby localities. Methods of counting the birds and of sampling their grain and clover food supply have been published (Murton *et al.* 1964).

During the first six winters battue shoots were held from late January until early March. In the following three years there was no organized shooting and only a few pigeons were killed by the gamekeeper; these can be ignored. In November 1967, some experimental shooting was begun and continued until December 1970 by Mr W. H. Edgar, one of the Ministry of Agriculture's Regional Pests staff, an ardent and highly competent pigeon shooter. It is pertinent to record that Mr Edgar rates as a top-class decoy gunner.

For the first twelve months Mr Edgar shot pigeons under our directions at sites at Carlton and nearby districts where we knew pigeons fed regularly. Either artificial pigeon decoys or dead pigeons were set-out 30 m from a shooting hide (bales of straw, camouflaged netting or cut branches) on a standard equal-sided grid at 1-m centres. From five to 200 decoys were used in separate trials. The dead pigeons were preserved by injecting them with formalin and dried either with their wings closed in a feeding posture, or with their wings open as if flying. Artificial pigeons, dead pigeons with their wings closed or dead pigeons with their wings open were used as decoys. An observer was stationed, usually in a vehicle, at a sufficient distance from the gunner not to disturb wild pigeons, but close enough to make accurate records. All wood-pigeons flying over, alone or in flocks, which passed within sighting range of the decoys were noted. The number which responded by dipping towards the decoys and/or attempting to settle, the number shot at and the number killed were recorded. Records were kept of man-hour and cartridge expenditure.

Following the termination of these experiments in September 1968, Mr Edgar was provided with all the cartridges he required and freedom of the study area and was given the task of eradicating the local wood-pigeons to the best of his ability. This phase of the work finished in October 1969 and there was relatively little shooting in the area until September 1970. Because this was an official study Mr Edgar shot pigeons as often and whenever he considered it worthwhile.

EFFECT OF SHOOTING AND FOOD STOCKS ON POPULATION SIZE

Effect of food supplies

Fig. 1 shows the changes in population size in relation to food stocks and the amount of shooting. Although some results were published in 1964 (Murton *et al.* 1964) records collected subsequently have not been published. It is, therefore, desirable to establish that the number of juveniles surviving until December depends on the amount of grain persisting on the stubbles in late autumn (Fig. 2) but that adult numbers are uninfluenced by this food supply (Fig. 3). This is because the adults can more readily turn to clover when cereals disappear. It has been shown for the first six years, that adult and juvenile numbers combined were related to grain stocks. For this purpose the 'grain index' was

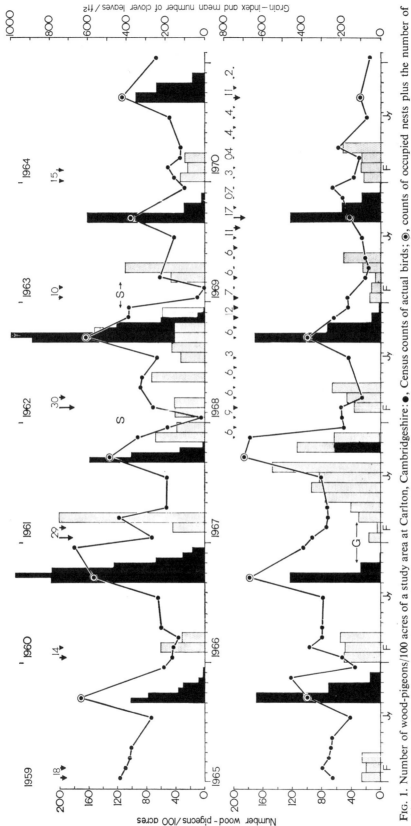

FIG. 1. Number of wood-pigeons/100 acres of a study area at Carlton, Cambridgeshire: ●, Census counts of actual birds; ◉, counts of occupied nests plus the number of chicks known to be fledged. Length of arrows indicates number of pigeons shot per month; numbers referring to the total killed/2 months. All shooting up to 1964 was of birds returning to roost and from 1967 onwards by a decoy gunner. Histograms refer to the food supply during critical seasons. The grain index is the product of the mean density of cereal grains/ft² throughout the study area and the percentage of area devoted to cereals and is shown by dark shaded histograms. The mean number of clover leaves/ft² throughout the area is depicted by light shaded histograms. During prolonged periods of snow cover (S) birds temporarily left the area to feed on nearby brassica crops. Grain (G) was abundant during winter 1966–67.

234

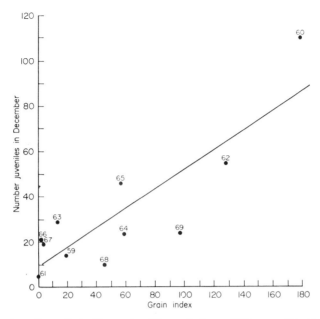

FIG. 2. Number of juvenile (< 12 months old) wood-pigeons/100 acres of the Carlton study area in early December in relation to the late November grain index (product of the mean number of cereal grains/ft^2 on all fields with grain and the percentage acreage of the study area devoted to cereals). $r_9 = 0.852$; $P < 0.01$; $y = 8.47 + 0.43x$.

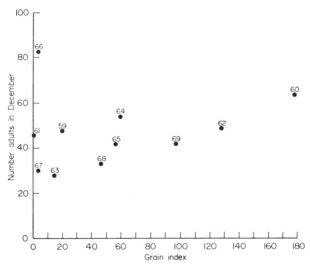

FIG. 3. Number of adult wood-pigeons/100 acres early December in relation to the late November grain index. $r_9 = 0.215$; n.s.

235

calculated as the mean number cereal grains/ft^2 on all fields multiplied by the percentage of the study area under cereals. An index of total quantity was important since pigeons and other species collect cereal grain, until virtually none is left. In preliminary studies winter pigeon numbers were related to the 'clover index' which was calculated in the same way as the 'grain index'. Subsequently, it was found that the actual density of clover leaves provided a more useful measure of the winter food supply by influencing the rate at which pigeons can obtain sufficient nutrients and clover stocks become limited when a threshold density is reached (Murton, Isaacson & Westwood 1966). Moreover, the birds select from the sward and eat the most nutritive leaves; only under adverse feeding conditions do they take weed leaves (Murton, Isaacson & Westwood 1971). Unfortunately, it is not possible to identify, in the field, the leaves preferred by the pigeons and so

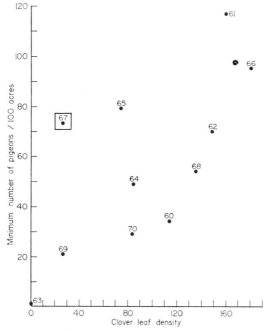

Fig. 4. Minimum number of wood-pigeons/100 acres at Carlton in winter (February–March) in relation to lowest clover leaf density recorded over the same period. $r_9 = 0.684$; $P < 0.02$; $y = 19.4 + 0.39x$. In 1967 the birds did not depend on clover due to large quantities of grain on stubbles. Omitting 1967 gives $r_8 = 0.812$; $P = 0.01–0.001$; $y = 4.6 + 0.5x$.

total leaf density serves as an indication of their availability. During the study the clover acreage declined but there were winters in which leaf density was high on the remaining fields. The minimum pigeon population in late February or early March, over eleven winters, has been related to the lowest 'clover index' over the same period, confirming preliminary studies. A better correlation is obtained by using the clover leaf density, and Fig. 4 shows that the minimum total population in late February or in March was related to the lowest clover leaf density over the same period. The mortality occurring between the end of the breeding season in September and the minimum population in March can be represented as the difference between the logarithms of the two counts; negative log values indicate an increase in numbers due to immigration. The rate of juvenile loss from September until February/March shows a density-dependent relationship with the size of the post-breeding population (Fig. 5). Although the slope of the regression ($b = 1\cdot87 \pm 0\cdot49$) suggests an over-compensating density-dependent mortality factor, it is not significantly different from unity ($t_9 = 1\cdot77$; n.s.). Changes in adult numbers were not significantly related to density (Fig. 6), but could have been except for three years. In 1963 there was an exceptionally hard winter and the shooting mortality was responsible for the unusually high rate of loss in 1968 and 1969. Changes in adult numbers involved immigration in three out of eleven years.

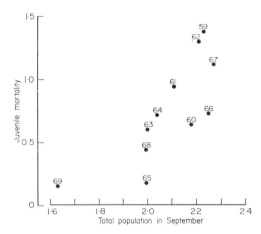

FIG. 5. Mortality of juvenile wood-pigeons in autumn and winter expressed as the difference between $\log_{10}$ population/100 acres in September and the minimum $\log_{10}$ population/100 acres in February or March. $r_9 = 0\cdot804$; $P < 0\cdot01$; $y = -3\cdot16 + 1\cdot87x$.

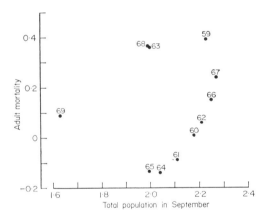

FIG. 6. Mortality of adult wood-pigeons in autumn and winter calculated as for the juveniles in Fig. 5. $r_9 = 0\cdot126$; n.s. Negative log values indicate that population size increased due to immigration.

Food supplies did not limit numbers between April and September for there was always more clover or cereal seed on sowings, ripening or ripe on the stalk, or wild weed seed, tree buds, and other food in excess of the amount demanded by the population; however, the ability of birds to breed in April and May was affected by woodland food supplies (Murton, Westwood & Isaacson 1974).

Effect of winter shooting at Carlton

Total populations at the start of winter (December) at Carlton are shown in Table 1 and Fig. 1. These populations, less natural losses occurring in early January, were available for shooting during the organized battue shoots during late January until early March or the experimental programmes of 1967–69. The percentages of the December totals which were shot and also the percentage change in number until April (when food stocks were not limited) which was not accounted for by shooting, are shown in Table 1. The summation of these losses and changes give the total percentage change in numbers from December until April. It is evident that the pattern of population change depended not on shooting but on other factors. The battue shoots were nullified by immigration, sometimes on a large scale. The results of the preceding section and those in Fig. 4, suggest that the amount of clover determined how many pigeons could live in the area and that if these were shot other birds moved in to fill the vacuum created.

Table 1. *Effect of shooting on changes in wood-pigeon numbers per* 100 *acres of the Carlton study area in winter*

	Total numbers in December	Total shot Dec. to Mar. (% in brackets) as minus value	Total numbers in April	Change in* numbers not due to shooting (% in brackets based on Dec. total)	Percentage change in numbers Dec. to Apr.
1958–59	117	18 (−15)	101	+2 (+1)	−14
1959–60	45	14 (−31)	59	+28 (+62)	+31
1960–61	72	29 (−40)	52	+9 (+12)	−28
1961–62	50	30 (−60)	88	+68 (+136)	+76
1962–63	104	9 (−9)	61	−34 (−32)	−41
1963–64	41	15 (−37)	32	+6 (+15)	−22
1964–65	79	0 (0)	68	−11 (−14)	−14
1965–66	52	0 (0)	79	+27 (+52)	+52
1966–67	104	0 (0)	72	−32 (−31)	−31
1967–68	52	19 (−37)	25	−8 (−15)	−52
1968–69	46	18 (−39)	21	−7 (−15)	−54
1969–70	66	3 (−5)	57	−6 (−9)	−14

* Out of 117 pigeons alive in December 1958, eighteen (15%) were shot, theoretically leaving ninety-nine. In April there were 101 birds so that two pigeons (1% of 117) must have moved into the area. Thus from 117 birds, −15% were shot, 1% were immigrants, hence the total population change between December and April was −14%.

The total percentage population change (y) was not correlated with the percentage of birds shot ($r_{10} = -0.159$; n.s.) but was correlated with the percentage change in numbers not due to shooting ($r_{10} = 0.901$; $P < 0.001$; $y = -19.13 + 0.81x$).

Immigration during winter probably involved surplus birds from nearby areas which would otherwise have died of food shortage. It was noticeable in the winter of 1964–65, following the abolition of the Government subsidy for battue shooting, that letters to the sporting journals expressed the presence of abnormally large numbers of dead wood-pigeons on roadside verges and the countryside. Presumably before 1964, many birds which might have died from food shortage or from other causes were being shot. This is substantiated from recoveries of ringed wood-pigeons marked under the British Trust for Ornithology scheme. Of 189 pigeons recovered during January–March 1958–64, 75% were shot. The bulk of the remaining 25% were found dead, while some birds died from injury, drowning, being killed by a cat and other miscellaneous causes. These records include a higher than average number in the found-dead category in consequence of exceptional mortality which occurred in the hard winter of 1962–63. From the same months in 1965–68, 241 pigeons were recovered of which 40% were in the found dead and miscellaneous category (60% were shot) ($\chi_1^2, = 9·91; P <0·01$).

Local movements also occurred during periods of snow as the birds could find un-covered fields of brassicae just outside the immediate census area. Immigration in May involved mostly juveniles which had migrated relatively long distances during the winter; a small proportion of the British population moves to France in early November and survivors return in April or May (Murton & Ridpath 1962; Murton, Westwood & Isaacson, unpublished). It is possible that the opportunity for long-distant migrants to return to the study area has increased since the abolition of intensive winter shooting. It is evident from Fig. 1 that the abolition of winter shooting did not lead to an increase in the local wood-pigeon population.

The shooting experiments November 1967 to October 1969 at Carlton

Clover density was exceptionally low during January–March 1969 (Fig. 4) and explains why the July breeding population was also low; the breeding population in 1970 and 1971 remained low and while leaf density was also fairly low in 1970 (Fig. 4), it was not meas-ured in 1971. But since shooting was discontinued in 1971 it did not explain the failure of the pigeon population to increase. In September 1967, there were 186 birds/100 acres (40·5 ha) following breeding (Fig. 1) of which 142 (76%) had vanished by July 1968. Thirty birds (21% of the 142) were shot over this period. Similarly of ninety-nine birds alive in September 1968, seventy-three (74%) were lost by the following July 1969 and shooting accounted for 55% (forty birds) of these: of the mortality occurring during the winter (the population declined from forty-six in January to twenty-one in April, Fig. 1) 72% was caused by shooting. There were forty-three birds/100 acres in September 1969 of which twenty-five (58%) were lost by the following July. During the same period twenty-seven pigeons were shot/100 acres. The exceptional adult mortality affecting the 1968–69 and 1969–70 cohorts (Fig. 6), suggests that very intensive shooting caused excessive mortality in years when population size was already low (see also Fig. 1), but only in 1968–69 was the shooter trying to eradicate pigeons. Although the total amount of late summer, autumn and winter mortality of adults was apparently increased by shoot-ing, there is no clear indication that the size of the subsequent breeding population was reduced (Fig. 1).

It might be argued that the shooting effort in 1967–68 could have been increased had not experiments been in progress. Even so, more birds were shot per hour in 1967–68 than in 1968–69 (cf. Tables 2 and 4), when the shooter was attempting to reduce numbers. If the shooting which was done after July 1969 is ignored, on the basis that a new population was now at risk following breeding, it can be calculated from the results shown in Table 2, that in 1968–69 it required about ten man-hours and nearly seventy cartridges to kill forty birds/100 acres. Table 2 gives the returns for the whole study area of 2647 acres (1061 ha) and these must be converted to the proportionate costing per 100 acres. Thus excluding travelling time and allowing a wage of £0.5/hour and a retail price of 5p/cartridge, it cost over £0.24 to kill each pigeon.

More pigeons are at risk immediately after the breeding season for population size is at first high and then declines (Fig. 1). Yet there was no consistent seasonal variation in the time required to shoot each bird nor in the expenditure of cartridges (Table 2). This

Table 2. *Number of pigeons shot and cartridges used by a decoy gunner at Carlton and other sites*

	Number pigeons shot	Man-hours expended	Cartridges /bird	Man-hours /bird
Carlton*				
Sept. 1968	78	20·5	1·7	0·26
Oct.	79	29·0	1·7	0·37
Nov.	168	46·8	2·1	0·28
Dec.	165	46·0	1·8	0·28
Jan. 1969	149	33·8	1·9	0·23
Feb.	30	7·0	1·6	0·23
Mar.	141	7·5	1·4	0·05
Apr.	33	7·0	1·7	0·21
May	23	11·0	1·4	0·48
June	140	30·5	1·5	0·22
July	72	22·0	1·6	0·31
Aug.	203	41·5	1·8	0·20
Sept.	365	86·3	1·7	0·24
Oct.	66	11·0	1·6	0·17
Total	1712	399·9 Mean	1·7	0·23
Carlton†	29	10·5	2·8	0·39
Vale of Evesham‡				
Roost	45	16·3	1·6	0·37
Decoying on clover fields	165	74·8 ⎫	2·0	0·45
Decoying on cabbage fields	597	377 ⎭		0·63
Walking round fields as in rough shooting	21	36	2·3	1·72

* Decoy shooting according to experiments detailed in text.
† Battue shooting by local guns at Carlton in 1969.
‡ By members of the West Midland Wood-pigeon Club (data from Murton & Jones 1973).

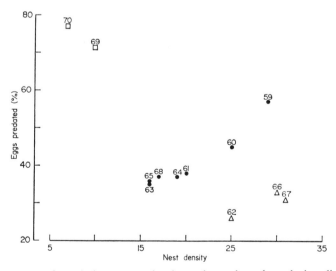

FIG. 7. Percentage of wood-pigeon eggs taken by predators throughout the breeding season in relation to the density of occupied nests/acre. Many adults were shot in 1969 and 1970 (□) during an experimental programme, while in 1962, 1966 and 1967 (△) jays and other predators were intensively slaughtered. In the remaining seasons conditions stayed constant and for these: $r_s = 0.957$; $P < 0.001$; $y = 9.8 + 1.5x$.

suggests that there was a limitation in the shooting technique. If the gunner was sited in a favourable place and pigeons were attracted to his decoys he enjoyed a successful session. But if after waiting a reasonable time no birds appeared the site was abandoned. In this way, the shooter tended to bias his prospects towards success. Table 2 gives comparative figures for the man-hour expenditure required to shoot pigeons in some other situations studied, these data representing the ability of average to good pigeon shooters.

During the main breeding season from July to September 1968, 154 pigeons were shot in the study area; 640 were killed in the same period in 1969 and 318 in 1970. This represents 14%, 96% and 61% respectively, of the adult breeding population in July. Shooting seems to have had no adverse effect in 1968, but in 1969 and 1970 the breeding success of the birds was seriously reduced (Fig. 7). Egg predation in Carlton wood was mostly from jays (*Garrulus glandarius* L.) who gain access to the eggs when the nests are left unguarded. Egg predation increases with the density of breeding pairs (see Fig. 7) and in 1969 and 1970 a low rate of predation should have been predicted. But the shooting of parent birds produced unguarded nests and the eggs were soon removed. In 1962, a new game-keeper was appointed and for one season he intensively killed predatory birds but this enthusiasm waned in the following year (see Lack 1966, p. 181). In 1966 and 1967 another game-keeper killed predators in Carlton wood and egg predation was lower than expected. An attempt was made to quantify these campaigns and occasionally the keeper revealed the number of corvids he had shot. But dead birds in the woods and on gibbets were also noted and it was evident that his records were not reliable. Birds of prey were also killed in the supposed interests of game preservation.

THE EFFECT OF USING DECOYS

For a given number of decoys the proportion of passing pigeons which respond by dipping in flight or attempting to alight declines as their flock size increases (Murton 1973). Thus single birds respond more readily to a given number of decoys than individuals in a flock of fifty. Increasing the number of decoys can increase the response of pigeons in the larger passing flocks but there are limitations (see below). Records combining the observations made when different numbers of decoys (1–200 dead pigeons with wings open or with wings closed) were used (Fig. 8), show how a smaller proportion of the flock responded as the size of the passing flock increased. As implied above a response is recognized as any deviation from the direct flight-path which could be expected in the absence of a decoy. The probability of shooting a bird which circles and attempts to settle with the decoys is obviously greater than that of shooting one which only dips in flight.

It is convenient to pool all degrees of response because defining categories is difficult, and to assume that the number of pigeons potentially at risk of being shot is a constant proportion of the total responding. Use of a double-barrelled twelve-bore shot-gun restricts the number of pigeons which can be shot to two, irrespective of the number responding at any time. Even so, the birds are only infrequently in a suitable position for long enough for the right and left barrels to be fired in quick succession at different birds, and it is more realistic to consider a maximum potential of about one bird per flock. Fig. 8 shows that if single birds were flying within the decoy area, 45% responded and of these 66% were shot, that is, 30% of all pigeons coming within range of the decoys were killed. When flocks of four were involved, 32% of the birds responded of which 25% were killed, representing only 8% of the pigeons potentially at risk. It is evident why shooters prefer situations where pigeons constantly arrive in small flocks.

The effect of varying the number of decoys on passing single pigeons, larger flocks being ignored (Table 3), avoids bias if social interaction leads to flock cohesion and group responses. Increase in the number of decoys from five to twenty-five resulted in an increase in the percentage of passing single birds which responded and this enabled a higher proportion to be shot. It made no difference to the proportion actually shot whether the decoys had closed or open wings. With more decoys there was no significant increase in the proportion of birds responding and there may even have been a decrease.

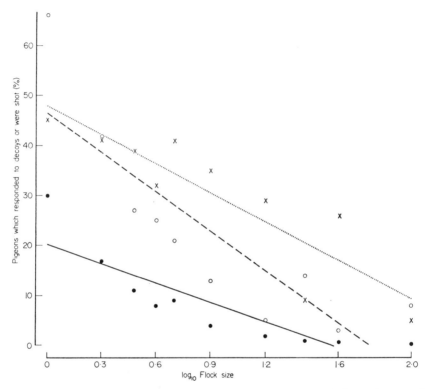

FIG. 8. Percentage of passing wood-pigeons which responded to dead pigeon decoys and were shot (records combined for experiments involving 5–200 decoys) in relation to $\log_{10}$ number of birds/flock. ×, Percentage of passing pigeons which responded by dipping or circling over the decoys or by trying to alight. $r_8 = -0.891$; $P < 0.001$; $y = 48.0 - 19.3x$. ○, Percentage of responding birds which were shot $r_8 = -0.848$; $P < 0.01$; $y = 46.5 - 26.2x$. ●, Percentage of birds at risk, that is, all those passing, that were shot. $r_8 = -0.865$; $P < 0.01$; $y = 20.2 - 12.9x$.

There were indications that individual pigeons were more attracted to medium numbers of decoys (which they presumably interpreted as feeding flocks) than to small numbers but they may have been repelled by very large flocks. That this was the case is shown by the response of passing pigeons in flocks, ranging in size from one to ten birds (Table 3, Fig. 9). A logarithmic relationship existed such that with five decoys, 7% of pigeons at risk were shot, 11% with ten decoys, 14% with twenty decoys, 19% with forty decoys and 23% (the maximum) with eighty decoys (Fig. 9). It is known from other studies in which no attempts were made to shoot the birds that wood-pigeons would land next to decoys with closed wings, whereas in the presence of many open-winged decoys, live pigeons

Table 3. *Response of single wood-pigeons to decoys and percentage which were shot according to number of decoys employed (data in parentheses refer to records when flocks of one to ten pigeons were at risk)*

| Number of decoys used | Number wood-pigeons passing which were at risk | Percentage of passing birds which: | | Number of pigeons shot which had not responded to the decoys |
		responded to the decoys	were shot	
5 WC*	17 (53)	29 (38)	12 (9)	0 (0)
15 WC	131 (760)	34 (31)	23 (10)	13 (28)
15 WC	76 (309)	50 (36)	25 (14)	3 (6)
25 WC	75 (300)	55 (43)	44 (17)	3 (6)
25 WO	49 (334)	65 (47)	43 (14)	2 (2)
40 WC	166 (776)	53 (60)	35 (18)	4 (8)
40 WO	92 (339)	48 (46)	33 (16)	4 (4)
80 WC	43 (199)	53 (51)	51 (28)	3 (4)
80 WO	22 (185)	55 (23)	50 (10)	1 (3)
100 WC	19 (116)	32 (35)	32 (13)	2 (2)
130 WC	30 (52)	63 (46)	40 (27)	0 (0)
200 WC	133 (489)	47 (40)	29 (16)	4 (8)
200 WO	23 (139)	35 (16)	17 (7)	0 (1)
15 A	169 (562)	31 (21)	20 (8)	11 (15)
40 A	95 (544)	44 (29)	19 (7)	6 (12)

* WC, dead wood-pigeons with wings closed; WO, dead wood-pigeons with wings open; A, artificial wood-pigeons.

which had initially responded would shy away and not attempt to settle (Murton 1973). Presumably decoys with closed wings simulate pigeons feeding in a safe site; small numbers with open wings perhaps give the impression of the short flights made by feeding birds, but large numbers in flight probably signal danger.

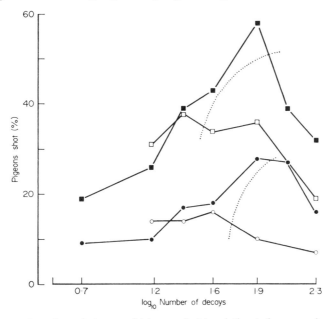

FIG. 9. Proportion of wood-pigeons which were shot in relation to $\log_{10}$ number of decoys (dead pigeons) used: solid symbols, decoys with closed wings; open symbols, decoys with open wings. Circles, percentage of passing pigeons killed; squares, total birds shot as percentage of number of passing flocks. Regressions calculated for the straight-line portions of the response graph and omit the points demarcated by the dotted lines. There is no difference in the response elicited by open- or closed-wing decoys and so these results are combined. Pigeons shot as a percentage of number of flocks at risk (squares): $r_5 = 0.971$; $P < 0.001$; $y = -7.4 + 32.7x$. Pigeons shot as a percentage of total number of birds at risk (circles): $r_6 = 0.877$; $P < 0.01$; $y = -3.8 + 14.3x$.

Artificial decoys produced a poorer response from the passing flocks than dead pigeons (Table 3). Comparing fifteen dead pigeons and fifteen artificial decoys shows that the latter resulted in 13% fewer pigeons being shot, and 46% fewer when forty decoys were used (Table 4).

In addition to the birds shot which responded to decoys, others were shot which passed by when the shooter was in his hide and would have been killed even if no decoys had been used. In the case when single birds were passing, an additional 11% were shot which had not responded to decoys and in flock sizes of one to ten birds combined, an additional 5% were shot (Table 3).

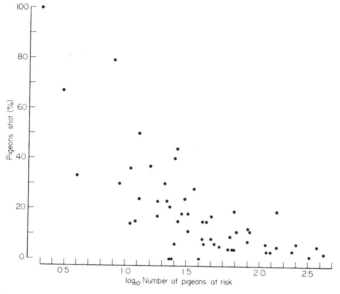

Fig. 10. Percentage of pigeons shot in relation to the $\log_{10}$ number passing within range of decoys/hour. Records combined for situations when fifteen or forty dead pigeon decoys with open or closed wings were used. $r_{53} = -0.724$; $P < 0.001$; $y = 63.5 - 28.1x$.

Sometimes flocks containing more than ten pigeons came in range of the decoys but although the total numbers of birds at risk was large the actual number of flocks was small. Since at most two birds could be shot per flock the sampling errors were large. Table 4 summarizes data dollected when fifteen, forty or 200 decoys were used. The response and shooting rates when dead pigeons with closed wings were used increased and declined as discussed above. Fifteen dead birds with open wings were more attractive to passing birds than fifteen dead birds with closed wings, but when forty decoys were used the response pattern was reversed. Artificial decoys of the kind mostly used by sportsmen were generally less effective than dead pigeons indicating a considerable visual acuity and ability to discriminate subtle cues by the pigeons flying overhead.

The number of pigeons killed per hour was positively correlated with the proportion responding to decoys and the proportion shot but sampling errors masked the relationship. Thus the number of birds and flocks passing per hour varied on different days so that conditions were not absolutely constant for all experimental situations. The data obtained during all separate shooting sessions involving fifteen or forty dead pigeons with wings open or closed are converted to the $\log_{10}$ number of birds passing per hour and the percentage of these which was shot (Fig. 10). The more birds passing per hour

244

Table 4. *Percentage of passing wood-pigeons, irrespective of flock size, which were shot according to the number of decoys used, 1967–68*

		Total time (h)	Total birds at risk	Mean flock size	Percentage responding to decoys	Percentage shot of birds at risk	Percentage shot of birds responding	Percentage shot of those shot at	Number birds passing per hour	Average time to kill one pigeon (h)
15	WC*	20·9	2296	6·7	19	5	28	74	110	0·17
15	WO	12·4	911	4·4	28	7	25	63	73	0·19
15	A	20·5	1088	3·7	18	6	34	73	53	0·31
40	WC	27·0	1220	3·7	56	12	22	66	45	0·18
40	WO	11·2	526	3·2	29	12	41	64	47	0·18
40	A	7·9	869	5·3	22	5	22	49	110	0·19
200	WC	15·3	617	2·5	36	17	47	75	40	0·15

* WC = dead wood-pigeons with closed wings; WO = dead wood-pigeons with open wings; A, artificial decoys. The differences in response rate between 15 WC and 15 WO ($\chi^2 = 31\cdot27$; $P<0\cdot001$), and between 40 WC and 40 WO, are significant ($\chi^2 = 106\cdot5$; $P<0\cdot001$).

the lower the percentage which was shot. This inverse density-dependence obviously, resulted from the fact that the shooter could have only two shots before reloading. But even if he had used a repeating gun there would have been a scaring effect from the first explosion causing the remaining birds to veer away. As might be predicted there was a poor correlation between the number of birds shot when expressed as a percentage of the total flocks passing per hour and regressed on the number of flocks passing per hour ($r_{53} = -0.272$; $P = 0.05$).

The time of day made little difference to the effectiveness of decoy shooting between 10.00 and 16.00 hours (Table 5). It appears, however, that pigeons did decoy less well before 10.00 hours and after 16.00 hours and shooting became less worthwhile in consequence. Early in the morning pigeons leave their roosts and depart on direct flight lines to feeding grounds which they have used the day before and they are not easily distracted. Similarly, in the evening the birds are motivated to get back to the roost.

Table 5. *Effect of time of day on efficiency of decoy shooting*

	Total no. birds passing	Number birds passing/h	Percentage passing birds responding to decoys	Percentage birds at risk which were shot	Average time (h) to kill one pigeon
Before 10.00 hours	758	84	12	5	0·23
10.00–12.00 hours	4718	78	28	7	0·18
12.00–14.00 hours	3046	66	27	11	0·14
14.00–16.00 hours	2624	61	30	9	0·19
After 16.00 hours	172	43	24	10	0·22

COMPARISON OF SHOOTING WITH OTHER METHODS OF KILLING PIGEONS AT CARLTON

Baits treated with alpha-chloralase as a stupefacient were used at Carlton to catch wood-pigeons for examination and in marking and release; over 3300 pigeons were captured in this way. Baits were mostly laid on feeding grounds where good captures could be expected and in general poor feeding places were avoided. Yet it is known that a lower proportion of juveniles is captured if baits are laid on fields where clover density is low and the mean weight of both adults and juveniles is lower than for birds caught on fields of high leaf density (Murton, Isaacson & Westwood 1971).

Comparable shot or stupefied samples for several years are combined in Fig. 11 to show how the estimated proportion of juveniles in the population varied seasonally according to the method of capture. Immediately after breeding neither method adequately sampled young birds as they remained in the woods and only came to consort with adults in the fields later in the autumn. It is possible that, compared with stupefying baits, shooting was biased towards the capture of inexperienced juveniles up until December. But the number of birds caught with baits was relatively small until this time. Food supplies had not reached a critically low level in January (Fig. 1) and on average the proportion of juvenile birds in shot and stupefied samples differed by only 7%, the shot samples containing more juveniles. The situation was reversed in February and stupefied samples contained 10% more young ($\chi^2_2 = 206.1$; $P < 0.001$). Clover stocks were usually at a minimum in February or March and young birds were concentrated on the better feeding grounds, which is where most trials with stupefying baits were conducted. Food supplies improved after March and differences depending on the method of capture were reduced.

246

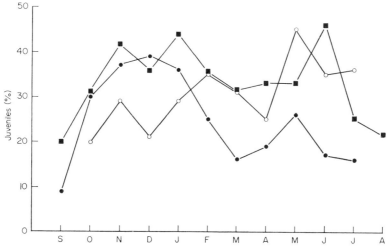

FIG. 11. Percentage of juvenile (<12 months old) wood-pigeons in shot or stupefied samples in monthly collections. ●, shot at Carlton during 1958–70; ○, caught with stupefying bait at Carlton during 1958–70; ■, ringed wood-pigeons which were shot and reported under the British Trust for Ornithology scheme during 1911–70.

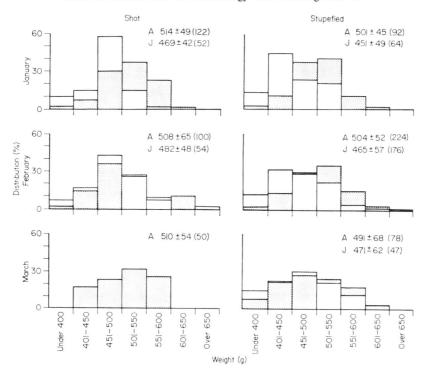

FIG. 12. Percentage weight distribution of wood-pigeons that were shot or captured with stupefying baits; 1964, 1969, 1970 records combined as comparable samples were obtained. stippled histograms, adults; open histograms, juveniles (<12 months old). Means ± S.D. (number in sample) are given. Significant differences between shot and stupefied juveniles were obtained in January ($t_{114} = 2\cdot107$; $P<0\cdot05$) and February ($t_{228} = 2\cdot251$; $P<0\cdot05$). There are differences in the frequency distribution of weights between shot and stupefied samples for adults in February ($\chi_4^2 = 13\cdot747$; $P<0\cdot001$) but not in January ($\chi_3^2 = 6\cdot051$) and March ($\chi_3^2 = 2\cdot998$). Juvenile shot and stupefied samples differed in January ($\chi_3^2 = 16\cdot466$; $P<0\cdot001$) but not in February ($\chi_3^2 = 7\cdot045$) or March (five juveniles only were shot, and are omitted from the histogram).

Both methods revealed an increase in the juvenile ratio in May when it is known from ringing recoveries that immigrants moved into the area. It is probable that immigrant juveniles favoured the pastures and leys where stupefying baits were localized. Those pigeons which fed in the woods and hedgerows which were less dependent on food supplies in the fields, were best sampled by shooting; the ratio of juveniles was much lower in shot samples from May until July. It is known from other studies (Murton 1965) that adults obtain territories in the woods in spring and that woodland rather than open arable farmland is the natural and favoured habitat of the species.

There was no difference in the mean weight of shot or stupefied adults in January but shot juveniles were, on average, 4% heavier than those caught with treated baits; the mean weight of shot juveniles was also higher in February (Fig. 12). In both months it is likely that the differences resulted from the fact that baits were mostly laid on fields of high clover density, where birds of low social status could establish themselves (cf. above and Murton *et al.* 1971). The mean weight of shot and stupefied adults did not differ in February but the variance of the former was significantly greater $F_{99/223} = 1\cdot240$; $P<0\cdot05$. Again it is likely that this was because the shot sample was drawn from a wider range of feeding habitats, for example, woodland, clover fields, fallows, old stubbles, than the baited birds. No differences in weight distribution were found in the case of pigeons examined in March (Fig. 12).

Although many trials with stupefied baits have been conducted records were not normally kept of the man-hour expenditure involved. But from January to March 1969, when Mr Edgar was shooting as many pigeons as he could in the study area (see Table 1) A.J.I. caught pigeons in the same area using baits treated with alpha-chloralose and recorded the costs involved. Excluding the time taken to walk from vehicle to field, also omitted from the shooting calculations, a total of 132 wood-pigeons was caught during 13·5 man-hours for which 80 kg of treated tic beans were used on two fields; pigeons were caught on only one of the sites. There is no reason why bait should not normally be distributed on many more fields, but in this case we did not want to interfere with the freedom of the shooter. This was, therefore, a conservative estimate of the efficiency of baiting procedures and the results compare the efficiency of two experts. The shooter required 0·23 man-hours to kill each pigeon but the baiting techniques needed only 0·1 man-hours. The tic beans plus alpha-chloralose used cost 8p/pigeon, giving a total cost of 13p/bird. This is nearly half of the cost to shoot a bird. The total cost of shooting or use of baits includes the time involved in reaching and leaving the site and carrying equipment and pigeons; the time of spreading bait is also included but the cost of erecting a shooting hide is not. Evidently baiting is a cheaper method of catching and killing pigeons than shooting. From a crop protection viewpoint, shooting has the additional advantage that vulnerable fields can be guarded by the scaring effect of the gunner.

NATIONAL EFFECTS OF CHANGES IN SHOOTING POLICY

Alterations in the seasonal pattern of mortality caused by changes in shooting policy can be judged at national level from the recoveries of birds ringed under the British Trust for Ornithology scheme (Fig. 13). Also, since the age at recovery was known the proportion of pigeons shot each month that were less than 12 months old can be delimited (Fig. 11). There was a consistent tendency for a higher proportion of juveniles to be killed nationally than at Carlton. This was probably because we were conscious of the need to avoid bias and relatively few shooters attempted to sample all habitats in the study area. But nationally many inexperienced guns are involved and these are not allowed to shoot in game preserves and probably concentrate too much on marginal habitats. Moreover, sites such as cabbage fields, where pigeons cause economic damage, are marginal habitats and they attract young birds displaced from more favoured areas. After March, juveniles which had completed the moult could not always be identified on plumage criteria and so some were probably incorrectly classified as adults when they were in fact less than 12 months old. Obviously if subjects were ringed as nestlings, their age on recovery was accurately known and the ringing recoveries are free from this bias.

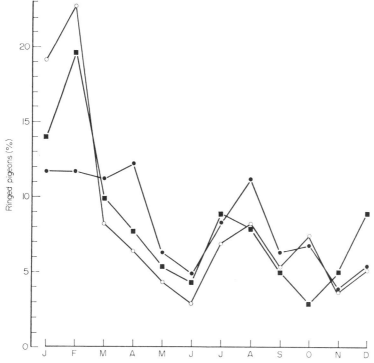

Fig. 13. Percentage distribution of ringed wood-pigeons which were shot; ●, shot between 1911 and 1952 (205 birds); ○, shot between 1953 and 1964, i.e., years of winter battue shoots (376 birds); ■, shot 1965–70 after support for winter battue shoots was withdrawn but subsidized cartridges remained available (413 birds).

Prior to 1953, there was a slight peak in shooting mortality in August, presumably because farmers, game-keepers and their associates shot birds at harvest and as they flighted to the stooked corn. The shooting pressure did not vary much between September and March, and employees on the estates were mostly involved. Thus pigeons will have been killed incidently during partridge shoots and pheasant drives over this period while gamekeepers probably contributed most of the remaining birds. The contribution from specialist decoy gunners was likely to have been small but consistent and such guns may have caused the peak in birds killed in April as wood-pigeons decoy well to the spring sowings.

Official support for the organized battue shooting of birds returning to roost was motivated by the belief that concerted efforts by many people would disturb the birds and keep them on the move causing more to be at risk of shooting. The subsidy scheme introduced in 1953 was administered through the County Pests Officers, who encouraged these evening shoots. But game interests did not allow strangers on the estates until after the pheasant shooting season and so battue shoots were concentrated into the period from mid-January until early March: thereafter, the light evenings brought counter attractions and also the onset of the pheasant breeding season. Fig. 13 shows that during the period 1953–64, 41% of all pigeons shot were killed in January and February, compared with only 23% before the introduction of the subsidy scheme. The subsidy was withdrawn from battue shooting in 1965 but half-price cartridges could still be obtained for other methods until 1969, through the Rabbit Clearance Societies. Although battue shoots were officially discouraged in favour of 'lone-wolf' decoy guns, to some extent, people have continued to follow the habits of the previous ten years as Fig. 13 shows. The current pattern of shooting mortality will doubtless be found to have changed again when sufficient records have accumulated for further analysis.

DISCUSSION

Although the studies described here had an economic purpose, one aspect of the research has theoretical implications in the context of the natural control of animal populations. It has been suggested that various behavioural conventions, including the flock habit and territorial activity serve to limit population size before resources become absolutely limiting (Koskimies 1955; Kalela 1957; Wynne-Edwards 1962). Thus the peck order or dominance hierarchy noted in feeding flocks has been viewed as mechanism for self-regulation of the population enabling resources to be distributed to best advantage and over-exploitation prevented. A contrary argument in the case of the wood-pigeon asserts that the flock habit maximizes population size for it improves the survival expectation of the individual (Murton, Isaacson & Westwood 1971). The amount of clover determined the number of pigeons which could live and survive at Carlton in winter. Shooting killed some birds which would otherwise have eaten food before dying and in this way resources were conserved to better advantage for the survivors. It follows that an efficient self-regulating mechanism should have achieved the same kind of result, but no such effect was seen. Winter mortality was the key-factor determining the way in which numbers fluctuated from year to year, while in turn the food supply determined the amount of winter mortality. Therefore, shooting at the level investigated must have reduced mortality rather than increased it. We suggest that natural selection has failed to produce a mechanism bringing the same benefits to the population as artificial culling because no means exist whereby the individual bird can be sacrificed for the benefit of the group.

Shooting for crop protection can only be justified in those circumstances where pigeons are prevented from attacking a vulnerable crop, and to a large extent the crop protection value of shooting depends on it acting as a scaring mechanism. It seems likely that more efficient and less costly scaring mechanisms are available. Paradoxically, because battue shooting reduced winter competition and allowed more birds to survive until spring it probably increased the risks of crop damage once the winter season of limiting resources was passed. In addition, winter battue shooting was more costly in man-hours and cartridge expenditure than decoy shooting (Table 2).

The scale of mortality due to shooting achieved to date, has been insufficient to hold population size below the level determined by food resources. If population control were made an objective more efficient ways of killing pigeons should be adopted. Alternatively, from a sporting viewpoint the wood-pigeon could be managed as a valuable resource, in which case the past level of shooting was below the optimum for maximum exploitation; perhaps an increase of one-half to three-quarters of the past annual shooting effort could have been tolerated without detriment to stocks. However, the decline in numbers of this species, first noted in 1968, has continued so that in 1973 the breeding population was about one-quarter of the level pertaining during the early years of the study. The decline has been the result of changes in arable farming methods which have led to a loss of leys and pastures and hence of clover stocks. The role of shooting in these changed circumstances has yet to be defined.

ACKNOWLEDGMENTS

The study would have been impossible without the splendid co-operation of Mr W. H. Edgar—we know he enjoyed his task even if at times we frustrated his prospects of achieving a good bag. We thank Dr J. P. Dempster for critically reading a draft of this manuscript, his suggestions for its improvement being gratefully accepted.

SUMMARY

(1) A wood-pigeon (*Columba palumbus*) population and its clover and grain food supply was censused from 1958 until 1970. During the first six years, winter battue shoots were held between late January until early March and large numbers of birds were killed as they returned to roost. No shooting occurred during the next three years and then an intensive experimental programme of decoy shooting by one man was monitored throughout the last three years.

(2) Shooting did not increase the total amount of winter mortality above the level experienced in the absence of shooting. The number of wood-pigeons in autumn and winter was determined by the amount of grain on cereal stubbles, or clover on leys and pastures, respectively, and immigrants moved in to take advantage of any unexploited food resource.

(3) There was no increase in pigeon numbers following abolition of battue shoots in 1965. Ringing records show that a higher proportion of recovered pigeons were found dead instead of being shot, suggesting that birds which previously were shot before dying of food shortage now succumbed for natural causes.

(4) In 1968–69 the average cost in terms of man-hours and cartridges for an expert decoy gunner to kill one pigeon was £0.24. It cost £0.13 to kill a pigeon with stupefying baits (0.10 man-hours/bird instead of 0.23 man-hours for shooting). For shooting to affect population size, a cost of about £0.50/bird would probably be realistic, assuming sufficient guns were available.

(5) For a given number of dead pigeon-decoys the percentage of passing pigeons at risk which responded, decreased as flock size increased as did the percentage shot. Ignoring any scaring benefit, decoy shooting is most effective as a means of killing pigeons when single birds or small flocks are at risk. An increase in the number of dead pigeon decoys with closed wings, to about eighty or, with open wings to about forty, led to an increase in the percentage response from live birds and hence numbers shot, but with more decoys pigeons were repelled. Within the ranges defined (0–80 and 0–40) there was no difference in the effectiveness of dead pigeons with closed or open wings. It is estimated that 7% of live pigeons at risk are killed with five closed-wing decoys, 14% with twenty such decoys and 23% (the maximum) with eighty decoys. Artificial decoys were 13–46% less useful than dead pigeons depending on the number used.

(6) A comparison is made of the age and weight distribution of shot wood-pigeons with those captured by the use of stupefying baits and differences are discussed. Variations in the seasonal pattern of shooting mortality consequent on changes in official policy and bounty incentives are examined by an analysis of those recoveries of ringed birds which had been shot.

REFERENCES

Colquhoun, M. K. (1951). *The Wood-Pigeon in Britain*. H.M.S.O., London.

Kalela, O. (1957). Regulation of reproduction rate in sub-arctic populations of the vole *Clethrionomys rufocanus* (Sund.). *Suomal.-ugr. Seur. Aikak.* Ser. A, IV, No. 34, 60 pp.

Koskimies, J. (1955). Ultimate causes of cyclic fluctuations in numbers in animal populations. *Papers on Game Research* (*Helsinki*), No. 15, 29 pp.

Lack, D. (1966). *Population Studies of Birds*. Clarendon Press, Oxford.

Murton, R. K. (1965). *The Wood-Pigeon*. Collins, London.

Murton, R. K. (1973). The use of biological methods in the control of vertebrate pests. *Biology in Pest and Disease Control* (Ed. by D. Price-Jones & M. E. Solomon). Blackwell Scientific Publications, Oxford. (In press.)

Murton, R.K. & Jones, B.E. (1973). The ecology and economics of damage to Brassicae by wood-pigeons *Columba palumbus*. *Ann. appl. Biol.* **75**, 107–22.

Murton, R. K. & Ridpath, M. G. (1962). The autumn movements of the wood-pigeon. *Bird Study*, **9**, 7–41.

Murton, R. K., Isaacson, A. J. & Westwood, N. J. (1966). The relationships between wood-pigeons and their clover food supply and the mechanism of population control. *J. appl. Ecol.* **3**, 55–96.

Murton, R. K., Isaacson, A. J. & Westwood, N. J. (1971). The significance of gregarious feeding behaviour and adrenal stress in a population of wood-pigeons *Columba palumbus*. *J. Zool. Lond.* **165**, 53–84.

Murton, R. K., Westwood, N. J. & Isaacson, A. J. (1964). A preliminary investigation of the factors regulating population size in the wood-pigeon. *Ibis*, **106**, 482–507.

Murton, R. K., Westwood, N. J. & Isaacson, A. J. (1974). Factors affecting egg-weight, body-weight and moult of the woodpigeon *Columba palumbus*. *Ibis*, **116**, 1–22.

Wynne-Edwards, V. C. (1962). *Animal Dispersion in Relation to Social Behaviour*. Oliver & Boyd, Edinburgh.

COMPETITIVE EXCLUSION BETWEEN THE RODENT GENERA *MICROTUS* AND *CLETHRIONOMYS*

Austin W. Cameron

Comparative studies of the faunas occurring on islands and adjacent mainland areas have revealed instances of what have been interpreted as examples of competitive exclusion in a number of vertebrate groups, particularly birds (Amadon, 1953; Lack, 1942; Mayr, 1942, 1963; Serventy, 1951) and reptiles (Brown and Marshall, 1953; Underwood, 1962). In these cases it has been found that closely related forms with similar habits may occur sympatrically on a mainland area but often only one species has succeeded in becoming established on an adjacent island, because, it is assumed, of the poverty of available ecological niches. It further appears, in many instances, that the particular species which first reaches an island is the one which will become established there and once it has done so it can apparently prevent subsequent colonization by other closely related forms.

Similar cases of competitive exclusion on islands have not been reported upon in detail for mammals, and it therefore seems desirable to place on record what appears to be a clear-cut example of ecological competition between the Holarctic rodent genera *Microtus* (North America: meadow vole; Britain: short-tailed vole) and *Clethrionomys* (North America: red-backed vole; Britain: bank vole). North American data apply only to *Microtus pennsylvanicus* and *Clethrionomys gapperi* due to the lack of detailed information on other species of these genera. The data presented here are based primarily on field studies carried out by the writer at various times over a 10-year period; otherwise, material has been drawn from the published works of other zoologists.

On the mainland of temperate North America where both genera occur, *Microtus pennsylvanicus* is essentially a grassland form whereas *Clethrionomys gapperi* is virtually confined to forested, or at least, scrubby areas. In peak years of population density, *Microtus* may invade open woodlands in small numbers and may even occur in isolated grassy areas which are completely surrounded by forest. Scrubby areas, especially in swamps, may be invaded at such times. *Clethrionomys*, on the other hand, seems never to invade exclusively grassy areas, regardless of population density. This is not to imply that *C. gapperi* is incapable of living in grassland habitats, but no instance is known to the writer where this is the case.

That *Microtus* may well be restricted to grasslands on the North American continent because it is excluded from the woodlands by *Clethrionomys* is quite apparent from the fact that on large, ecologically diversified islands such as Newfoundland where *Clethrionomys* is absent, *Microtus* occurs commonly throughout the woodlands as well as the grasslands (Cameron, 1958). Twenty-seven of the 43 specimens collected on the island were taken in forested areas; one specimen was collected in a mature spruce woodland 20 miles from the nearest known grassland area.

Similarly, *Microtus* was found to be most abundant in upland coniferous woodlands on the Magdalen Islands (Quebec) in the summer of 1959. Thirty-six of the 50 specimens collected were taken in woodlands. *Clethrionomys* does not occur there but the deer mouse, *Peromyscus maniculatus*, is native and presumably a limited degree of competition does exist between it and *Microtus* when the latter is at a peak in population density, as was the case in the summer of 1959 (Cameron, 1962a).

On a number of smaller inshore islands in eastern Canada studied by the writer, *Microtus* was also found in heavily forested areas, but in all cases *Clethrionomys* was absent. This was found to be true of Bonaventure Island (Gaspé Peninsula) and Ile-aux-Coudres (St. Lawrence River estuary). The 11 *Microtus* collected on the latter island were taken in mature coniferous woods typical of the habitat occupied by *Clethrionomys* on the mainland. Mac-Kay (1963) likewise found that *Microtus* is both a forest and grassland species on the main island of the Grand Manan Archipelago, New Brunswick. Here, as in the instance cited above, *Clethrionomys* is not part of the insular fauna.

Considering that *Clethrionomys* is absent from all the offshore islands in eastern North America, such as Newfoundland, Anticosti, and the Magdalens, the question naturally arises as to whether this is due to a failure in migration or to exclusion by already firmly established populations of *Microtus*. Since *Clethrionomys*, unlike *Microtus* and *Peromyscus*, has not colonized a single offshore island in eastern North America, and very few on the West Coast, it seems reasonable to conclude that this microtine is less adept at crossing saltwater barriers than the other two species.

Fortunately, the distribution of the two genera in the British Isles throws considerable light on the problem. In contrast to the situation in North America, *Clethrionomys* does occur on a number of offshore islands, on several of which it is the only microtine. *Microtus* is more widely distributed and occurs on approximately 75% of the islands, including the Orkneys and some of the Outer Hebrides (Barrett-Hamilton and Hinton, 1910–1921; Corbet, 1961). Except for the Scottish islands of Mull and Bute, which are separated from the mainland by narrow, shallow channels, on none of the islands do the two genera occur together.

Corbet (1961) is of the opinion that these islands were already separated from the mainland at the time of the retreat of the last ice sheet, or, in any case, that conditions were such that no rodents could have lived in the area when land connections were present. On this basis he expresses the view that all rodents now occurring on these islands were obliged to cross the water gaps between the islands and the mainland.

In the view of most mammalian taxonomists, only one species of bank vole, *Clethrionomys glareolus*, occurs in the British Isles, where it is widely distributed throughout England, Wales, the Lowlands of Scotland, the valleys of the Scottish Highlands, and on certain islands. Two species of *Microtus* occur in Britain, *M. arvalis*, which is confined to the Orkneys and the island of Guernsey, and *M. agrestis*, which is found throughout England, Scotland, and Wales and on some of the islands of the Hebrides group. Conflicting theories have been put forth to explain the restricted distribution of *arvalis*, some workers assuming that it is a relict form once widely distributed in Britain but subsequently replaced by *agrestis*, a later invader (Barrett-Hamilton and Hinton, 1910–1921), while others suppose that it was introduced to these islands by man (Corbet, 1961). Where *Clethrionomys* and *Microtus* occur together, the former is found chiefly in woodlands, hedgerows, and areas of low shrubs, whereas the latter is most common in rough grasslands and damp meadows.

Two of the islands in the Inner Hebrides provide naturally occurring experimental conditions pertinent to this problem, as the writer found while engaged in field studies there in 1962. Skye and Raasey are neighboring islands separated by a channel less than a mile in width at its narrowest point. Ecologically, the two islands appear identical. Yet, Skye is inhabited only by *Microtus agrestis* and Raasey only by *Clethrionomys glareolus*. There is nothing to suggest that conditions on either island especially favor the microtine which inhabits it.

A similar situation, with regard to these microtines, is to be found on the islands of Jersey and Guernsey. Guernsey is inhabited only by *Microtus arvalis* and Jersey only by *Clethrionomys glareolus*. The writer did not personally visit these islands, but all available information on their ecology would lead one to conclude that they do not differ sufficiently to favor either one microtine or the other.

In addition to the situation on Skye and Raasey and on Jersey and Guernsey, it might be mentioned that *Clethrionomys glareolus* occurs on the island of Skomer, whereas *Microtus* is absent, although present on the nearby coast of Wales.

Considering the distribution of microtines on the offshore islands of Great Britain, the fact seems inescapable that *Clethrionomys* is capable of preventing *Microtus* from colonizing an island which it has reached first and on which it has become firmly established. Likewise, *Microtus* seems capable of excluding *Clethrionomys* under similar circumstances. Corbet (1961) expresses such a view in his paper on the insular distribution of British mammals.

As previously mentioned, *Clethrionomys* is absent from all the larger offshore islands in eastern North America, and from many of the smaller inshore islands obviously only recently severed from the mainland. It is considered likely that this microtine is absent from such large, offshore islands as Newfoundland, Anticosti, and the Magdalens because these islands are believed not to have had postglacial land connections with the mainland (Cameron, 1958) and *Clethrionomys* was not successful in crossing the water barriers. *Microtus*, on the other hand, has reached both Newfoundland and the Magdalen Islands, but how this was achieved is now only a matter for speculation. Natural rafts or floating ice have been suggested as possibilities.

The situation with regard to Bonaventure Island and Ile-aux-Coudres differs in that these islands were severed from the mainland only recently and both are connected to it by ice bridges for at least 3 months of the year. Since *Clethrionomys* is common in the wooded areas of the mainland immediately adjacent to the islands,

there is every reason to suppose that this microtine was present prior to the disappearance of the land connection. Both islands have rather extensive coniferous–deciduous woods which do not appear to differ significantly from those on the neighboring mainland where *Clethrionomys* is common (Cameron, 1953). Other "islands," which are still connected to the mainland by land bridges, such as Cheticamp Island in Nova Scotia, are inhabited by both species. If the land connection is ecologically unfavorable to the species, it may be that *Clethrionomys* disappears before the island is completely severed from the mainland (Cameron, 1962b), but there is no evidence for this.

It is interesting that *Clethrionomys* should be absent from small coastal islands lying less than 2 miles offshore but present on those still connected by some sort of land bridge. It seems likely that both *Microtus* and *Clethrionomys* were present on the islands while they were connected to the mainland, but after the land bridges had disappeared, the competition between the two increased in severity and *Microtus* eventually replaced *Clethrionomys*. This suggests that *Microtus* is the more aggressive of the two, or that it has some slight advantage over its rival under the particular conditions that obtain in a restricted area. On islands that are largely forested, it might be expected that *Clethrionomys* would have the advantage, but apparently this is not so. Unfortunately, we know far less about the ecology of *Clethrionomys* than we do about *Microtus*, and there may be unknown factors involved that are not directly associated with interspecific competition.

Of interest, also, is the fact that *Clethrionomys* has successfully colonized a number of offshore islands in Europe but has failed to do so in eastern North America. Corbet (1961) supposes that *Clethrionomys* and *Microtus* were carried to the British offshore islands by man, but if so one would expect them to occur on such islands as Ireland, Rhum, and Lewis. Most zoogeographers favor the theory that they reached the islands by natural means (Steven, 1953). The writer, likewise, rejects the idea that man was responsible for the dispersal of small mammals to the islands in eastern Canada (Cameron, 1958).

Two salient facts emerge from the data presented above bearing on the ecological interaction between *Microtus* and *Clethrionomys*: (1) the competition between species of the two genera is sufficiently strong that one of them can establish a "beachhead" on an island and thus prevent the other from successfully colonizing it, as is evident from the insular distribution of both species in the British Isles, and (2) that on an island where *Clethrionomys* is absent, *Microtus* will appropriate the ecological niche normally occupied by species of that genus as studies on five North American islands have demonstrated. On the basis of these facts, it is quite evident that *Microtus pennsylvanicus* is largely restricted to grasslands because it is excluded, through ecological competition, from woodlands by *Clethrionomys gapperi*. It is postulated that *Microtus* would appropriate the ecological niche now occupied by *Clethrionomys* were the latter to disappear in the temperate parts of North America where is occurs.

SUMMARY

On the mainland of North America the two microtine rodents, *Clethrionomys gapperi* and *Microtus pennsylvanicus*, exist in close proximity in woodlands and grasslands, respectively, and exhibit no obvious competition. That ecological competition does exist between the two genera, however, and with considerable severity, is evident from studies made by the writer both in Europe and in North America.

The distributional pattern of the two genera on the coastal islands of Great Britain is indicative of a strong ecological competition between the two microtines. Some islands are inhabited by *Microtus*, others by *Clethrionomys*, but on none of the offshore islands do both occur together.

Since pairs of islands, such as Skye and Raasey, and Jersey and Guernsey, which are ecologically very similar, have different microtines inhabiting them, it can only be concluded that the particular genus which now occurs on a given island was the first to reach it. It is suggested that whichever reached the island first established a "beachhead" and thereby prevented its rival from becoming established. Only species which are in strong competition can exclude one another in this way.

On ecologically diversified islands in North America, such as Newfoundland, the Magdalen Islands, and Bonaventure Island, where *Clethrionomys* is absent, it was found that *Microtus* can appropriate the ecological niche normally occupied by *Clethrionomys*. On this basis it is suggested that on the North American mainland *Microtus* is absent from the woodlands because this ecological niche is occupied by *Clethrionomys* and not because it cannot adapt to such an environment.

From the foregoing it is evident that in those situations where suitable habitat is at a premium, a strong ecological rivalry arises between species of the genera *Microtus* and *Clethrionomys* such that one can effectively exclude the other.

ACKNOWLEDGMENTS

Grateful acknowledgment is made to the British Council for the financial assistance which made it possible to carry out field studies on the Scottish islands. Thanks are also due to the Redpath Museum, the National Research Council of Canada, and the National Museum of Canada for the financial support which enabled the writer to carry out his studies in North America and the British Isles.

Thanks are due to A. J. Tomlinson of the Redpath Museum for his assistance in collecting material in the field and subsequent processing in the laboratory.

LITERATURE CITED

AMADON, DEAN. 1953. Remarks on the Asiatic hawk-eagles of the genus *Spizaetus*. Ibis, **95**: 492–500.

A. W. Cameron

Barrett-Hamilton, Gerald E. H., and M. A. C. Hinton. 1910–1921. A history of British mammals. Gurney and Jackson, London.

Brown, W. C., and J. T. Marshall. 1953. New scincoid lizards from the Marshall Islands, with notes on their distribution. Copeia, **1953**: 201–207.

Cameron, A. W. 1958. The mammals of the Trois Pistoles area and the Gaspé Peninsula, Quebec. Nat. Mus. Canada Bull., **128**: 168–188.

——. 1958. Mammals of the islands in the Gulf of St. Lawrence. Nat. Mus. Canada Bull., **154**: 165 p.

——. 1962a. Mammalian zoogeography of the Magdalen Islands Archipelago, Quebec. J. Mamm., **43**: 505–514.

——. 1962b. Mammalian dispersal in relation to an artificial land bridge. Can. Field-Naturalist, **76**: 142–146.

Corbet, G. B. 1961. Origin of the British insular races of small mammals and of the "Lusitanian" fauna. Nature, **191**: 1037–1040.

Lack, David. 1942. Ecological features of the bird faunas of British small islands. J. Animal Ecol., **11**: 9–36.

MacKay, A. A. 1963. A comparative zoogeographical study of the mammals occurring on the islands of the Grand Manan Archipelago, New Brunswick. Unpublished Report, Dept. Zool., McGill Univ.

Mayr, Ernst. 1942. Systematics and the origin of species. Columbia Univ. Press, New York.

——. 1963. Animal species and evolution. Belknap Press of Harvard Univ., Cambridge.

Serventy, D. L. 1951. Inter-specific competition on small islands. Western Austral. Nat., **3**: 59–60.

Steven, D. M. 1953. Recent evolution in the genus *Clethrionomys*. Symposia for the Soc. Exp. Biol. (Evolution), Cambridge, Vol. **7**: 310–319.

Underwood, Garth. 1962. Reptiles of the eastern Caribbean. Caribbean Affairs, New Series, No. 1, Dept. of Extra-Mural Studies, Univ. of the West Indies.

INTERSPECIFIC TERRITORIES OF BIRDS

GORDON H. ORIANS AND MARY F. WILLSON[1]

Abstract. Territories of birds, usually defended against conspecific individuals, are some-times defended against individuals of other species. Since such behavior is demanding both of time and energy, natural selection should favor ecological divergence, the establishment of overlapping territories, and the reduction of aggression. Lack of divergence in modes of exploitation could mean that insufficient time has elapsed for the changes to be completed or that the environment imposes some limitation preventing the evolution of the required degree of divergence. Such environmental limitation can be predicted in (a) structurally simple environments, (b) when feeding sites are strongly stratified in structurally complex vegetation, or (c) when the presence of other species in the environment prevents divergence in certain directions. The known cases of interspecific territoriality in birds are analyzed and shown to be largely in accordance with these predictions, although several cases of overlapping territories in situations where interspecific territoriality has been predicted provide relationships worthy of further study. We suggest that Darwinian selection at the level of the individual permits an understanding of the known structure of avian communities and that there is no need at present to invoke new selective mechanisms at the level of the community or ecosystem.

INTRODUCTION

Most birds defend territories against conspecific individuals but some species also defend territories against individuals of other, usually closely related species. Since territories are multipurpose areas, it has been difficult to evaluate the evolutionary significance of various uses of them, but interspecific territorial behavior is a simpler phenomenon to interpret than intraspecific territorial behavior because none of the functions primarily concerned with reproduction, e.g., formation and maintenance of the pair and prevention of inbreeding, can be of much importance in such situations. Lanyon (1959) has suggested that interspecific territoriality may prevent the forma-tion of mixed pairs but this is unlikely (Johnson 1963 : 190).

Momentary aggression resulting from mistaken identity is commonly observed in birds, and it has been suggested that interspecific territorial aggression may be merely the result of a bird misidentifying an intruder as one of his own spe-cies. Several types of evidence indicate that erro-neous identification is probably inadequate as a general explanation of interspecific territorial ag-gression. First, some of the known cases involve species with strikingly different sizes and/or plumage patterns. Also, Weeden and Falls (1959) have demonstrated that discrimination of neigh-bors by males of one territorial species is fine enough to permit recognition of individual neigh-bors and Marler and Isaac (1960a and b) have shown that sufficient variability is present in the songs of a number of species to permit such discriminations. Many cases of interspecific territoriality appear to involve stable systems of sustained aggression that are difficult to dismiss on the basis of misidentification.

Territorial behavior is currently of theoretical interest since some investigators find concepts of group selection more attractive as explanations than natural selection operating through differential reproductive success of the individuals comprising an interbreeding population. For example, Wynne-Edwards (1962, p. 395) has suggested that two potentially competing populations have evolved interspecific territorial behavior in cooperation with each other so as to prevent mutual overexploitation of a common food supply. Group selection, under a variety of names, e.g., interdeme selection, community selection, selection for stability, ecosystem selection, etc., currently has widespread support (Dunbar 1960; Emerson 1960; Huxley 1962; Mather 1961; Slobodkin 1961). Although the results of this kind of selection might be useful for the populations concerned, the concept has been rejected by others (Fisher 1941; Lack 1954, p. 22; Rensch 1959, pp. 10-13) on the grounds that no adequate mechanism for such a process is known.

Although further work on possible mechanisms of group selection may be desirable, it is possible to study the evolution of territorial behavior in terms of natural selection by making predictions from selection and comparing them with present information.

Recently Johnson (1963 pp. 193-196) has considered the evolution of interspecific territoriality from the point of view of releasing mechanisms, and we shall not expand on his excellent treatment. Rather, our analysis will be directed toward ecological aspects of the subject.

Predictions from Natural Selection

Since conspicuous advertising by territorial males probably results in increased predation rates and requires increased energy intake while reducing the time available for feeding, resting, preening, and care of the offspring, the advantages of holding a territory presumably must outweigh these disadvantages. Defense of a territory against individuals of other species also demands increased expenditure of time and energy. Since individuals of other species are, in general, no threat to pair formation and mating, the exclusion of other species from territories strongly suggests that securing an adequate quantity of some limited resource has given selective advantage to the behavior.

Nestsites may be limited, particularly for hole-nesting species but securing a nestsite should be most easily achieved by aggression centered on the nestsite. Since we shall consider only cases where relatively large areas are defended, this leaves food as the most likely factor for it is the only other unsharable environmental resource likely to be generally in short supply for birds.

The potential impact of ecologically similar species upon each other's food supply is difficult to assess quantitatively. Measurement of the total amount of food present in an area and of the fraction consumed by the birds is but a small part of the required information. Of particular importance, perhaps, is the effect upon reproductive success of the rate at which food can be delivered to the nestlings. Feeding rates are influenced by many factors, including the abundance and availability of food, nutrient content of food items, time available for hunting, manner of searching, and so on.

If the ranges of two previously allopatric species begin to overlap, at least four outcomes of the initial contact are possible. (1) Barriers to interbreeding may not have been established, so that hybridization swamps the differences between the two populations. (2) One species may competitively eliminate the other. (3) The species may exclude each other from parts of the area, dividing the available terrain between them by means of habitat selection and/or interspecific territorial defense. (4) The species may persist sympatrically with overlapping territories.

Interspecific aggression may be expected when populations of two species of birds come into contact for the first time (Hamilton 1962; Johnson 1963, p. 199). Indigo (*Passerina cyanea*) and Lazuli buntings (*P. amoena*), whose zone of contact has been expanded by recent human activities (Wells 1958), and some species whose ranges are believed to have come in contact since the retreat of Pleistocene glaciation (Rand 1949) have been reported to be interspecifically aggressive. Initial aggression may be expected even if plumage divergence has been considerable, as in the case of the buntings, for any new intruder might profitably be considered to be a potential competitor. However, if the species are so different that the effort required for their mutual exclusion is not compensated by increased access to resources, interspecific aggression should, in time, decrease and disappear. When the species coming into contact are different enough ecologically to maintain overlapping territories, selection may favor morphological divergence to reduce the probability of mistaken identity, but since this possibility is not

TABLE I. Interspecific territoriality among birds of simple vegetation[a]

Vegetation type	Species	Location	References
Marshes	*Agelaius phoeniceus - Xanthocephalus xanthocephalus*	West. U.S.	Linsdale 1938; Fautin, 1940; this paper
	Agelaius phoeniceus - A. tricolor	California	Orians and Collier 1963
	Agelaius phoeniceus - Quiscalus quiscula	Wisconsin	Nero 1956; J. Wiens, in prep.
	Acrocephalus scirpaceus - A. schoenobaenus	England	Brown and Davies 1949
Grasslands	*Euplectes hordeaceus - E. nigroventris*	Tanganyika	Fuggles-Couchman 1943
	Sturnella magna - S. neglecta	Wisconsin	Lanyon 1956
	Cassidix major - C. mexicanus	Texas, La.	Selander and Giller 1961
	Corvus corone - C. monedula, C. frugilegus	England	Coombs 1960
Deserts	[a]*Oenanthe monarcha - *[a]*O. leucopyga - *[a]*O. lugens*	Egypt	Hartley 1949
	*Oenanthe lugens - *[a]*O. hispanica - *[a]*O. deserti*	Egypt	Hartley 1950
	Oenanthe pleschanka - O. oenanthe	Ukraine	Stresemann 1950
	Oenanthe hispanica - O. oenanthe	Aegean Is.	Stresemann 1950
	[a]*Monticola solitarius - *[a]*Oenanthe leucopyga*		
	[a]*O. lugens - *[a]*O. pleschanka*	Egypt	Simmons 1951
Tundra	*Stercorarius pomarinus - S. parasiticus*	Alaska	Pitelka, Tomich, & Treichel 1955 a & b
	Pluvialis squatarola - P. dominica	N.W. Terr.	Drury 1961
Shore lines	*Charadrius hiaticula - C. dubius - C. alexandrinus*	England	Simmons 1956
	Charadrius hiaticula - C. dubius	England	Armstrong 1952
		Denmark	Rosenberg and Nielsen 1957

[a]Nonbreeding territories.

central to our concern we shall not consider it further.

If individuals of two species upon first coming into sympatry are interspecifically territorial, and if ecological divergence and subsequent overlap of territories are favored by selection, explanations must be found for stable systems of interspecific territoriality. One possible explanation is that gene flow from the respective centers of the ranges of two species experiencing initial contact may prevent divergence, both ecological and behavioral, in the region of sympatry (Selander and Giller 1963). However, since many cases of interspecific territoriality involve species with extensive range overlap, this cannot account for all cases.

Conversely, it is possible that species may have evolved different enough releasers during their isolation that they do not respond aggressively to each other even though their degree of ecological overlap is sufficient to give selective advantage to interspecific territoriality. In these cases interspecific aggression would be expected to evolve but if the species are largely allopatric, gene flow from the areas of allopatry might prevent mutual exclusion from evolving. Careful studies of closely related species of similar ecology but with overlapping territories are needed to elucidate this problem. If gene flow is preventing interspecific territoriality from evolving, breeding success should be on the average lower for pairs whose territories broadly overlap those of the close relative. No data of this sort appear to be available.

Another possibility is that the nature of the environment may limit the types of efficient foraging patterns, thus reducing the possibilities for sufficient divergence to permit overlap in territories. MacArthur (1961) has presented a theoretical argument that some of the conceivable foraging adaptations must be more wasteful of time than others. Thus, two species with similar food requirements are not likely to forage through the same environments capturing, say, only particular species of insects, for any individual of either species that picked up all insects of suitable size should be able to gather more food per unit time. MacArthur has predicted that the most efficient foraging specializations for birds should involve distinctive, species-specific patterns of moving through different strata of the vegetation. Recent evidence indicates that the foraging patterns of birds conform to this prediction (Hartley 1953; MacArthur 1958; MacArthur, MacArthur, and Preer 1962).

Conditions Promoting Interspecific Territoriality

If environmental features restrict ecological divergence, interspecific territoriality may be maintained (a) when the structure of the vegetation is simple, (b) when species are adapted to exploit stratified food sources in complex vegetation, or (c) when other species are already exploiting similar resources in a diversified habitat. We shall now examine these cases in detail.

260

Structural simplicity of vegetation

Laboratory studies of competition have shown that coexistence is usually impossible for ecologically similar species in very simple, homogeneous environments (Gause 1934; Park 1954). Although natural environments are never as simple as laboratory conditions they may nonetheless be relatively simple with respect to the ecology of the species exploiting them. Many cases of interspecific territoriality involve species breeding in structurally simple vegetation such as marshes, grasslands, tundra, deserts, and shore lines (Table I). In these habitats most species of birds are dependent upon the air-water or air-ground interface for their major food supply. Since only a limited number of methods of exploitation are therefore possible, cohabitation should be more difficult.

Our work has primarily concerned relations between blackbirds breeding in structurally simple marsh vegetation. In western North America the red-winged blackbird (*Agelaius phoeniceus*) and the yellow-headed blackbird (*Xanthocephalus xanthocephalus*) are common and frequently breed in the same marshes. Of the two, the redwing has a widespread geographic range and is more ubiquitous in marshes within its range than is the yellowhead.

The data presented here were obtained during the 1961 and 1962 breeding seasons at Turnbull National Wildlife Refuge, Cheney, Washington. The refuge includes about 1,533 acres of open water, and about 2,462 acres of marshland, mostly in the form of potholes underlain by lava. The dominant emergent plants are cattails (*Typha*) and bulrushes (*Scirpus*).

Most marshes on the refuge support breeding populations of both species of blackbirds, and in every case the territories are mutually exclusive. Redwing territories are established by late March and typically encompass all available emergent vegetation. In mid- and late April the redwings are evicted by the incoming yellowheads from parts of the marshes, usually those with deeper water and sparser vegetation (Figs. 1, 2, and 3). Interspecific aggression, although common during this period, is not usually of the intensity characteristic of intraspecific encounters, probably because the species are genetically well isolated. Furthermore, conspecific males are sometimes attacked in areas where males of the other species are not molested, perhaps because they are capable of fertilizing the females of the territory owners. Areas defended by yellowheads against other yellowheads but not against redwings are indicated by arrows in Figures 1, 2, and 3.

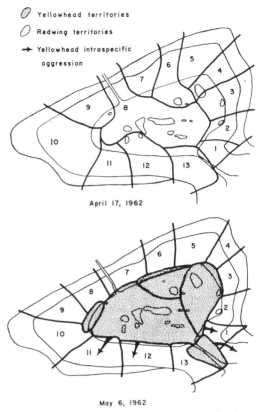

FIG. 1. Breeding territories of redwings and yellowheads. MacDowell Lake, Turnbull National Wildlife Refuge, Cheney, Washington.

Redwings frequently foraged on newly established yellowhead territories without being chased, but trespassing decreased and chasing increased as nesting began. Other observers (Linsdale 1938; Fautin 1940) have reported interspecific territoriality between these two species, so that the phenomenon is probably widespread throughout the area of sympatry. There is no reason to believe that the present situation is resulting from recent contact. Since the food brought to the nestlings of both species is very similar (Willson and Orians 1963) the competition necessary for the maintenance of interspecific territoriality is apparently present.

Yellowheads are dominant over redwings when they meet at feeding grounds off the breeding territories. In 53 out of 55 encounters observed at an artificial feeding station during April 1962, male yellowheads displaced male redwings. The outcomes of the remaining two cases were uncertain. Yet, in territorial interactions dominance is

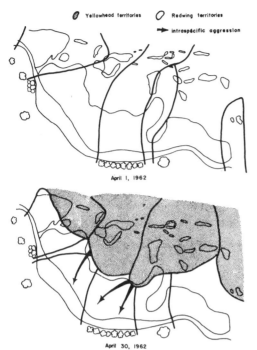

FIG. 2. Breeding territories of redwings and yellowheads, Thirty Acre Meadow, Turnbull National Wildlife Refuge, Cheney, Washington.

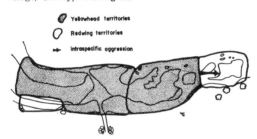

FIG. 3. Breeding territories of redwings and yellowheads. MacDowell Lake, Turnbull National Wildlife Refuge, Cheney, Washington.

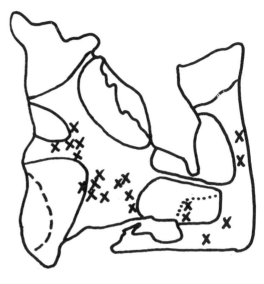

May 10, 1962

FIG. 4. Breeding territories of marsh wrens and locations of redwing nests, Foster's Island, Seattle, Washington. The dashed line indicates the actual closest border of the contracted wren territory at the time of construction of the closest redwing nest. The dotted line indicates the border of the wren territory at the time of construction of the two redwing nests. The subsequent expansion of the wren territory was accompanied by much interspecific strife. Data on marsh wren territories were provided by Jared Verner.

related to the nature of the vegetation, since redwings are dominant over yellowheads on the peripheries of most marshes. All cases of stable interspecific territoriality probably involve slight differences in habitat selection, as shown for the blackbirds, and for meadowlarks (Lanyon 1957). Presumably selection favors strong aggression especially in those parts of the habitat to which a species is best adapted because the benefits to be realized from aggression increase in relatively better habitats.

We have also noted strong interspecific aggression by both redwings and yellowheads toward

long-billed marsh wrens (*Telmatodytes palustris*) in several areas of Washington and British Columbia. Although the territories are not completely exclusive, nests and feeding areas are strongly segregated (Fig. 4). Marsh wren territories at Turnbull were compressed when yellowheads arrived and expanded into former yellowhead territories when the yellowhead breeding season was over. Fautin (1940) in Utah and Nero (1956) in Wisconsin recorded the same phenomenon. All redwing nests located within wren territories failed, usually very early in the nesting cycle (Verner, pers. comm.). The only known successful yellowhead nest near an active wren nest at Turnbull resulted in the wrens' desertion. A complicating factor is that wrens puncture unguarded eggs of blackbirds. At Turnbull in 1962, at least 21 of 260 sets of eggs (8%) were thought to have been destroyed by wrens. Therefore aggression toward wrens may be advantageous be-

TABLE II. Interspecific territoriality among birds with stratified feeding in complex habitats[a]

Method of feeding	Species	Location	References
Large ground arthropods taken from elevated perches	[a]*Lanius collurio* - [a]*L. nubicus*	Egypt	Simmons 1951
Arthropods taken in flight from elevated perches	*Otus trichopsis* - *O. scops* *Empidonax hammondii* - *E. oberholseri* *E. wrightii*	Arizona, Mexico California	Marshall 1957 Johnson 1963
Ground-dwelling vertebrates taken from elevated perches or flight	*Buteo jamaicensis* - *B. lineatus*	Michigan Maryland California	Craighead & Craighead 1956 Stewart 1949 Dixon 1928
	Bubo virginianus - *Strix varia*	Kansas	Baumgartner 1939
	Strix varia - *Tyto alba*	Michigan	Wilson 1938
	Asio otus - *Otus asio* - *Aegoluis acadicus*	Michigan	Wilson 1938
	[a]*Buteo lagopus* - [a]*Falco mexicanus*	Nebraska	Bennett 1938
Ground foragers	*Zonotrichia albicollis* - *Melospiza melodia*	Ontario	Kendeigh 1947
Arthropods taken from large trunks and branches	*Centurus aurifrons* - *C. carolinus*	Texas	Selander & Giller 1959
	Centurus aurifrons - *C. uropygialis*	Mexico	Selander & Giller 1963
	[a]*Centurus carolinus* - [a]*Melanerpes erythrocephalus*, [a]*Dendrocopos pubescens*, [a]*Parus bicolor*	Maryland	Kilham 1958 a & b
Flower feeders	*Calypte anna* - *Selasphorus sasin*	California	Legg & Pitelka 1956
	[a]*Calypte anna* - [a]*Selasphorus sasin*	California	Pitelka 1951 Trousdale 1944
	[a]*Calypte costae* - *Archilochus alexandri*	Arizona	Bene 1952
	[a]*Hylocharis leucotis* - *Eugenes fulgens*, [a]*Lampornis clemenciae*, [a]*Cynanthus latirostris*	Mexico	Moore 1939
	[a]*Calothorax lucifer* - [a]*Archilochus alexandri*, [a]*Selasphorus platycercus*	Texas	Fox 1954
	[a]*Selasphorus rufus* - [a]*Stellula calliope*	Wyoming	Armitage 1955

[a] Nonbreeding territories.

cause of its effects in reducing the loss of eggs rather than because of competition for food. However, it is, in turn, possible that the habit of puncturing eggs has evolved in wrens because they feed on a wide variety of small invertebrates and, hence, may overlap considerably in food requirements with other, mostly small passerines.

Interspecific territoriality should be looked for in such groups as the Old World larks where habitat segregation is marked (Mountfort 1958), and might be expected among surface-feeding aquatic species. Although colonies of gulls (Lewis 1941; Emlen 1956) and terns (Pemberton 1922) are species-specific, they may be adjacent, and detailed studies of foraging areas of birds from these colonies have not been made.

Stratified feeding in structurally complex habitats

Species with specializations for feeding on resources concentrated at a given level in the vegetation may find divergence difficult even in structurally complex vegetation. For example, interspecific aggression is recorded between species that hunt large, ground-dwelling arthropods by flying down from elevated perches; between ground-foraging species; between large raptors dependent upon ground foraging rodents; and between species foraging on tree bark (Table II).

We have tentatively included *Otus asio* and *O. trichopsis* in the list of interspecifically territorial species despite Marshall's somewhat contradictory statements (1957:76). Johnson (1963:193) has interpreted Marshall's data as indicating overlapping territories. But Marshall, although reporting that territories may overlap, states that *trichopsis* took over territories of *asio* after the latter had been shot for specimens, thus indicating mutual avoidance.

However, by no means all species foraging in these ways are interspecifically aggressive. Woodpeckers may exploit their food sources in several ways (Burt 1930), several species of large raptors in Africa are reported to have overlapping territories (Brown 1955), and the ground foraging Brown and Abert towhees (*Pipilo fuscus* and *P. aberti*) overlap with no aggression in Arizona (Marshall 1960). The factors making overlap possible for these species are poorly understood and more information on foraging behavior is required.

In temperate vegetation the location of flowers tends to be seasonally stratified and no North American hummingbirds are known to have overlapping foraging or breeding territories. This situation is complicated, however, by the insectivorous habits of some hummingbirds. An examination of floral diversity and overlap of hummingbird territories in the tropics might be rewarding, since with the profusion of epiphytes and prevalence of cauliflory it may be possible for the birds to specialize on different strata in the vegetation. Observations of fruit-eating musophagids in Africa (Moreau 1958) and of habitat selection among Australian meliphagids (Keast 1961) suggest that interspecific territoriality may occur in these groups also. See also Ripley (1959) for aggression between meliphagids and nectariids.

Evidence suggests that several species of wrens, all foragers on fallen trees and low tangles of vegetation, may be interspecifically territorial (Bent 1963, p. 190; Brooks 1934, 1947; Henderson 1931; Miller 1941; Sutton 1930; Newman 1961), but data are fragmentary and nest sites may be limited for these birds.

Prior Presence of Other Species Exploiting the Same Resources of the Environment

The ability of a species to diverge from a competitor is not only influenced by the structural complexity of the habitat and, hence, the number of efficient foraging methods possible, but also by the number of sympatric species of similar ecologies. Two species competing in a given habitat with an impoverished avifauna can more easily evolve sufficient differences to coexist permanently than the same two species in a similar habitat with a full complement of avian species.

For example, in western European forests as many as six species, including five subgenera, of titmice (*Parus*) can be found together in the same woods, foraging in mixed parties outside the breeding season and having overlapping territories during the breeding season (Gibb 1956). By contrast only two subgenera occur in North America and no more than two species can be found together. Moreover, all members of the *Poecile* group except *P. hudsonicus* and *P. atricapillus,* and all members of the *Baeolophus* group are largely allopatric (Dixon 1961). Two cases of interspecific territoriality are known and others suspected (Murie 1928; Dixon 1954; Brewer 1963; our observations on *P. atricapillus* and *P. gambeli* at Turnbull). In western Europe titmice dominate the forest canopy, only one of the large number of warblers (Sylviidae) being a canopy feeder, whereas in North America the titmice share the canopy with many species of warblers (Parulidae) and vireos (Vireonidae). The genus *Parus* apparently evolved in the Old World, invading the New World more recently (Snow 1954). In North America it encountered an avifauna already containing groups of species adapted for gleaning insects from the foliage of trees. The presence of these other species apparently restricted the evolutionary possibilities for parids on this continent, and being unable to diverge ecologically, they continue to find selective advantage in interspecific territoriality. Conversely, interspecific territoriality in European warblers (Howard 1913; Raines 1945) may be related to the restricting influence of the dominant titmice in the canopy (Table III).

TABLE III. Interspecific territoriality among species with ecologic range narrowed by the presence of ecologically similar species in different families

Species	Location	References
Parus inornatus - P. wollweberi	Arizona	Dixon 1950; Marshall 1957
Parus atricapillus - P. carolinus	Illinois	Brewer 1963
Sylvia atricapilla - S. borin	England	Howard 1913; Raines 1945

DISCUSSION AND CONCLUSIONS

Interspecific territoriality appears to be common in circumstances where one would predict, on the basis of natural selection at the level of the individual, that the achievement of the required degree of divergence should be most difficult. Moreover, among species of simpler vegetation we have found no cases of coexistence of large numbers of closely related species with overlapping territories, as occur among insectivorous birds of forests (Hartley 1953; MacArthur 1958). We therefore suggest that competitive interactions of individuals of the species living together provide a sufficient basis for understanding current knowledge of avian community structure. Acquisition of more complete data may necessitate modification of this statement but at the present there is no need to invoke group selection mechanisms.

For several reasons interspecific territoriality among birds may be much more common than currently recognized. Abundant evidence indicates that in the absence of a normal component of a community another species often occupies the habitat, suggesting that most species are prepared to expand ecologically, but are continually held in check by competition with other species. Moreover, surplus populations of sexually mature individuals are probably characteristic of many species of birds (Carrick 1963; Hensley and Cope 1951; Stewart and Aldrich 1951; Orians 1961). If the territorial system of a species prevents certain individuals from breeding in optimal areas, they should be expected to attempt to breed in habitats used by ecologically similar species, and, hence, aggression should occur.

Failure to observe interspecific aggression may be owing to a general bias introduced into most ecological investigations by time and energy considerations affecting the investigator. Typically investigators wish to maximize the amount of useful information obtained per unit of time expended and thus study species in optimal habitats, where the birds are most numerous. Strong selective pressure for ecological divergence in areas of sympatry may lead to divergence of habitat selection, thus reducing the arena of interspecific aggression to intermediate habitats. Thus, the literature of avian ecology pertains largely to populations in optimal habitats where interspecific aggression is less likely.

Finally, recent drastic changes in the earth's vegetation caused by human activity have resulted in many shifts in distributional range of species, so that the number of newly established contacts between formerly allopatric species may be large. Moreover, many range changes are probably still occurring in response to postglacial vegetation shifts. If it is true that interspecific aggression is often to be expected initially, there should be a number of cases of recently initiated aggression that might profitably be studied at this time.

Our analysis has proceeded from the assumption that the food resources of the territory give selective advantage to the expenditure of time and energy in interspecific territory defense. Since the predictions were relatively successful we suggest that more effective exploitation of food supplies may be a major function of territoriality in general, although certain important exceptions to our predictions warrant further investigation. Since the possible functions of interspecific territoriality are fewer than those of intraspecific territoriality, the former may prove of increasing usefulness in the study of the evolution of territorial behavior and of the complex ecological question of "How different is different enough?" to permit sympatry.

ACKNOWLEDGMENTS

The ideas presented here have been clarified through discussion with Frank A. Pitelka and Robert H. MacArthur. Personal observations were generously provided by Jared Verner on wrens and blackbirds. The original data presented here were obtained during research supported by National Science Foundation Grant G-17834 to Orians and a National Science Foundation Cooperative Graduate Fellowship to Willson.

LITERATURE CITED

Armitage, K. B. 1955. Territorial behavior in fall migrant rufous hummingbirds. Condor 57: 239-240.

Armstrong, E. A. 1952. The distraction displays of the little-ringed plover and territorial competition with the ringed plover. Brit. Birds 45: 55-59.

Baumgartner, F. M. 1939. Territory and population in the great horned owl. Auk 56: 274-282.

Bene, F. 1942. Costa hummingbird at Papago Park, Arizona. Condor 44: 282-283.

Bennett, W. W. 1938. A prairie falcon and American rough-legged hawk fight. Wilson Bull. 50: 57.

Bent, A. C. 1963. Life histories of North American nuthatches, wrens, thrashers and their allies. U. S. Nat. Mus. Bull. 195: xi + 1-435.

Brewer, R. 1963. Ecological and reproductive relationships of black-capped and Carolina chickadees. Auk 80: 9-47.

Brooks, M. 1934. Some changes in the breeding birds of Upshur County, West Virginia. Wilson Bull. 46: 243-247.

———. 1947. Interrelations of house wren and Bewick's wren. Auk 64: 624.

Brown, L. H. 1955. Supplementary notes on the biology of the large birds of prey of Embu District, Kenya Colony. Ibis 97: 38-64, 183-221.

Brown, P. E., and M. G. Davies. 1949. Reed-warblers. Foy, East Molesey, Surrey. 127 pp.

Burt, W. H. 1930. Adaptive modifications in the woodpeckers. Univ. Calif. Publ. Zool. 32: 455-524.

Carrick, R. 1963. Social and ecological factors in population regulation of the Australian magpie, *Gymnorhina tibicen*. Proc. XVI Int. Congr. Zool. 3: 339-341.

Combs, C. J. F. 1960. Observations on the rook *Corvus frugilegus* in southwest Cornwall. Ibis 102: 394-419.

Craighead, J. J., and F. C. Craighead, Jr. 1956. Hawks, owls and wildlife. Harrisburg, Pa.: Stackpole. Pp. xix + 1-443.

Dixon, J. B. 1928. Life history of the red-bellied hawk. Condor 30: 228-236.

Dixon, K. L. 1950. Notes on the ecological distribution of plain and bridled titmice in Arizona. Condor 52: 140-141.

———. 1954. Some ecological relations of chickadees and titmice in central California. Condor 56: 113-124.

———. 1961. Habitat distribution and niche relationships in North American species of *Parus*. Pp. 179-216. In W. F. Blair (ed.), Vertebrate speciation, Austin, Texas: Univ. of Texas Press.

Drury, W. H. 1961. The breeding biology of shorebirds on Bylot Island, Northwest Territories, Canada. Auk 78: 176-219.

Dunbar, M. J. 1960. The evolution of stability in marine environments. Natural selection at the level of the ecosystem. Am. Naturalist 94: 129-136.

Emerson, A. E. 1960. The evolution of adaptation in population systems. Pp. 307-348. In S. Tax (ed.) Evolution after Darwin, vol. 1, The evolution of life.

Emlen, J. T., Jr. 1956. Juvenile mortality in a ring-billed gull colony. Wilson Bull. 68: 232-238.

Fautin, R. W. 1940. The establishment and maintenance of territories by the yellow-headed blackbird in Utah. Great Basin Nat. 1: 75-91.

Fisher, R. A. 1954. Average excess and average effect of a gene substitution. Annals of Eugenics 11: 53-63.

Fox, R. P. 1954. Plumages and territorial behavior of the Lucifer hummingbird in the Chisos Mountains, Texas. Auk 71: 456-466.

Fuggles-Couchman, N. R. 1943. A contribution to the breeding ecology of two species of *Euplectes* (bishop-birds) in Tanganyika Territory. Ibis 83: 311-326.

Gause, G. F. 1934. The struggle for existence. Baltimore: Williams and Wilkins. Pp. ix + 163.

Gibb, J. A. 1956. Territory in the genus *Parus*. Ibis 98: 420-429.

Hamilton, T. H. 1962. Species relationships and

adaptations for sympatry in the avian genus Vireo. Condor 64: 40-68.

Hartley, P. H. T. 1949. The biology of the mourning chat in winter quarters. Ibis 91: 393-413.

———. 1950. Interspecific competition in chats. Ibis 92: 482.

———. 1953. An ecological study of the feeding habits of the English titmice. J. Animal Ecol. 22: 261-288.

Henderson, G. 1931. Incompatability of house and Carolina wrens. Wilson Bull. 43: 224-225.

Hensley, M., and J. B. Cope. 1951. Further data on removal and repopulation of the breeding birds in a spruce-fir forest community. Auk 68: 483-495.

Howard, H. E. 1913. The British warblers. Part 8. London: Porter.

Huxley, J. S. 1962. Higher and lower organization in evolution. J. Royal College of Surgeons of Edinburgh 7: 163-179.

Johnson, N. K. 1963. Biosystematics of sibling species of flycatchers in the Empidonax hammondii-oberholseri-wrighti complex. Univ. Calif. Publ. Zool. 66: 79-238.

Keast, A. 1961. Bird speciation on the Australian continent. Bull. Mus. Comp. Zool. 123: 305-495.

Kendeigh, S. C. 1947. Bird population studies in the coniferous forest biome during a Spruce Budworm outbreak. Dept. Lands and Forests, Ont., Div. Res., Biol. Bull., No. 1.

Kilham, L. 1958a. Sealed-in winter stores of red-headed woodpeckers. Wilson Bull. 70: 107-113.

———. 1958b. Territorial behavior of wintering red-headed woodpeckers. Wilson Bull. 70: 347-358.

Lack, D. 1954. The natural regulation of animal numbers. Oxford: Clarendon Press. Pp. viii + 1-343.

Lanyon, W. E. 1956. Territory in the meadowlarks, genus Sturnella. Ibis 98: 485-489.

———. 1957. The comparative biology of the meadowlarks (Sturnella) in Wisconsin. Publ. Nuttall Orn. Club 1: 1-67.

———. 1959. The behavioral, ecological and morphological characteristics of two populations of alder flycatcher, Empidonax traillii (Audubon) [Review of article by Robert Stein]. Auk 76: 110-111.

Legg, K., and F. A. Pitelka. 1956. Ecologic overlap of Allen and Anna hummingbirds nesting at Santa Cruz, California. Condor 58: 393-405.

Lewis, H. F. 1941. Ring-billed gulls of the Atlantic coast. Wilson Bull. 53: 22-30.

Linsdale, J. M. 1938. Environmental responses of vertebrates in the Great Basin. Am. Midland Naturalist 19: 1-206.

MacArthur, R. H. 1958. Population ecology of some warblers of northeastern coniferous forests. Ecology 39: 599-619.

———. 1961. Population effects of natural selection. Am. Naturalist 95: 195-199.

MacArthur, R. H., J. W. MacArthur, and J. Preer. 1962. On bird species diversity. II. Prediction of bird census from habitat measurements. Am. Naturalist 96: 167-174.

Marler, P., and D. Isaac. 1960a. Physical analysis of a simple bird song as exemplified by the chipping sparrow. Condor 62: 124-135.

———, ———. 1960b. Song variation in a population of brown towhees. Condor 62: 272-283.

Marshall, J. T. 1957. Birds of pine-oak woodland in southern Arizona and adjacent Mexico. Pac. Coast Avif. 32: 1-125.

———. 1960. Interrelations of Abert and brown towhees. Condor 62: 49-64.

Mather, K. 1961. Competition and cooperation. Pp. 264-281, in Mechanisms in biological competition. Symposia of the Society for Experimental Biology X v, Cambridge Univ. Press.

Miller, E. V. 1941. Behavior of the Bewick wren. Condor 43: 81-99.

Moore, R. T. 1939. Habits of white-eared hummingbirds in northwestern Mexico. Auk 56: 442-446.

Moreau, R. E. 1958. Some aspects of the Musophagidae. Ibis 100: 67-112, 238-270.

Mountfort, G. 1958. Portrait of a wilderness. London: Hutchinson. Pp. 1-240.

Murie, O. J. 1928. Notes on the Alaska chickadee. Auk 45: 441-444.

Nero, R. W. 1956. A behavior study of the red-winged blackbird. II. Territoriality. Wilson Bull. 68: 129-150.

Newman, D. L. 1961. House wrens and Bewick wrens in northern Ohio. Wilson Bull. 73: 84-86.

Orians, G. H. 1961. The ecology of blackbird (Agelaius) social systems. Ecol. Mono. 31: 285-312.

———, and G. Collier. 1963. Competition and blackbird social systems. Evolution 17: 449-459.

Park, T. 1954. Experimental studies of interspecies competition. II. Temperature, humidity, and competition in two species of Tribolium. Physiol. Zool. 27: 177-238.

Pemberton, J. R. 1922. A large tern colony in Texas. Condor 24: 37-48.

Pitelka, F. A. 1951. Ecologic overlap and interspecific strife in breeding populations of Anna and Allen hummingbirds. Ecology 32: 641-661.

———, P. Q. Tomich, and G. W. Treichel. 1955a. Ecological relations of jaegers and owls as lemming predators near Barrow, Alaska. Ecol. Mono. 25: 85-117.

———, ———, ———. 1955b. Breeding behavior of jaegers and owls near Barrow, Alaska. Condor 57: 3-18.

Raines, R. J. 1945. Notes on the territory and breeding behavior of blackcap and garden-warbler. Brit. Birds 38: 202-204.

Rand, A. L. 1949. Glaciation, an isolating factor in speciation. Evolution 2: 314-321.

Rensch, B. 1959. Evolution above the species level. New York: Columbia Univ. Press. Pp. xvii + 1-419.

Ripley, S. D. 1959. Competition between sunbird and honeyeater species in the Moluccan Islands. Am. Naturalist 93: 127-132.

Rosenberg, N. T., and B. P. Nielsen. 1957. Iag'ttagelser af vadefugle isger af Lille Praestekrare (Charadrius dubius curonicus Gm.); vel. Søndersø, Nordsjaelland, 1954. Dansk Orn. Foren. Tidskr. 57: 65-73.

Selander, R. K., and D. R. Giller. 1959. Interspecific relations of woodpeckers in Texas. Wilson Bull. 71: 107-124.

———, ———. 1961. Analysis of sympatry of great-tailed and boat-tailed grackles. Condor 63: 29-86.

———, ———. 1963. Species limits in the woodpecker genus Centurus (Aves). Bull. Am. Mus. Nat. Hist. 124: 213-274.

Simmons, K. E. L. 1951. Interspecific territorialism. Ibis 93: 407-413.

———. 1956. Territory in the little ringed plover Charadrius dubius. Ibis 98: 390-397.

Slobodkin, L. B. 1961. Growth and regulation of animal populations. New York: Holt, Rinehart, and Winston. Pp. viii + 1-184.

Snow, D. W. 1954. The habitats of Eurasian tits (*Parus* spp.). Ibis 96: 565-585.

Stewart, R. E. 1949. Ecology of a nesting red-shouldered hawk population. Wilson Bull. 61: 26-35.

———, and J. W. Aldrich. 1951. Removal and repopulation of breeding birds in a spruce-fir forest community. Auk 68: 471-482.

Stresemann, E. 1950. Interspecific competition in chats. Ibis 92: 148.

Sutton, G. M. 1930. The nesting wrens of Brooke County, West Virginia. Wilson Bull. 42: 10-17.

Trousdale, B. 1954. Copulation of Anna hummingbirds. Condor 56: 110.

Weeden, J. S., and J. B. Falls. 1959. Differential responses of male ovenbirds to recorded songs of neighboring and more distant individuals. Auk 76: 343-351.

Wells, P. V. 1958. Indigo buntings in lazuli bunting habitat in southwestern Utah. Auk 75: 223-224.

Willson, M. F., and G. H. Orians. 1963. Comparative ecology of red-winged and yellow-headed blackbirds during the breeding season. Proc. XVI Int. Zool. Congr., Vol. 3: 342-346.

Wilson, K. A. 1938. Owl studies at Ann Arbor, Mich. Auk 55: 187-197.

Wynne-Edwards, V. C. 1962. Animal dispersion in relation to social behavior. Edinburgh: Oliver and Boyd. Pp. xi + 1-653.

ALTITUDINAL ZONATION OF CHIPMUNKS (*EUTAMIAS*): INTERSPECIFIC AGGRESSION

H. Craig Heller

Abstract. Eutamias alpinus, E. speciosus, E. amoenus, and *E. minimus* are contiguously allopatric on the eastern slope of the Sierra Nevada, California. This paper is part of a study of the factors determining the lines of contact between these contiguously allopatric populations. Overlapping fundamental niches and nonoverlapping realized niches indicate that competitive exclusion has occurred. Patterns of intra- and interspecific aggression are described for these four species. The aggressive dominance of *alpinus* and *amoenus* explain the limited realized niches of *speciosus* and *minimus*. Hypotheses regarding the evolution of the patterns of aggressive behavior observed in these species are suggested. Aggression has been selected for in *alpinus* and *amoenus* because of a seasonal, potentially limiting food supply which is economically defendable. Aggression has not been selected for in *minimus* because it is not metabolically feasible to engage in aggressive interactions in the hot sagebrush desert. Aggressive behavior has not been selected for in *speciosus* probably because of predator pressure and the seasonal abundance of food in its habitat.

Altitudinal zonation of plant and animal species has been described for many localities since the classic work of C. Hart Merriam on San Francisco Mountain (1890). The present investigation is concerned with the causes of and maintenance of the altitudinal zonation of four species of western chipmunks along the Yosemite transect of the Sierra Nevada, California. The zonation of the animal species along this transect has been extensively documented by Grinnell and Storer (1924).

Altitudinal zonation is a special case related to the general question, why is a particular organism limited to the habitats in which it is found? This question takes on a great deal of interest in the case of closely related species whose ranges are contiguous but not overlapping, i.e. contiguous allopatry (Miller 1967). Contiguously allopatric species have a line of contact between them, and the maintenance of this line must be due to the effects of the environment on the species and/or the effects of the species on each other. Hutchinson's terminology (1957) of realized and fundamental niches facilitates clear visualization of the situation. If the fundamental niches of two contiguously allopatric species do not overlap, the line of contact between them must represent a physical or physiological barrier to both species. To have completely different fundamental niches, the species must have striking differences in physiology, morphology, and/or behavior. On the other hand if the fundamental niches of two contiguously allopatric species overlap but their realized niches do not, competitive exclusion has probably occurred. Competitive exclusion can be the result of exploitation competition or, as in this study, interference competition (sensu Miller 1967).

The work described in this paper is part of an analysis of the factors which determine the altitudinal zonation of four closely related, morphologically similar, contiguously allopatric species. This paper concerns the role of interspecific aggression in delimiting the lines of contact between the species and the evolution of these patterns of aggressive behavior.

MATERIALS AND METHODS

The four species of western chipmunks used in this study, *Eutamias alpinus* Merriam, *E. speciosus frater* J. A. Allen, *E. amoenus monensis* Grinnell and Storer, and *E. minimus scrutator* Hall and Hatfield (Hall and Kelson 1959), were live trapped on an east-west transect of the Sierra Nevada, California, through Yosemite National Park, 38° N latitude. The taxonomy and specific habitats of the chipmunks of the Sierra Nevada have been described by Johnson

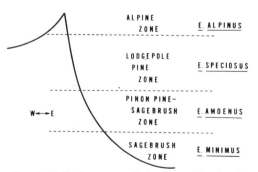

Fig. 1. Stylized transect of the Sierra Nevada, California, 38° N lat showing the zonation of dominant vegetation and the altitudinal ranges of the four *Eutamias* species.

(1943). The eastern slope of the Sierra Nevada was selected as the study area because it is a steep fault scarp with extremely well-defined life zones ranging from alpine to sagebrush desert (Grinnell and Storer 1924, Klyver 1931). In this area the chipmunk species are separated altitudinally according to the major plant life zones (Fig. 1). The animals were brought into the laboratory in September 1966, 1967, and 1968, caged individually as previously described (Heller and Poulson 1970), and maintained under constant conditions of 16° ± 2°C and a photoperiod of 12L:12D. Food in the form of sunflower seeds (27% protein) and Purina rat chow (23% protein) as well as water were available ad libitum.

Apparatus for the observation of behavioral interactions

Two observation chambers were built and used to observe intra- and interspecific patterns of aggression and dominance. Each chamber (Fig. 2) consists of a long runway (2.5 m × 20 cm × 10 cm) at either end of which there is a nest compartment and in the

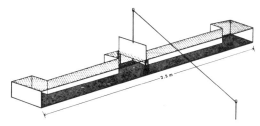

FIG. 2. The apparatus for the observation of behavioral interactions. The runway is 2.5 m long with a plexiglass front and a wire mesh top. A sliding partition divides the apparatus into two equal halves each with a feeding compartment and a nest compartment.

center there is a feeding compartment. The whole apparatus is divided into two equal halves by a sliding wood partition. The top of the chamber is covered with wire mesh, and the front of the runway is a hinged plexiglass cover. The observation chambers were placed in a room isolated from all other activities of the laboratory, and all observations were made from behind a black curtain.

Procedure for behavioral interaction experiments

Before each experiment the observation chamber was washed, clean sawdust was spread on the bottom, and food and water were provided in the center compartment. The weights and breeding conditions of the animals chosen for the experiment were recorded and, with the center partition down, each animal was introduced into its half of the apparatus through a door in the nest compartment. The animals were then left undisturbed for 1–3 days until they freely moved

with upright posture in the runways. They were then deemed acclimated, and the observer raised the center partition from behind the curtain. The movements of the animals to the food area and to the other half of the runway were noted while the partition was up. Behavioral interactions, mostly describable as attacks, chases, and retreats, were recorded. The animals were not always active, so long periods with no interactions often passed. After each 15-to-30-min observation period the animals were again separated by the center partition. Dominance was declared if during one observation period at least five attacks by one animal resulted in retreats by the other animal. A run was scored as "no aggression" if frequent contacts but no agonistic behavior occurred between the animals. If no or few contacts occurred after several observation periods, the run was discontinued and not scored.

Cover transects

The structure of the habitat was believed to be an important source of selective pressure involved in the evolution of the different patterns of aggressive behavior observed in the four species, and measurements of cover were therefore made. The amounts of cover available in the natural habitats of the four species were determined by using a tape to place random 30-m transects across the habitats and recording the percentage of each transect that fell over logs, shrubs, rocks, and roots.

RESULTS

The behavior of the animals in the apparatus clearly reflected their aggressive interactions and dominance relationships. Attacks, retreats, and chases occurred frequently. An intimidated animal would limit its activity and crouch or huddle in a corner, avoiding any direct head-on encounters with its opponent. An aggressive animal would rapidly extend its movements to the other half of the apparatus and frequently seek encounters with the other animal by approaching it closely. If an aggressive animal were approached, it would not avoid direct head-on encounters, but would lower its head, smooth back its ears, and stare directly at the other animal, often growling at the same time. A nonaggressive, nonintimidated animal would approach another animal freely and permit itself to be approached. If both animals were nonaggressive, they would characteristically rub noses and then smell each other's anal region. Attempted mountings were often observed between nonaggressive individuals regardless of sex or breeding condition.

Intraspecific aggression

Conspecific pairs were tested to establish whether or not intraspecific aggression occurs and to compare

TABLE 1. Intraspecific aggression

Species	Aggression	No aggression	Probability[a] of occurrence by chance
Eutamias alpinus	6	0	.02
Eutamias speciosus	3	5	.36
Eutamias amoenus	9	0	.01
Eutamias minimus	3	7	.17

[a]Based on one-tailed sign test.

TABLE 2. Patterns of interspecific aggression in *Eutamias*

Species combination	Outcome			Probability of occurrence by chance	
	Dominance		No Aggr.	Aggr.	Dom.
	alpinus	speciosus			
alpinus ♀ vs. speciosus ♀	7	1	1	< .02	< .04
alpinus ♂ vs. speciosus ♂	7	0	1	< .04	< .01
alpinus ♂ vs. speciosus ♀	2	2	1	< .19	< .69
Totals	16	3	3	< .01	< .01
	speciosus	amoenus			
speciosus ♀ vs. amoenus ♀	1	7	0	< .01	< .04
speciosus ♂ vs. amoenus ♂	0	3	3	< .66	< .13
speciosus ♂ vs. amoenus ♀	0	5	0	< .03	< .03
Totals	1	15	3	< .01	< .01
	amoenus	minimus			
amoenus ♀ vs. minimus ♀	7	1	1	< .02	< .04
amoenus ♂ vs. minimus ♂	1	1	3	= .05[a]	< .75
amoenus ♀ vs. minimus ♂	5	0	0	< .03	< .03
Totals	13	2	9	< .15	< .01

[a]No aggression occurred in a significant proportion of runs in this combination.

the extent to which it occurs in the four species. Only female/female and female/male combinations were used in order to maximize the probability of aggressive interactions (explanation under "Interspecific aggression"). The null hypothesis was that there is an equal probability in each run of aggressive or nonaggressive interactions. Of course, biologically, any occurrence of aggression may be significant. This null hypothesis was only used to reveal significant differences in the data. The data were analyzed using a one-tailed sign test (Owen 1962). All four species showed intraspecific aggression (Table 1). Aggression occurred in all *Eutamias alpinus* and *E. amoenus* runs, but not in a significant proportion of *E. speciosus* and *E. mimimus* runs. Using two-by-two contingency tables to detect interspecific differences in the levels of intraspecific aggression, the species fall into two groups: the highly aggressive *alpinus* and *amoenus* and the less aggressive *speciosus* and *minimus*.

Interspecific aggression

The data obtained from interspecific pairs are presented in Table 2 according to species combination and sex of the individuals. Each of the three interspecific combinations tested consisted of species which come into contact in nature (Fig. 1). Each run represents a different pair of individuals. A total of 14 *minimus*, 10 *amoenus*, 15 *speciosus*, and 12 *alpinus* were used. Only runs in which both animals acclimated fully were scored. The outcome of a run was scored in one of three categories: one or the other individual was dominant, or no aggressive interactions occurred.

Two null hypotheses were used to reveal significant differences in the data, and they were tested with a one-tailed sign test (Owen 1962). The first null hypothesis was that there is an equal possibility of aggressive or nonaggressive interactions in each pairing of individuals. The probabilities are listed in the column titled "Aggression" (Table 2). The second null hypothesis was that where aggressive interactions occur, both individuals of the pair have an equal possibility of being dominant. The probabilities are listed in the column titled "Dominance" (Table 2).

The totals for all *alpinus* versus *speciosus* runs show that the occurrence of aggressive interactions

and the dominance of *alpinus* over *speciosus* are significant ($P < .05$). In both male/male and female/female combinations aggression occurs and *alpinus* is aggressively dominant to *speciosus*. Aggression and dominance were not statistically significant in the *alpinus* male versus *speciosus* female combination. A few more runs may have revealed that aggression occurred in a significant number of cases, but the more interesting finding is that *alpinus* males are not consistently dominant over *speciosus* females even though they are dominant over *speciosus* males, and *alpinus* females are dominant over *speciosus* females. This is a reflection of the qualitative observation which applies to all of the species; aggression is more intense in the females than in the males. This observation is supported by field accounts that the home ranges of female *quadrimaculatus* (Storer, Evans, and Palmer 1944), *amoenus* and *minimus* (Sheppard 1965) are more exclusive (i.e. nonoverlapping) than the home ranges of the males of the respective species. The combination of *alpinus* female versus *speciosus* male was not tried; but, from the above evi-

H. C. HELLER

dence for (a) the aggressive dominance of *alpinus*
when paired with *speciosus* individuals of the same
sex, and (b) the higher levels of aggressiveness in
females of a species in comparison to the males, it
would be expected that *alpinus* females would be
dominant over *speciosus* males.

The totals for all *speciosus* versus *amoenus* runs
indicate that aggressive interactions occur in a significant proportion of runs and that *amoenus* is dominant. When females were paired with females, the
occurrence of aggressive interactions was significant
with *amoenus* dominant. When males were paired,
however, aggressive interactions did not occur in a
significant proportion of runs, but when they did
occur *amoenus* was dominant. *E. amoenus* females
were dominant over *speciosus* males.

The total data from the *amoenus* versus *minimus*

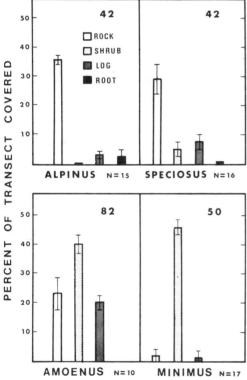

FIG. 3. The available low cover in the habitat of each
species. The *E. alpinus* data are averaged from 15 30-m
transects, the *speciosus* data from 16 30-m transects, the
amoenus data from 10 30-m transects, and the *minimus*
data are from 17 30-m transects. Two standard errors
are indicated to each side of the mean, and the total
per cent of the transect falling over low cover is indicated in the upper right of each set of histograms. The
diversity of cover in each habitat (H = $-\Sigma p_i \log_e p_i$) is
as follows: *alpinus*, H = .50; *speciosus*, H = .92; *amoenus*, H = 1.05; *minimus*, H = .30.

combinations do not permit the conclusion that aggressive interactions occur in a significant number of
encounters, but when aggression does occur *amoenus*
is dominant. Aggressive interactions occur when
amoenus females are paired with *minimus* females,
and *amoenus* is dominant. Very little aggression is
noted when males of this combination are paired,
and the data from these trials permit the conclusion
that nonaggressive interactions occur significantly
($P = .05$) between males of these two species.

Natural cover

Descriptions of the kind and amount of low cover
available in the habitat of each species are presented
in Figure 3. The habitat of *E. amoenus* offers the
most utilizable and diverse cover. In addition to the
categories noted, this habitat also contains numerous
piñon pine trees (*Pinus monophyla*) which *amoenus*
frequently climbs and forages under. The habitat
of *minimus* offers much less utilizable cover than that
of *amoenus* (50% in comparison to 82%), and the
cover is much less diverse, more dispersed, and consists primarily of bushes of sagebrush and a few other
desert shrubs.

The habitats of *alpinus* and *speciosus* both have
about 42% cover, the majority of which is rocks;
however, there is a qualitative difference. The habitat of *speciosus* has mostly large boulders separated
by open ground. The habitat of *alpinus* is very
broken boulder fields and very little open ground.
A stretch of boulder fields offers many more escape
routes and much more protection from predators
than would the same length of solid rock. In addition
to the low ground cover represented in Figure 3,
speciosus habitat also contains numerous evenly
spaced lodgepole pines (*Pinus contorta*) which this
species often climbs to considerable heights. *E. alpinus* habitat includes clumps of whitebark pine
(*Pinus albicaulis*) which the animals occasionally
visit but they do not appear to spend much of their
foraging time there.

DISCUSSION

The populations of the four chipmunk species considered in this study are contiguously allopatric. This
spatial distribution is often assumed to be the result
of competitive exclusion (Blair et al. 1957). However, a pattern of contiguous allopatry may also result from an environmental discontinuity presenting
a physical or physiological barrier to dispersal or just
facilitating habitat selection. As pointed out by Hutchinson (1957) and Miller (1964, 1967), in order to
invoke competition as a primary cause of contiguous
allopatry, it is necessary to demonstrate that where
the two species are in contact the realized niche of
at least one of the species is less than its fundamental
niche.

Two lines of evidence can be used to speculate on the degree of overlap of the fundamental niches of the *Eutamias* species: (1) comparisons of their physiological adaptations to sources of environmental stress, and (2) the habitats they occupy in other parts of their ranges where they are in contact with different or no other congeners.

Studies on the physiological adaptations of the four species (Heller 1970) have shown a great deal of overlap between the species. The most marked differences are between *E. minimus* and the other three species. The early morning peak activity of *minimus* is made necessary by the thermal stress and aridity of its habitat. Placing a thermometer a few millimeters under the soil surface fully exposed to the sun in the *minimus* habitat in early to midafternoon revealed temperatures as high as 57°–60°C while similar measurements in the *amoenus* habitat showed highs of 48°–52°C. Large, overlapping patches of shade from piñon pines in the *amoenus* habitat make movements across fully exposed soil unnecessary, but the small evenly dispersed patches of shade from sagebrush in *minimus* habitat make travel over fully exposed areas unavoidable. It is likely that *alpinus, speciosus,* and *amoenus* are physiologically unable to colonize the arid, hot desert where *minimus* is found (Heller 1970). The reluctance of *amoenus* to hibernate (Cade 1963, Heller and Poulson 1970) would severely limit this species in the alpine habitat. In no other case do the data support a conclusion that the species considered here are restricted to their respective habitats because of physiological limitations.

The variety of habitats occupied by *speciosus, amoenus,* and *minimus* in other parts of their ranges also suggests rather broad overlaps in their fundamental niches. Sheppard (1965) has reviewed accounts of habitat descriptions for 8 subspecies of *amoenus* and 13 subspecies of *minimus*. The *amoenus* subspecies occupy habitats from the very open coniferous forest-sagebrush habitat, typical of the present field area, through open deciduous forest, to alpine habitats. *E. minimus* subspecies occupy habitats ranging the full spectrum from arid sagebrush desert to alpine fell fields. As with *amoenus,* this entire range of habitats may be encompassed by a single subspecies. For instance, *E. minimus scrutator* extends from the field area of the present study at the base of the eastern fault scarp of the Sierra Nevada, across the hot, arid Owens Valley to the lower elevations of the White Mountains. This subspecies is absent from the piñon pine belt of the White Mountains, which extends from lower treeline to (on most slopes) upper treeline, and is occupied by *Eutamias panamintinus*. *E. minimus* reappears above the upper treeline and occupies the entire alpine zone where it is the only chipmunk species present.

E. speciosus is much more restricted in geograph-

ical distribution than either *amoenus* or *minimus* (Johnson 1943) and is only found in association with open coniferous forests. However, I have observed *speciosus* penetrating far into the habitat of *amoenus* where cover is very dense, i.e. along stream courses.

E. alpinus has a very limited range; it is found only in the alpine and Hudsonian zones of the Sierra Nevada, California, and it is in contact with other chipmunk species on all edges of its range. There is no opportunity to see what habitats *alpinus* would occupy if it were not in contact with another species. On the line of contact, the habitat utilized by *alpinus* interdigitates with that of *speciosus* wherever open rocky spaces penetrate into the lodgepole pine forest (personal observation, Grinnell and Storer 1924, Johnson 1943). There is no reason, however, to suspect that *alpinus* is physiologically prevented from occupying the Canadian zone (Heller 1970).

Interspecific aggression

The lines of contact between the four *Eutamias* species on the eastern slope of the Sierra Nevada may be partially determined by interspecific aggression. The upper range limit of *minimus* may be determined by aggressive interactions with the dominant *amoenus* which is at the limit of its fundamental niche where the piñon pine belt grades into the arid, hot sagebrush desert (Fig. 1). Similarly, the aggressive *amoenus* may determine the lower range limit of *speciosus,* while, at the upper edge of its range, *speciosus* is limited by the aggressively dominant *alpinus*.

The same dominance relationship between *minimus* and *amoenus* as described here exists elsewhere in their ranges. Sheppard (1965) studied these two species in western Alberta where *amoenus* is found in forested areas up to treeline, but never in the alpine zone which was occupied in some areas by *minimus*. *E. minimus* also occupied the forested areas wherever *amoenus* was absent. Sheppard found that *amoenus* was aggressively dominant over *minimus* in laboratory experiments similar to those described herein.

The most difficult questions are left to answer. What determines the upper range limit of *amoenus* and the lower range limit of *alpinus*? Of course genetically determined habitat preference, as demonstrated by Wecker (1963) for *Peromyscus maniculatus,* is likely to play a significant contemporary role, but if so, what were the selective pressures which led to this habitat preference? What environmental factors result in selective pressure for aggressiveness? Why are high levels of aggressiveness adaptive behavior patterns in *alpinus* and *amoenus* habitat but not in *minimus* and *speciosus* habitat?

Evolution of aggressive behavior in Eutamias

It is not yet possible to give conclusive answers to

the questions posed above, but some hypotheses can be formulated which point to the types of field data which are still required. The clearest, most generally applicable evolutionary framework for the consideration of aggressive territoriality has been presented by Brown (1964). Brown simply reasons that selection will favor aggressive territorial behavior as long as that behavior achieves goals which maximize individual survival and reproduction. Aggressive behavior would be a superfluous energy expenditure unless it secured for the organism some ecological requisite which is in short supply, e.g. food, nest site, or a receptive mate. Additionally, for selection to favor aggressive behavior, the object around which it is centered must be physically and economically obtainable or defendable by aggressive behavior. Brown's reasoning is quite applicable to the chipmunks which are the subject of this paper.

It is important to understand the common strategy of the chipmunks for dealing with the seasonality of their environment if one is to appreciate the selective pressures upon them. The four species in the present study are facultative hibernators (Heller and Poulson 1970). Their above-ground environments are uninhabitable for a considerable portion of the year, and the animals must retire to underground hibernacula which they stock with a sufficient amount of food for the winter months. The growing season and, therefore, the time available to breed and gather a winter food supply is limited. I suggest that selection operates, especially in years of low food production and/or long winters, to maximize the net yield of food for the winter.

Territoriality in E. alpinus.—The adaptive value of a territory is clear in the case of *alpinus*. The proportion of the alpine habitat which supports vegetation is small and the alpine growing season is short. Hence, the food supply is sparse and available for only a limited time. There is reason to assume that *alpinus* can economically defend a territory. Since the animals emerge from their hibernacula while the habitat is still largely snow covered, they have an opportunity to establish territories and dominance relationships in advance of the period of maximal food availability. A supply of food is thereby assured with the minimum sacrifice of foraging time for aggressive interactions. Bold displays and extensive behavioral interactions do not make *alpinus* seriously vulnerable to predation because the rocky nature of the habitat means that escape routes and refuges are always readily accessible. Also, the line of sight at ground level is severely limited in the alpine boulder fields making it practically impossible for a predator to stalk the rapidly moving *alpinus*. The lack of tree cover in the alpine habitat means that aerial predators can be seen at a considerable distance.

Territoriality in E. amoenus.—An important seasonal food supply is economically defendable in the case of *amoenus*. In the field study area, piñon pine is an important source of seeds for winter consumption by *amoenus*. This seed crop is not ripe, however, until early fall, and when available it is harvested rapidly. The territories established by *amoenus* early in the season probably guarantee an adequate share in the important piñon pine crop. Even where the habitat of *amoenus* does not include piñon pine, it may not build up its winter food caches until fall. Broadbooks (1958) documented the diversity of the diet that this species eats and caches in eastern Washington. His observations of animals' activities and his data from excavated burrows indicate that the animals did not cache food in their nests until fall. It is not clear whether the food carried into the burrow in the fall was taken from smaller caches or whether it came directly from foraging trips.

The structure of *amoenus* habitat enables this species to engage in extensive behavioral interactions. Large, contiguous patches of shade from the piñon pines allow it to be active all day in a rather hot, arid environment, and the presence of abundant ground-level cover (Fig. 3) reduces vulnerability to predation.

Low level of aggression in E. minimus.—The behavioral pattern of extreme aggressive territoriality is probably not adaptive in the habitat of *minimus*. Competition for a limited, seasonal food supply conceivably exists in this species' habitat, but territory is not economically defendable. The activity of *minimus* is largely limited to the early morning hours. This activity pattern is a response to aridity, high ambient temperature, high soil surface temperature, and exposure to solar radiation (Heller 1970). It is probably metabolically infeasible to engage in extensive behavioral interactions in the sagebrush desert habitat of *minimus* because any excess activity adds to the heat load the animals must dissipate, and the few hours the animals are above ground each day must be spent gathering food.

Low level of aggression in E. speciosus.—In *speciosus* habitat territory is defendable but there is no adaptive value in so doing. The vegetation in this habitat is abundant and diverse and does not show the effects of summer drought as much as in the other three habitats. It appears that food is seldom if ever limiting for *speciosus* but supporting data are not available. Hence, it would not be economical for this species to decrease its foraging time to engage in behavioral interactions.

The extremely secretive nature of *speciosus* suggests that predation may be a selective pressure operating on this species. The other three species are very obvious and vociferous in comparison to *speciosus*. Even in areas where many *speciosus* were trapped they were seldom seen or heard. Behavioral displays and interactions in the open forest habitat where low ground cover is not abundant (Fig. 3) and escape routes are widely separated would enhance the vulnerability of *speciosus* to predation.

Effects of speciosus *on* amoenus *and* alpinus.— The aggression of *amoenus* and *alpinus* is ineffective in limiting the activity of *speciosus* wherever it can take cover in dense vegetation or in trees which it readily climbs. Where creeks cross the piñon pine-sagebrush zone, they are bordered by dense growths of aspen, willow, and Jeffrey pine. *E. speciosus* is found all the way down to the tips of these narrow prongs of dense vegetation even though *amoenus* is abundant in the piñon pine-sagebrush surrounding the prongs. In areas of dense vegetation aggression is ineffective in excluding *speciosus* and repeated encounters with this species are probably detrimental to *amoenus* and *alpinus* in that their foraging time is decreased. Similar cases of aggression being disadvantageous to the aggressor have been reported by Pitelka (1951), Ripley (1959, 1961), Orians and Collier (1963), and a theoretical treatment has been offered by Hutchinson and MacArthur (1959).

Habitat selection.—The fundamental niches of *alpinus* and *amoenus* include the habitat of *speciosus*, but the presence of *speciosus* may reduce their success in this habitat by repeatedly eliciting their aggression but not being excluded by them. There should thus be selective pressures on *alpinus* and *amoenus* either to increase the effectiveness of their aggression or to evolve preferences for those habitats in which their aggression is effective in excluding *speciosus*. The only ways in which the effectiveness of aggression could be increased would be to increase the number and/or the duration of the encounters with *speciosus*. This strategy would decrease the foraging time of the aggressor and therefore is less economical than habitat selection. There should also be strong selective pressures for *speciosus* to avoid those habitats in which it can be excluded by the aggressive species.

Conclusions

Interspecific aggression and possibly habitat selection are of far greater importance than physiological adaptations in determining the lines of contact between altitudinally zoned, contiguously allopatric *Eutamias* species. I have argued that interspecific aggression is an extension of intraspecific territoriality which has been selected for in *alpinus* and *amoenus* because of properties of the cover in their habitats and the seasonality and defendability of a limited food supply. Territoriality is not adaptive if potentially limited resources are not economically defendable. Hence, intense aggressiveness is not adaptive in *speciosus* habitat because of predation and food abundance, nor in *minimus* habitat because of the physiological

stress it would entail. To complete the explanation of the sharp altitudinal zonation of these species, it seems necessary that the aggressive species have evolved preferences for habitats in which aggression is adaptive, and the nonaggressive species have evolved preferences for those habitats from which they will not be excluded. The predicted patterns of habitat selection remain to be investigated.

Acknowledgments

The advice and criticisms of Thomas L. Poulson were invaluable in the course of this work. N. Philip Ashmole, G. Evelyn Hutchinson, and Richard S. Miller provided stimulating discussion and critically read the manuscript. The expert help of Vincent Salerno with laboratory work, and the untiring assistance of Mr. and Mrs. Gary Colliver with field work are very much appreciated. I am grateful to Yosemite National Park for permission to do field work. This work was supported in part by an N.D.E.A. Title IV Fellowship, an N.S.F. Traineeship, funds from the Department of Biology, Yale University, and N.S.F. Grant GB6212 awarded to Thomas L. Poulson.

Literature Cited

Blair, W. F., A. P. Blair, P. Brodkorb, F. R. Cagle, and G. A. Moore. 1957. Vertebrates of the United States. New York: McGraw-Hill Book Co., Inc. 819 p.

Broadbooks, H. E. 1958. Life history and ecology of the chipmunk, *Eutamias amoenus*, in eastern Washington. Misc. Publ. Museum of Zool., U. of Mich. **103**: 1–41.

Brown, J. L. 1964. The evolution of diversity in avian territorial systems. The Wilson Bull. **76**: 160–169.

Cade, T. J. 1963. Observations on torpidity in captive chipmunks of the genus *Eutamias*. Ecology **44**: 255–261.

Grinnell, J., and T. I. Storer. 1924. Animal life in the Yosemite. Berkeley: University of Calif. Press. 752 p.

Hall, E. R., and K. R. Kelson. 1959. The mammals of North America, Vol. I. New York: Ronald Press Co. 546 p.

Heller, H. C. 1970. Altitudinal zonation of chipmunks (*Eutamias*): Interspecific aggression, water balance, and energy budgets. Ph.D. dissertation, Yale University, University Microfilms, Ann Arbor, Mich.

Heller, H. C., and T. L. Poulson. 1970. Circannian rhythms: II. Endogenous and exogenous factors controlling reproduction and hibernation in chipmunks (*Eutamias*) and ground squirrels (*Spermophilus*). Comp. Biochem. Physiol. **33**: 357–383.

Hutchinson, G. E. 1957. Concluding remarks. Cold Spring Harbor Symposia on Quantitative Biology **22**: 415–427.

Hutchinson, G. E., and R. H. MacArthur. 1959. On the theoretical significance of aggressive neglect in interspecific competition. Amer. Naturalist **93**: 133–134.

Johnson, D. H. 1943. Systematic review of the chipmunks (genus *Eutamias*) of California. U. Calif. Pub. Zool. **48**: 63–148.

Klyver, F. D. 1931. Major plant communities in a transect of the Sierra Nevada mountains of California. Ecology **12**: 1–17.

Merriam, C. H. 1890. Results of a biological survey of the San Francisco Mountain region and desert of the Little Colorado, Arizona. N. Amer. Fauna 3. 136 p.

Miller, R. S. 1964. Ecology and distribution of pocket gophers (Geomidae) in Colorado. Ecology **45**: 256–272.

Miller, R. S. 1967. Pattern and process in competition. Adv. Ecol. Res. **4**: 1–70.

Orians, G. H., and G. Collier. 1963. Competition and blackbird social systems. Evolution **17**: 449–459.

Owen, D. B. 1962. Handbook of Statistical Tables. Reading, Mass.: Addison-Wesley Publishing Co., Inc. 580 p.

Pitelka, F. A. 1951. Ecologic overlap in hummingbirds. Ecology **32**: 641–661.

Ripley, S. D. 1959. Competition between sunbird and honeyeater species in the Moluccan Islands. Amer. Naturalist **93**: 127–132.

Ripley, S. D. 1961. Aggressive neglect as a factor in interspecific competition in birds. Auk **78**: 360–371.

Sheppard, D. H. 1965. Ecology of the chipmunks *Eutamias amoenus luteiventris* (Allen) and *E. minimus orocetes* Merriam, with particular reference to competition. Ph.D. dissertation, University of Saskatchewan. (L. C. Card No. Mic 66-9605) 229 p. Univ. Microfilms. Ann Arbor, Mich. (Dissertation Absts. **27**: 1663).

Storer, T. I., F. C. Evans, and F. G. Palmer. 1944. Some rodent populations in the Sierra Nevada of California. Ecol. Monogr. **14**: 165–192.

Wecker, S. C. 1963. The role of early experience in habitat selection by the prairie deer mouse, *Peromyscus maniculatus bairdi*. Ecol. Monogr. **33**: 307–325.

INFLUENCE OF JACKRABBIT DENSITY ON COYOTE POPULATION CHANGE

FRANK W. CLARK [1]

Abstract: May coyote (*Canis latrans*) population densities were estimated by three methods on a 700-square-mile study area astride the Utah–Idaho state line during 1966 to 1970. Indices of coyote populations in the spring, summer, and fall of the same years, and in the winter of 1963 to 1966, collectively, provided trend information for the period 1963 to 1970. An estimate of the percentage of female coyotes breeding in 1969 was obtained from a February collection of 19 carcasses in a region surrounding the study area. Estimates of litter sizes and percentages of females breeding in the western third of Utah were obtained from records of the Division of Wildlife Services. Coyote food habits were studied from stomach contents of 186 animals collected in the winters of 1967–68, 1968–69, and 1969–70; and from 111 scats collected year-round, 1966–69. Coyotes in the study area from 1966–70 may have numbered somewhere near 200 or more animals in the 5 years of study. The population declined from its highest index value in 1963 to one-seventh of that value in 1968, then increased substantially in 1969 and 1970. These changes appear to have been correlated with the density of black-tailed jackrabbits (*Lepus californicus*) the previous year. The causal mechanism may in part have been the effect of jackrabbit density (jackrabbits comprised three-fourths or more of the coyote diet during the period of study) on the coyote reproductive rate, both in terms of litter size and percentage of females breeding. Although most of the observed coyote mortality was man-induced, it represented only a part of the total; hence, the pattern and causes of mortality remain largely unknown. Long-range coyote density appears to be partly a function of the size of the food base, with artificial control doubtlessly playing a part. In this region, where the biota is relatively simple, the jackrabbit constitutes a major part of the food base and therefore is a partial determinant of coyote density. The physiological or behavioral links, or both, are unknown at present.

This paper summarizes part of the findings of a long-term study of coyote populations being conducted on a 700-square-mile study area in northwestern Utah and south-central Idaho. Coyotes in this area have fluctuated markedly from 1963 to 1970, the period for which we have data. The purpose of this paper is to explore the circumstances of these changes and their possible interactions with population changes of black-tailed jackrabbits. The study was conducted in the eastern edge of the Great Basin where jackrabbits are a prominent herbivore, historically subject to marked population changes (Palmer 1897, Nelson 1909:128).

Coyotes in the locale of the study area are subject to heavy, man-induced mortality.

Control efforts by personnel of the U. S. Bureau of Sport Fisheries and Wildlife, Division of Wildlife Services, include annual baiting with sodium monofluoroacetate (Compound 1080), trapping of nuisance animals, and den hunting in the spring. Coyotes are shot from planes in winter by sheep ranchers in the region, especially in the Utah portion of the study area. Some bounty and fur trapping is carried out by individuals, and miscellaneous losses occur from highway kill, chance shooting by game bird hunters, and other factors. Probably due at least in part to these efforts, coyote densities are low in this area by comparison with other North American populations (Knowlton 1972).

Despite this intensive control, coyote numbers appeared to vary markedly during our period of study, including a three- or fourfold increase from the late 1960's to 1970.

I thank F. Knowlton for his advice, encouragement, and assistance during this

---

[1] Editor's note: Frank W. Clark died August 21, 1971, while camping in the mountains of Idaho. This paper is presented as a memorial to him and his efforts in the Curlew Valley coyote studies. Dr. F. H. Wagner is responsible for the final preparation of this report.

F. W. CLARK

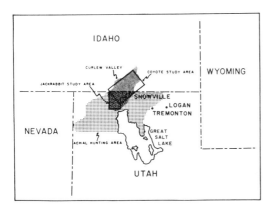

Fig. 1. Location of the coyote and jackrabbit study areas in Curlew Valley and the aerial hunting area.

project. D. Donahoo and his staff in the Utah office of the Division of Wildlife Services provided generous assistance and cooperation in locating data in their files. M. Robinson and the late F. Nelson of the Pocatello, Idaho District, and V. Montgomery from the Northern Utah District of the Division willingly contributed much time for advice and field assistance for den hunting and setting traplines. Many Utah State University students helped with the study, notably J. K. Morgan, H. Goulden, G. Elder, G. Whitney, and D. Gylten. I thank the *Tremonton Flyers* who provided coyote carcasses. L. C. Stoddart gave advice on the manuscript.

Finally, and importantly, the project was supported financially by the Research Division of the U. S. Bureau of Sport Fisheries and Wildlife and by the Utah State University Ecology Center through research grants to F. H. Wagner. Support of the rabbit studies is detailed by Wagner and Stoddart (1972).

METHODS

Study Area

The 700-square-mile coyote study area (Fig. 1) is rectangular, with the long axis

oriented approximately northeast–southwest. About four-fifths of the area is situated in Curlew Valley, an intermountain basin of roughly 1,200 square miles with its southern end terminating at Great Salt Lake. The remaining one-fifth includes a portion of Pocatello Valley, the first valley east of northern Curlew Valley.

The area lies within what is generally termed the northern or *cold* desert region of the United States (Odum 1959:405). Sagebrush (*Artemisia tridentata*) vegetation type dominates over half the area, with lesser shrub types, including shadscale (*Atriplex confertifolia*) and greasewood (*Sarcobatus vermiculatus*), in the valley bottoms. The lower altitudes of the mountains surrounding Curlew Valley and the few small hills within the valley are dominated by juniper (*Juniperus osteosperma*), often with an understory of sagebrush. Roughly 15 percent of the area—primarily in Idaho—is under cultivation; cereal grains and irrigated alfalfa are the chief crops. A comparable area had been cleared of brush and seeded to exotic grasses for livestock.

Annual precipitation varies from 10 to 12 inches at the southern part of the area to 14 to 16 inches at the northern, falling mostly between fall and spring, much of it as snow. Summer is the dry season. Mountains and hills occupy roughly 30 percent of the area, mostly with altitudes below 6,500 feet.

Approximately 40 percent of the area is privately owned; the remainder is public land administered either by the U. S. Forest Service or the U. S. Bureau of Land Management. Except for the cultivation, the area is rangeland grazed by limited numbers of sheep in winter and spring and by cattle year-round.

The study area was defined after a search for coyote dens in May 1966. A circle with a 6-mile radius was circumscribed on a map of the area around each den that was found. A circle of this size was believed, by federal trappers advising us in the study, to enclose the movements of young in summer during the early months of their foraging activities. A rectangle was then drawn to enclose these circles, and this rectangle became the 700-square-mile study area in which capture–recapture population estimates were to be based on pups caught and ear-tagged during the denning operation.

Coyote Census Techniques

Estimating Absolute Density.—Three methods were used to estimate absolute density of coyote pups in the study area: Bailey's (1951) modification of the Petersen Index (Petersen 1896), a minimum-count method, and a subjective estimate.

First samples for the Petersen Index were taken by digging coyote pups from their dens, ear-tagging, and releasing the pups during each May of the 5 years of field study. Dens were located by the use of a slow-flying Piper Supercub 135 and systematically covering the study area at altitudes of 100 to 200 feet. When a coyote or possible den was sighted, a more careful search of the vicinity was made at lower altitudes.

The second sample for the Petersen Index was obtained by trapping coyotes in the study area during 4 weeks in August and September. In 1966, 100; in each of 1967 and 1968, 200; and in each of 1969 and 1970, 150 square miles were randomly selected from the study area, and one trap was set at a point likely to attract coyotes in each square mile. The location of each set, all within access of passable roads so that they could be checked from a vehicle, was based on the judgment of experienced federal trappers in 1966 and on our own judgment in the next four summers.

Each set consisted of one staked No. 3 double-spring Oneida–Victor steel trap

buried about 18 inches from a bush, fence post, or clump of grass on which a scent bait was placed. In 1966 and 1969, when an animal such as a rabbit was found dead in a trap, it was buried at the site for additional bait. Each set was checked about every 3 days in 1966 and about every 2 days in 1967–70. (On the advice of personnel of the Division of Wildlife Services, traps were checked at this frequency to minimize human activity around them and maximize success.) About halfway through each trapping period, each set was rescented once with coyote urine.

The minimum-count method consisted of summing the total number of pups handled during the denning operation and the number of unmarked pups captured during the trapping program each year. Because all pups on the area were obviously not handled, this provided a conservative, but unchallengeable, estimate of the pup population.

The subjective estimate was made by attempting to judge the number of coyote litters raised on the study area each year and multiplying by the average litter size reported by personnel of the Division of Wildlife Services (below). The number of litters was approximated by summing (1) litters dug or observed during the spring denning program, (2) recently active but vacated dens found during the aerial search, (3) dens or pups reported by other persons (ranchers, federal-agency employees, and students) traveling afield in the study area, (4) litters located by stimulating the pups to respond vocally to amplified, tape-recorded coyote howls, and (5) unmarked pups trapped in areas remote from known den sites. These data were plotted on a map of the study area to reduce the chance of counting a den more than once.

The three methods (Petersen Index, minimum-count method, and subjective estimate) provided estimates of the total number of young produced on the area. These estimates were expanded to include adults and thus provide estimates of the total population. Postwhelping age ratios of coyotes vary, on the basis of population samples taken by different workers, from around 50 percent juveniles (Rogers 1965, Gier 1968:54) to the 75 percent found by the present study in carcass collections made in winter (described below). These carcass collections may overestimate the young because of pup dispersal and possible collecting bias. I have taken, for purposes of this study, a conservative 66:33 for the young:adult ratio and have added (to the pup estimates) one adult for each two pups, to provide estimates of the entire coyote populations.

Measuring Population Trends.—Four methods were used to obtain relative indices of the postbreeding coyote population on the study area each year: (1) the success rate of our May aerial den-hunting operation (dens found per flying hour); (2) the success of our summer trapping program expressed as coyotes captured per 1,000 trap days; (3) the rate of scat collection during late fall on a 40-mile route (number of scats obtained per week); and (4) the success of aerial coyote hunters during the winters of 1963–66 (number of coyotes shot per hour of flying time).

Measuring Coyote Reproductive Parameters

Measurements of Litter Size.—The number of litters dug during the denning season each year was too small (five or less in 3 of the 5 years) to permit meaningful comparison. Accordingly, estimates of mean annual litter sizes were based on data obtained from the Utah files of the Division of Wildlife Services. Division field personnel file regular activity reports giving the number

of coyotes taken and the dens dug, along with other phases of their activities. Each worker reports the number of pups found per den. Some workers autopsy females killed in late winter, spring, and early summer and report the number of fetuses found in utero and the number of placental scars observed. These data provide samples for annual estimates of mean litter size. We calculated means from the fetal counts, since litters at dens and placental scars may be subject to biases.

We used the Division's statewide data in the analyses, because, in Utah, roughly two-thirds of the Division's personnel operate within the Great Basin portion of the state in which the study area is located, and a somewhat larger fraction of the total control takes place here. Hence, a majority of the *statewide* reports represent coyotes within this ecologically uniform region. Any year-to-year changes shown by these records should, in my opinion, roughly parallel the changes occurring in our coyote study area.

Percentage of Females Breeding.—Data on this parameter come from two sources, the first being the records of the Division of Wildlife Services. We recorded the total number of adult coyotes killed by Division personnel each spring and halved these totals to estimate the number of adult females killed. [Young and Jackson (1951: 76) observed coyote sex ratios at about 50:50, based on large samples taken throughout the range of the species.] These estimates of females were then divided into the number of females reported to be carrying fetuses or the uterine scars for the respective years, and the resulting quotients were converted to percentages, which thereupon became indices of the percentage of females bearing young. These figures are not estimates of the actual percentage of females bearing young, because all trappers do not record, and some trappers do not always record, the breeding status of the females they handle. I assume, however, that the rate of recording was sufficiently constant from year to year for the percentages to be used as annual indices.

I obtained 41, 61, and 84 coyote carcasses during the winters of 1967–68, 1968–69, and 1969–70, respectively, from aerial coyote hunters operating within the area shown in Fig. 1. These animals were weighed, sex and age determinations made, stomachs removed, and reproductive tracts examined. Most of the carcasses in 1967–68 and 1969–70 were collected in December and January, too early to detect reproductive activity. In 1968–69, 19 of the carcasses were collected during the first 3 weeks of February. Reproductive tracts of these 19 females were examined to determine what percentage would likely have reproduced. Pregnancy was judged by the presence of fetuses or implantation sites, and ovulation was determined by the presence of corpora lutea or of ovulation pores on the surface of the ovaries. Probable ovulation was judged by the presence of follicles exceeding 2 mm in diameter.

Coyote Food Habits

Stomachs of the 186 coyotes collected during the three winters were analyzed by emptying their contents into a basin, washing with water, and identifying the material to species, when possible.

Seasonal variations in the coyote diet were determined from 111 scats collected within the study area. In the fall of 1966, 70 miles of ranch roads, throughout the western portion of the study area, were cleaned of all coyote droppings. Thereafter, the route was travelled about every 3–4 weeks to collect coyote scats that accumulated between visits. However, snow conditions prevented vehicular travel by December 1966, and the route was reduced to

40 miles in the southwest portion of the study area. These 40 miles were visited periodically throughout the fall of 1970.

Scats were examined by breaking apart the dried material by hand, separating the constituents by washing through metal screens, and identifying the items as accurately as possible. Identification was aided by a collection of bones and skins of animals known to occur in the study area. Only a sample of hair from each scat was identified. Identification was made microscopically by comparison with hair in the collection so that trace items were less likely to appear in the results.

RESULTS

Correlation Between Jackrabbit Numbers and Coyote Trends

Absolute Coyote Density.—The three methods used to estimate absolute coyote density provided a range of estimates within which the true densities probably fell. The Petersen Index (Table 1) provided the highest values. Any differential mortality of tagged pups between spring and summer trapping, and any movement bias (differential emigration of tagged animals or immigration of untagged animals, or both) would tend to inflate the estimates. Several observations are available to evaluate these possible biases.

We found two ear-tagged pups dead a few days after they had been caught. However, we eventually recovered 31 percent of 144 pups ear-tagged and released at dens. And we also recovered at least one pup each from 75 percent of tagged litters, suggesting at least some survival in most litters. Garlough (1940) reported eventual recovery, over a 9-year period, of 67 percent of pups ear-tagged at dens in New Mexico; and recovery, over a 2.5-year period, of 49 percent of a Wyoming sample. Since many

Table 1. Population estimates for the 700-square-mile study area, by the Petersen Index.[a]

YEAR	TOTAL MARKED (M)	TOTAL TRAPPED (C)	MARKED TRAPPED (R)	POPULATION ESTIMATES	
				Pups ($P_B \pm$ SD)[b]	Total ($P_B + 50$ percent)[c]
1966	27	26	1	364 ± 202	546
1967	21	34	3	184 ± 77	276
1968	8	9	0	– –	–
1969	53	21	4	233 ± 80	349
1970	35	33	2	397 ± 189	595
Total or mean	144	123	10	295	442

[a] The notation is that of Bailey (1951) where P_B is the population parameter being estimated.

[b] $P_B = \dfrac{M(C+1)}{(R+1)}$. $\text{SD} = \dfrac{M^2(C+1)(C-R)}{(R+1)^2(R+2)}$.

[c] Correction of pup estimates for a juvenile–adult ratio of 66:33.

animals obviously die in situations unobserved by humans or where tags are not seen, these observations suggest to us that three-fourths or more of den-tagged pups survived an initial tagging experience.

We trapped between mid-August and mid-September at a time when, according to trappers of the Division of Wildlife Services, pups were beginning to move about and hunt, but only within a relatively short distance of the den areas. In their experience, any marked extension of home ranges or early dispersal occurred later in the fall or in early winter. The 10 pups tagged at dens and recaptured during summer trapping (Table 1) were taken an average of 2.5 miles (SD $\pm$ 1.3) from their spring den sites, and the greatest spring–summer movement was 5 miles. Our observations indicate limited movement of young animals at this time of year in this area. The Petersen Index estimates may exceed the true population values, but I do not believe the overestimate is extreme, and the values may approximate the population size.

The minimum estimates (Table 2), based on the number of pups handled during denning and later during trapping, provide a lower range of values. Since the time spent in searching for dens varied between years (the flying time in 1968 and 1969 was 2.5 times that spent in 1966), as did the

Table 2. Minimum-count population estimates for the 700-square-mile study area.

YEAR	NUMBER OF PUPS TAGGED AT DENS			NUMBER OF UNTAGGED PUPS TRAPPED			TOTAL NUMBER OF PUPS HANDLED		ADJUSTED + 50 PERCENT[d]
	Actual[a]	F_1[b]	Adjusted	Actual	F_2[c]	Adjusted	Actual	Adjusted	
1966	29	2.5	72	23	2.2	51	52	123	185
1967	21	1.4	31	31	1.2	37	52	68	102
1968	8	1.0	8	9	1.0	9	17	17	25
1969	64	1.0	64	17	1.3	22	81	86	129
1970	39	1.2	49	31	1.5	46	70	95	143
Mean	32		45	22		33	54	78	117

[a] These values differ slightly from those in Table 1, because some pups were taken into captivity rather than being tagged and released; and some pups were seen but were not caught near the dens.

[b] F_1 is a correction factor that increases in 1966, 1967, and 1970 because of the greater flying time in 1968 and 1969 (Table 4).

[c] F_2 corrects all other years upward because of the greater trapping effort in 1968 (Table 4).

[d] Correction of pup estimates for a juvenile–adult ratio of 66:33.

281

trapping effort (1968 effort was 2.2 times 1966 effort), some correction seems in order. The corrected values differ materially (50 percent or more) from the actual number handled only in the 1966 values. Since undoubtedly not all of the pups in the valley were handled, probably by a substantial margin, these estimates are clearly conservative.

Thus, the true densities undoubtedly fell within the range bracketed by the minimum and Petersen estimates (Fig. 2), perhaps near the subjective estimates (Table 3). However, even the subjective estimate may be conservative. The minimum estimates range around 50 to 60 percent of the subjective estimates, and it seems problematical that 50 to 60 percent of the pups in the study area were handled. The striking values are the extremely low ratios of tagged pups in the summer trapping (Table 1). During 5 years of denning, 144 pups were tagged at dens. In those same years, 123 were caught in late summer, and only 10 of these were tagged. If the supposition is correct that movement bias and mortality were nominal, the coyote population in the 700-square-mile study area may have ranged between 200 and 500 during the period of study (Table 1). Conservatively, coyote numbers would appear to have been within the lower part of this range (Table 3).

Annual Coyote Population Trends.—Re-

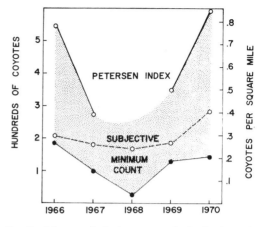

Fig. 2. Estimates of absolute coyote density in the study area, 1966–70. There is no Petersen Index value for 1968, because no marked animals were recaptured in that year.

sults of the four indices for determining relative coyote abundance in the study area are shown in Table 4. The value for each of these indices in 1966 was set at 100, and values for the years 1967–70 and 1963–65 were recalculated relative to the 1966 base of 100. The new relative values for each year were then averaged to provide a single, relative index value for each year. In this manner, four indices in 1966 and three for 1967–70 were utilized rather than relying on each individually; a separate 1963-to-1966 index was equated with the later ones. Ultimately, a 1963-to-1970 index for the species in the area was developed.

Table 3. Subjective population estimates for the 700-square-mile study area.

Year	Number of Dens Dug With Pups	Additional Number of Den Areas Located[a]	Total Number of Dens	Litter Size[b]	Total Number of Pups	Total + 50 Per-cent[c]
1966	5	15	20	6.9	138	207
1967	5	13	18	6.7	121	181
1968	3	14	17	6.6	112	168
1969	9	12	21	5.9	124	186
1970	12	13	25	7.6	190	285
Mean	7	13	20	6.7	137	205

[a] See text for derivation.
[b] Mean number of fetuses reported by personnel of the Division of Wildlife Services. See text.
[c] Correction of pup estimates for a juvenile–adult ratio of 66:33.

282

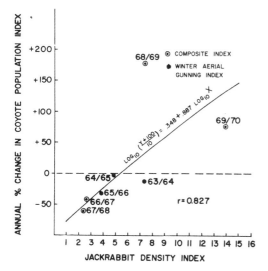

Fig. 3. Relationship between the 1963-to-1969 fall jackrabbit density (first date for each point) and rates of change in the annual coyote population index of the following year (second date) for Curlew Valley. The correlation is significant at the 0.05 probability level. Jackrabbit data are from Wagner and Stoddart (1972).

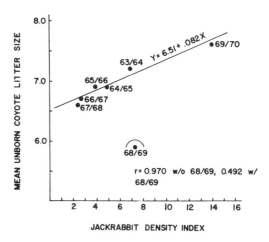

Fig. 4. Relationship between the 1963-to-1969 fall jackrabbit density (first date for each point) and mean, annual coyote litter size the following spring (second date). The correlation is significant at the 0.01 probability level without the 68/69 value but not significant with this value included in the test. Jackrabbit data are from Wagner and Stoddart (1972).

The resultant values suggested a continuous population decline from 1963 to 1968, then an increase in 1969 and 1970. The low population in 1968 may have been only about one-fourth the level for 1966 and somewhat less than one-seventh the value for 1963. The Petersen Index values (Fig. 2), which should be independent of the indices, followed the same trends for 1966–70.

Correlation Between Jackrabbit Numbers and Coyote Population Trends.—The 1963-to-1970 annual percentage change in the coyote population indices was plotted against an index of the population density of jackrabbits in Curlew Valley (Wagner and Stoddart 1972: Fig. 1) the preceding fall (Fig. 3). The scatter suggested a posi-

Table 4. Composite coyote population indices for Curlew Valley and vicinity, 1963 to 1970[a].

Year	Spring Den Hunting			Summer Trapping			Fall Scat Collection			Winter Aerial Hunting			Mean Index
	Hours Flown	Dens per Hour	Relative Index	Trap Days	Coyotes per 1,000 Trap Days	Relative Index	Number of Weeks Scats Accumulated	Number of Scats per Week	Relative Index	Hours Flown	Coyotes per Hour	Relative Index	
1963										5	0.80	174	174
1964										25	0.68	150	150
1965										46	0.67	147	147
1966	14	0.36	100	3,088	9.1	100	4	12.0	100	43.5	0.46	100	100
1967	24	0.21	58	5,641	6.7	74	4	5.8	43				58
1968	35	0.08	22	6,798	1.3	14	5	4.0	33				23
1969	35	0.31	86	5,189	4.6	51	3	6.7	56				64
1970	28	0.43	119	4,550	7.0	77	5	14.6	122				106

[a] See text for details on techniques.

tive relationship, which, if real, is probably curvilinear, because the function must be limited by some maximum rate of increase of which the species is genetically capable. Although it was impossible to say what the true relationship was from seven points, the equation $\text{Log}_{10} Y = a + b \, \text{Log}_{10} X$ was fitted as a preliminary approximation. This curve provided an r value of 0.827, significant at the 0.05 probability level.

Coyote Litter Size.—A plot of the mean, annual number of unborn fetuses per female coyote reported by personnel of the Division of Wildlife Services suggested a positive correlation with jackrabbit density (Fig. 4). The scatter included one point that deviated significantly from the others (1969). When this point was included, the relationship was not statistically significant; but without it, the remaining six points could be fitted with a straight line and an r value of 0.970, which was significant at the 0.01 level, obtained.

Percentage of Females Breeding.—A plot of the calculated index of the percentage of females breeding for 1964 to 1970 also suggested a positive correlation with jackrabbit density (Fig. 5). When given a preliminary fit with the equation $\text{Log}_{10} Y = a + b \, \text{Log}_{10} X$, the r value became 0.762, and the relationship was significant at the 0.05 probability level.

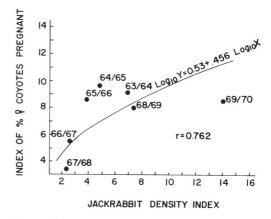

Fig. 5. Relationship between the 1963-to-1969 fall jackrabbit density (first date for each point) and annual index of percentage of female coyotes breeding (second date—see text for derivation). The correlation is significant at the 0.05 probability level. Jackrabbit data are from Wagner and Stoddart (1972).

Reproductive tracts of 19 female coyotes taken in the general vicinity of the study area February 1–11, 1969, were examined for evidence of reproductive activity (Table 5). At least 12 percent of the juveniles and 67 percent of the adults in this sample were pregnant. Since these dates are early in the period during which the animals breed, the ultimate number becoming pregnant was probably higher.

Some clue to the ultimate percentage becoming pregnant can be obtained by determining the percentage of females in

Table 5. Breeding condition of 19 female reproductive tracts collected in the Curlew Valley vicinity, February 1–11, 1969.

REPRODUCTIVE CONDITION	JUVENILES			ADULTS			TOTALS		
	Number	Percent	Cumulative Percent	Number	Percent	Cumulative Percent	Number	Percent	Cumulative Percent
Embryos or placentation sites	2	12	12	2	67	67	4	21	21
Corpora lutea present	5	32	44	1	33	100	6	32	53
Ovulation[a]	2	12	56	0	0	100	2	10	63
Probable ovulation[b]	4	25	81	0	0	100	4	21	84
No reproductive activity[c]	3	19	100	0	0	100	3	16	100

[a] Ovulation pores observed on surface of ovaries.
[b] Large follicles (>2 mm) along the margin of ovaries.
[c] Follicles all too small (<2 mm) to indicate probable ovulation.

284

F. W. Clark

Table 6. Frequency of food items in winter coyote stomachs from Curlew Valley vicinity.

Food Item	Percent Frequency of Occurrence		
	1968 (41)[a]	1969 (61)	1970 (84)
Jackrabbits	72[b]	85	95
Mice (*Microtus* sp. and *Peromyscus* sp.)	13	22	2
Other rodents	3	5	2
All rodents	16	26	3
Deer	6	0	0
Game birds	3	0	0
Other birds	0	3	3
Domestic turkey	10	0	0
Cattle	16	0	2
Sheep	6	0	2
All livestock	28	0	3
Vegetation	0	3	2
Unidentified materials	3	3	2
Empty stomachs[c]	22	33	21

[a] Total number of stomachs examined in parentheses.
[b] Percentages of stomachs containing food.
[c] Percentages of total stomachs examined.

this sample that had ovulated. All of the adults and 44 percent of the young animals examined had ovulated. This still underestimated the percentage of ovulators because of the early collection dates, and some additional clue to the eventual ovulation rate can be gained by adding the number pregnant, the number having ovulated, and the number likely to ovulate, as indicated by the presence of large graafian follicles (>2 mm in diameter). This sum was 81 percent in the young animals, 100 percent in the adults, and 84 percent of the total sample.

According to Knowlton's (1972) Texas sample, some 87 percent of ovulating animals become pregnant. If this is the case in Utah, and if the sample was representative, as high as 87 percent of the adults bred in 1969. No less than 49 (0.87 × 56) and perhaps as high as 70 percent (0.87 × 81) of the young animals bred (Table 5), and

the same two statistics for the entire female population were 55 (0.87 × 63) and 73 percent (0.87 × 84) for 1969. According to Gier (1968:49), a high reproductive rate for a coyote population might be 60 percent of the females breeding. Since his population approached a 50:50 age ratio, this presumably implied somewhere around 55 percent of the yearling females breeding if nearly all of the adults bred. Hence, the percentage in the present study, though based on a small sample, suggested a high female reproductive rate, especially among the young, for this year of high rabbit numbers.

Coyote Food Habits

Analyses of coyote stomachs collected in winter (Table 6) showed jackrabbit remains to be the most frequent food item in the winter diet. This species occurred in slightly over half of all stomachs; and in 72, 85, and 95 percent, respectively, of stomachs containing food items in 1968, 1969, and 1970. Domestic animals (probably carrion, in the case of the cattle) were second in importance in 1968 and rodents were third. In 1969, rodents were second to jackrabbits and were very nearly the only other food items. In 1970, jackrabbits were so strongly predominant in the diet that the next most important items—rodents, birds, livestock—were present in little more than trace amounts.

Frequency of occurrence tends to overestimate the importance of different food items in the diet, since such values for each food component usually exceed 100 percent in total. Percentage of stomach contents by weight or volume must total 100. Because a mouse or rabbit gets equal frequency values in a stomach, the degree to which frequency of occurrence overestimates volumetric occurrence is nearly always greatest in small food items such as rodents, and

Table 7. Percentage frequency of occurrence of food items in scats of Curlew Valley coyotes.

| | SEASON | | | | |
MATERIAL	Spring ($n = 6$)	Summer ($n = 30$)	Fall ($n = 69$)	Winter ($n = 6$)	TOTAL ($n = 111$)
Jackrabbit	60	70	77	82	77.4
Rabbit					
(*Sylvilagus* sp.)	0	5	6	2	5.2
All lagomorphs	60	75	83	84	79.6
Mice (*Microtus* sp. and					
Peromyscus sp.)	20	11	9	5	9.9
Other rodents	2	11	5	0	4.6
All rodents	22	16	14	5	14.5
Birds	0	1	0	2	0.4
Vegetation	0	1	0	0	0.3
Unidentifiable material	18	7	3	9	5.2

least in larger items such as lagomorphs (Sperry 1941, Ferrel et al. 1953:333, Fichter et al. 1955:16, Gier 1968:14). Consequently, frequency-of-occurrence values for lagomorphs may range from 67 to 90 percent of their volumetric percentage, whereas the rodent volume is materially overestimated by such parameters.

Lagomorphs, primarily jackrabbits, made up roughly three-fourths or more of the diet in terms of volume consumed in the three winters for which data were available. Rodents made up substantially less, ranging from no more than 3 percent to perhaps as high as 10 to 20 percent.

Analyses of the year-round scat samples (Table 7) showed much the same picture, with lagomorphs (mostly jackrabbit) averaging about 80 percent occurrence over the year and rodents about 15. This again probably implied that rabbits constituted something approaching 75 percent of the year-round diet by volume, whereas rodents made up perhaps 10 percent. No other identifiable material occurred in any significant amount. The high percentage of jackrabbits characterized years of low rabbit density (1966–68) as well as years of substantial numbers (1969–70).

DISCUSSION

The long-range goal in population ecology is to learn the pattern of influences operating on animal populations that are eventually expressed as demographic characteristics: long-term mean density, maintenance of equilibrium, and fluctuations. These patterns ultimately must be described mathematically so that the quantitative importance of different influences can be assessed, and so that changes that will result from both natural and man-made alterations in the pattern can be predicted.

One of the most successful approaches to this goal has been the development of a predictive model for population fluctuations of spruce budworms (*Choristoneura fumiferana*) by Morris (1963:31). This investigator developed an equation expressing the contribution of reproductive rate and survival rates at different stages in the life history to the annual rates of change in the budworm population. The reproductive and survival rates are then isolated, and each is studied as a dependent variable of the various environmental factors affecting it. The functional relationships between each factor and population parameter are expressed in the form of equations, and all functions are then integrated into a single predictive model. The various factors can be measured at any given time, programmed into the model, and a prediction made on the population trend. The approach can include artificially applied control as well as natural limiting factors.

This approach can serve as a prototype, which, with some modification (Wagner 1969), can be used in other species. The evidence presented here for coyotes in the Utah–Idaho region, limited though it may be, has been set forth as a beginning toward this general goal. Density of jackrabbits, an important part of the coyote food base in this area, appears to be one independent variable operating either through the coyote reproductive or mortality rate, or both, to influence the rate of population change.

Analyses of the relationships between jackrabbit densities and two parameters affecting the reproductive rate—litter size and percentage of females breeding (Figs. 4 and 5)—suggest some form of positive relationship between both parameters, relationships that have previously been suggested or observed by other authors (Criddle and Criddle 1923, Murie 1940:24, Gier 1968:79). The data in the present report are too few to discern the form of the functions; and until more data permit clearer definition of the function, it will not be possible to make predictions with any degree of accuracy.

To what extent the observed population changes have been influenced by variations in mortality, including those associated with the food base, is unknown at present, because the knowledge of mortality is fragmentary. One pup, dead of unknown causes, was found at a den site in 1969, and two were found at an abandoned den in the spring of 1967. There is thus some evidence

of early pup mortality. Gier (1968) has suggested that disease and parasites, food shortage, and occasional killing by adults take a sizable toll of the young.

I saw no evidence of coyote mortality, once the animals reached near-mature size in late summer and fall, other than that caused by man. Of 51 returns from dead animals tagged in both spring and summer, all but one were from man-induced mortality—20 from winter aerial hunting, 17 shot by hunters or ranchers, 4 killed by miscellaneous accidents, 2 by 1080 poison, 1 by a *coyote getter* (cyanide gun), 6 by steel traps, and 1 by unknown causes.

However, tag returns constituted only 30 percent of the tagged animals. Since the annual mortality rate probably ranges somewhere between 50 and 75 percent (as judged by the winter age ratios), obviously, only a part of the total mortality was observed. Further, based on tag returns, the mortality that was observed was of a type that would be more likely to come to our attention than mortality not associated with human activity. Hence, the mortality pattern is a moot point at this stage and needs intensive study. Probably the most promising approach to assessing the causes and magnitude of loss, including the influence of artificial control, is telemetry.

In any event, coyote populations in this area appear to have fluctuated with the density of jackrabbits (Figs. 3 and 6). According to personnel of the Division of Wildlife Services, this relationship may not be entirely causal, the increases of 1969 and 1970 having coincided with some relaxation in the intensity of coyote control over the western United States. However, the 1963-to-1968 decline obviously does not fall under this proviso, nor do the reproductive correlations for the entire 1963-to-1970 period (Figs. 4 and 5). Hence, some fluctuation of coyote populations with jackrabbit numbers appears real. For this to occur, jackrabbits must constitute a major portion of the diet, as indicated by the food habits data. Most coyote food habits studies show either rodents or lagomorphs as the major dietary item. Lagomorphs most often predominate in the Plains States (Fichter et al. 1955, Ellis and Schemnitz 1958, Gier 1968:12) and in the arid, intermountain region, as shown by this study and by the samples from desert areas in California (Ferrel et al. 1953).

In general, coyote food habits tend to reflect the composition of the prey base, because the animal distributes its feeding activity over what is available within its physical capabilities (Fichter et al. 1955, Knowlton 1964). Hence, although in Curlew Valley we do not yet have any estimates of rodent biomass, which we can compare with our measured jackrabbit biomass, one could postulate that the ratio follows the order of magnitude shown by the coyote food habits: perhaps of the order of three or four jackrabbit units of weight per one unit of rodents. The Great Basin biota is a relatively simple one in comparison with that of southern U. S. deserts (Pianka 1966, Wagner 1970). The jackrabbit appears to be markedly dominant over other coyote food items in this region, and changes in jackrabbit densities could logically be expected to effect changes in coyote numbers. Where the biota is more complex, the coyote feeds over a wider range of food types (Knowlton 1964). Changes in numbers of any one food species do not result in such profound changes in the total food base, and coyote populations may not vary with changes in the density of a single prey species.

An additional question that needs study is the link between food abundance and the response of the reproductive system. That link could be a nutritional one, as Gier

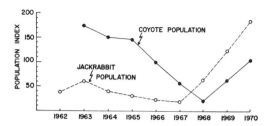

Fig. 6. Coyote and jackrabbit annual population trends for Curlew Valley, 1962 to 1970, as shown by population indices. Coyote data are from Table 4; jackrabbit data are from Wagner and Stoddart (1972).

(1968) and others have suggested. The relative frequency of jackrabbit in the diet appears to have increased between 1968 and 1970 (Table 6) in parallel with the jackrabbit population increase. However, weights of the 186 carcasses obtained from aerial gunners were not statistically different in the three winters. If the coyotes in 1968 were suffering any nutritional inadequacy, it apparently was not severe enough to affect body weights. Any influence on reproduction would have had to be more subtle. The other possible link between food abundance and reproductive effort would be behavioral, such as the epideictic mechanisms suggested by Wynne–Edwards (1962:16–17) and such as Mech (1966) pondered for the timber wolf (*Canis lupus*). At present we have no evidence for this possibility in the coyote.

Whatever the link may be, the reproductive rate and changes in coyote population seem to have varied with the food base, and that base depends importantly in this area on the jackrabbit population density. As the food base increases, coyote populations increase (Figs. 3 and 6), and it would seem to follow that any long-term increase in mean level of the food base would result in an increase in the mean level of the coyote population. Hence, the food level plays at least some role in determining the long-term, mean coyote density. The influence of food may be substantial, inasmuch as the coyote level appears to have varied by a factor of as much as seven between 1963 and 1968 (Table 4). This is not to suggest that predator-control efforts do not play a part in determining mean coyote density, but it is probable that both food and control enter into the equation. Their relative importance will not be known until we know more about the magnitude and causes of mortality, until we experimentally manipulate these factors in order to see the magnitude of population responses to such manipulation, and until we can discern the functional relationships between reproduction and mortality on the one hand and food and control on the other.

LITERATURE CITED

BAILEY, N. T. J. 1951. On estimating the size of mobile populations from recapture data. Biometrika 38(pts. 3–4):293–306.

CRIDDLE, N., E. CRIDDLE, AND S. CRIDDLE. 1923. The coyote in Manitoba. Canadian Field-Naturalist 37(3):41–45.

ELLIS, R. J., AND S. D. SCHEMNITZ. 1958 (1957). Some foods used by coyotes and bobcats in Cimarron County, Oklahoma 1954 through 1956. Proc. Oklahoma Acad. Sci. 38:180–185.

FERREL, C. M., H. R. LEACH, AND D. F. TILLOTSON. 1953. Food habits of the coyote in California. California Fish and Game 39(3):301–341.

FICHTER, E., G. SCHILDMAN, AND J. H. SATHER. 1955. Some feeding patterns of coyotes in Nebraska. Ecol. Monographs 25(1):1–37.

GARLOUGH, F. E. 1940. Study of the migratory habit of coyotes. U. S. Bur. of Sport Fisheries and Wildl., Denver Wildl. Research Center. 5pp. Typed.

GIER, H. T. 1968. Coyotes in Kansas (revised). Kansas State Coll. Agr. Expt. Sta. Bull. 393. 118pp.

KNOWLTON, F. F. 1964. Aspects of coyote predation in south Texas with special reference to white-tailed deer. Ph.D. Thesis. Purdue Univ. 208pp.

———. 1972. Preliminary interpretations of coyote population mechanics with some management implications. J. Wildl. Mgmt. 36(2):369–382.

MECH, L. D. 1966. The wolves of Isle Royale. Fauna of the Natl. Parks of the U. S., Fauna Ser. 7. 210pp.

MORRIS, R. F. 1963. 6. The development of a population model for the spruce budworm through the analysis of survival rates. Pages 30–32. In R. F. Morris [Editor], The dynamics of epidemic spruce budworm populations. Mem. Entomol. Soc. Canada 31. 332pp.

MURIE, A. 1940. Ecology of the coyote in the Yellowstone. Fauna of the Natl. Parks of the U. S., Fauna Ser. 4. 206pp.

NELSON, E. W. 1909. The rabbits of North America. U. S. Dept. Agr., Bur. Biol. Survey, N. Am. Fauna 29. 314pp.

ODUM, E. P. 1959. Fundamentals of ecology. 2nd ed. W. B. Saunders Company, Philadelphia and London. 546pp.

PALMER, T. S. 1897. The jack rabbits of the United States. Revised ed. U. S. Dept. Agr., Div. Biol. Survey Bull. 8. 88pp.

PETERSEN, C. G. J. 1896. The yearly immigration of young plaice into the Limfjord from the German Sea. Dept. Danish Biol. Sta. for 1895. 6:1–77.

PIANKA, E. R. 1966. Species diversity and ecology of flatland desert lizards in western North America. Dissertation Abstracts 27(1):334-B–335-B.

ROGERS, J. G., JR. 1965. Analysis of the coyote population of Dona Ana County, New Mexico. M.S. Thesis. New Mexico State Univ. 36pp.

SPERRY, C. C. 1941. Food habits of the coyote. U. S. Dept. Interior Fish and Wildl. Serv., Wildl. Research Bull. 4. 70pp.

WAGNER, F. H. 1969. Ecosystem concepts in fish and game management. Pages 259–307. In G. M. Van Dyne [Editor], Ecosystem concepts in natural resource management. Academic Press, London and New York. 383pp.

———. 1970. Plant species diversity of U. S. deserts as indicated by plant lists given for the proposed validation sites in the Biome Research Design. Appendix I, pages 3.3-136–3.3-139. In Desert biome reports. International Biological Program, Analysis of Ecosystems. R–71. 1.-1–4.3-5pp.

———, AND L. C. STODDART. 1972. Influence of coyote predation on black-tailed jackrabbit populations in Utah. J. Wildl. Mgmt. 36(2):329–342.

WYNNE–EDWARDS, V. C. 1962. Animal dispersion in relation to social behaviour. Oliver and Boyd, Edinburgh and London. 653pp.

YOUNG, S. P., AND H. H. T. JACKSON. 1951. The clever coyote. The Stackpole Company, Harrisburg, Pennsylvania, and the Wildlife Management Institute, Washington, D. C. 411pp.

REPRODUCTIVE RESPONSES OF SPARROWS TO A SUPERABUNDANT FOOD SUPPLY

TED R. ANDERSON

Do passerine birds raise as many young as they can adequately nourish? Considerable debate has surrounded this fundamental question in evolutionary ecology, particularly as it relates to the determination of clutch size (Wynne-Edwards 1962, Lack 1968, Skutch 1967, Ricklefs 1968, 1970). A clutch of eggs represents the commitment of an individual (or a pair) at one point in time to the production of the next generation. As such, the size of that commitment can be assumed to represent a variable which is very powerfully acted upon by natural selection. Lack (1947) first proposed that clutch size in altricial species of birds is adjusted evolutionarily to produce the maximum number of surviving offspring. He further proposed that food is the primary factor responsible for limiting the number of young that a pair can raise successfully. The clutch size of a species in a particular locality is therefore adapted to reflect the average food supply available for feeding the young in that locality.

Cody (1966) modified Lack's hypothesis by identifying other factors that might impinge on the ability of birds to raise the maximum number of young. The two major factors that he identified, predation and competitive ability, operate particularly in the tropics. He concluded, however, that in temperate regions food is probably of overriding importance in determining the number of young that can be raised.

The hypothesis that in temperate zone passerines reproduction is food-limited has been tested to date principally by artificially manipulating brood size (by the addition and sub- traction of young from a brood at hatching) and the comparison of survival rates in normal and manipulated broods. Lack's hypothesis predicts that the mean number of young surviving from the normal-sized broods will exceed that of either larger or smaller broods. The results of these experiments (some with very small samples) have been inconclusive, some supporting Lack's hypothesis (Rice and Kenyon 1962, Perrins 1964), and others finding increased productivity from super- normal-sized broods (Nelson 1964, von Haart- man 1967, Hussell 1972, Jarvis 1974). This experimental method, however, fails to dis- tinguish between the possibility that brood size is adjusted to the average food supply and the possibility that the foraging methods and rates of the adults are adapted to the normal brood size (Hussell 1972).

Experimental manipulation of the driving variable in this proposed system, food avail- able to the population for nourishing the young, has posed rather intractable problems. Two studies have been reported on the effects of an artificially supplemented diet on the clutch size and reproductive success of free- living individuals of two passerine species. Nutcracker (*Nucifraga caryocatactes*) females fed by P. O. Swanberg showed an increase in clutch size (Lack 1954). Yom-Tov (1974) reported that Hooded Crow (*Corvus corone*) pairs with experimentally supplemented diets showed no increase in clutch size, but did show improved hatching and fledgling suc- cess that he attributed to the indirect effects of the additional food in reducing predation. The present paper reports the results of a

TABLE 1. Comparisons of mean clutch size, fledging success and mean interval between successive clutches (first clutch successful) of the House Sparrow and the European Tree Sparrow between the emergence year of the 13-year periodical cicadas (1972) and non-emergence years.

	House Sparrow		Tree Sparrow	
	1969–71, 1973	1972	1969–71, 1973	1972
Clutch Size				
Number of Clutches	60	25	22[a]	12
Mean Clutch Size	5.10	5.12	5.14	5.83
Difference	$t = 0.1215$		$t = 2.5897^e$	
Fledging Success				
Number of Broods	32	10	9	4
Proportion Fledging	0.627	0.829	0.591	0.550
Difference	$X^2 = 5.790^d$		$X^2 = 0.003$	
Interval Between Clutches				
Number of Intervals	36	14	24	10
Mean Interval (Days)	38.0	36.6	36.7	34.2
Difference	$t = 1.5665^b$		$t = 1.9613^c$	

[a] Clutches from high density years of 1971 and 1973 only (mean clutch size varied inversely with breeding density in this species [Anderson 1973, in press], and 1972 was also a high density year).
[b] $0.05 < P < 0.10$.
[c] $0.025 < P < 0.05$.
[d] $0.01 < P < 0.025$.
[e] $0.005 < P < 0.01$.

natural experiment involving a superabundant food supply available to breeding populations of two species of sparrows.

METHODS

From 1968 through 1973 I studied and compared the ecologies of the House Sparrow (*Passer domesticus*) and the European Tree Sparrow (*P. montanus*) near St. Louis, Missouri (Anderson 1973, 1975, in press). I was primarily attempting to identify factors which limit the distribution of the introduced European Tree Sparrow, which has a very circumscribed range in North America. Concurrent population studies of the two species served as a cornerstone for the comparative study, and these included the determination of various fecundity parameters of the populations.

During the course of the study (in 1972) there was a local emergence of Brood XIX of the 13-year periodical cicadas, *Magicicada tredecim*, *M. tredecassini* and *M. tredecula*. Broods of periodical cicadas emerge synchronously during May and June of every 13th or 17th year, and are present locally in extremely high but uneven densities. They are much more abundant, however, than the "dog-days" cicadas that occur widely every year in late summer. Despite local variations in abundance, periodical cicadas represent a superabundant food supply for insectivorous species during the period of their emergence, assuming that other species of insects have a relatively constant unit-area biomass from year to year. Periodical cicadas are also conspicuous and are described as being "predator-foolhardy" (Lloyd and

Dybas 1966), scarcely avoiding predators. They can be captured readily by hand, for instance.

The study area was located in a highly cultivated portion of the floodplain between the Mississippi and Missouri rivers near Portage des Sioux, Saint Charles County, Missouri. The study site (site B in Anderson 1973) was a farmstead with a large breeding population (60–80 pairs) of sparrows of both species. During 1972 the cicadas emerged in the vicinity of the study area as early as 15 May, and were extremely numerous on the study site on 22 May. They remained common there through the first week of June, and were last seen there on 15 June. Periodical cicadas at the study site did not attain the tremendous densities that occurred elsewhere. Samples of nestling food from both species of sparrows, obtained by the "pipe-cleaner" method (see Orians 1966), contained cicadas, and I observed adult sparrows capturing flying cicadas by sallying from a perch.

The effects of a superabundant food supply on the following reproductive parameters of the two sparrows were examined, and comparisons made between 1972 and the four non-emergence years of the study: (1) clutch size, for clutches initiated from 20 May to 3 June (clutch size varies seasonally in both species (Anderson 1975) which allows for comparison only between comparable periods in the different years); (2) fledging success, expressed as the proportion of the young hatched from clutches initiated from 3 May to 18 May which survive to leave the nest (mean clutch initiation—hatching intervals for the House Sparrow and the European Tree Sparrow were 14.1 and 14.9 days, respectively, and nestling periods were 14.8 and 14.0 days, respectively, at the study area (Anderson, in press)); (3) nestling weight;

and (4) interval between successive clutches at a nest site, where the first clutch was initiated between 16 April and 10 May and was successful.

Based on Lack's hypothesis that reproduction in altricial species of birds is limited primarily by food, I made the following predictions concerning changes in these reproductive parameters in response to a superabundant food supply:

Clutch size: (1) If clutch size is a more-or-less genetically predetermined trait that is adjusted by natural selection to reflect average conditions of food availability, no change would be expected, or (2) if clutch size is responsive directly to food availability during the egg laying period, it should increase.

Fledging success: Fledging success should increase.

Nestling weight: (1) The rate of development should increase resulting in a more rapid attainment of fledging weight, and/or (2) weight at fledging should be greater.

Interval between successive clutches: If the rate of development of the young is increased and/or if the time to secure sufficient energy to produce a second clutch is reduced, the interval should be shorter.

Because the direction of all the responses can be predicted by the hypothesis, one-tailed *t*-tests and X^2 tests were used in the analysis.

RESULTS

The mean clutch size of the House Sparrow for the emergence year was not significantly different from that for the same period in the non-emergence years (table 1). The mean clutch size of the European Tree Sparrow in the emergence year, however, was significantly higher than that of the two non-emergence years with similar high densities of breeding tree sparrows, 1971 and 1973. Mean clutch size varied inversely with breeding density in this species (Anderson 1973, in press), as has been observed in many other species of birds (see Klomp 1970). The different responses of the two species may be the result of different selective regimes operating on the two species with respect to reproductive commitment. The House Sparrow, with a rather stable, dense population, may be under the influence of *K*-selection (MacArthur and Wilson 1967), which would favor the adoption of a clutch size which is not responsive to temporary fluctuations in the food supply (assuming that the population is not being controlled by predators). The European Tree Sparrow, however, is much less common than

the House Sparrow, and its population density is also less stable, at least in parts of its range (Barlow 1973). This species may therefore be under the influence of *r*-selection, with the result that it may exhibit a facultative response in clutch size to variations in the food supply.

Fledging success in the House Sparrow was significantly greater during the emergence year than in the comparable periods of the non-emergence years (table 1). Fledging success in the European Tree Sparrow was not significantly different. The samples for this species were very small, however, with only four broods observed during 1972.

Only five broods of House Sparrows whose nestling periods occurred during the cicada emergence were weighed near the time of fledging. The mean weights of each of these five broods (one with four young, two with five and two with six) are compared in figure 1 with the mean weights ($\pm 2 s_{\bar{x}}$) of young of the same ages weighed throughout the course of the study. In four of the five instances the mean weight of the brood was significantly higher than the mean weight of young raised under normal circumstances. The two broods of six young were the only House Sparrow broods of that size to fledge during the course of the study (in at least 18 other broods in which six young hatched, plus one brood of seven young, less than six young survived to fledge).

The mean interval between successive clutches was significantly shorter in the emergence year than in the non-emergence years in the European Tree Sparrow (table 1). It was also shorter in the House Sparrow, although not significantly so.

DISCUSSION

These results generally conform to the expectations derived from Lack's hypothesis, and hence further support it. They do not, however, constitute conclusive evidence with respect to the validity of that hypothesis for the two species. The question of whether or not feeding rates are adapted to the average brood size is left unanswered, as the superabundant prey in this case were much larger

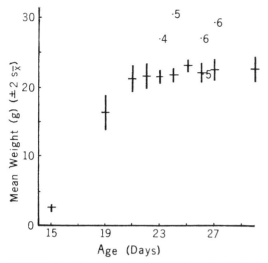

FIGURE 1. Mean weights of five broods of House Sparrows (with the number of young in the brood recorded beside the mean) raised during the emergence period of periodical cicadas plotted with the mean weights of nestlings of the same age raised under normal conditions (age plotted in days from initiation of the clutch [see Anderson 1973]).

than the average prey fed to the young under normal conditions (Anderson, in press). A carefully designed experiment in which brood sizes were manipulated and feeding rates were monitored in conjunction with a superabundant food supply at the population level, such as an emergence of periodical cicadas, would be most instructive.

ACKNOWLEDGMENTS

I thank R. Andrews, J. A. Mulligan and O. Sexton for their helpful advice and criticism, S. Steinhof and family for their patient hospitality during the study, and St. Louis University and McKendree College for financial assistance.

LITERATURE CITED

ANDERSON, T. R. 1973. A comparative ecological study of the House Sparrow and the Tree Sparrow near Portage des Sioux, Missouri. Ph. D. diss. St. Louis Univ.

ANDERSON, T. R., 1975. Fecundity of the House Sparrow and the Tree Sparrow near Portage des Sioux, Missouri, USA. Int. Stud. Sparrows 8:6–23.

ANDERSON, T. R. Population studies of European sparrows in North America. Occas. Pap. Mus. Nat. Hist. Univ. Kans. No. 70, in press.

BARLOW, J. C. 1973. Status of the North American population of the European Tree Sparrow, p. 10–23 In S. C. Kendeigh [ed.], A Symposium on the House Sparrow (Passer domesticus) and European Tree Sparrow (Passer montanus) in North America. Ornithol. Monogr. No. 14.

CODY, M. L. 1966. A general theory of clutch size. Evolution 20:174–184.

HUSSELL, D. J. T. 1972. Factors affecting clutch size in arctic passerines. Ecol. Monogr. 42:317–364.

JARVIS, M. J. F. 1974. The ecological significance of clutch size in the South African Gannet (Sula capensis Lichtenstein). J. Anim. Ecol. 43:1–17.

KLOMP, H. 1970. The determination of clutch-size in birds. Ardea 58:1–124.

LACK, D. 1947. The significance of clutch-size. Ibis 89:302–352.

LACK, D. 1954. The natural regulation of animal numbers. Clarendon Press, Oxford.

LACK, D. 1968. Ecological adaptations for breeding in birds. Methuen, London.

LLOYD, M. AND H. S. DYBAS. 1966. The periodical cicada problem. II. Evolution. Evolution 20: 466–505.

MACARTHUR, R. H. AND E. O. WILSON. 1967. The theory of island biogeography. Princeton Univ., Princeton.

NELSON, J. B. 1964. Factors influencing clutch size and chick growth in the North Atlantic Gannet, Sula bassana. Ibis 106:63–77.

ORIANS, G. H. 1966. Food of nestling Yellow-headed Blackbirds, Cariboo Parklands, British Columbia. Condor 68:321–337.

PERRINS, C. 1964. Survival of young Swifts in relation to brood-size. Nature (Lond.) 201: 1147–1148.

RICE, D. W. AND K. W. KENYON. 1962. Breeding cycles and behavior of Laysan and Black-footed Albatrosses. Auk. 79:517–567.

RICKLEFS, R. E. 1968. On the limitation of brood size in passerine birds by the ability of adults to nourish the young. Proc. Natl. Acad. Sci. (U.S.A.) 61:847–851.

RICKLEFS, R. E. 1970. Clutch size in birds: outcome of opposing predator and prey adaptations. Science (Wash. D.C.) 168:599–600.

SKUTCH, A. F. 1967. Adaptive limitation of the reproductive rate of birds. Ibis 109:579–599.

VON HAARTMAN, L. 1967. Clutch-size in the Pied Flycatcher. Proc. 14th Int. Ornithol. Congr., 155–164.

WYNNE-EDWARDS, V. C. 1962. Animal dispersion in relation to social behaviour. Hafner, New York.

YOM-TOV, Y. 1974. The effect of food and predation on breeding density and success, clutch size and laying date of the Crow (Corvus corone L.). J. Anim. Ecol. 43:479–498.

EXPERIMENTS ON POPULATION CONTROL BY TERRITORIAL BEHAVIOUR IN RED GROUSE

ADAM WATSON AND DAVID JENKINS

INTRODUCTION

Male red grouse (*Lagopus lagopus scoticus* (Lath.)) contest for territory each autumn, and some males are successful while others fail to secure territories. This paper describes experiments undertaken to test whether males which were not occupying territories could become territorial if the established territory owners were removed; that is to say, whether the number of breeding males was being limited simply by the territorial accommodation available or by some deficiency in the unsuccessful birds.

Previous research consisted of counts of the grouse on 100–120 ha study areas on heather (*Calluna vulgaris* L. (Hull)) moorland in north-east Scotland, with more detailed studies of the behaviour of individually marked birds on smaller parts of these areas (Jenkins, Watson & Miller 1963, 1967). Territorial behaviour, courtship and pair formation are described by Watson & Jenkins (1964). The population studies showed that there were many more grouse in autumn, even after the grouse shooting was over, than in the following spring. The behaviour studies showed that grouse populations from October to May consisted of (a) cocks which courted hens and defended territories, plus hens paired with them (territorial birds), and (b) non-territorial birds which did not defend territories, show courtship, pair up, or breed. Classes (a) and (b) both included birds less than 1 year old (called 'young' in this paper) and older birds. On average, 52% of the August population later became non-territorial over the autumn and winter and died before the next April–May (Jenkins *et al.* 1967), whereas both young and old territorial grouse survived the winter well and bred next summer. Consequently we postulated (Jenkins *et al.* 1967) that possession of territory was essential for breeding, and that territorial behaviour in autumn greatly limited the size of the next spring's breeding stock.

These hypotheses were open to the criticism that although territorial behaviour was associated with the population changes, it might not really be preventing the non-territorial grouse from taking territories. The crux was to find if they would take territories and breed when vacant ground was made available. If they did not, the hypotheses would be refuted. One might then explain the presence of non-territorial birds simply by suggesting that they were immature individuals, as in many other species where some individuals do not breed till 2 years old or more.

STUDY AREAS

Experiments before 1962 were done at Glen Esk in Angus, and subsequent experiments at Kerloch in Kincardineshire. The experimental areas at Glen Esk were on parts A1 and C (32 and 57 ha), separated by the 20 ha control area on part A2 and by a few fields (Fig. 1). All three areas were at about 230 m altitude. They were covered mainly by heather, which occurred in a patchwork of different ages due to fairly regular rotational burning in many small fires.

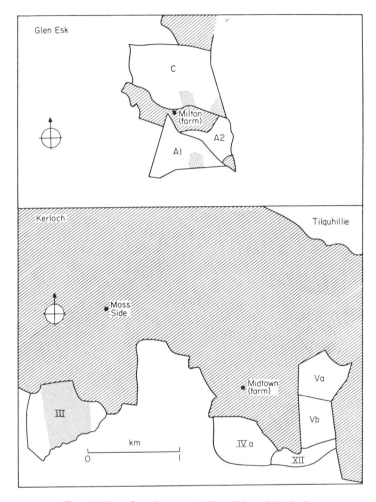

FIG. 1. Map of study areas at Glen Esk and Kerloch.
Notes: (a) The hatched areas show fields, scrub and woodland, and the rest is heather moorland, (b) the stippled areas indicate where removal experiments were done involving only part of a study area.

At Kerloch, the 40 ha experimental and the 32 ha control areas at parts V and IVa were on fairly uniform unburned heather at about 150–200 m altitude. Part IVa had a few boggy places, but was mostly dry and well drained like part V. Both areas were little grazed, except the south end of part V and the northern section of part IVa which were heavily grazed by cattle and sheep. The breeding stock of grouse on parts V and IVa remained fairly stable at twenty-three to twenty-seven and twenty-one to twenty-two birds in spring 1962 and 1963 before the experiments began, and was twenty-seven to thirty birds at part IVa during the 2 years of experiments, 1964–65.

Two other experimental areas at Kerloch were used less often. The 43 ha part III and the 12 ha part XII were mostly dry and well drained but with a few boggy places. They were covered mostly with heather that was fairly uniform and unburned, but heavily grazed by sheep and cattle.

METHODS

A Land Rover was used as a mobile hide for making total counts (i.e. censuses) of all red grouse present (Jenkins *et al.* 1963) on the experimental and control areas, for studying their behaviour, and for shooting selected birds with a 0·22 in. rifle. The work began at Glen Esk, with three small experiments where grouse were caught in wire traps with funnel

Table 1. *Total numbers of individual territorial cocks removed and subsequently replaced, and of non-territorial cocks on nearby areas available for replacement*

	No. of territorial cocks		
Experiment	Removed (i.e. number at beginning)	Replaced (i.e. number at end)¶	No. of non-territorial cocks† on nearby areas of 1 km² (excluding control areas)
1	10§	10	23*‡
2	13	15	39*
3	10	9	45*
4	5	5	45*
5	15	11	39
6	5	4	37
7	2	1 (temporary removal)	26
8	3	0 (temporary removal)	12
9	3	0	7
10	4	0	5
11	4	3	5
12	3	2	5
13	2	0	2

* In August–September (Experiments 1–4) the status of young birds was not yet known before removals were begun, and some would have become territorial in October in the absence of removals. These figures are therefore not exactly comparable with the rest. The young were not sexed, and the number of cocks in these cases is estimated by dividing the total number of young by two.

† The total number of individual non-territorial birds visiting or resident during counts over the two weeks before removals were begun was higher than the number seen on any one count. Many birds were not known individually, so these figures are minima, and the actual number available would be higher. The numbers of non-territorial cocks available on the experimental and control areas are in Appendix Table A.

‡ Unusually low figure because of poor breeding success.

§ See text, Experiment 1.

¶ Includes additional replacement in April–May, after earlier experiments up to March (see Fig. 2).

entrances, kept captive for a few days, and then released. This method was intended to answer two questions with each bird: was it replaced, and did it regain its territory after release? Subsequent experiments at Kerloch involved removing part or all of the population on certain areas by shooting. In some experiments we shot only the young cocks, and in others both young and old cocks. In later experiments all grouse of both sexes were shot, to avoid the possibility that newcomers might adjust their territory size to the areas used by hens left unshot.

The experiments were preceded by a study of the numbers and social status of all red grouse on the experimental and control areas, and on adjacent ground 150 m all around. The same work was also being done on nearby study areas of at least 1 km² and ranging up to 2 km²; this provided useful data on the number of birds available in nearby ground (Table 1). In different years 50–95% of the birds on these areas were individually marked with numbered plastic back tabs. Most unmarked birds were individually recognizable by variations in their plumage, using detailed field sketches of each bird. We knew which newcomers had formerly occupied neighbouring territories or had previously been without territories, which of them had previously been territorial and had later lost their territories before the shooting, and also which of them were previously unknown and with uncertain status because they had come from outside the areas being studied. Only one of these previously unknown birds was a cock but eleven were hens (Table 2); this was because more hens were unmarked and not recognized by plumage. At least 3 days of preliminary study were needed to discover the numbers and social status of all birds before each spring experiment and 1 week before each autumn one. In fact, all experiments except Experiment 1 were preceded by several weeks or months of work, during which the size of territories occupied by the birds was also measured. Shooting-out took at least 1 day but usually 2–3 days, and in Experiment 5, 2 weeks were needed. It was fairly easy to shoot most birds in the first few hours but increasingly difficult to shoot the remainder. Usually a whole day was needed to shoot the last one or two, and sometimes longer. As a result of this delay, replacement began before all the existing birds had been shot in Experiments 1, 2, 3 and 5, but any newcomers that appeared during this period were also shot. In Experiments 2, 3 and 5 it was impossible to shoot one particularly wary cock even during several days' attempts.

In spring, the breeding of hens was checked as a routine on experimental and control areas, by finding nests and young. In a few rare cases where neither were found, the characteristic large 'clocker' droppings of the incubating hen indicated that she was breeding.

RESULTS

For ease in understanding the results, the experiments are described not in the order in which they were done, but grouped instead according to season. This is because it became clear after the experiments were done that the pattern of replacement varied seasonally (Fig. 2). Subsidiary details are given in the Appendix. Seasonal changes in behaviour are briefly described at the beginning of each seasonal section, to give some background to the experiments. Fuller details about the annual cycle of behaviour are given in Jenkins *et al.* (1963, 1967).

A. *July–September*

During this period, old cocks (i.e. cocks that had bred that year and had been reared in some previous year) showed territorial behaviour only in the early morning, defending territories in the same place and of approximately the same size as in the previous winter and spring. They usually joined their families for the rest of the day. The families sometimes broke up as early as mid-August but usually in late September or early October,

297

Table 2. *The age and previous status of cocks taking territories and new hens paired with them, on experimental areas after shooting*

Period of shooting			August–early October			November–December			February–June		
Previous status			Juveniles* (non-territorial)	Moved from a former territory	Unknown	Non-territorial	Moved from a former territory	Unknown	Non-territorial	Moved from a former territory	Unknown
Cocks	Number of new territorial cocks	Young	46	0	0	9	1	1	8	0	0
		Old	–	11	0	2†	1	0	1†	1	0
	Total		46	11	0	11	2	1	9	1	0
Hens	Number of new paired hens	Young	23	0	0	1	0	4	2	0	3
		Old	–	8	2	1†	1	1	0	1	1
	Total		23	8	2	2	1	5	2	1	4

* Most young birds were in family parties in August–September, and if no old birds were shot they did not take territories till early October. Hence their social status could not usually be classified till October, but none of them had a territory prior to the shooting.

† Non-territorial old birds had been territorial in the previous year but had lost their old territories at the annual reshuffle of territories in October, and hence were now equivalent to non-territorial young which had failed to get territories in October. Birds which had moved from a former territory had held a territory elsewhere at the time of the shooting, but moved to colonize the vacant areas after a shooting. There are some replacement figures consequent on a removal experiment in an earlier period, e.g. the February–June data include April–May replacements long after Experiment 6 in November–December, and the August–October data include replacements long after Experiments 9, 10 and 13.

mainly as a result of aggressive encounters among the young birds (Watson & Jenkins 1964).

Experiment 1—early August 1965—complete removal

This was done on part V at Kerloch where there was a breeding stock of seven cocks and seven hens in June. Most of their eggs and young were collected; and all the remaining adults and young were shot from 1 to 3 August. On 3 August an extra pair with their brood had appeared; and two young cocks and an old cock were already showing territorial behaviour before all the original resident birds had been shot. All the newcomers were shot, leaving the whole area vacant. Two days later, two pairs with broods,

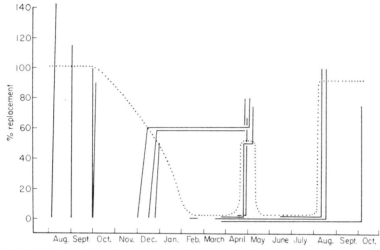

FIG. 2. Seasonal variation in the rate and extent of replacement of cock grouse taking territories following thirteen removal experiments; each solid line refers to one separate experiment.

Notes: (a) The percentage replacement is based on the final number of territorial cocks divided by the initial number. The data therefore exclude any replacement cocks which took territories and were themselves shot before an experimental shooting was completed. The results fall into five main sets—August–October, November–December, February–March, April–June and the next August–October. The dotted line indicates the approximate replacement for each set, adding up the percentage replacement for each experiment and taking a mean for each set. (b) The horizontal lines in spring and summer indicate no replacement, but are separated for clarity. (c) The second December experiment was run only for 3 days. (d) The first August result is probably artificially high because of the low breeding stock left after two earlier experiments. The replacement rate was only 100%, based on the breeding stock before the earlier experiments and this figure is used in calculating the mean for the dotted line. The April mean figure includes two experiments with nil replacement. (e) The steepness of the lines indicates the rate of replacement.

four single young cocks and a group of young (four cocks, six hens) were on part Va and none on Vb. Six cocks were showing territorial behaviour 4 days later and ten cocks occupied the whole of part V from 7 days later until October, pairing up with eight young and two old hens. This suggested an increase over the territorial stock of seven cocks in June, but the June figure was lower than usual following experiments 11 and 12 in March and April. In fact the number of territorial cocks before these spring experiments was ten—the same as in August–October 1965.

On the control area at part IVa, the territorial stock on 1 August consisted of sixteen cocks and fourteen hens paired up with them. The old cock that moved to the vacant ground on the experimental area was no longer on part IVa after 3 August, but all the remaining twenty-nine territorial birds stayed on IVa during the period of shooting and colonization (1–10 August) on the experimental area.

Experiment 2—late August 1963—removal of old cocks only

In August 1963 the population on part V at Kerloch comprised fourteen territorial old cocks, thirteen old hens paired up with the old cocks, sixteen young cocks, twenty-three young hens and two other young which were probably cocks. None of the young cocks showed territorial behaviour in August, and all were submissive to the fourteen old cocks. On 30–31 August, thirteen of the old cocks were shot but the fourteenth escaped. By 2 September, fourteen of the young cocks and one additional old cock which had moved from a territory outside the area had taken territories. The thirteen old hens were all paired up, and one young hen also. The size and shape of the new territories were similar to the old, except on part Vb (Fig. 1) where two small extra territories were held by unmated cocks (all the others were paired up). The number of cocks taking territories on Va was similar to the number available. Seven old cocks were shot, and seven young cocks plus one surviving old cock were left. All seven young cocks took territories and the cock that escaped took an eighth territory. However on Vb where six old cocks were shot and eleven young cocks were left, only seven young cocks took territories plus one old cock from outside the area.

On the control area at part IVa there were no changes in the territorial stock of eleven adult pairs during the period of shooting and colonization (end of August–beginning of September) on the experimental area.

Experiment 3—late September 1964—removal of all cocks and some hens

There were eleven old-established territories on part V at Kerloch, still remaining from the spring, and the population now consisted of eleven old cocks, ten young cocks, fourteen old hens and ten young hens. Ten old cocks and all ten young cocks were shot on 29–30 September. This was before the young showed any territorial behaviour. Six old hens and five young hens were also shot. On 1 October after the shooting there were one old cock, eight old hens, five young hens, and no young cocks (i.e. no immediate replacement occurred). Next day, two young cocks from elsewhere and two old cocks which had deserted their former territories elsewhere were already showing territorial behaviour, the latter two being already joined by two old hens of previously unknown status. These six birds were also shot.

Colonization continued rapidly, with five new territorial cocks at 3 days, seven at 4 days, and nine from 7 days onwards. Seven of these nine new cocks were young and the two old ones had left their former territories outside the area. Including the unshot original old cock, the territorial population of ten cocks and eleven hens was slightly lower than before shooting.

On the control area at part IVa there were no individual changes in the stock of fourteen territorial cocks and eleven hens paired up with them during the period of shooting and colonization on the experimental area (end of September–beginning of October).

Experiment 4—late September 1964—complete removal

Five old cocks and four old hens living on the 12 ha part XII at Kerloch—the entire population there—were shot on 30 September, concurrent with experiment 3 on the adjacent part V. This was before any young birds showed territorial behaviour. No grouse were present on 2 October, but 3 days later the whole area was occupied by four new pairs of young birds and one pair of old birds. All neighbouring pairs were still present. The control for this experiment was the same as for the concurrent experiment 3.

Conclusions

1. Young cocks showed territorial behaviour in early and late August (Experiments 1 and 2) on vacant ground, but not before mid-September (and not usually before early October) on the control area where territories were still occupied by old birds in August–September. Hence young birds were capable of territorial behaviour earlier than they usually showed it, but were presumably inhibited by the presence of the more dominant old birds.

2. The previous territorial density was reached within 2 days when all young cocks were left unshot (Experiment 2), but more slowly when both young and old cocks were shot (Experiments 1, 3 and 4).

3. Forty-six of the new territorial cocks were young birds (Table 2) but eleven old cocks left their former territories outside the area and moved to the vacant ground, in two cases accompanied by their hens and young (these figures include replacements in August–October long after Experiments 9, 10 and 13). There were similar results with the hens that colonized.

4. Newcomers settled to about the same territorial density as before shooting, whether all the formerly resident cocks and hens were shot or not.

5. A total of sixty-four vacancies for territorial birds was made during these experiments (including one natural disappearance, in Appendix, Experiment 3), and the total number of replacements was seventy-two. On the control area there was only one individual change out of an original total of seventy-nine territorial birds, during the periods of shooting and colonization on the experimental area. This single case involved a cock that moved to the experimental area. Table 2 shows ninety replacements, but this includes replacements in August-October long after Experiment 9, 10 and 13.

B. *November–December*

Many young cocks first challenged the old cocks and took new territories in late September–early October and many young hens paired up at this time (Watson & Jenkins 1964). A new pattern of territories was then established. Old birds which lost their territories were then equivalent to those young birds that failed to pair up or get territories in the first place. Territorial behaviour occurred only in the morning, and non-territorial birds fed freely on these territorial areas in the afternoon (Jenkins *et al.* 1963).

Experiment 5—late November 1963—removal of all cocks

Fifteen new cocks took territories on part V at Kerloch after experiment 2 and one of the previous old cocks escaped shooting. These fifteen colonizing birds were all shot on 15–29 November, leaving one old territorial cock. None of the fourteen hens paired up with them was shot.

The first immigrant cock showed territorial behaviour on 29–30 November, another after 3 days, four after 5 days, five after 6 days, seven after 10 days and nine after 14 days. Seven colonists were young cocks and two were old cocks which had been evicted from their territories outside the area in October. The shooting lasted 2 weeks, but ten of the previous territories were already vacant by 17 November. Since most of the vacant territories were filled only from 7 to 16 December, most of the new birds took 3–4 weeks to show territorial behaviour, although they had often been seen on the area earlier.

Including the single old cock that escaped shooting, there were ten territorial cocks from 12 December 1963 to April 1964, and sixteen hens paired with them from late December to March. One territorial old cock disappeared in early April, and in early May three non-territorial young cocks occupied new territories. The eventual summer stock was twelve cocks and fourteen hens, which all bred.

On the control area at part IVa, the only changes in the territorial stock of sixteen cocks and thirteen hens during the period of shooting and colonization on part V (mid-November–mid-December) were that two hens disappeared in late November and were replaced by two hens of previously unknown status.

Experiment 6—mid-December 1964—complete removal

All five pairs (four of young birds and one of old) on part XII at Kerloch were shot on 16 December. Next day one previously non-territorial young cock showed territorial behaviour, but numbers built up more slowly than after Experiment 4 on this area in September 1964, with one territorial cock after 3 days, two after 7 days and three after 12–14 days. Four young hens of previously unknown status paired with these three cocks after 12–14 days. In late April a non-territorial young cock occupied an extra territory and was later joined by a young hen of unknown status, thus bringing the breeding stock of nine birds almost to the previous year's level of ten. On the control area at part IVa, there were no changes in the territorial stock of fifteen pairs during the period of experiment and colonization in late December.

Experiment 7—late December 1960—temporary removal

At Glen Esk on 22 December, two young cocks A and B were trapped on the same afternoon and removed from territories 400 m apart on part C. Their hens were not removed. By next morning, a previously non-territorial young cock had occupied A's territory and paired up with hen A; and a neighbouring territorial cock N had enlarged its own territory to include B's territory and was courting hen B. Cocks A and B were released after $2\frac{1}{2}$ days, having lost only 3% of their weight. They were seen next morning fighting with and driving out the invaders, and they chased them away for 400–600 m, far beyond their territories. A and B courted and formed pairs with their former hens on the same morning.

On the control area at part A2, the size and individual membership of the territorial stock remained at the same five pairs during the period of experiment in late December.

Conclusions

After the annual competition for territories in October, the pattern of replacement on experimental areas was different from that in August–September. Replacement was rapid when only two individuals were removed (Experiment 7), but when all the cocks were shot on a large area (Experiment 5), or all birds on a large area (Experiment 6), territorial occupation of the whole area by newcomers took 2–4 weeks instead of 2–7 days as in August–September, and the number of territories over winter was smaller than before shooting. However in two experiments extra non-territorial cocks took territories months later in late April–early May, bringing the eventual number of territories nearly to what it was before shooting. Table 2 shows that most newcomers taking territories after these experiments were previously non-territorial young birds, but two were old birds which moved from territories held elsewhere at the time of the shooting and three were non-territorial old birds which had lost their former territories earlier at the annual competition for territories.

To sum up, compared with an original total of twenty-eight territorial vacancies, twenty-two new birds took territories. By contrast, out of an original total of sixty-nine territorial birds on the control areas, only two died or disappeared during the periods of shooting and colonization, and both were replaced.

C. *February–late March*

Territories were defended all day long during this period, and non-territorial grouse were evicted whenever they were discovered by the territory owners. The non-territorial birds were forced to spend most of their time on grassy undefended areas where heather was scarce and where many of these birds were found dead in poor condition subsequently during the spring (Jenkins *et al.* 1963). Fewer non-territorial birds were still alive from February to the spring than in the autumn and early winter (Table 1, Appendix Table A).

Experiment 8—late February 1961—temporary removal

At Glen Esk, three young cocks, C, D and E with adjacent territories on part A1 were taken into captivity on 22 February. Next morning, all three territories were divided among their neighbours. In each case the captive bird's hen paired up bigamously with one of the neighbours. No new birds were able to occupy the old territories. The captive cocks were released after 7 days, when they had lost only 2, 7, and 6% of their weight. Two mornings later they had regained their hens and former territories.

On the control area at part A2, the same six territorial cocks and hens were present throughout the second half of February during the period of experiment.

Experiment 9—mid-March 1961—temporary removal

At Glen Esk, three neighbouring young cocks with adjacent territories totalling 2·9 ha were captured on 16 March. Cocks F and G were put in $2 \times 1 \times 1$ m cages on their own territories, and cock H in a garden 8 km away. The vacant 2·9 ha were completely occupied next morning by three neighbouring territorial cocks. The now unattached hens G and H paired up bigamously with two of the neighbouring cocks and the third unattached hen F disappeared. The two neighbours now occupying the ground round the two cages spent much time on the cage roofs, dominating the former territory-owners inside even though these were still within their old territories. Cock H escaped after 7 days (Appendix), having lost only 4% of its weight, but did not return to its territory, presumably because it was too far away. Cocks F and G were released after 10 days. Cock F, which had lost only 4% of its weight in captivity, reoccupied most of its old territory next day. It also regained its previous hen, which had earlier disappeared. Cock G, which had lost 15% of its weight, showed no territorial behaviour after release and hid from the other cocks, even on its former territory. After 4 days it moved to grass fields 400 m away and died later, at the beginning of April. Territories G and H were retained by the two neighbouring territorial cocks that had earlier taken them over, and hens G and H paired up bigamously and bred with these two cocks. No new bird colonized before mid-August, when three young cocks took territories on this area in mid-August and paired up with three young hens.

On the control area at part A2, the territorial stock remained stable with the same six cocks and six hens throughout the period of experiment, i.e. the second half of March and early April.

Experiment 10—26–28 March 1963—removal of all cocks

Four old territorial cocks with adjacent territories were shot on part III at Kerloch (Fig. 1), leaving 15 ha vacant and four unattached hens. All four hens disappeared and none paired up bigamously with territorial cocks in the surrounding 80 ha. The area remained vacant of new territorial birds till October, when three new pairs of young birds colonized it. On the control area at part IVa, there were no individual changes in the territorial stock of ten cocks and ten hens during the period of experiment between 20 March and 20 April.

Experiment 11—late March 1965—removal of most birds

The breeding stock on part Va at Kerloch after experiment 5 was five territorial cocks and five hens. Two pairs, two paired territorial cocks and a non-territorial young cock were shot from 28 to 31 March; one of the paired cocks' hens disappeared, and the other paired bigamously with the sole remaining cock. This cock now expanded his territory to occupy about one third of the vacant ground. No new birds had taken territories by 20 April, although two non-territorial young cocks were seen on each visit. These two non-territorial cocks eventually took territories on the still vacant part of Va in the last week of April. Only one was joined by a hen, which was the same bird that disappeared after the shooting in late March. Up to 21 April when experiment 12 began, the five territorial cocks and five hens on the adjacent part Vb were present but did not occupy the vacant ground on Va. In addition, a third new cock took a territory on the vacant ground in early May, although it was an old bird that had lost its previous territory in October 7 months before.

On the control area at part IVa, the territorial stock remained stable with the same fifteen cocks and fifteen hens throughout the period of shooting and colonization between 28 March and 21 April.

Conclusions

No replacement occurred within a month after four shooting experiments from February to late March, although a total of sixteen vacancies was made and non-territorial birds were available in each case. One pair moved from a former territory but this was on the experimental area (Appendix, Experiment 10). Partial recolonization eventually occurred after only one experiment (no. 11). Possible reasons for this are given in the Discussion. No changes occurred on the control areas out of an original total of sixty-four territorial birds. This was the only set of experiments where the status quo immediately after the shooting experiments was maintained for at least 3 weeks on both experimental and control areas.

D. Mid-April–June

Territorial defence declined greatly just before and during the breeding season (most clutches were begun in late April), and after the end of April it occurred only early in the morning.

Experiment 12—21–24 *April* 1965—*removal of most birds*

Three pairs were shot out of a stock of five pairs on part Vb. Only one non-territorial bird had been seen on six counts in March and none during counts in April. A week later two new non-territorial young cocks took territories there and a young and an old hen of unknown status joined them and bred. A fourth hen was shot on the nest on 18 May and next day a previously non-territorial young hen from elsewhere had paired up with the mate of the hen that was shot. The new hen bred later. Replacement at such a late date was interesting, since most hens were far on in incubation by then, the mean hatching date in that year being 27 May (Jenkins *et al.* 1967).

As in Experiment 11, the territorial stock on the control area at part IVa remained stable during the period of shooting and colonization in late April and May.

Experiment 13—10 *June* 1964—*removal of all cocks*

One old and one young territorial cock were shot on part XII at Kerloch. There were no replacements until 1–5 August, when two young cocks showed territorial behaviour, and were joined by an old hen and a young hen from outside the area. The territorial stock on the control area at part IVa stayed at fourteen cocks and thirteen hens throughout June.

Conclusions

There was only partial replacement after Experiment 12 in late April, none after two natural disappearances in April (Appendix, Experiments 5 and 10) and none after Experiment 13 in June (five replacements in all for April–June out of an original total of eleven territorial vacancies). There was also partial replacement in April–May following the incomplete replacement after Experiments 5, 6 and 11 which were done earlier in the winter. The gap in replacement after these three experiments totalled sixteen, and there were ten new territorial birds in April–May. A few non-territorial birds were sometimes present during the breeding season, and in Experiment 12 one of them paired up with a territorial cock and bred. There were no changes in the control area, out of an original total of fifty-seven territorial birds.

MAIN CONCLUSIONS

The null hypothesis being tested was (a) that areas partially or wholly depopulated by shooting would not be recolonized, and (b) that individuals which had previously been non-territorial would all remain so and would not breed; in other words that the status quo occurring immediately after each of the thirteen removal experiments would continue. In fact neither result was found on the experimental areas except in three experiments in February–March and one in June, yet the status quo was almost wholly maintained on control areas where no shooting was done. Including the pair that moved in Experiment 11 (see conclusions for that section), a total of 111 new birds colonized to take territories by mid-summer, compared with 119 vacancies made experimentally. Yet on the control areas, where 269 territorial birds were present before the experiments, there were only three individual changes during the period of removals and colonization on the experimental areas. One moved to colonize a vacancy on an experimental area, and the other two disappeared and were themselves replaced. Whatever their previous status, all hens that were paired up with territorial cocks in May were known to breed (see Methods, last paragraph) on experimental and control areas.

Three main conclusions from these results are:

1. The size of breeding stocks was determined by territorial behaviour. Only territory owners bred, and birds failing to get territories in autumn did not occupy territories and breed unless there were subsequent vacancies through the removal of territory owners. The ultimate fate of birds that were still non-territorial in winter was therefore irrelevant to the size or regulation of the spring breeding stock. In fact most of them died after being forced to live largely off the moor (Jenkins *et al.* 1963), but even if they survived to the summer, which was rare (Table 1, Appendix Table A), they did not breed and so were not part of the breeding population.

2. In most experiments the shooting of the required number of birds took at least several days to complete. During this period, surviving territorial cocks whose neighbours were removed enlarged their territories, sometimes to meet other territorial birds from beyond. This implies that some previous pressure prevented these birds from enlarging their territories earlier. Similarly, increases in the number of non-territorial grouse during the period of colonization following a removal experiment (Appendix Table A) also suggest a greater previous pressure against settling.

3. The number of territory owners in spring on each experimental area was usually about the same as before shooting, showing that this form of population regulation results in a stability suited to some local feature of each area.

DISCUSSION

The main problem raised is why the final territorial or breeding density in the spring after most shooting experiments was similar to that before the experiments (Table 1). Newcomers took territories of a similar size to those held previously on the area, whether or not some or all the previous birds were shot. Hence the territory size of the newcomers could not have been adjusted to that of the previous owners. These results would not be surprising if population density in spring and the brood size of fledged young were similar all over the adjacent areas of moor, but in fact these varied greatly on different parts of the moor in the same year, and in different years on the same area (Jenkins *et al.* 1967). Presumably the newcomers' territory size related to some habitat feature which did not change during the experiment. It was certainly not limited by the number of birds available on nearby areas (Table 1) or on the experimental and control areas (Appendix Table A).

Speed and level of replacement reached

There was some seasonal variation, illustrated in Fig. 2. After experiments in August–September, the number of territorial grouse rose to the same level as before shooting— i.e. replacement was complete. Replacement was less complete after experiments in November–December, and remained incomplete over the winter. Although the number of non-territorial grouse did fall off over the winter many were still present in November–December (Table 1, Appendix Table A). The reason for this incomplete replacement is uncertain, but may possibly be that colonization in November–December proceeded with a slow succession of birds, compared with simultaneous or more rapid succession in earlier experiments. (Van den Assem (1967) found by experiment that more male sticklebacks (*Gasterosteus aculeatus* L.) can be accommodated in simultaneous introductions than in successive ones.) Replacement was least complete after experiments in February, March, April and June. Most non-territorial birds had by then died but some were present and yet did not take territories. Perhaps their capability for showing territorial behaviour was also important, as discussed below.

In August–September young cocks quickly took territories, often on the same day as the previous owners were shot. These were the most dominant young cocks. After October, when birds separated into distinct social classes, only a few birds that had been non-territorial before the experiments showed territorial behaviour immediately afterwards, and most showed it very gradually over a few weeks during which they increasingly spent more time on the area. Only two out of twenty cocks previously known to be non-territorial showed territorial behaviour on the first day. By contrast all fourteen cocks which left their former territories to move into vacant ground showed vigorous territorial behaviour from the time they were first seen there.

Clearly after October most non-territorial birds were incapable of showing territorial behaviour at once, even on vacant areas where all competition had been removed by the shooting of all the more dominant established birds. Possibly they could re-adjust to the new situation only slowly because they were not aggressive enough. There is some evidence that the gonads of most non-territorial cocks were smaller than those of territorial cocks after October–November, and this aspect is being studied further.

Up to January, vacant territories were usually colonized by previously non-territorial cocks, but in February–March they were partitioned among neighbouring territorial cocks which enlarged their former territories. Non-territorial cocks did try to settle but were excluded. This was probably because the established cocks that had defended their territories only on fine early mornings up to January expelled newcomers at all times of day and in almost all weathers in February–March (Jenkins et al. 1963, 1967). It cannot be simply that the non-territorial intruders were weak, since individuals which had failed to occupy vacant territories in February–March sometimes managed to take territories in late April–May, when fewer non-territorial birds still survived (Table 1, Appendix Table A) and when their condition would if anything be poorer. Furthermore areas with a lower stock after Experiments 5 and 6 in November–December and after two of the four later experiments in February–April were colonized almost up to the pre-shooting level by non-territorial birds in late April–early May. Non-territorial birds only rarely took new territories in April–May in undisturbed populations. A likely reason for this partial replacement is that newcomers which would probably have been ejected in February–March had more chance of settling in late April–May when territorial behaviour was declining and was largely confined to the early morning.

Reaction of hens

Hens whose mates were removed usually associated with incoming cocks that were previously non-territorial, or joined up bigamously with neighbouring territorial cocks. They did not continue to live on an area if no cocks were present, even in cases where they had lived on certain territories for 6 months or more. After Experiment 5 when cocks were shot in late November and the hens were left unshot, some hens paired bigamously with the newcomers and the excess of hens over the winter was bigger than was recorded (Jenkins et al. 1963, 1967) in undisturbed populations. However after Experiments 10 and 11, some hens which had been paired up for 6 months disappeared after their mates were shot and did not associate with other cocks on the area or on adjacent ground nearby.

Visits by birds living mainly elsewhere

Territorial hens did not stay on an area if all territorial cocks were shot, but some returned on the first day when their former mates or new territorial cocks appeared (Experiments 9, 10 and 11). This immediate return suggests that they had visited their old territories occasionally during the period since they disappeared, otherwise they would not have known that new cocks had arrived. Yet they were not seen when we visited their former territories during this period, and so must have been spending most of their time elsewhere. By contrast, hens that were paired up were consistently seen on territories in spring. Non-territorial birds must also have paid occasional visits like this. The Appendix Table A shows that few or no non-territorial birds were on the experimental areas during counts before some of the experiments, yet larger numbers usually appeared as soon as vacant ground was made available. Larger numbers did not appear on the control areas at these times. Furthermore, non-territorial birds which came to the experimental areas during the period of colonization did not stay there after the experiment, by which time the vacant ground was either occupied by newcomers or else divided up by previous territorial residents left unshot. Clearly they must have been moving about and visiting these areas occasionally, but started spending much time there—and thus being seen by us—only when the territory owners were removed. Even territorial cocks with territories elsewhere must have been moving and occasionally visiting other areas, or they could not so often have left their former territories and moved so quickly up to 1 km to colonize the new areas (see next paragraph). This must have happened even at times when territory owners were observed to be very sedentary and largely confined to their territories (e.g. early August, late March).

Leaving old territories

Table 1 shows that some grouse which colonized vacant areas had been occupying territories elsewhere at the time of the shooting, but moved in to the new areas quickly. Most of these birds had bred successfully on their former territories, in two cases for 2 and 3 years running, and some moved 1 km to the new ground. None of these birds was seen being evicted from its former territory. Probably they all left spontaneously, since no evictions of old cocks and hens were ever observed till late September–early October. Movements of territorial grouse to new territories occurred at all times from August to April. This was not expected and if no birds had been marked we might erroneously have assumed that all newcomers were previously non-territorial. The reason for these desertions is unknown. Possibly any large vacant area is more attractive than a former territory, provided the vacant space is much larger than the old territory (which was invariably the case with these experiments).

Management implications

The main implications for management are that established old territorial grouse which get shot in August–September will be quickly replaced by young birds. Any local areas (up to at least 52 ha) where the stock gets wholly wiped out will be quickly colonized, and presumably much larger areas where the stock is less heavily shot would also fill up quickly. Therefore local variations in density due to differences in shooting pressure would probably even out later on. Very heavy shooting in November–December is not advisable, since it would probably lead to lower breeding stocks in the next spring. Similarly the gamekeepers' habit of shooting single cock grouse in November–December, usually when they are on their territories, could lead to lower breeding stocks if it were done intensively. However at present these practices of late shooting are seldom important since organized large-scale shooting is rarely done after the end of September.

ACKNOWLEDGMENTS

We are grateful to Professor V. C. Wynne-Edwards for comments on the manuscript. Grouse were shot out of season under licence from the Nature Conservancy.

SUMMARY

1. Thirteen experiments over 6 years, involving the removal of red grouse from certain study areas at every season, showed that the size of breeding stocks was determined by territorial behaviour.

2. The numbers, location and social status of nearly all birds were known on and around the experimental and control areas. Most birds were marked, and with most newcomers it was known whether they were territory owners attracted from elsewhere or were previously part of the non-territorial population.

3. Non-territorial birds took territories and bred only after vacancies were provided by the experimental shooting or temporary removal of territory owners. Territorial cocks whose neighbours were shot invariably enlarged their territories; thus implying some previous pressure against this. The number of territories in the following spring on the experimental areas usually rose to about the same level as before the shooting, whether some or all the previous territorial birds were shot and irrespective of the number of non-territorial birds available. By contrast, hardly any changes occurred on the control areas.

4. Most newcomers were non-territorial young birds, but a few were non-territorial old birds that had previously lost their former territories. Some old birds which were occupying territories elsewhere at the time of the shooting left their old territories and moved up to 1 km to take new territories on the vacant ground.

5. As early as the beginning of August, young cocks took territories on vacant ground, but their territorial behaviour was delayed till October if old-established birds were still present. Replacement was rapid and complete after experimental shootings in August–September. It was slower and incomplete after experiments in November–December, but eventually became almost complete in April–May. It was slowest and incomplete after shooting in February–April and June. Non-territorial birds were still available after October, but only a few of them reacted by showing territorial behaviour on vacant ground immediately after a shooting.

REFERENCES

Jenkins, D., Watson, A. & Miller, G. R. (1963). Population studies on red grouse, *Lagopus lagopus scoticus* (Lath.) in north-east Scotland. *J. Anim. Ecol.* **32,** 317–76.

Jenkins, D., Watson, A. & Miller, G. R. (1967). Population fluctuations in the red grouse *Lagopus lagopus scoticus*. *J. Anim. Ecol.* **36,** 97–122.

Van den Assem, J. (1967). Territory in the three-spined stickleback *Gasterosteus aculeatus* L. *Behaviour*, Suppl. xvi, 1–164.

Watson, A. & Jenkins, D. (1964). Notes on the behaviour of the red grouse. *Br. Birds*, **57,** 137–70.

APPENDIX

This Appendix adds subsidiary details to the main text. Table A gives data on non-territorial birds before and after the experiments, showing particularly that their number increased during the period of colonization following the removal of territorial birds.

Experiment 1

On 3 August the extra pair and their two young came from 100 m outside part V. The old cock that took a territory on 3 August moved 1 km from the control area, where it had had a territory at least since spring 1962. On 5 August, two new pairs with broods of three and four young moved at least 1 km from their former territories. On 10 August seven young and three old cocks had territories (including an old cock which moved 500 m from its former territory).

On the control area, thirty adults and twenty young stayed till late September, except for one old cock that moved to the experimental area and one old hen that disappeared in September. There was no change in territory ownership till early October, when the first young cocks showed territorial behaviour. The territorial stock over winter was fifteen cocks and thirteen hens.

Experiment 2

The same fourteen adult cocks and thirteen hens were on part V from April to August 1963 when thirteen old cocks were shot. A young cock reared on the area showed territorial behaviour and courted a widowed hen 2 h after her previous mate was shot. Immediately after all the shooting, another old hen left to pair up with a cock 400 m outside the area, but returned 3 days later to pair up with the young cock which had taken her former mate's territory. An old cock moved from its former territory $\frac{1}{2}$ km outside and was joined next day by its mate. The twenty-six non-territorial young reared on the area associated as remnant family parties with the old hens, but these groups broke up between 11 and 18 September and by 1 October only seven non-territorial birds were left.

On the control area, there were eleven adult pairs in April and August 1963, with twenty-three young in August. In mid-September, one old hen disappeared, the families broke up, and many young went into flocks. The first young cocks took two extra territories from 14 September onwards (early October is usually the earliest for this) but there were no major changes till early October. The eventual territorial stock from early October to April 1964 was sixteen cocks and thirteen hens.

Experiment 3

Before the experiment, a territorial old cock on part V disappeared in the summer and was replaced in mid-August by a young cock that took the same territory and paired up with the old cock's previous mate. This showed that, as in experiments 1 and 2, young cocks can show territorial behaviour in August if old cocks are removed.

The first two old cocks which took territories after the experiment moved from former territories 400 m outside the area, and were joined by two old hens of previously unknown status; and the second two old cocks moved with their hens from territories 1 km away. Three of the eleven paired hens were young birds from outside. The remaining five young hens became non-territorial.

Table A. *Changes in total numbers of individual* non-territorial grouse available during removal experiments*

	Experimental areas						Control areas					
	No. before the experiment		Maximum change during period of territory colonization		Nett change after the experiment		No. before the experiment		Maximum change coincident with colonization on experimental area		Nett change after the experiment	
Experiment	Cocks	Hens	Cocks	Hens	Cocks	Hens	Cocks	Hens	Cocks	Hens	Cocks	Hens
1	2† (0)	2† (0)	+14	+16	+3	+6	20†	20†	0†	0†	0†	0†
2	18†	23†	+2	+2	−6	−4	12†	11†	0†	0†	0†	0†
3	10† (0)	10† (5)†	+3	+2	+3	0	35†	35†	0†	0†	−7†	−7†
4	0	0	+3	+3	+1	0	35†	35†	0†	0†	−7†	−7†
5	2	7	+7	+5	0	−1	9	36	−1	−1	−1	0
6	0	2	+2	+4	0	0	11	27	−2	−3	−3	−4
7	0	0	+2	+2	0	0	1	6	+1	−2	+1	0
8	2	3	+3	+2	+1	+1	2	6	+1	−1	0	0
9	2	3	+4	+1	0	−1	2	3	0	+1	0	−1
10	1	0	+1	0	0	0	2	3	+1	0	+1	0
11	2	2	+2	+1	0	0	0	0	0	0	0	0
12	2	0	+3	+1	0	0	0	0	0	0	0	0
13	0	0	+1	0	0	0	2	0	0	0	0	0

* See footnote symbol (†) in Table 1.

† In August–September (Experiments 1–4), the status of some young birds—and in some cases on the control areas their sex also—were not known before removals were begun. These figures are therefore not exactly comparable with the rest.

Notes. 1. Numbers before the experiment were checked during counts in the two weeks before shooting began. ( ) Shows number after last removal and before first replacement, if this number was different. Numbers during the period of colonization were checked up to the date of last replacement. If no replacement occurred, numbers were checked during the two weeks after the last removal. Numbers after the experiment were checked during the two weeks following the period of colonization.

2. In Experiments 7, 8, 9 and 13, when only a small part of an experimental area was made vacant, the figures show the number of birds on that part and not on the entire area.

Conclusions. (a) The number of non-territorial birds increased on experimental areas during the period of territory colonization following the removal of territorial birds, while there was no change on control areas.

(b) On experimental areas, the nett change was usually less than the maximum change, suggesting that some limit was placed on the number of non-territorial grouse able to settle.

On the control area, fourteen territorial cocks and thirteen hens had thirty-five young on 1 August, and in mid-August one old hen died and another disappeared. Up to 8 October the remaining fifty grouse were present, although the families broke up after late September. By 16 October there were many changes in territory ownership and the territorial stock increased slightly to sixteen pairs, but the total number of grouse did not change.

Experiment 5

An additional non-territorial young cock occupied a vacant territory on the same morning as the owner was shot, and was itself shot later. No others took territories in the 2 weeks of shooting, although up to nine non-territorial cocks were seen at a time. Two of these cocks took territories 1 and 2 weeks after the shooting was over. Two more colonists were old cocks which had been evicted from their former territories outside the area in October and had since been living as non-territorial birds on the control area. The young cock which colonized 3 days after the experiment moved from a territory 1 km away, but all the other young cocks were previously non-territorial.

Of the sixteen hens that were paired up over winter, twelve were from the original territorial stock of fourteen hens. Another two were an old hen and a young hen which had previously been non-territorial about 1 km away, one was an old hen which moved from a former territory 500 m away and one was an old hen of unknown status. Four of these sixteen hens disappeared in early March.

One territorial old cock disappeared from the experimental area in early April, and its mate paired with a non-territorial young cock which had moved in from the control area 1 km away by 7 April. On 9 April this new cock was driven away by a neighbouring territory owner which then occupied the vacant territory and paired up bigamously with the extra hen. This new young cock was again left without a territory but it continued to live on the experimental area, and when territorial behaviour declined in early May before breeding, it occupied a territory there and was joined by a young hen whose previous status was unknown. In early May, two other non-territorial young cocks from the control area also occupied territories on part V (experimental area). One of them paired with a previously non-territorial young hen, raising the breeding stock from ten cocks and twelve hens, to twelve cocks and fourteen hens. These all bred and except for one hen all survived the summer.

On the control area, the same sixteen territorial cocks, plus thirteen hens paired up with them, were present from early October 1963 to April 1964. Up to four non-territorial cocks and two hens visited part IVa until April–May, when some of them managed to take territories on the experimental area at part V. In early April, one territorial old cock disappeared and was replaced by another previously non-territorial old cock, and an old and a young territorial cock disappeared in early May.

Experiment 6

The second colonist was an old cock which moved from its original territory 200 m outside the area. The other two colonizing cocks were young birds—one previously non-territorial and the other of previously unknown status.

On the control area, the territorial stock in early December was sixteen pairs. Two territorial cocks and one hen which had entered our traps were killed by stoats (*Mustela erminea* L.) there on 13 and 15 December. In one case the territory was annexed by two neighbouring cocks, in the other by a previously non-territorial cock which paired up with the single unattached hen. The territorial stock stayed at fifteen pairs from December to April.

Experiment 8

When released at noon, the captive cocks flew out of sight and had not returned by evening, but next morning they were all back. Only cock C, which had lost least weight, regained its hen, and none fully regained its original territory. Two mornings later, all three had regained their hens and former territories. In early February before the experiment, one territorial hen disappeared on the control area and was replaced by a previously non-territorial hen.

Experiment 9

Cock H, which escaped in good condition after 1 week in captivity in a garden, did not return to its former territory 8 km away. It showed territorial behaviour 2 days running on the nearest moorland 400 m away, but was driven out by local territorial cocks. On the third day it was seen at the garden and in nearby fields, and next day appeared among poultry at a farmyard, where it was found dead in poor condition 4 days later.

A total of eight different non-territorial cocks and four hens visited the experimental area in March and early April, three cocks in late April and two cocks up to August, but none occupied the ground made vacant. At the beginning of March, before the experiment, a territorial cock on the control area gave up its territory which was divided up by three neighbouring territorial cocks.

Experiment 10

Two hours after cock I was shot, his hen had paired up bigamously with a neighbouring territorial cock J. By next morning cock J and another neighbour K had annexed about half the vacant ground and all of it by 6 days later. These two cocks and a third neighbour L were then shot, leaving four unattached hens.

Next morning the nearest territorial cock M and its mate deserted their territory and moved 300 m to cock I's territory. Cock M was then shot but flew off wounded in one foot and its hen disappeared within 1 h. This left 15 ha vacant and four unattached hens. All of these hens disappeared, none pairing with other territorial cocks in the surrounding 80 ha. A fifth previously unmated territorial cock disappeared in late March.

In the next week, cock M was seen twice in a nearby undefended bog, where it hid, did not call and flew weakly with a trailing leg; but by the eighth day it had recovered and flew around the first vacant territory giving many loud calls. Next morning it was associating with its original hen, although she had not been seen there since the shooting. It had about 30% more ground than on its former territory and about 10% more than the original owner I.

On the control area, one unmated young territorial cock gave up its territory in early March and was not replaced. This was before shooting began on the experimental area.

Experiment 13

One of the old territorial cocks that enlarged its territory after the June experiment was killed by a bird of prey about 19–20 September, and by 24 September a young cock had occupied the vacant ground and next day paired up with a young hen.

Reproduced from the *Journal of Animal Ecology* 37:595–614, 1968, with permission of the British Ecological Society.

SOCIAL BEHAVIOR AND BREEDING SUCCESS IN CANADA GEESE (*BRANTA CANADENSIS*) CONFINED UNDER SEMI-NATURAL CONDITIONS

BY NICHOLAS E. COLLIAS AND LAURENCE R. JAHN

An attempt is being made to reestablish the Canada Goose as a breeding bird in Wisconsin. This is being done by use of large, outdoor enclosures adjacent to appropriate habitat, in which wing-pinioned adults are maintained. The resulting young birds are not wing-pinioned but are allowed to fly over the surrounding fence, in the expectation that they will settle and breed in the adjoining marshlands. The present study was carried out in an eleven-acre enclosure at the Horicon Marsh Wildlife Refuge, Wisconsin. The main objective was to ascertain to what extent and in what ways loss of productivity in the Canada Goose population at the various stages of the breeding cycle was related to social behavior. With this objective, a detailed study of the social behavior of marked individuals was made.

The set-up and the general plan of the study were established by Jahn, while most of the observations were made by Collias, who also prepared and organized the report. This study was financed by the Wisconsin Conservation Department with federal aid in Wildlife Restoration funds under Pittman-Robertson Project W-6-R. We wish to express great appreciation to Cyril Kabat, Research Coordinator, and James Hale, Chief Game Biologist, of the Wisconsin Conservation Department, for permission to publish the data. Kabat also provided much help and useful advice at the outset of the project. We are grateful also to the other personnel of the Wisconsin Conservation Department who aided this study. We wish to thank Mrs. Elsie Collias for preparation of the illustrations.

Observations on the behavior of Canada Geese in the Mississippi Valley have been reported by Johnson (1947), Elder and Elder (1949), Hanson and Smith (1950), and by Kossack (1950), while Balham (1954) has made a study of the behavior of Canada Geese at the Delta Waterfowl Research Station in Central Canada. In the Western States, Canada Geese often concentrate on islands to nest; losses from intraspecific strife have been reported (*cf.* Hammond and Mann, 1956). Considerable information on the migratory behavior of Canada Geese, a topic not covered here, is available in Hochbaum's recent book (1955).

METHODS

In the spring of 1952, when this study was effected, the enclosure at Horicon contained 38 adult males and 34 adult females, including three pairs known to have bred the preceding spring. There were also a good many wing-pinioned Mallards present, while various kinds of ducks often visited the enclosure from the adjoining marshlands.

In general, adult male geese were distinguished by a red plastic collar fastened by means of snaps around the neck, and also by an aluminum government band on the right leg. The adult females were distinguished by a white collar, and had an aluminum band on the left leg. The young from each of the preceding two years were similarly and distinctively marked as age classes.

The adult birds were also marked for individual recognition with colored airplane dope painted on the white cheek patch and on the white flanks in various combinations. A given individual was designated by reading first the color of its face, secondly that of its flanks. For example, Male YR, refers to a male with a yellow face and red flanks. Male Y– refers to a male with yellow face, but with flanks unpainted. Young birds as well as adults could also be identified as individuals under favorable conditions by reading the numbers on the leg band with the aid of a 35-power telescope.

In an attempt to increase productivity, artificial nesting sites were provided, made of brush and covered with marsh hay. These sites were located on and about the six-acre pond and labelled as shown on the accompanying map (Fig. 1). The food consisted of a specially prepared diet put up in pellet form, of a calcium source in the form

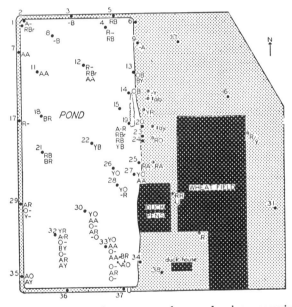

FIGURE 1. Diagram of the eleven-acre enclosure, showing successive territorial occupants of specific nest sites, March-May, 1952. Artificially provided nest sites are numbered and indicated by black dots; a nest built by a female in some other locality is indicated by a dot in a circle. Letter designations refer to males, unless otherwise indicated. The stippled area is land.

of crushed oyster shell, of an abundant supply of greens, as well as various natural forms of aquatic and terrestrial growing vegetation. The pellets and oyster shell were fed to the birds from hoppers. A wheat field was planted in the enclosure at such a time that the young wheat plants became available for grazing by goslings as well as adults.

Observations were commenced on March 14, 1952 and were terminated on May 29, 1952. The actual observations were made from two to four days a week, and ranged from 4 to 13 hours a day, as a rule covering about 8 hours a day. In March there was a total of 70½ hours of observation, in April, 101½, and in May, 104½. The total number of hours of observation forming the basis of this report was 276½.

BREEDING BEHAVIOR

Pair formation. Many of the adult geese were apparently paired at the time when observations began on March 14. However, only three pairs were marked and known from the preceding spring; these were R x W, R/Y x W/Y, and R/G x W/G. Of these, Male R x Female W had been checked also during the fall and early winter and it was noted that they remained together as a consistent pair throughout, together with their young of the 1951 hatch. However, many of the adult geese were seen gradually to form pairs with the advent of the 1952 breeding season.

The sexes have similar plumage in Canada Geese, but the female is smaller and differs characteristically from the male in behavior. She is less aggressive, has a very different voice (see p. 486 *infra*), and often tends to hold her head lower. No doubt these characteristics aid sex recognition.

Successful pair formation in the competition for mates depended both on *specific preferences* and on aggressive *dominance relations* between individuals. One or the other factor might be more important in particular instances. *Preferences* were indicated by persistent tendency of a bird to follow a specific individual. *Dominance* was expressed by defense of the vicinity of the female with special reference to potential or actual sex rivals.

Selection of nest sites. The female usually selects the nest site, leading the male about on exploratory jaunts, getting up on nest islets, and poking about inspecting these heaps of branches, twigs and hay with her beak. But when a desirable nest heap was already occupied by other birds, the male would forge ahead to take the lead in driving the other birds away, and if he was successful the female might then mount the potential nest site and inspect it.

The search for a suitable nest site might take one to many days, depending in part on the availability of good nest sites and in part on the dominance status relative to competitors for specific sites. Male AR and his mate got a late start and were rather low in dominance. They found most of the desirable nest sites already occupied. One morning they were seen to visit nine different nest sites in the space of an hour, being evicted from most of these sites by birds that had already laid claim to the sites in question.

Some birds preferred to build their own nests along the shore,

316

constructing them of dried and dead weed stalks, and largely ignored artificial nests still unoccupied. Two of the artificial nest heaps overturned when the ice melted and the birds showed no interest in them until marsh hay was placed on them.

Nest sites were selected both before and after the ice melted from the pond.

Both of the two pairs whose nesting sites of the preceding year were known nested at about the same location in 1951 and 1952.

Establishment of territories. Once a nesting site was selected both members of the pair generally stayed close by. Their claim was announced to all other geese by loud honking and other threatening actions, particularly by the male, whenever intruders came near. Typically, the male would sally forth at an intruder in the vicinity, with neck outstretched and head held low. If the intruder stood his ground or came closer, a fight would probably ensue, in which the territorial owner was usually, but not always, the winner. Should he lose, the intruding pair, if searching for a nest site, evicted the resident pair, or if not in need of a nest site, but having asserted their domination, merely continued on their way, perhaps pausing a few minutes to inspect the nest of the vanquished pair. As a rule the owner of a territory successfully drove off intruders without the necessity of a fight; often merely a honking defense sufficed. The intruder would move away, sometimes with the neck fluffed out, whereas the more aggressive bird always kept his neck feathers smooth and appressed. On returning to the female, the male would both honk and utter his snoring vocalization, and the female would chime in with her distinctive voice, her short staccato honks or yips alternating with the louder, longer and more resonant honks of the male. The honking duet was also given as intruders approached, but the snoring sound was more likely to be given after the encounter. The retreating birds were far less likely to vocalize than was the winner, and frequently fell silent.

A special display was often engaged in by the male with respect to intruders. With neck stretched up he would abruptly flip his beak upwards, simultaneously rolling the head, showing off to advantage the white cheek patches. This head-flipping, which possibly serves a threat function, seems to indicate indecision, since it was generally seen at the moment when a bird was likely to change from one behavior pattern to another, for example, from standing in one spot to charging an intruder, or to flight from an enemy. Head-flipping was characteristic of the males, but was only occasionally seen in females. This action was strongly associated with display of the white cheeks, which are a brighter, clearer white in the spring than in the fall. Perhaps this peculiar display, which has a warning connotation as well as threat and mild alarm, evolved from shaking mud from the beak preparatory to flight.

Sometimes when the observer or a goose approached a territorial bird, its body plumage was abruptly raised, and if the intruder passed at too great a distance to provoke an active attack, the plumage was again appressed after a vigorous shake, as if the bird had "shaken off" a state of tension.

A human intruder was treated in much the same way as were intruding geese by a territorial male. A female on her nest frequently would not honk, but rather hiss repeatedly at a man coming close to her. The male would not only honk and flip his head, displaying his white cheeks, but he would also pump his head up and down just as the female might do. This pumping display (also done against geese) indicates incipient attack, and consists of a vacillation between lowering the head with the base of the neck drawn back slightly to facilitate striking out and a return to a resting position, perhaps not unmixed with fear of the intruder. On a closer approach of the intruder the head pumping would begin to include another component in which the lowered head was thrust out in the direction of the intruder, and finally, should the man persist in his approach to the nest, some ganders would actively attack. The black and blue bruises inflicted by the strong jaws and blows of the powerful wings demonstrated the potency of the male in defending his home and mate.

The role of dominance in the establishment of nesting territories was most clearly demonstrated by instances of circular dominance relations. Thus, in a contest over Nest Site 33 that went on for several days, Male BR would drive off Male AO and his mate; Male BR would then be driven off by Male AA, and in turn Male AA and his mate would be driven off by Male AO (Fig. 1). This cycle would be repeated indefinitely, until some male dominant to all three, such as Male O–, would come along and take over the nest site.

Repeated evictions and repeated attempts at reestablishment on a given nest site, covering a period of time anywhere from a few minutes to several weeks before such attempts were given up, were the rule for birds of relatively low dominance status. The resulting picture was a complex network of movements and shifting ownerships of the more heavily contested nest sites. Figure 1 shows the number of successive owners of different nest sites laying more than momentary claim to these nest sites.

Size of territories varied greatly with the individual bird. Some of the males defended more than one of the artificial nest sites, especially where the nest sites were close together (Fig. 2). In every case the great majority of the territorial defenses of a male centered about the nest site of the female.

The size and shape of territories changed with time and circumstances. At first Male YO defended not only the future nest site of his mate (Nest Site 26), but occasionally he defended the four neighboring nest islets as well. Later, as these islands came to be occupied by other pairs he restricted his defenses to his own nest islet. In contrast, Male RO, which wedged in between two powerful and

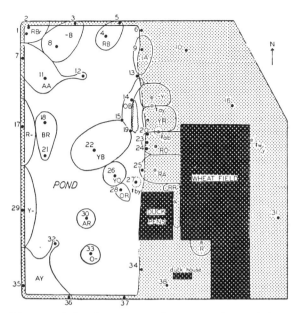

FIGURE 2. Diagram of the eleven-acre enclosure, showing established goose territories on May 1, 1952. Artificial nest sites (black dots) are numbered, ganders are named by letters. Territories of unpaired females are shown by dotted lines about the nest site. The stippled area is land.

established males, for a time did not even "dare" to honk, and his female was often driven from her nest during the egg-laying period. But in a few weeks his territory had enlarged considerably, and he soon honked at and later fought with his neighbors, defeating one of them. In general, after a bird defeated its neighbor in a fight the territorial boundary moved in the direction of the loser's ground.

The sound of honking served to excite the aggression of the territorial males. One peculiar case gave a clear example of this. Whenever any geese would honk just outside the bounds of his territory, a certain male would thereupon often attack and drive from her eggs an unpaired female which had her nest at the edge of his territory. The disturbed honking of his own female frequently excited the aggressiveness of a male, and might lead to fights between otherwise relatively peaceful neighbors.

In the pre-egg stage territorial activity was greatest in the early part of the morning . But this extra activity in the early part of the morning was only slightly, although consistently, greater than at other times of day. As the season progressed, this slight early morning peak advanced to still earlier hours, as did the sunrise.

Defense of territories about the nest sites by both male and female, but particularly by the male, continued until the eggs hatched, and the young left the nest, after which time the parents seemed to lose all interest in territorial defense.

The importance of the male in territorial defense was made evident

319

by cases in which there was no male to defend the nest site. Female W/Y lost her mate by death late in her incubation period, and although she had been sitting very steadily up to the time the male was lost, her eggs failed to hatch. The reason was that with loss of her guardian she became subject to the domination and disturbance of other pairs as well as of unpaired males, who drove her repeatedly from her eggs, resulting in death of the embryos, presumably from chilling.

DOMINANCE ORDER

These birds show a dominance order which centers in good part over competition for food. In competing for food one bird would advance at another, often honking at the same time, and as it came near, the aggressor would lower its head nearly to the ground, and with the long neck outstretched, except for its basal portion curved back ready to strike, the bird would charge with open threatening jaws at the goose it intended to displace or keep away from the food. Should the bird which was attacked retreat it was adjudged to be subordinate. No interaction was tabulated unless one bird was definitely the aggressor, and the other definitely retreated. Rarely, a bird

TABLE 1

DOMINANCE ORDER OF 38 MALE CANADA GEESE AT HORICON MARSH
IN THE BREEDING SEASON OF 1952

Domination-subordination ratios (d:s) are shown for various degrees of breeding success. The d:s ratio for any given male refers to the number of birds dominated (d) and the number of birds to which that male was subordinate (s).

Males which held territory:

Mate hatched out goslings (aver. d:s ratio of males, 15:7)

Male	d:s ratio	Male	d:s ratio
R	19:1	YR	16:7
AY	31:1	–Y	12:9
–B	18:2	RR	8:7
Y–	21:3	RB	10:10
YO	21:7	–A	8:9
RA	12:4	RO	9:11
OB	15:5	OR	7:9
R–	19:7	BR	7:20

Eggs of mate lost (aver. d:s ratio of males, 7:11)

BY	5:2	–R	5:17
R/Y	12:9	Red-breast	2:12
YB	11:15		

Mate did not lay eggs (aver. d:s ratio of males, 8:10)

O–	14:8	AA	6:8
–O	18:14	A–R	3:5
AR	11:12	AB	3:7
AO	8:10	A–	1:19

Males which failed to hold territory and to pair effectively (aver. d:s ratio, 3:13):

OO	6:12	YA	2:11
YY	3:12	BB	2:13
BA	3:13	OA	1:10
B–	4:14	OY	0:9
R/G	4:19		

threatened failed to retreat, and ordinarily a fight for dominance then ensued in which the contestants attempted to seize and hold each other by the base of the neck with the beak, meanwhile repeatedly administering powerful blows at each other with the wings. A fight attracted the attention of and excited other geese, some of which would honk, while those nearby were likely to orient themselves towards and watch the contestants.

The dominance hierarchy that resulted was reinforced by aggressive-submissive interactions at food, and was habitual and consistent as a rule, although some 18 reversals were observed during the breeding season, probably often due to competition for mates. It was not always possible to separate aggressive competition for food from defense of the vicinity of the mate, since early in the breeding season at least, mates ordinarily accompanied each other to the food area.

Both male and female adults as well as younger birds had their place in the dominance order. However, males almost never attacked their mates. Since the dominance of the male over other males seemed crucial for nesting success, emphasis was placed on ascertaining the dominance order of the males as shown in Table 1. The number of paired relationships possible among the 38 males of this table was 703, as calculated by the formula, n(n — 1)/2, and of these relationships there were observed 345, or about half.

Circular dominance relations were not uncommon. Thus, Male R dominated Male AY, which dominated Male R/Y, which in turn dominated Male R.

The female and young birds of a family to a considerable extent shared in the male's dominance, although when they were not in his immediate vicinity their status was likely to be altered, especially when they attempted to attack ganders.

Role of Behavior in Reducing Breeding Success

The factors reducing productivity in the breeding colony at Horicon were almost entirely factors connected with social behavior. Predation and mortality from parasitism were apparently nil, although the pen was surrounded merely by a fence enclosing one corner of the marsh. (However, two adults died from unknown causes.) Flooding was not a factor in loss of any nests, nor was weather the cause, directly or indirectly, of any losses, although the birds were just as exposed to the elements as they would have been had there been no fence about them.

One pair of two-year-old birds successfully hatched out six goslings on top of a muskrat house in the marsh some 150 yards south of the enclosure. This pair is not included in this account which refers entirely to conditions within the breeding pen.

Factors reducing productivity at each stage of the breeding cycle. With respect to success in breeding, the geese may be grouped into five categories: (1) pairs that hatched out goslings, (2) pairs that laid and incubated eggs, but failed to hatch young, (3) pairs that held territory but failed to lay and incubate eggs, (4) pairs that failed to establish territory, and (5) geese that failed to pair normally.

Table 2 summarizes the gains and losses within the breeding pen during the breeding season of 1952. There were 73 adult birds on hand at the start of the breeding season; also included in the tabulation are one pair of two-year-olds that laid and incubated eggs, and a couple of two-year-olds, each of which paired with an adult bird, making a total of 77 breeders to be considered. Within the pen, 16 pairs hatched 71 goslings.

TABLE 2

GAINS AND LOSSES OF CANADA GEESE IN THE BREEDING PEN AT HORICON MARSH, DURING THE BREEDING SEASON OF 1952 (TO MAY 29TH)

	Gains	Losses	Per cent loss
Adults present at start	77		
Adult mortality		3	4
Eggs laid (23 clutches)	133		
Eggs lost:		62	44
Dropped eggs		6	
Clutches lost (seven)		35	
Infertile eggs of successful pairs		10	
Inviable embryos of successful pairs		11	
Goslings hatched (by 16 pairs)	71		
Gosling mortality		5	7

It may be seen from Table 2 that egg loss was the greatest source of loss, considering gross age categories, since only 4% of the adults and only 7% of the goslings were lost (to May 29, 1952), whereas 44% of all eggs laid were lost.

It is useful to consider the relative losses in *theoretical* breeding potential that occurred at different stages of the breeding cycle, since this type of consideration helps us to decide just where and when most of productivity is lost. Table 3 shows the different percentage losses at each stage of the breeding cycle, assuming a clutch size of 5 eggs. This table brings out the importance of factors concerned with failure to lay eggs, at least in nests. Over half the birds assumed to be capable of breeding failed to make nests in which they laid and incubated eggs; one-fifth of the birds failed even to pair up effectively. The nine pairs that failed to lay eggs in nests were involved in unusually frequent territorial clashes, and most of them were unable to maintain stable territories for any length of time. Four of the 5 pairs (and perhaps all 5) that lost their clutches did so because of disturbance to the female from other geese, related to a lack of effective male defense. It would seem that over half the loss in breeding potential could be ascribed to factors having to do with territory, *i. e.*, to lack of effective territorial establishment or defense (Table 3). The possible alternative is that many of the females that were sufficiently motivated to defend territories and to copulate, for some reason were not sufficiently in breeding condition to lay eggs. These two explanations are not completely antithetical.

If we take 5 eggs as a general figure for average clutch size, the 41 males and 36 females present should have raised 180 goslings, instead of only 66 (to May 29), as their theoretical breeding potential. Tak-

TABLE 3

RELATIVE LOSSES IN THEORETICAL BREEDING POTENTIAL AT VARIOUS STAGES IN THE
BREEDING CYCLE, ASSUMING THAT EACH PAIR OF ADULTS COULD
HAVE RAISED FIVE GOSLINGS

	Numbers lost	Per cent of total
Failure to pair effectively		
(11 males and 5 females, equivalent to five pairs)	25	20
Failure to lay and incubate (9 pairs)	45	37
Loss of entire clutch during period of incubation		
(5 pairs)	24	20
Inviable and infertile eggs in nests otherwise successful	21	17
Gosling mortality	5	4
Adult mortality	3	2
Totals	123	100

ing into account a slight adult mortality, it may be calculated $(123/180 \times 100)$ that about 70% of the theoretical increase in population was lost (Table 3).

Although failure to lay eggs, as well as loss of eggs once laid, was the most important source of loss in productivity, the breeding potential was frittered away to a greater or lesser extent at all stages of the reproductive cycle. It is pertinent to consider in more detail the various mechanisms involved at each step in the cycle, insofar as these mechanisms could be observed or deduced.

Geese (including Males R, R–, AY, Y–, YR, and R/Y) with a previous history of rearing families successfully, were among those likely to succeed again. But we did not know the breeding history of many pairs. Part of the reason for the success of experienced birds was their relatively high dominance status (Table 1).

The evidence that high rank of the male in the dominance hierarchy during late winter and early spring increases the chances of an individual male and his mate to breed successfully is shown in Table 1.

Twenty per cent of the loss in breeding potential came from failure of some birds to pair effectively (Table 3). As Table 1 indicates, part of this reason was probably due to low dominance status. Factors of individual preference and fixation were also important, being true of both males and females.

For some weeks, Female –Y trailed after Male –Y, which was already closely attended by Females AY and OA; he preferred (often followed) and paired with Female OA. Both Females AY and OA dominated Female –Y, and occasionally would drive her back away from the vicinity of the male. Female –Y eventually stopped following this or any other male, but Female AY laid, and for 35 days incubated, a clutch of infertile eggs at the edge of the territory of Male –Y x Female OA. But the male never defended Female AY directly from other males; he occasionally drive her off her eggs himself.

The same type of situation but in the opposite sex, was manifested by Male –O, which persistently maintained his interest and fixation with respect to the apparent mate of Male AO. Eventually he defeated Male AO in this competition, but so late in the season that none of these three birds managed to breed.

Unisexual attachments among seven males, as well as in two of the females may also have acted to delay normal pairing with the opposite sex, until advance of the season made successful breeding impossible.

Male RY and Female AB showed very little interest in specific individual geese, for unknown reasons.

Male OO became attached to the keeper, and thereafter made no attempt to pair with any goose.

Only one of the unpaired geese, Female –A, was seen to copulate.

Thirty-seven per cent of the loss in breeding potential was due to failure of nine pairs to lay and incubate eggs (Table 3).

One of these pairs included a non-territorial adult male which was wing-pinioned, but paired with a free-flying two-year-old female. The latter bird often flew off with a two-year-old male, leaving her adult male alone much of the day. The other 8 pairs (including Males O–, AR, AO, –O, AA, AB, A–R, A–, and U), although they defended territory, seemed unable to hold a stable territory for any length of time, and shifted about a good deal from place to place (Fig. 1). In these pairs one female, AR, was first mated to Male AO, and then to Male –O. Male O– was the most dominant male of these pairs that defended territory but did not lay, and was probably capable of holding territory long enough to breed, but his mate, Female O–, refused to accept the nest site (33) that he defended most often. This nest site, although it appeared to be suitable in terms of construction and materials, and seemed to be popular with many pairs (Fig. 1), was located in the main line of traffic of the geese going to and from the feeding area from various parts of the pond.

Part of the reason for failure to lay eggs might have been due to fixation on specific nest sites, involving considerable and often unsuccessful competition, until with advance of the season the physiological state of the birds changed in a direction unfavorable to egg-laying. Furthermore, pairs that were most often displaced from nest sites were also the ones that generally did not lay eggs. These evictions were related to low dominance. The domination-subordination ratio per male was 7:11 for 13 males evicted from at least one nest site at which they had spent most of one day or more trying to establish themselves, whereas the d:s ratio was 15:7 for 16 males which were never so evicted, and which for the most part bred successfully.

Failure of normally paired geese to lay eggs was not due to lack of copulation. There were observed 21 copulations by 11 pairs that failed to lay and incubate eggs, for an average of 1.9 observed copulations per pair, and 10 of these 11 pairs were seen to copulate. In contrast, for 21 pairs that laid eggs which were incubated, there were observed 24 copulations, an average of only 1.1 observed copulations per bird, and only 14 of the 21 pairs were seen to copulate.

Inadequate diet or lack of food does not seem a likely explanation for failure of some birds to lay eggs. At least the food was provided in some abundance, and was adequate for egg-laying by many of the females, as well as for a high egg production by the many Mallard ducks maintained for this purpose within the same large enclosure. All of the Canada Geese dominated the Mallards, and had precedence to food over all ducks.

Perhaps the six dropped eggs found belonged to birds not able to maintain a stable territory, but attempting to lay in some other bird's territory, since all of the six dropped eggs were found within occupied territories in which the resident female laid a full clutch of her own. Furthermore, females were seen on two occasions to be repeatedly attacked by males, just before the female laid an egg in her own nest at the edge of the territory of the attacking male.

Twenty per cent of the loss in breeding potential was due to loss of the entire clutch by five pairs of birds (Table 3).

Four of these five clutches were lost as a result of evictions of the pair from its territory or of the female (of Male R/Y, who died) from her nest by more dominant birds. The fifth clutch, that of Male YB x Female B–, was lost with the death from unknown causes of the female, after three weeks of incubation. Although not observed, possibly dominance by other geese was involved here also, since the male coincident with the death of the female, lost all of his tail feathers. This phenomenon was noted in the breeding season, only when a male had lost a severe fight and was pursued by the victor, which would often seize the tail feathers of the retreating loser, sometimes pulling out some of these feathers. One of the evictions involved a two-year-old pair. A few days after the male had been beaten and the female evicted temporarily from her nest by a neighboring male, the nest was observed to be deranged and the eggs were out of the nest. The two-year-old female rolled one of these eggs toward herself, but since she was standing to one side of the nest, the egg rolled into the water instead of into the nest cavity. Soon afterwards the dominant pair came and displaced them from the nest, and shortly after this the remaining egg was seen sinking in the water.

Seventeen per cent of the loss in breeding potential was due to infertile and inviable eggs in nests from which goslings were hatched. Ten such eggs were infertile, while eleven contained embryos that had died in the egg.

There is a suggestion in the data that relatively infrequent coition contributed to the occurrence of the infertile eggs. Eight females laid infertile eggs (not including unpaired females), and only two of these eight females were seen to copulate, for a total of only three copulations. On the other hand, eleven of the females that hatched out goslings, laid only fertile eggs, and all of these eleven females were seen to copulate, for a total of 17 copulations.

The occurrence of inviable embryos showed no connection with inattentiveness of the female during incubation, as measured by the number of times a female was seen to be absent from her nest and eggs, once she had begun steady incubation, as checked at the beginning of each hour of observation. Nine females that had at least one dead embryo in the clutch, were seen to have only 9 such absences from the nest during the incubation period, whereas 7 females with no dead embryos had 12 absences. There may however be some relationship between the clutch size and inviable eggs, and the data suggest further investigation of this idea to be worthwhile. Thus, 8 of the 9 females with one or more inviable eggs each had 6 or more eggs in her full clutch, the average clutch size for these females being 6.4 eggs. In contrast, 6 of 7 females with no dead embryos each laid 5 or fewer eggs, the average clutch size being only 4.9 eggs.

Only four per cent of the loss in breeding potential (to May 29) was due to gosling mortality, including 5 dead goslings. Three of these were from one nest, of which two were found dead on the nest on the date of hatching; the other one made it to shore, but was very weak and was finally abandoned by its parents, which went away with their remaining three goslings. Then another family came along and one of the adults and one of the goslings of this family bit the helpless and abandoned gosling. The latter was then put in a brooder where it later died. Another gosling was found with its head caught in a wire fence and when extricated proved unable to walk and later died in the brooder. The fifth dead gosling was found dead in the weeds along the shore; the cause of death was unknown.

Only two per cent of the loss in breeding potential was in terms of adult mortality, although 2 of the 3 deaths of adults resulted indirectly in loss of an entire clutch. Both of these two deaths, one of a male and one of a female, were due to unknown causes. The remaining death was of an adult male gander, killed by a rival male competing for the same female.

Factors having a regulatory effect on population density. Some factors take an increasing percentage of a population as density increases (Nicholson, 1935), while certain other factors take a decreasing percentage as density increases. This latter type was probably not operating in the present case, since the geese were already too crowded. It refers to such things as Darling's (1952) idea of a threshold of numbers that must be reached to provide sufficient social stimulation to facilitate breeding in some species of birds. It was indeed observed that sexual display and coition, like most of the activities of the geese, were contagious, tending to spread from one pair to another, but, as previously pointed out, those pairs that failed to lay eggs were seen to copulate more often than those that did lay eggs. This observation of course does not exclude the possible importance of social stimulation to facilitate breeding at lower population densities than that with which we were concerned.

A limited number of nest sites for which the birds compete would be expected to exert density-dependent effect with increase in numbers of birds. Amount of shoreline may be an important factor in providing suitable nest sites for effective breeding. A number of pairs chose to build nests on the shore, before some of the artificial islet nests were occupied. This included most of the more dominant pairs. Ten of 16 nests on or near the shore produced goslings, but only 5 of 12 islet nests produced goslings. It seems likely that in the event of disturbance eggs on islet nests are more likely to be lost by rolling out of the nest into the water. Suitability of the available nest materials is of course important, and islet nests with branches and twigs, but temporarily without marsh hay, generally found little favor.

Increase in the number of nest sites has a limited influence, since, beyond a certain degree of crowding, the territorial space requirements of the birds begin to act as a limiting factor. Aggressive behavior of this type was probably the most important cause of population limitation in the breeding colony under the crowded conditions that existed. Many of the territorial males defended more than one of the artificial nest sites (Fig. 2), effectively preventing other geese from becoming established thereon.

Dominance operated as a density-dependent factor in conjunction with fixation on or preference for a given nest site. The more crowded the population, the more chances there are for two pairs to compete for the same nest site. As Figure 1 shows, some of the nest sites changed occupants and owners repeatedly during the breeding season.

All of these factors operate jointly with seasonal factors that regulate the time of the breeding season, probably including such things as gradual change in the relative lengths of day and night, as well as temperature and other factors. Subordination to dominating geese, inability to establish a foothold against the resistance of territorial incumbents, unsuccessful fixations on certain nest sites or on certain individuals as potential mates, all serve to delay, and by delay may finally prevent entirely, effective breeding by many individuals.

SUMMARY

The breeding behavior, vocalizations and dominance order of Canada Geese (*Branta canadensis*) confined under semi-natural conditions at Horicon Marsh, Wisconsin, are described in some detail, with special reference to social interactions between individually marked birds.

Pair formation depends both on specific preferences and on dominance relations between individuals. The nest site is selected by the female of a pair; she is escorted in the search by the more aggressive male. Repeated attempts at establishment on suitable nest sites and repeated eviction by more dominant birds is the rule for birds of relatively low dominance status.

When regular incubation begins, copulation ceases. After hatching, the goslings usually spend a day in the nest before leaving. During their first week goslings are apt to become lost, and are readily adopted into some other family. However, the early development of aggressiveness against strangers by the goslings, as well as by their parents, tends to preserve the integrity of each family.

Loss in productivity of the breeding colony was very largely due to the territorial behavior of the birds themselves resisting the crowded conditions. In the breeding season of 1952 at the Horicon Marsh colony, about 70 per cent of the theoretical or potential increase was lost. In turn, this loss was traced mainly to (1) failure of birds to pair effectively, (2) failure to lay and incubate eggs, and (3) to loss of the clutch once laid, all generally as a result of domination by other birds.

LITERATURE CITED

BALHAM, R. W. 1954. The behavior of the Canada Goose (*Branta canadensis*) in Manitoba. Unpublished thesis, University of Missouri.

COLLIAS, N. E. 1950. Hormones and behavior, with special reference to birds and to the mechanisms of hormone action. *In* Steroid Hormones. Edited by E. Gordon. University of Wisconsin Press, Madison, pp. 277–329.

COLLIAS, N. E. 1952. The development of social behavior in birds. Auk, **69**: 127–159.

COLLIAS, N. E., and E. C. COLLIAS. 1956. Some mechanisms of family integration in ducks. Auk, **73**: 378–400.

DARLING, F. F. 1952. Social behavior and survival. Auk, **69**: 183–191.

ELDER, W. H., and N. L. ELDER. 1949. Role of the family in the formation of goose flocks. Wilson Bull., **61**: 133–140.

HAMMOND, M. C., and G. E. MANN. 1956. Waterfowl nesting islands. Jour. Wildl. Manag., **20**: 345–352.

HANSON, H. C., and R. H. SMITH. 1950. Canada Geese of the Mississippi Flyway, with special reference to an Illinois flock. Bull. Ill. Nat. Hist. Survey, **25**: 59–210.

HOCHBAUM, H. A. 1955. Travels and traditions of waterfowl. Univ. Minnesota Press, Minneapolis. 301 pp.

JOHNSON, C. S. 1947. Canada Goose management, Seney National Wildlife Refuge. Journ. Wildl. Manag., **1**: 21–24.

KOSSACK, C. W. 1950. Breeding habits of Canada Geese under refuge conditions. Amer. Midl. Nat., **43**: 627–649.

NICHOLSON, A. J. 1933. The balance of animal populations. Journ. Animal Ecol., **2**: 132–178.

TINBERGEN, N. 1940. Die Übersprungbewegung. Zeitsch. f. Tierpsych., **4**: 1–40.

THE RELATIONSHIP BETWEEN ADRENAL WEIGHT AND POPULATION STATUS OF URBAN NORWAY RATS

JOHN J. CHRISTIAN AND DAVID E. DAVIS

It has been proposed that changes in the size of animal populations exert density-dependent effects on the physiology of individuals in these populations (Christian, 1950). Theoretically, the magnitude of the physiological alterations would increase with increases in population size until there is a cessation of population growth followed by a decline or, in extreme cases, a population crash. Emphasis was placed on the adaptive reactions of the pituitary-adreno-cortical and reproductive systems to density-dependent stimuli which were presumably sociopsychological in nature. Therefore these stimuli would be effective throughout the history of a population, changing only in magnitude with changes in population size. Environmental hardships, such as food shortages and disease, of necessity would be imposed on and additive to this basic response to density.

A direct relationship between adrenal weight and population density was demonstrated in the laboratory with albino and wild house mice in populations of fixed size (Christian, 1955a, b). A similar relationship was demonstrated in freely growing populations of wild house mice maintained in the laboratory (Christian, 1956). Increases in adrenal weight resulted primarily from cortical hypertrophy. Subsequently it was shown that the adrenal weights of wild Norway rats decreased following an artificial reduction of population (Christian and Davis, 1955). Finally, the subordinate rats of a group, as determined by losing fights, exhibit increased adrenocortical activity with eventual cortical hypertrophy (Barnett, 1955). The latter work suggests a sociopsychological mechanism by which population density might be related to adrenal activity in rats.

None of these experiments has demonstrated a corresponding relationship between population density and adrenal weight in natural populations. The present experiments were designed to examine natural populations for such a relationship.

The opinions or assertions contained herein are the private ones of the writers and are not to be construed as official or reflecting the views of the Navy Department or the naval service at large.

METHODS AND PROCEDURE

The rats (*Rattus norvegicus*) in 21 blocks of Baltimore City were used. Each city block is effectively an island and its rats form a discrete population unit, since immigration and emigration of rats is negligible or absent (Davis, 1953). The rats obtain their food from the abundant and relatively constant supply of garbage available in the back yards. Harborage is found in and around houses, fences, trash piles, and old buildings, and its availability remains fairly constant unless a housing rehabilitation program is in progress. These city blocks provide numerous discrete populations of rats ideal for the study of population phenomena under natural conditions. The quantitation of environmental factors is still a major problem, however, which has been discussed in detail by Davis (1953) along with the effects of environmental variation on rat populations. Food and harborage were believed to be adequate in all of the blocks used in the present experiment.

Each block population selected for study had a long history of repeated censuses by the method of Emlen, Stokes, and Davis (1949). This method cannot reliably detect population changes of less than 10 per cent. This degree of insensitivity is unimportant in the present experiment, since relatively large changes in population usually were used, and for the most part these were produced artificially or stimulated by trapping. The histories of the rat populations in these blocks were used to estimate maximum values for the populations as well as to assign a stage of growth for each population, whenever a

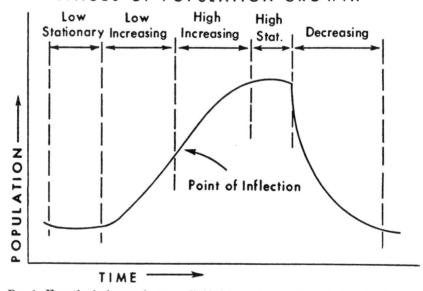

FIG. 1. Hypothetical growth curve divided into stages of population development as described in the text. Each population of rats was placed in one of the five population stages at the time of collecting each sample.

sample was taken, by estimating in which portion of a hypothetical growth curve the population lay immediately prior to trapping. The growth curve used (Fig. 1) was composed of a sigmoid positive increasing portion succeeded by a high stationary phase of indefinite length and finally a decreasing phase, and broadly conformed to the general growth form of populations (Allee, Emerson, Park, Park, and Schmidt, 1949). Experience has shown that such a general curve is sufficiently close to the observed facts so that its various stages may be applied to rat populations, even though it is not precisely defined at present. The curve was divided somewhat arbitrarily into the following stages: low stationary, low increasing, high increasing, high stationary, and decreasing as shown in Figure 1. One of us (D. E. D.) assigned every population to one of these stages each time it was sampled. The same author also made all of the censuses for this study.

Bimonthly censuses were made of each population for at least a year prior to the start of the present program in March, 1952. The following procedure was followed between March, 1952, and February, 1953. The population was estimated and a week later approximately 50 per cent of the rats were trapped, and another census was made about two weeks later. The rat populations were initially selected so that they were high increasing, high stationary, or decreasing, and were large enough for adequate sampling. Six weeks later another census was made and another sample trapped, providing samples in the low stationary and low increasing categories. Another sample was trapped at varying intervals of time later, depending on the history of the particular population. The dates of trapping, population stages, and other pertinent data are given in Table 1. The assigned population stages can be considered only reasonably close approximations because of the limitations of quantitating the various factors of the environment and of the population itself for natural populations.

Subsequent to February, 1953, samples were taken and stages assigned without necessarily repeating the procedure following the initial trapping for the earlier populations. Block populations were programmed for further study which in some instances had to be abandoned because of the inability to obtain samples of adequate size. These blocks are self-evident in Table 1.

The weight in decigrams, length from the tip of the nose to the base of the tail in centimeters, and reproductive status were determined for each rat in the laboratory. The carcass was placed in 10 per cent neutral formalin. At a later date the weights of the paired adrenal glands, paired thyroid glands, pituitary gland, and thymus were obtained on torsion balances to the nearest 0.1 milligram for all but the pituitary, which was weighed to the nearest 0.01 milligram. Representative sections of these glands and of the various visceral organs of rats from the first group of populations studied were taken for microscopic study. They were prepared by routine paraffin imbedding and stained with hematoxylin and eosin. Four rats with obvious pathological conditions that might affect the adrenal weight were discarded from further consideration. Three rats had adrenal medullary tumors and one had a renal abscess.

TABLE 1.—*Dates of collection, preceding estimates of population size, and the sizes of the sample trapped of male and female Norway rats from Baltimore city blocks together with the mean adrenal values (see text) for each sex, grouped according to population stage*

Block no.	Date trapped	Pre-trap popn. est.	No. of females, >100 gm. in sample	Adrenal wt. as mean % of ref. values	No. of males, >100 gm. in sample	Adrenal wt. as mean % of ref. values
\multicolumn{7}{c}{Low Stationary Populations}						
070421	May 52	45	7	95.81	3	130.07
070513	Oct. 52	48	7	103.29	8	97.45
140158	May 52	10	0	—	2	105.85
140220	May 52	48	12	89.92	7	118.57
140222	May 52	45	14	100.01	9	105.05
140226	June 52	47	10	89.25	5	124.84
140344	June 52	20	2	91.55	6	114.88
\multicolumn{7}{c}{Low Increasing Populations}						
070421	Dec. 52	85	4	96.90	8	90.69
070426	Nov. 52	120	15	95.07	23	79.69
080750	May 52	15	4	92.48	2	84.15
140111	Nov. 52	43	12	79.67	7	84.93
140118	May 52	47	3	69.03	2	80.00
140132	Feb. 53	75	4	76.20	7	92.09
140138	July 52	59	15	98.63	14	102.31
140201	May 52	63	10	110.52	14	101.35
140222	Dec. 52	75	19	95.61	13	93.58
140222	Feb. 53	76	8	96.51	9	102.11
140226	Oct. 52	66	5	100.72	4	92.68
140332	Feb. 53	44	3	101.37	2	92.95
\multicolumn{7}{c}{High Increasing Populations}						
070410	May 52	46	5	102.64	0	—
070410	Dec. 52	88	9	105.82	11	93.51
070421	Mar. 52	90	13	103.64	17	101.69
070506	Oct. 52	43	5	81.80	3	97.63
140111	Dec. 53	150	6	92.23	0	—
140118	Mar. 52	77	9	96.32	7	99.13
140118	Mar. 53	100	22	101.52	19	102.37
140158	Nov. 52	34	11	107.96	2	79.85
140201	Jan. 53	88	13	122.94	20	99.09
140201	Dec. 53	135	0	—	6	104.42
140220	Jan. 53	90	15	100.32	16	110.89
140222	Dec. 52	90	0	—	5	93.82
140344	Jan. 53	35	5	91.88	0	—
140134	Dec. 53	140	6	94.78	0	—
\multicolumn{7}{c}{High Stationary Populations}						
070411	Mar. 52	35	8	93.79	2	119.65
070505	Mar. 52	49	6	110.15	7	88.70
070513	Feb. 53	63	16	124.89	8	79.21
110403	Dec. 53	80	0	—	6	137.40
140132	Oct. 52	45	10	79.36	3	114.63
140138	Nov. 51	75	17	86.39	11	111.74
140220	Mar. 52	81	15	107.06	12	118.66
140222	Apr. 52	75	13	110.01	13	98.28
140226	Apr. 52	67	4	107.50	11	115.25
\multicolumn{7}{c}{Decreasing Populations}						
070410	Mar. 52	153	25	117.65	38	102.98
080750	Mar. 52	30	8	102.19	4	94.88
140158	Mar. 52	35	17	112.54	3	112.33
140201	Mar. 52	92	20	119.28	14	102.18
140322	Apr. 52	81	18	109.01	12	114.68
140322	June 52	58	12	97.17	5	108.16
140344	Apr. 52	58	13	114.95	14	130.69

Microscopic study was abandoned after February, 1953. Leptospirosis, Salmonellosis, and infestations of *Capillaria* are exceedingly common in the rats of Baltimore City. Studies by Davis (1951) indicate that the prevalence of Salmonellosis and Leptospirosis is the same for increasing, stationary, and decreasing populations; so that these diseases would not affect the present study. The same holds true for Capillariasis in rats weighing more than 199 grams. The vast majority of rats in this study were above this weight, and none was used that weighed less than 100 grams. The collection of thyroid, thymus, and pituitary weights was abandoned at the same time as the microscopic studies.

The rats varied from 100 to more than 600 grams; hence it was necessary to find a relationship between adrenal weight and body size which would permit the use of rats of every size in any sample, as the number of rats in most samples would not permit further subdivision into weight classes. Several transformations of the data were tried and the best straight line relationship was found to be the logarithm of the adrenal weight on the body length exclusive of the tail. A regression of the logarithm of the adrenal weight on length was determined for each sex, using over 1000 urban and rural rats from a variety of population densities, to obtain a standard line for reference. With few exceptions the rats in the present study comprised the urban rats used in determining these regressions. The equations for the regressions and their graphical representations are given elsewhere (Christian and Davis, 1955). There was no detectable difference between the urban and rural rats in the relationship of the logarithm of adrenal weight to length for either sex. A reference adrenal weight was determined for each body length for each sex from the regressions, and the adrenal weight of each rat in the study was converted to a percentage of the reference value for the appropriate length and sex. A mean value was determined from the individual percentages for each sex in every sample trapped (Table 1).

The unit of measurement used throughout this study is the mean value of the particular organ for the rats trapped in each block. Analyses of variance (Snedecor, 1946) were used throughout this study for evaluating the data unless otherwise specially noted.

RESULTS

Adrenal glands.—The adrenal values, given as the means of the individual percentages of reference weights for each sex and sample, are grouped according to the stage of population growth (Table 1) together with the sample sizes for each sex and the estimated number of rats in the population immediately prior to trapping. The mean adrenal values for each sample are shown plotted against the appropriate assigned stage of population growth (Fig. 2). The mean value for each sex and stage and its standard error are also shown.

There was a significantly greater variation in the mean adrenal values between stages than within stages of population growth for each sex (Females: $P < 0.02$; males: $P < 0.001$), indicating that changes in adrenal weight (relative to body length) are associated with the stages of population development.

333

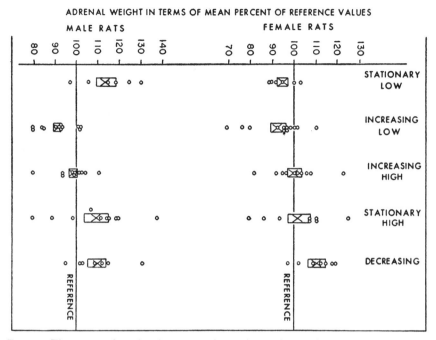

FIG. 2.—The mean adrenal value for each sex for each sample (shown as a circle) of Norway rats plotted on the population stage. The mean adrenal value for each population stage is also shown (as an X) with its standard error.

It is apparent that the adrenal glands of male and female rats responded alike to all stages of population except the low stationary (Table 2, Fig. 2). There was a progressive increase in the mean adrenal value from both sexes starting with the low increasing populations, progressing through the high increasing and high stationary stages, and ending with an overall 18 per cent increase in adrenal value in the decreasing populations. The mean change in adrenal weight value was approximately 6 per cent per stage of population (Fig. 2).

The adrenal glands differed markedly with respect to sex in their response to low stationary population status. The adrenal values of the female rats from these populations were essentially the same as those from low increasing populations and were therefore close to the lowest weights observed. On the other hand, the highest mean adrenal weight value of the male rats was for the low stationary stage, exceeding the mean adrenal value for the decreasing stage, although not significantly. It is quite apparent that there is a fundamental difference with respect to sex in the stimuli to the adrenal cortices in low stationary populations of urban rats.

The population stages have been arranged, in Table 3, in such order that, according to the hypothesis proposed in this paper, the mean adrenal weights would be expected to increase from left to right. It will be observed that this is the case with only one exception. Moreover, since the various rows of the table confine the results to very small time intervals, the effect noted within

J. J. Christian & D. E. Davis

Table 2.—*Mean relative weights of the adrenal, thymus, thyroid and pituitary glands for each stage of population for Norway rats from Baltimore City blocks*

Stage of population	Sex	Number of samples	Paired adrenal wt. as mean % of ref. values ± std. error	Mean thymus wt., mg/100 gm. ± std. error	Mean pituitary wt., mg/100 gm. ± std. error	Mean paired thyroid wt., mg/100 gm. ± std. error
Low stationary	F	6	94.97 ± 2.35	117.0 ± 40.3	4.48 ± 0.25	12.30 ± 0.72
	M	7	113.82 ± 4.41	71.7 ± 12.4	4.29 ± 0.88	11.44 ± 1.39
Low increasing	F	12	92.73 ± 3.43	85.0 ± 9.2	3.91 ± 0.30	12.40 ± 0.48
	M	12	91.38 ± 2.31	59.2 ± 8.8	2.79 ± 0.02	11.79 ± 0.72
High increasing	F	12	100.15 ± 2.94	80.6 ± 12.1	4.11 ± 0.62	11.68 ± 0.65
	M	10	98.24 ± 2.62	76.8 ± 14.6	2.77 ± 0.07	12.06 ± 0.44
High stationary	F	8	102.39 ± 5.23	73.1 ± 11.5	4.48 ± 0.49	12.79 ± 0.80
	M	9	109.28 ± 5.40	70.9 ± 13.4	3.91 ± 0.56	11.94 ± 0.76
Decreasing	F	7	110.40 ± 3.90	58.0 ± 16.7	4.38 ± 0.54	12.47 ± 0.77
	M	7	109.41 ± 4.35	53.7 ± 9.9	3.50 ± 0.49	12.40 ± 1.12

Table 3.—*The mean adrenal value of both sexes for each population stage and month of capture. Months represented by only one population stage and all low stationary populations have been excluded*

	Low increasing	High increasing	High stationary	Decreasing
October	92.8	89.7	97.0	—
November	84.8	93.9	99.6	—
December	94.2	97.4	137.4*	—
February	91.7	—	102.1	—
March	—	100.8	106.3	108.0
April	—	—	107.8	117.3

* Represents a single value.

any single row is independent of seasonal change. Thus if there is any seasonal effect it does not affect the trends noted within the rows of this table. Low stationary populations were omitted because of the marked difference between male and female adrenal weights. Months represented by a single population stage were likewise omitted.

Thymus gland.—There was a suggestive decrease in the weights of the thymus glands of female rats from low stationary through decreasing population stages (Table 2, Fig. 3). The variation in thymus weight with population stage was not significant, nor was the difference between the extremes of the means. There was no suggestion of a pattern of weight change with population stage in the thymus glands of male rats. The thymus weights of the two sexes did not differ significantly.

Pituitary gland.—The mean pituitary weight relative to body weight (milligrams/100 grams) with its standard error is given for each population stage

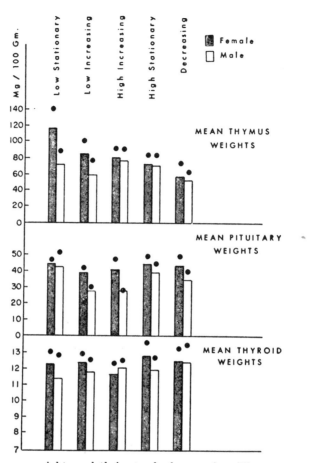

Fig. 3.—The mean weights and their standard errors in milligrams per 100 grams of body weight of the thymus, thyroid, and pituitary glands of Norway rats plotted for each population stage for each sex.

for each sex (Table 2). The relative pituitary weights were consistently greater in the female than in the male rats (P < 0.01) (Table 2, Fig. 3). The relative pituitary weights of the female rats showed no significant variation with population stage. The variation with population stage in the relative weights of the male pituitary glands appeared to parallel roughly the changes in adrenal weight (Fig. 3), but these changes were without significance. However, regressions of male mean adrenal values on relative pituitary weight and vice versa had slopes significantly different than zero (P < 0.001) suggesting positive relationship between the weights of the adrenal and pituitary glands of the male rats.

Thyroid gland.—There was no detectable relationship between thyroid gland weight and population stage (Table 2). The weights of the thyroid glands from male and female rats were not significantly different.

DISCUSSION

Intraspecific competition has been assigned a major role in regulating and limiting population growth (Allee, Emerson, Park, Park, and Schmidt, 1949). It has been shown that such competition between animals of the same species becomes more pronounced as populations increase and is manifested by decreased reproduction, growth, and survival (Davis, 1949; Calhoun, 1950). It is generally assumed that food, harborage, or other environmental necessities impose the limits on population growth and that intraspecific competition is to a large extent the medium through which these factors operate. It was suggested, however, that population growth might be limited purely by social competition in spite of an abundance of all of the usual environmental necessities (Christian, 1950). Presumably such sociopsychological pressures, as indeed they would have to be, would act as density-dependent stimuli to the pituitary-adrenocortical axis producing a progressive enlargement of the adrenal cortex and reduction in reproduction as the population increased. A point finally would be reached when a failure of reproduction would result in a failure of population growth. The animals in such a population presumably would be extremely susceptible to any additional insult. A decline in population might be expected to result from an additional burden which was beyond the ability of the animal to cope with it.

In order to verify such an hypothesis it was necessary to show that there is a density-dependent adrenocortical response independent of supplies of food, water, and harborage. Experiments in the laboratory with fixed and freely growing populations of white and wild house mice established the existence of such a mechanism, using the weights of the adrenal glands and reproductive organs as indicators (Christian, 1955a, b, 1956). The amount of adrenocortical tissue was shown to be positively related to the level of population. The present experiments are an extension of experiments with laboratory populations designed to establish whether adrenal weight (as a measure of cortical mass) was related to population status under natural conditions.

There was a positive relationship between the weights of the adrenal glands adjusted for body length and stages of population growth for urban Norway rats. There was a progressive increase in adrenal weight in both sexes as population status progressed from low increasing, through high increasing and high stationary, to decreasing. The adrenal glands in decreasing populations were 18 per cent heavier than in low increasing populations. These changes in adrenal weight occurred over and above any possible seasonal variation, although a seasonal effect could not be ruled definitely in or out. So far these data fit our hypothesis and coincide with the results of experiments in the laboratory, as increases in adrenal weight occurred with stages of population growth in spite of an excess of the usual environmental necessities. The marked difference between the sexes in their adrenocortical responses to low stationary populations is difficult to interpret. One would expect a decrease in adrenal weight following a decrease in population and the release of density-dependent social pres-

337

sures resulting in very low adrenal weights in low stationary populations. Apparently this is true for female rats, but not for males. The reason for male rats attaining their greatest adrenal weight in low stationary populations is not known. It may be that there is considerable strife among the males in these populations, perhaps resulting from reestablishing their social orders following a decrease in population. If so, it is hard to explain why the adrenal weights of male rats decreased following an artificial 50 per cent reduction in population size (Christian and Davis, 1955). However, the changes in adrenal weight in these experiments were on the whole predictable from the assumption that density-dependent sociopsychological factors operate as stimuli to the pituitary-adrenocortical system. Evidence that such social factors exist in rats has been presented by Barnett (1955) and Calhoun (1950). Frank (1953), in discussing his studies on experimental crashes in *Microtus* populations, has suggested that such a mechanism is operative, but that a final additional insult is necessary to initiate a precipitous crash with the syndrome of hypoglycemic shock when a population attains a peak level.

The alterations in adrenal weight in the present experiments were attributed to changes in adrenocortical mass. The adrenal medulla of rats does not contribute to changes in adrenal weight (Rogers and Richter, 1948), consequently changes in weight must result entirely from changes in cortical mass. Furthermore, adrenal weight was shown to be directly related to cortical mass and in turn to population size in mice (Christian, 1955b, 1956).

The apparent decrease in the weights of the thymus glands of female rats with increasing population density (and adrenal weight), although not significant, is suggestive of the thymico-lymphatic involution usually associated with increased adrenocortical function (Selye, 1950). A direct relationship between the weights of the pituitary and adrenal glands was seen in the male, but not in the female rats. This difference cannot at present be explained.

Throughout these experiments there was a considerable degree of variability which may have obscured the significance of changes in the weights of some of the organs. Unfortunately such variability is unavoidable with the presently available unprecise techniques for working with wild populations and their environment. The greatest error occurs in the stationary populations where estimation of the population status is least critical. Rapidly increasing or decreasing populations are usually clearly defined, but slowly changing populations may be erroneously classified as stationary, as their changes may be too small to be detected by the methods used. However, such errors in classification would do no more than place the population in one category higher or lower than its correct one. It is assumed that any such errors which may have been made are randomly distributed and have little effect on the final results.

The variability in adrenal weight throughout the experiment (Table 1) prompted further thought on the population mechanics of these rats. The population of rats in each block is composed of discrete colonies that tend to merge as the population increases, whereas they remain quite discrete at low levels of population. It may be that each colony acts as a discrete population in its effect on the adrenal cortex; for example, one colony may be a dense population while another in the same block may be just the opposite. Grouping such diverse colonies into a single value for each block would tend to increase the variability in the results. This problem needs to be examined further, as a preliminary analysis suggests that each colony indeed acts as a discrete population unit. Any colony effect in the present experiments has been overridden by the use of a large number of populations and population samples.

SUMMARY AND CONCLUSIONS

There was a significant relationship between the weights of the adrenal glands relative to body length and population status in 49 samples of Norway rats from 21 blocks in Baltimore City. The adrenal glands of both sexes increased regularly in weight as the population status progressed along a hypothetical growth curve in successive stages from low increasing, through high increasing and high stationary, to decreasing stages. The adrenal glands in decreasing populations were approximately 18 per cent heavier than in populations that were in the low increasing stage. Male and female rats reacted differently to populations in the low stationary category. The adrenals of male rats were heaviest in these populations, while those of the female rats were essentially the same weight as in low increasing populations. The changes in adrenal weight with population status were on the whole consistent with the concept that there is a density-dependent sociopsychological stimulus to the pituitary-adrenocortical system that may be a major factor in the regulation of population growth. The changes in adrenal weight could not be attributed to seasonal variation.

There was a significant positive relationship in male rats between the relative weights of the pituitary and adrenal glands which was not observed in the female rats. A decline in the weight of the thymus gland of female rats with increasing population density and adrenal weight was suggestive but not significant. No relationship was found between population status and the pituitary glands of male rats or the thyroid glands from either sex.

It is concluded that there is a density-dependent stimulus to the pituitary-adrenocortical system of wild Norway rats that operates independently of season or supplies of the usual environmental necessities.

LITERATURE CITED

Allee, W. C., A. E. Emerson, O. Park, T. Park., and K. P. Schmidt. 1949. Principles of animal ecology. W. B. Saunders Co., Philadelphia.

Barnett, S. A. 1955. Competition among wild rats. Nature, 175: 126.

Calhoun, J. B. 1950. The study of wild animals under controlled conditions. Ann. N. Y. Acad. Sci., 51, Art. 7: 1113–1122.

Christian, J. J. 1950. The adreno-pituitary system and population cycles in mammals. Jour. Mamm., 31: 247–259.

———. 1955a. Effect of population size on the weights of the reproductive organs of white mice. Amer. Jour. Physiol., 181: 477–480.

———. 1955b. Effect of population size on the adrenal glands and reproductive organs of male mice in populations of fixed size. Amer. Jour. Physiol., 182: 292–300.

————. 1956. Adrenal and reproductive responses to population size in mice from freely growing populations. Ecology, 37: 258–273.

CHRISTIAN, J. J. AND D. E. DAVIS. 1955. The reduction of adrenal weight in rodents by reducing population size. Trans. 20th North Amer. Wildlife Conf.: 177–189.

DAVIS, D. E. 1949. The role of intraspecific competition in game management. Trans. 14th North Amer. Wildlife Conf.: 225–231.

————. 1951. The relation between the level of population and the prevalence of Leptospira, Salmonella, and Capillaria in Norway rats. Ecology, 32: 465–468.

————. 1953. The characteristics of rat populations. Quart. Rev. Biol. 28: 373–401.

EMLEN, J. T., A. W. STOKES, AND D. E. DAVIS. 1949. Methods for estimating populations of brown rats in urban habitats. Ecology, 30: 430–442.

FRANK, F. 1953. Untersuchungen über den Zusammenbruch von Feldmausplagen (*Microtus arvalis* Pallas). Zool. Jahrb. (Systematik), 82: 95–136.

ROGERS, P. V. AND C. P. RICHTER. 1948. Anatomical comparison between the adrenal glands of wild Norway, wild alexandrine, and domestic Norway rats. Endocrinology, 42: 46–55.

SELYE, H. 1950. Stress. Acta, Inc., Montreal.

SNEDECOR, G. W. 1946. Statistical methods. Iowa State College Press, Ames.

ADVERSE EFFECTS OF CROWDING ON LACTATION AND REPRODUCTION OF MICE AND TWO GENERATIONS OF THEIR PROGENY[1]

JOHN J. CHRISTIAN AND COBERT D. LEMUNYAN

ABSTRACT

Each of 7 populations of 20 male and 20 female mature mice (isolated since weaning) was placed in a 13 in.×18 in. cage for 6 weeks which constituted experimental crowding. No young were born during this period. The mice were established as pairs after crowding, one pair per cage. High mortality of males during crowding restricted the number of pairs available to 88, of which 68 had litters and 56 pairs weaned litters after segregation into pairs. Weights of progeny were obtained at birth and each of the 56 litters was matched and half litters switched with one of equal size and age born to a female which had remained isolated. Weights of the young were obtained weekly for three weeks. The mean weights at birth of progeny of previously crowded and of isolated mice did not differ. Young nursed by crowded females were 15% lighter at weaning than those nursed by isolated mice (P <0.001). The weights of progeny did not differ significantly with respect to which mother bore them or to whether they were nursed by foster or by their own mothers. The mean weight of progeny nursed by crowded or by isolated mothers decreased with increasing litter size. Progeny from litters of 6 or more nursed by crowded mothers weighed significantly less (17%) than those nursed by isolated females, but the weights did not differ significantly for litters of 5 or less.

Young nurtured by crowded mice were paired and their litters similarly matched and half litters exchanged with ones of similar age and size born to isolated mothers. Progeny nurtured by females in turn nurtured by crowded mothers weighed 8% less than their controls (P <0.06). They averaged 18% lighter than their controls for litters of 8, 9 and 10 (P <0.005) but were not significantly lighter in smaller litters.

It was concluded that suppressed growth of progeny nurtured by crowded mothers, persisting for at least 2 generations, was due to quantitatively and/or qualitatively deficient lactation resulting from crowding. Such attenuation of the effects of crowding may explain the long-continued decline in natural populations following peak levels and a precipitous crash in numbers.

An eighth population of 10 male and 10 female mice was sacrificed after 6 weeks of crowding and compared with 10 littermate segregated pairs for reproductive function. Uterine implantation scars were present in all females of both groups, but only 3 of the crowded females bore litters or ever appeared grossly pregnant, whereas all of the segregated females bore litters. The number of implantations per mouse and number of young per litter were significantly less in the crowded females. It was concluded that crowding resulted in intra-uterine mortality and probably diminished fertility, explaining why none of the mice in the preceding 7 populations ever appeared pregnant during crowding and why almost half never bore litters, even after segregation.

THE importance of reproduction to the growth and survival of a population is in its ability to produce reproductively competent individuals (1). A decline or failure in the productivity[1] of a population therefore may result from (a) decreased fertility,[1] (b) failure of the zygotes to implant properly, (c) increased postimplantational intra-uterine mortality, (d) post-parturient failure to survive, or (e) failure of the young to mature properly. Deficient lactation could produce mortality of the nursing young directly by starvation or indirectly by inanition with a resultant decreased resistance to disease or environmental exigencies. The developmental stage at which reproductive failure occurs is unimportant in terms of the immediate population, but is important if the adverse effects are such that the progeny are permitted to survive with diminished reproductive competency.

Decreased productivity in mammalian populations associated with increased population density has been demonstrated with house mice and voles in the laboratory with voles and Norway rats under natural conditions (2–13). Data collected from natural populations of other species suggest a similar relationship (14, 15, 16). Investigators agree that decreased productivity is associated with a cessation of population growth, but there is no general agreement on the causes for the diminished productivity. Several mechanisms have been implicated and any or all of them could participate in reducing productivity coincident with increasing population density. A decline in the activity of the reproductive organs occurs in response to increased population density (7, 10, 11, 12). House mice from populations of high density exhibit increased prenatal mortality (12). Increased mortality of young prior to and immediately following weaning has been associated with increased density in several studies (4, 5, 6, 8, 9, 12, 17). Mortality during nursing may be due to altered maternal behavior (6, 9) or to deficient lactation (12, 18). Young house mice and red-backed voles from populations of high density either fail to mature or their maturation is significantly delayed (12, 13). Thus increased mortality of the young associated with increased population density occurs at all stages of fetal and postnatal development. It is possible that all of these forms of mortality are attributable to a common mechanism: The physiological

---

[1] Productivity is defined for the present purposes as the production of reproductively competent recruits for a population. Fertility is used in a restrictive sense meaning the ability to produce viable ova and sperm capable of producing viable zygotes. Fecundity is defined as the ability to give birth to living progeny. Productivity obviously includes fertility, fecundity and lactational competency.

responses to intraspecific competition and its sequelae (10, 11, 12, 19, 20, 21, 22, 23).

Intra-uterine or postparturient factors adversely affecting the ability of surviving progeny to reproduce would seriously affect the future of their populations. Inadequate nutrition during nursing or intra-uterine physiological derangements conceivably could produce such manifestations. Chitty (17) observed that the progeny of voles from dense populations were more susceptible to disease and less resistant to various stressors. He first suggested that such diminished resistance might result from intra-uterine physiological derangements but later proposed that inadequate maternal lactation probably accounted for the changes in the progeny. His proposal was supported by limited experiments with voles in which he was able to demonstrate diminished growth in the progeny nursed by previously crowded mothers (18). He was unable to demonstrate any prenatal effects. Christian (12) suggested that there was a suppression of lactation in house mice from dense populations since no change in maternal behavior was observed and the stomachs of nursing young were devoid of milk. The progeny in these experiments were stunted, weaned early, and most were unable to survive the immediate postweaning period. Furthermore the survival rate of nursing progeny was inversely related to the logarithm of the number of mice in the population.

Increased population density produces adrenocortical hypertrophy, decreased activity of the reproductive organs, decreased reproductive performance, and other endocrine changes usually associated with pituitary-adrenocortical stimulation (10, 11, 12, 23). The magnitude of these changes is related to the logarithm of the population size (12, 23). It was logical to suppose that lactation would reflect the altered endocrine functions brought about by increased population density, as a variety of stressful stimuli may diminish lactation (24).

The following experiments were designed to show (a) whether crowding female mice results in a subsequent lactational deficiency, and if so (b) how it affects subsequent generations, and (c) to determine at what developmental stages reproductive losses may occur in mice as a result of crowding.

METHODS[2] AND PROCEDURE

Effects of previous crowding on lactation

A standard procedure (diagrammed in Fig. 1) was used for all experimental populations. Twenty male and 20 virgin female albino mice of the NMRI strain were taken at maturity (about four weeks after weaning) and placed in a $13'' \times 18'' \times 7''$ cage for six weeks. Food in excess of usage was distributed over the bottom of the cages and water was available from several sources to avoid competition for these items. This pro-

[2] The authors are indebted to Mr. James S. Reid and Robert Tenney, HN, for technical assistance and to Mr. William Cochran for statistical advice.

EXPERIMENTAL PLAN AND RESULTS AS FOLLOWS:

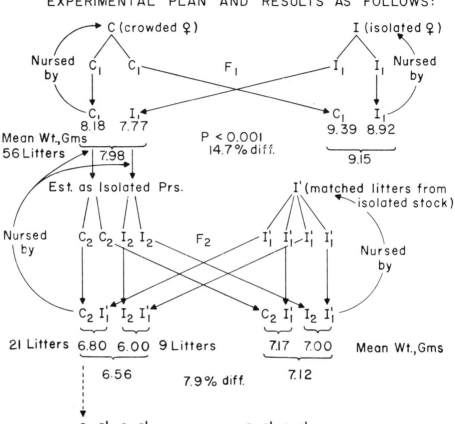

FIG. 1. Effects of maternal crowding on lactation. Seven populations of 20 pairs of mice each crowded for six weeks, then established as single pairs. Mean weight per half litter used as the unit of measurement.

cedure constituted experimentally crowding the mice. Seven such populations were used (Table 1). None of the females in these populations appeared grossly pregnant nor were any litters born during the period of crowding. In no population did all of the males survive crowding. Females occasionally succumbed but the number dying was much smaller than for the males. It has been shown previously that deaths can rarely be attributed to fighting *per se* (10–12), and in any event fighting essentially ceases after the first day or two of crowding.

The mice surviving six weeks of crowding were segregated in pairs, and each pair put in a cage of its own. These segregated pairs were checked daily for litters. When a litter was born, it was weighed *in toto*, the number of young counted and each one marked by toe clipping. Half of this litter was then exchanged with half of one of the same size, age, and parity belonging to a mother which had been segregated since weaning with her mate. Therefore a previously crowded female nursed half of her own and half of a litter born by an isolated mother, and vice versa. The pups were then individually

TABLE 1. Summary of the survival and productivity of mice
crowded 20 pairs to a cage for 6 weeks

Note that the data for three populations were combined for experiment 2. The variation in the number of pairs surviving crowding is due to the differences between populations in the numbers of males which survived the 6 weeks of crowding. See the text for a discussion of this variation in the mortality of males. Note also the general agreement between the percentages surviving and the percentages of the surviving pairs which had litters.

Expt.	No. pairs crowded	No. pairs after 6 wks. crowding	% pairs surviving crowding	No. pairs having litters	% surviving prs. having litters	No. litters weaned	% litters weaned	Mean pup wt.		Wt. of pups crowded as % of isolated
								Raised by crowded mother	Raised by isolated mother	
1	20	13	65	7	54	5	71	6.20	8.08	77
2	60 (3×20)	44	73	36	82	29	81	7.79	8.95	87
3	20	6	30	4	67	2	50	7.30	8.48	86
4	20	8	40	5	63	4	80	8.38	8.82	95
5	20	17	85	16	94	16	100	8.59	9.94	86
Total	140	88		68		56		38.26	44.27	
Mean (per pop.)	20	12.6	63	9.4	77	8.0	86	7.65	8.85	86.4

weighed weekly for three weeks. The mean weight per pup was determined each time for the four half-litters: (1) born and nursed by crowded females, (2) born and nursed by isolated females, (3) born to crowded and nursed by isolated females, and (4) born to isolated and nursed by crowded females (see Fig. 1). The mean weight per infant per half-litter was the unit of measurement, but the 56 degrees of freedom available for statistical analyses were determined by the number of matched whole litters. The effect of crowding the mothers on the weights of the infants at birth was determined for 51 of the 56 pairs of litters.

Effects of crowding on lactation in the second generation

Progeny nursed by crowded females were segregated in pairs at weaning and the entire procedure repeated for another generation, except that none was ever crowded to determine the effects on the F_2 generation. The litters of the progeny were pair-matched with litters of isolated females and half-litters switched between the two mothers, one experimental and one control. The procedure is outlined in Figure 1, but it was carried to the F_2 generation for only the first four populations and, with inevitable losses in the progress of the experiment, only 30 matched pairs of litters from the F_2 generation were available for measurement.

Effects of crowding on reproduction

A progressive loss of productivity with each stage of the reproductive process was suggested by the data in Table 1. There appeared to be a relationship between the number of pairs surviving crowding and the number having litters. The failure of the females to reproduce during crowding did not appear to be due to inadequate male fertility, as twenty-four of the fifty litters from the first four experiments were born between three and four weeks following removal from the crowded conditions (Table 2). This indicates

TABLE 2. Distribution of litters born following crowding for the
first four experiments with respect to the number of days
after removal from crowded conditions

	Days after removal from crowded cages											
	21	22	23	24	25	26	27	28	29–35	36–42	43–49	50–67
Number of litters born	1	1	8	0	4	5	3	2	11	2	7	5

that the males had mature sperm and were capable of fertilizing the females during the first estrus following crowding. Furthermore, these males were distributed so that each crowded population contained at least one of them. These results, coupled with an absence of grossly apparent pregnancies during crowding, raised the question of whether decreased fertility, increased intra-uterine mortality or both were responsible for the reproductive failure. If the females became pregnant during crowding, but lost their young *in utero*, deficient male fertility is automatically ruled out as a contributing cause. The following experiment was designed to explore the above questions.

Forty mice, 20 littermate pairs of the same age, were individually caged at weaning. Six weeks later, each of 10 pairs was segregated, one pair to a cage. The remaining mice were put in a single cage, which constituted experimental crowding. Littermate pairs were divided equally between the crowded and segregated groups. The mice were checked daily for litters or for grossly apparent pregnancy in the case of the crowded females. When a crowded female appeared grossly pregnant, it was removed and placed in a cage of its own. The others remained in the crowded group. All of the mice were sacrificed six weeks after the beginning of crowding. The reproductive tracts of the females were examined for embryos and implantation scars.

RESULTS

Infant weights at weaning, F_1 generation

The effects of crowding female mice on the mean weights of their progeny at birth and at weaning are summarized in Table 3. Mice nurtured by crowded females weighed 14.7% less at weaning than those nursed by females which had remained in segregated pairs (P <0.001). Pups born to crowded mothers tended to weigh more at weaning than those born to isolated mothers, irrespective of which female nursed them, but the difference was not significant (P <0.10). The mean weights of pups raised by their own mothers did not differ from those of pups raised by foster mothers (P <0.90). There was no significant difference (P <0.40) in mean weights of pups at birth between those born to crowded and those born to isolated females.

TABLE 3. COMPARISONS OF THE WEIGHTS OF YOUNG MICE IN THE F_1 GENERATION ACCORDING TO THEIR BIRTH OR NURTURING

Comparisons were made using the mean infant weight for each whole litter. See Figure 1 and text for the method of obtaining the whole litter values.

	No. of litters	Mean pup weight ±S.E. at weaning in grams	P diff.
Nursed by crowded female	56	7.84 ±0.22	
Nursed by isolated female	56	9.09 ±0.20	<0.001
Born to crowded female	56	8.80 ±0.18	
Born to isolated female	56	8.31 ±0.19	<0.10
Nursed by own mother	56	8.55 ±0.19	
Nursed by foster mother	56	8.59 ±0.09	<0.90
		at birth	
Born to crowded mothers	51	1.74 ±0.049	
Born to isolated mothers	51	1.78 ±0.055	<0.40

Weights at weaning vs. litter size, F_1 generation

Since the above comparisons disregarded litter size, it is worth examining the differences in weight at weaning with respect to litter size between the mean weights of pups raised by isolated and those raised by crowded females. These data are summarized in Table 4. The data for litters of 2, 3 and 4 young were combined because of the limited number of litters of these sizes. The number of litters of a given size raised by isolated females is not always equal to the number raised by crowded females, even though the litters were matched for size at birth (Table 4). These inequalities resulted from occasional differences in the survival of pups between a litter raised by isolated and one raised by the crowded female of a matched pair. The mean weights of the pups decreased with increasing litter size regardless of whether they were raised by crowded or by isolated females (Table 4, Fig. 2).

The mean weights of pups raised by crowded mothers were less than for their controls raised by isolated mothers for litter sizes of 5 or under, but the differences were small and not significant. However, in litters of 6 or more (except for litters of 9, which may be due to inadequate numbers for the degree of difference observed), the pups raised by crowded mice were significantly lighter at weaning than those raised by isolated mice. The mean weight of pups from litters of 6 or more raised by crowded females was 83% of the mean weight of pups from litters of the same sizes

TABLE 4. MEAN WEIGHTS OF MOUSE PUPS OF THE F_1 GENERATION RAISED BY ISOLATED OR BY CROWDED MOTHERS AND GROUPED ACCORDING TO LITTER SIZE

Each given mean value and its standard error were calculated from the mean pup weights for the individual litters. P values were calculated using Student's t test with the numbers of whole litters determining the number of degrees of freedom. Unequal numbers of litters for litter sizes of 5, 6, 7 and 8 were brought about by a differential mortality of the young between those raised by isolated or by crowded mothers, as all litters were paired for size and age at birth.

Litter size at weaning	Nursed by female	No. litters	Mean weight ±S.E. in grams	P diff.
2, 3, 4	crowded isolated	6 6	9.89 ±0.74 10.73 ±0.30	N.S.
5	crowded isolated	11 12	8.75 ±0.37 9.37 ±0.44	N.S.
6	crowded isolated	19 17	7.73 ±0.30 9.55 ±0.25	<0.0001
7	crowded isolated	5 4	7.12 ±0.39 8.77 ±0.33	<0.02
8	crowded isolated	7 9	6.28 ±0.55 7.93 ±0.31	<0.02
9	crowded isolated	5 5	7.90 ±0.46 8.73 ±0.80	N.S.
10	crowded isolated	3 3	5.80 ±0.44 6.92 ±0.22	<0.06

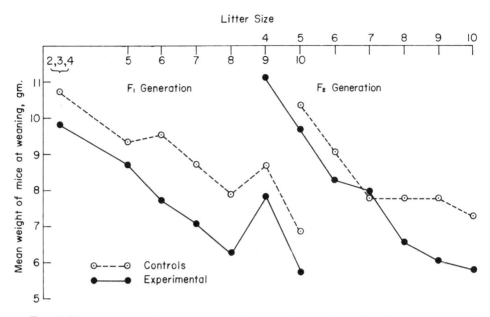

FIG. 2. Mean weights of progeny raised by crowded and by isolated mothers plotted against litter size (F_1 generation) and for progeny of mice raised by crowded mothers (F_2 generation). Mean values derived from the mean weights for each litter.

raised by isolated females, whereas in litters of 5 or less the mean weights of young raised by crowded females was 95% of that of young raised by isolated females. Regressions were fitted to the weights of infants on litter size. The slopes of regressions of the weight of the pups on litter size was -0.498 for those raised by crowded mice and -0.419 for those nursed by isolated mice, showing a more rapid decrease in weight with increasing litter size for pups nursed by crowded females than in their controls.

Weights at weaning, F_2 generation, and variations with litter size

Pups raised by females which in turn had been raised by crowded females weighed 8% less than their controls raised by isolated females ($P < 0.06$). The difference between the means was of questionable significance, but when the differences are examined with respect to litter size (Table 5, Fig. 2), it is clear that pups nursed by females which had been nursed by crowded mice weighed less than their controls for litters of 8 ($P < 0.05$), and 9 and 10 combined ($P < 0.05$). The weights of weaning mice from litters of 5, 6 and 7 did not differ significantly with respect to which mouse nurtured them, although the mean weights of progeny nursed by mice which were in turn nurtured by crowded females were less than those of their controls in every instance. If the data for litters of 8, 9 and 10 are combined, the mean weight of pups nursed by females which in turn were nursed by crowded females was 17.8% less than their controls ($P < 0.005$). There were no significant differences in the weights of progeny in the F_2

TABLE 5. MEAN WEIGHTS OF MOUSE PUPS OF THE F_2 GENERATION
GROUPED ACCORDING TO LITTER SIZE

The females bearing and raising these progeny were raised either by crowded or isolated mothers. See text and legend for Table 3 for details.

Litter size at weaning	Nursed by mother which in turn had been nursed by females	No. of litters	Mean pup wt. ±S.E. in grams	P diff.
4	crowded	2	11.14 ± 0.26	
	isolated			
5	crowded	2	9.67 ± 0.57	< 0.40
	isolated	2	10.36 ± 0.14	
6	crowded	9	8.29 ± 0.63	< 0.30
	isolated	10	9.09 ± 0.27	
7	crowded	2	8.00 ± 1.70	< 0.90
	isolated	2	7.80 ± 0.10	
8	crowded	8	6.60 ± 0.31	< 0.05
	isolated	8	7.80 ± 0.45	
9–10	crowded	7	5.86 ± 0.31	< 0.05
	isolated	8	7.44 ± 0.66	
8, 9, 10	crowded	15	6.26 ± 0.23	< 0.005
	isolated	16	7.62 ± 0.38	

generation with respect to the true parentage of mice in the F_1 generation. Therefore, the important factor in determining the differences in weights of progeny at weaning in the F_2 generation was whether or not the mouse nurturing them had been nursed by a crowded female.

The effects on the weights of the young are less marked in the F_2 than in the F_1 generation. The differences in mean weight between the experimental and control pups were significant only for litters of 8, 9 and 10 in the F_2 generation whereas litters of 6 or more weighed significantly less than their controls in the F_1 generation.

The litters measured may represent bias towards minimizing the effects of crowding as it is conceivable that these were produced by the females least affected by crowding.

Effects of crowding on reproduction

The results of crowding 10 male and 10 female mice in a single cage on reproductive performance, measured by live births, embryos, and uterine implantation scars, are summarized in Table 6. The presence of implantation scars showed that every female became pregnant, but that only 3 of the crowded females bore litters during the period of crowding or later. Therefore there was a marked intra-uterine mortality of implanted embryos. The fact that every female mouse became pregnant, even though she may have failed to carry the pregnancy to term, shows that the effect was not primarily on the fertility of the males. The intra-uterine loss

TABLE 6. SUMMARY OF DATA ON PRODUCTIVITY OF MICE CROWDED 10 PAIRS
TO A CAGE COMPARED TO THEIR 10 CONTROL PAIRS

Note that all of the females became pregnant but that the crowded females exhibited a marked intra-uterine loss of young, reduction of implantation sites, reduction of litter size, and significant delay until the birth of first litters compared to the controls. Crowding produced a 75% loss in the number of young born.

	No. of pairs	No. litters born	Mean No. days to litter birth	Mean No. progeny per litter ±S.E.	No. females with placental scars	Mean No. scars per female
Crowded females	10	3	40 ± 1.0	7.67 ± 0.33	10	6.90 ± 1.37
Isolated females	10	10	26 ± 1.5	9.00 ± 0.75	10	11.00 ± 0.47

apparently occurred during the first half of gestation as none of the 7 without litters, but with implantation scars, ever appeared grossly pregnant. Apparently there also was some preimplantation loss in the crowded females as the mean number of implantation scars was significantly reduced from the control values obtained from the isolated littermate controls. It is not known whether the preimplantation loss was due to a failure of some of the fertilized ova to implant properly or to a reduced number of fertilized ova. A decrease in the fertility of the females is suggested by the 14 days greater mean time lapsing between exposure to males and the birth of the three litters of crowded mice compared to their isolated controls. These results suggest that crowding produced a serious loss of young due to intra-uterine mortality and probably to some decrease in fertility in female mice. These results probably explain the reason for the diminished productivity of crowded females in the preceding lactation experiments.

DISCUSSION

The above experiments demonstrate the adverse effect of crowding on lactation and reproduction in female albino mice, confirming and extending Chitty's observations on voles (18). Progeny raised by crowded females were adversely affected as were their progeny in turn.

It might be thought that crowding interfered with adequate nutrition of the females and that a resulting nutritional deficiency was responsible for the effects on the progeny. Several facts argue against such a suggestion. First, it has been shown that crowding has little if any effect on the body weight of adult albino mice (10, 11). Second, food in the form of pellets was generously spread all over the floor of the cage, so that any mouse was almost always in contact with food. There was therefore no competition for food or space at a feeding site. Daily observation further indicated that there was no interference with feeding or competition for food. Third, lactation began not less than three weeks after the mice were removed from the crowded cage (Table 2); so that there were three or more weeks of living in segregation with abundant food before lactation began. Finally, the young of crowded mothers tended to weigh more at birth than those of isolated mothers and grew normally when nursed by isolated mothers. It therefore does not seem likely that the effects on the lactation of the crowded mothers, and hence on their offspring, can be attributed to inadequate nutrition.

Crowding apparently has no effect on the growth of young *in utero*, as there were no significant differences in weight at birth between the young of crowded and those of isolated mothers. Genetic effects are apparently ruled out by the fact that mice born to crowded and raised by isolated females actually tended to be heavier than those born to and raised by isolated mothers, and that mice born to isolated and raised by crowded females were smaller. Whether or not the young were raised by their own or a foster mother made no difference in their weights. Therefore the deleterious effects of crowding on the two succeeding generations of progeny must be attributed to inadequate lactation on the part of the originally crowded female and not to intra-uterine or genetic factors.

A difference in maternal behavior between previously crowded and isolated females was not detected in the course of daily observations. However, no detailed measurements were made to substantiate or disprove the impressions gained by the routine observations of maternal behavior. Brown (6) and Southwick (9) reported that interference with nursing and nest construction by other mice in the population was responsible for the deficient maternal behavior in their experiments. Interference by other mice was excluded from our experiments during the period of lactation by maintaining the mice as segregated pairs after crowding.

The only remaining alternatives to explain the decreased weight of young raised by crowded mice are quantitative and qualitative deficiences in the milk. The present experiments were not designed to distinguish between these two alternatives. One or both may have been operative, but a quantitative deficiency seems more likely, as in earlier experiments the stomachs of the young mice contained little or no milk when sacrificed (12).

Why females raised by previously crowded mice should in turn raise progeny smaller at weaning than their controls can only be conjectured. A specific factor in the milk is unlikely, and genetic factors have been ruled out. An explanation for the diminished size of the young mice in the F_2 generation could be that the effect of inanition resulting from deficient lactation affects the progeny of the first generation in such a manner that they, in turn, do not lactate adequately.

It has been noted that in every crowded population the number of mice at the end of six weeks of crowding was less than the original number, due mainly to the death of males, as fewer females than males died (Table 1). The number of male deaths varied from 3 to 14 per population, as shown by the number of pairs alive after crowding. The number of deaths is in a real sense a measure of the degree of social strife within a given population, and the amount of strife is not necessarily a function of the absolute number of mice in a population. The aggressiveness of particular individuals as well as the degrees of difference in dominance and subordinance between the various members of the population are major factors in determining the amount of intraspecific strife in a given population. The bases for these statements will not be discussed here, as they have been covered in greater detail elsewhere (3, 8, 9, 12, 18, 20, 23, 25). It should be mentioned, however, that we have observed that the degree of stress engendered in a given population coincides with the amount of social strife better than with the actual number of animals (23). While no measurements of aggressive behavior or strife were made in the present experiments, it was noted that the amount of fighting observed corresponded to the degree of mortality, and these observations were consistent with those made on all of our experimental populations to date. It should be emphasized that fighting is rarely a direct cause of death (10, 11, 12, 23).

There was a direct correspondence between the number of pairs which survived crowding and the number of these which bore litters (Table 1). Evidently the amount of strife resulting in a given mortality rate affected reproduction in the surviving pairs to a comparable degree. The litters available for measurement were produced by less than half (68/140) of the crowded females, and not all of these litters survived until weaning. It is suggested that those females which produced young were physiologically less affected by crowding and therefore the least stressed. This suggestion is further supported by earlier experiments in which the dominant females in a group of mice have been reported to be better producers than their subordinate sisters (2, 3). Corresponding to these findings we have noted that adrenal weight, used as an index of stress, is least in dominant and greatest in subordinate mice (25). The present experiments offer some evidence that females having the largest litters were less affected by crowding than others. The differences between the mean weights of pups raised by crowded and those raised by isolated mothers were not proportionately as great for litters of 9 and 10 as they were for litters of 6, 7 and 8 in the F_1 generation (Table 4). These data suggest that females capable of producing large litters were also more capable of adequately nurturing their young than females bearing somewhat smaller litters. The results from the experiment with ten pairs of crowded mice show that reproductive failure in females surviving crowding is due primarily to intra-uterine mortality and secondarily to diminished fertility. All of the mice in this experiment became pregnant during the period of crowding, but only 3 gave birth to litters, and the mean size for these 3 litters was significantly less than for their controls. The onset of the first pregnancy also was considerably delayed compared to the control mice.

These experiments indicate that crowding can decrease productivity in female house mice by decreasing fertility, increasing intra-uterine mortality, and causing deficient lactation which results in diminished growth of the young. The young are themselves affected so that they in turn have smaller progeny, apparently as a result of deficient lactation. Data from populations of house mice in the laboratory (12) indicate that adversely affected progeny are less able to survive and reach maturity. Therefore crowding, or high population density, affects productivity immediately by decreasing fertility and increasing prenatal mortality, and at long range by depressing lactation with subsequent detrimental effects on the survival and productivity of progeny. It is likely that the severity of the effects is related to the degree of social strife and less closely to the actual number of animals interacting with one another (23). The experimental evidence indicates that recovery of reproductive competence from the effects of a period of high population density would necessarily be slow, possibly lasting several generations.

REFERENCES

1. Cole, L. C.: *Quart. Rev. Biol.* **29**: 103. 1954.
2. Crew, F. A. E. and L. Mirskaia: *Biol. Generalis* **7**: 239. 1931.
3. Retzlaff, E. G.: *Biol. Generalis* **14**: 238. 1938.
4. Calhoun, J. B.: *Science* **109**: 333. 1949.
5. Davis, D. E.: *Ecology* **32**: 459. 1951.
6. Brown, R. Z.: *Ecol. Monogr.* **23**: 217. 1953.
7. Strecker, R. L. and J. T. Emlen, Jr.: *Ecology* **34**: 375. 1953.
8. Clarke, J. R.: *Proc. Roy. Soc. B.* **143**: 68. 1955.
9. Southwick, C. H.: *Ecology* **35**: 627. 1955.
10. Christian, J. J.: *Am. J. Physiol.* **182**: 292. 1955a.
11. Christian, J. J.: *Am. J. Physiol.* **181**: 477. 1955b.
12. Christian, J. J.: *Ecology* **37**: 258. 1956.
13. Kalela, O.: *Ann. Acad. Sci. Fennicae. A. Biologica* **34**: 1. 1957.
14. Errington, P. L.: *Jour. Wildlife Mgt.* **18**: 66. 1954.
15. Leopold, A. S., T. Riney, R. McCain and L. Tevis, Jr.: Cal. Div. of Fish and Game, Game Bull. No. 4, p. 1. 1951.
16. Buechner, H. K. and C. V. Swanson: Trans-North. Am. Wildlife Conf. **20**: 560. 1955.
17. Chitty, D.: *Ecology* **35**: 227. 1954.
18. Chitty, D.: "The numbers of man and animals," Ed. J. B. Cragg and N. W. Pirie, Oliver and Boyd, Ltd., Edinburgh, pp. 57. 1955.
19. Christian, J. J.: *Jour. Mammal.* **31**: 247. 1950.
20. Christian, J. J.: *Am. J. Physiol.* **187**: 353. 1956.
21. Christian, J. J. and D. E. Davis: *Trans. North. Amer. Wildlife Conf.* **14**: 225. 1955.
22. Christian, J. J. and D. E. Davis: *Jour. Mammal.* **37**: 475. 1956.
23. Christian, J. J.: In press.
24. Selye, H.: *Rev. Canad. Biologie* **13**(4): 377. 1954.
25. Davis, D. E. and J. J. Christian: *Proc. Soc. Expt. Biol. and Med.* **94**: 728. 1957.

Reproduced from *Endocrinology* 63:517–529, 1958, with permission of the Endocrine Society and the Williams and Wilkins Co.

Regulation of numbers in the Great tit (Aves: Passeriformes)

JOHN R. KREBS

The census data of the Great tit collected by Perrins (1965) and others in Marley Wood near Oxford are analysed for density-dependence. Clutch size and hatching success are density-dependent and sufficiently so to regulate the population at the observed level (assuming that there is in addition a fairly large density-independent mortality). There may also be some weak density-dependent mortality outside the breeding season. The density-dependent variations in clutch size are probably in the main due to shortage of available food and density-dependent hatching failure is caused by predation. Territorial behaviour has been shown experimentally to determine breeding density, and may produce a density-dependent effect outside the breeding season. These three factors are responsible for regulation of the Great tit population in Marley Wood.

Introduction

The Great tit is one of the best studied species of bird in terms of its population ecology (e.g. Lack, 1966; Perrins, 1965; Kluijver, 1951; 1967; Dhondt & Hublé, 1968; Vilks, 1966) and yet little is clearly understood about the factors determining its abundance. This paper presents a re-analysis of the census data of the Great tit collected in Marley Wood, near Oxford (see Lack, 1966 and Perrins, 1965 for details) with a view to clarifying some of the factors and processes determining numbers of the Great tit.

The analysis of density-dependence

Perhaps the most important theoretical concept of population ecology is that of density-dependence (for definition see Solomon, 1958 and Varley, 1958). The fact that, where records are available, populations remain relatively stable in relation to their potential rate of increase and the fact that it has not been possible to simulate such stability in a model population without incorporating density-dependence (Richards & Southwood, 1968) is a strong indirect argument in favour of the idea that natural populations are regulated* by density-dependent factors (density governing as used by Nicholson, 1954). However, density-dependent processes are not always easy to demonstrate as acting on natural populations (Reddingius, 1968). Varley & Gradwell (1960, 1963, 1968) have developed a simple method for testing population data for density-dependence and for recognizing the action of *key factors*, that is to say, the largest section of the annual mortality (usually, but not always density-independent) which is responsible for short-term fluctuations in numbers. The prime interest of isolating the key factor(s) is that this enables predictions about population change.

Varley & Gradwell's method consists simply of expressing mortalities (k values) as the $\log_{10}$ of the ratio of the populations before and after the particular mortality in question has acted:

$$k = \log_{10} \frac{\text{initial population}}{\text{final population}}.$$

A separate k value can be calculated for each stage within the annual cycle at the start and end of which censuses (or samples) are taken. The total annual mortality, K, is the sum of the separate mortalities $k1$, $k2$, $k3$, etc. If the k values are plotted against time (Fig.

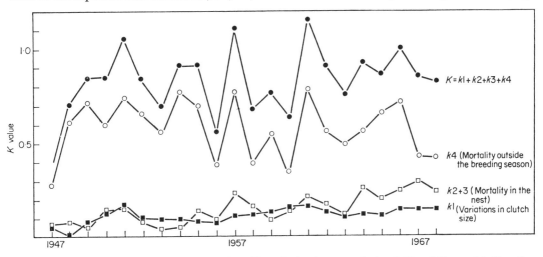

FIG 1. K values 1947–68, see text for explanation of how the k values are calculated. $k2$ and $k3$ are added together for clarity. $k4$ is the largest section of the annual mortality and its fluctuations parallel those of total K, i.e. it the key factor.

* It is important to note that the terms "regulation" and "regulate" in this paper are used in a restricted sense, referring only to the influence of *density-dependent* processes on the population. The terms do not refer to any density-independent factors which may cause year to year fluctuations in numbers, or remove a constant proportion from the population each year. "Regulation" refers to the processes which compensate for disturbances from a particular level of abundance, but the level of abundance at which the population is regulation may vary greatly according to numerous features of the environment. Thus the overall abundance is influenced by (i) regulatory processes (which are density-dependent and stabilizing); (ii) density-independent factors, causing short term fluctuations; (iii) the general nature of the habitat, which determines the level about which the population fluctuates and is regulated.

1), a graphical estimate is obtained of which mortality acts as the key factor (i.e. is largest and parallels fluctuations in K). In Fig. 1 this is clearly $k4$. Density-dependence is tested by plotting the k value against the $\log_{10}$ of the population on which the mortality acts (Fig. 2). A significant positive slope indicates density-dependence. A lack of correlation may mean that there is no density-dependence, or that a density-dependent effect is being masked by inaccuracies in the population samples, or large density-independent factors. If the data from which the k values are obtained are not direct counts of the population, but estimates based on samples, a further test is necessary to prove the density-dependent relationship suggested by plotting the k value on its initial population (Southwood, 1966; Varley & Gradwell, 1968). The test consists of calculating two regressions, of log initial population on log final population and of log final population on log initial population. If both of these regressions produce slopes which are significantly different from a slope of $b = 1$, and on the same side of unity, density-dependence is proved. All the density-dependent effects shown below are based on direct counts of the population.

As far as the Great tit is concerned, the basic census data consist of direct counts of (i) number of breeding birds, (ii) number of eggs laid, (iii) number of eggs hatching, (iv) number of young fledging and (v) number of breeding birds in the following year. In some years an estimate of the population outside the breeding season has been made (see later). From these census data, the following mortalities (k values) were calculated:

(i) The "mortality" which operates before the eggs are laid, in other words yearly variations from the potential maximum average clutch size. The potential maximum average clutch size was obtained by adding a small amount to the maximum observed annual average (maximum observed $= 12{\cdot}3$, estimated maximum potential $= 12{\cdot}5$). (It does not matter for the subsequent calculations how much is added on.)

$k1$ ("Clutch size variations")* is expressed as:

$$\log\left[\frac{(\text{potential max. clutch}+2)N}{(\text{obs. clutch}+2)N}\right]$$

where N is the number of breeding *pairs*.

(ii) The mortality which operates between the eggs being laid and the eggs hatching out:

$$k2 \text{ ("hatching failure")} = \log\left[\frac{(\text{clutch}+2)N}{(\text{hatching birds}+2)N}\right].$$

(iii) Mortality operating on the young in the nest, after hatching and before fledging:

$$k3 \text{ ("nestling mortality")} = \log\left[\frac{(\text{hatch}+2)N}{(\text{fledg.}+2)N}\right].$$

(iv) Mortality operating outside the breeding season, between the time the young leave the nest and the following breeding season:

$$k4 \text{ ("mortality outside the breeding season")} =$$

$$\log\left[\frac{\text{summer pop. in year 1}}{\text{breeding pop. in year 2}}\right] (\text{summer pop.} = [\text{fledg.}+2]N).$$

* The addition of 2 is to allow for the presence of adult birds in the population.

As mentioned above for some years it is possible to divide $k4$ into:

$$k4.1 \text{ (``autumn mortality'')} = \log\left[\frac{\text{summer pop.}}{\text{winter pop.}}\right]$$

and

$$k4.2 \text{ (``winter mortality'')} = \log\left[\frac{\text{winter pop.}}{\text{breeding pop.}}\right].$$

This division of $k4$ is not based on direct counts of the population, but on a sample.

Lack followed Kluijver (1951) in showing that clutch-size and fledging success are weakly density-dependent, but both writers argued that this was not sufficient to regulate the population (Lack, 1966: 74–75). The main regulating mortality and the key factor mortality were considered to occur outside the breeding season, the former probably in winter and the latter in autumn.

The k value analysis confirms the conclusion that clutch size is density-dependent (Fig. 2(a)). Hatching success is also density-dependent, but mortality of young in the nest is not density–dependent (Fig. 2(b),(c)); (this is in agreement with Lack's finding that overall mortality in the nest is density-dependent). Mortality outside the breeding season ($k4$) shows a barely significant density-dependent effect (Fig. 2(d)) which is entirely dependent on the point for one year (the first year of the study—1947). If this is omitted from the data, the other 21 points show no sign of density-dependence at all. It might be argued that, from a biological point of view, a relationship which cannot be shown to occur in 21 out of 22 cases cannot be very important. As mentioned above, the calculations of $k1$, $k2$, $k3$ and $k4$ are based on direct counts of the population rather than samples, and it is therefore not strictly necessary to perform a further test on the density-dependent relationships shown in Fig. 2(a),(b),(d). However, the further test (see above) constitutes a more rigorous method of showing density-dependence than the one shown in Fig. 2. When this test was carried out on the data shown in Fig. 2, it confirmed that $k1$ and $k2$ are density-dependent, whilst the suggested density-dependence in $k4$ was not confirmed. This is a further indication that the strong density-dependence effect in $k4$ shown in Fig. 2(d) is spurious.

The first step in assessing the possible importance of density-dependence in $k4$ is to find out what effect the other density-dependent factors (which have been clearly demonstrated) have on the population. The easiest way of assessing this is to use the calculated density-dependent values to simulate the population and to compare what happens if $K4$ is assumed to be respectively density-dependent and density-independent. The simulation was run by starting from an arbitrarily chosen value for the number of breeding pairs, adding to the $\log_{10}$ of this number a fecundity factor ($\log_{10}$ potential max. clutch$+2$) and then subtracting successively the various k values, to obtain a breeding population for the following year. This process was repeated until the resulting breeding population was the same in successive "years". The density-dependent k values were calculated for each population on which they acted from the regression equations, and density-independent mortalities were counted as constants (taking the average observed values). This simulation does not introduce any new data, but illustrates graphically the effects of the k values shown in Fig. 2. The simulations with and without $k4$ as a density-dependent factor are shown in Fig. 3. (The simulation shown started at 60 pairs, the stable density would be

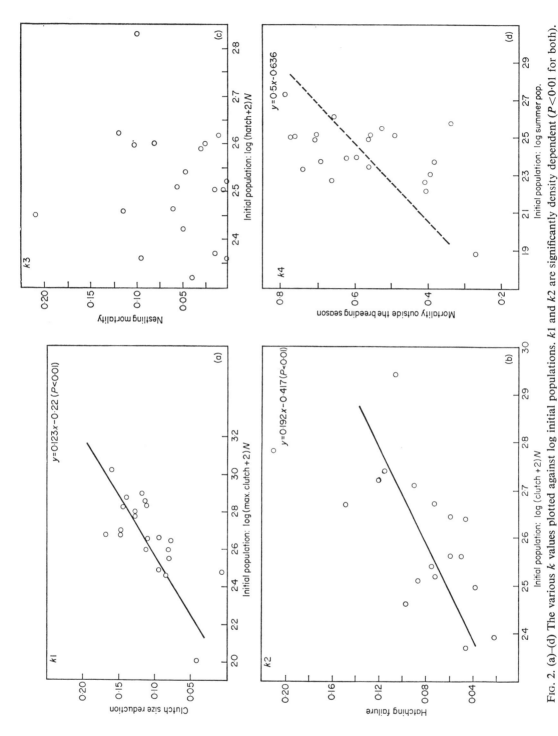

FIG. 2. (a)–(d) The various k values plotted against log initial populations. $k1$ and $k2$ are significantly density dependent ($P<0.01$ for both). For discussion of density dependence in $k4$ see text.

In calculating $k1$, $k2$ and $k3$, relays and second broods were excluded. In some years so many clutches were interfered with for experimental purposes that it was not possible to obtain an average hatching success. These years were omitted from the calculations of $k2$.

the same starting from any value.) The observed population in Marley Wood increased gradually over the first ten years or so (having started off at an exceptionally low density) and since then has fluctuated considerably about a mean of 45 pairs. Both simulations give a reasonable value for the stable population level. With $k4$ as density-dependent, the population stabilizes out at 37 pairs, and with $k4$ counted as a constant, at 44 pairs. The latter is a little nearer to the observed stable level, but not sufficiently so to reject the idea of

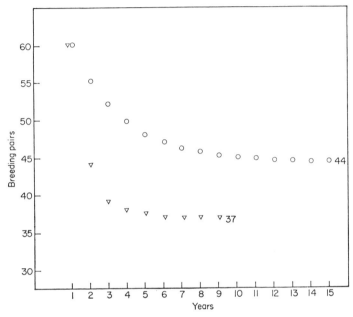

FIG. 3. Population simulations with $k4$ as density dependent ($\triangledown$), and density independent ($\bigcirc$). Both stabilize out at levels similar to the observed stable mean. In this particular simulation the starting density was 60 pairs. The stable level would be the same starting from any density.

$$k4 = \log \left[\frac{\text{summer pop. in year 1}}{\text{breeding pop in year 2}} \right]$$

density-dependence in $k4$. The simulations show, however, that even if there were *no density-dependence in* $k4$, the population would be approximately as observed in the wild, thus there is no *necessity* to postulate density-dependence in $k4$. There are, in addition, some indirect arguments against there being any strong density-dependence in $k4$. The observed population has fluctuated considerably during the 22 years of study (minimum breeding population 7 pairs, maximum 86 pairs). If all the annual mortality were density-dependent (i.e. if there were no disturbing factors acting on the population), the population would be completely stable from year to year; if $k4$ were really as strongly density-dependent as the regression line in Fig. 2(d) suggests, a large part of the annual mortality would be density-dependent and we would expect the observed population to be much more stable than it has in fact been. Thus there are good *a priori* grounds for saying that if there is any density-dependence in $k4$, it is weak. As mentioned earlier, if a k value contains a weak density-dependent effect and a stronger density-independent one, the former may be masked and not show up in a statistical analysis based on rather limited data. If this were true in the case of $k4$, it might be expected that if we divide $k4$ into two parts (see above)—autumn and winter mortality—that any weak density-dependence would show up in one of the subdivisions. The two parts of $k4$ ($k4.1$ and $k4.2$) are plotted on their initial populations in Fig. 4(a),(b) neither shows any suggestion of density-dependence.

A striking difference between the two simulations in Fig. 3 is that the one with stronger density-dependence stabilizes out much more rapidly. Therefore it should in theory be possible to infer something about the strength of density-dependent factors operating on the real population by noting how quickly it returns to the stable level after a big disturbance. In practice, however, there have been only two really big disturbances, one at the start of the study, when the population was at seven pairs, and one in 1961, when the population rose to 86 pairs. The "return"* to the stable level took about ten years after the first disturbance, and only one year after the second. Since one would predict that on some occasions a random density-independent factor would more or less cancel itself out from one year to the next, the available data do not really distinguish between strong and weak density-dependence on the basis of the speed of compensation for a disturbance. The initial increase of the population between 1947 and 1957 is further complicated by the fact that during this period the number of nest boxes in the area was increased. Boxes were first put up in 1947 and more were added in 1951.

Thus the statistical analysis fails to demonstrate conclusively that there is any density-dependent mortality operating on the Marley Wood population outside the breeding season. Some evidence, however, suggests that there is density-dependent disappearance outside the breeding season. When territorial pairs in mixed woodland were shot in the spring (mid-March), they were rapidly replaced by new birds (Krebs, in press): this showed that some aspect of territorial behaviour limits the breeding density of Great tits in mixed woodland. On the simple hypothesis that territory sizes are fairly constant from year to year, it would be expected that this territorial limitation would be density-dependent. Thus there is an apparent conflict, territory has been shown experimentally to limit breeding density and might be expected to do so in a density-dependent fashion, yet the k value analysis fails to show density-dependence at the time of year when the territorial limitation operates (late winter—early spring) (Fig. 4(b)). The apparent conflict could be due to two factors: either territory does not limit breeding density in a constant fashion, but to a different level each year; or any density-dependent effect that territory has on the population does not show up in the analysis because the data are inadequate. Probably both these factors are involved: (i) Territory size in the Great tit is variable from year to year and probably has a weak density-dependent "restraining" effect on the population rather than a strong density-dependent "limiting" effect. (This, together with the factors causing year to year fluctuations in territory size, are discussed in Krebs (in press)). A weak density-dependent effect of territory would be consistent with the conclusion of the earlier discussion, namely that there is unlikely to be any strong density-dependent mortality outside the breeding season. (ii) the effects of territory on the population should be revealed in Fig. 4(b), where winter "mortality" (in fact emigration) is plotted on the initial winter population. The winter population is estimated by an indirect method (Lack, 1966:

* Since the population prior to 1947 was not known, it is not strictly correct to talk of a "return" to a stable level, since it is possible that the stable level of the population was very different before and after 1947.

59 and 67), which is likely to be inaccurate. Thus it is not surprising that a weak density-dependent effect in $k4.2$ is masked by large sampling errors involved in estimating the winter population.

The results of the k value analysis may be summarized as follows: the observable density-dependence in $k1$ and $k2$ (mortality acting during the reproductive period) is enough to regulate the population at approximately the observed level. There may also be a weakly

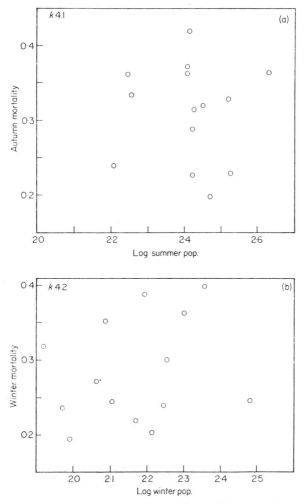

FIG. 4. Division of $k4$ into autumn (a) and winter (b) mortality. Neither part shows any density dependence.

density-dependent effect outside the breeding season ($k4$) which is not, however, demonstrated conclusively in the analysis. Experiments have shown that territory determines breeding density; this is evidence in favour of a density-dependent effect outside the breeding season. This conclusion is in contrast to the widely held view that bird populations are primarily regulated by mortality outside the breeding season.

Pennycuick (1969) has analysed the Marley Wood data and concluded that the Marley population is regulated by density-dependent mortality of juveniles after leaving the nest (k4.1), which the author claims (on p. 395) "... agrees with Lack's (1966) conclusion that survival of the young after leaving the nest is the most critical stage for *regulation* of numbers...". Lack himself, however, clearly stated (1966: 73–74): "While the critical factor influencing the annual *fluctuations* in the breeding population of the Great tit in Marley Wood has been the juvenile mortality ... there is no evidence that this mortality has varied with density.... Hence the density-dependent regulation of the Great tit population has evidently been brought about by some different factor". The reason for Pennycuick reaching her erroneous conclusion is that in her Fig. 3 she plotted percentage juvenile survival on total summer population (equivalent to Fig. 4(a)), but in fitting in a line to the points, she assumed that as density approaches 0, per cent survival approaches 100, which is equivalent to assuming the mortality to be density-dependent. There are several other errors in the paper; for example, it is not possible to show density-dependence in k4.2 as Pennycuick claimed, nor is winter mortality related to the beech mast crop (Lack, 1966; Krebs, in press).

Factors responsible for density-dependent mortality

The previous section was concerned with trying to isolate the density-dependent mortalities; this section contains a discussion of the proximate factors actually responsible for producing density-dependence in the field.

Density-dependent variations in clutch size (k1)

Perrins (1965) reviewed the proximate factors influencing clutch size in the Great tit. Apart from the density effect, he showed that date of breeding, age of female, and nature of habitat have an influence on the annual variations in mean clutch size. Perrins also found that food availability had an apparent effect on clutch size (Perrins, 1965: Fig. 10), but that when clutches were compensated for date and population density, the correlation with food supply disappeared. In fact Perrins (1965: Fig. 10) referred to availability of food *after* the eggs have been laid, but this probably also gives an index of food availability *at the time* at which the female is laying eggs. Thus any influence of immediate availability of food on clutch size seems to be related to date or density. Density could influence the availability of food for the female to make eggs simply by greater depletion of the food supply at higher density of birds. This however seems unlikely, since the abundance of insect food is increasing rapidly at the time of egg laying. An alternative mechanism by which density could influence the availability of food, might be that at higher densities the birds spend more time defending their territories (Krebs, in press) and less time collecting food—especially the male who at this time of year supplies a considerable quantity of food to the female (Royama, 1966). A third possibility would be that at higher densities the female predicts that there will be less food for feeding the young and reduces her clutch size accordingly. In this case food would be the ultimate factor influencing clutch size variations, and some other factor related to density (for example frequency of territorial interactions) would act as the proximate factor. Since date of breeding is not related to breeding density (Fig. 5), it seems unlikely that the density-dependent variations in clutch size are a result of birds laying later in high density year.

The age ratio of the breeding population varies significantly with density; at higher densities there is a greater proportion of first year females in the population (Fig. 6). Perrins (1965) showed that first year females lay on average 0·6 eggs less per clutch than older birds. Thus the variation in the age ratio of the population will produce an automatic

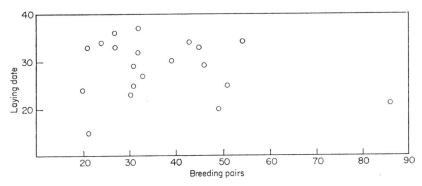

FIG. 5. Graph of mean date of first egg (1 = 1 April) against breeding population: no significant relationship.

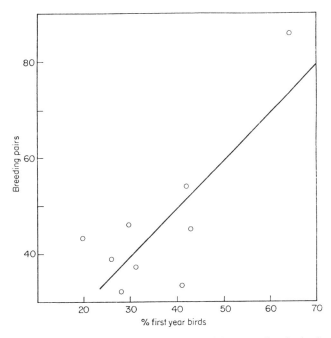

FIG. 6. Relationship between breeding density and proportion of first year females in the population ($p < 0.05$).

density-dependent depression in average clutch size. An estimate of how much this age factor contributes to the total density-dependence of clutch size was made as follows: (i) the slope of the regression line in Fig. 6 was used to calculate the proportion of first year females in the population at the various observed densities (direct counts of the age ratio have been made only since 1960). (ii) As mentioned above, Perrins found that first year

363

females lay on average 0·6 eggs per clutch less than adults, thus a population of 100% first year birds would show an average depression in clutch size due to age alone of 0·6 eggs, as compared with a population with no first year birds. The clutch size depression for different age ratios (corresponding to different densities) was calculated as follows:

If p = proportion of first year birds laying a clutch of $c-0·6$ eggs each,
and $1-p$ = proportion of adult birds laying a clutch of c eggs each;
the mean clutch of the population = $c-0·6p$.

The average depression in clutch size over 22 years due to the age factor was only 0·155 eggs per clutch, whilst the average value of $k1$ was 1·29 eggs. Therefore the age factor comprises only 12% of the total density-dependent clutch size effect. (In fact the age ratio contribution may be considerably less than 12% since the slope of the regression of Fig. 6 is strongly influenced by one point.)

The final factor influencing annual clutch size is the nature of the habitat. Perrins (1965, plate facing p. 626) found that if he divided Marley Wood subjectively into "good" and "bad" areas, there was a highly significant difference in clutch size between the two types of area. Assuming that the birds prefer to settle in areas in which they are likely to breed most successfully, it would be expected that birds would prefer to settle in the "good" habitats described by Perrins. This, however, did not appear to be so when direct observations were made (Krebs, in press). Because of this apparent paradox, the "good" and "bad" clutch size areas described by Perrins were re-examined as follows: rather than dividing the wood into good and bad areas on *a priori* grounds, the positions of boxes with "good" and "bad" average clutch sizes over a number of years (1960–68) were plotted on a map and then tested to see if they fell into clumps of "good" and "bad" areas. The procedure for obtaining "good" and "bad" boxes was to calculate the average clutch size, corrected for age, date (between years) and density for each box; (second clutches were excluded). The distribution of average clutch sizes was such that approximately half of the boxes had an average clutch size of between eight and nine and the remainder were equally divided between those with an average clutch of more than nine and those with an average clutch of less than eight. Thus it was decided to call boxes with an average corrected clutch size of more than nine "good" and those with an average less than eight "bad". The proportion of eggs hatching and fledging in the two areas was not significantly different—thus birds in the good areas were not laying "too many" eggs and suffering proportionately greater subsequent loss of young in the nest. When these boxes were plotted on a map (Fig. 7), they showed statistically significant clumping into good and bad areas, but these areas did not agree with Perrins' divisions (see Appendix for further details of "good" and "bad" areas). Evidence that the birds did actually prefer the areas found to be good in terms of clutch size (as described above) is that the settling density was higher in good areas than in bad both in terms of number of birds per hectare, and proportion of nest boxes occupied (Fig. 8).

These differences in habitat quality within Marley Wood could influence the density-dependent variations in clutch size if, at higher densities, a greater *proportion* of birds bred in the "bad" areas. This would have the effect of reducing the average clutch size of the population as density increased. Figure 9 shows that the proportion of birds breeding in the "bad" areas does increase with increasing density, but that the effect is small and thus contributes little to the density-dependent clutch size variations. Figure 9 also shows that a weak *buffer effect* (Kluijver & Tinbergen, 1953) is operating between the good and

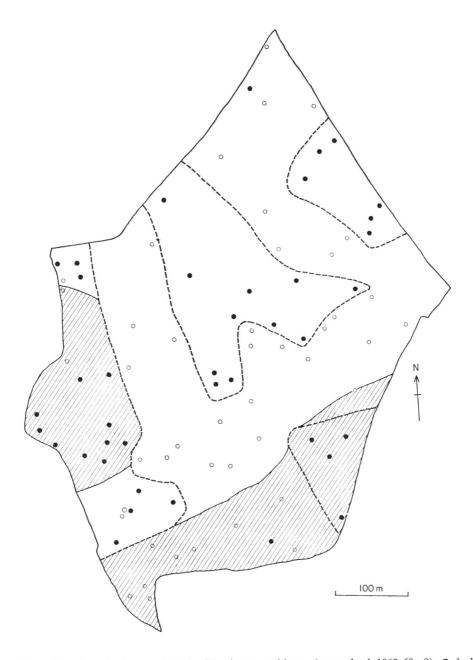

FIG. 7. Map of good and bad areas of Marley Wood: ○, good boxes (mean clutch 1960–68 <9); ●, bad boxes (mean clutch 8). Clumping of boxes into good and bad areas was tested with χ^2 test ($p < 0.02$), the null hypothesis being that the number of boxes with a nearest neighbour of the "same type" $= (a+b)^2+(c+d)^2/N$. (a, number of good boxes with good nearest neighbour; b, number of good with bad; c, number of bad with bad nearest neighbour; d, number of bad with good. $N = a+b+c+d$.) The cross-hatched areas are those described as "good" by Perrins (1963).

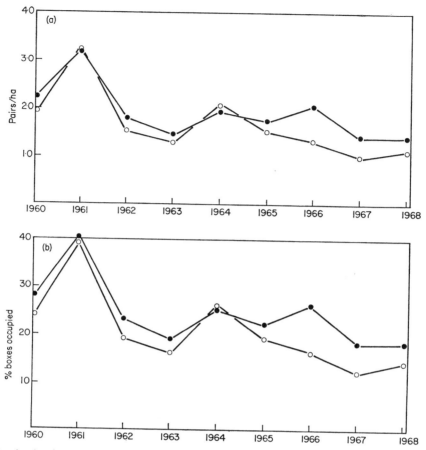

FIG. 8. Graphs showing that birds (a) settled at a higher density and (b) occupied a higher proportion of boxes in good areas ($p<0.01$ in both cases). ○, Bad areas; ●, good areas.

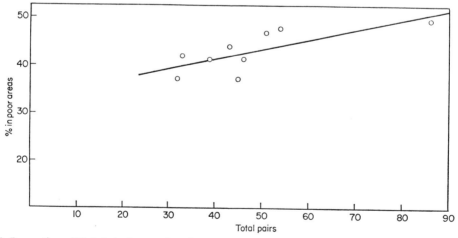

FIG. 9. Proportion of birds in bad areas plotted against total population, showing a weak buffer effect ($p<0.05$) within Marley Wood.

366

bad areas of Marley Wood; birds presumably settle up to a certain limit in the good areas, and later settlers "spill over" into the bad areas.

Summarizing, it can be shown that the age ratio of the population makes some contribution to the density-dependence of clutch size, but its effect is small; there is a weak buffer effect operating between good and bad areas of the wood, but again this contributes only a small amount to the total density-dependence of $k1$; probably some factor associated with availability of food for the female to make eggs is responsible for the remaining density-dependence of clutch size.

Density-dependent variations in hatching success ($k2$)

The analysis of factors responsible for $k2$ are more straightforward, since the causes of mortality have been directly measured in the field. Failure of eggs to hatch is due to three factors, which, in order of magnitude, are predation (largely by the weasel *Mustela nivalis*), abandonment of clutches, and infertility of eggs. Abandonment is caused either by attempted predations whilst the female is on the nest, by human interference or by a sudden spell of cold wet weather during the laying period. If abandonment was clearly caused by an attempt predation, it was counted as predated in the analysis below.

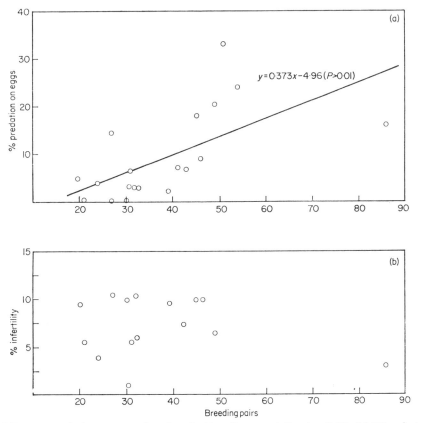

Fig. 10. (a) Per cent predation on eggs plotted against breeding population ($p < 0.01$). (b) Other factors causing "mortality" of eggs (infertility etc.) plotted against breeding population: no significant relationship.

Figure 10 shows that predation on eggs is clearly density-dependent, whilst other contributions to $k2$ are not density-dependent. Surprisingly, predation, also by *Mustela nivalis*, on the young is not density-dependent (Fig. 11). This is possibly because at the stage

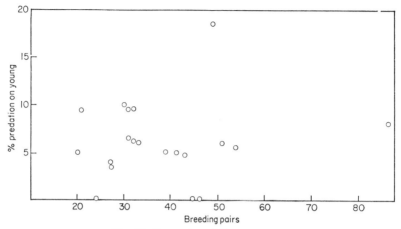

FIG. 11. Per cent predation on young.

when the young are in the nest, the ground vegetation has grown up and weasels no longer hunt visually for nest boxes, but only predate nests in which the young are begging loudly (Perrins, 1963: 99–107). Predation at the egg stage is not only density-dependent between years, but also within each year nests close together stand a higher chance of being predated than more spaced-out nests (see Krebs, in press).

Density-dependent mortality outside the breeding season (k4)

As discussed above, territorial behaviour has been shown to determine the breeding density of Great tits in mixed woodland. This is most likely to be the factor responsible for any density-dependent "mortality" (in fact emigration) outside the breeding season.

Summary

Analysis of the census data of the Great tit collected in Marley Wood since 1947 shows that clutch size and hatching success are density-dependent. Mortality outside the breeding season is the key factor responsible for annual fluctuations, and may contain a weakly density-dependent effect.

The density-dependent effects of clutch size and hatching success are sufficient in themselves to regulate the population at the observed level. Thus it is not necessary to postulate any regulating mortality other than that occuring in the breeding season, but there may still be some weakly density-dependent mortality outside the breeding season.

The main factors responsible for population regulation are availability of food at the time of egg-laying (or some factor which correlates with, and enables prediction of subsequent food availability for the young), and predation of eggs (mainly by weasels). Spring territorial behaviour has been shown experimentally to determine breeding density and this may produce a weak density-dependent effect contributing to regulation of the population.

J. R. KREBS

I am indebted to Dr J. M. Cullen for his advice and criticism at all stages of this work. I am most grateful to Mr G. R. Gradwell, Dr M. P. Hassell and Professor G. C. Varley for their advice concerning the analysis of population data. The analysis would not have been possible had I not been allowed free access to the data at the Edward Grey Institute, for this I am indebted to Dr C. M. Perrins and earlier workers (Dr J. Gibb and Dr D. F. Owen) who collected the data. Dr J. M. Cullen, D. G. Dawson, Dr D. Lack, F.R.S., R. J. O'Connor and Dr C. M. Perrins and Professor G. C. Varley kindly read and offered valuable comments on earlier drafts of this paper. Financial support was received from the Science Research Council.

REFERENCES

Dhondt, A. A. & Hublé, J. (1968). Fledging date and sex in relation to dispersal in young Great tits. *Bird Study* **15**: 127–134.
Kluijver, H. N. (1951). The population ecology of the Great tit. *Ardea* **39**: 1–135.
Kluijver, H. N. (1967). Territory and regulation in a population of Great tits. Paper read at D.O.G. meeting, Heligoland. September 1967.
Kluijver, H. N. & Tinbergen, L. (1953). Territory and the regulation of density in titmice. *Archs néerl. Zool.* **10**: 266–287.
Krebs, J. R. (In press). Territory and breeding density in the Great tit, *Parus major* L. *Ecology*.
Lack, D. (1966). *Population studies of birds.* Oxford: Clarendon Press.
Nicholson, A. J. (1954). An outline of the dynamics of animal populations. *Aust. J. Zool.* **2**: 9–65.
Pennycuick, L. (1969). A computer simulation of the Oxford Great tit population. *J. Theor. Biol.* **22**: 381–400.
Perrins, C. M. (1963). *Some factors influencing brood-size and populations in tits.* D. Phil. thesis, Oxford University.
Perrins, C. M. (1965). Population fluctuations and clutch-size in the Great tit, *Parus major*, L. *J. Anim. Ecol.* **34**: 601–647.
Reddingius, J. J. (1968). *Gambling for existence.* Ph.D. thesis, Gröningen.
Richards, O. W. & Southwood, T. R. E. (1968). The abundance of insects: introduction. *Symp. R. ent. Soc. Lond.* No. 4: 1–7.
Royama, T. (1966). A re-interpretation of courtship feeding. *Bird Study* **13**: 116–129.
Solomon, M. E. (1958). Meaning of density-dependence and related terms in population dynamics. *Nature, Lond.* **181**: 1778–1781.
Southwood, T. R. E. (1966). *Ecological methods.* London: Methuen.
Varley, G. C. (1958). Meaning of density-dependence and related terms in population dynamics. *Nature, Lond.* **181**: 1778–1781.
Varley, G. C. & Gradwell, G. R. (1960). Key factors in population studies. *J. Anim. Ecol.* **29**: 399–401.
Varley, G. C. & Gradwell, G. R. (1963). The interpretation of insect population changes. *Proc. Ceylon Ass. Advmt Sci.* **18**(D): 142–156.
Varley, G. C. & Gradwell, G. R. (1968). Population models for the winter moth. *Symp. R. ent. Soc. Lond.* No. 4: 132–142.
Vilks, E. K. (1966). [Migrations and territorial behaviour of Latvian tits and nuthatches from ringing data]. *Trudy Inst. Biol. Akad. nauk Latvian SSSR* No. 27: 69–88 (Russian, English summary).

Appendix

Further comments on the "good" and "bad" areas of Marley Wood

The "good" areas were quite diverse, including some areas of dense hazel understorey, an area of tall elms, and some areas with oaks and fewer secondary storey trees. In order to see if it was possible to relate the different quality areas to particular types of vegetation, the map shown in Fig. 7 was superimposed on various vegetation maps of Marley Wood, but no correlation between quality of area and tree type (or simple combination of tree types) was found. It is possible that the particular tree species is less important than some measure such as volume of foliage or diversity of plant species (since both of these measures presumably relate to insect abundance).

The fact that areas with a canopy layer and an understorey layer were on the whole better than areas with only one or the other suggests that "total volume of foliage" may in fact be an important measure. (No attempt was made to measure this in detail.) The good areas derived from the method just described included areas similar to those "preferred" by the birds when settling, but puzzlingly, some apparently very similar areas came out as bad.

To check that the good and bad area divisions did not merely reflect areas in which birds tended to lay early or late within each year (late clutches are on average smaller), a map similar to that shown in Fig. 7 was constructed for laying dates. The "early" and "late" boxes did not tend to fall into particular areas, thus the clutch-size-area-effect was not caused by differences between the areas in laying date. The fact that early and late boxes did not fall into clumps suggests that the factor influencing laying date is extremely local to the box. This local feature is unlikely to be the availability of food immediately around the box, since the female wanders over the whole territory collecting food at the time of egg laying. A possible box-specific factor influencing laying date would be temperature of the box. The female roosts in the box just before the start of laying and it is possible that if the box becomes cold at night, the onset of laying is delayed because the female used her food reserves to maintain her body temperature. Some preliminary measurements suggested that the temperatures inside "early" boxes was higher than ambient but was not higher in the case of "late" boxes (R. J. O'Connor, pers. comm.).

Direct comparison between the good and bad areas obtained in the present analysis and those obtained by Perrins is not completely justifiable, since the two analyses were based on different years. When data from earlier years (1947–58) were analysed by plotting good and bad boxes, good and bad areas were again obtained, but these were somewhat different from the 1960–68 areas, and they were also more similar to Perrins' areas. The data for earlier years however are less reliable since the ages of females were not recorded, and thus it was not possible to correct the clutches for this factor before plotting them on the map.

Reproduced from the *Journal of Zoology, London* 162:317–333, 1970, with permission of the Zoological Society of London.

DEVELOPMENT OF BIG GAME MANAGEMENT PLANS THROUGH SIMULATION MODELING

CARL J. WALTERS

JACK E. GROSS

Abstract: Current and future demands on wildlife resources require greater levels of stewardship from the wildlife manager. More complex demands and inevitable compromises will require more sophisticated management plans whose attributes are alternative paths of action and estimates of the consequences. The core of needed management plans is visualized as question banks and data-processing models. Simulation models permit premanagement experimentation in terms of *what if* games. Examples of what if games are discussed to illustrate critical population conditions, sensitive management parameters, alternative objectives, consequences of environmental catastrophes, and procedures for developing objective measures for management performance. This paper attempts to show how information generated from a complex of variables can be channeled into the decision-making process.

Wildlife managers are experiencing increasing difficulty in maintaining the stewardship expertise that is required to cope with the increasing complexity of administration of wildlife resources. Managers are frequently unequipped to objectively outline compromise management plans for controversial issues or to develop arguments against activities that may be incompatible with the wildlife resources. The problems are partially due to difficulties in interpreting relevant data, in developing sound, decision-making criteria, in outlining alternative management plans, and in evaluating the consequences of compromise plans. The intent of this paper is to illustrate how simulation modeling can be used to develop comprehensive and detailed management information that may help to solve current and future management problems.

This research was conducted under a cooperative contract with the Division of Wildlife Refuges and the Division of Wildlife Research, Bureau of Sport Fisheries and Wildlife. We are indebted to C. V. Baker, L. Paur, and M. Taylor for their help in the development of this model.

PERSPECTIVE

Management plans in this paper are visualized as question banks that produce a profile of alternative plans and their consequences for a variety of management problems. A bewildering variety of problems face the present and future wildlife manager. Thus, it becomes increasingly difficult to convey comprehensive and detailed information to the decision maker, with the traditional written and verbal report. Thus, data-processing programs that combine and manipulate data to produce relevant information for specific management problems will be helpful. Such plans are visualized as open-ended management games that can be conducted to the limit of the manager's imagination.

The manager can use management-plan models to experiment with what if games and to make useful *conditional predictions* such as: if estimates of . . . are accurate, then we can expect . . . to happen; or, if . . . is true, then estimates of . . . cannot be accurate; or, what would happen to . . . if . . . were to occur. It may often be as useful to be able to say what is not likely to happen as it is to say what is likely to happen.

To gain insight to management, the development of a model does not necessarily require an understanding of the effects of factors such as social aggression, food supply, disease, and predation on a population.

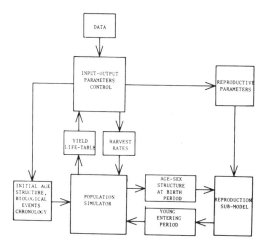

Fig. 1. Compartmental illustration of information control and processing and categories of information required for simulation.

With applied management in mind, it would in most cases be difficult and probably irrelevant to try to model the processes that directly influence the dynamics of a particular wildlife population. However, the effects of those processes can be modeled indirectly. Quade (1966) stated: "A model is a simplified, stylized representation of the real world that abstracts the cause-and-effect relationships essential to the question studied."

The procedure for producing management information involves a feature of modeling that Holling (1966) termed realism. Realism is the insight into a system's behavior that can be provided by a model whose basic features mimic the real world. Realism is not necessarily prediction in the sense of describing the behavior of a system at some time in the future. Rather, it can be prediction of how some part of the system will behave if another part of the system is known to behave in a certain way.

We have developed a general simulation model for the analysis of single-species populations that is based on interactions of density, specific natality rates, and specific

mortality rates. The basic information-processing framework of the model is shown in Fig. 1. Mathematical derivations are described by Gross (1970).

The computer program is a bookkeeping procedure to perform calculations and to keep track of indices. The program accepts a set of age-specific natality rates, age-specific mortality rates, initial age structure, initial sex structure, age-specific weights, age-specific antler classes, and a harvest regime. The program generates output information including numbers of animals harvested, quality of animals harvested, biomass of animals harvested, and forage required to produce the foregoing yields. Information on population size and sex and age structure is generated for output and for running the program for as many years as desired. Relationships among numerical yield, value yield, biomass yield, forage requirements, and harvest regime are determined by repeatedly simulating the population while varying harvest rates and sex-specific hunting effort.

EXAMPLE FOR THE SIMULATION MODEL

An example of the application of the simulation model can be illustrated using data that Teer et al. (1965) obtained from the white-tailed deer (*Odocoileus virginianus*) herd in the Llano Basin of Texas. We are not suggesting a management plan for this deer herd; we are merely using the data from the Llano Basin as an example for analyzing real-world data through simulation modeling.

Two components necessary for the model's operation are patterns of natality rate and mortality rate. Teer et al. (1965) estimated constant mortality rates for fawns and adults over time and found statistically significant, inverse relationships between population density and natality rates in yearling and adult females (Table 1). All

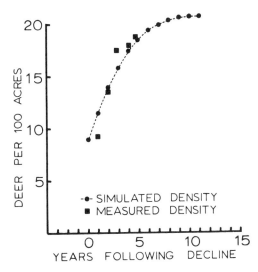

Fig. 2. Recovery of Llano Basin white-tailed deer herd after a population decline, superimposed on simulated population recovery calculated by demographic simulator from vital statistics and life-history data from the same herd (original data from Teer et al. 1965).

simulation analyses in the present paper use these basic data.

To show the general descriptive ability of the model, a simulated trend of population growth, based on the data in Table 1, was compared with the actual recovery of the Llano Basin herd after a population decline (Fig. 2). However, closely corresponding simulation curves of population density over time were obtained with values different from those in Table 1. Thus, there is no unique or least-squares set of natality

and mortality values to describe a specific population change. In one sense, the simulation model is like a polynomial curve: it can be altered to fit data to any desired degree of precision. However, despite the lack of uniqueness of data sets, the ability of the model to generate general patterns of response has potential usefulness for management.

When many parameters can be used to analyze or manage a population, it is meaningful to ask which parameter(s) most strongly controls or alters the behavior of the population over time. For example, one might want to know whether, for the example deer population, it is more important to have accurate data on patterns of natural mortality rates than to have accurate data on patterns of natality rates. A partial answer to this question is suggested in Fig. 3. High and low mortality-rate slopes, coupled with normal natality-rate slopes, produced stabilized population densities, but a high mortality-rate slope, coupled with a high natality-rate slope, produced an oscillating population. In some cases, the stability of simulated populations was more sensitive to changes in yearling natality-rate patterns than in adult natality-rate patterns. Thus, a simulation as in Fig. 3 would suggest to the manager that his first priority for data collection should go to reproductive information, and secondly that he should prevent the population from de-

Table 1. Specific natality rate and specific mortality rate estimates for white-tailed deer in the Llano Basin (Teer et al. 1965).

PARAMETER	AGE GROUPS		
	Fawns	Yearlings	Adults
Instantaneous natural mortality rates	0.256	0.151	0.151
Conception rates as a function of density	0	$Y = 1.23 - 0.035X$	$Y = 1.12 - 0.021X$
Ovulation rates as a function of density	0	$Y = 2.15 - 0.056X$	$Y = 2.48 - 0.058X$

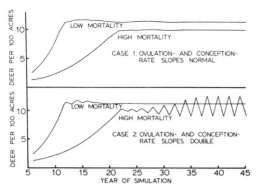

Fig. 3. Simulated behavior of white-tailed deer population density under two combinations of mortality rates and two patterns of reproductive-rate slopes (original data on reproductive rates from Teer et al. 1965).

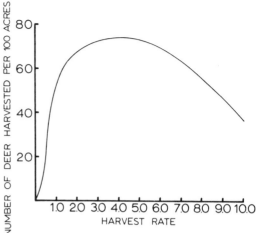

Fig. 4. Simulated curve of yield obtainable with different harvest rates from a white-tailed deer population. The curve was obtained from a 40-year simulation with a 60:40 buck: doe ratio maintained in the harvest (harvest rate is the proportion of population harvested annually expressed as instantaneous annual values).

veloping the natality rates and mortality rates that produce instability.

When the simulation model is used to analyze various management plans with the aim of determining maximum yield (numbers harvested), it is not necessary to explicitly examine annual net production. Long-term yield can be expressed directly as a function of harvest rates (percentage of the herd killed by sex-class). For example, a yield curve is shown for cases in which harvest rates are constant each year (Fig. 4). The overall yield curve could be broken down to give separate curves for blocks of years. If harvest rates are varied from year to year, total yield over all years could be expressed as a multidimensional response surface with each independent variable axis representing the harvest rates for one year (or for a short series of years). Methods are available for seeking maxima on such multidimensional surfaces (Wilde 1964, Walters 1969).

A typical simulation problem might occur when the management decision has been made to increase harvest rate from a low value, where the herd size has stabilized, to a higher harvest rate. A manager might want to know the consequences of this change in management strategy. For example, how would gross production, net production, and population size change after the higher harvest rate was initiated? The simulated effects of a change in harvest rate from 15 percent to 30 percent are shown in Fig. 5. The population size drops sharply to about half its original value and after about 13 years becomes stable again. Gross production in the population at first increases, then drops below the gross production established at the original harvest rate. Yield increases sharply at first, then gradually drops and after about 13 years becomes stabilized at a higher value than before the change in harvest rate was initiated. The peak yields are maintained only for a few years after the harvest rate is changed. After population density becomes stable, annual yield remains higher than before the change in harvest rate, despite the fact that gross production is lower than before the change.

374

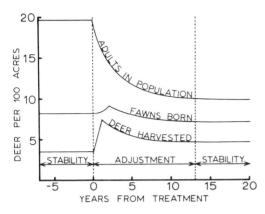

Fig. 5. Simulated response of the number of deer in the population, the number of fawns born, and the number of deer killed in a white-tailed deer population after the annual kill is changed from 15 to 30 percent (original data from Teer et al. 1965).

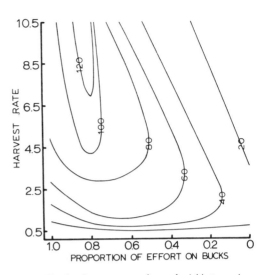

Fig. 6. Simulated response surface of yield to various combinations of harvest rate (proportion of population harvested annually expressed as instantaneous values) and proportion of the effort on bucks (figures on isopleths are numbers of deer harvested per 100 acres in 40 years—original data from Teer et al. 1965).

A simulation model that produces information such as illustrated in Fig. 5 is advantageous for two reasons. First, an indication of the consequences of a management plan can be obtained in a few seconds, whereas in the real world the results could not be obtained for 13 years. Even if response studies of such intervals were possible, the outlay of manpower and money would be prohibitive under current management philosophies. Second, several hundred such simulations can be produced for the manager in 2–3 minutes. Such computational powers allow the manager to explore a wide variety of possibilities or suspected impossibilities. A profile of simulations can be generated to provide the manager not only with an estimate of the consequences of a management plan, but also to provide an idea of the consequences if the simulated management plan is in error or if it cannot be developed in the real-world population.

Isopleth diagrams are useful for examining the effects on populations of nonlinear interactions between variables. For example, the interaction of harvest rate and proportion of hunting effort on bucks produces a yield isopleth (long-term yield plotted as a contour map) that suggests a 20 percent kill (equal to an instantaneous harvest rate of about 9.5) with 80 percent of the kill effort directed to bucks (Fig. 6). Points on the surface of the isopleth diagram in Fig. 6 were generated by simulating the population 36 times with 40 years in each simulation.

The isopleths in Fig. 6 reflect an important characteristic of unequal harvest effort on the sexes. An imbalanced effort on the sexes may produce unexpected changes in age and sex ratios and thus unexpected changes in gross production and net production. The interactions between age-specific natality rates, harvest rates, and proportion of effort on bucks seem to be so complex that a detailed understanding of population behavior developed by such procedures as isopleth analysis would be necessary before the manager could design

375

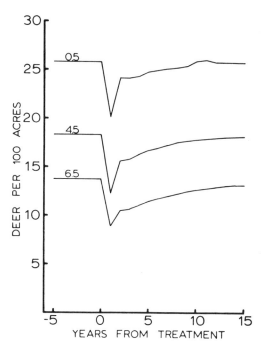

Fig. 7. Simulated population-size history after a loss of the fawn crop under three instantaneous-value harvest rates: 0.5, 4.5, and 6.5. Simulation executed with 60 percent proportion of effort on bucks (original data from Teer et al. 1965).

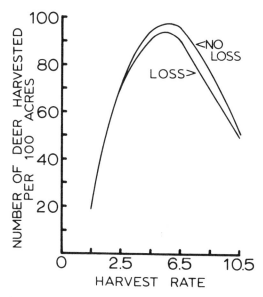

Fig. 8. Simulated yields from two white-tailed deer populations, one suffering a loss of the fawn crop and one with no loss of the fawn crop. Yields obtained from a 40-year simulation with 60 percent proportion of effort on bucks. Harvest rates are instantaneous values (original data from Teer et al. 1965).

reasonably precise, goal-oriented management plans.

Fig. 6 also illustrates the lack of fixed sensitivity for the parameters of harvest rate and proportion of effort. At higher ranges of values, the maintenance of maximum or near-maximum yield is highly sensitive to the changes in the proportion of effort on bucks. In order to achieve maximum yield, the proportion of effort on bucks must be maintained at about 0.8. In the same situation, the harvest rate could vary from 7.5 to 10.5 without materially changing the maximum yield. Conversely, at lower harvest rates and high proportion of effort on bucks, the proportion of effort can vary almost over the entire range without materially changing the yield, but the harvest

rate becomes the sensitive variable for the maintenance of a given yield.

Sensitivity simulations such as the foregoing analyses of harvest rate and proportion of effort can be valuable because of the frequently imprecise control that managers can maintain over populations. Through simulation, the manager may be alerted that he must maintain a certain combination of harvest parameters in order to keep one relatively uncontrollable parameter from causing undesirable consequences. Likewise, sensitivity analyses could suggest a research or inventory priority by showing what parameters should be more accurately measured in the population.

The consequences to management of population catastrophes can also be examined with simulation modeling. As an example, the simulated effects of harvest

Table 2. Arbitrary relative quality values assigned to age-classes of white-tailed deer (bucks and does), based on expected number of antler points.

SEX	AGE-CLASS									
	1	2	3	4	5	6	7	8	9	10
Bucks	1	2	3	4	4	4	4	4	4	4
Does	1	1	1	1	1	1	1	1	1	1

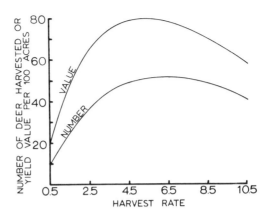

Fig. 9. Simulated yield and quality value obtained from a white-tailed deer population under various harvest rates. Quality values for antler classes are listed in Table 2. The yield and quality values were obtained from a 40-year simulation with a 60 percent proportion of the effort on bucks. Harvest rates are instantaneous values (original data from Teer et al. 1965).

rates on the recovery of the example population after a single total loss of the fawn crop are shown in Fig. 7. The herd takes longer to regain its original density the more heavily it is hunted. Thus, if the goal of a management plan is to maintain a population density at some previously determined level, quick recovery after a loss of the fawn crop could be attained by reducing the harvest rate. But when the 40-year yield is plotted as a function of the harvest rate for two cases—one simulation without a loss of the fawn crop and one simulation with such a loss—practically identical yield curves are obtained (Fig. 8). In particular, the harvest rates that provide maximum yield for the two cases are so close that for practical purposes they can be considered the same. Thus, if a long-term management plan designed to produce maximum yield was being followed, the manager need not alter management strategy in the face of occasional (10–15 years) net production failures.

A final example of the use of simulation modeling to evaluate harvest plans illustrates the effects of quality constraints on harvest rates. Arbitrary relative values for bucks and does of each age-class were assigned according to the number of antler points, with animals having no antlers receiving a value of 1 (Table 2). As shown in Fig. 9, maximum long-term value yield is obtained by using lower harvest rates than those that would give maximum numerical yield.

Perhaps the most valuable ultimate benefit provided by simulation modeling is the development of quantitative information that can serve as performance measures or management goals for population manipulation. The following equations illustrate how new management insights may be developed.

Consider the Llano Basin deer population in which the natural mortality rate of juveniles (young-of-the-year) is m_1 and natural mortality rate of yearlings and adults is m_2. Then we can write net production for the population, P, for a year as

$$P = B(N) - m_2 N - m_1 B(N), \quad (1)$$

where N is the number of animals at the start of the biological year (just before the young are born) and $B(N)$ is to be read as total births, B, as a function of N. P equals the potential numerical yield for the year.

To find the population size that will produce optimum numerical yield, we differentiate (1) with respect to N to give

$$dp/dN = (1 - m_1) [dB(N)/dN] - m_2. \quad (2)$$

377

Equation (2) implies that an optimum breeding-population size of

$$dB(N)/dN = m_2/(1 - m_1) \text{ (for } N = N_{opt}). \quad (3)$$

Thus, the population is at optimum-numerical-yield size when the slope of the curve of total births equals the slope of the curve of total deaths divided by the survival rate of animals during their first year of life. Since $B(N)$ is the product of N times the specific birth rate, $b(n)$, (3) becomes

$$[db(N)/dN] \ N_{opt} + b(N) = \quad (4)$$
$$m_2/(1 - m_1) \text{ (if } N = N_{opt}).$$

Equation (4) indicates that a population of density N_0 is close to optimum-numerical-yield size if (at density N_0) the sum of the birth date $b(N_0)$, plus the rate of change of the specific birthrate at that density times N_0, is equal to $m_2/(1 - m_1)$.

The problem is to estimate the rate of change of birthrate with respect to density. To estimate this rate of change requires birthrate information from a range of densities. Estimates of absolute densities are not necessary if density indices represent the same proportion of the population each year. The following data are needed for two consecutive years: density indices T_1 and T_2 for breeding-population density, estimates of birthrates b_1 (for T_1) and b_2 (for T_2), and estimates of natural mortality rates m_1 (for T_1) and m_2 (for T_2). If T_1 and T_2 are not greatly different,

$$N_1[db(N)/dN] = N_2[db(N)/dN] \quad (5)$$
$$= (b_2 - b_1)/(T_2 - T_1),$$

where T_2 is taken to be the larger of the two density indices. By substituting the last term of equation (5) into equation (4), if

$$(b_2 - b_1)/(T_2 - T_1) + b_2 > m_2/(1 - m_1), \quad (6)$$

then the population size represented by T_2 is below the density where optimum nu-

merical yield would occur, and the population should be allowed to increase. Similarly, if

$$(b_2 - b_1)/(T_2 - T_1) + b_2 < m_2/(1 - m_1), \quad (7)$$

then the population size represented by T_2 is above the density where optimum numerical yield would occur, and the population should be reduced. Limitations of this procedure are that (1) density indices may not represent the same proportion of the population from year to year, and (2) the specific birthrate (b) may vary from the expected density dependent value due to year-to-year changes in environmental factors.

Since a regression of specific birthrates on density was determined for the Llano Basin deer herd (Table 1), $db(N)/dN$ can be estimated as the slope of the regression line if it is assumed that the birthrate decreases linearly with density over the observed density ranges. For purposes of illustration, the data in Table 2 were condensed into a single regression of young per density. If a and b are the intercept and slope, respectively, of the birthrate-density line, solving (4) for optimum population sizes gives

$$N_{opt} = \frac{1}{2a} - [b - m_2/(1 - m_1)]. \quad (8)$$

For example, assuming $m_1 = .236$ and $m_2 = .149$,

$$N_{opt} = \frac{1}{2(0.0995)}[2.73 - 0.149/(1.0 - 0.236)]$$
$$= 16.97 \text{ deer per 100 acres.}$$

Given the estimate of population size as to optimum numerical yield of 16.97 deer per 100 acres, the optimum numerical yield (if hunting is not selective by sex or age of animals) can be calculated as

$$Y_{opt} = N_{opt} \ (1 - m_1) \ (a - b \ N_{opt}). \quad (9)$$

Thus, for the Llano Basin population

$$Y_{opt} = 16.97 \ (1.0 - 0.236) \ [2.73 - 0.0995(16.97)] = 13.47$$

deer per 100 acres.

We have implicitly assumed in the above equations that the specific birthrate can be represented by an overall population value and that the effects of density on the birthrate are the same from year to year. If these assumptions are not too severe, equations (8) and (9) can be used to obtain a reasonable approximation of a target population size from which the optimum numerical yield can be obtained. If a population is managed so that N_{opt} animals are present just before the young are born in one year, and if Y_{opt} animals are killed that same year, then equations (8) and (9) will account for natural mortality and insure that N_{opt} animals are present before the birth of young the next year. Y_{opt} will be the maximum sustained annual harvest.

DISCUSSION

Simulation modeling can be used to analyze a wide variety of population phenomena other than the ones described above. The amount of information that can be generated depends essentially on the problems for which answers are sought. Phenomena associated with changes in sex and age structure can be easily attached to the model, as can social and economic evaluations of simple management regimes. More complex analyses require correspondingly more complex means of summarizing and displaying results. Likewise, simulation models, for multiple species, now under development will permit analyses of complex management plans wherein one species is managed for trophies, another for numerical yield, and yet another for optimum protein (biomass) production—all to be managed

simultaneously for optimum use of a given land space.

We have glossed over the problem of how to vary hunting effort over time to maintain a population that is resilient to occasional catastrophic mortality agents or to management regimes that go awry. Some situations suggest that the manager need not be too concerned about short-term population perturbations (Fig. 8). However, every situation requires its own specific analysis, because each is the result of a different combination of events. The fact that every situation is a dynamic process is the reason why simulation models must eventually come into common use. We have found in our simulation studies that it is manifestly impossible to select *the* harvest rate, *the* population size, or *the* sex ratio as ideal for any big game management plan. As more precise management plans are demanded by more intensive use of wildlife species, alternative or multiple-goal objectives must be developed for the decision maker.

The model should give essentially the same results as the dynamic linear programming model of Davis (1967) for low herd densities. Since optimization under the linear programming model is relatively simple, we recommend its use in the analysis of the best management policy for growing populations. The manager could then use a more complex model, such as the one we have described, to decide on a management regime for larger populations in which specific natality rates or specific mortality rates have begun to respond to density.

LITERATURE CITED

Davis, L. S. 1967. Dynamic programming for deer management planning. J. Wildl. Mgmt. 31(4):667–679.

Gross, J. E. 1970. Program anpop: a simulation modeling exercise on the Wichita Mountains

National Wildlife Refuge. Colorado Cooperative Wildl. Research Unit Progr. Rept. 133pp. Mimeo.

HOLLING, C. S. 1966. The functional response of invertebrate predators to prey density. Memoirs Entomol. Soc. Canada 48:1–86.

QUADE, E. S. 1966. Systems analysis techniques for planning–programming–budgeting. Pages 1–31. *In* Executive orientation in planning, programming, and budgeting workshop. U.S. Bur. Budget and U.S. Civil Serv. Comm.,

Washington, D.C.

TEER, J. G., J. W. THOMAS, AND E. A. WALKER. 1965. Ecology and management of white-tailed deer in the Llano Basin of Texas. Wildl. Monographs 15. 62pp.

WALTERS, C. J. 1969. A generalized computer simulation model for fish population studies. Trans. Am. Fisheries Soc. 98(3):505–512.

WILDE, D. J. 1964. Optimum seeking methods. Prentice-Hall, Inc., Englewood Cliffs, New Jersey. 202pp.

ADDITIONAL READINGS

GENERAL

Andrewartha, H. G., and L. C. Birch. 1954. *The distribution and abundance of animals*. Univ. of Chicago Press. 782 pp.

Cole, L. C. 1954. The population consequences of life history phenomena. *Quar. Rev. Biol.* 29:103–137.

Keith, L. B. 1974. Population dynamics of mammals. *XI Int. Congress of Game Biologists*, Stockholm.

Kluijver, H. N. 1951. The population ecology of the great tit, *Parus m. major* L. *Ardea* 39:1–135.

Lack, D. L. 1954. *The natural regulation of animal numbers*. Clarendon Press, Oxford. 343 pp.

Watson, A. 1973. A review of population dynamics in birds. *Brit. Birds* 66:417–437.

Wynne–Edwards, V. C. 1962. *Animal dispersion in relation to social behavior*. Hafner Pub. Co., New York. 653 pp.

NATALITY

Barkalow, F. S., Jr. 1962. Latitude related to reproduction in the cottontail rabbit. *J. Wildl. Manage.* 26:32–37.

Conaway, C. H. 1971. Ecological adaption and mammalian reproduction. *Biol. of Repro.* 4:239–247.

Coulson, J. C., and E. White. 1961. An analysis of the factors influencing the clutch size of the kittiwake. *Proc. Zool. Soc.*, London, 136:207–217.

Crossner, K. A. 1977. Natural selection and clutch size in the European starling. *Ecology* 58:885–892.

Fretwell, S. D. 1969. The adjustment of birth rate to mortality in birds. *Ibis* 111:624–627.

Klomp, H. 1970. The determination of clutch size in birds: A review. *Ardea* 58:1–124.

Perrins, C. M., and P. J. Jones. 1974. The inheritance of clutch size in the great tit (*Parus major* L.). *Condor* 76:225–229.

Recklefs, R. E. 1970. Clutch size in birds: Outcome of opposing predator and prey relations. *Science* 168:599–600.

Safriel, U. N. 1975. On the significance of clutch size in nidifugous birds. *Ecology* 56:703–708.

MORTALITY

Brownie, C., D. R. Anderson, K. P. Burnham, and D. S. Robson. 1978. *Statistical inference from band recovery date — A handbook*. U. S. Fish and Wildl. Serv., Resource Pub. No. 131. Washington, D. C. 212 pp.

Cook, R. S., M. White, D. O. Trainer, and W. C. Glazener. 1971. Mortality of young white-tailed deer fawns in south Texas. *J. Wildl. Manage.* 35:47–56.

Coulson, J. C. 1960. A study of mortality of the starling based on ringing records. *J. Anim. Ecol.* 29:251–271.

Deevey, E. S., Jr. 1947. Life tables for natural populations of animals. *Quar. Rev. Biol.* 22:283–314.

Lack, D. 1946. Do juvenile birds survive less well than adults? *Brit. Birds* 39:258–264.

Spinage, C. A. 1972. African ungulate life tables. *Ecology* 53:645–652.

DISPERSAL

Dobson, F. S. 1979. An experimental study of dispersal in the California ground squirrel. *Ecology* 60:1103–1109.

Gaines, M. S., A. M. Vivas, and C. L. Baker. 1979. An experimental analysis of dispersal in fluctuating vole populations: Demographic parameters. *Ecology* 60:814–828.

Herzog, P. W., and D. A. Boag. 1978. Dispersion and mobility in a local population of spruce grouse. *J. Wildl. Manage.* 42:853–865.

Lidicker, W. Z. 1962. Emigration as a possible mechanism permitting the regulation of population density below carrying capacity. *Amer. Nat.* 46:29–33.

Myers, J. H., and C. J. Krebs. 1971. Genetic, behavioral, and reproductive attributes of dispersing field voles *Microtus pennsylvanicus* and *Microtus ochrogaster*. *Ecol. Monogr.* 41:53–78.

Thompson, D. C. 1978. Regulation of a northern grey squirrel (*Sciurus carolinensis*) population. *Ecology* 59:708–715.

AGE AND SEX COMPOSITION

Johnson, D. H., and A. B. Sargeant. 1977. *Impact of red fox predation on the sex ratio of prairie mallards.* U. S. Fish and Wildl. Serv., Wildl. Res. Rep. 6. Washington, D. C. 56 pp.

Mech, L. D. 1975. Disproportionate sex ratios in wolf pups. *J. Wildl. Manage.* 39:737–740.

Paulik, G. T., and D. S. Robson. 1969. Statistical calculations for change-in-ratio estimators of population parameters. *J. Wildl. Manage.* 33:1–27.

Trivers, R. L., and D. E. Willard. 1973. Natural selection of parental ability to vary the sex ratio of offspring. *Science* 179:90–92.

POPULATION GROWTH

Brewer, R., and L. Swander. 1977. Life history factors affecting the intrinsic rate of natural increase of birds of the deciduous forest biome. *Wilson Bull.* 89:211–232.

Caughley, G. 1970. Eruption of ungulate populations, with emphasis on the Himalayan thar in New Zealand. *Ecology* 51:53–72.

Eberhardt, L. L. 1970. Correlation, regression, and density dependence. *Ecology* 51:306–310.

Slade, N. A. 1977. Statistical detection of density dependence from a series of sequential censuses. *Ecology* 58:1094–1102.

Tanner, J. T. 1966. Effects of population density on growth rates of animal populations. *Ecology* 47:733–745.

POPULATION FLUCTUATION

Batzli, G. O., and F. A. Pitelka. 1971. Condition and diet of cycling populations of the California vole, *Microtus californicus*. *J. Mammal.* 52:141–163.

Bulmer, M. G. 1974. A statistical analysis of the 10-year cycle in Canada. *J. Anim. Ecol.* 43:701–718.

Cole, L. C. 1951. Population cycles and random oscillations. *J. Wildl. Manage.* 15:233–252.

Horn, H. S. 1968. Regulation of animal numbers: A model counter-example. *Ecology* 49:776–778.

Mueller, H. C., and D. D. Berger. 1967. Some observations and comments on the periodic invasions of goshawks. *Auk* 84:183–191.

Pimentel, D. 1968. Population regulation and genetic feedback. *Science* 159:1432–1437.

Ricker, W. E. 1954. Effects of compensatory mortality upon population abundance. *J. Wildl. Manage.* 18:45–51.

Wiens, J. A. 1966. On group selection and Wynne–Edwards' hypothesis. *Amer. Sci.* 54:273–287.

Wynne–Edwards, V. C. 1965. Self-regulating systems in populations of animals. *Science* 147:1543–1548.

WEATHER

Gilbert, P. F., O. C. Wallmo, and R. B. Gill. 1970. Effect of snow depth on mule deer in Middle Park, Colorado. *J. Wildl. Manage.* 34:15–23.

Kluyver, H. N. 1952. Notes on body weight and time of breeding in the great tit, *Parus m. major* L. *Ardea* 40:123–141.

ADDITIONAL READINGS

Severinghaus, C. W. 1972. Weather and the deer population. *The Conservationist* 27:28–31.
Stafford, J. 1971. The heron population of England and Wales, 1928–1970. *Bird Study* 18:218–221.
Wagner, F. H., C. D. Besnady, and C. Kabot. 1965. *Population ecology and management of Wisconsin pheasants.* Wis. Cons. Dept. Tech. Bull. No. 34. 168 pp.

PREDATION AND EXPLOITATION

Anderson, D. R., and K. P. Burnham. 1976. *Population ecology of the mallard. VI. The effect of exploitation on survival.* U. S. Fish and Wildlife Service Resource Pub. 128. Washington, D. C. 66 pp.
Balser, D. S., H. H. Dill, and H. K. Nelson. 1968. Effect of predator reduction on waterfowl nesting success. *J. Wildl. Manage.* 32:669–682.
Cain, S. A., J. A. Kadlec, D. L. Allen, R. A. Cooley, M. H. Hornocker, A. S. Leopold, and F. H. Wagner. 1972. *Predator Control — 1971 report to the Council on Environmental Quality and the Department of Interior by the advisory committee on predator control.* Univ. of Michigan Press, Ann Arbor. 207 pp.
Davis, D. E., J. J. Christian, and F. Bronson. 1964. Effect of exploitation on birth, mortality, and movement rates in a woodchuck population. *J. Wildl. Manage.* 28:1–9.
Errington, P. L. 1945. Some contributions of a fifteen-year local study of the northern bobwhite to a knowledge of population phenomena. *Ecol. Monogr.* 15:1–34.
Errington, P. L. 1963. The phenomenon of predation. *Amer. Sci.* 51:180–192.
Hirst, S. M. 1969. Predation as a regulating factor of wild ungulate populations in a Transvaal Lowveld nature reserve. *Zool. Afr.* 4:199–231.
Holling, C. S. 1959. The components of predation as revealed by a study of small-mammal predation of the European pine sawfly. *Can. Entomol.* 91:293–320.
Hornocker, M. G. 1970. An analysis of mountain lion predation upon mule deer and elk in the Idaho primitive area. *Wildl. Monogr.* 21:1–39.
Luttich, S., D. H. Rusch, E. C. Meslow, and L. B. Keith. 1970. Ecology of red-tailed hawk predation in Alberta. *Ecology* 51:190–203.
Pimlott, D. H. 1967. Wolf predation and ungulate populations. *Amer. Zool.* 7:267–278.
Pitelka, F. A., P. Q. Tomich, and G. W. Treichel. 1955. Ecological relationships of jaegers and owls as lemming predators near Barrow, Alaska. *Ecol. Monogr.* 25:85–117.
Roseberry, J. L. 1979. Bobwhite population responses to exploitation: Real and simulated. *J. Wildl. Manage.* 43:285–305.
Schnell, J. 1968. The limiting effects of natural predation on experimental cotton rat populations. *J. Wildl. Manage.* 32:698–711.

INTERSPECIFIC COMPETITION

Brown, J. H. 1971. Mechanisms of competitive exclusion between two species of chipmunks. *Ecology* 52:305–311.
Crowell, K. L. 1973. Experimental zoogeography: Introduction of mice to small islands. *Amer. Nat.* 107:535–558.
Hartley, P. H. T. 1953. An ecological study of the feeding habits of the English titmice. *J. Anim. Ecol.* 22:261–288.
Joule, J., and D. L. Jameson. 1972. Experimental manipulation of population density in three sympatric rodents. *Ecology* 53:653–660.
Koplin, J. R., and R. S. Hoffman. 1968. Habitat overlap and competitive exclusion in voles (*Microtus*). *Amer. Midl. Nat.* 80:494–507.
MacArthur, R. H. 1958. Population ecology of some warblers of northeastern coniferous forests. *Ecology* 39:599–619.
Miller, R. S. 1964. Ecology and distribution of pocket gophers (*Geomyidae*) in Colorado. *Ecology* 45:256–272.
Morris, R. D., and P. R. Grant. 1972. Experimental studies of competitive interaction in a two-species system. IV. *Microtus* and *Clethrionomys* species in a single enclosure. *J. Anim. Ecol.* 41:275–290.

383

Murray, B. G., Jr. 1976. A critique of interspecific territoriality and character convergence. *Condor* 78:518–525.

Rosenzweig, M. L., and P. W. Sterner. 1973. Habitat selection experiments with a pair of coexisting heteromyid rodent species. *Ecology* 54:111–117.

Selander, R. K. 1966. Sexual dimorphism and differential niche utilization in birds. *Condor* 68:113–151.

Williams, J. B., and G. O. Batzli. 1979. Competition among bark-foraging birds in central Illinois: Experimental evidence. *Condor* 81:122–132.

INTRASPECIFIC COMPETITION

Daniel, M. J. 1963. Early fertility of red deer hinds in New Zealand. *Nature*, London, 200:380.

Flowerdew, J. R. 1972. The effect of supplementary food on a population of wood mice (*Apodemus sylvaticus*). *J. Anim. Ecol.* 41:553–566.

Murton, R. K., A. J. Isaacson, and N. J. Westwood. 1966. The relationships between wood-pigeons and their clover food supply and the mechanism of population control. *J. Appl. Ecol.* 3:55–96.

Myers, K., and W. E. Poole. 1962. A study of the biology of the wild rabbit, *Oryctolagus cuniculus* (L.), in confined populations. III. Reproduction. *Aust. J. Zool.* 10:225–267.

Smith, M. C. 1971. Food as a limiting factor in the population ecology of *Peromyscus polionotus* (Wagner). *Ann. Zool. Fennici* 8:109–112.

Stenger, J. 1958. Food habits and available food of ovenbirds in relation to territory size. *Auk* 75:335–346.

Yom–Tov, Y. 1974. The effect of food and predation on breeding density and success, clutch size and laying date of the crow (*Corvus corone* L.). *J. Anim. Ecol.* 43:479–498.

BEHAVIOR

Best, L. B. 1977. Territory quality and mating success in the field sparrow (*Spizella pusilla*). *Condor* 79:192–204.

Brown, J. L. 1969. Territorial behavior and population regulation in birds: A review and re-evaluation. *Wilson Bull.* 81:293–329.

Calhoun, J. B. 1952. The social aspects of population dynamics. *J. Mammal.* 33:139–159.

Dunford, C. 1977. Behavioral limitation of round-tailed ground squirrel density. *Ecology* 58:1254–1268.

Harris, M. P. 1970. Territory limiting the size of the breeding population of the oystercatcher (*Haematopus ostralegus*)—A removal experiment. *J. Anim. Ecol.* 39:707–713.

Klomp, H. 1972. Regulation of the size of bird populations by means of territorial behavior. *Netherlands J. Zool.* 22:456–488.

Krebs, J. R. 1971. Territory and breeding density in the great tit, *Parus major. Ecology* 52:2–22.

MacRoberts, B. R., and M. H. MacRoberts. 1972. Social stimulation of reproduction in herring and lesser black-backed gulls. *Ibis* 114:495–506.

Manuwal, D. A. 1974. Effects of territoriality on breeding in a population of Cassin's auklet. *Ecology* 55:1399–1406.

Rabb, G. B., J. H. Woolpy, and B. E. Ginsburg. 1967. Social relationships in a group of captive wolves. *Amer. Zool.* 7:305–311.

Victoria, J. K., and N. E. Collias. 1973. Social facilitation of egg-laying in experimental colonies of a weaverbird. *Ecology* 54:399–405.

PHYSIOLOGICAL STRESS

Bailey, E. D. 1966. Social interaction as a population-regulating mechanism in mice. *Can. J. Zool.* 44:1007–1012.

Christian, J. J. 1950. The adreno-pituitary system and population cycles in mammals. *J. Mammal.* 31:247–259.

Christian, J. J., and D. E. Davis. 1964. Endocrines, behavior, and populations. *Science* 146:1550–1560.

Louch, C. D. 1958. Adrenocortical activity in two meadow vole populations. *J. Mammal.* 39:109–116.

Selye, H. 1946. The general adaptation syndrome and the diseases of adaptation. *J. Clin. Endocrin.* 6:117–230.

384

ADDITIONAL READINGS

ASSESSING THE IMPORTANCE OF VARIOUS FACTORS

Blank, T. H., T. R. E. Southwood, and D. J. Cross. 1967. The ecology of the partridge. I. Outline of population processes with particular reference to chick mortality and nest density. *J. Anim. Ecol.* 36:549–556.

Bobek, B. 1980. A model for optimization of roe deer management in central Europe. *J. Wildl. Manage.* 44:837–848.

Connolly, G. E., and W. M. Longhurst. 1975. *The effects of control on coyote populations: A simulation model.* Univ. of Calif. Div. of Agric. Sci. Bull. No. 1872. 37 pp.

Lobdell, C. H., K. E. Case, and H. S. Mosby. 1972. Evaluation of harvest strategies for a simulated wild turkey population. *J. Wildl. Manage.* 36:493–497.

Watson, A. 1971. Key factor analysis, density dependence, and population limitation in red grouse. In P. J. den Boer and G. R. Gradwell (eds.), *Dynamics of populations*, pages 548–559. Centre for Agric. Pub. and Document., Wageningen.

Zarnoch, S. J., R. G. Anthony, and G. L. Storm. 1977. Computer simulated dynamics of a local red fox population. In R. L. Phillips and C. Jonkel (eds.), *Proceedings of the 1975 Predator Symposium*, pages 253–268. Univ. of Montana, Missoula.